ADVOCATES

The Penthouse, Tower Business Centre
Tower Street, Swatar BKR4013, Malta
T: (+356) 2557 2300
E: info@csb-advocates.com
www.csb-advocates.com

Gaming Law

Jurisdictional comparisons   **Second edition 2014**

General Editor:

Julian Harris, Harris Hagan

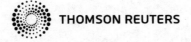
THOMSON REUTERS

General Editor:
Julian Harris

Commissioning Editor
Emily Kyriacou

Commercial Director
Katie Burrington

Freelance Senior Editor
LIsa Naylor

Design and Production
Dawn McGovern

Editing and Typesetting
Forewords

Published in July 2014 by European Lawyer Reference Series,
100 Avenue Road, London NW3 3PF
part of Thomson Reuters (Professional) UK Limited
(Registered in England & Wales, Company No 1679046.
Registered Office and address for service:
Aldgate House, 33 Aldgate High Street, London EC3N 1DL)

A CIP catalogue record for this book is available from the British Library.

ISBN: 9780414034679

Contents

Foreword Julian Harris   v

Introduction Philip Graf, Chairman, Gambling Commission, Great Britain   ix

Alderney Julian Harris & John Hagan Harris Hagan   1

Australia Jamie Nettleton, Justine Munsie & Jessica Azzi Addisons   17

Austria Walter Schwartz & Raffaela Wallerstorfer Schwartz Huber-Mede   35
und Partner Rechtsanwälte OG

Belgium Pieter Paepe Astrea   49

Brazil Fabio Kujawski & Fernanda Bezerra BKBG – Barretto Ferreira, Kujawski, 65
Brancher Sociedade de Advogados

Colorado (USA) Roger M. Morris Esq & Sean McGuinness Esq   79
Lewis Roca Rothgerber LLC

Cyprus Alexia C. Couccoullis Constantinos N. Couccoullis and Associates   91

Czech Republic Jan Kozubek & Veronika Žánová   101
Law Office Becker and Poliakoff

Denmark Nina Henningsen & Mikkel Taanum Horten   117

Estonia Silja Elunurm Law Firm Indela & Elunurm   135

France Diane Mullenex & Annabelle Richard Pinsent Masons LLP   151

Germany Dr Joerg Hofmann, Matthias Spitz, Danny Engelhardt & Martin Jarrett 171
Melchers Law

Gibraltar Peter Montegriffo & Nyreen Llamas Hassans   189

Greece Constantinos N. Couccoullis & Alexia C. Couccoullis   199
Constantinos N. Couccoullis and Associates

Ireland Rob Corbet & Chris Bollard Arthur Cox   211

Isle of Man Miles Benham MannBenham Advocates Limited   229

Israel Yehoshua Shohat Gurtler, Itzhak Shragay & Ariel Yosefi   237
Herzog Fox & Neeman Law Office

Italy Quirino Mancin SCM Lawyersi   247

Japan Ko Hanamizu Anderson Mori & Tomotsune   259

Luxembourg Michaël Kitai Bonn Steichen & Partners   271

Macau Luis Mesquita de Melo MdME Lawyers   289

Malta Dr Andrew Zammit, Dr Lynne Satariano & Mr Josef Cardona   313
CSB Advocates

Mexico César Morales Galán Bufete Carrillo Gamboa, S.C.   329

Monaco Diane Mullenex & Annabelle Richard Pinsent Masons LLP   345

The Netherlands Dr Alan Littler & Justin Franssen   353
Kalff Katz & Franssen Attorneys at Law

Nevada (USA) Dan R. Reaser, Mark A. Clayton & Robert D. Faiss   371
Lionel Sawyer & Collins

New Jersey (USA) Guy S. Michael Michael and Carroll   387

Ontario (Canada) Michael D. Lipton, Q.C., Kevin J. Weber & Jack I. Tadman   399
Dickinson Wright LLP
Panama Herbert Young Rodriguez & Lizi Rose Archer   417
Blandon & Young Attorneys
Romania Ana-Maria Baciu, Oana Albu & Lucian Barbu   429
Nestor Nestor Diculescu Kingston Petersen
Singapore Lawrence Quahe & Yeo Khung Chye Quahe Woo & Palmer LLC   447
South Africa Garron Whitesman Whitesmans Attorneys and A G Consulting   473
South Korea Jeffrey D. Jones, Hyun Ho Eun, Jin Ho Song, Michael S. Lee,   489
Mi-Ryoung An, John K. Kim & Junhee Choi Kim & Chang
Spain Santiago Asensi & Alla Serebrianskaia Asensi Abogados SLP   501
Sweden Dr Ola Wiklund Hansen Advokatbyrå KB   517
Switzerland Luka Müller-Studer & Andreas Glarner MME Partners   535
United Kingdom Julian Harris & John Hagan Harris Hagan   549
Contact details   569

Foreword

Julian Harris

In the foreword to the first edition of this book, I touched on the controversy to which the subject of gambling gives rise and the differences in approach across jurisdictions, often according to differing traditions, moral and religious views and its potential for harm. Such questions, and indeed arguments, have been prevalent for as long as gambling has existed, and continue today. Nevertheless, gambling continues to grow as a popular form of adult entertainment and states still see it as an opportunity to raise revenue and create economic growth and jobs.

When the first edition was published in September 2012, much of the western world remained firmly in the grip of economic recession and the newer land-based jurisdictions of Macau and Singapore had overtaken even the casino metropolis of Las Vegas in terms of revenue. Whilst online gambling remained a major growth area, all of the USA was still a closed market to legal, regulated operators, and much of Europe was in the hands of state monopolies. Even in the short time that has elapsed since then, there have been substantial developments and changes that make a new edition timely. Whilst gambling is still the subject of debate, growth continues and more jurisdictions are perceiving and addressing the need for consumers to be protected but enabled to gamble in a properly regulated, legal environment.

In land-based casino gambling, whilst the first true resort casino project proposed by Las Vegas Sands in Spain now appears unlikely, Cyprus looks set to be the first to market in Europe, whilst in Asia, Japan is taking the first tentative steps to legalise casinos. It seems unlikely that these two jurisdictions will be anything other than trailblazer locations for further growth on both continents. Japan has a hitherto untapped substantial market and a rich customer base. They may have been buoyed by the example of Singapore, which is an extraordinary example of how firm, but astute, measured and sophisticated regulation be strict and firm, yet can march hand in hand with extraordinary commercial success. If Cyprus proves that resort casinos can work in Europe, and can form a base for substantial tourist and convention growth, other European jurisdictions may well follow its lead.

The face of online gambling globally changed fundamentally with the grant of online licences, albeit limited ones, in Nevada, New Jersey and Delaware. This was perhaps the inevitable consequence of the *volte face* by the US Department of Justice when, in December 2011, it released an opinion reversing its previous long-held view stating that the Wire Act of 1961 did not apply to casino gaming. Whilst two of the three US states that have issued licences are relatively small, in population at least, there are already signs that they will quickly be followed by others, and certainly more quickly than it took land-based casino gaming to spread across most of the USA.

This does not mean that the arguments about online gaming in the USA do not continue. The Coalition to Stop Internet Gambling, led and backed by Sheldon Adelson, is calling for Congress to ban online gambling in its entirety, sighting it as a threat to US national security. He therefore places himself firmly in opposition to the position taken by the American Gaming Association. It is difficult to envisage his argument succeeding; the remainder of the US casino industry is backing and entering the online market. There is no reason to suppose that the US experience will be any different from that which pertains in Europe, namely, that online gambling creates a new and different market, that it does not therefore damage the casino industry, that further jobs and state revenue can be created, and that online gaming can not only be properly controlled and regulated, but that regulation is easier, given that every single transaction can be recorded for eternity.

Whilst in Europe there has been no fundamental change in online gambling similar to that seen in the USA, the UK has followed the trend set by other member states (Italy, France, Spain and Denmark) of moving to a point-of-consumption licensing regime, as explained in the UK chapter. This trend will continue, with the Netherlands and others coming on line during the coming year. Meanwhile, at the EU level, the European Commission's Action Plan, unveiled in November 2012, set up an expert group of European jurisdictions to forge cooperation between member states with coordinated measures and strategies. Further, in September 2013, the European Parliament adopted a report on online gambling in the internal market by an overwhelming majority and, in November 2013, the European Commission launched formal infringement proceedings against six member states – Belgium, Cyprus, the Czech Republic, Lithuania, Poland and Romania – and two reasoned opinions against Sweden for failing to comply with European law. These are the first series of decisions in relation to the outstanding complaints and infringement cases against more than 20 member states. The European Commission has closed some of the complaints in relation to member states; however, cases again France, Germany, Greece, Hungary and the Netherlands remain open. Whilst a European online gambling licence is likely to remain no more than a dream for years to come, this is a step in the right direction.

It remains a pressing question on both sides of the Atlantic the extent to which the commercial viability of regulated online gambling can be achieved by cooperation between states and between regulators. This has to go much further than the exchange of information, and progress has been made with the multi-jurisdictional business form for applications, which was developed by the International Association of Gaming Regulators. The form seeks to standardise the general information, track record and compliance records that businesses are required to provide to regulators as part of their application for a licence. The aim is to reduce the burden on those that may apply to multiple jurisdictions as the form will be portable. The UK will be the first state to use this approach. There remains the need for much greater cooperation, not least in relation to pooling of liquidity, where the first tentative steps are being taken by forward-looking jurisdictions, such as Alderney and Denmark. The experience of US states, where poker is the only or main permitted product, is very likely to force the pace. Those with small populations will need to address this issue if their nascent online industry is to survive, let alone prosper.

These developments and others are addressed in this second edition. Once again, my partner, John Hagan, and I have been ably assisted by two of our regulatory specialist solicitors, Melanie Ellis and Bahar Alaeddini, in developing a standard format that can be applied to all of the international jurisdictions covered in this book, in order to aid comparison of particular subjects across jurisdictions.

For the second edition, some new and important jurisdictions have been added, including Alderney, which was an unfortunate and glaring omission from the first edition. This chapter has been contributed by my firm, though I would like to thank Andre Wilsenach, Executive Director, and Philip Taylor, In-house Counsel at the Alderney Gambling Control Commission, for their helpful review and editing.

I am grateful, as ever, for the enormous support we have received throughout from all those at Thomson Reuters, but particularly Emily Kyriacou, Kate Burrington, Nicola Pender and Chris Myers, and of course to our fellow specialist contributors from each jurisdiction, all of whom have worked hard to meet our demanding requirements and tight deadlines.

As before, this book is not intended to be a detailed textbook guide to the often complex licensing regime relating to gaming. Instead, and I hope more realistically, our aim has been to provide a useful broad guide to the legal and regulatory framework for gaming and a comparison of the varied approaches to this fascinating area of law between jurisdictions throughout the world. In drawing on the knowledge and expertise of the principal gaming lawyers from each jurisdiction, readers also have a useful directory of firms in important jurisdictions, all of whom will I know be willing to provide further guidance where necessary.

Julian Harris, Partner
June 2014

Introduction

Philip Graf, Chairman, Gambling Commission, Great Britain

Even in the twenty-first century, different societies and cultures take different views on gambling and the balance to be struck in terms of protecting individuals – from prohibition to one of *caveat emptor* and the right of adults to decide how dangerously to live. There are differences, too, in how societies handle market forces and any failures or adverse external impacts, such as problem gambling or money laundering. Some societies adopt a 'polluter pays' approach, and expect the industry to fund both regulation and the costs of preventing or treating problem gambling, as we do in Great Britain. Some use tax to compensate or mitigate effects, as do France and Norway. Some use controls or restrictions and others try prohibition – although it is fair to say that prohibition is very much on the retreat in a world of internet and smart phone access.

Some see competition as a powerful force to help the consumer – resulting in lower prices and helping to foster innovation. Others fear competition as a pressure on operators to cut corners and consider that limiting market access, whether to state monopolies or to a limited number of well-established companies, is the way to ensure responsible gambling. Protection of domestic suppliers may also play a part. Whatever the approach, regulation is a trade-off between the perceived costs and benefits, and it inevitably has a cost that eventually falls on the consumer and/or the tax payer as well as shareholders.

Broadly speaking, regulatory policy across the world has moved from seeing gambling as a sin which had to be prohibited, through accepting it as vice that needed to be controlled and to some extent exploited for the employment and revenue it could generate, to – in some countries, but by no means all – seeing gambling as a legitimate but risky leisure activity for adults. However, even in countries with a long tradition of sports betting and casino gaming, such as Great Britain, there is considerable ambivalence about whether gambling can in fact be provided safely and unease about the possible implications of technological innovation and widespread availability of high stake/high reward gambling – whether in a casino or at a bookmaker's, on the pc at home or in your pocket in the form of a smart phone, or on easily accessible gambling machines on the high street.

The exact nature of gambling law and regulation in any jurisdiction reflects its own specific cultural and political history, and the balance currently struck between that state's interest in the commercial and fiscal contribution of the industry, its concern to protect those who might come to harm and how far it considers that it should abrogate individuals' right to risk harm in the pursuit of entertainment. This second edition of *Gaming*

Law details the similarities and differences in the ways jurisdictions have struck the balance, while the changes since the last edition indicate that the combination of financial pressures, technological development and the increasingly international nature of commerce and media is leading gambling provision in different countries to converge. There is increasing recognition that the internet and the development of high-speed broadband and smart phones and tablets fundamentally change the context in which jurisdictions approach gambling regulation. Across the world, jurisdictions are responding to these challenges by moves towards legalising and regulating remote gambling (ie via the internet), but the way in which this is done varies hugely from place to place – as does the speed of change.

The European Commission has been active in encouraging collaboration between regulators in Europe, but harmonisation appears some way off. While there is consensus on many practical aspects of regulation, member states are not yet close enough in terms of their social, economic and fiscal objectives in relation to gambling for mutual recognition of regulatory regimes or agreement on tax rates. Countries in Europe, and now in the United States and elsewhere, are adopting domestic licensing or point-of-consumption regimes that enable the jurisdiction to provide a consistent approach to consumer protection within its boundaries and to tax the revenues generated by its consumers. While this undoubtedly imposes additional costs on the multinational operator obliged to seek licences in each jurisdiction, it enables the domestic regulator to support and enforce consistent high standards from its licensees – and to do so with less risk of those standards being undermined by rival attractions of other jurisdictions with less stringent fiscal or regulatory demands.

Great Britain's own very recent conversion to domestic licensing is already adding to the pressure on those software operators who have supplied software or operating platforms to those competing with licensed operators to choose whether to supply the legal or illegal market. Similarly, the requirement for B2B operators to obtain a Commission licence if they wish to continue to provide facilities for gambling to those in Britain, for example by providing a poker platform, is helping to reinforce player protection measures. Domestic licensing provides the access and relationship needed if regulators and law enforcement bodies in different jurisdictions are to be able to collaborate in detecting suspicious activities and maintaining and developing good player protection measures. Ironically, the move to domestic licensing by helping enforce national licensing regimes and making undercutting by less responsible competitors more difficult may provide some additional impetus to efforts to agree international standards for responsible gambling and for combating money laundering and sports betting corruption.

Alongside the trend to a more liberal approach to gambling provision and the growing acceptance that the criminal and societal risks from remote gambling are better tackled by control and regulation than by prohibition, there is also a move away from the highly prescriptive, heavily policed regulatory framework put in place decades ago to drive organised crime out of gambling. Some countries with a developed consumer protection and financial services infrastructure are moving towards a more principles and risk-based regulatory structure that focuses regulation and the associated compliance and enforcement effort on those higher impact issues and operators potentially posing the greatest potential threat to the public interest. By using the general legal framework for law enforcement and consumer protections so far as possible and making the gambling-specific regulatory regime one that minimises regulatory burdens so far as is consistent with the need to keep gambling fair and safe, responsible operators can be given more scope to develop and market their products; this, in turn, leaves much less opportunity for illegal competitors to gain market share.

In Great Britain the reforming gambling legislation of 2005 and 2014 (the Gambling Act 2005 and the Gambling (Advertising and Licensing) Act 2014, respectively) assumed what came to be called the Hampton principles of good regulation: proportionality, accountability, consistency, transparency and targeting. These principles were established as the basic tests of whether any regulation is fit for purpose in the UK following a review by Sir Philip Hampton in 2005 on how to reduce unnecessary administration in business without compromising the UK's regulatory regime. In applying these principles to gambling, the Gambling Commission seeks to work with the gambling industry and other stakeholders in a partnership in which the Commission, on behalf of the public, sets the standards that operators should secure in terms of public protection, but so far as possible leaves it for the operator to decide how best to achieve those standards.

Operators are better placed than regulators both to identify current and emerging risks to the safe and crime-free provision of gambling and to work out the most effective ways to mitigate those risks. For this reason, we license both operators and key individuals within an organisation. It is people that make policies and processes work effectively. We hold those key individuals personally accountable for what their organisation does and who they employ to do it – not just or even primarily the compliance director – and we expect boards to put responsible gambling policies, whether keeping crime out or protecting players, at the heart of their commercial and strategic decision making, and make them key to the acceptability and long-term sustainability of their business.

However, in Britain, as in most jurisdictions, much of the current regulatory framework contains hard-wired, highly prescriptive provisions which severely constrain innovation, eg controlling electronic gaming machines or data provision. Such controls tend to focus operators' attention more on tick box legal compliance and pushing regulatory boundaries than on developing more responsible gambling provision. Further, the greater visibility of gambling that comes with liberalisation and treating it as a normal leisure activity has led to renewed concern in Britain, and in a number of other countries, about the potential risks from gambling and its longer term impact on society, and to concomitant calls for tighter regulation. Such calls reflect widespread concern at the potential harm players can come to on the higher stake/higher prize machines, especially if easily accessible, despite the little evidence so far of any increase in harm from gambling. The regulatory requirements on gaming machines, deriving as they typically do from experience in the mid- to late twentieth century, contrast with the approach usually adopted to regulating remote gambling offering similar virtual gaming products. The result is a continuing tension between the remote and non-remote regulatory framework in most countries. However, the technological developments that are putting pressure on traditional bricks and mortar regulation also offer opportunities for more effective risk mitigation across the board. The complete audit trail available in remote gambling and the increasing power of data analytics enable law enforcement, regulators and operators to develop more effective ways of combating money laundering and sports betting corruption and better ways of reducing gambling-related harm.

With some notable exceptions, the industry has been slow to develop their capacity to use the data and computing power now available to them except for narrow commercial purposes. Growing revenues from an industry apparently focused on profits, no matter whether from recreational or problem gamblers, reinforces both public scepticism about the gambling industry and government nervousness about replacing controls aimed at nineteenth- and twentieth-century problems with those more suited to a digital, mobile twenty-first-century world.

We are now challenging the whole industry – both land-based and remote operators – through their boards to consider player protection on a par with commercial development. I see other regulators making the same challenge. Amongst other things, this means utilising the same tools and analytical approach that operators use to manage commercial opportunities and risks, to understand the risk to players or, in some cases, to understand the money laundering risk. This will help identify which players are more likely to be engaged in harmful gambling behaviour and help find ways of targeting player protection and assistance measures. If operators actively develop and market such player protection and crime prevention measures, regulators can then support the measures by incorporating them into regulatory expectations and help by fostering pan-industry collaboration on research and the development of best practice.

If the industry can demonstrate to opinion formers and to a sceptical and sometimes antagonistic public that innovation is being used to improve player protection and combat crime and not to exploit the consumer, then further editions of this volume should show regulation moving towards a more player-focused and data-driven approach reflecting the technological world we live in, less hamstrung by regulations tackling the last century's problems.

Alderney

Harris Hagan Julian Harris & John Hagan

1. OBJECTIVES AND STRUCTURE OF LEGISLATION

Alderney is part of the Bailiwick of Guernsey, comprising the three main islands of Guernsey, Alderney and Sark. The bailiwick is a self-governing dependency of the British Crown, but is effectively independent of the UK and EU. The government of Alderney is administered by the states of Alderney. Since 1948, the states of Guernsey have exercised financial and administrative responsibility for certain public services in Alderney. Alderney is not within the EU or the EEA.

In 1999, a general gambling law, the Gambling (Alderney) Law 1999 (the 1999 Law), was approved authorising the regulation of gambling through future ordinances. Section 1 of the 1999 Law established the Alderney Gambling Control Commission (the AGCC) and section 5 provided that all forms of gambling are unlawful except as provided by the provisions of any other legislation. The lawfulness of online gambling was established by various ordinances, including the Gambling (Interactive Gaming) (Alderney) Ordinance 2001, which implemented and permitted applications to be made to the AGCC for remote licences, and the Alderney eGambling Ordinance 2006 (superseded by the Alderney eGambling Ordinance 2009).

Initially, Alderney planned to regulate telephone betting; however, in 2001 it moved into the regulation of online gambling, commonly referred to by the AGCC as 'eGambling'. Alderney was amongst the first non-EEA jurisdictions to be whitelisted by the UK, following the implementation of section 331(4) of the Gambling Act 2005 on 1 September 2007. In practical terms, this meant that Alderney and other whitelisted jurisdictions were considered to have regulatory regimes of a sufficient standard to allow its operators to advertise and provide gambling services into the UK market without obtaining a UK operating licence. However, this is subject to imminent change following implementation of the UK Gambling (Licensing and Advertising) Act 2014. Please see 3.5 for a recent update in relation to Alderney's whitelisted status.

In an attempt to future-proof the regulatory landscape in Alderney and respond to technical innovation, the legislation was overhauled by the government in 2009. Some of the main advantages of operating in Alderney include:

- a technologically advanced and forward-thinking regime with two types of licences – a 'category one' or B2C licence, for an operator which uses either its own or someone else's platform and has the direct contractual relationship with the customer, and a 'category two' or B2B licence, for

an operator which manages the platform and any games approved to
run on that platform;
- seamless transfer of players to Alderney;
- multiple licensing;
- no gambling taxes;
- no corporation tax;
- no VAT;
- low income tax rates; and
- competitive and advanced data centres and networks.

The AGCC's key objective is to provide a regulatory environment which
offers robust, enlightened, active regulation while also being responsive
to the needs of a changing industry. In this way, the AGCC aims to
protect players, to ensure the continuing high reputation of Alderney as
a jurisdiction and to establish a regulatory environment which attracts
operators who seek a comprehensive and tightly controlled regime.

In February 2012, the AGCC celebrated its 100th licence and is now
widely regarded as a leading jurisdiction for the regulation of online
gambling.

The AGCC has good relationships with other regulators and has
been working hard to secure agreements with emerging European and
international licensing jurisdictions, particularly as a result of the rise in
licensing from a point of consumption perspective. Alderney's aim is to
house and regulate gambling servers for B2B operators, who will work with
B2C licensees (or obtain their own B2C licences) in target jurisdictions. In
May 2010, the AGCC signed a memorandum of understanding (MoU) with
the Kahnawake Gaming Commission to exchange information relating to
past, present and prospective licensees for the purpose of ensuring effective
regulation between both jurisdictions. Similar MoUs were signed with
Antigua and Barbuda (February 2010), the Nevada Gaming Control Board
(January 2011), the Danish Gambling Authority (June 2011), the Alcohol
and Gaming Commission of Ontario (January 2012), the Casino Regulatory
Authority of Singapore (October 2012), the British Gambling Commission
(February 2013) and the Maltese Lotteries and Gaming Authority (October
2013). In February 2014, the AGCC entered into an MoU with the
International Olympic Committee ahead of the Winter Olympics and
entered into an MoU with Fédération Internationale de Football Association
(FIFA) to protect the integrity of betting on football. The AGCC also entered
into an MoU with the European Sports Security Association (ESSA) in
December, 2011.

Furthermore, Alderney has been in the vanguard of jurisdictions
exploring the possibility of establishing pooling of liquidity across borders.
We anticipate early announcements here with both European and possibly
US jurisdictions. This is achievable, given the reputation of Alderney
as a jurisdiction trusted by other jurisdictions, and would enhance its
attractiveness to operators.

2. FRAMEWORK OF LEGISLATION

The most important pieces of Alderney eGambling legislation consist of:
*   the 1999 Law;
*   the Alderney eGambling Ordinance 2009 (the 2009 Ordinance); and
*   the Alderney eGambling Regulations 2009 (the 2009 Regulations).

In addition, there are two pieces of Guernsey legislation which affect Alderney eGambling licensees. These are:
*   the Alderney eGambling (Operations in Guernsey) Ordinance, 2006; and
*   the Alderney eGambling (Operations in Guernsey) (Amendment) Ordinance, 2010.

These permit the holders of Category 1 and Category 2 eGambling licences to locate their servers in data centres located on the island of Guernsey. This enables those licensees to benefit from the greater connectivity available on Guernsey.

2.1 What is the legal definition of gambling and what falls within this definition?

Section 20 of the Gambling (Alderney) Law 1999 provides the definitions of key concepts.
*   '"Gambling" is defined as all forms of betting, gaming and wagering and any lottery.
*   "Gaming" means the playing of a game of chance for winnings in money or money's worth, whether any person playing the game is at risk of losing any money or money's worth or not, but does not include the making of bets by way of pool betting.
*   "Game of chance" includes a game of chance and skill combined and a pretended game of chance or of chance and skill combined, but does not include any athletic game or sport.
*   "Lawful gambling" means any form of gambling made lawful under section 6 of the 1999 Law.
*   "Pool betting" means bets made by a number of persons:
    (a) on terms that the winnings of such of those persons as are winners shall be, or be a share of, or be determined by reference to, the stake money paid or agreed to be paid by those persons, whether the bets are made by means of a totalisator, or by filling up and returning coupons or other printed or written forms, or in any other way; or
    (b) on terms that the winnings of such of those persons as are winners shall be, or shall include, an amount (not determined by reference to the stake money paid or agreed to be paid by those persons) which is divisible in any proportions among such of those persons as are winners; or
    (c) on the basis that the winners or their winnings shall, to any extent, be at the discretion of the promoter or some other person.
*   "Winnings" includes winnings of any kind.'

2.2 What is the legal definition of online gambling and what falls within this definition?

Section 30(1) of the Alderney eGambling Ordinance 2009 defines 'eGambling' as gambling where the gambling transaction with an eGambling licensee or Category 2 associate certificate holder is effected remotely by a customer by means of a telecommunication device. A Category 2 associate certificate is for B2B activities, where the operator is the foreign-based equivalent of a Category 2 eGambling licensee and based outside Alderney.

Section 1 of the Alderney eGambling Ordinance 2009 provides that online gambling is not unlawful where:

- the transaction is not effected by, with or through a young person;
- the transaction is organised or promoted by or with the holder of a Category 1 eGambling licence; and
- the transaction is effected by or with the holder of a Category 2 eGambling licence or a Category 2 associate certificate holder (formerly known as a 'foreign gambling associate certificate').

A young person is defined in section 20 of the 1999 Law as a person who has not attained the age of eighteen.

2.3 Please set out the different gambling products identified by legislation.

Licensees in Alderney are able to offer multiple products with one eGambling licence from the AGCC. This includes bingo, casino and betting products.

2.4 Please list the different requirements for each gambling product, including legal classifications for each; for example, is poker a game of skill or game of chance?

The AGCC publishes guidelines for the preparation of an internal control system which set out the regulatory and technical requirements in respect of each type of game. These can be found on the AGCC's website.

2.5 Explain the system of regulation of gambling; which regulatory or governmental body is responsible for the supervision of gambling? Which body issues licences? Which body examines enforcement powers? Is there any limit on the number or duration of available licences?

The AGCC is the regulatory authority tasked with ensuring and maintaining the integrity of the online gambling industry in Alderney. Its objectives are to protect the reputation of Alderney as a first tier eGambling jurisdiction by seeking to ensure that:

- all electronic gambling on Alderney is conducted honestly and fairly;
- the funding, management and operation of electronic gambling on Alderney remains free from criminal influence; and
- electronic gambling is regulated and monitored so as to protect the interests of licensees' customers as well as the young and vulnerable.

Further, section 2 of the 1999 Law provides that the duties of the AGCC include:

- granting such licences as may be necessary to a person applying to provide and operate any form of gambling;
- supervising and controlling, including by way of inspection and the imposition of conditions, the conduct and operation of any form of gambling so licensed;
- investigating the character and financial status of any person applying for, or holding, a licence in Alderney;
- ensuring that all fees, royalties and other monies payable to the states by a person providing or operating any form of gambling are duly paid and accounted for; and
- performing such other functions as are assigned to the AGCC by this law or by ordinances made thereunder.

The operational responsibilities of the AGCC are divided into two: (i) licensing activities; and (ii) compliance activities. Licensing involves the investigation of new applicants to determine they are fit and proper, as well as the maintenance of all required records regarding licensees and certificate holders. As part of stage 1 of the application process, the applicant and its key personnel are subject to probity checks. In relation to compliance, and as part of stage 2 of the application process, the AGCC will approve the licensee's gambling equipment, internal controls and operating procedures.

Licences and certificates are granted for an indefinite period. There is no limit to the number of licences which can be granted.

The AGCC specifies provisions and conditions that apply to different categories of licences and certificates. These are set out in the Alderney eGambling Regulations 2009. Part I, chapter II relates to the conditions attached to Category 1 eGambling licences, chapter III relates to Category 2 eGambling licences and chapter IV relates to temporary eGambling licences. Part II, chapter I relates to the conditions attached to the associates providing core services and chapter II relates to Category 2 eGambling licensees. Part III, chapter II relates to conditions attached to hosting certificates and part IV, chapter III relates to conditions attached to key individual certificates.

Section 13 of the 1999 Law sets out the offences and penalties. In addition to the criminal offences contained in the 1999 Law, the AGCC can bring regulatory proceedings where provisions of either the 2009 Ordinance or the 2009 Regulations have been breached. Section 12 of the 2009 Ordinance sets out the circumstances under which the AGCC may take action and what sanctions may be applied. The AGCC has a range of sanctions, including requiring the licensee or certificate holder to rectify the issue, issuing a formal caution, imposing a financial penalty, suspending the licence or certificate, or, if circumstances require, revoking a licence or withdrawing a certificate.

3. ONLINE GAMBLING

3.1 To what extent can online gambling be offered in your jurisdiction? Are licences available and, if so, for which gambling products? Please describe briefly the licensing process, who may apply, whether licences are limited in number and, if no licences are available, whether it is legal for online gambling to be offered. In the case of EU jurisdictions, please state whether there are any issues as to the legality of the local law at EU level. Please refer to any relevant cases at ECJ level and explain any measures taken or pending by the European Commission.

Licences

Licences and certificates are broadly divided by the scope of the activities that they cover, which are either B2C or B2B in nature.

The licences available in Alderney are:

- a Category 1 eGambling licence for B2C activities, where the operator organises and prepares the customer to gamble including, the contractual relationship, registration, verification and fund management;
- a Category 2 eGambling licence for B2B activities, where the operator is effecting gambling transactions located within an approved hosting centre in Alderney/Guernsey; and
- a temporary eGambling licence.

It is possible to obtain one or both Category 1 and Category 2 licences, depending on the business model. A Category 1 eGambling licensee could work in conjunction with a number of Category 2 eGambling licensees or Category 2 associate certificate holders, who would host games on their server and players would be sent to the Category 2 eGambling licensee or Category 2 associate certificate holder wherever situated.

A Category 1 licence holder could subsequently apply to also hold a Category 2 licence and vice versa. As investigations will have already been carried out, the timescale and cost of the application is likely to be reduced.

Both categories of licences can only be held by an Alderney registered company. However, the company no longer needs to be formed before the application is made to the AGCC, providing a commitment is given to form an Alderney registered company during the application process and before a licence is issued.

A temporary eGambling licence allows the licensee to conduct a gambling transaction under limited circumstances, including using the licence for no longer than 29 days continuously or for an aggregate of 59 total days of use within any six month period. Upon the 30th day of continuous use, or upon the 60th day of aggregated use within any six month period, the Commission will require the licensee to apply for a Category 1 eGambling licence and/or Category 2 eGambling licence within 42 days. A temporary licence would be applicable to an operator using Alderney servers for disaster recovery purposes.

Certificates

The certificates available in Alderney are:
- a Category 2 associate certificate for B2B activities, where the operator is the foreign-based equivalent of a Category 2 eGambling licensee and based outside Alderney;
- a core services provider associate certificate for a third party entity with which an eGambling licensee or Category 2 associate certificate holder contracts directly for the provision of gambling software, player fund deposit or company management.
- a hosting certificate for the accommodation of gambling equipment, which must be suitable, secure and meeting the AGCC's technical standards; and
- a key individual certificate.

In addition to partnering with a Category 2 eGambling licensee, Category 1 eGambling licensees can also work with a Category 2 associate certificate, formerly known as a foreign gambling associate certificate, for the purpose of that entity effecting gambling transactions with the customer.

A key individual is a person who is, or will be:
- someone who occupies or acts in a managerial position;
- someone who carries out managerial functions; or
- someone in a position to control or exercise significant influence over the operations.

Regulation 4(a) of the 2009 Regulations sets out the general conditions applicable to a Category 1 eGambling licence and how compliance with section 1(3) of the 2009 Ordinance can be met.

As of 31 December 2013, there were 52 registered licensees, consisting of 38 holders of Category 1 licences and 37 holders of Category 2 licences, of whom 22 were holders of both Category 1 and Category 2 licences. In addition, there were 11 Category 2 associate certificates in issue. There were also 34 core services associate certificates in issue, nine hosting certificates and one temporary eGambling licence.

Licensing process

The Alderney application and approval process can be divided into three parts: suitability, fair games and adequate processes. These processes can be run in parallel or in series. The AGCC states that live activation is routinely achievable within six months of initial application. This is, of course, dependent on the speed at which the applicant progresses through the process.

Unless by special agreement with the AGCC, gambling servers must be located within Alderney or Guernsey at hosting premises approved by the AGCC by way of a hosting certificate. Where hosting premises outside the Bailiwick of Guernsey are approved, the premises do not need to hold a hosting certificate. The AGCC will expect, at a minimum, that disaster recovery capability is sufficient to ensure protection of customer entitlements and audit ability up to the point of the disaster. Any disaster recovery plan may contemplate continuation of part or all of the business outside the Bailiwick of Guernsey in other licensed jurisdictions.

STAGE 1

1. submission of the corporate application form and supporting documents;
2. submission of the key individual certificate applications;
3. payment of an initial investigation deposit of £10,000; and
4. the formation of an Alderney registered company.

Following receipt of the application, the AGCC will arrange a meeting with the applicant to facilitate a better understanding of:

- the business plan and proposed eGambling operations;
- potential business and executive associates;
- the corporate entities involved in the application; and
- person who may need to submit applications for key individual certificates.

If the application is successful, a licence will be issued on payment of the relevant licence fee, and the licensee will proceed to 'stage 2'.

STAGE 2

AGCC approval of:

1. internal control system (ICS);
2. gambling equipment; and
3. capitalisation status.

1. ICS

The AGCC assesses a licensee's conformity with the law and regulation by assessing the correct application of procedures as set out in the licensee's ICS, which must be approved as part of the application process. The ICS, defined as *'a system of controls and administrative and accounting procedures used by an eGambling licensee for the conduct of eGambling'*, is a detailed document following the AGCC's prescribed sections covering:

Section 1: the corporate structure and staffing;
Section 2: accounting systems;
Section 3: customer registration, verification, banking and management;
Section 4: eGambling; and
Section 5: computer controls.

The ICS is designed to allow a licensee to describe how it proposes to mitigate the risks associated with its business, including protection of customer funds, disaster recovery and protection of customer funds. For more information, please see the AGCC's Technical Standards and Guidelines for Internet Gambling Systems:

http://www.gamblingcontrol.org/userfiles/file/ICSG%20Version%203_4_FINAL. pdf

Once an ICS is approved, the AGCC will expect the licensee to adhere to the provisions and controls it contains. Any changes to an approved ICS will require AGCC approval.

2. Gambling equipment

In relation to the gambling equipment, all equipment used to operate games must be located in approved premises in either Alderney or Guernsey. This essentially means that the game server, player databases and transaction databases must be in the jurisdiction. It is not necessary for any personnel or any back office functions to be located in Alderney or Guernsey.

Gambling transactions can only lawfully be effected at 'approved premises', which means premises controlled by the holder of a hosting certificate. It is usual for eGambling licence holders to use premises provided by hosting certificate holders such as Cable & Wireless Guernsey, Itex (Guernsey) Limited and BM IT Limited.

3. Capitalisation status

Licensees are required to hold capital, subject to a liquidity adjustment in respect of investment in fixed assets, equal to or exceeding the sum of qualifying overheads, arising using the formula below, using the relevant account groupings as they appear in reports specified in Schedule 18 and submitted pursuant to Regulation 242(2) of the 2009 Regulations:

Shareholders' funds minus an adjustment equal to the total of fixed assets must meet or exceed the quarterly reported value of net gaming yield minus operating profit, excluding the cost of affiliate fees (as approved by the Commission).

Once their licence has been granted, licensees will be required to submit monthly and quarterly financial and operational reports, which include information relating to player activity, suspicious transactions, significant player deposits or losses. Licensees are also required to have their financial accounts audited every year.

Within 12 months of live activation of the site, and annually thereafter, the AGCC will visit the main operational centre of the licensee to check that the relevant licence conditions are being upheld and that the approved games and internal control systems in use are those that have been previously approved. The AGCC's inspection will examine a broad range of the licensee's operations including: corporate structures, staffing and staff training; financial reporting; player registration, verification and associated banking procedures; anti money laundering/combating financing of terrorism procedures; game fairness and player protection; security policies and procedures; and operation of approved games and gambling equipment.

The annual licence fee will be payable on or before the anniversary of the grant of the licence.

Timing

The application process in Alderney generally takes approximately three to six months from receipt of the full application and fee.

Costs

There is no application fee, but investigation costs totalling around £5,000–10,000 are payable. Upon application, a deposit of £10,000 is made, from which these costs are drawn. The unused balance of these investigation costs is refunded to the applicant or licensee. Each key individual application will require an initial deposit of £1,000.

Deposits	eGambling licence	Core services, Category 2 eGambling certificate and hosting certificate
Initial deposit	£10,000	£5,000
Supplementary deposit	£5,000	£5,000
Modification fee	£100	£100
Approval of ICS	£10,000	
Changes to ICS	£5,000	
Approval of gambling equipment	£5,000	
Inspections of operations	£7,500	
Special investigations	£5,000 (£2,000 supplementary deposit, if required)	

Annual licensing fees in Alderney range from £35,000 to £140,000 per year, depending on the gross gambling yield (GGY), as set out in the table below.

Licence or Certificate	Description	Fee
Category 1 eGambling licence	For a new licensee in Alderney, for its first year	£35,000
Category 1 eGambling licence (Band A)	After the first year of operation where GGY less than £1 million	£35,000
Category 1 eGambling licence (Band B)	After the first year of operation where GGY equals or exceeds £1 million but is less than £5 million	£70,000
Category 1 eGambling licence (Band C)	After the first year of operation where GGY equals or exceeds £5 million but is less than £7.5 million	£100,000
Category 1 eGambling licence (Band D)	After the first year of operation where GGY equals or exceeds £7.5 million	£140,000
Category 2 eGambling licence	Annual fee (fixed)	£35,000
Category 2 associate certificate	Annual fee (fixed)	£35,000

Core services associate certificate	Annual fee (fixed)	£10,000
Temporary eGambling licence	Annual fee (fixed)	£10,000

3.2 Is there a distinction between the law applicable to B2B operations and that applicable to B2C operations?

There is a distinction between B2C and B2B operators. Regulation 3 of the Alderney eGambling Regulations 2009 provides that *'a Category 1 eGambling licence permits a Category 1 eGambling licensee to contract with customers to organise and prepare the customer to gamble … [including] entering into an agreement with the customer, registration and verification of the customer, engaging in financial transactions with the customer and the management of the customer's funds, offering or promoting gambling to the customer and such other actions that the Commission determines to be activities that may only be carried out by a Category 1 eGambling licensee'.*

Regulation 5 of the Alderney eGambling Regulations 2009 provides that *'a Category 2 eGambling licence permits a Category 2 eGambling licensee to effect gambling transactions … [including] striking a bet, housing and recording the random element or gambling transaction outcome, operating a system of hardware and software upon which the gambling transaction is conducted and for the avoidance of doubt, "effecting a gambling transaction" does not include engaging in a financial transaction with the custom'.*

Section 3.1 above contains further information in relation to B2C and B2B activities in Alderney.

3.3 What are the consequences for B2C or B2B operators who are active in your jurisdiction without having obtained or applied for the required permits, licences and approvals? What penalties and enforcement powers are available in respect of the illegal operators? Please outline any significant domestic decisions or enforcement actions that have been taken by the relevant authorities in recent years.

Section 13 of the 1999 Law, as amended by the Gambling (Amendment) (Alderney) Law 2001, provides that any breach will in the case of a first offence be subject to a maximum fine of £25,000, up to six months' imprisonment, or both. In the case of a second or subsequent offence, the maximum penalties are a maximum fine of £50,000, two years' imprisonment, or both.

Section 12 of the Alderney eGambling Ordinance 2009 provides that the AGCC may take regulatory action where:

- an eGambling licensee or a certificate holder is no longer a fit and proper person;
- an associate of an eGambling licensee or a certificate holder is not, or is no longer, a fit and proper person to be associated with the operations of the licensee or certificate holder;

- an eGambling licensee or a certificate holder has contravened a provision of the gambling legislation, or a condition attached to the eGambling licence or certificate in question; or
- a temporary eGambling licensee is no longer licensed or properly licensed in another jurisdiction to conduct eGambling operations.
Sanctions available to the AGCC include:
- issuing a direction to rectify;
- issuing a written caution;
- imposing a financial penalty of up to £25,000, which can be suspended; and/or
- suspend the licence or certificate; or
- revoke the licence or certificate.

Before a 'direction to rectify' is made, the AGCC can also issue a 'proposal to rectify'. In practical terms, this is an opportunity to rectify the regulatory breach within a specified period without the need for a regulatory hearing. A direction to rectify can also be issued without holding a regulatory hearing.

The most notable regulatory action taken by the AGCC was in 2011 in relation to Full Tilt Poker, which was operated by four Alderney licensees. On 15 April 2011, a date now known in the industry as 'Black Friday', authorities in New York announced an indictment naming 11 individuals, including two connected to Full Tilt Poker, relating to illegal gambling, bank fraud and money laundering. On the same day, the Full Tilt Poker domain was seized by the US Department of Justice (DoJ) and various bank accounts relating to Full Tilt Poker companies were restrained. The DoJ accused the Alderney licensees of defrauding online poker players out of $440m (£289 million) and giving misleading statements about the extent of its funds.

Three of the four licences were revoked with the fourth (non-operational licence) remaining suspended and, in addition to an internal review that was conducted by the AGCC, an independent review of the AGCC's actions was conducted in 2012 by Peter Dean, a former chairman of the UK Gambling Commission, to identify possible improvements. Whilst the review highlighted that the AGCC fulfilled its statutory obligations and that its actions were appropriate, timely and fair, it also highlighted lessons to be learnt in relation to player protection, procedure for regulatory hearings, relations with licensees and resources. Measures subsequently implemented are set out in section 3.5 below.

In February 2014, the AGCC withdrew the Category 2 associate certificate belonging to Bubble Group BV following a regulatory hearing.

3.4 What technical measures are in place (if any) to protect consumers from unlicensed operators, such as ISP blocking and payment blocking?

ISP blocking and payment blocking measures are not currently in place.

3.5 Has the legal status of online gambling changed significantly in recent years and, if so, how?

On 25 July 2012, following publication of the Alderney eGambling (Amendment) Regulations 2012 (the 2012 Regulations) and following recommendation made by Peter Dean during his review following the Full Tilt Poker case referred to at 3.3 above, the AGCC introduced a requirement for licensees to adhere to revised financial ratios in order to provide assurance of the financial health of the remote gambling operations. This equates to maintaining a sum equivalent to three months' operating costs (see above for the calculation). In addition, the 2012 Regulations require Category 1 eGambling licensees (and their associates holding customer funds) to hold funds standing to the credit of registered customers in accounts that are segregated from those used to operate the business of the licensee. The segregation requirement can be waived only where a written guarantee has been provided which is considered adequate by the AGCC. A Category 1 licensee must also inform registered customers of the risks associated with their funds in the event of its (or its relevant associates') insolvency.

A further significant change relates to Alderney's whitelisted status under the UK Gambling Act 2005. Following the implementation of the *Gambling (Licensing and Advertising) Act 2014, which introduced a point of consumption regime in the UK, Alderney licensees will no longer be able to transact with customers in Great Britain without holding a licence from the UK Gambling Commission. This, in effect, abolishes the whitelist system. However, Alderney licensees will be eligible for transitional rights.* The UK Gambling Commission has indicated that existing Alderney licensees will be able to retain their servers in Alderney and obtain a UK licence.

3.6 Whilst acknowledging the inherent difficulty in predicting developments in gambling law, what are the likely developments in online gambling in your jurisdiction, both short term and long term? Are any specific amendments under consideration? Have there been any recent political developments, or do you envisage any in the near future? Are any specific amendments under consideration? Are they likely to be adopted and, if so, what is the time scale?

The AGCC is currently embarking on a programme of legislative change which aims to set out effective information sharing gateways with other competent authorities, make changes necessary to deal with issues arising from the British Gambling (Advertising and Licensing) Bill and make amendments necessary for AML/CFT best practice, and will implement the revised hearing process suggested by Peter Dean in his review of Full Tilt Poker.

3.7 Is the law the same in relation to mobile gambling and interactive gambling on television? If not, are there any headline differences?

The legislation is also applicable to mobile gambling and interactive gambling on television.

4. LAND-BASED GAMING
4.1 Please describe the licensing regime (if any) for land-based gaming, and what products are included. Please set out what licences are available, and the licensing regime for them.
Alderney has legislation to regulate land-based gambling in the form of the Gambling (Bookmakers) (Alderney) Ordinance, 2002. Until January 2014, Alderney had one land-based bookmaker. He has now retired.

4.2 Please set out any particular limitations or requirements for (eg. casino) operators, such as a ban on local residents gambling.
N/A.

4.3 Please address the questions in 3.5 above, but in relation to land-based gaming.
N/A.

5. TAX
5.1 Please summarise briefly the tax regime applicable to both land-based and online gaming.
There is no corporate tax, gambling duty or VAT in Alderney. Income tax is at 20%, with a maximum charge of £200,000 per year on Guernsey-sourced income and a maximum charge of £110,000 on non-Guernsey income. More than 90 days in Guernsey will establish residency and 180 days will establish sole or principal residency.

The corporate tax regime for Guernsey and Alderney companies has been approved by the EU. Under this regime ('zero-10'), companies with non-resident shareholders are not liable for any corporate tax, so the effective rate for a foreign-owned company is 0 per cent. In order to benefit from the 0% corporate tax regime, a licensee must demonstrate that (i) it is resident in and managed and controlled from the bailiwick; and (ii) its main permanent establishment that generates all or the majority of group profits is in the bailiwick.

6. ADVERTISING
6.1 To what extent is the advertising of gambling permitted in your jurisdiction? Again, this should cover both land-based and online gaming. To the extent that advertising is permitted, how is it regulated?
Regulation 4(c) of the Alderney eGambling Regulations 2009 provides that any advertising carried out by, or conducted on behalf of, a Category 1 eGambling licensee must:
- be truthful;
- not be distasteful;
- not promote gambling by, with or through persons under the age of 18 years, and this factor must be taken into account when determining media selection and placement of the advertising;

- not encourage people to engage in excessive participation in eGambling that would be socially irresponsible or could result in harm to them or others;
- not imply or convey any message that a person's status, general abilities or social success can be attributable to gambling;
- not challenge or dare people to participate in eGambling;
- not, having regard to the expected returns to customers through eGambling, promote or suggest any unrealistic expectation of winning;
- not bring into disrepute the Island of Alderney, the AGCC or, in any broader context, the Bailiwick of Guernsey; and
- comply with any requirements relating to the content or nature of advertising imposed in the jurisdiction covering the target market for that advertising.

Similar provisions apply to temporary eGambling licensees (Regulation 8(1)(c)). In addition, Category 2 eGambling licensees and Category 2 associate certificate holders are bound by the same conditions, notwithstanding they are unlikely to come under direct advertising (Regulations 6(c) and 60(b), respectively).

7. SOCIAL GAMING

7.1 We believe this to be a growing area. Please decide under what criteria social gaming is permitted in your jurisdiction. If games are free to play or if there is no prize, are they legal without a licence? Please address circumstances where virtual currency is used and can be won: ie currency which is of no monetary or other value, save for as credits to take part in games. The answer should address the question whether game credits or virtual money can be exchanged for other prizes. Is any change to regulation in the area proposed or envisaged?

Whilst the AGCC has noted regulatory interest in social gaming, it has not issued any formal guidance in relation to the issue.

Australia

Addisons Jamie Nettleton, Justine Munsie & Jessica Azzi

Gambling was substantially liberalised in most Australian states and territories in the 1990s. Subsequent years saw not only a surge in gambling expenditure and industry growth, but also adverse impacts on many Australians and their families. The resulting backlash within the community led to the first independent national public inquiry into the gambling sector which was conducted by the Productivity Commission in 1999.

Since then, there have been significant changes in the gambling industry and the regulatory environment, with a greater policy focus on community awareness and harm minimisation.

1. OBJECTIVES AND STRUCTURE OF LEGISLATION

Australia is a federation. Legislative power is divided between the federal government (with jurisdiction over the entirety of Australia) and eight principal state and territory governments (with jurisdiction over discrete geographical areas of Australia).

Traditionally, gambling legislation had been the exclusive preserve of state and territory governments both before Federation in 1901, and subsequently, mainly because the Commonwealth constitution does not give the Commonwealth power expressly to regulate gambling. The long history of gambling in Australia resulted in each state and territory developing a unique regulatory regime reflecting local legislative, economic and social policy which has varied over time.

In 2001, the federal government enacted the first federal law specifically focused on the gambling sector, the Interactive Gambling Act 2001 (Cth) (the IGA), which relates to interactive gambling. In 2012, the federal government passed legislation (known as the National Gambling Reform Laws) that put in place measures to reduce the harm from poker machines. These measures included restrictions in respect of withdrawals from ATMs at gaming venues and the requirement to put in place for slot machines (known in Australia as poker machines or EGMs) procedures for mandatory pre-commitment. However, in March 2014, the recently elected federal government repealed the National Gambling Reform Laws. In place of these laws, the federal government introduced the Gambling Measures Act 2012 (Cth), which sets out the federal government's commitment to work with states/territories to achieve a voluntary pre-commitment scheme.

Accordingly, when considering Australia's gambling laws, regard must be had first to federal law (which prevails to the extent of any inconsistency with state or territory legislation) before turning to state and territory law. Given the breadth of the regulatory roles of government generally and the number of governments and agencies involved, the Australian policy environment relating to gambling is highly complex.

At the federal level, the IGA prohibits operators from providing prohibited interactive gambling services to persons in Australia and in certain designated countries. (No other countries have been designated yet.) Aside from the IGA and the Gambling Measures Act, there is no legislation at federal level which regulates gambling.

State gambling law remains of relevance in determining how gambling is regulated in Australia. This is illustrated well in respect of online gambling. The fact that an activity is not prohibited under the IGA does not mean it is permitted necessarily in each state and territory. Indeed, state/territory laws apply to gambling activities, both online and offline, with different effects.

For example, in New South Wales, the Unlawful Gambling Act 1998 (NSW) (the NSW UGA) is relevant. While the NSW UGA is not drafted specifically with reference to the internet, the position of the New South Wales authorities is that the legislation applies to both online and offline activities. In Victoria, on the other hand, the Gambling Regulation Act 2003 (Vic) (the Vic GRA) is a very detailed (and lengthy) statute. It regulates many forms of gambling; for example, it contains provisions relating respectively to offline activities and to online activities.

The complexity of Australian gambling regulation is illustrated further by the existence of different regulatory models depending on the form of gambling involved: in almost every state and territory, there exists different regulatory regimes for casinos, slot machines, wagering/sports betting, lotteries and miscellaneous forms of gambling.

The bipartite regulatory regime exists due, in essence, to the fact that Australian policymakers took the view that online gaming represented a new type of gambling activity for which new legislation at the federal level had to be developed. In contrast, the regulation of online wagering and sports betting is considered an 'expansion' of the existing legal framework and, as a consequence, legislation regulating telephone and physical wagering and sports betting at the state/territory level has either been only slightly amended, or not amended at all. However, this model may be subject to change in the near future in light of growing recognition that a consistent approach nationally is required towards the regulation of the promotion of online wagering. This is a departure from the current regulatory regime in which online wagering is regulated generally by state and territory laws.

2. FRAMEWORK OF LEGISLATION
2.1 What is the legal definition of gambling and what falls within this definition?
Gambling in Australia encompasses the staking of money on uncertain events driven by chance (in whole or in part), with the potential to win a prize. (Gambling is differentiated from investment activity which is regulated separately (with limited overlap) on the premise that gamblers as a group will lose over time and that gambling is intended to be a recreational activity.)

Gambling comprises many categories, ranging from activities considered of lesser harm, such as lotteries (which covers scratch cards ('scratchies')) to wagering/sportsbetting, electronic slot machines ('pokies'), and casino games like roulette or blackjack. Each of these categories is regulated separately in most Australian states and territories.

2.2 What is the legal definition of online gambling and what falls within this definition?

Online gambling is defined in the IGA by reference to 'interactive gambling services' with those interactive gambling services directed to persons present in Australia being 'prohibited interactive gambling services' with various exceptions. An 'interactive gambling service' is defined in section 5 of the IGA and comprises any form of gambling service that is provided in an interactive manner. This includes services provided over the internet.

Gambling services include games of chance and games of mixed chance and skill. Excluded from the scope of prohibited interactive gambling services are:

- wagering services (except to the extent that they are in-play wagering services);
- lotteries (except to the extent that they are instantaneous); and
- services provided over the telephone.

The IGA operates concurrently with the relevant state and territory laws (on the basis that the IGA prevails to the extent of any inconsistency). This means that, if an internet gambling service is exempt under the IGA, it may still fall within a prohibition contained in a state or territory law. Conversely, the relevant service may be prohibited under the IGA even if licensed or authorised under a state or territory law. In particular, state and territory legislation continues to be of significance in relation to the regulation of gambling over the internet in the following ways:

- through the licensing of Australian-based interactive gambling providers; and
- through limitations concerning the manner in which permitted interactive gambling services can be provided or promoted to persons present in Australia. For example, there are a number of controls over the manner in which online wagering services can be provided and advertised, such as the restrictions under state and territory law on the provision and advertising of free bets or inducements to bet.

Gambling laws in all Australian states and territories have provisions prohibiting various forms of online gambling activity unless licensed.

2.3 Please set out the different gambling products identified by legislation.

Australian gambling laws differentiate, in general terms, between games of skill and games of mixed skill and chance (which includes games of chance).

Games of skill are regulated only to a limited extent. For example, skill-based games played for prizes must meet certain criteria when forming the basis of a trade promotion.

Games of mixed skill and chance played for a prize are regulated in all states and territories, except South Australia. Unless expressly permitted, the supply and promotion of those games, whether land-based or online, are prohibited unless provided by a licensed provider (where available). In South Australia, for a game to be prohibited, it must be a game entirely of chance.

To understand the manner in which these regulations apply, it is necessary to consider various categories of games.

Australian states and territories have enacted laws which contain specific legislation for the following products:
* wagering/sportsbetting;
* casino games (including poker);
* slot machines;
* lotteries;
* keno; and
* two-up.

The IGA differentiates between the following gambling products provided online:
* gaming, which includes casino games (for example, blackjack, baccarat, roulette), poker and electronic slot machines;
* wagering, which includes betting on racing, sports betting and betting on the outcome of events; and
* lotteries, including keno.

Online gaming products fall within the scope of prohibited interactive gambling services, while wagering services (except for in-play betting on non-racing events) and lotteries services (except for instantaneous games) are excluded from the scope of the prohibitions in the IGA.

2.4 Please list the different requirements for each gambling product, including legal classifications for each; for example, is poker a game of skill or game of chance?
Land-based gambling regulations
Poker
Whether poker is a game of mixed skill and chance has not yet been the subject of a determination of an Australian court. However, in *Police v Jones, Police v Ravesi* [2008] SAMC 62 it was found that participation by players in a Texas Hold'Em Poker tournament did not constitute unlawful gaming under the South Australian law, on the basis that poker is not wholly a game of chance. Although the outcome of this case was dependent on the specific wording of the South Australian statute (which prohibited games only to the extent that they are wholly of chance, a position different to other Australian states and territories, which prohibit games of mixed skill and chance), it is indicative of the view taken by most Australian authorities that poker should be treated differently from other games when considering whether unlawful gambling has taken place.

In most states, the authorities permit poker tournaments to be conducted in licensed venues subject to compliance with published guidelines.

In some Australian jurisdictions, poker is deemed unlawful (principally because it is considered to be a game that should only be organised by, and played in, the locally licensed casino).

Betting
Various prohibitions relating to betting exist in the legislation of all Australian states and territories. This legislation includes prohibitions relating to:
* the conduct of betting houses or betting places;
* betting in public places;
* the advertising of betting and betting places;
* the possession of instruments of betting;
* cheating in betting; and
* betting with and by minors.

The sole exception to these prohibitions exists where the relevant conduct is permitted expressly by relevant legislation, for example, where the relevant conduct falls within the scope of the rights conferred on a locally licensed party (eg the totalisator which, in most states/territories, has the exclusive right to conduct off-course betting) or on-course bookmakers.

Casino games
In all Australian states and territories, the conduct of casino operations and gaming in a casino must be conducted in accordance with applicable laws. Otherwise, casino gaming is prohibited.

Slot and other machine gaming
Given the repeal of the National Gambling Reform Laws, the regulation of slot machines remains exclusively the legislative preserve of Australian states and territories.

Except in Western Australia, each state and territory has legislation governing the supply and operation of slot machines in licensed venues (eg pubs and clubs).

There are major differences in policy parameters and technical specifications with each jurisdiction having its own regulatory arrangements justified by harm minimisation policies relevant to that jurisdiction.

There are also differences among the states and territories in the processes for obtaining approval for slot machines and the manner in which they must be made available for sale to, and supplied to, venues. Also, manufacturers are required to engage an approved testing facility to undertake independent verification of all software and systems.

Except in Western Australia, this regulatory framework comprises:
* licensing of suppliers of slot machines (and key personnel);
* approvals of slot machines;
* regulation of linked jackpots;
* licensing of venues and limits on gaming in those venues; and
* accounting and taxation requirements.

Moreover, all jurisdictions have some type of cap on gaming machine numbers and most of them have restrictions on the daily operations of slot machines in clubs and hotels, with required shutdown periods ranging from around 4 to 10 hours. The restrictions prescribe the times of day and/or the duration of the period, in which slot machines are either required to be shut down or permitted to operate. Casinos are exempt from these restrictions and, generally, are permitted to operate their gaming facilities 24 hours a day.

Victoria is the only jurisdiction to introduce a state-wide pre-commitment scheme. This scheme is set out in the Gambling Regulation Amendment (Pre-commitment) Act 2014 (Vic), which was enacted in February 2014 pursuant to the now-repealed National Gambling Reform Laws. The Victorian pre-commitment scheme will remain in effect irrespective of the repeal of the National Gambling Reform Laws.

Lottery

Legislation in all jurisdictions permits the conduct of prescribed types of lotteries by persons who fulfil the relevant licensing requirements. Most of the licences granted in any state or territory are exclusive. There are restrictions on the supply and promotion of lotteries by unlicensed providers.

Keno

In New South Wales, Queensland, Tasmania and Victoria, the conduct of the game of keno is regulated by statute.

Keno in New South Wales and Tasmania comes under the ambit of the public lotteries and gaming operators legislation respectively, whereas in Victoria keno is regulated by the general gambling legislation.

In Queensland, the licensing and authorisation of keno operators and the conduct of the game of keno is regulated by legislation which deals exclusively with keno.

There is no dedicated legislation permitting or regulating keno in the remaining jurisdictions. In the Australian Capital Territory, keno is declared to be an unlawful game and, in the Northern Territory, it is a scheduled prohibited game, but keno is allowed and regulated in those jurisdictions under the lotteries legislation, as 'keno' comes within the statutory definition of a 'lottery'. This is also the position in South Australia.

Online gambling regulation
Online wagering

According to section 8A(1) of the IGA, online wagering (eg, betting on a horse race, a greyhound race, a sporting event, an event or series of events) is not prohibited in Australia. However this exception only covers wagering that contemplates a bet being accepted online before an event has started. Services that provide for wagering after the event (but not racing events) has commenced (in-the-run betting) and services that provide for wagering on contingencies within an event (other than a race) (microbetting) are prohibited by section 8A(2) of the IGA.

Generally speaking, most Australian states and territories provide a licensing regime for wagering and sports betting operators. The licensed online wagering operators mostly fall into three principal categories:

- the exclusive totalisator licensee in each state and territory (which has been extended to permit that operator to provide fixed odds betting services); or
- corporate bookmakers licensed principally in either Northern Territory or Norfolk Island; or
- a betting exchange.

Online gaming
Casino games (blackjack, baccarat, roulette)
The IGA prohibits interactive gambling services (principally online casino games) being provided to people physically located in Australia. To the extent that online gaming falls outside the ambit of the IGA, state and territory legislation applies.

In most states and territories, there is a prohibition on conducting an unlawful game (which covers most casino games) unless conducted by and played in a casino.

Poker
At the federal level, the IGA does not refer expressly to poker.

While there are no express references to poker in the IGA, the view has been taken by the authorities that poker would be construed in a similar manner to blackjack, that is, as a game of mixed chance and skill. This view was confirmed in two determinations of the Australian Communications and Media Authority (ACMA) in 2011 relating to the broadcast of advertisements for free-play poker sites.

Accordingly, notwithstanding the existence of contrary arguments, there is a significant risk that the provision of a service which enables players present in Australia to participate in an online poker site amounts to the provision of a prohibited interactive gambling service in contravention of the IGA and certain state and territory laws.

For example, in July 2013, Apple removed a poker app (which allowed Australian residents to play online poker games with real money) from the Apple iTunes store. The Department of Broadband, Communications and the Digital Economy (now called the Department of Communications) (the Department), confirmed that Apple had removed the app after the Department raised concerns with Apple that the app was in breach of the IGA.

In its final report released on 12 March 2013 relating to its review of the IGA (Final Report), the Department recommended that the IGA be amended to provide for a trial for five years to allow the provision of online tournament poker services to Australian residents. However, on the same day, the federal government announced that it would not pursue the trial until national minimum standards for harm minimisation and consumer protections had been established. No further developments have occurred since (see section 3.5 below).

At the state/territory level, the legislation in some states/territories, such as NSW, expressly deems poker to be an unlawful game. It is likely that this legislation, even where it does not expressly contemplate online gaming, would be interpreted by the regulators to apply to both land-based and online poker.

Keno
The lottery services exception contained in section 5 of the IGA includes keno. However, the Explanatory Memorandum of the IGA states that the relevant minister has a reserve power to impose further conditions in connection with the lottery services exemption. To date, the Minister has not exercised this power and keno services are provided online by at least one licensed gambling operator.

Despite this, there is a risk that the Minister's discretion would be exercised if the relevant game were considered to be a highly repetitive or frequently drawn form of keno-type lottery or other form of lottery.

Bingo
The IGA prohibitions do not extend to certain 'excluded services', which include internet lotteries: section 5(3)(ae) of the IGA. An excluded lottery service does not include scratch lotteries or other instant lottery services provided online: section 8D of the IGA.

Although it appears that the lottery services exception includes keno, the position is less clear in relation to bingo.

The IGA does not refer expressly to bingo and whether, to the extent that it is provided online, it would be classified as a prohibited interactive gambling service or would be considered as a lottery and therefore fall within the lottery services exception.

However, in a report released in December 2011, the Joint Select Committee on Gambling Reform (JSCOGR) expressed the view that bingo is prohibited by the IGA.

Nevertheless, little guidance exists as to whether the bodies charged with the enforcement of the IGA, including the Department, ACMA and the Australian Federal Police (AFP), share this view.

Virtual slot machines
Gambling services prohibited under the IGA include online versions of electronic slot machines. A more recent issue being considered is whether online games that replicate features of slot machines are caught by the IGA (see section 7).

Lotteries
Online lotteries and the online sale of lotteries are not prohibited by the IGA. However, online scratch or instant lotteries and betting on the outcome of scratch or instant lotteries are not permitted. As noted above, the Minister has the discretion under the IGA to make regulations to ban highly repetitive or frequently drawn forms of keno-type lottery or similar types of lottery that are provided to customers using interactive communications networks or media.

2.5 Explain the system of regulation of gambling; which regulatory or governmental body is responsible for the supervision of gambling? Which body issues licences? Which body examines enforcement powers? Is there any limit on the number or duration of available licences?

Gambling regulation is jurisdiction-specific, with each state and territory having its own regulatory authority responsible for the regulation of gambling and for the issue of licences (where available) in their jurisdiction.

At the federal level, the government is responsible for the IGA.

3.   ONLINE GAMBLING

3.1 To what extent can online gambling be offered in your jurisdiction? Are licences available and, if so, for which gambling products? Please describe briefly the licensing process, who may apply, whether licences are limited in number and, if no licences are available, whether it is legal for online gambling to be offered. In the case of EU jurisdictions, please state whether there are any issues as to the legality of the local law at EU level. Please refer to any relevant cases at ECJ level and explain any measures taken or pending by the European Commission.

The IGA, which regulates interactive gambling services that have an Australian customer link (ie gambling services being provided to persons present in Australia), contains two principal prohibitions:

* a prohibition on the provision of prohibited interactive gambling services to persons present in Australia (the 'Operational Prohibition'); and
* a prohibition on the publication/broadcast of prohibited interactive gambling service advertisements (the 'Advertising Prohibition').

A defence to the Operational Prohibition exists if the provider did not know and could not, with reasonable diligence, have ascertained that the service had an Australian-customer link. Accordingly, if an operator of a site outside Australia providing prohibited interactive gambling services takes certain steps to prevent persons present in Australia from accessing the site, a defence might be available.

The IGA targets the supply of online gambling, rather than its demand. It prohibits the *provision* of online gambling services to customers in Australia, but does not outlaw Australians from accessing online gambling services. Nor does it prevent Australian-based companies from providing online gambling services to customers in other countries. Further, although the IGA contains provisions that would prohibit the provision of gambling services to persons in designated countries, no country has ever been designated.

As stated above, the IGA treats betting and gaming differently. Online betting is essentially exempt from the IGA, meaning that only restrictions at the state and territory level apply to these services. Online gaming, on the other hand, is essentially prohibited insofar as services are provided to persons physically located in Australia.

Accordingly, the IGA does not prohibit the provision of online wagering (eg on a horse race, a greyhound race, a sporting event, an event, or series of events) in Australia. However, at the date of writing this chapter, this exception only covers wagering on an event (other than a racing event) that contemplates a bet being accepted online before an event has started. Online services that provide for wagering on a sports event after the event has commenced (on the outcome of that event (in-play betting) and/or 'microbetting', that is, wagering on contingencies within a sports event) are prohibited by section 8A(2) of the IGA.

However, if an activity is not prohibited by the IGA, it may nevertheless require a licence at the state and territory level. Generally speaking, most of the states and territories provide a licensing regime for wagering and sports betting operators. Sports betting licences are often also held by the relevant jurisdiction's licensed totalisator and licensed bookmakers.

Wagering operators (whether or not licensed in any Australian jurisdiction) which accept bets on Australian racing or major sports must obtain approval from the relevant racing body.

In respect of racing, the wagering operators must apply for approval from each racing body to publish race field information relating to that particular form of racing. Approval is subject to the payment of race field fees (ranging from 10 per cent of gross profits to 2 per cent of turnover) set out in terms and conditions which have statutory effect under legislation in each state and territory. Other obligations are imposed to assist in maintaining the integrity of the racing code. These approaches are required by statute, in the case of most racing events and other sporting events held in Victoria. (At the time of writing, a bill to enact similar legislation in NSW had recently been introduced.) Failure to comply with these terms and conditions may result in the approval being withdrawn and an offence being committed.

Despite the various prohibitions contained in the states and territories laws, it is still possible for an operator to obtain a licence in certain Australian jurisdictions to conduct online gaming. However, even if a licence were obtained, the provision of those services to persons present in Australia would be prohibited by the IGA (save to the extent they fall within one of the exceptions).

3.2 Is there a distinction between the law applicable to B2B operations and that applicable to B2C operations?

Generally speaking, yes. Most of the prohibitions (and the licences) contained in Australian gambling legislation are directed at B2C operators.

There is no licensing system specifically for B2B operators. Generally, an approval process exists for suppliers of certain categories of services to online gambling operators (eg gaming software providers). Also, certain types of arrangements, such as revenue share arrangements, may require specific approval by the relevant regulator. This issue has recently received significant attention from the Northern Territory Racing Commission (NTRC), the licensing body in the Northern Territory responsible for granting a licence to many of the major Australian corporate bookmakers. The NTRC's view is that any affiliate arrangement between a corporate bookmaker and an affiliate which involves a revenue share payment (typically in respect of any bets made by customers introduced to the bookmaker by the affiliate) requires the NTRC's prior approval.

3.3 What are the consequences for B2C or B2B operators who are active in your jurisdiction without having obtained or applied for the required permits, licences and approvals? What penalties and enforcement powers are available in respect of the illegal operators? Please outline any significant domestic decisions or enforcement actions that have been taken by the relevant authorities in recent years.

Providing a prohibited interactive gambling service to persons present in Australia without having obtained the required licences and approvals constitutes a breach of the IGA. There is a risk that any party who 'aids and abets' the provision of a prohibited interactive gambling service would be considered an accessory.

3.4 What technical measures are in place (if any) to protect consumers from unlicensed operators, such as ISP blocking and payment blocking?

There are currently no technical measures mandated by Australian laws to protect Australian consumers from unlicensed operators.

3.5 Has the legal status of online gambling changed significantly in recent years and, if so, how?

No. The Final Report included a number of recommendations that, if adopted, would have liberalised Australian online gambling significantly and strengthened the enforcement of the IGA. For example, in respect of liberalisation, the Department recommended the relaxation of the prohibition on in-play wagering (subject to a ban on microbetting) and the trial of a five year pilot to allow for the provision of online tournament poker services to Australian residents. However, on the same day that the Final Report was released, the Minister for Broadband, Communications and the Digital Economy released a statement announcing that the federal government would not be pursuing these recommendations until agreement was reached in respect of a nationally consistent approach to harm minimisation and consumer protection.

Subsequently, the government changed following the federal election in September 2013. The newly elected Coalition Government had been critical of the former government's position and took the position that the current laws in respect of online gambling have not been adequately enforced. Contrary to the Department's recommendations that online gambling should be liberalised, the Coalition issued a policy paper which indicated that they supported tightening online gambling restrictions. (See section 3.6 for further information.)

In 2013, the advertising restrictions on online wagering operators were strengthened (see section 6.1).

3.6 Whilst acknowledging the inherent difficulty in predicting developments in gambling law, what are the likely developments in online gambling in your jurisdiction, both short term and long term? Are any specific amendments under consideration? Have there been any recent political developments, or do you envisage any in the near future? Are any specific amendments under consideration? Are they likely to be adopted and, if so, what is the time scale?

There is considerable uncertainty about the future direction of Australian gambling regulation. Since the Department's Final Report was released in March 2013, there has been a change in the Australian federal government. During their election campaign, the Liberal–National Coalition (the Coalition) released the Coalition's Helping Problem Gamblers Policy (the Gambling Policy). The Gambling Policy sets out the Coalition's position in response to a number of gambling issues, one of which is the regulation of online gambling. The Gambling Policy indicates that the Coalition is concerned about the growth of online gambling and will be looking to tighten restrictions on online gambling on the basis that the current laws are not being adequately enforced. Of particular note is the suggestion that the Coalition is not supportive of any future liberalisation of online gambling and will be investigating methods of strengthening the enforcement of the IGA to ensure Australians *'are protected from illegal online gambling operators'*.

However, since the federal election in September 2013 to the date of writing, the Coalition Government has not undertaken any action or made any public statements in respect of online gambling.

Match-fixing and cheating at sports betting has attracted attention recently. A number of states/territories (NSW, Victoria, South Australia, the ACT and the Northern Territory) have passed legislation which introduces offences for match-fixing and cheating at sports betting. At the time of writing, a bill to put similar legislation in place is before the Queensland Parliament. These laws have received considerable media attention and are likely to be enforced by regulators and law enforcement agencies. For example, in September 2013, a number of players and the head coach of a semi-professional soccer team in Victoria were arrested and pleaded guilty to offences under the Victorian match-fixing laws. In April 2014, the Australian head of the match fixing syndicate involved in fixing the results of these matches also pleaded guilty.

Further, in January 2014, Melbourne police charged a man for allegedly 'courtsiding', that is, transmitting tennis scores directly from his courtside seat to his UK based employer. The relevant offence under the Victorian legislation is *'engaging in conduct that would corrupt a betting outcome'*. Interestingly, this prosecution has now been withdrawn.

3.7 Is the law the same in relation to mobile gambling and interactive gambling on television? If not, are there any headline differences?

Section 5(3) of the IGA expressly excludes from the definition of interactive gambling services a telephone betting service via a standard voice call and services that have a designated broadcasting link.

Therefore, in order to lawfully provide a telephone betting service, the operator must deal with customers wholly by way of voice calls. The terminology used is archaic and there is some uncertainty as to the scope of this exception.

4. LAND-BASED GAMING
4.1 Please describe the licensing regime (if any) for land-based gaming, and what products are included. Please set out what licences are available, and the licensing regime for them.

The licensing regime for land-based gambling is jurisdiction-specific and differs, depending on the relevant category of gambling.

In all jurisdictions, regimes are in place for the licensing or registration of on-course bookmakers and their clerks and/or agents and/or employees. Provision is also made for the cancellation or suspension of a licence or registration in prescribed circumstances.

The conduct of totalisator betting is subject to legislative control. In most states and territories, an exclusive licence has been granted to conduct totalisator betting in that jurisdiction. These licences have different terms.

Legislation in each jurisdiction provides for the licensing of casinos and the licensing of particular casino employees. Until recently, a monopoly licence model applied in New South Wales, with Echo Entertainment Group Ltd (Echo) holding the sole casino licence in the state. However, in mid-November 2013, despite efforts by Echo to extend the exclusivity of its agreement, the NSW Government indicated that it had approved James Packer's Crown Resorts Ltd's (Crown) proposal to operate a second casino in Sydney. Legislation was passed in late November 2013 to enable an operator 'approved' by the government to apply for a licence. At the time of writing, the regulator had received an application from Crown and was in the process of investigating the applicant's probity. Similarly, in Queensland, the Queensland government has indicated that it will be granting up to three new casino licences. Media reports suggest that 18 companies have formally expressed interest in these new licences. Crown has again been the front runner in expressing interest in this area.

Finally, in all jurisdictions, separate licences or authorities are required for the supply and operation of slot machines. The only exception is Western Australia, where slot machines are not permitted except in the casino. In all jurisdictions, the slot machines legislation also provides for the licensing of repairers of slot machines and testing agents. Legislation in most jurisdictions also provides for the licensing of specified employees in relation to slot machines. In Queensland, South Australia and Victoria, there is also statutory provision for the licensing of monitoring operators.

Lotteries are also separately regulated with specific legislation in most states. Again, in most states, an exclusive licence has been granted to conduct a public lottery. In certain jurisdictions, there are also provisions to enable charitable lotteries to be conducted.

4.2 Please set out any particular limitations or requirements for (eg casino) operators, such as a ban on local residents gambling.

Save for online gaming services, which cannot be provided legally to persons present in Australia, there are few limitations that exist on operators in respect of the persons to whom services can be provided.

The restrictions that exist fall into the following categories:

- Minors: all states and territories have an express prohibition on gambling services being provided to minors (persons under 18 years of age).
- Excluded Persons: there are mechanisms under the laws of all states and territories which enable persons to exclude themselves from specific categories of gambling. For example, mandatory self-exclusion procedures apply to cover gaming or betting in casinos, clubs and with wagering operators. These vary from jurisdiction to jurisdiction.
  In Tasmania, there is also provision for third party exclusion, namely the ability of an interested party to require an operator to exclude a nominated person from utilising gambling services which that operator provides.
- Interested Persons: persons involved in the management of a gambling operator are expressly prohibited from participating in gambling services provided by that operator.

Victoria has introduced the Gambling Regulation Amendment (Pre-commitment) Act 2014, which requires all slot machines to be linked to a state-wide pre-commitment system by 1 December 2015.

However, unlike certain overseas jurisdictions, there is no express prohibition or restriction on casinos, for example, concerning the ability of local residents to enter facilities and make bets.

4.3 Please address the questions in 3.5 above, but in relation to land-based gaming.

Given the repeal of the National Gambling Reform Laws in March 2014, there has been little change (if any) to the regulation of land-based gaming at the federal level. The National Gambling Reform Laws would have made significant changes to the requirements for slot machines, most notably requiring pre-commitment mechanisms, and eventually all slot machines, to be linked to a state-wide pre-commitment system.

Victoria has introduced the Gambling Regulation Amendment (Pre-commitment) Act 2014, which requires all slot machines to be linked to a state-wide pre-commitment system by 1 December 2015. This legislation will continue to apply irrespective of the repeal of the National Gambling Reform Laws.

5. TAX
5.1 Please summarise briefly the tax regime applicable both to land-based and online gaming.

In addition to the taxes which are payable generally by gambling operators as a business conducting business in Australia, namely income tax and GST, there are a number of taxes or imposts which are payable specifically by gambling operators. The taxes payable relate specifically to the relevant category of gambling and differ considerably between the various states and territories. Gambling taxes represent a material source of revenue for the states and territories, comprising approximately 9.5 per cent of their revenues in recent years.

Among the taxes which are payable by gambling operators are the following:
- direct gambling taxes;
- licence fees: in some cases, licence fees represent a one-off payment for exclusive rights, for instance, the Star casino paid $100 million in respect of the grant of exclusivity for a 12 year period from November 2007, while Tabcorp paid $410 million to the Victorian government in respect of its wagering and betting licence in March 2012 for a 12 year period and will pay $75 million to the NSW government to extend its exclusive licence and monopoly on NSW retail totalisator betting until 2033; and
- mandatory community contributions, such as the requirement to make contributions through a responsible gaming levy;
- the requirement of wagering operators to pay fees in respect of use of race fields and sports fixture information.

The level of taxation between types of gambling varies quite markedly. Lotteries and pools are generally taxed at the highest level, followed by slot machines and casino gaming.

6. ADVERTISING
6.1 To what extent is the advertising of gambling permitted in your jurisdiction?
The extent to which advertising of gambling is permitted depends to a considerable extent on the category of gambling involved. There is a lot of concern about the dangers of gambling and there are a number of controls over the manner in which gambling can be promoted.

Reflecting these concerns, an extensive array of rules provide guidance on how gambling products can be advertised in Australia. The IGA contains an express prohibition on the broadcast or publication of interactive gambling service advertisements in Australia. This has the effect of making it illegal for advertisements relating to offshore gaming operators to be advertised in Australia.

In each state/territory, gambling advertising is subject to various legislative restrictions. For example, most states and territories have legislation which places restrictions on the manner in which wagering can be advertised. All states and territories contain legislation prohibiting the advertising of unlawful gaming services. Authorities take the view that these prohibitions apply to the promotion of services provided by operators based outside Australia. More generally, trade practices and consumer protection laws, which apply at both the federal and state/territory levels, prohibit misleading and deceptive conduct. This is particularly relevant for wagering operators seeking to promote open account offers which are typically subject to numerous qualifications.

Additionally, advertisements are also subject to industry codes of conduct (eg codes specific to lotteries), an advertising industry code (which applies to all advertisements targeting Australians) and, depending on the form of the advertising, a media code of conduct (eg codes specific to television advertising – see below).

Restrictions include, for example, restrictions on operators from overstating the chances of winning and targeting gambling advertising at children. Further, there are controls on the timing of any gambling advertisements on broadcast media, the nature of the promotions in respect of certain types of gambling (for example, casinos can only promote themselves as entertainment destinations), as well as the necessity for the inclusion of mandatory harm minimisation messages.

The advertising of wagering services was the subject of significant media attention in 2013. In May 2013, the federal government announced that it would legislate a ban on the advertisement of live odds unless the industry took action to eliminate such advertisement during the broadcasting of sporting events. Subsequently, the broadcasting industry introduced new codes relating to the promotion of 'live odds' advertising, effectively removing the need for the federal government to introduce legislation.

South Australia has gone one step further and has introduced new requirements relating to wagering advertisements that target residents of that state. For example, the mandatory harm minimisation message must be included in any television commercial (TVC) that is greater than 15 seconds in duration so that the message occupies at least 25 per cent of the screen space for at least one-sixth of the duration of that TVC. Alternatively, the message must occupy 100 per cent of the screen space for at least one-tenth of the duration of that TVC. Each of the harm minimisation messages must also be spoken at the same time as the relevant image appears on the screen. These requirements came into effect on 1 March 2014.

7. SOCIAL GAMING
7.1 We believe this to be a growing area. Please decide under what criteria social gaming is permitted in your jurisdiction. If games are free to play, or if there is no prize are they legal, without a licence? Please address circumstances where virtual currency is used and can be won: ie currency which is of no monetary or other value, save for as credits to take part in games.

The IGA prohibits the supply of interactive gambling services to persons resident in Australia. For a virtual game to constitute a gambling service, it must have all of the following characteristics:
- be a game of chance or of mixed chance and skill;
- involve consideration; and
- be played for money or anything else of value.

Online social games are distinct from gaming in that they are often free to play and are not played for any monetary prizes or anything else of value. Accordingly, on this basis, it is arguable that online social games do not constitute a gambling service and can be provided legally.

Despite this, concerns have been expressed about social games to the extent that they feature casino-style or gambling-like content. For example, in October 2011, the ACMA was contacted by Senator Nick Xenophon (an Australian politician who is frequently involved in discussions of gambling regulation and who generally takes an activist stance on the protection of problem gamblers) in connection with a 'free' online game available on Facebook and other social media sites which offers games such as blackjack and roulette.

In response to Senator Xenophon's request, the ACMA published a letter expressing its view confirming that these activities are not in breach of the IGA because they do not constitute gambling. This view was reached on the basis that the third element required in order to have an unlawful game is not met as it is not possible to win 'money or anything else of value' through playing the game and 'there is no facility to convert or cash out the 'virtual' currency accumulated during play into 'real' currency'. However, had all the elements of a gambling service existed, the provision of the game would be in contravention of the IGA and unlawful.

While this conclusion is not binding on the ACMA and does not constitute a legal precedent, it provides guidance to the suppliers of similar games, as well as the platforms (such as Facebook) used to distribute these games, that the supply of games of this nature to Australian residents is not prohibited by the Act.

Further, the Department confirmed this position in its Final Report, concluding that *'the distinction between these [online social] games and gambling is that there is no cash prize on the outcome and no cash at risk during the game'*.

However, there remains concern that the widespread availability of these games on social media encourages minors to gamble (as many of these sites allow any user 13 years or older to register). For example, in May 2013, Senator Xenophon introduced the Interactive Gambling Amendment (Virtual Credits) Bill 2013 (the Virtual Credits Bill) into the Federal Parliament. This Bill sought to amend the definition of 'gambling service' in the IGA to state that *'anything else of value'* now includes *'virtual credits, virtual coins, virtual tokens, virtual objects or any similar thing that is purchased within, or as part of, or in relation to, the game'*.

The Virtual Credits Bill was referred to the JSCOGR for further review. In its Final Report, released in June 2013, the JSCOGR recommended that the Virtual Credits Bill should not be passed and was supportive of the Department's findings. The JSCOGR acknowledged that there was a significant lack of research and empirical evidence in the area of online social games and stated that, before any legislation is passed, further independent research is required to assist with the development of effective policy.

Accordingly, whilst a number of government departments and bodies have confirmed that online social games are legal and distinguishable from gambling and online gaming, there remains a risk that a stronger stance from Australian regulators will be taken in relation to the availability of virtual games if the Australian community becomes sufficiently concerned.

The authors would like to thank other members of the Addisons Media and Gambling Team for their assistance in writing this chapter.

Austria

Schwartz Huber-Medek und Partner Rechtsanwälte OG
Walter Schwartz & Raffaela Wallerstorfer

1. OBJECTIVES AND STRUCTURE OF LEGISLATION
Structure
Article 10(1)(4) of the *Bundes-Verfassungsgesetz* or B-VG (the Federal Constitutional Act of Austria) allows the federal legislator to establish monopolies. On this constitutional basis, a national gaming monopoly was founded by section 3 of the *Glücksspielgesetz* or GSpG (Austrian Gaming Act). Gaming is regulated by the GSpG which, depending on the gaming product, splits the jurisdiction between the federal state and the nine Austrian provinces:
- the lottery market is monopolised; one lottery licence is issued to *Österreichische Lotterien Gesellschaft* m.b.H.;
- the casino market is organised as an oligopoly as there are 15 casino licences available. Three additional licence may be granted for running a poker salon;
- slot machines are partly regulated by the federal state, partly by some of the nine Austrian provinces; and
- the sports betting market, limited to a combination of up to 10 individual bets, is regulated by the nine Austrian provinces.

Objectives
Governments subject gaming operators to certain requirements, restrictions and guidelines. Among others their objectives are:
- ensuring that the operations as well as the corporate and the shareholder structures of gaming operators do not violate security standards and ensure proper gaming;
- reducing the level of risk that gamers are exposed to, as studies show that gaming can become a psychologically addictive and harmful behaviour in some people;
- reducing the risk of gaming operations being used for criminal purposes, eg money laundering or fraud; and
- ensuring certain cash flows from gaming taxation to the government.

2. FRAMEWORK OF LEGISLATION
2.1 What is the legal definition of gambling and what falls within this definition?
Games of chance
The Austrian gaming monopoly covers all 'games where the decision on the result exclusively or predominantly depends on chance' (section 1(1) GSpG).

This means that in a game of chance, aleatory moments do not exclusively need to be material; to a certain extent, the outcome of the game may also be influenced by the participants. Such a game will only become a 'game of chance' which is subject to the gaming monopoly if the outcome of the game is determined by an absolute majority of aleatory moments.

Pursuant to section 1 in conjunction with section 3 GSpG, the Austrian gaming monopoly generally includes all games of chance. The federal government assigned only the organisation of 'lottery games' (*Bestimmte Lotterien*) and of 'casino games' (*Spielbanken*) to private individuals by granting licences (sections 14 and 21 GSpG). Furthermore, the GSpG stipulates the assignment of the organisation of 'other lottery games' (*sonstige Ausspielungen*) to private individuals.

Section 1(2) GSpG lists several games as games of chance: roulette, optical roulette, poker, blackjack, two aces, bingo, keno, baccarat, baccarat chemin de fer and their different variations.

Although the games of chance not mentioned in the relevant licence decrees or in section 1(2) GSpG are currently not managed, all rights related thereto are still reserved to the federal government within the scope of the monopoly. Pursuant to section 1(2) the federal minister of finance may list further games as games of chance via ordinance.

Games of chance, operated, organised, offered or commercially made available by an entrepreneur where gamers or others have to place a stake to participate in the game with the entrepreneur's or someone else's promise of possible winnings (*Ausspielung*) may only be organised on the basis of a national licence. Otherwise they are illegal games of chance (*verbotene Ausspielungen*).

Games of skill
Games of skill are not subject to the gaming monopoly. Typical games of skill are chess, tarot, bridge and the popular card game '*Schnapsen*'. The question if a game is a game of chance subject to the gaming monopoly or a game of skill may be answered after a case-by-case analysis.

Sports betting
The jurisdiction for sports betting is distributed among the federal state of Austria and the provinces: pursuant to Article 15(1) B-VG, the provinces are responsible for the legislation and its enforcement in the field of totalisator and bookmaker bets (*VfSlg* 1477/1932 '*Sammlung der Erkenntnisse und Beschlüsse des Verfassungsgerichtshofs*') (collection of the major findings and decisions of the Austrian Constitutional Court), however, pursuant to Article 10(1)(4) B-VG in conjunction with section 7 GSpG, 'sports toto' (pools) is subject to the gaming monopoly. The Austrian Federal Minister of Finance, who is responsible for the gaming monopoly, assumed in an official communication that sport bets up to a combination of 10 individual bets are not subject to the gaming monopoly. Thus sports betting is subject to the original (not merely derivative) legislative and executive powers of the nine Austrian provinces (*VfSlg* 1477/1932).

2.2   What is the legal definition of online gambling and what falls within this definition?

The GSpG also applies to online gaming services. Hence, online games are subject to the Austrian gaming monopoly.

Section 12a(1) GSpG defines electronic lottery games as games of chance. In electronic lottery games, the gaming contract is concluded via electronic media (telephone, fax, internet etc). The decision on the result has to be made centrally (*zentralseitig*) and has to be provided via electronic media.

The special characteristic of electronic lottery games is that the legislator does not define these games of chance with regard to their contents; they are rather defined only by the conclusion, not, however, through the games' content.

Thus, any game of chance constitutes an electronic lottery, if '*the player participates directly in the game via electronic media and the decision on the result of the game is made by a central system and provided via electronic media*'. These legal conditions are regularly fulfilled by games of chance offered online. They may therefore only be organised by the licencee of the single lottery licence. Thus, there is a monopoly on online games of chance as part of the lottery monopoly.

2.3   Please set out the different gambling products identified by legislation.

Please see section 2.4.

2.4   Please list the different requirements for each gambling product, including legal classifications for each; for example, is poker a game of skill or game of chance?

Poker

Poker holds a special position. It was disputed over a long period of time whether this game was a game of chance or a game of skill. By the amendment of the GSpG in 2010, poker has been included in Section 1(2) GSpG. It was thereby established that poker, regardless of whether it depends predominantly on chance or on skill, is deemed a game of chance before the law, which may only be organised on the basis of a national licence. In addition, the Federal Minister of Finance had the possibility to grant an additional poker casino licence provided that '*it is limited to the exclusive organisation of a poker salon without bank in live gaming*' (section 22 GSpG – Nov 2010).

On 27 June 2013, the Constitutional Court repealed section 22 GSpG – Nov 2010, which provided that only one poker licence can be granted, as unconstitutional (VfGH 27 June 2013, G 26/2013). In the same decision the Constitutional Court also repealed the word 'poker' in section 1(2) GSpG – Nov 2010 as unconstitutional. Hence, poker was no longer deemed a game of chance before the law. This means that each variant of the game had to be examined to determine whether the variant depends predominantly on chance or on skill. If a variant of the game was qualified as a game of chance, it could only be operated by the authorised concessionaire. However, if a variant of poker was qualified as a game of skill, a trade licence was necessary.

With the Tax Amendment 2014, the Gambling Act was amended again. With this amendment, poker was restated in section 1(2) GSpG. This means that, regardless of whether poker depends predominantly on chance or on skill, it is deemed a game of chance before the law (again), which may only be organised on the basis of a national licence. In addition, the Federal Minister of Finance has the opportunity to grant three licences for running poker salons *'without bank in live gaming'* (section 22 GSpG).

Sports betting
According to the relevant definitions provided by the provincial acts there are two different ways to provide sports betting: a bookmaker is a person who accepts sport bets on a commercial basis, and a totalisator is a person who negotiates sport bets on a commercial basis. Sports betting is not defined as a game of chance and for this reason sports betting is regulated by the legislators of the nine provinces. It is possible to get licences; the number of these licences is not limited.

The form of how to conclude a betting agreement is not subject to any legal restrictions. Apart from the placing of bets in the presence of both parties on the bookmaker's or totalisator's premises (the so-called 'betting office'), a betting agreement can also be concluded by phone, letter, email and a 'mouse click' on the internet.

Betting (other than sports betting)
The organisation of bets for other reasons than sports events (for example on the outcome of elections) is not governed by law, however, neither is it expressly prohibited. According to the prevailing opinion, these so-called 'society bets' are subject to the relevant regulations of some of the provinces (see *Schwartz/Wohlfahrt*, ecolex 2001, 51).

Casino games
Casino games are games of chance which are only allowed in casinos (*Spielbanken*) pursuant to section 21 GSpG. A 'casino' is a gaming house where the public may participate in hazards. Contrary to lottery games, the GSpG provides no exhaustive list of casino games. Section 22(7)(3) GSpG expressly states that the individual games of chance played in the casinos have to be mentioned in the licence decree.

Slot and other machine gaming
Slot machines providing games of chance are governed by different regulations:
- slot machines may be used in the (15) casinos without applicable limits as to stakes or winnings. These slot machines currently generate the largest turnover in casinos; and
- slot machines may be set up outside casinos only if it is permitted by the relevant provincial legislator.

Lottery games

Lottery games are games of chance where the respective gain is calculated according to the totalisator principle. This means that the amount of the actually distributed gains is directly proportional to the stakes actually made by the participants. The organiser of games of chance that work according to this principle virtually incurs no financial risk.

Sections 6 to 12b GSpG provide an exhaustive list of lottery games: lotto; pools; bonus game; instant lotteries; class lottery; number lotto; lotto with running numbers; electronic lotteries; bingo and keno are expressly referred to as lottery games. Only the organisation of these lottery games can be assigned to private individuals by granting a licence.

The lottery licence includes the right to operate electronic lotteries. They may therefore only be organised by the licencee of the lottery licence.

Other gambling products: lottery games without pecuniary reward

Sections 32 to 49 GSpG provide specific regulations for 'lottery games without pecuniary reward' (*Lotterien ohne Erwerbszweck*). These 'lottery games without pecuniary reward' are other number lotteries (*sonstige Nummernlotterien*); tombola games (*Tomobolaspiele*); originally charity lottery games at fairs (*Glückshäfen*); and hoax lottery games (*Juxausspielungen*). 'Other number lotteries' are defined as lottery games in which the tickets are earmarked with consecutive numbers and in which publicly drawn tickets win. 'Tombola games' are lottery games in which each tombola ticket has three different sequences of numbers, each consisting of five different numbers from the sequence of number from 1 to 90. The tombola tickets whose combinations of numbers are winning combinations pursuant to the rules of the game win; the numbers of these combinations are determined in a public draw. 'Originally charity lottery games at fairs' (*Glückshäfen*) are lottery games in which the gamblers find out if their tickets are winning tickets or if they are blanks through drawing or through contributing to the drawing process. 'Hoax lottery games' (*Juxausspielungen*) are lottery games in which each ticket is a winning ticket, the gamblers draw lots to find out what they win.

2.5 Explain the system of regulation of gambling; which regulatory or governmental body is responsible for the supervision of gambling? Which body issues licences? Which body examines enforcement powers? Is there any limit on the number or duration of available licences?

Casino and lottery games

The Federal Minister of Finance is responsible for the GSpG as well as for the relevant regulatory authority. He grants the licences for lotteries and casinos games. This allocation of competence may be historically explained and is based on the fact that the Austrian gaming monopoly initially pursued mainly objectives of fiscal policy. Practice shows that the Federal Ministry of Finance is striving to preserve the gaming monopoly and intends to allow change only if it involves an increase in the tax revenue. The lottery market is organised as a monopoly as there is only one licence available; in contrast to the lottery monopoly, the casino market is organised as an oligopoly, with 15 casino licences being available. Both the lottery licence and the casino licences are limited to a maximum of 15 years (see § 14 Abs 4 Z 1 GSpG and § 21 Abs 7 Z 2 GSpG).

Provincial games with slot machines and sports betting
The licences for sports betting and provincial games with slot machines are granted by the nine provincial governments. The provincial governments are responsible for the granting of the licences as well as for the regulatory authorities. A licence for provincial games with slot machines can only be granted for a maximum of 15 years and three licences can be granted at most per federal state (section 5 Abs 1 GSpG). As is the case with sports betting, the numbers of licences are not limited; anyone who meets the legal requirements has the legal right to be granted a licence. The duration of a licence for sports betting is determined by the relevant federal state law.

3. ONLINE GAMBLING
3.1 To what extent can online gambling be offered in your jurisdiction? Are licences available and, if so, for which gambling products? Please describe briefly the licensing process, who may apply, whether licences are limited in number and, if no licences are available, whether it is legal for online gambling to be offered. In the case of EU jurisdictions, please state whether there are any issues as to the legality of the local law at EU level. Please refer to any relevant cases at ECJ level and explain any measures taken or pending by the European Commission.
The licence for lottery games pursuant to section 14 GSpG includes the right to offer any gambling product online (see section 2.2). There is only one licence available (section 4.1).

Currently, there is no harmonisation of the gambling law. That means that – as long as the European Court of Justice does not find a common regulation – each member state has its own regulations concerning (online) gambling and sports bets, and has to rely on the case law of the European Court of Justice.

The ECJ-ruling *Ömer and Dickinger* (ECJ 15/09/2011, C-347/09) has affected Austria. Jochen Dickinger and Franz Ömer, who are Austrian nationals, are the founders of the multinational online games group bet.at-home.com AG. They hold gambling licences in Malta through various subsidiaries. Through a server in Linz, Austria, they also offered games of chance (online casino games) in Austria without holding an Austrian licence. The District Court of Linz eventually referred to the ECJ for a preliminary ruling on the question of whether the national obligation to hold a licence was compatible with the fundamental freedoms under the law of the EU. The ECJ concluded that – due to the different level of protection and technical requirements – no duty of mutual recognition of authorisations could exist. In addition, the ECJ held that, even if national gambling constituted a restriction of the freedom to provide services, such a monopoly was justified for overriding reasons in the public interest, such as a high level of consumer protection. Furthermore, the ECJ affirmed that advertising must remain measured and strictly limited to what is necessary.

3.2 Is there a distinction between the law applicable to B2B operations and that applicable to B2C operations?

The service provider's responsibility depends on the services it provides to the actual online gambling provider. Operating, organising, offering or commercially making available illegal games of chance is subject to administrative penalties (section 52(1)(1) GSpG); so is supporting illegal games of chance by soliciting participation in the game and/or commercially placing internet links (section 52(1)(6) GSpG). Moreover, whoever advertises or facilitates the advertisement of illegal games of chance is subject to prosecution (section 52(1)(9) GSpG). Such administrative offences are, in the case of (1), subject to fines of up to EUR 60,000 and, in the cases of (6) and (9), subject to fines of up to EUR 22,000.

3.3 What are the consequences for B2C or B2B operators who are active in your jurisdiction without having obtained or applied for the required permits, licences and approvals? What penalties and enforcement powers are available in respect of the illegal operators? Please outline any significant domestic decisions or enforcement actions that have been taken by the relevant authorities in recent years.

See section 3.2.

Pursuant to section 52(1)(1) GSpG, whoever operates games of chance possibly commits an offence against the GSpG. Such violations are punishable with fines of up to EUR 60,000. Pursuant to section 53 GSpG, objects which are used for intervening in the gaming monopoly may be subject to forfeiture. Furthermore, the authorities can order, pursuant to section 54 GSpG, a confiscation of intervention objects and facilities on suspicion that the objects which are used to intervene in the gaming monopoly of the state are also used to commit continued offences against the bans set out in section 52(1) GSpG.

Upon justified suspicion that games of chance are being operated or executed as a business activity, thereby violating the GSpG, and upon a justified assumption that these activities will be continued, the authorities, without previous procedure but not without having requested a stop of the games of chance operated or executed against the provisions of the GSpG, are entitled to order the complete or partial shut down of the business on the spot (section 56a GSpG). According to this provision, not only the internet provider is punishable by administrative penalty regulation if games of chance abroad are accessible via his/her web server (which is always the case unless the providing is completely stopped), but also the developer of web pages offering a link to an operator of games of chance abroad.

Intentional offences against the ban on participating in illegal online gambling will be fined up to EUR 7,500 and negligent offences will be fined up to EUR 1,500. Austrians abroad are allowed to participate in games of chance not executed in Austria and to visit a casino. The ban on participating in games of chance not executed in Austria also applies to online games of chance (eg online casinos). Participating in online games of chance not executed in Austria is punishable if the stake is made in Austria.

Section 168 of the *Strafgesetzbuch* (*StGB*) (Criminal Code) defines the legal element of a crime. Whoever operates a game where gain and loss exclusively or predominantly depend on chance or which is expressly illegal and whoever supports get-togethers for the purpose of operating such a game in order to make financial profits for himself/herself or others will be punished with a term of imprisonment of up to six months or fined with up to 360 daily rates unless the game is executed only for non-profit purposes and amusement and if small amounts of money (under EUR 10) are involved. Whoever takes part in such games in order to make profits is also punishable.

3.4 What technical measures are in place (if any) to protect consumers from unlicensed operators, such as ISP blocking and payment blocking?

There are no technical measures in Austria to protect consumers from unlicensed operators. However, in 2013, the European Parliament adopted a resolution on online gambling. In this resolution the European Parliament clarified that it is necessary to take action against illegal gambling operators. Such measures would be: payment blocking, blacklists, whitelists etc. So far, these measures have not been implemented in Austria.

3.5 Has the legal status of online gambling changed significantly in recent years and, if so, how?

The legal status of online gambling has not changed significantly in recent years.

3.6 Whilst acknowledging the inherent difficulty in predicting developments in gambling law, what are the likely developments in online gambling in your jurisdiction, both short term and long term? Are any specific amendments under consideration? Have there been any recent political developments, or do you envisage any in the near future? Are any specific amendments under consideration? Are they likely to be adopted and, if so, what is the time scale?

Recently, the Gaming Law in Austria was amended by the Tax Amendment Act 2014. The most important changes were:

- 'poker' has been included in section 1(2) GSpG again. This means that poker – regardless of whether this game depends predominantly on chance or on skill – is deemed a game of chance before the law, which may only be organised on the basis of a national licence;
- in the amendment of the GSpG it is provided that the Federal Minister of Finance has the opportunity to grant three poker casino licences provided that 'they are limited to the exclusive organisation of a poker salon without bank in live gaming';

- if an act fulfils both the elements of section 52 GSpG and the elements of section 168 of the Criminal Code, the act should only be punished after the provisions of section 52 GSpG. Such administrative offences are, in the case of section 52(1)(1) GSpG, subject to fines of up to EUR 60,000 and, in the case of (2) to (11), subject to fines of up to EUR 22,000. Several discussions about whether this provision is unconstitutional or not are currently ongoing; and
- there is a new section 52(2) GSpG which grades penalties depending on the severity of the intervention (number of gaming machines and other infringing objects) or frequency of intervention (in the event of repeated infringement) and a minimum fine control.

This amendment contains no novelty in relation to online gambling. The Constitutional Court has clarified that it has no objections that online gambling is a part of the lottery licence (*VfSlg* 19.717). There is no change of the online gambling legislation planned for the near future.

3.7 Is the law the same in relation to mobile gambling and interactive gambling on television? If not, are there any headline differences?

Section 12a(1) GSpG defines electronic lottery games as games of chance. In electronic lottery games, the gaming contract is concluded via electronic media (telephone, fax, internet etc). Hence it does not matter which game of chance is offered; the sole decider is if the gaming contract is concluded via electronic media.

Mobile gambling and interactive gambling on television are therefore electronic lottery games (section 12a GSpG) that may only be provided by the licencee for providing lottery games pursuant to section 14 GSpG.

4. LAND-BASED GAMING

4.1 Please describe the licensing regime (if any) for land-based gaming, and what products are included. Please set out what licences are available, and the licensing regime for them.

Sports betting

Betting services (bookmaker or totaliser) can only be provided by virtue of a permit issued by the respective provincial government which has local jurisdiction at the entrepreneur's business location. The applicant, both a natural person and a legal entity, complying with the legal requirements is legally entitled to obtain a permit to work as a bookmaker or totaliser.

Legal requirements apart from the existence of the personal requirements, such as legal capacity, for a legal entity are for example being registered in the companies register and/or proving the reliability of the persons authorised to represent the firm or subsidiary and/or proving their creditworthiness with a bank guarantee for a certain amount for each location.

The authority will issue a permit either for an indefinite period of time or a fixed term (approximately three to five years), such a decree will be extended if the statutory requirements are still maintained.

Betting (other than sports betting)
Currently, the organisation of society bets (see section 2.4) is only regulated
in Vorarlberg and in Styria because the relevant acts of these provinces do
not distinguish between sport bets and society bets.

Casino games
Pursuant to section 21(5) GSpG, only 15 licences for casino games can be
granted. A licence is only granted 'for the operation of a casino' at a certain
place in Austria.

Licences are only granted if the licencee is a stock corporation having
registered offices in Austria or the European Economic Area, if no
shareholder whose regulatory reliability is not guaranteed has a dominant
influence, and if a share capital of at least EUR 22 million is paid up. In
addition, managers have to be appointed who have the qualities and
experience necessary for a proper operation of the business due to their
previous training and who are not subject to any reason for exclusion (eg
criminal record). Finally, due to the circumstances (in particular experience,
skills and his/her own funds), the licencee must justify the expectation that
he/she will run the licence in the best way (section 21(2) GSpG). In addition,
the licencee has to provide a security of at least 10 per cent of the share
capital, a security which serves as satisfaction of claims that may be asserted
by gamblers and as a guarantee for governmental gaming taxes and has to be
deposited with the federal minister of finance (section 21(7)(2) GSpG).

Twelve casino licences, divided into a 'city package' (Bregenz, Graz,
Innsbruck, Linz, Salzburg, Vienna) and a 'rural area package' (Baden, Bad
Gastein, Kitzbühel, Kleinwalsertal, Seefeld, Velden), were granted to Casinos
Austria AG for a period of 15 years (until 2027 and 2028, respectively).
These casinos may offer French roulette, baccarat, baccarat chemin de fer,
blackjack, pay-outs by gaming machines, American roulette, punto banco,
wheel of fortune, poker, red dog, and sic bo. For the three additional casino
licences (Vienna west, Vienna north, Lower Austria), which were created by
an amendment of the GSpG in 2010, the deadline for the application has
already expired. The licencing is expected soon.

Slot and other machine gaming
Provincial laws have been issued in Lower Austria, Upper Austria,
Burgenland and Carinthia. In these federal provinces – except Carinthia –
the licences granted for 'provincial games with slot machines' are legally
binding. However, the licensing will be reviewed by the courts of public law.
These 'provincial games with slot machines' are also about to be permitted
also in Styria. The federal provinces of Salzburg, Tyrol and Vorarlberg will
continue to prohibit slot machines. It is currently a matter of controversy
whether slot machines should be allowed in Vienna, but it is likely that
Vienna will ban them.

Even where 'provincial games with slot machines' are permitted, stringent
regulations apply, eg: (i) limits as to stakes and winnings (salons/single
machines: maximum stakes per game: EUR 10/EUR 1; maximum winnings

per game: EUR 10,000/EUR 1,000); (ii) minimum playing period (salons/ single machines: one second/two seconds); (iii) cool-down phase (salons/ single machines: after two hours of consecutive gaming, the machine shuts down/only three hours of gaming per player per day); and stringent player protection.

Minimum requirements for applicants are: there must be no dominant influence from any shareholder whose regulatory reliability is not guaranteed; and paid up share capital of at least EUR 8,000 per slot machine. It requires a way of operation and a corporate structure that allows proper regulatory supervision as well as an engineering evaluation that guarantees the player's protection and distribution of profits. In addition, managers have to be appointed who have the qualities and experience necessary for a proper operation of the business due to their previous training and who are not subject to any reason for exclusion (eg criminal record). A licence can only be granted for a maximum of 15 years.

Lottery games

Pursuant to section 14(6) GSpG, only one licence – ie one licence that allows the organisation of all lottery games referred to in sections 6 through 12b GSpG – can be granted. The licence has to be limited in time and may only be granted to a corporation if the licencee is a stock corporation having registered offices in Austria or the European Economic Area; there is no dominant influence from any shareholder whose regulatory reliability is not guaranteed; and if a share capital of at least EUR 109 million is paid up. In addition, managers have to be appointed who have the qualities and experience necessary for a proper operation of the business due to their previous training and who are not subject to any reason for exclusion (eg criminal record). Finally, due to the circumstances (in particular experience, skills and his/her own funds), the licencee must justify the expectation that he/she will run the licence in the best way (section 14(2) GSpG). In addition, the licencee has to provide a security of at least 10 per cent of the share capital, a security which serves as satisfaction of claims that may be asserted by gamblers and as guarantee for governmental gaming taxes and has to be deposited with the federal minister of finance (section 14(4)(2) GSpG).

In October 2011 the only existing licence for lottery games was granted for 15 years to *Österreichische Lotterien Gesellschaft m.b.H.* Pursuant to section 14(6) GSpG, further licences for lottery games cannot be granted.

Other gambling products: 'lottery games without pecuniary reward'

The right to carry out 'lottery games without pecuniary reward' can be transferred to other persons through a permit by the federal state of Austria (section 36 GSpG). Such a permit can only be given to legal entities based in Austria for the performance of 'tombola games', 'originally charity lottery games at fairs' and 'hoax lottery games' with a gambling capital of up to EUR 15,000 where the event does not serve to gain earnings. Such a permit can also be given to legal entities based in Austria and which deserve to be promoted because of their actions serving the general public for the performance of 'tombola games', 'originally charity lottery games at fairs' and 'hoax lottery games' with a higher gambling capital as well as for other number lotteries – where the event strives to serve specific charitable, churchly or non-profit purposes within the borders of Austria.

4.2 Please set out any particular limitations or requirements for (eg casino) operators, such as a ban on local residents gambling.

Some conditions to ensure player protection accompany the casino licences.

Only adults who have provided adequate proof of identity (official photo ID) and are not subject to any form of entry ban can be permitted to enter and gamble in a casino. It is forbidden for visitors to use technical equipment to gain an unlawful advantage.

The licensee monitors the frequency of visiting casinos and gambling intensity. If individuals may be identified who are potentially at risk of threat to their minimum subsistence income, the casino has to carry out credit checks. If this is not possible, or if necessary, specially trained employers of the casino will have a counselling interview with the person concerned. If the individual continues its gambling habits or refuses to provide information, the licensee has to ban the person from visiting the casino – either for an unlimited period or for a certain time. Violating that law, the casino is liable for an individuals' threatened minimum subsistence income and needs to compensate – limited to the minimum living wage.

Furthermore the casino needs to monitor and to report to the *Österreichische Geldwäschemeldestelle* (Austrian Financial Intelligence Unit or AIFU) any suspicious incidents particularly with regard to money laundering and terrorist financing.

4.3 Please address the questions in 3.5 above, but in relation to land-based gaming.

One of the most significant changes concerning land-based gaming occurred in the year 2010. The 2010 Gambling Amendment Act strengthened the protection of minors and players as far as gambling machines are concerned. Gaming arcades and gambling machines set up at individual locations are still subject to stringent provisions governing the protection of players and the regulatory rules of the Austrian provinces.

This amendment introduced new provisions concerning the (previous) area of 'minor gambling with gambling machines'. The provincial legislators, within a legal frame provided by the federal legislator, are at liberty to allow certain 'provincial payouts with gambling machines' and to provide that the right to operate such provincial payments may be transferred by way of a licence to companies organised under private law. The maximum number of such licences depends on the population, and not more than three licences per province may be granted. In addition, the provision specifies the requirements to be met by an applicant (type of company, quality of managing director) and the underlying conditions applicable to the protection of players (regulations concerning the equipment of an outlet, minimum distance to other outlets), as well as regulations concerning the duration of games (duration of individual games, maximum amount of stakes and gains, cooling phase). Furthermore, the obligation to prevent money laundering, previously only applicable to federal licensees, was extended to include gambling machines, and regulatory minimum regulations were stipulated.

5. TAX
5.1 Please summarise briefly the tax regime applicable both to land-based and online gaming.
The basis of assessment for gaming taxation is the annual gross gaming income, which consists of stakes wagered less the pay-outs for winnings during a calendar year.

Lottery games are taxed with 18.5 per cent up to 27.5 per cent; electronic lottery games are taxed at 40 per cent. The gaming tax for slot machines is 30 per cent or, if subject to provincial law, 10 per cent. Slot machines in a provincial legislation that does not grant any licences for slot machines are taxed at 25 per cent. The gaming tax rate for casinos is 30 per cent less statutory VAT for earnings from the operation of slot machines. Betting within Austria is subject to a 2 per cent gaming tax calculated on the basis of amounts wagered. Any other games that are not subject to the monopoly are excluded from gaming taxation.

The Austrian provinces are not allowed to tax licensees who operate games exclusively under federal laws.

6. ADVERTISING
6.1 To what extent is the advertising of gambling permitted in your jurisdiction? Again, this should cover both land-based and online gaming. To the extent that advertising is permitted, how is it regulated?
Games of chance organised for a fee may be advertised, provided that these are games of chance for which a licence under the GSpG has been issued. When advertising these games, 'a responsible standard must be observed' (section 56(1) GSpG). Games of chance that have not been licensed under the GSpG may be marketed, provided that these are casino games from a casino that is located and appropriately licensed in a member state of the European Economic Area. The federal minister of finance may issue a permit for marketing such casino games (section 56(2) GSpG), provided that the statutory provisions for the protection of players that are applicable in that member state of the European Economic Area at least correspond to the relevant Austrian provisions.

Marketing other games of chance is inadmissible and constitutes a criminal offence. Whoever advertises or facilitates the advertisement of illegal games of chance is subject to prosecution (section 52(1)(9) GSpG). Such administrative offences are subject to fines of up to EUR 22,000.

7. SOCIAL GAMING

7.1 We believe this to be a growing area. Please decide under what criteria social gaming is permitted in your jurisdiction. If games are free to play or if there is no prize, are they legal without a licence? Please address circumstances where virtual currency is used and can be won: ie currency which is of no monetary or other value, save for as credits to take part in games. The answer should address the question whether game credits or virtual money can be exchanged for other prizes. Is any change to regulation in the area proposed or envisaged?

Games of chance that are not organised as pay-outs pursuant to section 4 Abs 1 GSpG may legally be played without a licence – if they are played as a pastime and for minimal sums of money. This provision covers games mostly organised within families or friends. In order to be classified as a pay-out, a game must have players or other parties who place a stake on the one side and a business owner, other players or parties who hold out the prospect of a pecuniary benefit on the other side. So, if the players do not have to place a stake and they can only win credits to take part in additional games, it cannot be qualified as a pay-out. In Austria the Administrative Court has decided that if players can only win credits to take part in additional games, a game cannot be considered as offering pecuniary benefits (VwGH 10.11.1980, 571/80). Beyond that, they must be played as a pastime and for minimal sums of money.

As the GSpG does not make any distinction between money and entities of monetary value, in online games of chance where virtual currency is used and can be won it must not be possible to exchange game credits or virtual money for other prizes – otherwise it is an illegal game of chance only allowed for the licensee of the lottery concession.

Tournaments of card games are allowed – if per tournament and person not more than EUR 10 has to be paid to participate and not more than EUR 1,000 may be won, if not more than 100 players participate and if the tournament is held not more than once per quarter in a tavern or restaurant (*Wirtshauspoker*).

Belgium

Astrea Pieter Paepe

1. OBJECTIVES AND STRUCTURE OF LEGISLATION

The regulatory landscape for games of chance consists of a number of
different legal acts. The most important acts are the federal act of 7 May
1999 regarding games of chance, wagers and the protection of the players
(the Gaming Act), the federal act of 31 December 1851 regarding lotteries
(the Lotteries Act) and the federal act of 19 April 2002 to rationalise the
functioning and the management of the National Lottery (the National
Lottery Act).

For private operators, the most important piece of legislation is the
Gaming Act. Whereas online games of chance were prohibited before 2011,
the Belgian legislator modified the Gaming Act in 2010 in order to put in
place a strict licensing regime for online games of chance and bets. However,
the Gaming Act excludes lotteries from its scope of application. Lotteries are
regulated by the Lotteries Act.

2. FRAMEWORK OF LEGISLATION

2.1 What is the legal definition of gambling and what falls within this definition?

Gaming Act

Article 2, 1° of the Gaming Act defines *'games of chance'* as *'any game by which
a stake of any kind is committed, the consequence of which is either loss of the
stake by at least one of the players or a gain of any kind in favour of at least one
of the players, or organisers of the game and in which chance is a factor, albeit
ancillary, for the conduct of the game, determination of the winner or fixing of
the gain'*. A game of chance therefore requires the presence of the following
elements:

* a game;
* a stake of any kind;
* a loss or a gain; and
* chance playing a role, however minimal, in the outcome of the game.

Because there must be a stake of some kind, games which are completely
free cannot qualify as a game of chance within the meaning of the Gaming
Act.

A *'wager'* is defined as a specific sub-category of games of chance: *'a game
of chance in which each player wagers an amount that generates a gain or loss
that does not depend on an act of the player, but depends on the realisation of
an uncertain event happening without the intervention of the players'* (Article 2,
5° of the Gaming Act). The Gaming Act explicitly distinguishes *'totalisator'*
(mutual bets) (*'bet for which an organiser acts as the intermediary between*

various players who play against each other and in which the bets are collected and distributed among the winners, after deduction of a percentage to cover the taxes on gambling and betting, the costs of the organisers and the profits they gain from it') from *'odds betting' ('bet in which a player places stakes on the result of a certain act, in which the amount of earnings is determined according to fixed or conventional odds and in which the organiser is personally liable to pay winnings to players')*.

Considering the broad definition of games of chance, the Belgian legislature has explicitly excluded certain games from the definition of games of chance:

- the practice of sports;
- games in which the only stake offered to the player or wager is to continue the game free of charge up to a maximum of five times; and
- card games or board or parlour games played outside class I and II gaming establishments (see below) and games operated in attraction parks or by industrial fairgrounds in connection with carnivals or trade or other fairs and on analogous occasions, as well as games organised occasionally, and at most four times a year, by an association having a social or charitable purpose or by a non-profit association for the benefit of a social or philanthropic project, requiring only a very limited stake and that can procure for the player or wager only a low-value material advantage.

In addition, the Gaming Act explicitly states that it does not apply to lotteries within the meaning of the Lotteries Act and Articles 301–303 of the Belgian Criminal Code. The same provision adds that the Gaming Act does also not apply to the public lotteries and the games as meant by Article 3, §1, paragraph 1 of the National Lottery Act.

Lotteries Act and the National Lottery Act
A lottery is any *'transaction offered to the public meant to procure a gain by means of chance'* (Article 301 of the Criminal Code). Three remarks are presented to explain the definition of a lottery. First, and most importantly, the essence of a lottery is that the loss or gain is exclusively determined by chance, without any active involvement or intervention of the player. In other words, the skill of a player cannot have any influence on the result of the lottery. Secondly, free transactions can also qualify as a lottery. The definition of Article 301 of the Criminal Code does not require that the player commits a stake. Thirdly, a lottery must be offered to the public.

2.2 What is the legal definition of online gambling and what falls within this definition?
The Gaming Act only applies to games of chance, which are not explicitly excluded from its scope (see above). The Gaming Act does not recognise the concept 'online games of chance', but only *'games of chance offered through an instrument of the information society'*. An instrument of the information society is understood to be *'electronic equipment for the processing (including digital compression) and storage of data which is entirely transmitted, conveyed*

and received by wire, by radio, by optical means or by other electromagnetic means' (Article 2, 10° of the Gaming Act). Games of chance offered through an instrument of the information society therefore include games of chance on the internet. With the use of the term 'instruments of the information society', the Belgian legislature wanted to take make sure that the Gaming Act would also apply to games of chance and bets offered through new technologies, which may not yet be known.

We explain below in more detail that the National Lottery Act allows the National Lottery to organise public lotteries, games of chance, wagers and games. For all these services, the National Lottery Act explicitly states that the National Lottery can make use of instruments of the information society.

2.3 Please set out the different gambling products identified by legislation.
Gaming Act
The Gaming Act itself does not identify any specific gambling products. Instead, it states, for each category of licence, that the holders can offer those games of chance that are enumerated in a royal decree (ie an act of the executive power):

- Casinos (class I games of chance establishments/licence A): a royal decree of 19 July 2001 enumerates the games of chance that can be offered in casinos. These games are subdivided in two categories. The first category of games comprises table games (baccara, big wheel, blackjack, poker, chemin de fer, craps, mini punto banco, midi punto banco, maxi punto banco, French roulette, American roulette, English roulette, sic bo and bingo); the second category comprises automatic games (reel-slot-type games, video-slot-type games, wheel-of-fortune-type games, horse races with several terminals where at least 12 players can take place, keno-type games and interactive poker games). Casinos can therefore offer poker both as a 'table game' and as an 'automatic game'. In addition, casinos have the right to organise one poker tournament per year, in close cooperation with the Gaming Commission.

- Gaming arcades (class II games of chance establishments/licence B): a royal decree of 26 April 2004 establishes the list of the games of chance that can be offered in gaming arcades. There are two categories of games: automatic games without players' cards and automatic games with players' cards. In the category of automatic games without players' cards, there are five types of games: blackjack, horse bets, dice games, poker games and roulette. There is currently only one game of chance that B-licence holders can offer as an automatic game with players' cards, namely interactive poker.

- Class III games of chance establishments or bars (licence C) are premises where drinks, of whatever nature, are sold to be consumed on the spot and where at most two games of chance are offered, namely bingo and one-ball.

- Class IV games of chance establishments (licence F1). Bets can be organised on sports events, on horse races and other (non-sporting) events. It is prohibited to organise wagers on an event or activity contrary to public order or morality. It is also prohibited to organise wagers on events or acts the outcome of which is already known or for which the uncertain act has already occurred.

The Gaming Act lists the ways in which bets on horse races can be offered:

- totalisator betting (mutual bets) on horse races that take place in Belgium and are organised by a racing association approved by the competent federation;
- totalisator betting (mutual bets) on horse races taking place abroad under conditions set by the king;
- fixed or conventional odds betting on horse races that take place in Belgium and are organised by a racing association approved by the competent federation; and
- bets on horse races that take place abroad, either in accordance with the results of totalisator betting, or by the conventional odds to which the parties refer.

Lotteries Act

Article 1 of the Lotteries Act states that all lotteries are prohibited. There are nevertheless certain limited exceptions to this general prohibition, namely for lotteries *'exclusively intended for religious or charitable purposes, to promote industry and art or any other purpose in the general interest'*: these lotteries must obtain a licence (depending on their catchment, at local, provincial or national level).

National Lottery Act

The National Lottery Act itself does not identify any specific games, but identifies the categories of games that the National Lottery can offer. According to Article 6, §1, 1°–3° of the National Lottery Act, the National Lottery's statutory purposes include:

- organising public lotteries;
- organising games of chance and wagers; and
- organising games.

The National Lottery has been granted a monopoly on offering public lotteries. The same provision specifies that these services should be offered *'in the general interest and in accordance with commercial methods'*. However, the National Lottery cannot freely decide which games, games of chance, wagers or public lotteries it will offer; a royal decree must set the forms and (general) rules for each of them.

The organisation of public lotteries, games of chance, wagers and games are public services. For all these services, the Lotteries Act explicitly provides that the National Lottery can make use of instruments of the information society.

2.4 Please list the different requirements for each gambling product, including legal classifications for each; for example, is poker a game of skill or game of chance?

Poker

Poker is considered as a game of chance provided that the several legal requirements for such a qualification (see above) are present:

- it is a game;
- there is a stake of some kind;
- there is a loss or a gain; and
- chance plays a role, even minimal, in the outcome of the game.

With regard to the fourth condition, the Belgian legislature wanted to prevent discussion about whether a game qualifies as a games of chance or a game of skill. As soon as chance plays a minimal role, and even though the skills of a player largely determine the outcome of a game, the game is qualified as a game of chance. It follows that poker is generally considered to be a game of chance.

Gaming Act

For every class of games of chance establishment (I–IV), a royal decree determines the operating rules of the games of chance and the bets that can be offered (see also section 4.2 below).

2.5 Explain the system of regulation of gambling; which regulatory or governmental body is responsible for the supervision of gambling? Which body issues licences? Which body examines enforcement powers? Is there any limit on the number or duration of available licences?

The Gaming Act attributes in essence three tasks to the Belgian Gaming Commission. The first task is advisory: on request from a concerned minister or Parliament, the Gaming Commission provides advice about legislative or regulatory issues concerning the Gaming Act. The second task is to grant licences. The Gaming Act is premised on the prohibition of offering games of chance. Certain games of chance can be offered as exceptions to this general prohibition, but only if the required licence is obtained. The Gaming Commission is responsible for granting these licences. The Gaming Commission's third task is supervisory: the Gaming Commission is responsible for monitoring the compliance with the Gaming Act and controls the licences that have been granted.

The number of licences available is limited, and the licences are granted for a limited period of time. This is discussed in more detail below.

3. ONLINE GAMBLING

3.1 To what extent can online gambling be offered in your jurisdiction? Are licences available and, if so, for which gambling products? Please describe briefly the licensing process, who may apply, whether licences are limited in number and, if no licences are available, whether it is legal for online gambling to be offered. In the case of EU jurisdictions, please state whether there are any issues as to the legality of the local law at EU level. Please refer to any relevant cases at ECJ level and explain any measures taken or pending by the European Commission.

Since 1 January 2011, the date of entry into force of the amended Gaming Act, there is an explicit legal framework for offering online games in Belgium; before that date, online games of chance were prohibited. The Belgian legislature has set up a closed licensing system: offering online games of chance and bets requires an online licence (licence A+ for online casinos, licence B+ for online gaming arcades and licence F1+ for online bets). The number of online licences available is limited to 9 A+ licences, 180 B+ licences and 35 F1+ licences (initially only 34 F1+ licences). In addition, an online licence requires a mandatory physical connection to the Belgian territory: only those operators licensed to operate in the real world (and holding a principal licence A, B or F1) can obtain a licence to offer the same games of chance and bets online (an additional A+, B+ or F1+ online licence). The Belgian gambling legislation thus introduces a parallelism between the offline and online licences.

The following scheme summarises the online licensing system:

Additional licence	Description	Principal licence	Numerus clausus?	Situation in January 2014
A+	Online casino	A	9	8 active A+ licences
B+	Online gaming arcade	B	180	30 active B+ licences
F1+	Online bets	F1	35	13 active F1+ licences

In 2010, a case was initiated before the Belgian Constitutional Court in order to contest the constitutionality of several provisions of the Gaming Act. One of the arguments invoked was that the online gambling legislation violated the freedom to provide services, as protected by Article 56 of the Treaty on the Functioning of the European Union. In its judgment of 14 July 2011, the Belgian Constitutional Court dismissed the arguments set forth by the requesting parties and held that the online gambling legislation does not violate the freedom to provide services.

In November 2013, the European Commission addressed a letter of formal notice to the Belgian authorities requesting information on the Belgian legislation restricting the supply of gambling services. In addition, the Commission raised questions about the transparency of the Belgian legal framework, in particular with regard to the rules governing the legal conduct of online gambling business and in view of the grant of a betting licence through royal decree to the National Lottery.

3.2 Is there a distinction between the law applicable to B2B operations and that applicable to B2C operations?

B2B operators should hold an E licence. The following activities are subject to an E licence requirement: sale, rental, supply, making available, import, export, manufacture, maintenance, reparation and equipment of games of chance. The Gaming Act does not distinguish between land-based games of chance and online games of chance. It also follows that all undertakings providing one of these services to an A+, B+ or F1+ licence holder should obtain an E licence.

3.3 What are the consequences for B2C or B2B operators who are active in your jurisdiction without having obtained or applied for the required permits, licences and approvals? What penalties and enforcement powers are available in respect of the illegal operators? Please outline any significant domestic decisions or enforcement actions that have been taken by the relevant authorities in recent years.

Gaming Act

The Gaming Act contains a very broad prohibition clause. Not only is it prohibited to *'operate in any place, in any form and in any direct or indirect manner, games of chance or gambling establishments without a license'*, but it is also prohibited to participate in illegal (ie offered without a licence) games of chance, facilitate the operation of illegal games of chance, advertise illegal games of chance or recruit for illegal games of chance if it should be known that said game of chance or a gambling establishment is not authorised under the Gaming Act. All these acts are punishable with criminal sanctions.

The operation of illegal games of chance can be sanctioned with a prison sentence of six months to five years and/or with a fine of EUR 600–600,000. Persons guilty of breaching a prohibition to participate in and facilitate the operation of illegal games of chance, or advertising or recruiting for illegal games of chance, are liable to imprisonment for a period of one month to three years and/or a fine of EUR 156–150,000. In particular cases (recidivism or if the infringement involves a person younger than 18 years), these sanctions can de doubled.

The Gaming Act also provides that it is prohibited for any person to participate in any game of chance on the result of which, by its nature, he could have a direct influence. A violation of this provision can give rise to a prison sentence of six months to five years and/or with a fine of EUR 600–600,000.

The Gaming Act contains also an administrative sanctioning mechanism. If the Public Prosecutor, within a time period of six months from the day of receipt of the original of official report, does not communicate to the Gaming Commission or informs it that, without calling into question the existence of the infringement, it will not prosecute the facts, the Gaming Commission has the power to impose administrative sanctions. If, however, the Public Prosecutor, also within a time period of six months from the day of receipt of the original of the official report, informs the Gaming Commission that it will prosecute the facts or that no sufficient elements to prosecute are available, the Gaming Commission cannot impose an administrative sanction. The Gaming Commission can impose an administrative fine corresponding to the minimum and maximum amounts of the criminal fine. The administrative fine must be imposed by reasoned decision. The notification of that decision prevents a criminal prosecution for the same facts. The Gaming Act contains a specific procedure to legally challenge an administrative fine.

Lottery Act
Article 1 of the Lottery Act stipulates that all lotteries are prohibited. Article 302 of the Belgian Criminal Code provides that organisers, entrepreneurs, directors, representatives and agents of lotteries which are not legally allowed will be punished with a prison sentence of eight days to three months and with a criminal fine of EUR 50–3,000. In addition, the moveable property staked in the lottery can be seized.

3.4 What technical measures are in place (if any) to protect consumers from unlicensed operators, such as ISP blocking and payment blocking?
The Gaming Commission publishes on its website a blacklist of prohibited gaming websites. In January 2014, the domain names of 84 websites were included in the blacklist.

The blacklist is supplied to all Belgian internet service providers, most of which will block access to the websites (DNS blocking). In addition, the Gaming Commission has concluded a protocol with Febelfin (a Belgian non-profit-making association representing the interests of banks and financial institutions). On the basis of this unpublished protocol, Belgian banks and financial institutions are requested to block payments from and to blacklisted operators. In March 2014 it was reported in the Belgian press that, for the first time, payments and accounts regarding one of the blacklisted operators have effectively been blocked.

3.5 Has the legal status of online gambling changed significantly in recent years and, if so, how
On 1 September 2011, the regulatory framework applicable to online games of chance was completed by the entry into force of two royal decrees. The first royal decree lays down the form of the additional licence and how application for an additional licence must be submitted and verified, while the second enumerates the quality requirements to be met by the applicant for an additional licence.

The first royal decree requires the applicant to enclose with its application a plan containing the name of the website, the structure of the website, the place where the website will be administered, the points of contact and the responsible party for the administration of the website. Applications will be treated within a period of six months starting from the application. The second royal decree contains obligations with regard to the applicant's creditworthiness, the security of payment transactions between the operator and the players, the operator's policy with regard to the accessibility of games of chance for socially vulnerable groups, a complaint procedure, advertisement policy and fiscal obligations. In addition, the royal decree states that the applicant is responsible for a permanent data connection between the website and the Gaming Commission.

However, the regulatory framework applicable to online games of chance is not yet complete. The Gaming Act enumerates several other conditions that should be detailed in royal decrees (see below). This further increases the legal uncertainty in a field that is already subject to much contestation.

3.6 Whilst acknowledging the inherent difficulty in predicting developments in gambling law, what are the likely developments in online gambling in your jurisdiction, both short term and long term? Are any specific amendments under consideration? Have there been any recent political developments, or do you envisage any in the near future? Are any specific amendments under consideration? Are they likely to be adopted and, if so, what is the time scale?

The first development that is generally expected to take place is of a regulatory nature. With the entry into force of the amended Gaming Act on 1 January 2011, the basic and fundamental outlines of the Belgian online gaming policy were set. However, the Gaming Act requires the passing of a number of executive acts (royal decrees) for completion. With regard to online games of chance and bets, Article 43/8, §2 of the Gaming Act provides that royal decrees should regulate the following matters:

(1) the quality conditions of the operator applying for a additional licence, which should at least cover the creditworthiness, the safety of payment transactions between the operator and the player, the policy of the operator regarding access to games of chance by socially vulnerable groups, the policy regarding complaints, rules on advertising and compliance with all fiscal obligations;

(2) the conditions under which games can be offered (covering at least the registration and identification of the player, age control, the games offered, the rules of the game, payment methods and the distribution of prizes);

(3) the methods for monitoring and controlling the games operated, covering at least the condition that the servers where the data are stored and through which the website is administrated have to be located in a permanent establishment in Belgium;

(4) the games that can be operated; and

(5) the rules on information *vis-à-vis* the players about the legality of the games of chance offered through a service of the information society.

Only the royal decrees with regard to point (1) have been issued. This means that important executive measures are still lacking. It is generally hoped that these executive measures will be adopted and published in the near future. In April 2014 Belgium notified by the European Commission of three draft royal decrees: a draft royal decree regarding the conditions under which games of chance may be offered through information society tools, concerning at least the registration and identification of the player, age verification, the games offered, the rules of the games, the method of payment and the prize distribution method; a draft royal decree regarding the list of games that may be operated by holders of a supplementary licence through the use of information society tools; and a draft royal decree regarding the monitoring and control procedures for games of chance operated via authorised websites. These three drafts are the texts that will implement Article 43/8, §2, 2°–4° of the Gaming Act.

A second development may come from the possible conflict between the online gaming legislation and EU law. In November 2013, the European Commission wrote a letter of formal notice to Belgium to address the restrictions of the supply of gambling services. In addition, the Commission raised questions about the transparency of the Belgian legal framework. If the Court of Justice of the European Union were to ultimately decide that the Gaming Act violates EU law, the Belgian legislator would have no other choice but to alter the Gaming Act.

Finally, the Belgian gaming landscape is currently also being investigated by the Belgian Competition Authority, which is investigating whether the National Lottery infringes the Belgian Competition Act. Several competitors had filed complaints with the Belgian Competition Authority concerning SCOOORE!, the football betting service offered by the National Lottery.

3.7 Is the law the same in relation to mobile gambling and interactive gambling on television? If not, are there any headline differences?

The Gaming Act provides for the explicit regulation of media games. A *'media game'* is *'a game of chance operated via the media'*. A provider of media games should obtain a G1 or G2 licence.

4. LAND-BASED GAMING
4.1 Please describe the licensing regime (if any) for land-based gaming, and what products are included. Please set out what licences are available, and the licensing regime for them.

The following scheme summarises the various land-based gaming licences, as laid down in the Gaming Act:

Licence	Description	Numerus clausus?	Situation in January 2014	Duration
A	Gaming establishment of type I: casino	9 available licences	9 active licences	15 years – renewable
B	Gaming establishment of type II: gaming arcades	180 available licences	178 active licences	9 years – renewable
C	Gaming establishment of type III: bars	No	1849 (in 2012)	5 years – renewable
D	Exercising a professional activity within gaming establishments of type I, II or IV	No	1087 (in 2012)	Duration not provided in the Gaming Act
E	Sale, rental, supply, making available, import, export, manufacture, maintenance, reparation and equipment of games of chance	No	194 active licences	10 years – renewable
F1	Gaming establishment of type IV: organisers of bets.	35	35 active licences	9 years – renewable
F2	Licence to take bets on behalf of an F1 licence holder	1000 fixed and 60 mobile	Not known	3 years – renewable
G1	Media games	No	Not known	5 years – renewable
G2	Media games	No	Not known	1 year

A *'casino'*, also known as a class I gaming establishment, is defined as an establishment *'in which are operated games of chance, whether or not automatic, that are authorised by the King and in which there are at the same time organised socio-cultural activities, such as shows, exhibitions, congresses and hotel and catering activities'*. The Gaming Act explicitly provides that there are only nine casinos allowed on Belgian territory and also enumerates the territories of the communes/cities where a casino can be operated: Blankenberge, Chaudfontaine, Dinant, Knokke-Heist, Middelkerke, Namen, Oostende, Spa and Brussels.

'*Gaming arcades*', also known as class II gaming establishments, are '*establishments in which only games of chance authorised by the king are operated*'. Their number is limited to 180.

The licensing system for bets distinguishes between the organisation of bets and the acceptance of bets. An organiser of bets must hold an F1 licence. The maximum number of F1 licences has been set at 34 for the period from 1 January 2011 until 1 January 2020. A royal decree of 20 July 2012 nevertheless added that an additional F1 licence could be granted to the National Lottery. Class IV gaming establishments are places exclusively permitted to accept bets on behalf of an F1 licence holder. The acceptance of bets requires to acceptor to hold an F2 licence. It is prohibited to accept bets outside a class IV gaming establishment. There are, however, a limited number of exceptions to this prohibition. A class IV gaming establishment can be fixed or mobile. A fixed class IV gaming establishment is a permanent establishment, clearly demarcated, where bets are offered. A royal decree determines that a maximum of 1000 fixed class IV gaming establishments can be licensed. A mobile class IV gaming establishment is a temporary establishment, also clearly demarcated, where bets are offered during and at an event, a sports game or a sports competition. A maximum of 60 mobile class IV gaming establishments are allowed.

4.2 Please set out any particular limitations or requirements for (eg casino) operators, such as a ban on local residents gambling.

Persons younger than 21 years are prohibited from accessing a casino or a gaming arcade. Bets are prohibited for minors (less than 18 years). The same age requirements apply for online games of chance and bets. The Gaming Act contains additional prohibitions to access casinos and gaming arcades for particular persons (eg magistrates).

Casino (class I gaming establishment)

A royal decree of 3 December 2006 contains the operating rules and additional requirements concerning the accounting and control of games of chance that can be offered in class I gaming establishments. A royal decree of 15 December 2004 provides that class I (and II) gaming establishments must have an access register. A royal decree of 23 May 2003 lays down the rules for the supervision and control of the games of chance offered in casinos, including control through an IT system. All casinos must have a local area network (LAN), which must be connected with the LAN of the Gaming Commission.

Gaming arcade (class II gaming establishment)

The operating rules for the automatic games of chance that can be offered in class II gaming establishments are laid out in a royal decree of 8 April 2003. A royal decree of 23 May 2003 sets out the rules for supervising and controlling the games of chance offered in class II gaming establishments. This includes the control through an IT system, whereby the class II gaming establishment has a LAN that is connected with that of the Gaming Commission.

Bars (class III gaming establishment)
A royal decree of 11 July 2003 lays down the operating rules for the games of chance that can be offered in class III gaming establishments.

Bets (class IV gaming establishment)
A number of royal decrees of the same date (22 December 2010) lay down detailed rules regarding bets. These royal decrees set out, for example, the rules regarding the operation of bets, the conditions for organising mutual bets on horse races taking place abroad and the rules regarding the automatic games of chance that can be offered in class IV gaming establishments.

4.3 Please address the questions in 3.5 above, but in relation to land-based gaming.
The main change of land-based gaming is that the regulation of land-based bets has been incorporated into the Gaming Act. Whereas bets were hitherto regulated by separate legal acts (namely, the federal act of 26 June 1963 regulated sports bets other than bets on horse races, while the Code on Taxes Equated to Income Taxes regulated horse racing bets), the regulation of bets has been laid down in the amended Gaming Act, which entered into force on 1 January 2011. As a consequence, the Gaming Commission has become competent to grant the licences required to organise bets and to take on bets.

5. TAX
5.1 Please summarise briefly the tax regime applicable to both land-based and online gaming.
The gaming and betting tax is generally levied on the gross amount of the sums that have been staked. Particular games of chance are explicitly excluded from the scope of application of the gaming and betting tax. One of these exceptions is 'permitted lotteries'.

As a general rule, the tax rate is 11 per cent, to be calculated on the gross amount of the sums staked. There are, however, many specific tax regimes. These can be summarised as follows.

Online games of chance and bets
The three regions (ie the three federated entities Walloon Region, Flemish Region and the Region of Brussels-Capital) have the competence to determine the tax rates applicable to online games of chance and bets. While these regions could have set different tax rates, in practice they have set the same tax rate of 11 per cent of the actual gross margin realised with the game of wager, ie the gross amount of the sums staked minus the profits that have actually been distributed.

Bets

In the Flemish Region and the Region of Brussels-Capital, bets on horse races, dog races and sports events, taking place in Belgium or in an EEA member state, are taxed at a rate of 15 per cent, calculated on the actual gross margin realised with that wager. Bets on horse races, dog races and sporting events taking place outside the EEA are taxed at a rate of 15 per cent on the gross amount of the sums or stakes involved. In the Walloon Region, bets are generally taxed at a rate of 15 per cent on the actual gross margin realised upon the bet.

Casino games

In the Flemish Region, the tax applicable to casino games is as follows:
- baccarat: 5.30 per cent of the banker's winnings;
- roulette without zero: 3 per cent of the punter's winnings;
- other casino games: 33 per cent of the gross gaming revenue, but 44 per cent on the portion of the gross gaming revenue exceeding EUR 865,000.

In the Walloon Region, the tax applicable to casino games is as follows:
- baccarat: 4.80 per cent of the banker's winnings;
- roulette without zero: 2.75 per cent of the punter's winnings;
- other casino games: 33 per cent of the gross gaming revenue up to EUR 1,360,000 and 44 per cent on the portion of the gross gaming revenue exceeding that amount.

In the Region Brussels-Capital, the tax applicable to casino games is as follows:
- baccarat: 4.80 per cent of the banker's winnings;
- roulette without zero: 2.75 per cent of the punter's winnings;
- other casino games: 33 per cent of the gross gaming revenue, but 44 per cent on the portion of the gross gaming revenue exceeding EUR 865,000.

6. ADVERTISING

6.1 To what extent is the advertising of gambling permitted in your jurisdiction? Again, this should cover both land-based and online gaming. To the extent that advertising is permitted, how is it regulated?

The Gaming Act explicitly prohibits advertising for a game of chance or a gaming establishment if it should be known that said game of chance or a gambling establishment is not authorised under the Gaming Act. A violation of this prohibition can give rise to criminal sanctions (see section 3.3 above).

Regarding online games of chance and bets, Article 43/8, §2(e) of the Gaming Act stipulates that a royal decree should lay down rules regarding advertising. Articles 8 and 9 of the royal decree of 21 June 2011 says that the application for an online licence should clearly explain the advertising policy that will be implemented. The same royal decree stipulates that an operator should observe a 'certain reluctance' in its advertisements.

7. SOCIAL GAMING
7.1 We believe this to be a growing area. Please decide under what criteria social gaming is permitted in your jurisdiction. If games are free to play or if there is no prize, are they legal without a licence? Please address circumstances where virtual currency is used and can be won: ie currency which is of no monetary or other value, save for as credits to take part in games. The answer should address the question whether game credits or virtual money can be exchanged for other prizes. Is any change to regulation in the area proposed or envisaged?

The Belgian Gaming Commission follows the development of social games closely. If a social game qualifies as a game of chance (see section 2.1 above for the constituent elements of the definition of a game of chance), the Gaming Act applies. It follows that offering such social games is prohibited, unless the Gaming Commission has granted a licence to do so.

The Gaming Commission has explored whether it is possible to issue specific rules regarding social gaming. A representative of the Gaming Commission has set out that this specific regulation could exist in a double-track system, whereby social games could be offered without a licence (with a limit of EUR 100 per month) or with a licence (for which the Gaming Commission would publish a list of applicable games). There is currently no specific regulation in force that regulates social games.

Brazil

BKBG – Barretto Ferreira, Kujawski, Brancher
Sociedade de Advogados
Fabio Kujawski & Fernanda Bezerra

1. OBJECTIVES AND STRUCTURE OF LEGISLATION

The practice of gambling is dealt with by Decree Law 3688/1941, the Law of Misdemeanours (the Law). When the legislator drafted this law, the intention was to preserve social morality, expressing the standards envisioned and accepted at that time (1941) as well as suppressing those activities believed to be vile.

The Law forbids the practice of gambling, which is referred to therein as 'games of chance'. When the Law was created, the legislator's main purpose was to espouse the benefits of hard work, thereby condemning the practice of activities from which money could be easily earned and consequently, lost. In this respect, the government was seen to occupy a crucial role in gambling regulation, by valuing the useful behaviour of individuals and the preservation of family property and integrity, since the harm that can arise from gambling addiction can end up not only ruining an entire family structure but also lead to the perpetration of crimes to uphold the addiction. This was the *mens legis* at that time.

According to the Law, those who establish or exploit games of chance in a public place or place accessible to the public, by means of the payment of an entry fee or otherwise, commit a misdemeanour.

The penalties for those that exploit games of chance in Brazil are imprisonment of three months to one year and a fine. For land-based premises, the movable assets are also confiscated. The penalty is increased by one-third if a minor is either employed or participates as a bettor in the game. A fine is also assessed on the players.

The conduct forbidden by Article 50 of the Law consists of establishing or exploiting games of chance. For the purposes of determining the criminal type, 'establishing' means providing access to a game of chance, while 'exploiting' means making a profit out of third parties' participation in the game. The profit that the law forbids does not relate only to money, but also to any economic advantage (for example, through brand exposure).

Nowadays, despite ongoing changes in the perception of the family structure and principally, in the definition of morality over time, the prohibition on gambling in Brazil remains. Nevertheless, over the years there has been continuous pressure from different economic and social sectors to soften these provisions and prohibitions.

The main aspect that should be analysed in order to determine whether or not a certain game represents a 'game of chance' is the element of luck as the prevailing factor for the result of the game. The greater the preponderance of this factor, the greater the chance that it will fall into the legal prohibition in the Law.

Since the statute that governs games of chance was enacted in the early 1940s and has not been modified since then in this respect, there is no differentiation between land-based and online gambling. The existing statute shall be interpreted as encompassing both. The law forbids the establishment of the means or provision of access to games of chance. This should be construed as any kind of means, including in the virtual world.

In addition to the criminal implications for the entity that exploits a game of chance, there is an important civil consequence concerning the debts that are incurred by those that participate in such games. The Brazilian Civil Code sets forth that gamblers and bettors cannot be compelled to pay debts that originate from gambling and betting. Since the nature of these games conflicts with the legal system, no value or protection is given to the results and effects of such games. Therefore, there is no legitimacy for the creditor or gaming company in collecting those debts through the judiciary branch. However, if the gambler or bettor pays the debt voluntarily, he/she cannot go to court and seek recovery of the amounts paid. Also, if a person loans money for gambling/bets, he/she cannot file a lawsuit to recover the amounts loaned in case of lack of payment.

While the gambling legal framework has remained unchanged for more than 70 years, some developments have taken place with respect to the analysis of which games are considered misdemeanours, notably concerning poker (please refer to answer to question 2 below). Case law in Brazil remained steady until the last decade, in the sense of prohibiting most - if not all - games in which the luck element was important for the determination of the winner. Case law has recently shown a tendency towards a more flexible approach with respect to poker.

2. FRAMEWORK OF LEGISLATION

2.1 What is the legal definition of gambling and what falls within this definition?

Article 50, paragraph 3, of the Law provides three different situations in which a given activity will be considered gambling, namely: (i) the exclusive or preponderant dependence on luck for the determination of the final result of the game; (ii) horse racing in non-official places; and (iii) betting on other kinds of sports.

Therefore it can be perceived that in most cases gambling qualifies as a game of chance whose elements rely ultimately on luck, risk and the profit-making purpose. However, whenever a certain game depends on skill or dexterity, it does not qualify as a game of chance. Therefore, the crucial part of this analysis is to demonstrate whether or not the user/customer can influence the result of the game with his/her ability.

There are some games in which luck is the only element that determines the winner, meaning that no other factor is even considered. For these games, the Law is clearly applicable. In some other cases, though, a combination between luck and the ability of the player may exist; in which case the preponderance of the luck element for the result of the game may be disputable. Since the Law states that games of chance are those depending exclusively or preponderantly on luck, in these disputable cases, the restriction established by law may or may not apply. Whenever gaming companies face this debate regarding the games they develop, we advise that an unbiased expert opinion on the game rules be issued in order to demonstrate the company's good faith with respect to the game offering. Another measure is to seek *ex ante* a legal remedy in order to obtain a court decision determining that a particular game does not fall into the category of 'game of chance' (and, therefore, is not embraced by the Law).

Brazilian case law is silent when it comes to the explanation of the minimum legally admissible standard for one to be able to consider a game as not preponderantly dependent on luck and, therefore, adherent to the provision of Article 50 of the Law. Notwithstanding, in a recent decision of the Court of Justice of the State of Rio Grande do Sul (*TJRS, Mandado de Segurança (Writ of Mandamus) n. 70025424086*), the judge rapporteur affirmed that as the Law forbids the preponderance of luck, but does not require the preponderance of skill, a game that requires skill and luck from the players should not be deemed illegal. However, although this position is not prevalent in our case law, it represents an interesting precedent.

2.2 What is the legal definition of online gambling and what falls within this definition?

There is currently no legal definition of online gambling in Brazilian legislation. The relevant characteristic is determining whether the luck element is preponderant for the result of the game. If it is, most likely the game will be considered illegal *vis-à-vis* the Law.

2.3 Please set out the different gambling products identified by legislation.

Poker

There is no explicit legal reference to poker qualifying it as a game of chance. In spite of the existence of judgments where the game of poker is classified as a game of chance and, therefore, a misdemeanour offence prohibited by Article 50 of the Law, there are recent judgments and decisions where certain games, whose results depend on the skill of their players, do not have the essential characteristics to be classified as games of chance, thereby ruling out the possibility of a misdemeanour. In this respect, poker is usually targeted as the main point of a discussion attempting to prove that there are games and activities that, although commonly known as games of chance, do not actually rely on luck but on the player's skills for the achievement of successful results. The Institute of Criminal Matters of the Public Security Secretariat of the State of São Paulo has already issued two reports, one in 2007 and another in 2011, supporting this argument.

Another relevant expert opinion that analysed the luck element in poker (Texas Hold'em – TH) was issued by Professor Roberto Molina de Figueiredo on 23 November 2006. According to the Professor: *'That is to say, in poker (whether conventional or TH), assuming that the players are homogeneous, the expected profit is always zero, inasmuch as the return expected from the game is equal to that of the bet. In spite of this, the real games, whether online or in poker houses rarely end this way.*

This occurs because the players are never homogeneous, ie, they always possess different skill levels. In principle, the player who knows the probability of each event and that uses more than one strategy, in accordance with the profile of the other players, is at an advantage. This advantage, although small, will cause the more skilled player, in the long term, to have a significantly greater gain, as we will see in the next model.

But how does one more precisely define 'skill'? What is skill in the context of TH? And more, would it be possible to estimate the relative importance of this factor, in contrast with the luck factor?

In section II.3 we made a brief study of the probabilities at different phases of the game, in accordance with the cards until then received. Well now, the mere knowledge of these probabilities at each moment of the game is already an advantage factor for the player. Thus, the first and most fundamental skill required for a good TH player is the mathematical domain of the probabilities; he/she must have a safe expectation of his/her real chances.

But the probabilistic calculation alone does not solve the question. Although this skill (that of rapidly calculating the probabilities) is an enormous advantage in 'live' games, in the case of online games it is possible to rely on plug-in type games, that is, programs that practically calculate in real time the probabilities of each step, including indicating to the player what the 'best' action at that time is (FOLD, CALL or RAISE). In a virtual table on the internet it is very likely that the majority, if not all, the players rely on some auxiliary program for the calculation of probabilities, which, in a certain way, would put them on an equal footing in relation to this aspect. Nevertheless, although many online players use poker odds calculator programs, not all of them will be successful. The fact is that the assessment of the probabilities is only one among many relevant aspects in TH, and, certainly, not the most important.

Poker is, in any of its modalities, above all, a game that requires a constant assessment of the opponents, their reactions, standards of behaviour in different situations, the boldness with which the opponent bets, etc. It has already been said that all that a good TH player should do is 'getting into your opponent's heads, analysing how they think, figuring out what they think you think, and even determining what they think you think they think'.

In other words, Poker is a game in which, to be victorious, it is necessary, to in addition to the capacity of making rapid mathematical calculations, be able to 'read' the hidden intentions of the opponent, and at the same time dissimulate its own intentions. It would not be an overstatement to classify Poker in general (and especially TH, in which this component appears to be even more important) as a psychological assessment game.'

'It is not our objective to describe all the possible strategies in the game studied here, nor would we have the competence for such. What we wanted to point out, with some examples, is the importance of the skill factor in TH. It seems clear that nobody will be a winner in TH, depending exclusively on the 'luck' factor. It is no accident that a relatively small number of players always appear in the first places of the ranking. Certainly they are the best, the most skilled. On this point, TH is no different from other games, even those considered of 'pure skill', such as tennis, golf, etc.'

'Considering that TH, like other types of Poker, is always played in long-haul sessions, we may safely affirm that skill is decisive to define the winner. Note that this conclusion is valid both for 'live' TH and for online games, since, basically, the only

information not available in games on the internet is the visual. All the other, that is, the estimate of the odds, history of the opponent's actions, etc., continue available.'

As can be perceived, there are sound arguments to be made that poker is not a game of chance, and therefore should not be encompassed by the restrictions provided for by the Law.

Betting (other than sports betting)
There is no explicit legal reference to betting other than sports betting. However, case law unanimously indicates that any type of activities that include monetary betting and that depend on the luck factor characterise a 'game of chance' and are therefore prohibited.

Sports betting
The Law determines a straightforward prohibition on sports betting, except for horse races on official race tracks. Online horse race betting was considered illegal by a court decision published in October 2013.

Casino games
There is no explicit legal reference to casinos or roulette, but case law unanimously indicates that casino games such as roulette, slots and other types of games that depend on the luck factor characterise 'games of chance' and are therefore prohibited.

Slot and other machine gaming
There is no explicit legal reference to slot or machine gaming either, but case law unanimously indicates that such activities and other types of electronic games that depend on the luck factor characterise 'games of chance' and are therefore prohibited.

Bingo
Another interesting factor concerning gambling in Brazil refers to the legality of bingo. Currently, this activity is prohibited due to the lack of express permission for its practice, although Brazil has had in the past laws authorising the exploitation of bingo. The exploitation of bingo activities was previously regulated by Law 8,672/1993, which permitted the exploitation of bingo by athletic entities for the purposes of creating an alternative source of sports income, provided that they were duly authorised by the Brazilian authorities. This activity was later regulated by Law 9,615/98 (the Pelé Act), which revoked Law 8,672/1993. The National Institute for Sports Development was then created, which was responsible for the supervision of the bingo activity.

Two years after its enactment, the Pelé Act was expressly revoked by Law 9,981/00 with respect to its Articles 59 to 81, which regulated the exploitation of bingo in Brazil, including the criminal provisions, and established that bingo should only be exploited, directly or indirectly by Caixa Econômica Federal (CEF), a Federal Savings Bank. No further laws governing the exploitation of bingo by private entities have been issued since then. In addition, right after the enactment of Law 9,981/00, Provisional Measure 2,049-24, which was further edited by Provisional Measure 2,216-37, was issued and ratified the provisions of Law 9,981/00 as regards the exclusive authority of the federal government to exploit bingo through CEF. In 2004, Provisional Measure 168/2004 was enacted in order to expressly forbid the exploitation of bingo in Brazil. However, this provisional measure was rejected by the Brazilian Senate because it did not comply with the requirements of relevance and urgency that are required for the enactment of provisional measures.

Due to the expiration of Provisional Measure 168/2004, some states issued laws regarding the exploitation of bingo within their territories and several private entities began to exploit bingo again on their business premises. Notwithstanding the existence of state laws, the exploitation of bingo was the target of police operations and caused private entities and associations to pursue writs of mandamus allowing for these business activities. Some writs of mandamus were granted by the lower courts but were denied by the higher courts based on precedent 02 of the Supreme Court of Justice which says that the states do not have the power to regulate bingo and lotteries.

Currently, there are several bills under consideration with the aim of regulating the legality of bingo in the Brazilian jurisdiction. The most relevant of them, PL 2944/2004, justifies its proposal based on the controversy that regardless of consideration by many Brazilian court decisions and scholars classifying bingo as a leisure activity, it remains legally prohibited due to the provisions of the Law, which considers it as a game of chance. The bill aims to properly regulate the exploitation of bingo, in such a way as to also ban from the market those entities that do not have the means to operate transparently (in terms of accounting and tax matters), or comply with proper hygiene and safety standards generally required for the exploitation of this activity. This bill also states that part of the income raised from bingo shall be further earmarked for the funding of specific social policies such as public health and safety. Therefore, in addition to stimulating the creation of jobs, the concept is that this activity should also help to subsidise other relevant social areas. It is noteworthy that while bingo was expressly allowed in Brazil, several hundreds of places were created for the practice of this activity, and consequently, job positions.

Lottery
Decree-Law 204/1964 provides that the exploitation of the lottery activity constitutes a public service that shall be performed solely and exclusively by the Government through CEF, which is the body in charge of granting to private entities the right to sell lottery tickets to individuals, as provided by Decree-Law 759/1969.

Any other gambling products identified by legislation
Not applicable.

2.4   Please list the different requirements for each gambling product, including legal classifications for each; for example, is poker a game of skill or game of chance?
Please refer to answers to questions 2.1 and 2.3 above.

2.5   Explain the system of regulation of gambling; which regulatory or governmental body is responsible for the supervision of gambling? Which body issues licences? Which body examines enforcement powers? Is there any limit on the number or duration of available licences?
The body in charge of issuing licenses for lotteries is CEF, as previously mentioned. Those interested in selling lottery tickets must participate in a bid organised by CEF for the purposes of granting the right to exploit federal lottery products and services, including the Federal Lottery, Instantaneous Lottery, Mega-Sena, Dupla-Sena, Quina, Lotomania, Lotogol, Loteca and Lotofácil. The parties that are selected to be grantees of federal lottery products and services are subject to the payment of a Permission Fee in the amount of R$ 10,000.00. There are several other bodies that are responsible for preventing and repressing illegal gambling, such as the Ministry of Justice, Federal Police and Federal Prosecutors' Office (*Ministério Público*).

CEF, upon study of market potential, determines areas such as neighbourhoods, municipalities and cities where licences can be issued, as well as the number and terms of such licences. There is no specific limitation on the number or duration of licences available, since this is a discretionary process organised by CEF. In any case, each bid invitation establishes certain criteria and term limitations.

3.   ONLINE GAMBLING
3.1   To what extent can online gambling be offered in your jurisdiction? Are licences available and, if so, for which gambling products? Please describe briefly the licensing process, who may apply, whether licences are limited in number and, if no licences are available, whether it is legal for online gambling to be offered. In the case of EU jurisdictions, please state whether there are any issues as to the legality of the local law at EU level. Please refer to any relevant cases at ECJ level and explain any measures taken or pending by the European Commission.
Considering the absence of a specific regulation regarding online gambling, the general rules of the Law apply. Despite the prohibition of such activities, games of chance are commonly found online or even advertised in different media (including TV broadcasters). In all cases analysed, neither the entity that promotes the game nor the ISP is based in Brazil. The payment mechanisms are generally credit card or payment enabler companies. There are several difficulties for the Brazilian government to effectively restrict the offer of online gambling in Brazil when the providers are outside of the country. Law enforcement concerning cyber crimes is not always very easily accomplished. The Brazilian government has entered into judiciary cooperation agreements with countries such as the United States of America, France, Spain and

Portugal for the purposes of enabling the exchange of information and identification of persons under investigation. The cooperation between the countries generally includes: (i) assistance for evidence production; (ii) the notification and hearing of suspects, testimonies and experts; (iii) carrying out search and seizure orders; (iv) the transfer of persons under custody for deposition; and (v) exchange of information regarding the laws of the signatory parties. The country requiring the assistance shall comply with the formalities set forth in each cooperation agreement such as providing the requirement in writing with detailed information of suspects and witnesses, describing the crime under investigation and the proceeding that shall be performed by the country receiving the request.

There is no specific licensing procedure for online gambling for all reasons explained in previous answers.

3.2 Is there a distinction between the law applicable to B2B operations and that applicable to B2C operations

The criminal implications brought by the Law apply to all entities that participate in the chain, either directly or indirectly. Therefore, from a criminal law standpoint, there is no distinction between B2B or B2C arrangements. With respect to commercial and civil law matters, some clarifications are important. Since the debts incurred by the players cannot be judicially collected (please refer to answer to question 1), there is also no significant difference concerning the jurisdiction in which the game provider is established. If it were possible to collect the debts through the judiciary branch, the company contracting with the customers should preferably be present in the country where the players are located; this is because of the difficulty of prosecuting a person in Brazil from a foreign jurisdiction. Finally, for B2C operations, the Brazilian Consumer Protection Code shall apply. This Code confers several rights on customers that are not otherwise present in other types of commercial or civil relationships. Among such rights, we emphasise the strict liability regime, according to which any entity within the chain of entities involved in providing a certain service to a Brazilian consumer may be held jointly and severally liable for any losses and damages that such consumer may suffer. This liability may be imposed regardless of any direct relationship with the customer.

3.3 What are the consequences for B2C or B2B operators who are active in your jurisdiction without having obtained or applied for the required permits, licences and approvals? What penalties and enforcement powers are available in respect of the illegal operators? Please outline any significant domestic decisions or enforcement actions that have been taken by the relevant authorities in recent years.

Gambling under Brazilian laws, whether promoted by B2C or B2B operators, is forbidden by the Law. Breach of such regulations may subject the infringer to a penalty of imprisonment of three months to one year as well as the payment of a fine.

In addition, we cannot rule out the possibility that the competent governmental authority may attempt to block a website that is offering online gambling in Brazil by involving the ISP that hosts the content deemed illegal under local laws.

The majority of the court decisions on this matter deal with electronic machines that allow the practise of games of chance. In those cases, all such machines have been seized and their owners have lost ownership of them.

Moreover, in 2011 a bill of law (PLS 570/2011) aimed to expressly increase the penalty applied to online gambling operators. According to its provisions, those who establish, exploit or permit, through an international computer network, bingo, betting or any type of gambling not allowed in Brazil, regardless of any payment, would be subject to imprisonment (two to five years) and a fine. The referred bill remains under analysis by the Senate.

3.4 What technical measures are in place (if any) to protect consumers from unlicensed operators, such as ISP blocking and payment blocking?

The implementation of technical measures to prevent access of unlicensed operators by Brazilian consumers may sometimes depend on the issuance of a previous court order, as it may imply in content removal, blog, webpage, etc.

In addition to the specific removal request, Courts may determine that the Brazilian Internet Registration entity (Registro.br) suspend, cancel or even assign to a third party the infringing website registered in Brazil (.br).

The Brazilian judiciary recognises that the removal request has to be directed to the ISPs that host the illegal content, as directing the order to search engine websites will not be effective because the content will continue to be available in the web.

A change in the ISP DNS chart may also be requested. In this case, the DNS chart used by the ISP (in Brazil, the most common DNS chart is maintained by the Information and Coordination Group of .BR, NIC.br, an entity related to the Internet Management Committee of Brazil, CGI.br) may be amended to purposely change the IP address of the website in which the inappropriate content is hosted to a non-existent IP address or to another IP address website. Thus, if users located in Brazil try to access the original website where the inappropriate content is hosted, they will receive an error message from the browser or be redirected to another website.

Payment mechanisms may also be subject to restraining orders for blocking payments from illegal websites.

3.5 Has the legal status of online gambling changed significantly in recent years and, if so, how?

The legal status of online gambling has not changed significantly. However, recent case law seems to reveal a greater level of scrutiny as to the preponderant factors for determining the winner of the game, which is positive for the industry. If one can prove or convince that luck is not the prevalent factor, the game can be considered legal. Brazilian judges seem to be willing to understand those differences – which has not happened too many times in the past.

Furthermore, due to upcoming sports events, such as the Olympics and the World Cup, some members of the Brazilian Secretariat for Economic Monitoring have demonstrated an interest in developing legislation for sports betting in Brazil. However, no concrete action has been taken.

There is also a bill of law (PL 255/2009) that defines as a crime the facilitation of gambling exploitation through computer networks, which remains under evaluation at the Committee of Science, Technology, Innovation, Communication and Informatics (CCT) at the Brazilian Congress. The referred bill also encompasses access to gambling by mobile phone, digital TV and other technologies.

3.6 Whilst acknowledging the inherent difficulty in predicting developments in gambling law, what are the likely developments in online gambling in your jurisdiction, both short term and long term? Are any specific amendments under consideration? Have there been any recent political developments, or do you envisage any in the near future? Are any specific amendments under consideration? Are they likely to be adopted and, if so, what is the time scale?
Although there are no important developments, please refer to questions 3.1 and 3.5 above.

3.7 Is the law the same in relation to mobile gambling and interactive gambling on television? If not, are there any headline differences?
There is no distinction.

4. LAND-BASED GAMING
4.1 Please describe the licensing regime (if any) for land-based gaming, and what products are included. Please set out what licences are available, and the licensing regime for them
Not applicable.

4.2 Please set out any particular limitations or requirements for (eg casino) operators, such as a ban on local residents gambling.
Not applicable.

4.3 Please address the questions in 3.5 above, but in relation to land-based gaming.
Not applicable.

5. TAX
5.1 Please summarise briefly the tax regime applicable to both land-based and online gaming.
Considering that the gaming company is a Brazilian legal entity, the federal tax regime applicable both to land-based and online gaming could be either calculated in accordance with the Real Profit Method or Presumed

Profit Method. They contemplate different tax burdens and calculations, as follows:

Real Profit:

- Corporate Income Tax: 15 per cent on adjusted net profit, plus an additional rate of 10 per cent on any income exceeding R$ 240,000.00 on an annual basis or R$ 20,000 on a monthly basis;
- Federal Contribution Tax on Net Profit: 9 per cent on adjusted net profit;
- Federal Social Contribution Taxes: 9.25 per cent on gross revenue (with the possibility to use credit with respect to certain costs and expenses authorised by law).

Presumed Profit (in the case of services in general, it is applied 32 per cent on gross revenue):

- Corporate Income Tax: 15 per cent on presumed profit, plus an additional rate of 10 per cent on any income exceeding R$ 240,000.00 on an annual basis or R$ 20,000 on a monthly basis;
- Federal Contribution Tax on Net Profit: 9 per cent on presumed profit;
- Federal Social Contribution Taxes: 3.65 per cent on gross revenue (without credit).

The Brazilian legal entity will be subject to Tax on Services which is a municipal tax that ranges from 2 to 5 per cent of the revenue, depending on the city where the service provider is located.

If the online gaming provider is a foreign company domiciled abroad, the remittances will be subject to the following:

- Withholding Income Tax: 15 per cent. The IRRF taxpayer is the foreign recipient of the payments, but the IRRF is withheld and paid by the Brazilian payer. Please note that the IRRF will be levied at a rate of 25 per cent if the foreign recipient is established in a low-tax jurisdiction, or favoured by a privileged tax regime in accordance to the Brazilian tax legislation;
- Import PIS/COFINS: 9.25 per cent. The taxpayer is the Brazilian payer. In certain cases, Import PIS/COFINS may generate credits that may offset PIS/COFINS taxes due in subsequent transactions;
- Municipal Service Tax: levied at a rate of between 2 and 5 per cent, depending on the municipality in which the Brazilian payer is located. Brazilian law determines that ISS is levied on the importation of services, and that it is payable by the foreign company.

It is worth mentioning that depending on the activities to be performed by the gaming company, state VAT (generally levied at a rate of 18 per cent depending on the state where the user is located) may be assessed.

Nevertheless, it is also worth mentioning that the Contribution for Intervention in the Economic Domain might be levied at a 10 per cent tax rate on any amount paid, credited, delivered, employed or remitted abroad as technical services, or in connection with technical or administrative assistance service agreements, being the burden borne by the Brazilian payer.

6. ADVERTISING

6.1 To what extent is the advertising of gambling permitted in your jurisdiction? Again, this should cover both land-based and online gaming. To the extent that advertising is permitted, how is it regulated?

To the extent that gambling and games of chance are prohibited in Brazil basically due to their reliance exclusively and preponderantly on luck, there has recently been considerable discussion about the specific types of games including poker, since many understand that its results depend largely on the player's skills. In this regard, in September 2010, a decision rendered by CONAR, the Brazilian Self-Regulation Advertising Counsel, added more ground to this discussion by allowing a poker advertisement on a Brazilian television network because, according to the judging counsellor's understanding and in consideration of the inclusion and acceptance by the International Olympic Committee of poker as a 'mind sport', the issue regarding the legality of poker games has already been surpassed. Nevertheless, the decision also made reference to betting in such activities, reaffirming the position that advertising campaigns which make reference to betting and monetary values should not be permitted. Please note that CONAR is not a governmental entity and therefore, its decision is not binding *vis-à-vis* the Brazilian courts. Nevertheless, the position of the entity is respected in the media and advertising circles.

In any case, advertising of online games (the games allowed by the applicable law) is governed by some provisions of the Brazilian Consumer Code (in connection to false advertising and the omission of relevant consumer information, for example), by CONAR's Self-Regulation Code and by some rules issued by the Ministry of Justice (in connection to age rating).

With respect to age-rating rules, any entity promoting, distributing, licensing or selling games should rate the games in accordance with the rules established by the Ministry of Justice. If the promoted game is not duly rated, the distributor can be fined by the Federal Prosecution Office (which will act with the Ministry of Justice) and, depending on the case, the distribution of unrated games may even be prohibited by a court order.

Currently, there are two procedures for rating games: (i) the regular procedure (previous analysis); and (ii) the self-rating procedure exclusively applied to electronic games digitally distributed in Brazil and already rated outside Brazil (as long as they were rated in accordance with the International Age Rating Coalition). In the second case, the applicant opting for the self-rating system does not need to submit documents/information to the Ministry of Justice – the applicant only assigns the desired age rating for the content, based on the certified foreign rate and the parameters set in the Official Rating System Manual provided by the Ministry of Justice.

7. SOCIAL GAMING

7.1 We believe this to be a growing area. Please decide under what criteria social gaming is permitted in your jurisdiction. If games are free to play or if there is no prize, are they legal without a licence? Please address circumstances where virtual currency is used and can be won: ie currency which is of no monetary or other value, save for as credits to take part in games. The answer should address the question whether game credits or virtual money can be exchanged for other prizes. Is any change to regulation in the area proposed or envisaged?

There is no specific regulation regarding social gaming in Brazil and therefore no licensing requirements or issues should arise as long as the game is deemed legal. Due to the provisions that forbid gambling in Brazil, the legality of bingo, casinos and the like in social networks, whether paid or free of charge, is questionable and may be risky. With respect to other types of games that are not framed as gambling, since luck is not the prevailing factor for the result of the game, the use of game credits or virtual money has no barrier in Brazilian legislation. Users are allowed to use money in order to acquire game credits as well as to exchange them for prizes.

Notwithstanding the above, there is a distinction between virtual currency and electronic currency. Electronic currency is regulated by the Brazilian Central Bank and is defined as resources kept in an electronic system, which allows its users to make payments in Brazilian Reais. Virtual currency refers to resources which are not kept in an electronic system and are not linked to a governmental entity. Game credits can be considered as virtual currency and, as such, are not regulated by the Brazil Central Bank. Nevertheless, on 19 February 2014 the Brazilian Central Bank published a brief letter on virtual currency, stating that, although this issue is not currently regulated, the Brazilian Central Bank is following the development of the use of virtual currency in order to take the applicable regulatory measures, if necessary.

Colorado (USA)

Lewis Roca Rothgerber LLC
Roger M. Morris Esq & Sean McGuinness Esq

1. OBJECTIVES AND STRUCTURE OF LEGISLATION
At the outset, it should be understood that the State of Colorado
distinguishes between 'gambling' and casino-style 'gaming'. The former,
with some exceptions, is illegal, and the latter has been constitutionally
authorised. 'Gambling' traditionally means placing a wager on an event
involving an element of chance. This activity has been illegal for many
years and remains prohibited today. See the discussion below in response
to question 2.1. Legal casino-style 'gaming' on the other hand, known in
Colorado as 'Limited Gaming', is a 20 plus year-old, ever-evolving activity.
With the privilege of the conduct of Limited Gaming, however, come
numerous constraints and limitations.

In 1990, lawful wagering activity in Colorado was limited to pari-mutuel
betting on horse and dog racing as well as participation in a state run
lottery that was itself legalised in 1983. Colorado's history as a centre of
gold and silver mining in the late 19th and early 20th centuries left it with
many virtual ghost towns that had struggled to find modern day success
as tourist attractions. Efforts in the late 1980s began to coalesce around
bringing back the era of saloons with gaming as an amenity to the overall
19th century experience and as a way of recreating the appeal of the 'Old
West'.

In November 1990, pursuant to a state-wide general election, the eligible
voters of the State of Colorado approved an amendment to the Colorado
Constitution to add a new section 9 to Article XVIII. That amendment
provided that Limited Gaming would become legal on 1 October 1991,
in three mountain towns in Colorado that had formerly thrived as
mining centres, namely Cripple Creek, Black Hawk, and Central City. The
amendment additionally provided other guidelines for the conduct of
Limited Gaming in the three towns, including the requirement that Limited
Gaming be conducted subject to the enactment of appropriate legislation by
the Colorado General Assembly.

Subsequently, in 1991, the Colorado General Assembly enacted the
Colorado Limited Gaming Act of 1991 (the Colorado Act), which includes
Colorado Revised Statutes (CRS), sections 12-47.1-101 *et seq*. The Colorado
Act, which has been amended by the legislature several times since its
original enactment, authorises Limited Gaming only in certain designated
commercial districts of Central City, Black Hawk and Cripple Creek,
Colorado. Limited Gaming consists of the games of poker, blackjack, slot
machines, roulette, and craps, each with maximum single bet of $100. Only

persons aged 21 or older may participate in Limited Gaming, and Limited Gaming is permitted to be offered to and played by customers of licensed casinos for 24 hours a day, seven days a week.

Limited Gaming is only allowed on premises licensed for that purpose, and the gaming-licensed premises of any building may not exceed 35 per cent of the square footage of the building and no more than 50 per cent of any floor of such building. There is no limitation on the size of any structure or total square footage devoted to Limited Gaming. However, the gaming-licensed premises of any casino must be physically located within the designated commercial district of one of the three above-referenced cities.

There are also two Indian casinos located in the south-western corner of Colorado. One is owned and operated by the Southern Ute Indian Tribe in Ignacio, Colorado. The other is owned by the Ute Mountain Ute Indian Tribe in Towaoc, Colorado. Both casinos offer slots, poker, blackjack, and other casino games. Such casinos are authorised by federal laws, in particular the Indian Gaming Regulatory Act, 25 U.S.C., sections 2701 *et seq*. This comprehensive set of laws regulating Indian gaming was enacted in 1988. These casinos' operations are under the jurisdiction of federal law, and oversight is provided by the National Indian Gaming Commission. Further information and description is available upon inquiry, but beyond the scope of this chapter.

2. FRAMEWORK OF LEGISLATION

2.1 What is the legal definition of gambling and what falls within this definition?

Gambling is defined in the Criminal Code at CRS sections 18-10-102 *et seq* to mean, '*...the risking of money, credit, deposit, or other thing of value for gain contingent in whole or in part upon lot, chance, the operation of a gambling device, or the happening or outcome of an event, including a sporting event, over which the person taking a risk has no control*'. This definition expressly excludes acts or activities otherwise expressly authorised by law which include, Limited Gaming, State-run lottery and pari-mutuel wagering on horse and dog racing. All unauthorised gambling in Colorado is a criminal offence both for the wagering player as well as the unlawful operator, referred to in the CRS as a 'Professional Gambler'.

Limited Gaming is both constitutionally and statutorily defined as, '*...the use of slot machines, and the card games of blackjack and poker as well as the table games of roulette and craps with all single bets being subject to a US $100.00 maximum*' CRS sections 12-47.1-103(19).

2.2 What is the legal definition of online gambling and what falls within this definition?

All Limited Laming must take place within a physical casino located within the cities of Blackhawk, Central City or Cripple Creek, and no online gaming is defined or permitted.

2.3 Please set out the different gambling products identified by legislation.

- Poker: defined in CRS sections 12-47.1-103(22) means *'a card game played by a player or players who are dealt cards by a dealer'*. Poker is allowed in all forms authorised by the Colorado Commission.
- Betting (other than sports betting): (i) pari-mutuel wagering – greyhound and horse tracks can be operated in Colorado subject to licence and regulation pursuant to CRS sections 12-60-101 *et seq*. This activity is regulated separately from Limited Gaming by the Colorado Racing Commission; (ii) simulcast pari-mutuel wagering – it is permitted to wager on horse and dog races in Colorado and throughout the United States at the physical location of a licensed facility authorised to accept such wagers. No such wagers may be made by use of a remote or mobile device or on the internet.
- Casino games: (i) blackjack is defined at CRS section 12-47.1-103(4) as a banking card game commonly known as '21' played by a maximum of seven players in which each player bets against the dealer; (ii) craps is defined at CRS section 12-47.1-103(5.7) as a game played by one or more players against a casino using two dice, in which players bet upon the occurrence of specific combinations of numbers shown by the dice on each throw; (iii) roulette is defined at CRS section 12-47.1-103(25.5) as a game in which a ball is spun on a rotating wheel and drops into a numbered slot on the wheel, and bets are placed on which slot the ball will come to rest.
- Slot and other machine gaming: 'Slot machine' is defined at CRS section 12-47.1-103(26)(a) as any mechanical, electrical, video, electronic, or other device, contrivance, or machine which, after insertion of a coin, token, or similar object, or upon payment of any required consideration whatsoever by a player, is available to be played or operated, and which, whether by reason of the skill of the player or application of the element of chance, or both, may deliver or entitle the player operating the machine to receive cash premiums, merchandise, tokens, or redeemable game credits, or any other thing of value other than unredeemable free games, whether the payoff is made automatically from the machines or in any other manner.
- Bingo: may only be offered as a charitable activity licensed to qualified operations by the Colorado Secretary of State pursuant to CRS sections 12-9-102 *et seq*.
- Lottery: a state-wide lottery was authorised by constitutional amendment in 1982 and legislation, CRS sections 24-35-201 *et seq* was enacted to commence ticket sales in January of 1983. The Lottery is a state monopoly and sells tickets only in physical facilities. Games include instant scratch tickets as well as intra and interstate large progressive prize draws. All proceeds from sales after vendor pay-outs and prizes go to the state.

Rules and regulations cover game operation and technical aspects. Each of the games or activities described above is subject to detailed regulation as to the exact nature of all aspects of play.

2.4 Please list the different requirements for each gambling product, including legal classifications for each; for example, is poker a game of skill or game of chance?

As previously mentioned, each of the gaming activities subject to licence by the State has specific rules and regulations governing their use. All are denominated games of chance by statute.

In the specific case of poker the Supreme Court of the State of Colorado has twice ruled specifically that poker is a game of chance. In 1952 in the case of *Ginsberg v Centennial Turf Club*, 252 P2d 926 the Court ruled that poker was a form of gambling as prohibited by the State's criminal code which only outlawed wagering on games of chance.

Again in 1989 in the case of *Charnes v Central City Opera House Association*, 773 P2d 546 in considering whether some element of chance was present in the game of poker the Court wrote, *'While poker...might involve some skill, these games certainly are contingent 'in part' upon chance, and when, as here, the games involve risking a thing of value for gain, they constitute a form of 'gambling' in its commonly understood sense'*.

2.5 Explain the system of regulation of gambling; which regulatory or governmental body is responsible for the supervision of gambling? Which body issues licences? Which body examines enforcement powers? Is there any limit on the number or duration of available licences?

The Colorado Act provides for the oversight and supervision of the Limited Gaming industry , and the issuance of the proper licences, by the Colorado Limited Gaming Control Commission (the Colorado Commission).

The Colorado Commission is the governmental authority with primary responsibility for the regulation of Limited Gaming activities in Colorado. The Colorado Commission consists of a five-member board appointed by the Governor. Its members serve at the pleasure of the Governor. The Commission customarily meets once each month on the third Thursday of the month, although, in its discretion, the Commission may meet more frequently. The Commission has plenary authority over gaming, and it is the Commission which promulgates the rules and regulations pursuant to the Colorado Act (collectively, the Colorado Gaming Regulations), located at 1 Colorado Code of Regulations, part 207-2. Under the Colorado Act and Gaming Regulations, the ownership and operation of Limited Gaming facilities in Colorado and all persons in any way associated with such facilities (eg, as a vendor, principal, lender, or owner) are subject to investigation and extensive regulation by the Colorado Commission in its discretion. Licences are issued for two-year periods.

The duties of the Colorado Commission have been delegated, consistent with the Colorado Act, in large part to the Colorado Division of Gaming (Division). The Division is an agency of state government within the Colorado Department of Revenue. Among its responsibilities the Division performs background investigations for the Colorado Commission, and the Division provides day to day oversight of the industry and is responsible for the enforcement of the laws. The Commission has also delegated to the Division the authority to issue certain approvals and licences.

In the case of pari-mutuel wagering on greyhound and horse racing all licenses are issued by the Department of Revenue Racing Commission.

The licensing function and all governance of the Lottery are also within the province of the Department of Revenue through the State Lottery Commission.

3. ONLINE GAMBLING

3.1 To what extent can online gambling be offered in your jurisdiction? Are licences available and, if so, for which gambling products? Please describe briefly the licensing process, who may apply, whether licences are limited in number and, if no licences are available, whether it is legal for online gambling to be offered. In the case of EU jurisdictions, please state whether there are any issues as to the legality of the local law at EU level. Please refer to any relevant cases at ECJ level and explain any measures taken or pending by the European Commission.

As recently as 2012 the Attorney General of Colorado, the state's chief law enforcement official has posted on the website of the Department of Law as well as that of the Colorado Gaming Commission its position that online gaming in all forms is illegal in Colorado. The Attorney General wrote: *'Internet gambling sites and telephone sports books are illegal under state and federal laws. Colorado law prohibits the transmission or reception of gambling information by any means. In addition, the Colorado Constitution allows only certain types of gambling, which does not include internet or telephone wagering'.* Statement of Attorney General John Suthers, originally published 31 August 2005 and currently maintained on the Department of Law website as the position of the Attorney General.

3.2 Is there a distinction between the law applicable to B2B operations and that applicable to B2C operations?

No.

3.3 What are the consequences for B2C or B2B operators who are active in your jurisdiction without having obtained or applied for the required permits, licences and approvals? What penalties and enforcement powers are available in respect of the illegal operators? Please outline any significant domestic decisions or enforcement actions that have been taken by the relevant authorities in recent years.

Two Colorado criminal statutes are violated by offering online gambling for wagers in Colorado. First is the gambling prohibition contained in CRS sections 18-10-101 *et seq*. Violations of this statute would be treated as professional gambling and prosecuted on a first offence as a misdemeanour and on subsequent offences as felonies as a repeat gambling offender.

More serious would be prosecution under the State's Organised Crime Control Act (COCA) 18-17-101 which classifies as a pattern of racketeering activity violations of the State's gambling prohibitions by an 'enterprise' which is defined as *'any individual, sole proprietorship, partnership, corporation, trust, or other legal entity'*. Violations of COCA are felonies and carry criminal and civil fines and forfeitures.

3.4 What technical measures are in place (if any) to protect consumers from unlicensed operators, such as ISP blocking and payment blocking?
None.

3.5 Has the legal status of online gambling changed significantly in recent years and, if so, how?
Not at all.

3.6 Whilst acknowledging the inherent difficulty in predicting developments in gambling law, what are the likely developments in online gambling in your jurisdiction, both short term and long term? Are any specific amendments under consideration? Have there been any recent political developments, or do you envisage any in the near future? Are any specific amendments under consideration? Are they likely to be adopted and, if so, what is the time scale?
As online gambling is currently illegal in Colorado, the initial step in any analysis of speculative or hypothetical activities and their regulation must be the legalisation of this activity. To the knowledge of the authors there is no organised Colorado-based effort underway to legalise online gambling in Colorado at this time. Grass roots legalisation efforts of small groups, such as individuals who play poker, may perhaps be presently hidden from public scrutiny, but exist nonetheless. Regardless, any such attempt at legalisation of online gaming will more than likely require the further amendment of the Colorado Constitution. The Colorado Constitution, in Article 18, section 9, prohibits Limited Gaming in all but the three cities named above. Online gaming would expand the gambling customer base to the entire state. Amending the Colorado Constitution, however, is a difficult process which would necessitate a majority vote of the state-wide electorate at the next state-wide election. State-wide elections are held in November of each even dated year.

Colorado, as do many of its neighbouring states, often legislatively mimics its peers. Therefore, examination of pending legislation legalising online gambling in other states (eg, Nevada) may provide some insight into the future possibilities for legalisation of online gaming in the Colorado market.

3.7 Is the law the same in relation to mobile gambling and interactive gambling on television? If not, are there any headline differences?
It is the same.

4. LAND-BASED GAMING
4.1 Please describe the licensing regime (if any) for land-based gaming, and what products are included. Please set out what licences are available, and the licensing regime for them.

Generally, any person or entity offering Limited Gaming to the public must hold a retail gaming licence. Those persons importing, selling, distributing, or manufacturing slot machines must hold a valid manufacturer and distributor gaming licence from the Colorado Commission. Licensing as an operator is also required for any person or entity providing goods or services to a casino based or calculated upon a percentage of adjusted gross proceeds (gross gaming revenue) received by that casino. Moreover, persons employed in the Colorado gaming industry must be individually licensed. The Colorado Commission may issue the following gaming licenses: (i) slot machine manufacturer or distributor; (ii) operator; (iii) retail gaming; (iv) associated equipment supplier; (v) support; and (vi) key employee. The retail gaming licence is required for the operation of a casino, and support and key licences are issued to individuals working in the gaming industry, as employees and managers, respectively. All these licences require renewal every two years by the Colorado Commission. Support and key employee licences only may also be initially issued and renewed by the Director of the Division in his discretion. Prior to initial issuance or renewal of any retail gaming (casino) licence, the Colorado Commission or the Division, if applicable, will first determine that: the licensee will operate in compliance with the statutes, rules and regulations governing the conduct of casino gaming in Colorado; the licensee is of good moral character; and the licensee is suitable to participate in the Colorado gaming industry. The Colorado Commission has broad discretion to condition, suspend for up to six months, revoke, limit or restrict a licence at any time and also has the authority to impose fines for any violations of the gaming laws. A retail gaming licensee may utilise slot machines on its own premises and is not required to hold an operator licence. No person may have an ownership interest in more than three retail licences.

The Colorado Act requires that every officer, director, and stockholder of a privately-held corporation – where such corporation is licensed or is an applicant for a licence – be of good moral character and be suitable for participation in the gaming industry. The same requirements apply to equivalent office-holders and owners of privately-held, non-corporate applicants. With respect to publicly-traded corporations and entities, all officers and directors (and for limited liability companies, their managers), and all persons holding a 5 per cent or greater beneficial ownership interest directly or indirectly on a pass-through basis, must be persons of good moral character and be suitable. These persons ordinarily must submit to a full background investigation conducted by the Colorado Division and the Colorado Gaming Commission. The cost of the background investigation is borne by the applicant. The Colorado Commission or the Division may additionally require any person having an interest, however limited or indirect, in a licence or a licensee to undergo a full background investigation for suitability and pay the cost of investigation in the same manner as an applicant. Limited disclosure forms are customarily required of those persons holding an equity interest under 5 per cent in a non-publicly traded licensee or applicant, or its parent companies.

In addition, all persons loaning monies, goods, or real or personal property directly or indirectly to a licensee or applicant, or having any interest in a licensee or applicant, or entering into any agreement with a licensee or applicant, must provide any information requested by the Division or Colorado Commission, and in the discretion of the Division or the Colorado Commission, these persons must supply all information relevant to a determination of any such person's suitability for licensure, and must submit to a full background investigation if ordered by the Colorado Commission. Failure to promptly provide all information requested, or to submit to a suitability or background investigation, may result in a finding of unsuitability, the denial of a licence application, suspension or revocation of an existing licence, termination of any lease, note arrangement, or agreement between the applicant or licensee and the person requested to provide the information, and other sanctions. Investigations for suitability, background, or any other reason may delay a licence application or the operation under any agreement with a licensee. All agreements, contracts, leases or arrangements in violation of the Colorado Act or the Colorado Gaming Regulations are void and unenforceable. Additionally, violations of the Colorado Gaming Regulations are criminal acts, and violators are subject to arrest, prosecution, and possible incarceration, as well as the payment of fines and costs.

Persons found unsuitable by the Colorado Commission may be required immediately to terminate any interest in, association or agreement with, or relationship to a licensee – regardless of any negative financial consequences to such persons. A finding of unsuitability with respect to any officer, director, employee, associate, lender or beneficial owner of a licensee or applicant may also jeopardise the licensee's licence or applicant's licence application. Licences, and their continuing validity, may be conditioned upon termination by a licensee or applicant of any relationship with unsuitable persons.

With limited exceptions applicable to licensees that are publicly-traded entities, no person, including persons who may acquire an interest in a licensee pursuant to a foreclosure or through federal bankruptcy proceedings, may sell, lease, purchase, convey or acquire any interest in a retail gaming or operator licence or business without the prior approval of the Colorado Gaming Commission.

Rule 4.5 of the Colorado Gaming Regulations provides for the licensing of publicly-traded corporations and entities (collectively, PTCs). The definition of a PTC for Colorado gaming purposes pursuant to Rule 4.5 may vary from the definition of the term under federal or state securities laws. In contrast to Regulation 420 (requiring prior Colorado Commission approval for transfers of direct or indirect ownership interests in a casino entity), Rule 4.5 permits such transfers; but those transfers are subject to approval by the Colorado

Commission after the fact.

According to Regulation 47.1-4.508, any person acquiring 5 per cent or more of the beneficial ownership of a PTC casino licensee or applicant (directly or indirectly) must, along with the applicant or licensee, notify the Division within 10 days of such acquisition. Upon acquisition of 10 per cent or more, such person must file an application for suitability with the Division within 45 days of the acquisition and undergo a comprehensive background investigation at such person's expense. For institutional investors, as defined in Rule 4.5, the necessity for filing for suitability occurs upon the acquisition of 15 per cent or more of the beneficial ownership, direct or indirect, of the casino licensee. Other persons called forward for a determination of suitability by the Colorado Commission or the Division have the time provided by the applicable agency in which to file their documents.

4.2   Please set out particular limitations or requirements for (eg casino) operators, such as a ban on local residents gambling.

In addition to those requirements provided in response to question 4.1 above, all casino operations must meet the operational standards of the Colorado Internal Control Minimum Procedures (ICMPs). The ICMPs are a comprehensive set of mandatory procedures which must be followed to comply with the operational and accounting requirements of the Colorado Act. The ICMPs are provided by the Division to the casino licensee in a standard form, and licensees may ask the Division to grant variances to the ICMPs when necessary for more efficient yet responsible operation. Failure to comply with the iCMPs is a violation of the Gaming Act and the Rules thereunder.

The three cities of Black Hawk, Central City, and Cripple Creek, Colorado each are authorised by the Gaming Act to impose a device fee on each gaming device (eg, slot machine, blackjack, roulette, craps and poker table). For example, the City of Black Hawk levies a yearly gaming device fee in the current maximum amount of $945, payable in monthly increments, per device. Black Hawk, and the other two cities also impose taxes and fees on other aspects of the businesses of gaming licensees, such as lodging, sales, parking, liquor licences and other municipal taxes and fees. The Colorado Commission has authority to assess a state gaming device fee as well, but currently there is no such fee.

The sale of alcoholic beverages in gaming establishments is subject to strict licensing, control and regulation by state and local (city) authorities. All gaming operations must comply with the Colorado Liquor Code, CRS sections 12-47-101 *et seq.* Gaming establishments serving alcoholic beverages must maintain valid state and city liquor licences for their operation. Legal hours for service and sale of alcoholic beverages are from 7:00 am through 2:00 am daily, and no one under age 21 may be served alcohol. Alcoholic beverage licences are renewable annually, revocable and non-transferable. State and local licensing authorities have full power to limit, condition, suspend or revoke any such licences for violations of the Liquor Code or the regulations thereunder. Violation of these state alcoholic beverage laws is a criminal offence, and violators are subject to criminal prosecution, incarceration and fines.

4.3 Please address the questions in 3.5 above, but in relation to land-based gaming.
It has not significantly changed.

5. TAX
5.1 Please summarise briefly the tax regime applicable both to land-based and online gaming.
The State of Colorado, as provided in the Gaming Act, imposes an annual gaming tax on the adjusted gross proceeds (AGP) from Limited Gaming. AGP is generally defined as the amounts wagered minus payments to players. For poker, AGP means those sums wagered on a hand retained by the licensee as compensation. The gaming tax is paid monthly, with licensees required to file returns by the 15th of the following month. Effective 1 July of each year, the Colorado Gaming Commission establishes the gaming tax rates for the following 12 months. In setting the tax each year the Colorado Commission holds public hearings and considers the needs of various private businesses and public agencies affected by Limited Gaming. The Colorado Gaming Commission may theoretically increase the gaming tax rate to as much as 40 per cent of AGP. Currently, however, the applicable gaming tax rates, which were amended in May 2012, and in effect on 1 July 2012, are: 0.25 per cent on AGP of up to and including $2 million; 2 per cent over $2 million of AGP up to and including $5 million; 9 per cent over $5 million up to and including $8 million; 11 per cent over $8 million up to and including $10 million; 16 per cent over $10 million up to and including $13 million; and 20 per cent over $13 million. A previous amendment to the Colorado Constitution, Amendment 50, limited future maximum gaming taxes to their 1 July 2008, levels, unless any such tax increase is approved by voters voting in a state-wide election. Those levels are, for the identical ranges of AGP as set forth above, respectively: .25 per cent; 2 per cent; 9 per cent; 11 per cent; 16 per cent; and 20 per cent respectively.

The Colorado gaming regulations are subject to amendment and interpretation by the Colorado Gaming Commission.

6. ADVERTISING
6.1 To what extent is the advertising of gambling permitted in your jurisdiction? Again, this should cover both land-based and online gaming. To the extent that advertising is permitted, how is it regulated?
There is no limitation on advertising for licensed Limited Gaming, greyhound or horse racing or lottery by any media so long as the advertisements are not deceptive.

7. SOCIAL GAMING

7.1 We believe this to be a growing area. Please decide under what criteria social gaming is permitted in your jurisdiction. If games are free to play or if there is no prize, are they legal without a licence? Please address circumstances where virtual currency is used and can be won: ie currency which is of no monetary or other value, save for as credits to take part in games. The answer should address the question whether game credits or virtual money can be exchanged for other prizes. Is any change to regulation in the area proposed or envisaged?

It is useful to distinguish online social gaming as those products are currently offered on social gaming websites from wager and prize activities. Online social gaming as it is generally structured and offered today in Colorado is an activity which does not fall under the criteria of prohibited gambling under Colorado law. Offering games that may require a payment for increased time on the game but offer no prize do not offend gambling prohibitions. Colorado State law allows 'social gambling' for real money among participants who have a 'bona fide social relationship' and in which all moneys wagered goes out in prizes. A 'bona fide social relationship' means that the parties must have an established social relationship based upon some other common interest other than the gambling activity. Further, participants cannot directly or indirectly participate in 'professional gambling', which is defined as *'aiding or inducing another to engage in gambling, with the intent to derive a profit therefrom'*. CRS sections 18-10-101 *et seq*. These two criteria – a bona fide social relationship and no profit motive – must be present for a gambling activity to be considered legal 'social gambling'.

When considering the world of online social gaming the threshold issue to be resolved concerns application of Colorado Criminal Code, CRS 18-10-101 *et seq*. Gambling is defined as *'risking any money, credit, deposit, or other thing of value for gain contingent in whole or in part upon lot, chance, or the operation of a gambling device'*. The statute defines a 'gain' as 'the direct realisation of winnings'; and 'profit' as 'any other realised or unrealised benefit, direct or indirect'.

It has been the position of the Colorado Courts to interpret these statutes to apply only to activity in which money or merchandise is at stake. In this regard in the 1988 case of *People v Baker*, 759 P 2d 26, the Court stated that 'gain' for purposes of the gambling statutes means a 'thing of value' as that phrase is applied in other subject areas.

The statutory definition of the phrase 'thing of value' in the Colorado Criminal Code. defines 'thing of value' as including *'real property, tangible and intangible personal property, contract rights, choses in action, services, confidential information, medical records information, and any rights of use or enjoyment connected therewith'*. CRS 18-10-102.

The Colorado Supreme Court distinguished free replay pin-ball machines (games of amusement) from pin-ball machines through which cash or merchandise could be redeemed for successful play in *Approximately Fifty-*

nine Gambling Devices v People ex rel Burke, 110 Colo. 82 (1942).

In *Bills v People*, 113 Colo. 326 (1945), the Colorado Supreme Court found that a 'suit club' in which members paid a weekly fee to gain the chance to win a free suit constituted an illegal lottery because consideration in the form of payment, the purchase of a suit, was required to enter and a merchandise prize was available.

In 1949 the Court found that where a game only awarded points and not cash or merchandise, it was a game of amusement and not a gambling device – *MacArthur v Wyscaver,* 120 Colo. 525 (1949). In an entirely consistent ruling the court in *Brownlee v Dept. of Revenue,* 686 P.2d 1372 (1984), held that a poker-themed mechanical game constituted a gambling device because payment was required to play and the credits won by successful play could be bet on future play or redeemed for cash from the establishment proprietor.

Finally in the Colorado Act governing Limited Gaming, the definition of slot machine specifically states that, *'any other thing of value other than unredeemable free games…'.*

Colorado is at present clear in the position that a 'thing of value' needs to be redeemable in a form other than spending more time on a game. Even a seemingly innocuous 'thing of value' can become a thing that turns one kind of inoffensive intangible benefit into one that violates the law. Caution is recommended in the design of any online social gaming scheme which: (i) moves away from pure 'time on the game' as a reward for pay or play; and (ii) incorporates more attractive redeemable prize credit. No change to these governmental determinations is likely in the near future.

Cyprus

Constantinos N. Couccoullis and Associates
Alexia C. Couccoullis

1. OBJECTIVES AND STRUCTURE OF LEGISLATION
In Cyprus, gambling market regulation is still non-existent. Cyprus does not yet have any land casinos unlike its counterpart Greece; however recent history has shown that when Cyprus decides to create foundations, it does so effectively.

Online gaming in Cyprus, is making over EUR 2.5 billion a year and is currently regulated by the Betting Law, which was amended in 2007 to comply with EU legislation for the free provision of services across borders.

Under the Law on Betting Houses, Gambling Houses and the Restriction of Gambling (Chapter 151 of the Statute Laws of Cyprus, as amended, most recently by Law No. 15(I) of 1998) land gambling in Cyprus is prohibited.

According to a letter from the General District Attorney responding to a question asked by the Police Chief, it is mentioned that halls licensed for offline sports betting may be considered legal when it comes to online sports betting, with the aim that, if an entity simultaneously holds an online licence issued by an EU jurisdiction along with the domestic offline one, then it could offer either online sports betting or online gaming games. The illegality of online gaming is questioned and, according to the said letter, gaming websites operating with a licence provided by an EU member state do operate legally and any potential illegalisation or prohibition of these activities may occur following the introduction of legislation by the government.

Today it is estimated that more than 200 venues exist in Cyprus providing online gaming and many of them do not have an EU member state licence, hence they operate illegally. It is estimated that illegal venues amount to 80 per cent of all halls operating in Cyprus. In the past two years, the police have conducted 1,400 raids, reporting 970 individuals and seizing around 7,500 computers. Thus regulation of Cyprus' gaming market would seem essential.

However there are provisions for 'offshore' betting services, given that the state can issue licences allowing foreign companies to be seated in Cyprus in order to provide betting services to players outside Cyprus. For online gambling sites it is still impossible to be licensed by the state but it is not illegal for licensed operators from other EU member states to be active in Cyprus.

In 2010 a bill was drafted that provided for the banning of online gambling and it was voted in 2012. As expected, Cyprus's Betting Act 2012 indeed provided a complete ban on online gambling in Cyprus. With the Act, games such as poker, casino games and sports exchange betting are banned and only traditional sports betting with online bookmakers and lotteries are allowed. Moreover, the Betting Act 2012 prohibits spread betting, dog racing and games of chance, and makes it an offence to advertise such activities. The Act repeals the previous betting legislation and provides for the establishment of a central National Betting Authority (NBA), which submits for approval to the Ministerial Council regulations concerning sports betting premises and online sports betting.

Moreover, a significant number of licensed betting offices (LBOs) that are operating online, bypassing the necessity of issuing Cypriot offline sports betting licences, are operating using EU jurisdiction licences either offline or online. The leading firm under this modulation is Stanleybet International, which has been operating in Cyprus since 2006 using a Maltese licence. Following this model of deployment, a network of LBOs of other European offline operators, like Typico, Betshop and Coral, are exploring the quite vast Cypriot market in terms of revenues from and enthusiasm for gaming.

However, Cyprus wishes to protect minors and earn the maximum profit possible from the legalisation of gambling. According to the bill, a national gambling regulator will be introduced as an independent body controlling the gambling industry. Moreover bookmaker licences will be issued with differentiated classes A and B – with both types being valid for two years – whereby class A is needed for land activities and class B is needed for online activities. Nonetheless casino games will still be prohibited. Legal entities wishing to apply for licences must be seated in Cyprus and legal entities wishing to apply for class B licences must use a backup server located in Cyrpus and connected with the state's central server. However, online betting will be banned.

There are no regulations on remote lottery offers. There is legislation on land-based lotteries such as the Lotteries Law (Chapter 74 of the Statute Laws of Cyprus), the Lotteries Regulations 1974, and the Law of Betting Houses, Gambling Houses and the Restriction of Gambling (Chapter 151 of the Statute Laws of Cyprus).

The Lotteries and Gaming Authority (LGA) is established under The Lotteries and Other Games Act and it is liable for issuing gaming licences and determining whether licensees are eligible persons to perform the functions related to gaming. However, casino related gambling is prohibited.

In 2007, the Cypriot government began preparing a bill that would impose a stricter set of rules for the licensing of online gaming. A previous bill had been submitted to Parliament in 2006, but it was soundly rejected by the parties involved.

2. FRAMEWORK OF LEGISLATION
2.1 What is the legal definition of gambling and what falls within this definition?
Cyprus moved closer to banning online gaming when the Cabinet approved a draft bill in March 2011. The bill outlaws online games such as roulette, poker, and slot machines, but allows licenses for sports betting outlets. It

also provides for the creation of a gaming board that will regulate betting within Cyprus. To ensure that the government does not incur loss of tax revenue, the bill designates that licensed gaming venues on the island will be taxed at 3 per cent of turnover instead of 10 per cent on gross profits. In order to indicate how serious the Cypriot government is concerning the banning, punitive measures are included, with fines of up to EUR 170,000 or a five-year prison term or both.

Section 2 of the Law related to Betting Houses, Gambling Houses and the Restriction of Gambling defines gambling indirectly, and *'being involved in gambling'* means *'playing or being involved in any game of luck or any game involving both luck and skill, for money or money's worth'*.

Pursuant to section 2 of the Collective Bets (Regulation and Taxation) Law 1997, a 'collective bet' is defined as *'... a bet held by a number of persons participating in the bet: (a) on the terms that the winnings shall be distributed or determined proportionally to the whole amount of the sums paid or agreed to be paid by the persons participating in the bet; or (b) on the terms that the winnings shall be or shall include a sum (not determined in relation to the sum paid or agreed to be paid by such persons) distributable in any proportion between such persons; or (c) on the basis that the winners or their winnings, to any extent, shall be determined in the unfettered judgment of the persons running the bet or any other person'*.

2.2 What is the legal definition of online gambling and what falls within this definition?

There is no legal definition of online gambling. According to a letter of the General District Attorney responding to a question asked by the Police Chief it is mentioned that halls licensed for sports betting may be considered legal when it comes to online betting. The illegality of online gambling is questioned and according to the letter, casinos operating with a licence provided by an EU member state do operate legally and any potential prohibition of these activities may only occur following the introduction of legislation by the government. Today in Cyprus it is estimated that more than 200 halls providing online gambling exist and many of them do not have an EU member state licence, hence they operate illegally. It is estimated that illegal halls amount to 80 per cent of all halls operating in Cyprus.

2.3 Please set out the different gambling products identified by legislation.

Pursuant to subsection 2(1) of the Lotteries Law, a lottery is *'any scheme for the distribution of prizes by drawing or by means which depend on chance'*. Arguably this definition includes bingo.

Poker is not mentioned at all however, other casino games are prohibited.

In Cyprus there is a law ratifying the Inter-Governmental Agreement between Cyprus and Greece concerning the Organisation of Football Prognostics (OPAP) and the Collective Bets (regulation and taxation) Law 1997 No. 75 (I)/97.

Pursuant to clause (b1) of section 15 of Law No. 71 of 1986, the Minister of Finance may issue a licence to the Cyprus Broadcasting Corporation to conduct lotteries broadcast on radio television. Pursuant to clause (b), the Minister of Finance may issue licences allowing fundraising lotteries for charitable purposes.

Pursuant to the Collective Bets Law 1997, pool betting is offered in Cyprus by 'collective bet companies', which can be seated abroad provided they have paid their share capital of EUR 175,000. Moreover 'receivers of collective bets' are people receiving, negotiating or engaging in collective betting as agents of a collective bet company. Pursuant to the Collective Bets Regulations 1998, after being issued a licence, persons can offer pool betting on football, basketball, or any other sport allowed by the government. This may also happen with horse racing provided Nicosia Race Club has authorised it first. People wishing to offer pool betting services on an 'offshore' basis are allowed to do so following the issuance of an appropriate licence pursuant to section 12 (1) of the Collective Bets Law 1997. Pursuant to section 12 (2), offshore companies are defined as companies seated incorporated, registered, managed and controlled in Cyprus, but owned exclusively by aliens offering pool betting services outside Cyprus on events held also outside Cyprus.

It is worth mentioning that in Cyprus, betting exchange companies operate which are believed to conduct essential gambling business, eg Betfair's gross profit amounted to EUR 2.5 billion when the total gross profit amounted to EUR 5.5 billion and the Nicosia Race Club suffered damage in 2011 for the first time ever.

2.4 Please list the different requirements for each gambling product, including legal classifications for each; for example, is poker a game of skill or game of chance?

In Cypriot legislation there are no requirements for any gambling product given that they are considered illegal. Poker is not considered at all.

2.5 Explain the system of regulation of gambling; which regulatory or governmental body is responsible for the supervision of gambling? Which body issues licences? Which body examines enforcement powers? Is there any limit on the number or duration of available licences?

Since gambling is considered to be illegal there is no government body responsible for gambling supervision or for issuing licences.

3. ONLINE GAMBLING

3.1 To what extent can online gambling be offered in your jurisdiction? Are licences available and, if so, for which gambling products? Please describe briefly the licensing process, who may apply, whether licences are limited in number and, if no licences are available, whether it is legal for online gambling to be offered. In the case of EU jurisdictions, please state whether there are any issues as to the legality of the local law at EU level. Please refer to any relevant cases at ECJ level and explain any measures taken or pending by the European Commission.

EU law makes it impossible for Cyprus to ban online gaming in the draft law it has prepared, given that such an action would be against the free movement of services. Nonetheless, justified restrictions on the free movement of services could be compatible with EU law under certain circumstances only. It remains to be seen whether the Cyprus legal framework when voted on will be compatible with EU law or not. However, the bill has provisions that may be found contrary to EU law, such as the obligation to be established in Cyprus, or having a server on the island.

There are licences for offline sports betting providers pursuant to the Collective Gambling Regulation Act 75 (I) 1997 which also impose taxes on the bets. According to the law a limited liability company registered in Cyprus according to the Companies Law Cap.113 operating exclusively as a betting company and accepting bets with a share capital of EUR 170,100, is able to apply to the Cyprus Ministry of Finance in order to obtain a licence to operate as a betting provider.

Remote gaming may be prohibited as far as it concerns gambling, however, as far as it concerns gaming only, the Remote Gaming Regulations are applicable. Remote gaming operators from Cyprus or from other states must be issued with a valid licence of the relevant class if they meet the relevant criteria, ie they must be limited liability companies seated in Cyprus, show business, financial and technical ability to operate the games and make sure that players' winnings are safeguarded. When the term gaming is used in these paragraphs, its meaning is different from gambling, given that when we say gaming we do not include gambling games, ie games of chance.

3.2 s there a distinction between the law applicable to B2B operations and that applicable to B2C operations?

There is no distinction between B2C and B2B operations.

There can be no gambling operators. However, there are classes concerning remote gaming, ie four different types:

Class 1 Remote Gaming Licence – is applicable for operators offering games based on recurring events whereas simultaneously the gaming risk is controlled by the operator.

Class 2 Remote Gaming Licence – is applicable for operators controlling risk based on a unique event using markets. With that licence, fixed odds betting games are covered along with pool betting.

Class 3 Remote Gaming Licence – is applicable for operators organising player-to-player games not participating in the risk and receiving merely a commission. This licence may cover betting exchanges, pools and poker providers of rooms.

Class 4 Remote Gaming Licence – is applicable for software vendors wishing to host and run remote gaming operators with any of the aforementioned classes. They are also not allowed to participate in the related risk of the games and they also are merely allowed to accept a commission.

3.3 What are the consequences for B2C or B2B operators who are active in your jurisdiction without having obtained or applied for the required permits, licences and approvals? What penalties and enforcement powers are available in respect of the illegal operators? Please outline any significant domestic decisions or enforcement actions that have been taken by the relevant authorities in recent years.

Criminal offences are introduced for companies providing gambling games in Cyprus without permission, and perpetrators face five years maximum imprisonment and a maximum fine of EUR 170,000. Casino games are banned under subsection 3(1) of the Law on Betting Houses. It is a criminal offence to play casino games and perpetrators may be punished by imprisonment or a fine up to EUR 1,700. It is also illegal and a crime punishable with imprisonment or a fine of EUR 2,550 maximum to produce, import, have, use or provide slot machines. No legislative exceptions to this prohibition exist whatsoever.

3.4 What technical measures are in place (if any) to protect consumers from unlicensed operators, such as ISP blocking and payment blocking?

Cyprus created an online gaming site blacklist and ISPs were required to block access to all of the sites on that list and 270 sites were placed on the blacklist. The blacklist was issued by the NBA and in 2013 it gave the ISPs 72 hours notice in order to block all sites offering unlicensed services in Cyprus or face fines of EUR 30,000. Included on the blacklist were many well-known European and International operator names, such as Bwin.party, which held 22 of the 270 domains, PokerStars, which held 11 domains on the blacklist, and Betfair. William Hill allegedly shut down its sports book in Cyprus before the drawing of the blacklist and did not offer online casino or poker; nevertheless, it was also included on the blacklist. Any citizens attempting to log on to the domains included on the blacklist view the NBA notice stating that *'access on this website is forbidden in accordance with the Gambling Law of 2012. For more information please visit the webpage of the National Gambling Authority www.nba.com.cy'*.

Pursuant to Article 54 of the Act, players must be registered and maintain an account with the gambling service provider. Pursuant to Article 58 of the Act, betting transactions can be executed only by credit cards, debit cards, electric transfer and electronic money; cash transactions are strictly prohibited. The providers are obliged to maintain a bank account in a bank or institution providing services in Cyprus, into which all amounts received from players are deposited for safekeeping.

3.5 Has the legal status of online gambling changed significantly in recent years and, if so, how?

It has not changed yet, since there is no legal status permitting online gambling.

3.6 Whilst acknowledging the inherent difficulty in predicting developments in gambling law, what are the likely developments in online gambling in your jurisdiction, both short term and long term? Are any specific amendments under consideration? Have there been any recent political developments, or do you envisage any in the near future? Are any specific amendments under consideration? Are they likely to be adopted and, if so, what is the time scale?

Article 12 of the Betting Act 2012 sets out two classes of authorised gambling services: class A and class B. Class A includes the provision of gambling services within licensed premises excluding any services falling within class B or horserace betting. Class B includes every form of electronic gambling with the exclusion of slot machines, lucky online casino games and horserace electronic betting. Gambling services may be provided exclusively by licensed persons or by their authorised representatives. Applications must be submitted to the Board and are subject to Board approval. The applicant must not have a criminal record that concerns a related crime and, in the case of individuals, s/he must be at least 25 years old. The applicant must prove the possession of adequate resources to secure the payment of players' winnings, the adequacy of systems of accounting and internal control and compliance with regulations for the protection of players set by the Board. Licences may last for one year or two years, and may be renewed on application subject to the approval of the Board pursuant to Article 24 of the Act. The Board can suspend or revoke a licence in the event of failure to comply with the required standards. The providers must show prescribed information on their website, including the registered name of the company, its registered address, the official number and date of the licence, and a statement that the use of the services by any minor is illegal under the Act. Moreover, class B services may be provided only through a website using a '.com.cy' domain name.

3.7 Is the law the same in relation to mobile gambling and interactive gambling on television? If not, are there any headline differences?

There are no provisions separating mobile gambling and interactive gambling on television.

4. LAND-BASED GAMING
4.1 Please describe the licensing regime (if any) for land-based gaming, and what products are included. Please set out what licences are available, and the licensing regime for them.

So far there have been many arguments related to legalisation of the gambling market. Contemporary Cypriot legislation draws a line between gambling and betting, whereby gambling means casino games and slot machines; and betting means putting money on the outcome of sporting events etc. However this differentiation continues given that gambling and betting activities are controlled by the Directorate of Coordination of the Computerisation of the Public Sector, while lottery games are controlled by the Directorate of Budget and Fiscal Control. Both Directorates are controlled by the Ministry of Finance. In Cyprus, lottery games can be operated by the Republic alone, although there is a sub-licence to OPAP, which originates in Greece. OPAP has formed a subsidiary organisation known as 'OPAP Cyprus' which controls lottery games and sport betting. OPAP entered Cyprus in 2003 following an agreement among both states and it nowadays has 162 betting shops. Horse racing bets can be provided only by the Nicosia Race Club.

In Cyprus there is a law ratifying the Inter-Governmental Agreement between Cyprus and Greece concerning OPAP and a Collective Bets (regulation and taxation) Law 1997 No. 75 (I)/97. OPAP Cyprus has 162 venues but not all belong to OPAP exclusively, given that many are linked with other providers eg Megabet and the same is valid for all its networks. This is why their exact number is debatable. OPAP games began operating in Cyprus in 1969 following the signing of the first interstate agreement among Greece and Cyprus concerning the operation of the famous then game of PROPO. In 1991, the Lotto began in 1992 Proto began, in 1996 Propo-Goal, in 1997 Joker made its first appearance. In 2001 a new agreement was signed between Greece and Cyprus and in 2002 the games of Extra 5 and Super 3 followed. In 2003 a new interstate agreement was signed between Greece and Cyprus founding OPAP Cyprus as we know it. It has to be mentioned that there was no tender for what OPAP now has in Cyprus.

Nowadays casinos and slot machines are still banned, however lottery, sports betting, horse racing and bingo may be allowed if a licence has been provided by the state. The same is valid for collective bets ie pool betting and fixed odds betting.

Moreover an illegal gambling market exists in Cyprus with many illegal shops inside coffee shops. A decline observed in horse race betting could be attributed to thriving illegal gambling activities within Cyprus. Though the law provides criminal offences for those managing an illegal shop where casino games are played, by punishing the perpetrators with imprisonment and a fine, the illegal marketing endures. The opening of land casinos in Cyprus is viewed by certain politicians as 'dangerous' for its population, disregarding the fact that illegal casinos exist within every neighbourhood. It is estimated that the gambling market had a EUR 2.5 billion turnover in 2008, with gross profit at EUR 400 million, while EUR 5 billion and gross profit of nearly EUR 1 billion was expected by 2012. Moreover it is estimated that Cypriots lose in casinos established within the Turkish part of the republic EUR 100 million every year.

In order to be granted a licence, betting companies must:

- be registered in Cyprus;
- have an agreement between the applicant company and the betting company stating that the applicant company is duly authorised by the betting company to act as its representative and accept on its behalf collective bets;
- the applicant submits a bank guarantee from a Cypriot Bank for an amount of money defined by the Minister of Finance but no less than EUR 340,000.
- the applicant shall submit a bank guarantee from a Cypriot Bank for an amount of money defined by the Minister of Finance but no less than EUR 51,260.

4.2 Please set out any particular limitations or requirements for (eg casino) operators, such as a ban on local residents gambling.

As already mentioned before, gambling games are prohibited.

4.3 Please address the questions in 3.5 above, but in relation to land-based gaming.

No land-based gaming in Cyprus has ever existed as it concerns games of chance; therefore there have been no changes whatsoever in recent years.

5. TAX

5.1 Please summarise briefly the tax regime applicable to both land-based and online gaming.

Taxation will be no more than 10 per cent. So far there is the Taxation of Horseracing Bets and Sweepstakes Law 1973 (Law No. 48 of 1973); Collective Bets (Regulation and Taxation) Regulations, No. 102 of 1998; and Law `6 (I) 2007 amending the Collective Bets (Regulation and Taxation) Law 1997.

As far as lotteries are concerned, there is no special tax on lottery revenues.

Since casinos are prohibited there are no taxes whatsoever on them. This also applies to gambling machines outside casinos.

As for betting, the OPAP operates in Cyprus via a local subsidiary company paying an important part of its revenue from betting however, there is no special tax levied on its activities. Pursuant to section 3 of the Taxation of Horseracing Bets and Sweepstakes Law 1973, tax is paid by players calculated at 10 per cent. Under section 8(2) of the Collective Bets (Regulation and Taxation) Law 1997, legal pool betting is subject to tax rate of 25 per cent. VAT is not levied on revenue flows generated by gambling activity in Cyprus with the exceptions of commissions retained by 'receivers of collective bets', 'assistant receivers of collective bets' and agents of the Nicosia Racing Club from the gross betting revenues, which have a VAT rate of 15 per cent.

6. ADVERTISING

6.1 To what extent is the advertising of gambling permitted in your jurisdiction? Again, this should cover both land-based and online gaming. To the extent that advertising is permitted, how is it regulated?

Given that gambling is prohibited, advertising is also prohibited.

7. SOCIAL GAMING

7.1 We believe this to be a growing area. Please decide under what criteria social gaming is permitted in your jurisdiction. If games are free to play or if there is no prize, are they legal without a licence? Please address circumstances where virtual currency is used and can be won: ie currency which is of no monetary or other value, save for as credits to take part in games. The answer should address the question whether game credits or virtual money can be exchanged for other prizes. Is any change to regulation in the area proposed or envisaged?

It remains to be seen whether the draft law will include provisions for social gaming. So far, however, it seems that no relevant provisions will be included.

Czech Republic

Law Office Becker and Poliakoff
Jan Kozubek & Veronika Žánová

1. OBJECTIVES AND STRUCTURE OF LEGISLATION
The Czech Republic gaming industry is regulated by:
* Act No. 202/1990 Coll., on lotteries and other similar games (the Act);
* Decree No. 223/1993 Coll., on gaming machines;
* Decree No. 285/1998 Coll., on terms of monitoring and record keeping in the casino; and
* Decree No. 315/1999 Coll., on the method of notifying competitions, sweepstakes and other events for prizes which are not consumer lotteries (together referred to hereinafter as the Legal Rules)

The above-listed Legal Rules, including the Act, were adopted after the collapse of the Iron Curtain in 1989. The original legal framework in this area was drafted using very liberal terminology, which caused an influx of gaming operators to enter the Czech market. Over the years, the Act has been amended on a number of occasions, however, the Legal Rules remain outdated and they do not address the requirements of the twenty-first century.

The general framework of the Legal Rules has remained unchanged for years. There are two principal reasons for this, as follows.

The municipal jurisdiction
According to the Act, the Czech state (relevant authorities exercising state power) is the only entitiy competent to decide on the issuance of the gaming licence. During the first decade of the twenty-first century, a dispute about gaming licences arose between the Czech state and the municipalities, as the Act does not give any scope for municipalities to influence the issuance of a licence to an operator seated in their territory. As one might expect, the Czech state has exercised its powers in accordance with the Act and not delegated any powers or consulted the municipalities when exercising those powers. This exercising of power led to a challenge by the municipalities in the Czech Constitutional Court in 2010 to decide whether the Act and/or the exercising of the Czech state's powers without involving the municipalities on the issuance of gaming licences was a breach of the Czech Constitution, ie should the municipalities be able to decide whether or not to permit the operation of games in their respective territories?

Prior to 2010, jurisprudence from judicial decisions of courts of first instance showed support for the Czech state's interpretation of the Act and the Legal Rules. During this period, the courts read the Czech Constitution restrictively, ie they considered the regulation of games not to be a matter of local importance and this right was not a constitutionally guaranteed right of the municipalities. Following the decision of the Czech Constitutional Court in 2010, this line of judicial authority changed significantly, as the Czech Constitutional Court decided that decisions on whether and where games parlours may be placed are a question of local order and therefore they fall under the municipal jurisdiction. The Act must therefore comply with this.

Practical application of the Czech Constitutional Court's decision in 2010 means that nowadays a gaming licence may be issued by the Czech state; however, it is only applicable to the municipality to which it is directed if that territory has not prohibited it.

Operator's seat
According to the Act, the licence to operate a game may be granted only (with one exception) to an operator that is a legal person and has its seat in the territory of the Czech Republic, with no foreign equity participation (direct or indirect through a third person). Such provision might be in conflict with the existing rules of the EU legislation, namely the Treaty on European Union and the Treaty on the Functioning of the European Union, as amended by the Lisbon Treaty of 2009. However, the regulation of games is a matter of public order and member states are given a high degree of discretion, it being understood that its regulation still shall comply with the principle of free circulation of the service in the single market. Therefore any limitation of such free circulation has to be adequate, effective and non-discriminatory. The General Court of the European Union has also outlined that limitation of free circulation due to financial reasons is not acceptable. A new bill on gambling operations modified this rule in a way which enabled foreign equity participation for the first time; however, the requirement to have a physical location in the territory of the Czech Republic remained in place.

A new bill on gambling operations
A new amendment to the Act was prepared in 2010 and passed through the legislative process, but was ultimately vetoed by the President. Due to the general elections in 2010 and objections of the European Union (regarding the requirement of a physical location in the territory of the Czech Republic), the draft bill on gambling operations has not been submitted to the Czech Parliament yet and there have been no major developments on the bill since since that time. However, a new government, nominated by the President in January 2014 (and approved by the Parliament in February 2014), intends to expedite work on adopting a completely new gambling law. It is, therefore, possible that the new Act could finally enter into force within two years.

2. FRAMEWORK OF LEGISLATION

2.1 What is the legal definition of gambling and what falls within this definition?

The Act includes a general definition of a lottery or similar games. Next to this general definition it also lists typical games as examples, by way of a non-exhaustive list. In practical terms, this means that any game which falls within the general definition shall be deemed to be a lottery or a similar game, even it is not listed as an example. It should be noted that the definition of gambling has been dramatically broadened, as from 1 January 2012.

A lottery or a similar game shall be deemed a game in which every physical person participates voluntarily after having paid a deposit (bet), the return of which is not guaranteed to the participant. Coincidence, a certain circumstance not known in advance or an occurrence defined by the operator within the issued game conditions determines a win or loss. It does not matter whether the game is operated by a mechanical, electromechanical, electronic or similar appliance.

A lottery or a similar game shall also be deemed a contest, survey or any other activity for prizes, whereby the operator undertakes to pay to the participants, determined by a draw or some other random selection method, prizes in cash, deposit books, securities, insurance etc and real estate, and in which participation is conditional upon the purchase of specific goods or services, the buying of some other product and documenting the purchase to the operator, the entering into a contract relationship with a provider of goods, services or some other product, or participation in promotion or advertisement events organised by the provider or operator, and also indirectly through a third party (hereinafter Consumer Lotteries). Consumer Lotteries shall also include contests, surveys and other activities for prizes in which the operator, under the aforementioned conditions, undertakes to provide to the participants performance in kind, services or prizescomprising goods and products, etc, provided the total sum of all in-kind prizes in all games organised by the operator exceeds CZK 200,000 (approx. EUR 8,000) in any calendar year and the value of a single prize exceeds the amount of CZK 20,000 (approx. EUR 820). Consumer Lotteries are prohibited and contests, surveys and other activities for prizes mentioned above, organised by a single operator, in which the sum total of in-kind prizes in a given calendar year does not exceed the amount of CZK 200,000 (approx. EUR 8,000) and the value of a single prize does not exceed the amount of CZK 20,000 (approx. EUR 820) shall be reported to the financial office of jurisdiction.

From 1 January 2012 activities aimed at putting lotteries and similar games into operation, including mediation, organisational, financial and technical and other services related to the operation of these games and their successful completion and billing, shall also be understood to be an operation of a lottery or other similar games. Also, performance of other activities which other laws impose on the operator shall be deemed to be an operation of a game.

2.2 What is the legal definition of online gambling and what falls within this definition?

The Act does not regulate online gambling explicitly. However, any type of gambling activity in the Czech Republic requires a valid licence issued by the Ministry of Finance (the Ministry). Generally, the Ministry does not issue licences in this area as it is convinced that no model on the internet can fulfil the legal requirements (eg the actual control of age). Conversely, the Act envisages that if the Ministry licenses a game operated via the internet, the registration of bettors for such a game may only be conducted at places where the applicant who applies for such a licence normally receives bets on a game licensed under this Act.

In 2008, the Ministry issued five licences to Czech companies (ie companies established under Czech jurisdiction and having seats in the territory of the Czech Republic) to allow them to operate sports betting on the internet. As of 1 November 2013, nine licences had been been issued to online sports betting operators (also only Czech Companies).

The new draft bill on betting games also allows issuance of a licence for the operation of betting games via the internet under certain conditions (eg participants shall register in a permanent game room after presentation of an ID card). As stated above, the draft bill has not been presented to the Parliament yet.

2.3 Please set out the different gambling products identified by legislation.

The Act explicitly defines:
* **monetary lotteries or lotteries for prizes in kind**, in which a given number of tickets bearing serial numbers are issued by the operator according to the Gambling Scheme. If the tickets are divided into a number of series, then each series must include the same number of lottery tickets and each ticket must bear an indication of both the serial number and the series. The sale price of the ticket of each series must be the same in every series. All tickets that have been issued are included in the draw;
* **tombolas**, in which only the tickets that were sold are included in the draw. The tickets are sold and the prizes are given on the day and at the place of the draw;
* **numerical lotteries**, in which neither the number of participants nor the amount of game surety is specified beforehand, with the amount of the game surety being taken as the multiplication of the issued tickets and the sale price per ticket. The prize is calculated from the number of winners and the aggregate deposits (wagers) by means of a ratio determined in advance, or, alternately, it can be calculated by means of a multiple of the deposit (wager), according to what number of digits were guessed by a participant from the limited number of digits that were drawn according to the Gambling Scheme;

- **instant lotteries**, in which, after paying the deposit, a participant learns, at the periods prescribed by the operator, whether he has won or not after removing the indicated section of the lottery ticket or lot that had been covered until the time of purchase;
- **Betting games**:
  - that are operated by means of electronic or electromechanically controlled gaming machines or other like devices;
  - in which the prize is conditional on successfully guessing the outcomes or order of sporting competitions or races, the amount of the prize depending on the ratio between the number of winners and the total amount of the deposit (wager) and the prize ratio, which is set in advance;
  - that are operated with the use of special types of token bearing the combination of 15 numbers in a numerical series from 1 up to 90, with neither the number of participants nor the game surety amount being known in advance. The drawing of lots takes place publicly with the use of a mechanical device and consists of the gradual drawing of lots with digits from 1 up to 90. The prize is calculated from the aggregate amount of deposits accordingly to the type of the winning, and in each round depending on the outcome of the drawing of lots. The terms and conditions of the game are stipulated in detail in the Gambling Scheme;
  - in which the prize is conditional on successfully guessing the outcomes or order of sporting competitions or races, or the successful guessing of the outcome of other events of public interest, providing that betting on such events is not in defiance of any ethical principles. The prize is directly proportional to the prize ratio at which the bet was accepted and the wager amount;
  - operated in gambling parlours specifically established for this purpose (casinos), including those operated with the use of mechanical devices, in which neither the number of participants nor the amounts wagered during any one run of the game is known beforehand, such as roulette, dice and card games, when the bettors play against the casino operator, or other games approved in the Gambling Scheme, as well as variations of these games. The prize is calculated from the deposited amounts or according to the terms and conditions that are set forth in the Gambling Scheme. Betting games under this point cannot be operated in mobile gambling parlours (casinos);
  - in which a win depends on guessing the order in which racehorses arrive at the post and the winnings depends on the proportion of the winners to the sum total of collected deposits and the proportion of winnings determined in advance, or the winnings is proportional to the odds at which the bet was made and the amount of the bet;
  - operated by means of a functionally indivisible technical device of a central lottery system, which is an electronic system consisting of

a central control unit, local control units and an unlimited number of connected interactive video-lottery terminals. The central control unit controls all the gaming processes, draws the results on the basis of chance, decides on all winnings and immediately displays these winnings on an interactive video-lottery terminal, manages bettors' deposits and performs all the administration connected with the course of the game. The central control unit must always be located in the Czech Republic. The interactive video-lottery terminal is operated directly by the bettor and serves merely as a display unit of the central lottery system; or

- operated via a technical device, which is an electronic system consisting of a central control unit with three gaming venues with fixed physical connections operated by bettors, with which it forms a functionally indivisible whole. This technical device offers bettors specific reel games displayed via at least three mechanically spun or electronically generated discs with different symbols, complemented by a bonus game. The technical device cannot be expanded by the addition of other gaming venues. The basic winnings are decided upon and the bettors' deposits are managed directly on site via either a technical device or one of the gaming venues;
- **lotteries and other similar games**, which are run by means of technical devices operated directly by the bettor or operated over the telephone, with neither the number of participants being determined in advance nor the amount that was wagered being known beforehand. The prize is calculated from the amount of the deposits or according to the terms and conditions set forth in the Gambling Scheme; or
- **tournament or cash betting games** operated using playing cards, where there is no predetermined number of participants, where the amounts bet are not known and where the participants pay a deposit (wager) or starting fee, the return of which to the participant is not guaranteed. The winnings are calculated according to the terms and conditions set forth in the Gambling Scheme. Betting games under this provision cannot be operated in mobile gambling parlours (casinos). These games are operated:
  - as board games during which bettors play against one another on gaming tables; or
  - via devices operated directly by the bettor (eg via the internet, interactive video-lottery terminals, local lottery systems, gaming machines).

2.4   Please list the different requirements for each gambling product, including legal classifications for each; for example, is poker a game of skill or game of chance?
N/A.

2.5   Explain the system of regulation of gambling; which regulatory or governmental body is responsible for the supervision of gambling?

Which body issues licences? Which body examines enforcement powers? Is there any limit on the number or duration of available licences?

Lotteries and other similar games may be operated legally only if a licence has been granted by the competent authority:

- the municipal authority under delegated powers in the case of tombolas with a surety of up to approx. EUR 1,800 and material with a lottery game with a surety of up to EUR 8,000; or
- the Ministry in any other cases.

A licence is granted if the operation of games is in compliance with other laws, provided that it does not disturb the peace and order, and provided that a proper operation of the games is provided for, including the necessary technical devices. The licence to operate games may only be granted to a legal entity having its registered office in the territory of the Czech Republic. The licence may not be granted to a Czech legal entity in which a foreign party holds an ownership interest or a legal entity in which such a company has an ownership interest.

The body which licensed the game shall withdraw the licence if there occur or become known any circumstances for which it would not have been possible to license the game or if it proves later that the data according to which the licence was granted are inaccurate.

The state supervision over the conformity with Act by the operators of games is exercised by:

- the municipalities in cases when they grant the licence for the operation of games;
- the regional offices in cases when they grant the licence for the operation of games;
- the competent financial office and the financial offices in the territorial districts in which the gambling premises are situated in cases when the licence for the operation of games is granted by the Ministry; or
- the Ministry.

The Act stipulates explicitly that a licence for the operation of gaming (slot) machines is granted for one calendar year, at most. The licence for the operation of odds betting is granted for 10 years, at most. The licence for operating a gambling business in gambling parlours specifically established for this purpose (casinos) is granted for 10 years, at most.

The body which licensed the games shall withdraw the licence if there occur or become known any circumstances for which it would not have been possible to license the games or if it proves later that the data according to which the licence was granted are inaccurate.

This common provision of the Act is very important in connection with the Constitutional Court decision stating that municipalities are empowered directly by the Constitution to regulate gambling in their territory by municipal decree. As the licence may be issued only if it is in conformity with all relevant legal regulation, ie by municipal decree as well, it practically means that licences may last for as long as the municipality allows it in its territory. Therefore the above-stated terms are rather relative.

The body that granted the licence for the operation of the games is obliged to check the games. The body exercising the state supervision powers may check at any time whatsoever whether the games are operated according to the terms and conditions specified in the licence and whether the applicable laws are complied with.

The operator of the games is obliged to enable the licensing body and the state supervision body to enter the business premises and to present the body with the accounting documents, accounting statement, reports, vouchers and other documents and records on data media, to enable the inspection of the operated games and technical devices, to supply information about the accounting transactions and to co-operate in the inspection. If so required by the nature of the matter, the licensing body and the state supervision body are free to seize the documents and hold themfor the time necessary to investigate and complete the case.

3. ONLINE GAMBLING

3.1 To what extent can online gambling be offered in your jurisdiction? Are licences available and, if so, for which gambling products? Please describe briefly the licensing process, who may apply, whether licences are limited in number and, if no licences are available, whether it is legal for online gambling to be offered. In the case of EU jurisdictions, please state whether there are any issues as to the legality of the local law at EU level. Please refer to any relevant cases at ECJ level and explain any measures taken or pending by the European Commission.

The Act does not expressly regulate online gaming; however, any type of gaming activity in the Czech Republic requires a valid licence issued by the municipal authority or the Ministry. Therefore, it could be said that, by implication, the Act can be said to regulate online gaming.

General conditions for the licence

A licence is granted if the operation of games is in compliance with other laws, provided that it does not disturb the peace and order, and provided that a proper operation of the lottery or game is provided for, including the necessary technical devices.

Generally, it can be said that games may be operated by either the state or a joint stock company with its registered office in the territory of the Czech Republic the subject of business of which is the operation of games and the shares of which are registered shares in their entirety; if the shareholder of such a company is another joint stock company, all the shares of this other company must also be registered shares. The Act stipulates the minimum amount of registered capital of the company (up to EUR 3.7 m), below which the amount must not fall during the validity of the licence. The prescribed amount of registered capital may only be paid in the form of cash contributions. The applicant must prove the origin of the funds used to pay the registered capital as part of proceedings on the approval of a game (eg by way of a set of tax returns from the Czech Republic as well as abroad). The registered capital must be paid prior to the filing of a licence application.

If the Ministry licenses a game operated via the internet, the registration of bettors for such a game may only be conducted at places where the applicant who applies for such a licence normally receives bets on games licensed under the Act.

To secure the receivables towards the government and municipalities, and the prizes payable to the bettors, the applicant is obliged to deposit, in a special bank or savings bank or loan cooperative account, a surety (of up to EUR 730,000).

The applicant for the licence to operate games, whether physical persons who hold the position of a statutory body of the applicant or who are one of its members, or physical persons who are shareholders or members of the applicant, must be persons having criminal integrity.

The operation of foreign games, including the sale of foreign gambling tickets, participation in betting abroad with wagers that are paid abroad, and the collection of wagers for betting games operated abroad or the mediation of wagers for betting games operated abroad, is prohibited. The operation of Czech games with wagers that are paid abroad is prohibited. The Ministry may grant an exemption from this ban in order to ensure mutuality. As such, the Ministry maintains that foreign-based online remote gambling operators offer their betting services in violation of the Act (ie without a licence) and, therefore, illegally.

3.2 Is there a distinction between the law applicable to B2B operations and that applicable to B2C operations?
No.

3.3 What are the consequences for B2C or B2B operators who are active in your jurisdiction without having obtained or applied for the required permits, licences and approvals? What penalties and enforcement powers are available in respect of the illegal operators? Please outline any significant domestic decisions or enforcement actions that have been taken by the relevant authorities in recent years.
Fines of up to EUR 370,000 shall be imposed by the respective state authority on the legal entity which operates a game without the appropriate licence or if such business is carried out in contradiction to the Act, the Gambling Scheme or the terms and conditions set forth in the licence.

The fine may be imposed within one year after the date when the body authorised to impose the fine learned of the breach of the duty or loss of the licence and within up to three years of the date when the breach of the duty or loss of the licence occurred. The fine is payable within one month after the date on which the resolution on its imposition came into power.

3.4 What technical measures are in place (if any) to protect consumers from unlicensed operators, such as ISP blocking and payment blocking?

The draft bill amendments that were approved in 2011 originally contained provisions concerning illegal online gambling. These provisions would have required internet service providers (ISPs) to block illegal games and their advertisement, and banks to proceed with blocking payments to foreign gaming sites. Under the draft amendments, those who do not comply would risk a fine of up to EUR 370,000. These provisions of the draft resulted in public scorn, and ISPs presented a petition to the Parliament signed by several thousand Czech citizens raising concerns about the internet censorship. As a result of the vigorous discussions over the planned blocking system, this part of the bill was separated from the broader regulation and was planned to be voted on at a later occasion. The date for this vote has not yet been announced.

Participation in betting abroad, with wagers that are paid abroad, and the collection of wagers for betting games operated abroad or the mediation of wagers for betting games operated abroad, is prohibited. The operation of the Czech lotteries and other similar games, with wagers that are paid abroad, is also prohibited.

A fine up to EUR 1,800 shall be imposed by the state supervision body on the physical person who is in an employment, membership or other like relation with the operator and the participant of odds betting and gambling in a casino if they acted in defiance of this Act or the licence for gambling operation or the Gambling Scheme.

3.5 Has the legal status of online gambling changed significantly in recent years and, if so, how?

From the very beginning the Ministry has not issue licences, as it was convinced that no model on the internet could fulfil the legal requirements (eg the actual control of age). In 2008, however, the Ministry issued five licences to Czech companies (established under Czech jurisdiction) which have been allowed to operate sports bets on the internet. As of 1 November 2013, nine licences have been issued to online sports betting operators (all are Czech companies).

The Act still does not regulate online business. The Act envisages only that if the Ministry licenses a game operated via the internet, the registration of bettors for such a game may only be conducted at places where the applicant who applies for such a licence normally receives bets on a game licensed under this Act.

Also, the new draft bill on betting games allows issuance of a licence for operation of games via the internet under certain conditions (eg participants shall register in a permanent game room after presentation of an ID card). As stated above, the draft bill has not been presented to the Parliament yet.

3.6 Whilst acknowledging the inherent difficulty in predicting developments in gambling law, what are the likely developments in

online gambling in your jurisdiction, both short term and long term? Are any specific amendments under consideration? Have there been any recent political developments, or do you envisage any in the near future? Are any specific amendments under consideration? Are they likely to be adopted and, if so, what is the time scale?

The current Czech regulatory framework is widely acknowledged to be outdated and does not impose sufficient regulation on the industry. The fact that the law has not changed substantially in the last 20 or so years means that new and effective regulation has long been overdue.

In general, regulation and compliance standards for gambling are relatively liberal in the Czech Republic. As the scope and complexity of the gambling industry grows, there has been increasing pressure on the Czech government to introduce a new regulatory framework, better suited to overseeing emerging technologies such as interactive gambling.

The government resolved in 2008 to engage in a broad legislative reform process to amend the country's gaming legislation and commenced a period of public consultation in May 2008. Although the consultation phase of the project concluded in 2008, the draft law was not submitted to the Czech Parliament. Many more attempts at reform followed, with a number of competing draft bill proposals materialising in the chamber since January 2009. Only one managed to progress to the final stages of the Czech legislative process, only to be vetoed by the President in a sudden twist of events.

The Czech government approved a new draft bill which it notified to the European Commission on 16 August 2012. The draft Act on Gambling Operations is to repeal the existing gambling law – Act No 202/1990 Coll., on lotteries and others such games, as amended.

The draft act would bring into effect, inter alia, the following changes:

- one of the biggest changes is thatforeign operators will, for the very first time, be allowed to participate in all forms of gambling, provided they satisfy the various requirements necessary to be granted a licence – eg they have the required registered capital, surety, debt-free status, good repute. Operators may be joint stock companies, foundation or endowment funds and, in relation to small-scale card tournaments only, the draft expressly authorises civic associations to obtain licences for these. The requirements for registered capital and surety will depend on the type of game of chance. In addition, certification from an appointed authorised person in respect of technical gaming equipment will also be required;
- to operate fixed-odds betting on the internet, operators will have to have a registered office in the Czech Republic, as players must be registered at a permanent gaming facility before they will be able to use the website. The draft proposal expressly mentions fixed-odds betting on the internet but contains no mention of card games. Card games on the internet were introduced in the 2011 amendments; however, they are now set to be left out of the new law. The operator must conduct registration of the participant at a fixed gaming area upon presentation of a valid ID;

- in relation to licensing, the new act will authorise the General Financial Directorate and its Specialised Tax Office to issue permits. For the purposes of ensuring a uniform authorisation regime, the directorate and its field offices will act together as administrative supervisory authorities; and
- games of chance will be divided into the following two groups:
  - authorised; and
  - notified games of chance (raffle and consumer games of chance).

The existing list of authorised games will expand to include small-scale tournaments and a new group of games which use technical gaming devices operated directly by the participant. They will also include current games operated using technical gaming devices which are already available in the gambling market.

The draft bill also proposes a dual authorisation procedure, which will consist of the following:

- a basic permit, which would be valid nationwide for the specific type of game of chance or type of technical gaming device. Such procedure is intended to verify the applicant's competences to be an operator of that particular game of chance; and
- a permit to operate and physically place the particular game of chance, eg a VLT (video lottery terminal) or AWP (amusement with prizes) machine, in the specific location at which the game of chance is to be operated. The Specialised Tax Office must take into account binding decrees issued by municipalities (eg those banning VLTs or limiting their number).

The proposed draft bill will also, for the first time, expressly distinguish between gaming facilities in which games of chance may be operated. These facilities are to be: gaming centres, gaming parlours, casinos, and sale and collection points.

Other provisions that would be introduced are the principles of responsible gaming, consisting of prevention and measures taken by the operator, including self-limiting measures by the participants in the game of chance.

The draft provides for a new type of 'special gambling tax', specifically, a tax on games of chance, which will be revenue for the state and municipalities.

The administrative supervision will also be tightened, with a new regime that differentiates between the various offences and imposes higher penalties for these.

It is virtually impossible to predict when, and in which concrete version, a new act on gambling will pass the Czech legislation process. General elections took place in the Czech Republic in November 2013, and a new government was appointed in February 2014. The Ministry of Finance will undoubtedly develop the above described draft and submit it to the government again. However, it is unlikely that this will occur in the very near future.

3.7   Is the law the same in relation to mobile gambling and interactive gambling on television? If not, are there any headline differences?
It is the same.

4.   LAND-BASED GAMING
4.1   Please describe the licensing regime (if any) for land-based gaming, and what products are included. Please set out what licences are available and the licensing regime for them.
N/A.

4.2   Please set out any particular limitations or requirements for (eg casino) operators, such as a ban on local residents gambling.
N/A.

4.3   Please address the questions in 3.5 above, but in relation to land-based gaming.
The Act does not differ between online gambling and land-based gaming. In every case the operator must obtain a licence under the same conditions (for general conditions please see above). Therefore everything stated above applies accordingly.

5.   TAX
5.1   Please summarise briefly the tax regime applicable both to land-based and online gaming.
Lottery operators are subject to a flat tax rate of 20 per cent of gross gaming revenues and are liable to a fee of CZK55 per day per VLT machine and other technical gaming machines. Starting from 1 January 2012, the operators are subject to an income tax of 19 per cent.

6.   ADVERTISING
6.1   To what extent is the advertising of gambling permitted in your jurisdiction? Again, this should cover both land-based and online gaming. To the extent that advertising is permitted, how is it regulated?
The Act only prohibits promotion, advertisement and support of the sale of games not licensed or reported under the Act. Violation of this provision is subject to a penalty in the amount of EUR 80,000.

The advertisement shall comply with the Act No. 40/1995 Coll., on the regulation of advertising, which is the general legal rule for advertising in the Czech Republic. The act on the regulation of advertising does not include special regulation of gambling advertising.

7.   SOCIAL GAMING
7.1   We believe this to be a growing area. Please decide under what criteria social gaming is permitted in your jurisdiction. If games are free to play or if there is no prize, are they legal without a licence? Please address circumstances where virtual currency is used and

can be won: ie currency which is of no monetary or other value, save for as credits to take part in games. The answer should address the question whether game credits or virtual money can be exchanged for other prizes. Is any change to regulation in the area proposed or envisaged?
In the Czech Republic any betting game or game of chance is characterised by four main characteristics, which must be met for the game to be considered a game and therefore governed by the Act. Those characteristics are:
* the voluntary participation of physical persons;
* a deposit (stake), return of which is not guaranteed;
* the existence of win and loss; and
* a coincidence or circumstance not known in advance that participant´s win or loss in the game depends on (ie it must be unpredictable).

A deposit represents an asset (including personal performance) which a participant spends for a specified purpose (ie in relation to a particular game), the return of which is not guaranteed to the participant. The fact that the return of the deposit is not guaranteed should be considered in connection with the existence of win and loss.

At present, the Ministry interprets the Act in a very broad way, basically considering any payment or personal performance directed to the operator as a deposit, regardless of its purpose or nature, or whether such payment may be returned or not. It applies the same approach to the evaluation whether or not there is win or loss. Such interpretation, however, has not been confirmed yet by the relevant court.

If social gaming meets the above criteria, it shall be deemed as a game and its operation requires a licence. If it does not meet one of the criteria, the Act does not apply.

As stated above, prohibited consumer lotteries are also understood as contests, surveys and any other activity for prizes, where the operator undertakes to pay the participants, determined by a draw or some other random selection method, prizes, and in which the participation is conditional upon (i) the purchase of specific goods or services; (ii) buying some other product and documenting the purchase to the operator; (iii) entering into a contract relationship with a provider of goods, services or some other product; or (iv) participation in promotion or advertisement events organised by the provider or operator, and also indirectly through a third party. Consumer lotteries also include contests, surveys and other activities for prizes in which the operator, under the aforementioned conditions, undertakes to provide to the participants performance in kind, services or prizes comprising goods and products, etc, provided the total sum of all in-kind prizes in all games organised by the operator exceeds CZK 200,000 (approx. EUR 8,000) in any calendar year and the value of a single prize exceeds the amount of CZK 20,000 (approx. EUR 800).

The financial limit of prizes limits significantly marketing activities based on the win principle. The new draft bill on gambling has acknowledged this, and proposes to raise the limit up to EUR 80,000.

It will be for the Czech courts to deal with the question how to interpret the term 'random selection'. In 2006 the Ministry issued a memorandum in order to help marketing specialists to prepare 'win' promotions without the risk of breaching the gambling law. However, this memorandum has not been followed by state authorities since 2013 and its rationale (relating to consumer lotteries) is rather unclear. The state authorities prefers the notion that every selection which depends only partially on a circumstance not known in advance (typically guessing questions, where 99 per cent of the answer may be derived and the remaining 1 per cent is influenced by chance) is random selection. The first judicial decisions on this question may be delivered towards the end of 2014, which may give some clarity to this area.

Denmark

Horten Nina Henningsen & Mikkel Taanum

1. OBJECTIVES AND STRUCTURE OF LEGISLATION

1.1 What is the current legal status of gambling in the jurisdiction?

Since 1 January 2012, the Danish gaming market has been partly liberalised. This part liberalisation has made it possible to offer gaming products such as online and land-based betting and online casino games to the Danish market. Lottery and bets on races with pigeons, horses and dogs were not liberalised and are still under the monopoly of the state-owned company Danske Spil A/S. The possibility of providing land-based gaming machines at gaming venues and land-based casinos was maintained with the new legislation.

The Danish gaming market is governed by the Danish Gaming Act, which covers both land-based and online gaming. The provision or organisation of games covered by the Danish Gaming Act is subject to duty under the Danish Gaming Duties Act.

A licence is required to provide both land-based and online gaming in Denmark, and parties wishing to provide gaming in Denmark must be prepared for a thorough application process – see sections 3 and 4 for further details regarding the licensing process.

The main purposes of the current Danish gaming legislation are:

- to maintain the consumption of gaming services at a moderate level;
- to protect young people and other vulnerable persons from being exploited through gaming or developing a gaming addiction;
- to protect players by ensuring that gaming is provided in a fair, responsible and transparent manner;
- to ensure public order; and
- to prevent gaming as a means to support crime.

2. FRAMEWORK OF LEGISLATION

The Danish Gaming Act is divided into different 'parts'. Part 1 sets out the purpose and scope of the Act. Part 2 contains various definitions. Part 3 deals with the various licences for the individual types of games, and Part 4 sets out the criteria for providing games. Part 5 contains the rules on duty of disclosure, sale and marketing. Part 6 contains the rules for approval of managers and staff. Part 7 contains different administrative provisions on fees etc. Part 8 sets out the requirements for the withdrawal and expiry of licences. Part 9 sets out the rules regarding supervision and exchange of information between the Danish Gaming Authority and other governmental bodies. Parts 10 and 11 contain the rules regarding complaints over decisions made by the Danish Gaming Authority and the possibilities of judicial review. Part 12 contains the penalty provisions and, finally, part 13 contains the entry into force of the Act and interim provisions.

2.1 What is the legal definition of gambling and what falls within this definition?

A 'game' is defined in the Danish Gaming Act as any activity that falls within one of the categories of: (i) lottery; (ii) combination game; or (iii) betting.

These three terms are defined as follows:

(i) Lottery: *'Activities in which a participant has a chance of winning a prize and where the probability of winning is solely based on chance'.*

(ii) Combination game: *'Activities in which a participant has a chance of winning a prize and where the probability of winning is based on a combination of skill and chance'.*

(iii) Betting: *'Activities in which a participant has a chance of winning a prize and where bets are placed on the outcome of a future event or the occurrence of a particular event in the future'.*

If an activity falls within one of the above-mentioned three categories, it is considered a game and thus the provision of such activities to the Danish market is thus considered provision of gaming services.

Lotteries

A game where the winner is chosen at complete random, for instance bingo or lottery, is solely based on chance and would therefore fall within category (i).

Combination games

In other games, skill may influence the outcome. For example, in poker the players are each dealt a hand consisting of a number of random cards which they in turn must decide how to play. Such games require both skill and luck which is why they fall within category (ii).

Betting

When betting on what team will win a certain match or whether it will gain entry to the finals etc, the bet concerns the outcome of a future event or the occurrence of a particular future event thus falling within category 3.

Skill games

Outside the range of the above-mentioned categories there are pure skill games such as most sports activities, computer games or quiz shows where the chance of winning is primarily based on skill. Skill games are thus not covered by the Danish Gaming Act and a licence is not needed.

2.2 What is the legal definition of online gambling and what falls within this definition?

Online gaming is defined as games that take place between a player and a gaming operator through the use of remote communication. See above under section 2.1 for further details on the definition of games.

Remote communication means communication that takes place without the player and the gaming operator meeting physically. It may include use of the internet, telephone, TV, radio, mobile telephone, videotext (micro-computer, TV screen) with a keyboard or touch screen, or electronic mail. The games thus have to be provided and take place from a distance (interactively).

Consequently, a game is not provided online if the parties meet physically in connection with the conclusion of the agreement.

2.3 Please set out the different gambling products identified by legislation.

The Danish Gaming Act identifies the following games:
- betting, including pool betting and betting exchanges;
- casino games, including baccarat, blackjack, poker, punto banco and roulette;
- lotteries, including class lottery and bingo;
- gaming machines; and
- pyramid schemes, the provision of which is illegal in Denmark.

2.4 Please list the different requirements for each gambling product, including legal classifications for each; for example, is poker a game of skill or game of chance?

As described above in section 2.1 gaming is an activity which falls within one of three categories.

(i)   Lottery

A lottery is an activity in which the participants have a chance of winning a prize and where the probability of winning is solely based on chance.

In the classic definition of a lottery the player pays a stake to the gaming operator and gets or chooses some numbers (or symbols, etc) whereupon the gaming operator makes a draw that decides whether or not the player wins. The drawing of numbers is randomised. The player's possible winnings depend on the number of participants in the lottery and the numbers chosen by the other players.

The definition of a lottery in the Danish Gaming Act includes games such as Lotto, Joker, class lotteries, bingo and scratch games. In such games the player does not have any possibility of affecting the outcome of the game by the application of skill or ability. Solely the element of chance (luck) decides the outcome of the game.

Lotteries that are subdivided into several classes with separate drawings in each class are called class lotteries. A class lottery is divided into one or more classes, each with its own separate draw. In a class lottery different ticket types are sold, eg whole tickets and half tickets. The player's stake and winnings are decided by the type of ticket bought.

As mentioned earlier, lotteries are still monopolised by the state-owned company, Danske Spil A/S, as the authorised provider.

(ii)   Combination game

A combination game is categorised as an activity in which a participant has a chance of winning a prize and where the probability of winning is based on a combination of skill and chance. The definition of combination games covers a number of different types of games, eg poker, backgammon, blackjack, rubber-bridge, whist and guessing competitions (eg where the competition is decided by a draw or a similar element of chance).

A combination game is therefore a generic term for the games whose outcome is decided by a combination of elements of chance, such as the dealing of cards, the throw of a dice, draws, etc and the player's skill/ability. Whether a game can be classified as a combination game does not depend on the proportion between chance and probability. If an element of chance is added to a game which otherwise is decided by skill only, ie by a draw being made between the most skilled players, the game can be described as a combination game, as the chance of winning in the game depends on a combination of skill and chance.

Casino games are described as a mixture of lotteries and combination games. Several casino games are decided purely by chance such as roulette, punto banco, baccarat and gaming machines (eg slot machines) offering cash winnings, while the chance of winning in other games depends to a greater or lesser extent on the player's skill, such as eg blackjack and poker.

(iii)   Betting

A licence to provide betting under the Danish Gaming Act is a licence to provide betting both online and from physical shops (land-based betting). Both 'regular' betting and betting exchanges are allowed.

As mentioned earlier, bets on races with pigeons, horses and dogs are still monopolised by the state-owned company, Danske Spil A/S, as the authorised supplier.

Online betting

Betting is an activity in which the participants have a chance of winning a prize and where bets are placed on the outcome of a future event or the occurrence of a particular event in the future.

The definition of betting includes betting on the result of future events and not on events which have already taken place. The event on which a bet is placed could be eg a football match, a tennis match, a general election or a song competition. Also bets placed on the occurrence (or not) of a particular future event are defined as betting. The definition therefore includes betting on events or occurrences which are not necessarily planned and will not necessarily occur. Examples of such betting are bets on 'whether the next prime minister will be a woman' or 'whether a particular tennis player will win a Grand Slam tournament in the next season' (binary bets).

It is not permitted to provide betting on the result of lotteries. Therefore, it is not possible for the holders of licences to provide betting on the result of lottery draws. Furthermore, it is not permitted to provide betting on the outcome of casino games where the probability of winning in the game is solely a matter of chance, eg roulette or gaming machines offering cash winnings.

Betting where the entire or parts of the winnings depend on the size of the total stake pool or are divided among the winners is called pool betting. In pool betting the size of a player's winnings depends on how the other players have placed their bets. In pool betting the players compete for the entire pool of stakes or for winnings whose size has been determined in advance. In pool betting, such as eg Tips12, Tips13 and Måljagt (products offered by Danske Spil A/S), the size of the first prize depends on the total revenue on the game and on the players' bets. If more players have bet on the correct outcome of all matches on the pools coupon, the first prize will be divided among these players.

Pool betting with fixed odds (ie the stake is multiplied by x) is not allowed, but in some forms of pool betting, current odds are calculated which show the size of the possible winnings when a bet is made.

Land-based betting
Land-based betting follows the same rules as online betting with the additional possibility of providing betting on the result of electronically simulated sporting events.

2.5   Explain the system of regulation of gambling; which regulatory or governmental body is responsible for the supervision of gambling? Which body issues licences? Which body examines enforcement powers? Is there any limit on the number or duration of available licences?
The Danish Gaming market is supervised by the Danish Gaming Authority, the Danish Ministry of Taxation and the Danish Consumer Ombudsman.

The Danish Gaming Authority
The Danish Gaming Authority is an authority placed within the Danish Ministry of Taxation. The Danish Gaming Authority is, *inter alia*, responsible for the administration and granting of licences for betting, land-based casino and online casino as well as the monitoring of the Danish gaming market.

The Danish Gaming Authority has published guidance in both Danish and English on its website: *www.spillemyndigheden.dk*. These documents vary from legal guidelines to technical descriptions, Q&As and newsletters.

The Danish Ministry of Taxation
A division under the Danish Ministry of Taxation called SKAT (the Danish Tax Administration) deals with the registration of licence holders, inspection and collection of gaming duties.

Furthermore, a department in the Danish Ministry of Taxation deals with legislative issues and handles matters in relation to European regulation.

The Danish Consumer Ombudsman
As far as marketing is concerned, the Danish Gaming Authority and the Danish Consumer Ombudsman have established informal cooperation in this regard as the Danish Consumer Ombudsman supervises the compliance with the Danish Marketing Practices Act.

3. ONLINE GAMBLING
3.1 To what extent can online gambling be offered in your jurisdiction? Are licences available and, if so, for which gambling products? Please describe briefly the licensing process, who may apply, whether licences are limited in number and, if no licences are available, whether it is legal for online gambling to be offered. In the case of EU jurisdictions, please state whether there are any issues as to the legality of the local law at EU level. Please refer to any relevant cases at ECJ level and explain any measures taken or pending by the European Commission.
Online gaming licences in Denmark
Two different types of online gaming licences are available in Denmark: (i) a betting licence; and (ii) an online casino licence. The betting licence covers both online and land-based betting, see section 4 below.

A Danish licence to provide betting and/or online casino grants the right to provide gaming to the Danish market.

As a starting point, the licence does not cover the provision of games to Greenland. However, the licence can be issued to cover Greenland at no extra cost. If the licence is to cover Greenland, the licence holder must ensure that specific information is available to players in Greenlandic.

Licences are granted for a term of five years and there is no restriction on the number of licences that may be granted to gaming operators who wish to provide gaming on the Danish market.

Note that if a game is provided for free (ie no stake or payment is needed to participate), the game may be provided without a licence.

The application fee is DKK 254,500 (approximately EUR 34,100) for each licence (2014 level); however, if the party applies for both a betting and a casino licence, the combined fee is DKK 356,300 (approximately EUR 47,750) (2014 level). For companies with an annual gross gaming revenue of less than DKK 1,000,000 (approximately EUR 133,500), a 'revenue-restricted' betting or online casino licence may be issued and the fee is DKK 50,900 (approximately EUR 6,800) per licence (2014 level).

Gaming operators have to pay an annual fee based on their gross gaming revenue, as well as a weekly gaming duty, see section 5 below for further details regarding the gaming duty.

Requirements for applicants
Both physical persons and companies may apply for a gaming licence in Denmark if the person or company meets the minimum legislative requirements.

Any person wishing to provide online gaming on the Danish market must:
• be at least 21 years old;

- not have a legal guardian;
- not be subject to insolvency proceedings;
- not have been convicted of criminal offences, which render it probable that the person will abuse the access to gaming; and
- not have any due debt to public authorities.

If the person does not live in Denmark or in another EU or EEA country, the person must have appointed a legal representative in Denmark.

Any company wishing to provide online gaming on the Danish market must:

- be established in Denmark or in another EU or EEA country or have an appointed legal representative in Denmark;
- the board and the directors must all meet the requirements for physical persons mentioned above.

A legal representative must be approved by the Danish Gaming Authority and must meet a number of requirements that are similar to the requirements for board members or executive officers mentioned above.

If these minimum requirements are met, the applicant must further prove that it can provide online gaming in a sound financial and professional manner.

The assessment is made by the Danish Gaming Authority based on a large number of documents, which the applicant is required to submit. The Danish Gaming Authority will consider the overall picture and, if they find that the necessary requirements are met, they will issue either a conditional or an unconditional licence. See below for a more detailed description of the application process.

To help applicants to get an overview of what is required the Danish Gaming Authority has published a Guide on betting and online casino.

The Guide lists 11 duties related to gaming which the applicant must demonstrate its ability to perform sufficiently:

'1. *Responsibility, risk and managerial prerogative relating to the operation of games.*
2. *Contracting with players.*
3. *Ownership of player data, including registration of players.*
4. *Player support.*
5. *Ownership of intellectual property rights relating to games.*
6. *Ownership of website/game client.*
7. *Operating the gaming system, including maintenance of hardware.*
8. *Owner or renter of the greater part of the gaming system (gaming infrastructure).*
9. *Control of collusion etc, money laundering and combat of the financing of terrorism.*
10. *Payment transfer services and underpinning of payment instruments.*
11. *Marketing of trademarks and/or games.'*

The licence holder may outsource some of these duties to third parties, which may be companies within the same group structure or external companies.

However, duties 1 and 3 above must always be performed by the licence holder and thus never be outsourced to a third party.

The Guide addresses three types of third parties – sub-contractors, white label partners and affiliates.

Sub-contractors may be used to perform some of the tasks mentioned above, for example, they may be a platform provider or a payment provider and must only maintain and perform a minority of the licence holder's tasks.

How many duties can be outsourced to sub-contractors will be decided on a case-by-case basis by the Danish Gaming Authority, but the licence holder must always have sufficient infrastructure to provide online gaming on a sound financial and professional basis.

If the sub-contractor is also a white label partner, the sub-contractor will normally be required to apply for an online gaming licence.

A white label partner is a third party marketing the licence holder's gaming products; it thus appears as if it is the white label partner itself that operates the gaming products, eg through their own marketing and by use of their own domain names.

A white label partner does not need a gaming licence provided that it:
- is not also a sub-contractor;
- does not have (significant) influence on the licence holders' operations or the gaming accounts;
- does not own the player database or the gaming system;
- does not have access to the player information, besides what is necessary for marketing of the gaming product; and
- does not have any relation to registered players other than that necessary for marketing of the gaming product.

The white label partner is not responsible for the gaming activities, but may become liable for breach of Danish marketing legislation. See section 6 below for further details regarding the Danish marketing rules.

White label partners may own the trade mark, which they use for branding their particular website. A list of domain names related to every specific licence holder, including the white labeller's own domain names, is available at the Danish Gaming Authority's website.

Prior to operating a white label, the contract between the licence holder and the operator of the white label, has to be approved by the Danish Gaming Authority.

Affiliates advertise for the licence holder's gaming products in other ways than white label partners, eg by use of banner commercials or by offline marketing sources, eg hotels, sports bars, cinemas etc.

Affiliates do not need a licence if they only advertise gaming products of one or more licence holders and do not:
- have any relation to the players;
- own any player or game data;
- do not own rights connected with the trade marks and sites they are marketing; and
- own parts of the gaming system used for the game or the site they are marketing.

As for the white label partners, affiliates may be liable for breach of Danish marketing legislation.

The application process

Any person or company wishing to apply for an online gaming licence in Denmark must submit three different forms – the main application, Annex A (personal statements) and Annex B (technical information).

The application and annexes must be filled out in Danish, but the related documentation may be in either Danish or English.

In the main application the applicant must provide legal and financial information about itself, including a description of the company structure. Further, the applicant must designate a number of key persons to be responsible for different areas, eg the gaming system, change management, etc.

In Annex A, executive directors and members of the board are required to submit personal information, including name, address, civil status and experience with gaming.

In Annex B, the applicant must provide detailed information about its technical capabilities and the gaming system. The applicant must perform a number of different tests and submit certificates proving that these tests have been carried out by accredited testing houses.

These three forms must be accompanied by an extensive amount of documentation, which can easily consist of thousands of pages, including (but not limited to):

*   criminal records and curriculum vitaes;
*   financial reports;
*   budget forecasts;
*   detailed descriptions of the applicant's policies and internal procedures;
*   detailed description of the gaming system;
*   third party guarantees;
*   bank declarations;
*   company chart;
*   list of sub-contractors;
*   white label contracts;
*   business plan;
*   licences from other countries.

After all of the necessary documentation has been submitted, the Danish Gaming Authority will evaluate the submitted documentation in cooperation with its designated accountancy.

The Danish Gaming Authority may choose to grant a full licence, grant a conditional licence or reject the application. An applicant failing to submit sufficient documentation or failing to live up to the requirements set by the Danish Gaming Authority will normally be given a chance to take remedial action by providing the missing information before the application is rejected.

There is no refund of the application fee, which will be forfeited if the application is rejected. If the applicant applies again, a new fee must be paid.

From the handing in of an application to the Danish Gaming Authority, the issue of a licence will normally take approximately three to six months, depending on the information provided by the applicant.

Other relevant information
The Danish Gaming Duties Act is currently under review by the European Court of Justice.

On 23 July 2010, the Danish trade organisation for gaming machines filed a complaint with the European Commission regarding the different taxation of online and offline gaming providers under the Danish Gaming Duties Act. On 20 September 2011, the European Commission found that the duties were not in conflict with European Union state aid rules.

The Danish trade organisation for gaming machines then filed a subpoena on 30 November 2011 against the European Commission in relation to its decision.

Even though this case is currently pending, the Danish Gaming Act entered into force on 1 January 2012, along with the Danish Gaming Duties Act.

At the time of writing (March 2014), there has been no further development in the case.

3.2 Is there a distinction between the law applicable to B2B operations and that applicable to B2C operations?
Online gaming operators contracting with players directly – either through their own website (B2C) or through a white label site – are required to hold an online gaming licence to provide gaming in Denmark.

Online providers who do not contract directly with players, but only provide services to gaming operators directly are not required to hold a licence.

3.3 What are the consequences for B2C or B2B operators who are active in your jurisdiction without having obtained or applied for the required permits, licences and approvals? What penalties and enforcement powers are available in respect of the illegal operators? Please outline any significant domestic decisions or enforcement actions that have been taken by the relevant authorities in recent years.
The Danish Gaming Act criminalises the provision of illegal gaming in Denmark.

'Illegal gaming' may be the provision of gaming services on the Danish market without a proper licence, but the term also includes the promotion of and advertising of such gaming.

Whether a gaming operator provides gaming to Danish players depends on the specific marketing of the gaming operator. The main criterion is not whether the gaming operator actually takes bets from Danish players, but whether the company markets itself towards Danish players, eg by having a website in Danish and/or carrying out marketing campaigns in Denmark.

Advertising for illegal gaming covers all types of advertising directed towards the Danish market. Even the mere reception of a sponsor payment from an illegal gaming operator may be seen as illegal gaming in rare circumstances.

If a party commits a breach of the Danish Gaming Act it may be fined or in very severe cases imprisoned.

3.4 What technical measures are in place (if any) to protect consumers from unlicensed operators, such as ISP blocking and payment blocking?

The Danish Gaming Authority has the means to require internet providers to block access to illegal gaming providers' websites once an injunction has been issued by a Danish Bailiff's Court. During 2012, the Danish Gaming Authority dealt with about 50 gaming providers operating illegal games on more than 100 websites. Most of these decided to comply with a request from the Danish Gaming Authority to stop providing the games. However, 20 websites had to be blocked by means of an injunction from Danish Bailiff's Courts.

The Danish Gaming Authority also has the means to require banks to block financial transactions from or to an illegal gaming provider once an injunction has been issued by a Danish Bailiff's Court. However, at the time of writing (March 2014), the Danish banks and the Danish payment service providers do not have the technical means necessary to block financial transactions.

3.5 Has the legal status of online gambling changed significantly in recent years and, if so, how?

The possibility of providing online gaming to Danish players has changed significantly with the entry into force of the new Danish Gaming Act on 1 January 2012. The entry into force of the Danish Gaming Act changed the provision of online gaming to Danish players from a monopolised to a partly liberalised online gaming market.

3.6 Whilst acknowledging the inherent difficulty in predicting developments in gambling law, what are the likely developments in online gambling in your jurisdiction, both short term and long term? Are any specific amendments under consideration? Have there been any recent political developments, or do you envisage any in the near future? Are any specific amendments under consideration? Are they likely to be adopted and, if so, what is the time scale?

The partial liberalisation of the Danish online gaming market is widely considered a success, and Denmark now has a well-functioning online gaming market. As of March 2014, there are 40 holders of betting and/or online casino licences (nine of which are income-restricted licences).

Financially, the partial liberalisation has also been a success for the Danish state. Thus, the gross gaming revenue for holders of betting and online casino licences was DKK 2,045,000,000 in 2012 (approximately EUR 274,500,000) and 2,375,000,000 DKK (approximately EUR 318,300,000) in 2013.

In addition, there are specific plans to amend the Danish Gaming Act and the Danish Gaming Duties Act. The draft amendments are expected to be published in the autumn of 2014 and come into force in 2015.

Since the legislation and guidelines were published, there have been only minor amendments, and the focus has mainly been on the interpretation of the legislation and guidelines. At the time of writing (March 2014), the Danish Gaming Authority has issued a public consultation regarding new and updated certification and technical documents. It is expected that these documents will come into force during the autumn of 2014, with amendments based on the received comments.

A player has to use an OCES-standard encryption, more specifically a Danish technical solution named NemID, when registering on a licence holder's gaming site. Furthermore, the player needs to use the NemID to log in every time he/she wants to play.

The Danish Gaming Authority is currently considering whether changes should be made in relation to the requirement for using NemID. This includes considering whether a more situational access could be used without compromising safety. Furthermore, it is considered whether an exemption should be made from the requirement to use NemID in case of a breakdown at NemID.

3.7 Is the law the same in relation to mobile gambling and interactive gambling on television? If not, are there any headline differences?

The law is in general the same in relation to mobile gaming and interactive gaming in Denmark; however, there is one exception in relation to mobile gaming.

The requirement for players to use NemID when logging on to play (see the answer to question 3.6 above), has not yet been adjusted to mobile telephones and other mobile platforms (eg tablet computers). Thus, it is possible for online gaming operators to obtain permission to provide gaming through such devices without the use of NemID.

This exception is only temporary ,and a solution where players have to use NemID when logging on to play through mobile solutions and other mobile platforms is expected during the first half of 2014.

4. LAND-BASED GAMING

4.1 Please describe the licensing regime (if any) for land-based gaming, and what products are included. Please set out what licences are available, and the licensing regime for them.

Land-based gaming licences may be granted for casino games and betting. Further, a limited licence covering only gaming machines or poker may be granted.

The land-based casino licence is valid for a term of 10 years and covers a variety of common casino games such as roulette, baccarat, poker, blackjack and gaming machines offering cash winnings.

See section 2 above for definitions of these games.

The betting licence covers both land-based and online betting, thus only one betting licence per operator is needed. See section 3 above regarding online betting.

A betting licence is valid for a term of five years.

A limited land-based gaming machine licence is granted on an individual basis and may be granted for an unlimited time period.

A limited land-based poker licence may be granted for gaming operators wishing to provide public poker tournaments from Danish premises only. A land-based poker licence is granted for a maximum of two years.

4.2 Please set out any particular limitations or requirements for (eg casino) operators, such as a ban on local residents gambling.

The requirements for the different licences mentioned in question 4.1 are described in detail in the executive orders relating to the Danish Gaming Act.

The operation of land-based casinos is heavily regulated in the executive order on land-based casinos. The regulation concerns:

- the premises;
- requirement of identification by use of ID;
- the use of electronic calculation;
- opening hours;
- registration of players;
- rules relating to the casino staff;
- the individual games;
- the exchange of gaming tokens and settlement;
- control of cash at the gaming tables, etc;
- gaming technology equipment;
- the tronce (tips);
- annual accounts and audit; and
- certain controlling measures (for instance the involvement of an independent third party controlling the activity at the premises at all times).

Land-based betting is less regulated than online betting. The players do not have to be registered in order to play, they do not need accounts, and the operator is not obligated to enable them to set betting limits. There is no ban on local residents' gaming.

However, when providing betting from a physical shop, there are requirements for sending a clear message to the customers that only players above the age of 18 are allowed to play, that gaming is potentially harmful, and that treatment for compulsive gaming is available. The information must be in Danish.

Furthermore, the manager of the place must satisfy certain requirements, eg be at least 21 years of age, not convicted of a crime that may involve a risk that the manager will abuse his access to working with games, and his conduct in general must not give reason to assume that the gaming establishment will not be run in a fully responsible manner.

With regard to gaming machines there are detailed requirements for the technical performance of the gaming machines in the Executive Order on gaming machines in gaming arcades and restaurants. Further the operators of gaming machines must comply with regulations regarding, for example, the premises and the staff at the gaming venues.

With regard to land-based poker licences, the gaming legislation contains regulations on the persons or companies providing the poker tournaments and restrictions on the number of tournaments that may be held. This poker licence may not be used for providing online poker.

4.3 Please address the questions in 3.5 above, but in relation to land-based gaming.

The passing of the Danish Gaming Act has to some extent changed the regime of land-based gaming. Accordingly, land-based betting was liberalised with the passing of the Danish Gaming Act in 2012. However, there has been no significant change in the legal status of land-based casinos except that land-based casinos are now governed by the Danish Gaming Act and the supervising authority is now the Danish Gaming Authority.

5. TAX

5.1 Please summarise briefly the tax regime applicable both to land-based and online gaming.

The Danish Gaming Duties Act contains the rules governing gaming duties. SKAT (the Danish Tax Administration) is responsible for ensuring that the gaming operators comply with the rules of the Danish Gaming Duties Act. All persons and companies holding a licence to provide gaming on the Danish market are required to notify their activities for registration.

The provision or organisation of games covered by the Danish Gaming Act is subject to duty under the Danish Gaming Duties Act. The calculation of the duty varies depending on the type of game.

Game	Percentage	Duty period
Betting (both online and land-based)	20 per cent of the gross gaming revenue, defined as received stakes minus paid out winnings (in the following "GGR")	Weekly
For betting exchanges (both online and land-based)	20 per cent of the amount charged in commission	
Online casinos	20 per cent of the GGR	Weekly
For poker and other cases where the gaming operator's profit is the commission charged	20 per cent of the amount charged in commission	
Land-based casinos	45 per cent of the GGR minus the amount of special tipping chips plus an additional 30 per cent on the part of the GGR that exceeds DKK 4.0 million (approximately EUR 538,000)	Calendar month

Physical gaming machines in restaurants or gaming arcades	41 per cent of the GGR For gaming machines in restaurants an additional 30 per cent on the part of the GGR that exceeds DKK 30,000 (approximately EUR 4,025) is added For gaming machines in gaming arcades an additional 30 per cent on the part of the GGR that exceeds DKK 250.000 (approximately EUR 33,600) is added plus DKK 3,000 (approximately EUR 400) per machine until 50 machines and DKK 1,500 (approximately EUR 200) per machine exceeding 50	Calendar month
<u>Non-profit lottery</u> Cash prizes Prizes consisting of goods or services (market value)	 15 per cent of the amount that exceeds DKK 200 (approximately EUR 27) 17.5 per cent of the amount that exceeds DKK 200 (approximately EUR 27)	15 days after the result of the lottery has been decided
<u>Prizes in connection with free games (i.e. games where no stake is paid)</u> Cash prizes Prizes consisting of goods or services (market value)	 15 per cent of the amount that exceeds DKK 200 (approximately EUR 27) 17.5 per cent of the amount that exceeds DKK 200 (approximately EUR 27)	15 days after the result of the game has been decided

Lottery and betting on races with pigeons, horses and dogs are, as mentioned earlier, under the monopoly of Danske Spil A/S. The tax regime applicable to such gaming is therefore not included in the above.

If the winnings are goods, it is the market value of the goods that is included in the gross gaming revenue. If the winnings exceed the stakes in a duty period and the gross gaming revenue becomes negative, no duty will be payable. If there is no or a negative gross gaming revenue for one period, the duty must be declared at DKK 0. Negative gross gaming revenue in one period cannot be carried forward for set-off against the positive gross gaming revenue of subsequent periods.

Free games, bonuses and the like are regarded not as stakes but as marketing expenses. Consequently, these costs and all other costs of the gaming operator that are not actual winnings for the players cannot be deducted when calculating the gross gaming revenue.

In addition to the tax duties described above, a licensed gaming operator must pay an annual fee for the licence. The size of this depends on the actual revenue, and is fixed in classes varying from DKK 50,900 (approximately EUR 6,800) (2014 level) to DKK 1,527,000 (approximately EUR 204,500) (2014 level).

Apart from taxes and fees, the gaming operator may also be liable to Danish income tax, depending on the particular circumstances. In 2014 the Danish company tax is 24.5 per cent, which will gradually be lowered to 22 per cent in 2016.

6. ADVERTISING

6.1 To what extent is the advertising of gambling permitted in your jurisdiction? Again, this should cover both land-based and online gaming. To the extent that advertising is permitted, how is it regulated?

The Danish rules regarding advertising of gaming (land-based and online) are divided into two categories: (i) the general advertising rules that apply to all marketing; and (ii) a specific set of rules that apply to gaming alone.

General marketing legislation

The central piece of marketing legislation in Denmark is the Danish Marketing Practices Act.

The Danish Marketing Practices Act includes provisions on comparative advertising, the use of misleading or false statements, and communication with customers (e.g. the players), etc.

The Danish Marketing Practices Act applies a very strict interpretation of the word 'free' when advertising. If the word 'free' is used, the product or service needs to be 100 per cent free and not subject to limitations.

Pursuant to the Danish Marketing Practices Act, direct marketing, eg newsletters or special offers to players, is generally illegal. Such marketing may, however, be used when dealing with pre-existing players as long as the player consented to it after being thoroughly informed of it when the player registered with the licence holder. The player should furthermore – both on registration and afterwards – have an easy and free option to decline further inquiries from the licence holder.

The Danish Consumer Ombudsman monitors advertising directed towards the Danish market and can on his own motion initiate investigations regarding the legality of marketing campaigns.

Specific gaming marketing legislation

In recognition of the fact that the provision of games is a sensitive area where aggressive marketing of gaming products may directly generate an excessive consumption and increased dependency on gaming, it has been necessary to impose limits on the marketing of games that go beyond the limits imposed by the provisions of the Danish Marketing Practices Act.

Thus, in addition to general marketing legislation, the Danish Gaming Act contains a number of specific rules relating to the marketing of gaming:

- the chance of winning must be presented in a correct and balanced way, thus the player will not get the impression that the chance of winning is greater than it actually is;
- gaming must be presented as a form of entertainment;
- gaming must not be directed towards minors or young people under the age of 18. This applies both to the communication and the choice of media;
- if a celebrity is used in an advertisement or in a marketing campaign, the celebrity must not imply that his participation in gaming has contributed to his success, unless this is actually true (eg poker celebrities); and
- marketing must not have content which implies that participation in gaming promotes social acceptance or is the solution to financial problems.

Considering the fact that the provisions of the Danish Gaming Act regarding marketing contain supplementary rules in relation to the general provisions of the Danish Marketing Practices Act, it will often be possible to judge cases regarding violation of the rules governing the marketing of games based on the rules of the Danish Gaming Act without it being necessary to involve the Danish Marketing Practices Act as well.

Further, the marketing of bonuses is regulated in the executive orders on the provision of both land-based and online betting, and on the provision of online casino. A bonus will typically be in the form of a welcome or loyalty bonus and will normally be a service, money or better odds (when betting). When marketing a bonus, the gaming provider must make sure that:

- all information regarding the terms of the bonus is available in a clear and unambiguous manner at the time when the offer is presented;
- the bonus is paid into the player's account immediately after the player meets the terms for receiving the payment;
- the player has at least 60 days to meet the terms of the bonus; and
- a bonus offer is not given to individual players on terms that are different from offers made to other players.

The Danish Gaming Authority has published a guide on the marketing of bonus offers by the provision of betting and online casino. It sets out how the Danish Gaming Authority will interpret the bonus provisions, and hence which practices the Danish Gaming Authority will regard as lawful.

In relation to the use of sales promotion measures when providing betting and online casino, the Danish Gaming Authority has also published a guide. The guide contains the Danish Gaming Authority's assessment of the licence holders' access to use sales promotion measures according to the gaming legislation.

Under the Danish Gaming Act, a national register of voluntarily excluded players, the ROFUS (which is an abbreviation of the Danish words for 'Register of Voluntarily Excluded Players') has been established. The register is maintained by the Danish Gaming Authority and it is the obligation of the licence holder to take measures to prevent further marketing material to be sent to a player who has excluded himself in the ROFUS register or on the licence holder's website.

Advertising illegal gaming is considered a criminal act under Danish law and is punishable by fine or in the worst cases, imprisonment. This applies to all parties who direct marketing towards the Danish market. Advertising in Danish will normally be considered to be directing services towards the Danish market, but marketing legislation might also apply to commercials and marketing campaigns in English directed towards the Danish market.

7. SOCIAL GAMING

7.1 We believe this to be a growing area. Please decide under what criteria social gaming is permitted in your jurisdiction. If games are free to play or if there is no prize, are they legal without a licence? Please address circumstances where virtual currency is used and can be won: ie currency which is of no monetary or other value, save for as credits to take part in games. The answer should address the question whether game credits or virtual money can be exchanged for other prizes. Is any change to regulation in the area proposed or envisaged?

Social gaming is often described as games consisting of structured activities which have contextual rules through which users can engage with one another. Social games are most often multiplayer and have one or more of the following features: turn-based; based on social platforms for providing users with an identity; and casual.

As mentioned in section 2 above, the Danish Gaming Act applies to all activities which fall under the legal definition of 'games'. Accordingly, if a social game is considered an activity constituting a lottery, a combination game or betting, and there is a prize to win, the Danish Gaming Act applies.

If the games covered by the definition above are provided for free (ie, no stake or payment have to be paid in order to participate), the games may be provided without a licence.

If a stake or payment is required to participate in a game, a licence is required in order to provide the game. As mentioned above in section 3, it is not possible to provide a game which falls under the definition of a lottery, as lottery is still kept under a monopoly.

The Danish Gaming Act is silent on the subject of when and if virtual currency can be given monetary value. It thus has to be decided on the basis of an interpretation of the Act based on a description of the specific set-up.

However it is clear that if virtual currency is used for winnings and stakes, but is of no monetary or other value, except as credits to take part in further games, such currency would under the Danish Gaming Act not constitute a prize or a stake.

In relation to marketing through social media, the Nordic Consumer Ombudsmen has issued a joint position available at *www. consumerombudsman.dk/Regulatory-framework/dcoguides/Social-media-marketing*.

Estonia

Law Firm Indela & Elunurm Silja Elunurm

1. OBJECTIVES AND STRUCTURE OF LEGISLATION

The gambling business in Estonia is relatively young. While Estonia was a part of the USSR, all types of the Gambling Activities except national lottery games were banned. The first attempts to organise a regulated market were made in 1994–1995, when the first Lottery Act and the first Gambling Act took effect. After implementation of said legislative acts, gambling became a licenced activity in Estonia, although we can say now that the regulation at this point was rather ambiguous. The aim of the regulation was to limit practically any kind of the Gambling Activity. The legislator did not see it as an acceptable business activity, which could also deliver an income to the state budget.

Estonia's gambling market has historically been dominated by terrestrial casinos, slot halls, betting premises and lotteries. The latest Gambling Act was adopted in 2008 and came into power at the beginning of 2009. The Act regulates the gambling industry in today's Estonia and also specifically addresses the status of online gambling, which has been regulated since 2010.

Today, the two main legal acts regulating gambling in Estonia are the Gambling Act and the Gambling Tax Act. In addition, the Advertising Act and Media Services Act must also be taken into account in respect of advertising and media services activities. Pursuant to the Gambling Act 2009, only 100% state-owned public limited companies (*aktsiaselts*) can organise lottery games in Estonia. Therefore, since the implementation of the Gambling Act 2009, AS Eesti Loto (established 1991) has enjoyed the status of a legal monopoly. There have been discussions of privatisation of AS Eesti Loto, especially during the years of the financial crisis in 2008–2009, but currently the topic is off the table.

In addition to the creation of a legal monopoly for lottery games and allowing remote gambling as a licenced activity, the latest Gambling Act clarified the list of gambling products allowed in Estonia. There are five types of the Gambling Activities currently identified by the law, namely:
- games of chance;
- games of skill;
- totalisators;
- betting; and
- lottery

Online gambling is not a type of gambling (there can be online games of chance or online games of skill) but, rather, a method of organising gambling. It is clear that, with the implementation of new Gambling Act,

Estonia started to consider gambling activity more as an acceptable business activity, which could also mean a new source of income for the state budget via gambling tax and licence fees. At the same time, the gambling regulations overall are quite strict by nature. There are considerable corporate share capital thresholds, which makes the entrance to the market rather difficult. Also, the verification and identification requirements of players are unique in Estonia, and inevitably require operators to develop customised IT solutions.

The general regulations of the Gambling Act and Gambling Tax Act apply to all different gambling products. Specific norms related to specific types of gambling game are also incorporated into the Gambling Act and Gambling Tax Act. Therefore it is quite simple to follow the current framework of law. However, it should also be noted that online gambling is regulated in greater detail according to the guidelines of the Estonian Tax and Customs Department (which is the supervisor of the gambling market, and also the issuer of activity and operating licences).

The Gambling Act of Estonia has the following structure:

Chapter 1 – General provisions

Chapter 2 – Gambling operator

    Division 1 – General requirements for the gambling operator

    Division 2 – Activity licence for organising gambling

    Division 3 – Operating permit for gambling

Chapter 3 – Organisation of gambling

    Division 1 – General requirements for the organisation of gambling

    Division 2 – Specifications for the organisation of gambling of different types

    Subdivision 1 – Special requirements for the organisation of games of chance, games of skill and lotteries

    Subdivision 2 – The organisation of commercial lotteries

    Subdivision 3 – Specifications for the organisation of gambling as remote gambling

Chapter 4 – Reporting of gambling operators and state supervision over the organisation of gambling

    Division 1 – Reporting of gambling operators

    Division 2 – State supervision of the organisation of gambling

Chapter 5 – Liability for violation of the Gambling Act

Chapter 6 – Implementing provisions

2. FRAMEWORK OF LEGISLATION

2.1 What is the legal definition of gambling and what falls within this definition?

Pursuant to the Gambling Act, gambling is a game that meets all the following criteria:

- it is a precondition for participating in a game that the player makes a bet;
- the player may win a prize as a result of the game; and

- the outcome of the game is partly or fully determined by an activity based on chance or depends on the occurrence of a previously unknown event.

It should be noted that a bet within the meaning of this act is a sum of money paid for participating in a game or a monetarily appraisable obligation undertaken to obtain the right to participate in gambling. A bet is not a fee for using a means of distance communication if it is not received by a gambling operator and does not exceed the amount usually paid for the use of such means of distance communication. At the same time, if coupons, vouchers etc have a monetary value and the person (or a third person) was obliged to make some kind of monetary contribution, this could be also considered as making a bet. A prize within the meaning of the Gambling Act is the right of a player, obtained as a result of gambling, to acquire money or another benefit with a monetarily appraisable value. So also can gifts or 'free tickets to enter' be considered as prizes in certain circumstances. The Gambling Act does not apply to:

- games of skill, the only possible prize of which is getting the opportunity to take part in the same game again;
- sports competitions;
- lotteries with the value of the prize pool of up to EUR 1,000; and
- commercial lotteries with the value of the prize pool of up to EUR 10,000.

2.2 What is the legal definition of online gambling and what falls within this definition?

Pursuant to the Estonian Gambling Act, online gambling is considered as remote (or distant) gambling. This term also encompasses the telephone and broadcasting media. A game is considered an online gambling game if the following two criteria are simultaneously met:

- the result is determined by an electronic device; and
- the player plays using an electronic communications device.

This means, for example, that online betting (if sports competitions are held between real human players) shall not be considered as online gambling, as the result is not determined by an electronic device. Such company should apply for a betting licence, not an online gambling one.

2.3 Please set out the different gambling products identified by legislation.

Estonian Gambling Act classifies the different gambling games as following:

The types of gambling are:

- **games of chance** – games, the outcome of which depends on chance and which are played by means of a mechanical or electronic device or by mediation of the organiser of the game. Poker, casino games, slot and other machine gaming are considered to be games of chance. Poker is not specifically named in the law;
- **lotteries** – games, the outcome of which depends on chance, where the prize pool constitutes up to 80 per cent of the selling price of the

circulation of the lottery tickets and the outcome of the game is not determined more than three times per 24 hours or it is determined by opening the ticket field on the lottery ticket (the Estonian regulations do not specifically name bingo; it is simply one type of lottery game);

- **totos and totalisator**– games, the outcome of which depends on whether an event bet on by the player does or does not occur or how it occurs, where the event bet on by the player is beyond the control of the gambling operator, the winning of a prize depends on whether the bet turns out to be true or not and the amount of the prize depends on the amount of the bet and the winning coefficient determined before the making of the bet (betting) or percentage of the total amount of the bets as determined by the gambling operator, the number of people who bet correctly and the amount of their bets (totaliser); includes general betting and also sports betting; and
- **games of skill** – games, the outcome of which depends predominantly on the physical skills, abilities or knowledge of the player, and which are played by means of a mechanical or electronic device.

2.4   Please list the different requirements for each gambling product, including legal classifications for each; for example, is poker a game of skill or game of chance?

Poker, casino games and slot machines as games of chance

Poker, casino games and slot machines are considered as games of chance. The main corporate requirements for organising games of chance are as follows:

- the share capital of the organiser (also if foreign company) needs to be at least EUR 1,000,000;
- the organiser needs to establish an additional reserve capital of at least one-third of the share capital; the additional reserve shall be formed by annually allocating at least one-seventh of the net profit to the additional reserve;
- members of the managing bodies of, and shareholders with qualifying holdings in, the organiser must comply with the following requirements:
  - the person must not have been punished for a crime;
  - the person must not have been a member of the managing body of a company which has significantly infringed the Gambling Act; and
  - the person must not have caused the insolvency of a company due to a grave error in management of the company;
- the organiser's only business activity should the organising of gambling games; the gambling operator may, however, engage in ancillary activities relating to the organisation of gambling in gaming locations, including catering, currency exchange, and the organisation of recreational and cultural events;
- the gambling operator shall ensure that it is possible to connect the electronic record-keeping and control system with the information system of the Estonia Tax and Customs Board in order to enable access

to the data required pursuant to the Gambling Act. The electronic record-keeping and control system is an electronic communications network connecting the gaming machines of the gambling operator or additional games of chance with other electronic gaming equipment used for the organisation of gambling or gaming equipment used for the organisation of remote gambling. A gaming table shall be connected with the electronic record-keeping and control system if settlements are performed at the gaming table or if the game is fully or partially organised by electronic means;

- the state fee for issuing activity licence for organising games of chance is EUR 47,933.73; and
- in addition to the licences for organising games of chance, the gambling operator should obtain from the rural municipality government or a city government written consent for opening a gaming location. The consent for opening a gaming location for a game of chance or toto is granted for 5–20 years. A rural municipality government or a city government may grant written consent for a shorter term than the one set out in the application.

There are specific requirements for the premises of the gaming location. A gaming location for games of chance may be situated only in:

- a separate building;
- a hotel, conference centre or recreational establishment; or
- a business building or shopping centre if it is not possible to enter the gaming location for games of chance through other premises of the business building or shopping centre and if there are no living quarters in the same building.

It is also required that the gaming location for games of chance, toto or games of skill may not be situated on an estate that is in use as a pre-school childcare institution, basic school, upper secondary school, vocational educational institution, hobby school, permanent youth camp, child welfare institution or youth work agency.

Betting and sports betting as betting products
Betting and sports betting are not specifically differentiated in the law. The main difference from the corporate requirements applicable to games of chance is that the share capital threshold is considerably lower: EUR 130,000.

All other listed corporate requirements, except the obligation to connect the electronic record-keeping and control system, apply.

The state fee for issuing activity licence for organising betting is EUR 31,955.82.

Lottery
The Gambling Act prescribes that lotteries may be organised by a public limited company the share capital of which amounts to at least EUR 1,000,000 and all of the shares of which are held by the Estonian state.

Thus the law prescribes a legal monopoly for a state-owned company. We therefore will not elaborate on the conditions in any more detail.

The Gambling Act also regulates commercial lotteries, which includes classical lotteries and instant lotteries that are organised by providers of goods or services for the promotion of the sale of goods or services or for advertising the goods, services or provider thereof. Commercial lotteries with a prize pool below EUR 10,000 shall not be regulated with the Gambling Act. The Gambling Acts specifically regulates commercial lotteries having prize pool more than EUR 10,000, with maximum prize pool of EUR 100,000. The main requirement is the obligation of the commercial lottery to register before it is initiated.

2.5 Explain the system of regulation of gambling; which regulatory or governmental body is responsible for the supervision of gambling? Which body issues licences? Which body examines enforcement powers? Is there any limit on the number or duration of available licences?

The company may organise gambling only after obtaining an activity and operating licence for each type of gambling activity. There are a number of different activity licences:

- an activity licence for organising games of chance;
- an activity licence for organising betting; and
- an activity licence for organising games of skill.

If the operator wishes to provide casino games and also games of skill in its gambling premises, it needs to obtain separate activity licences for such activities.

During the activity licence application process the trustworthiness and credibility of the gambling operator will be analysed. The applicant should submit thorough information about the financial situation of the company, and the financial status and economic interests of the major stakeholders and management. It is required to fulfil the share capital threshold requirements and also to prove the legal source of that money.

After the activity licence has been issued, the operating licence issuance procedure shall commence. During this process the compatibility of the specific gambling product with Estonian law shall be determined. It should be noted that operating licences are issued separately:

- for opening a gaming location at the address or on the ship indicated in the decision on the issue of the operating permit in order to organise one type of game of chance;
- for organising a toto or for opening a gaming location at the address or on the ship indicated in the decision on the issue of the operating permit in order to organise toto;
- for opening a gaming location at the address or on the ship indicated in the decision on the issue of the operating permit in order to organise a game of skill;
- for organising a type or subtype of gambling as remote gambling; and
- for organising a lottery, except a commercial lottery.

The Estonian Tax and Customs Board is the supervisory authority of gambling and also the issuer or licences. If, during the licensing procedure or during the activities of the operator, any disputes arise, then these will be reviewed by the administrative courts of Estonia.

Activity licences are issued for an unlimited term. It should be noted, however, that they are not transferable/assignable. The transfer of an activity licence can only take place via universal succession (legal division, merger, reorganisation of the entity's legal form). There is no limit prescribed by Estonian law as to how many activity licences might be issued in total for providing gambling services on the Estonian market.

An operating licence is issued for up to 20 years. A remote gambling operating licence is issued for only five years. There is no limit prescribed by Estonian law as to how many operating licences might be issued for different gambling products.

3. ONLINE GAMBLING

3.1 To what extent can online gambling be offered in your jurisdiction? Are licences available and, if so, for which gambling products? Please describe briefly the licensing process, who may apply, whether licences are limited in number and, if no licences are available, whether it is legal for online gambling to be offered. In the case of EU jurisdictions, please state whether there are any issues as to the legality of the local law at EU level. Please refer to any relevant cases at ECJ level and explain any measures taken or pending by the European Commission.

Online gambling has been allowed in Estonia since 2010. A company may organise remote gambling only after obtaining activity and operating licences. During the activity licence application process the trustworthiness and credibility of the gambling organiser will be analysed. The applicant should submit thorough information about the financial situation of the company, and the financial status and economic interests of the major stakeholders and management. It is required to have paid-in share capital to the amount of EUR 1,000,000 and it is necessary to prove the legal source of that money. During the operating licence process the compatibility of the remote gambling service process with Estonian law shall be determined. The main requirements here relate to server, software and reporting issues.

The state fees for obtaining Estonian licences are: EUR 47,933.73 for the issuance of an activity licence and EUR 3,195.58 for an operating licence. The activity licence will be issued for an unlimited term but will terminate upon the bankruptcy or liquidation of the company. The remote gambling operating licence will be issued for five years. The administrative procedure for obtaining the licences takes up to six months from the submittal of all the necessary documents and information.

It should be noted, however, that an online lottery is generally considered as online gambling (as the result is determined by an electronic device and the player plays using an electronic communications device). Therefore the legal monopoly of AS Eesti Loto does not include the online gambling market for lottery-like products. Online betting (real events–real time) is not considered to be online gambling, as the result is not determined by an electronic device.

There have not been and are no issues pending at EU level in respect of the legality of the local law.

3.2 Is there a distinction between the law applicable to B2B operations and that applicable to B2C operations?

Estonian law does not make such a distinction. It does not matter whether you are B2C operator providing services yourself via your website and directly to customers or whether you are operator providing services through a white label site run by a third party: the key is the legal relationship between the operator and the final customer. Such a company should obtain all the necessary licences for gambling activities.

The transfer of activities aimed at organising gambling is regulated in Estonian law is. A gambling operator may transfer such activities to another person only with the written consent of the Tax and Customs Board. The liability of a gambling operator for the organisation of gambling is non-transferable. The transfer of such activities cannot impede the internal control of the gambling operator or the ability of the Tax and Customs Board to monitor the compliance with the requirements established for the organisation of gambling by the Gambling Act. There are specific regulations for the transfer of essential activities. Essential activities aimed at organising gambling are such activities which, when omitted or when performed defectively, would significantly compromise the fulfilment of the legal requirements set upon the operator, its financial performance or the organisation of gambling by the gambling operator. Such essential activities shall not be transferred, unless:

- the obligations of the gambling operator to players do not change; or
- the conditions, the compliance with which was material in issuing the activity licence or operating permit for organising gambling to the gambling operator, neither change not cease to exist.

If the operators follow the notification procedure prescribed in law, and the Estonian Tax and Customs Board allows the transfer of some activities, for example, a white label online casino is run by third party contractor, then the latter is not considered as a gambling operator.

The law also clarifies that a local gambling operator has the right to intermediate prizes and bets received from gambling organised by a foreign gambling operator with no activity licence or operating permit in Estonia, as well as payments to the account of the foreign gambling operator for making a bet in such gambling. In that case, the intermediary of prizes, bets or payments transferred to the account of the foreign gambling operator for making bets is considered a gambling operator within the meaning of the Gambling Act, and the foreign gambling operator is considered a person to whom the activities aimed at organising gambling are transferred.

3.3 What are the consequences for B2C or B2B operators who are active in your jurisdiction without having obtained or applied for the required permits, licences and approvals? What penalties and enforcement powers are available in respect of the illegal operators? Please outline any significant domestic decisions or enforcement actions that have been taken by the relevant authorities in recent years.

The Gambling Act prescribes the following misdemeanours that might be applicable:

- the intermediation of bets and prizes in remote gambling by gambling operators that do not hold an activity licence or operating permit in Estonia, which carries a punishment to the legal person of a fine of up to EUR 2,600; or
- the organisation of prohibited gambling, which prescribes a fine of up to EUR 2,600 to the legal person.

In addition, the Estonian Penal Code prescribes criminal sanctions for economic activities without an activity licence. In such a case, the natural person offender is punishable by a fine of up to 300 fine units or by detention, and the legal person by a fine of up to EUR 32,000.

In addition to these measures, an operator who has been found providing illegal services shall be listed in the so-called blacklist of foreign operators. (This is the basis for ISP blocking; the list is available at *http://www.emta.ee/public/Kontroll/MTA_must_nimekiri_25.02.2014.pdf*.) If an operator is listed there, the due fulfilment of the corporate requirements may be evaluated much more strictly, as the Tax Department considers the list to be one element of inspecting the trustworthiness of the operator.

As a conclusion, however, it should be noted that, except for ISP blocking activity, the Tax Department has not taken any strong enforcement measures to fighting against illegal (unlicenced) gambling activities in Estonia.

3.4 What technical measures are in place (if any) to protect consumers from unlicenced operators, such as ISP blocking and payment blocking?

The provider of a publicly available electronic communication service providing internet access shall, on the basis of a precept of the Tax and Customs Board and by the due date set out in such precept, block the domain name of any illegal remote gambling operation specified in the precept in the domain name servers belonging to such service provider. The Tax and Customs Board updates the above-mentioned blacklist continually and, if necessary, sends out new precepts to implement the ISP blocking. The failure of the electronic communication service provider to implement the precept is considered a misdemeanour, and is punishable with a fine of up to EUR 2,600.

A payment service provider shall, on the basis of a precept of the Tax and Customs Board, stop the debiting and crediting of the account used for organising illegal remote gambling immediately after receipt of the respective precept. A payment service provider shall make available information regarding the funds in such account and monies received and paid during the period specified in the precept. In the case of there being funds in such account, the Tax and Customs Board shall publicly announce that the players may apply for repayment of such funds. If, after the repayments have been made, there are still funds in such account, then the Tax and Customs Board shall issue a precept to the payment service provider for debiting the account with such amount and transferring the funds to the state revenues. The failure of the payment service provider to implement the precept is considered a misdemeanour, and punishable with fine up to EUR 2,600.

3.5 Has the legal status of online gambling changed significantly in recent years and, if so, how?

As stated before, it has changed considerably, as before 2010 it was considered illegal. Additional amendments were made in 2012. Before the newest amendments in law took effect (in March 2012), the Gambling Act provided that the server containing the software used for the organisation of remote gambling must be located in Estonia and its possessor must ensure that supervisory officials have unobstructed access to the server. In practice, this norm was never enforced in its strictest sense. The Estonian Tax and Customs Board, as the supervisory authority, interpreted this norm itself and said in its guidelines that remote gambling services must be available through the web server located in Estonia and that the Estonian server must undergo compulsory verification checks (identification and authentication of a gambler, age of the player and restriction on playing games of chance). Although the Estonian Tax and Customs Board made such an interpretation, it was not validated with relevant legislation, creating an uncertain legal environment for the organisers.

The Estonian Tax and Customs Board requirement in respect of server could in practice be fulfilled by contracting with AS Sertifitseerimiskeskus, which is a local certification authority, providing certificates for authentication and digital signing to Estonian ID Cards. AS Sertifitseerimiskeskus would run identification and age limit checks (player should be older than 21 years) on the basis of players' ID cards. The check-up in regard of restrictions on playing games of chance could be completed through the X-road service platform. X-road is a platform-independent secure standard interface between databases and information systems that connect databases and information systems of the public sector. To be able to conclude a service agreement for using the X-road platform, the organiser of the remote gambling must register itself with the Estonian Tax and Customs Board.

Therefore, remote gambling operators did not have to run these compulsory checks itself (or have special systems for that or have its own server in Estonia), but simply implement the necessary functionalities and contracts with relevant service providers. (This, of course, applies only to Estonian residents who have a digital ID card.) The actual location of a gambling server was never the main question. Gambling reporting was also organised through the X-road service platform, whereby the organiser of the remote gambling should submit quarterly reports.

With the amendments enacted in March 2012, the following main changes were made:

- A gaming server can be located in another country only if there is legal basis and actual possibility for the local authority to co-operate with the Estonian authority. Such legal basis is considered to be proven if there is a bilateral cooperation agreement concluded between the respective countries or if the country of the location of the gaming server is a member state of the Budapest Convention on Cybercrime. In all other cases, a server located outside of Estonia will not be accepted. The implementation of this requirement has a considerable influence on the development of the remote gambling market in Estonia. Note that in such countries as Andorra, Ireland, Greece, Lichtenstein, Luxembourg, Monaco, Poland, Sweden and Turkey the relevant convention has not entered into force.
- The organiser of the remote gambling must ensure that supervisory officials have unobstructed access to the gaming server, and must allow them to monitor whether the organiser has completed the following checks: identify and authenticate the name and age of the player, verify whether the player has been entered into the list of restrictions on playing games of chance, and log files of the gaming sessions. The data mentioned should be stored for 5 years. This requirement can be easily fulfilled by using local e-services (certification service provided by AS Sertifitseerimiskeskus; and the X-road platform provided by Estonian Tax and Customs Board).
- It must be made clear that the age limit (21 years) is only applicable in respect of Estonian players; the remote gambling organiser can provide its services through the same gaming platform to other countries' players, taking into consideration the age limit applicable in the respective country.
- As of January 2012, reporting is made through an electronic accounting and control system (continuous data feed). This system must ensure the recording and storing of information in a manner that enables the calculation, at any moment, of the turnover of the organiser of gambling and the percentage of payments to the players from the amount of all stakes for each gambling machine, gambling table connected to the system and remote gambling. The Electronic Gambling Reporting System X-road services technical specification is also available in English.
- It is permissible to create players' accounts that can be used for playing in both online and terrestrial casinos.
- There were considerable amendments relating to the media services. Gambling organisers which do not have an Estonian licence are not allowed to advertise or sponsor programmes, or present their trade mark in any other way, in Estonian media.

3.6 Whilst acknowledging the inherent difficulty in predicting developments in gambling law, what are the likely developments in online gambling in your jurisdiction, both short term and long term? Are any specific amendments under consideration? Have there been any recent political developments, or do you envisage any in the near future? Are any specific amendments under consideration? Are they likely to be adopted and, if so, what is the time scale?

In respect of online gambling, there has not been any discussion of potential new amendments or requirements.

It should be noted however that advertising limitations, especially in respect of lottery has been under revision. Most probably advertising restrictions in respect of lottery activities will be removed. This however shall not encompass online lottery, which, as said before, is considered as online gambling.

3.7 Is the law the same in relation to mobile gambling and interactive gambling on television? If not, are there any headline differences?

There are no differences currently. However, it should be noted that such services are not widespread in Estonia.

4.   LAND-BASED GAMING

4.1 Please describe the licensing regime (if any) for land-based gaming, and what products are included. Please set out what licences are available, and the licensing regime for them.

The structure for the licensing regime is basically the same as that described above. An operator should obtain an activity licence and a specific operating licence for each gaming place. The following activity licences are available:
- an activity licence for organising games of chance;
- an activity licence for organising betting; and
- an activity licence for organising games of skill.

If an operator wishes to provide casino games and also (for example) games of skill in its gambling premises, it needs to obtain separate activity licences for such activities; if a betting service is also provided, an additional activity licence must be obtained. Activity licences are issued for unspecified terms. Operating licences are issued for 5–20 years, but not longer than the local municipality has given approval to run gambling place for. The administrative procedure for obtaining licences usually takes 2–3 months.

4.2 Please set out any particular limitations or requirements for (eg casino) operators, such as a ban on local residents gambling.

A gaming location for games of chance may be situated only in:
- a separate building;
- a hotel, conference centre or recreational establishment; or
- a business building or shopping centre if it is not possible to enter the gaming location for games of chance through other premises of the business building or shopping centre and if there are no living quarters in the same building.

The gaming location for games of chance, toto or games of skill may not be situated on an estate that is in use as a pre-school childcare institution, basic school, upper secondary school, vocational educational institution, hobby school, permanent youth camp, child welfare institution or youth work agency.

A detailed plan issued by the municipality may specify a district where no gaming location for a game of chance may be situated (i.e. residential areas).

A regulation of the council of a rural municipality or city council:

1. may establish a uniform restriction on the opening hours of the gaming locations for games of chance situated in the territory of the rural municipality or city government;
2. may prohibit the opening of a gaming location for games of chance situated in a separate building if the gaming location would be situated in the immediate vicinity of a pre-school childcare institution, basic school, upper secondary school, vocational educational institution, hobby school, permanent youth camp, child welfare institution or youth work agency; or
3. may specify the district which shall be deemed as in the immediate vicinity of the immovable specified in point 2 above.

4.3 Please address the questions in 3.5 above, but in relation to land-based gaming.

The main amendments were made in March 2012. The biggest changes relate to the requirement to implement an electronic accounting and control system (continuous data feed). The electronic accounting and control system must ensure the recording and storing of information in a manner that enables the calculation, at any moment, of the turnover of the organiser of gambling and the percentage of payments to the players from the amount of all stakes for each gambling machine, gambling table connected to the system and remote gambling. The Electronic Gambling Reporting System X-road services technical specification is also available in English.

An additional amendment has considerably reduced the administration of players' data for operators who provide both land-based gaming and online gaming services. As of 2012, it is permissible to create players' accounts that can be used for playing in both online and terrestrial casinos. This amendment has also considerably influenced the marketing options of operators via players' online accounts.

5. TAX
5.1 Please summarise briefly the tax regime applicable to both land-based and online gaming.

According to Gambling Tax Act, gambling tax is imposed on:
- gambling tables and gambling machines used for organising games of chance and gambling machines used for organising games of skill;
- amounts received from the sale of lottery tickets when lotteries are organised;

- winning pots when commercial lotteries are organised if the value of a winning pot exceeds EUR 10,000;
- amounts received as stakes in totalisators from which the winnings have been deducted;
- amounts received as stakes in games of chance and games of skill when remote gambling is organised from which the winnings have been deducted; and
- amounts of participation fees when tournaments of game of chance are organised.

Gambling tax shall be paid by organisers of gambling. The taxable period for gambling tax shall be one calendar month.

The rates of gambling tax are the following:
- EUR 1,278.23 per one gambling table;
- EUR 447.38 per one gambling machine;
- EUR 31.95 per one gambling machine of game of skill;
- 18 per cent of the turnover received from the sale of lottery tickets;
- 18 per cent of the winning pots when commercial lotteries are organised;
- 5 per cent of the net profit in case of totalisators;
- 5 per cent of the net profit in case of remote gambling; and
- 5 per cent the amounts of participation fees when tournaments of game of chance are organised.

6. ADVERTISING

6.1 To what extent is the advertising of gambling permitted in your jurisdiction? Again, this should cover both land-based and online gaming. To the extent that advertising is permitted, how is it regulated?

Advertising of gambling, gaming premises and organisers of gambling (hereinafter advertising of gambling) is prohibited, except:
- on the premises where gambling is organised;
- on board a water craft or aircraft used for the international carriage of passengers;
- in the building of a passenger terminal of an airport or port which provides international regular services;
- in a hotel where gaming premises are located;
- on the website of an organiser of gambling;
- advertising of lottery on the sales premises of lottery tickets or in television or radio programmes immediately before or after the programmes showing lottery draws or draw results, or between parts of such programmes; or
- advertising of toto at the time of holding the event at the place where the event is held, concerning the result of which bets can be made in toto.

The following are not deemed to be advertising of gambling:
- marking of gaming premises with the name of the undertaking, the trade mark, the type, name and opening hours of the gaming premises

on a building where the gaming premises are located or at the entrance of the gaming premises;
* communication of information to the public on the rules of the game, prize fund, potential winnings and use of income to be received from organisation in the case of lotteries to be organised and on the winning tickets, winning combinations and prizes in the case of draws held; or
* communication of information to the public on commercial lotteries. A commercial lottery is deemed to be the same as within the meaning of the Gambling Act.

7. SOCIAL GAMING

7.1 We believe this to be a growing area. Please decide under what criteria social gaming is permitted in your jurisdiction. If games are free to play or if there is no prize, are they legal without a licence? Please address circumstances where virtual currency is used and can be won: ie currency which is of no monetary or other value, save for as credits to take part in games. The answer should address the question whether game credits or virtual money can be exchanged for other prizes. Is any change to regulation in the area proposed or envisaged?

The Estonian legislator or the supervisory authority of gambling (the Estonian Tax and Customs Board) has not issued any guidelines or notice letters etc in respect of social media games or so-called 'freemium' games (meaning the app is free but players can fork out real money for extended features, bonus levels and extra fake coins to play with). There has also not been any investigation or dispute in respect of this matter that would have determined the practice and opinion of the Estonian Tax and Customs Board. This issue is therefore rather vague in the context of Estonian legal system.

On the basis of the definition of gambling, we could say that it is legal to allow players in Estonia to take part in social games as long as there is no monetary submission or receipt of monetarily appraisable goods or services. Such games are not considered gambling. Note that both conditions should be present. Such games are not considered gambling if making a bet is not a prerequisite for participating in the game (player participates for free), or if there is no prize that has a monetarily appraisable value.

France

Pinsent Masons LLP
Diane Mullenex & Annabelle Richard

1. OBJECTIVES AND STRUCTURE OF LEGISLATION

As France is a country of Christian-Catholic tradition, gambling has long been totally prohibited. The general ban on gambling is now stipulated in Article L.324-1 of the the French Code of Homeland Security relating to game of chance. Over the years, the ban has received several exemptions and several pieces of legislation have gradually authorised some gambling activities that have to be either offered in specific venues or provided by duly authorised operators.

Code of Homeland Security (the CHS): This Code, enacted on 1 May 2012, encompasses a significant part of the gambling regulations under French law. It provides for the major general prohibitions on gambling and set the principles applicable to the following gambling products:

Casinos: The CHS regulates casino games in sea, thermal and climatic resorts and in casinos operated on ships registered with the French international register authorised, subject to conditions, the operation of casinos in sea, thermal, climatic resorts and cities with more than 500,000 inhabitants with the exception of Paris.

Gaming clubs and houses: The law of 30 June 1923 relating to the budget for the year 1923 authorised some gaming clubs and houses to offer games of chance subject to authorisation by the Minister of Home Affairs. Furthermore, an Instruction dated 15 July 1947 on the regulation applicable to club games authorised gaming clubs to provide 'club card games' which is a special category of gambling that only includes bridge, poker, tarot and rummy.

La Française des Jeux: Article 136 of the Finance Law dated 31 May 1933 authorised the Government to create a national lottery. The national lottery is a legal monopoly in France operated by the incumbent operator La Française des Jeux. In addition, the Decree n°85-390 relating to the organisation and operation of sport forecasts games authorised La Française des Jeux to offer sports betting games.

Pari Mutuel Urbain (PMU): The law of 2 June 1891 relating to the organisation and operation of horse races authorised horse race companies to offer pooled betting (*pari mutuel*). The Décret n° 97-456 of 5 May 1997 relating to horse race companies and pooled betting provides that horse race companies may organise bets on their races and has entrusted the management of such bets to the PMU.

Greyhound race companies: Although greyhound races are not very popular in France, the Decree n°83-922 dated 20 October 1983 relating to greyhound racing companies authorised to organise pooled betting, authorised greyhound race companies to offer pooled betting on the races they organise.

Online gambling operators: The Law n°2010-476 dated 12 May 2010 opening to competition and regulating the online gambling and betting market provides that the online gambling authority, ARJEL (*Autorité de Régulation des Jeux en Ligne*) may deliver licences to operators for offering club games (although the law refers to club games, only poker is authorised), sports betting or betting on horses.

2.   FRAMEWORK OF LEGISLATION

2.1   What is the legal definition of gambling and what falls within this definition?

Traditionally, French law places gambling contracts into the 'random contracts' category which are mutually agreed conventions whose consequences, being profits or losses for one or both parties, depend on an uncertain event. In accordance with Article 1964 of the Civil Code, included in the aleatory contracts category are insurance contracts, life annuity contracts and games or wagers. For these last two, the uncertainty relies on the chance of winning or on the risk of bearing a loss.

With regards to gambling, the legal criterion which distinguishes it from other random contracts is the existence of a wager on chance, ie the fact that a party bets money on the chance of the other party, whereas in other random contracts, the money which is put at 'risk' is the consideration for a service.

However, recent changes in French law have tended to blur these frontiers, with skill games entering the scope of the prohibition against gambling products. The French legislator seems to have aligned the definitions for both online and land-based gambling products, with the new definition codified in Articles L.322-2 and L.322-2-1 of the French Code of Homeland Security. Pursuant to Article L.322-2 of the French CHS, games of chance shall mean *'any operation offered to public participation, regardless of the designation it may receive, in order to trigger the hope of a gain which would be acquired, even partially, through chance and for which the operator requires from participants a financial contribution'*. In addition, under Article L.322-2-1 of the French CHS, this definition covers *'games whose functioning relies on the know-how of the player'*, particularly skill games.

2.2   What is the legal definition of online gambling and what falls within this definition?

Article 10 of the law n°2010-476 sets out the definition of online gambling and betting as follows: *'any gambling game or betting performed exclusively through a service of online communication to the public'*. The Law further stipulates that an online gambling operator is any person offering to the public, on a regular basis, services of online gambling or betting with stakes having a monetary value and pursuant to terms and conditions that constitute a standard membership agreement.

The Law n°2010-476 only refers to sports betting, horse betting and club games. Nevertheless, the only club game authorised is poker. To date, there are no other gambling activities authorised under the Law n°2010-476.

2.3 Please set out the different gambling products identified by legislation.

See question 2.5 below.

2.4 Please list the different requirements for each gambling product, including legal classifications for each; for example, is poker a game of skill or game of chance?

As explained above, French law only authorises a limited number of gambling products, namely:

Poker
Poker is currently considered by the Law n°2010-476 as a game of chance and it is the most popular game in France. Poker can be offered by gaming clubs, casinos and online gambling operators.

Poker in casinos: Casinos have the right to offer four different types of poker: Casino Hold'em poker; Casino stud poker; Texas hold'em poker; and Omaha poker 4 high. The rules applicable to each category of poker are detailed in the order dated 14 May 2007 relating to the regulation applicable to games in casinos. Pursuant to the Order of 14 May 2007 poker can be played in casinos in the form of cash games or tournaments.

Casinos are strictly regulated venues, they must provide three different activities (entertainment, catering and games) and are not allowed to offer all casino games without limitation. They may only offer the types of games for which they have been granted their licence.

Poker in gaming clubs: The Instruction of 15 July 1947 provides that 'club card games' may be played in gaming clubs subject to a mere declaration with the regional representative of the state (*Préfet*). Gaming clubs shall be incorporated as non-profit organisations that have to abide by specific rules. As poker is defined by the Tax Code as a 'club card game' it counts therefore among the few card games that are authorised in gaming clubs and houses. The gaming activities offered by clubs must have an ancillary character. As a main purpose, gaming clubs shall pursue for instance a social, sporting, cultural, artistic or literary purpose.

Online poker: The law n°2010-476 has authorised online poker and introduced the principle of a 'club game' licence for online gambling operators delivered by the online regulatory authority ARJEL.

The Decree n°2010-723 relating to the categories of club games mentioned in Article 14 of the Law n°2010-476 and the principles governing their technical rules provides for the types of poker that can be operated online. As the scope of the Decree is very strict, only the following types of poker are authorised: Texas Hold'em Limit; Texas Hold'em pot limit; Texas Hold'em no limit; and Omaha Poker 4.

Such types of poker may be offered in the form of cash games or tournaments.

Lastly, in a court decision dated 20 July 2011, it upheld that poker is not a game of chance but shall be viewed as a game of skill. With this decision, the court has attempted to reverse a string of constant case law dating back to a Supreme Court decision of 1877. This decision is a low court decision and still isolated. If this trend were confirmed by other decisions, including on appeal and by the Supreme Court, it could mean that poker would no longer be regulated as a game of chance. As a result, in the future, it could become lawful to organise private poker games without authorisation.

Betting (other than sports betting)

As mentioned above, apart from sports betting, the authorised forms of betting in France are horse and greyhound betting. Greyhound betting is almost anecdotal and for the purpose of this review only horse betting (which can be provided online and land-based) will be addressed.

Land-based horse betting: As mentioned above, the Décret n° 97-456 provides that horse race companies may organise bets on their races and entrust the management of such bets to the PMU. The PMU is a special legal entity that was created by all horse racing companies to manage their betting activities. All horse racing companies authorised to organise bets are members of the PMU. The organisation of bets on horse races is therefore the monopoly of PMU. Horse betting organised by the PMU is regulated by the Order dated 13 September 1985 relating to the rules of urban pooled betting and to hippodromes.

Land-based horse betting is a pooled betting system according to which all the stakes concerning a certain type of bet are pooled and redistributed among the players. The rules concerning each type of bet are duly provided in the Order of 13 September 1985. As part of the general rules, minors are of course not allowed to place bets. Practically, bets may be placed at the appropriate counters located in the hippodromes, in the establishments located outside hippodromes and duly authorised for that purpose, by telephone (subject to conditions), or through an interactive terminal.

The Order dated 13 September 1985 provides for the different types of authorised bets, eg simple bets, coupled bets, first three horses, first four horses, first five horses etc. There are several different types of authorised bets all of which are duly regulated in the Order.

Online horse betting: Online horse betting is regulated by the Decree n°2010-498 dated 17 May 2010 relating to the definition of horse races on which online bets may be offered and to the general principles applicable to pooled betting.

Online horse betting operators may offer horse betting on races organised in France or abroad, provided that such races are listed on the official list approved each year by the Minister of Agriculture. The list, available from ARJEL, indicates all the bets that are authorised, that may be simple or complex bets. Complex bets are defined as bets for which players have to designate the horses ranked in the five first positions (no need however to find the right order of finish).

Online bets on horse racing may only be offered on the official results in relation to one or several authorised horse races. The official result of a race is defined as horses ranked in the positions which will receive prizes, limited to the five first positions.

Sports betting

Land-based sports betting: The Decree n°85-390 relating to the organisation and operation of sport forecasts games has authorised La Française des Jeux to offer betting games. Originally, the Decree n°85-390 only created a game called 'loto foot', which was halfway between a lottery and a pure betting game. The Decree offers the possibility to offer such forecast games on all sports and competitions.

The forecast games offered by La Française des Jeux are similar to a lottery and include several variants. Participants have to fill in a grid and forecast the results of games. Nowadays, there are three different forecast games offered: loto foot, Match of the day and 1N2, all of which are odds betting games. Players have only the possibility to play in all duly licensed points of sale and also online on the Française des Jeux website.

Online sports betting: Online sports betting is regulated by the Decree n°2010-483 of 12 May 2010 relating to competitions and types of sports results defined by the online gambling regulatory authority.

Bets may only concern certain sports, competitions and types of results as determined by ARJEL following consultation with the sport federations. The official list is available on ARJEL's website and ARJEL may decide from time to time to add new competitions or new types of results.

Under French law, organisers of sports competitions are considered as having a right over the competition they organise. Consequently, sports betting operators may only offer bets on the competitions for which they have entered into an agreement with the organiser of each competition. Pursuant to the Decree n°2010-614 dated 7 June 2010 relating to the conditions applicable to market the rights to organise bets in relation to a sports competition or event provides that any licensed operators requesting it have to be offered to sign such contracts. These contracts are reviewed by ARJEL and the French Competition Council (*Autorité de la concurrence*) and offer similar terms for all operators.

Casino games

The scope of authorised games is strictly circumscribed by the Decree n°59-1489. Casinos are allowed to offer slot machines and the following games (which may also be provided electronically):

Consideration games (*jeux de contrepartie*)	Club games (*jeux de cercle*)
- The boule	- Baccarat-chemin de fer
- The Twenty-three	- Limited bank Baccarat on two tables
- French roulette	- Open bank Baccarat on two tables
- American roulette	- The écarté
- English roulette	- Texas Hold'em poker
- Thirty-forty	- Omaha poker 4 high
- Blackjack	
- Craps	
- Punto banco	
- Casino Hold'em poker	
- Casino stud poker	

Casinos are limited by the scope of their licences. The game limits are set out by the decision granting the licence that determines, in particular, the number and type of games allowed, the duration of the licence, the opening times of the venue etc. In addition, the Minister of Home Affairs may authorise a casino to provide, from time to time, for experimentation purposes, new types of games of chance or new technical devices.

Furthermore, gaming clubs or houses may offer, subject to authorisation from the Minister of Home Affairs some games of chance, namely the Baccarat-chemin de fer, the Baccarat on two tables and the Multicolore.

Slot and other machine gaming

The French CHS provides that importing or manufacturing slot machines is prohibited. However, by way of an exemption, casinos are authorised to offer slot machines and other machines offering games of chance (together 'slot machines' as their regulation is the same) if such casinos offer at least one of the games mentioned in the Decree n°59-1489 dated 22 December 1959 on the regulation applicable to games offered in casinos located in sea, thermal and climatic resorts.

Slot machines are regulated by the Order of 14 May 2007 which sets out the way they shall be operated. The Order does not differentiate between categories of slot machines and the same rules apply to all machines.

The Decree n°59-1489 provides that the return rate to players applicable to slot machines cannot be less than 85 per cent. The applicable value of each unitary credit wagered in slot machines is determined by the operator of the casino and communicated to the Minister of Home Affairs (and to an authority appointed by the Minister of Budget) at least 15 days before the concerned slot machine is made available to the public. Any modification of the return rate to players or the applicable value of each unitary credit wagered has to be duly communicated to the Minister of Home Affairs and to an authority appointed by the Minister of Budget at least 15 days before the concerned slot machine is made available to the public. Casinos cannot operate such modifications to more than 50 per cent of their slot machines every year.

In addition, the law sets out a limit with regards to the credit which may be purchased from a slot machine. Such limit is equal to the maximum amount that a machine can pay without human intervention.

The configuration of gaming devices is highly evolving, with the French gaming authorities taking into account, for licensing, cloud-based gaming devices, provided that a sufficient level of data security and reporting is ensured.

Lottery

As a general principle, lotteries are prohibited. The new version of Article L.322-2 of the CHS defines prohibited lotteries as follows: *'Are presumed to be lotteries and forbidden as such: the sales of estate, goods or merchandise which are realized through chance, or to which have been added bonus or other benefits, due, even partially, to chance and, generally, any operation offered to public participation, regardless of the designation it may receive, in order to trigger the hope of a gain which would be acquired, even partially, through chance and for which the operator requires from participants a financial contribution'*. In addition, pursuant to the new Article L.322-2-1 of the CHS: *'This prohibition covers games whose functioning relies on the know-how of the player'*.

Recent changes have been made in the field of lotteries. The Consumer Right Law (enacted in February 2014) extends the list of prohibited lotteries to similarly organised skill games and subsequently restricts the scope of lotteries that can be organised in France, both as gambling products and as promotional media. Indeed, the (absolute) ban on lotteries is extended to all games open to the public meeting all of the following conditions:

- the outcome of the game is partially determined through chance;
- the game requires a financial contribution from the player, even when reimbursement is offered; and
- the game creates the hope for gain, regardless of its form or the nature of such gain.

However, there are a number of exceptions to this general prohibition of lotteries:

- lotteries exclusively for charitable acts, encouragement of arts or financing of sports non-profit (Article L.322-3 of the CHS);
- traditional bingo, also called 'poules au gibier', 'rifles' or 'quines' (Article L.322-4 of the CHS);
- lotteries in fairgrounds (Articles L.322-5 and L.322-6 of the CHS);
- lotteries on television and radio shows (Article L.322-7 of the CHS);
- the national lottery (Decree n°78-1067 dated 9 November 1978 relating to the organisation and operation of lottery games); and
- lotteries organised as promotional campaigns (Articles L.121-36 and following of the Consumer Code).

National lottery. Pursuant to Decree n°78-1067 dated 9 November 1978 relating to the organisation and operation of lottery games, the operation of the national lottery is granted to La Française des Jeux which is structured as a public limited liability company with regulatory powers. As such, Article 21 of the Decree provides that the CEO of La Française des Jeux shall monitor the application of the laws and regulations relating to games. For that purpose he shall draft the rules of the games and set out their technical features, terms and conditions of participation, amounts of the stakes, technical conditions for determining the winners and awarding winnings and prizes, terms relating to the payment/award of the winnings and prizes and time limits for claiming payments and prizes.

Lotteries organised as promotional campaigns. A specific regime applies to lotteries organised as promotional campaigns, which are regulated under Article L. 121-36 of the French Consumer Code.

From now on, Article L 121-36 of the French Consumer Code aims at covering *'trade practices implemented by professionals/businesses in the form of promotional operations which are likely to trigger the hope of a gain, whatever the modalities for the draw or for the intervention of chance may be'*.

Such promotional lotteries are valid as long as:

- if they are disconnected from the purchase of a product or a service, contestants can obtain a reimbursement for the expenses incurred in participating to the game, and are duly informed of such a reimbursement possibility in advance; and
- if participation to these lotteries is reliant on the purchase of a product or a service, the lottery does not constitute an unfair trading practice as construed under French law further to the implementation of the Unfair Commercial Practices Directive (2005/29/EC).

2.5 Explain the system of regulation of gambling; which regulatory or governmental body is responsible for the supervision of gambling? Which body issues licences? Which body examines enforcement powers? Is there any limit on the number or duration of available licences?

The regulation of gambling belongs to different governmental authorities or bodies, depending on whether it is land-based gambling or online gambling.

All land-based gambling which has been progressively authorised in France is centrally supervised by the Ministry of Home Affairs at a national level. Depending on the nature of the game at stake, various governmental or state representatives may additionally intervene at different levels, during either the licence application process or the enforcement process, mainly the *Préfet*, or national commissions or federations empowered with some regulatory prerogatives. Licences are all issued by the Ministry of Home Affairs.

Online gambling is regulated by a single governmental authority, the ARJEL, which was created upon the opening of the market in 2010. The ARJEL has full competence to issue licences, enforce online gambling regulations and fight against illegal gambling websites.

Regarding the number and duration of available licences, see sections 3.1 and 4.2.

3. ONLINE GAMBLING

3.1 To what extent can online gambling be offered in your jurisdiction? Are licences available and, if so, for which gambling products? Please describe briefly the licensing process, who may apply, whether licences are limited in number and, if no licences are available, whether it is legal for online gambling to be offered. In the case of EU jurisdictions, please state whether there are any issues as to the legality of the local law at EU level. Please refer to any relevant cases at ECJ level and explain any measures taken or pending by the European Commission.

An online operator can only offer gambling products in France, ie websites which target French residing customers, if it has been licensed by the ARJEL prior to the launch of any website.

Licences are available for the following three gambling products: poker, sports betting and horse betting. A licence must be sought individually for each one of the authorised gambling products. As such, an operator can be licensed to offer all three gambling products, but it will have to go through three licensing process to obtain three licences. A licensed operator can then operate several gambling websites with a single licence, provided that a licence has been granted for all the contemplated websites.

There is no requirement as to the form of incorporation of an online gambling operator. The law even provides for the hypothesis of an individual operating a gambling website.

The application procedure is similar for all three licences. Therefore, if an operator is willing to offer all three gambling products, it has to proceed three times with the licensing procedure.

The operator has to fill in a form which will be submitted to the ARJEL and which provides information on specific legal and financial elements and on technical features.

The application also contains an undertaking from the operator to give to all authorised agents of the ARJEL access to their premises, and in particular to the hosting facilities where the frontal is stored.

While reviewing the licence application, ARJEL may request any additional information and documents to operators. ARJEL's review may not last longer than four months. In the absence of a reply from ARJEL past this four-month delay, the licence is deemed to be denied.

Online operators have to pay a licence fee depending on the number of applications (EUR 5000 for one application, EUR 8000 for two applications and EUR 10,000 for three applications). In addition, operators have to pay a yearly fee of EUR 20,000, EUR 30,000 or EUR 40,000 (depending on whether operators hold one, two or three licences).

The licence is granted for a period of five years and may not be assigned. Every five years, operators have to renew their licence. There is no *numerus clausus*.

After the licence is granted, the operator is subject to a series of system verifications, compliance audits, and reporting requirements.

It must be noted that platform providers do not need to ask for a licence directly, but operators seeking a licence need to have the gaming software that they use approved by the ARJEL. In addition, all suppliers shall be mentioned in the licence application. Contracts concluded with suppliers also need to be provided when submitting the licence application. In the specific case of white label, a distinction must be drawn between the company owning the trade mark under which a gambling website is operated and the company actually operating the website, ie having full control of the gaming software, etc. In this case, white label operators need to seek a licence and become licensed operators, but trade mark owners do not need to be licensed.

Since the opening of the online gambling market, the European Commission has closed all proceedings against France. Some voices in the market claim that the French system may not be fully compliant with European rules, as all gambling products cannot be offered online (especially horse betting). This has been highlighted with the *Zeturf v Prime Minister* case (ECJ, Case C 212/08). In this case, *Zeturf* claimed that the French monopoly on online horse betting is contrary to freedom of services. However, the ECJ has ruled that such monopoly could be legitimate as long as it serves to protect consumer interests against excessive gaming and help the fight against money laundering. So far, the Commission has not given any indication of new concerns about the French regulatory framework.

3.2 Is there a distinction between the law applicable to B2B operations and that applicable to B2C operations?

B2B is absent from the scope of the Law n°2010-476. As such, ARJEL is the regulator of online gambling operators. ARJEL only answers to operators and not to players or providers of technical solutions. On this particular aspect, there is a noticeable difference between the French law and the English law that has created a specific licence for the providers of technical solutions.

This has raised a lot of issues in the French online gambling industry. As part of the monitoring and controlling powers of ARJEL, operators have to take certification audits: one technical audit of their frontal six months following the launch of their platform and one yearly and legal/financial certification audit each year on the anniversary date of the granting of their licence. Although most of the elements to be audited are in the hand of platform providers, the operator is the only debtor of the obligation of certification. As a result, this causes a number of difficulties in the certification process.

Concerning the white labelling, only operators providing the white label websites are liable for the services provided. In addition all domain names (even for the websites operated in white label) shall be listed in the licence application or later authorised by a decision of ARJEL and are thus assimilated only to one operator. The trade mark owner has no direct relationship with ARJEL.

3.3 What are the consequences for B2C or B2B operators who are active in your jurisdiction without having obtained or applied for the required permits, licences and approvals? What penalties and enforcement powers are available in respect of the illegal operators? Please outline any significant domestic decisions or enforcement actions that have been taken by the relevant authorities in recent years.

Operators who are active in France without having obtained or applied for the required permits, licences and approvals face sanctions including but not limited to:

- IP blocking of the illegal websites by ISPs at ARJEL's request;
- conviction for illegally offering of gambling products, ie up to three years' imprisonment and a fine up to EUR 90,000 (five times higher for companies). The conviction and the sanctions can be aggravated if the offence is committed through an organised group (up to seven years' imprisonment and a fine up to EUR 200,000); and
- a ban on applying for an online operator's licence, or for a land-based casino licence, for up to five years.

For example, on 28 June 2013, ARJEL sanctioned an online gambling operator for breach of its certification requirement imposed by Act No. 2010-476. The ARJEL Sanctions Committee sanctioned this operator to pay a fine amounting to EUR 20,000. Another example of a significant decision was in February 2014, when a company operating online gambling in France without the required licence was sanctioned to pay a fine amounting to EUR 300,000.

3.4 What technical measures are in place (if any) to protect consumers from unlicensed operators, such as ISP blocking and payment blocking?

According to Decree n°2011-2122 of 30 December 2011, the President of the Tribunal de Grande Instance of Paris may order an ISP blocking. In addition, pursuant to Article L.563-2 of the French Monetary and Financial Code, the Minister of Budget may, on a proposal from ARJEL, ban any movement or transfer of funds from unlicensed operators accounts (for a renewable period of six months).

3.5 Has the legal status of online gambling changed significantly in recent years and, if so, how?

The Consumer Right Law makes some amendment to the Law n°2010-476 of 12 May 2010. Most of these changes are based on the following points:

- the protection and guarantees of players' assets repayment;
- strengthening the fight against gambling addiction; and
- strengthening the fight against fraud, money laundering and terrorism.

However, the most significant changes are on the protection and guarantees of the repayment of players' assets.

Article 15 of Law n°2010-476 now includes a new paragraph that requires companies seeking approval as authorised online gaming or betting operators to justify the existence of a security, trust, insurance, escrow account or any other instrument or mechanism to ensure the repayment of all players' assets. Moreover, the scope of this guarantee is variable. The operator must adapt its guarantees of changes to players' assets and advise ARJEL of these variations. Furthermore, the regulator may, on its own initiative, require the operator to conduct these adjustments within a period fixed by the regulator itself.

Finally, the Consumer Right Law has a new Article 70 under which the authorised operators have a period of six months, from the publication of the law, to implement the guarantee of protection of players' assets. Otherwise, ARJEL could implement its sanction proceedings.

Since 2011, ARJEL has imposed these safeguards measures as an approval condition for new entrants. However, there was no basis on which to impose such measures on the operators approved before 2011.

Ultimately, the reaction of ARJEL and the adoption of these provisions constitute a response to the unfortunate 'Full Tilt Poker' affair, which was a result of the 'Black Friday' in 2011.

3.6 Whilst acknowledging the inherent difficulty in predicting developments in gambling law, what are the likely developments in online gambling in your jurisdiction, both short term and long term? Are any specific amendments under consideration? Have there been any recent political developments, or do you envisage any in the near future? Are any specific amendments under consideration? Are they likely to be adopted and, if so, what is the time scale?

Law n°2010-476 contained a review clause, pursuant to which an overview of the position of online gambling had to be made 18 months after implementation.

On that basis, four reports have been submitted by the following persons or entities during the second semester of 2011: (i) Senator François Trucy; (ii) Aurélie Filippetti and Jean-François Lamour (both Members of Parliament); (iii) ARJEL; (iv) the Government.

Several amendments to the Law n°2010-476 have been recently made; however, only a few effective changes should be noted.

The most significant change is the amendment of Article L.322-2-1 of the French CHS, which states that online skill games requiring a financial contribution from the player and triggering the hope of a gain which would be acquired are *de facto* illegal, because they cannot be licensed by ARJEL yet. The main purposes of this amendment was to prevent gambling offers getting around the applicable regulation and to ban what were considered as abusive practices. Nevertheless, this extension creates confusion between, on the one hand, those gambling offers the perceived intrinsic dangers of which may justify a strict regulatory framework and, on the other hand, other types of games of a 'purely entertaining' nature. Concerning the latter, the player's main interest does not originate in the hope of a gain, but in the mere entertainment of playing the game itself.

Moreover, one might expect some changes in the not too distant future concerning practical issues in relation to eg the identification of players, the creation of player accounts, the recording of transactions etc.

Furthermore, one can also expect at a later stage some tax changes and potentially an extension of the scope of the law to new games. More specifically, regarding tax changes, the taxation (currently based on the overall amount of stakes placed by players) could be based on the gross gambling revenue generated by the operators. This would in particular respond to a request from the operators who have regularly claimed that the taxation was too high and not calculated on the right base.

3.7 Is the law the same in relation to mobile gambling and interactive gambling on television? If not, are there any headline differences?

The Law n°2010-476 was designed to cover internet gambling in general but mobile gambling and interactive gambling on television have not been specifically addressed in the Law. However, some online gambling licensed operators have developed mobile gambling and interactive gambling offers. Such offers have not been deemed illegal by ARJEL, which has simply requested that the concerned operators shall submit their software for new approval in relation to such additional services. Hence, mobile gambling and interactive gambling on television have been considered as new applications of the gambling platform.

4. LAND-BASED GAMING

4.1 Please describe the licensing regime (if any) for land based gaming, and what products are included. Please set out what licences are available, and the licensing regime for them.

Please see below question 4.2.

4.2 Please set out any particular limitations or requirements for (eg casino) operators, such as a ban on local residents gambling.

The following gambling products can be offered as land-based:

- in casinos: casino games, poker, slot machines;
- in gaming clubs: club card games (including poker), games of chance (pool, baccarat);
- horse and greyhound racing betting;
- sports betting; and
- lotteries.

Sports betting and most lotteries fall under the monopoly of a state-owned corporation, La Française des Jeux. Therefore, the licensing regime for these two gambling products will not be further detailed.

The organisation of horse betting is limited to mutual betting, the organisation of which is completely devoted by licensed horse racing societies to a consortium called PMU. It is, *de facto*, subject to the monopoly of the PMU. As such, given the practical resonance that this chapter is aiming at, the licensing regime applicable to horse racing societies will not be further developed.

Therefore, this section will focus on the licensing regime for casinos and clubs. Some general restrictions exist as to the geographic area in which some gambling products may be offered. The main geographic restriction is that a gaming club cannot be opened in the same city where a casino is already implemented (Article 13 of the Order dated 15 July 1947 on the regulation of games in clubs).

Casinos

Obtaining a licence for a land-based casino is a long and complicated process.

The operator of a casino must seek to obtain a global licence for the whole activity conducted in a single place. There is a single licence for a single casino operator in a single place. As such, there is no distinct licence for the premises, the type of games which are offered, etc. Everything needs to be described in the authorisation submission. Aside from this 'main' licence for the casino operator, employees and suppliers of a casino must also be licensed.

Any additional licence that may be required from a casino operator will relate to liquor selling, etc, but will not relate to the gaming activity *per se*.

i.　　Licence for the casino operator

Authorisations for casinos are granted in consideration of the single establishment where games are to be played by the public, regardless of the entity operating it. A single entity could theoretically operate several casinos in different places.

There is no requirement as to the form of incorporation of the operator of a casino. The law even provides for the hypothesis of a casino owned by an individual.

Casinos need to be authorised by public authorities before starting operating. Such authorisation is granted by administrations in the form of a delegation of public service (similar to a concession). As such, the authorisation that is granted is necessarily temporary, subject to permanent control by administrations, subject to reporting duties, and the authorisation process is partly done in the form of a call for tenders.

Pursuant to Articles L.321-1 to L.321-3 of the CHS, casinos can be authorised in sea, thermal, climatic and touristic resorts and on cruise ships registered with the French international register.

The authorisation process is slightly different in these two cases.

ii.　　Licence for the casino employees

Casinos are free to hire whomever they want, however, employees in charge of gaming activities or enforcing regulatory obligations (ie employees who operate gaming tables, control entrance to the premises, the security manager, CCTV operation employees) shall be individually licensed prior to starting their work (Article 15 of the Order dated 14 May 2007). It shall be stressed that employees admitted to work in casinos can only be French or EU member state citizens.

Employees need to obtain a licence card. Such card is given to them after filing a specific application. The casino is responsible for filing with the Minister of Home Affairs a licence application for each one of the employees accompanied by the following documents:

- an individual application;
- a recent ID photograph;
- evidence that the employee benefits from his civil rights;
- a copy of the employee's criminal record from last than two months as of the date of the application.

Aside from this application, a list of the employees, stating their tasks, shall be sent to the head of the local central police department prior to the beginning of the employees' work (Article 19 of the Order dated 14 May 2007).

The licence card given to employees authorises them to work in all French casinos. In the event of a change of location of the casino, or if the employee starts working in a new casino, the police department in charge of controlling the new establishment validates the employees' licence cards for the new casino.

In order to maintain the casino licence, the casino director needs to provide to the administration specific information on such employees (Article 19 of the Order dated 14 May 2007), including a monthly report sent to the *Préfet* and the Minister of Home Affairs.

iii. Licence for suppliers
The Order dated 14 May 2007 provides for a set of rules for the regulatory licensing of slot machine builders included in Articles 68-2 through 68-9.

The following are subject to a licence from the Minister of Home Affairs: (i) the word trade marks of slot machine manufacturers; (ii) companies which are in charge of selling, setting up and maintaining slot machines; and (iii) companies which are in charge of technical supervision of machines, of specific payment systems.

The licence application shall be addressed by the manufacturer of the machines or the companies listed above. The application file shall contain a fact sheet on the company and technical information on the machines.

Licensed companies have exclusivity to provide specific services to casinos, such as customs formalities while importing machines, managing the transport of machines on the French territory, delivering and setting up machines in casinos, or maintenance.

The licence order of the Minister is strictly personal to the company and cannot be used by, nor transferred or assigned in any way to another entity. Any failure to comply with such exclusivity of the authorisation is a cause for withdrawal of the authorisation.

Gaming clubs
Pursuant to similar rules as those applying to casinos, gaming clubs must seek to obtain a single licence for the whole scope of their activity in a single place. This licence will describe, as per the authorisation that has been

submitted to the authorities by the operator, the authorised scope of activity for the specific gaming club.

To be licensed, gaming clubs need to be incorporated in the form of a non-profit association pursuant to the Law dated 1 July 1901 related to the contract of association (Article 47 of the Law of 30 June 1923 on the public budget for year 1923). The gaming activity that they offer must remain a side activity to other social, cultural or charitable activities.

The creation of such an association is completed by filing, prior to starting the activity, a declaration of creation with the *Préfet*. If such declaration is compliant with the law, the creation of the association is published in the Official Journal. The association only obtains legal capacity upon the publication of its creation in the Official Journal.

Clubs are free to hire whomever they want, but all employees, regardless of their functions, shall be licensed prior to their work. A similar licence application to the one for casino employees is required for gaming clubs' employees (Articles 21 and 22 of the Order dated 15 July 1947 on the regulation of games in clubs).

Authorisation from the Minister of Home Affairs is required for most gaming clubs (Article 1 of the Decree n°47-798 of 5 May 1947 on regulation of games in clubs; Article 47 of the Law of 30 June 1923 on the public budget for year 1923). The exception to this rule is very limited and briefly exposed at the end of this section.

The request for an authorisation is made by the 'director' of the club in two copies: one for the *Préfet*, the other one for the Ministry of Home Affairs. The two copies of the request are filed with the *Préfet* who transmits it to the Ministry which rules after receiving the opinion of the Special Commission for Games (*Commission Spéciale des Jeux*, whose duty is to review the authorisation requests and investigate the measures that will be implemented by the operator to prevent excessive gambling). The request itself can be made in the form of a letter where the club represents that and undertakes to:

- comply with the applicable regulations, and abide by any control or inspection;
- dedicate a specific percentage of the gross gaming revenue to the fulfilment of the purpose of the association (eg subsiding an activity falling under the purpose of the association);
- the club premises are independent from any restaurant, hotel, bar, café, nightclub that would be located in the same building or in an immediately neighbouring one, and have a separate entrance.

The request shall provide specific information and be accompanied by documents, including (a full list is available in Article 8 of the Ministerial Order dated 15 July 1947 on the regulation of games in clubs):

- the list of games offered in the club;
- the date and place of declaration of the association;
- the list of members of the board of directors;
- the list of members of the gaming committee;
- if any, a copy of the previous authorisation order:

- the articles of association of the club;
- the map of the club premises;
- the grounded opinion of the police department in charge of the surveillance of the club;
- a document presenting the purpose of the association and evidencing: (i) how the club actually helps the sector it belongs to; and (ii) how it is ensured that the gaming activity is not the sole or main purpose of the association;
- the opinion of the *Préfet* based on the general activity of the club and the guarantees given by its directors.

The authorisation can only be granted by a special decision of the Ministry. The absence of any response for a period of four months shall be interpreted as a denial of the authorisation (Article 1-1 of the Decree n°47-798 of 5 May 1947 on regulation of games in clubs).

The authorisation granted is strictly personal to the club, and cannot be used by, nor transferred or assigned in any way to another club or any other entity. Any failure to comply with such exclusivity of the authorisation is a cause for withdrawal of the authorisation.

Any modification of the name, headquarters of the club, or any change in the members of its board of directors, is interpreted by French law as the creation of a new club, and requires that the club requests a new authorisation.

Depending on the type of games that these clubs want to offer to their members, specific formalities can be additionally incurred. For instance, in the event electronic machines are to be used within the club, a specific authorisation shall be given for it (either by a specific mention on the authorisation if the request has been made while submitting the main authorisation, or by a distinct and specific authorisation (Article 1 of the Decree n°47-798 of 5 May 1947 on regulation of games in clubs).

The authorisation from the Ministry is not required in the case of gaming clubs whose members agree to play only club card games ('*jeux de commerce*') within the club. This qualification of '*jeux de commerce*' is tax subcategory for gambling products which is very specific and limited in scope. Instead, these clubs shall file a declaration with the *Préfet* of the county where they are established. This declaration shall be accompanied by almost the same information as the one accompanying the request for an authorisation.

4.3 Please address the questions in 3.5 above, but in relation to land-based gaming.

Regarding land-based gaming, there have been no significant changes in recent years. The latest changes concerned casino regulation, but they are not significant. These changes were made by the decree of 6 December 2013 amending the provisions of the Order dated 14 May 2007. This Order provides for various measures to modernise the regulation of games in casinos, especially by introducing rules to the lucky ladies game, the bad beat jackpot game, poker tournaments and electronic blackjack, and allowing the closure of slot machines before the table games.

5.   TAX
5.1   Please summarise briefly the tax regime applicable both to land based and online gaming.
VAT
According to Article 261 E of the French Tax Code, the operating revenue (*revenu d'exploitation*) related to the organisation of betting and gambling activities, whether land-based or online, are exempted from VAT. Casino games are also exempt from VAT.

This VAT exemption is not applicable to the earnings (*rémunération*) of gambling and betting operators and intermediaries (land-based and online) who take part in the organisation of lotteries, poker and horse betting.

The earnings on which VAT shall be paid is the amount remaining once the operators have paid their taxes and the winnings to players (Earnings = Operating Revenue - Taxes - Winnings paid out to players).

Other taxes
Different taxes are applicable depending on the betting and gambling activities. Furthermore, the taxation may either be based on the wagers or on the gross gaming revenue.

Casinos
Two tax levies exist, based on the gross gambling revenues of the casinos. One is paid to the state and 10 per cent of such tax is paid back to local authorities; the other one is paid to the local authorities and may not exceed 15 per cent of the gross gaming revenue of the casino.

In aggregate, both taxes may not exceed 80 per cent of the gross gaming revenue of the casino. In addition, several caps are also applicable to the above outlined tax levies.

A social contribution of 9.5 per cent is also due. It is based on 68 per cent of the gross gaming revenue of automated games. This social contribution amounts to 12 per cent when the winnings exceed EUR 1,500.

Gaming clubs
Special taxation is applicable to gaming clubs. The revenues of gaming clubs are gathered in the form of a pot (*cagnotte*) that is composed of the gross gaming revenue generated by the gaming clubs.

The taxation of gaming clubs is progressive and the following rates apply:
*   Up to EUR 30,490: 10 per cent;
*   between EUR 30,491 and 228,700: 40 per cent;
*   above EUR 228,701: 70 per cent.

Lottery
The tax for the National Centre for Sports is applicable. It amounts to 1.8 per cent of the wagers (limited to EUR 173.8 million/year). A 0.3 per cent tax (limited to EUR 24 million/year) is also applicable until 2015.

A social contribution amounting to 6.9 per cent must also be paid. It is calculated on the basis of 25.5 per cent of the wagers.

Horse betting

Taxation will be the same whether horse betting is land-based or online.

Tax Contribution	Social Security Contribution	Tax for companies organising races	Total
4.6 per cent	1.8 per cent	8 per cent	14.4 per cent

Online sports betting

Tax Contribution	Social Security Contribution	Tax for the National Centre for Sports	Total
4.6 per cent	1.8 per cent	8 per cent	14.4 per cent
5.7 per cent	1.8 per cent	1.8 per cent (limited to EUR 31 million/year) + 0.3 per cent (limited to EUR 24 million/year) until 2015	9.6 per cent

Online poker

Taxation of poker will differ whether poker player online or is land-based.

Activity	Tax Contribution	Social Security Contribution	Total
Online poker	1.8 per cent	0.2 per cent	2 per cent
Land-based poker	Please refer to taxation principles applicable to casinos and gaming clubs		

6.   ADVERTISING

6.1   To what extent is the advertising of gambling permitted in your jurisdiction?

The French CHS provides that any form of advertising for a house providing games of chance (*maison de jeux de hasard*) that has not received proper authorisation is prohibited. Hence, advertising is authorised for all other establishments or websites duly licensed or authorised pursuant to the applicable legislation. However, many rules restrict the possibility to advertise games of chance, in particular in relation to the protection of minors or the fight against addiction: for instance, any advertising for online gambling websites shall be duly identified as such and contain written or verbal warning messages depending on the support on which the advertising is offered. If the advertising is offered online, the warning message must contain a link to a website dedicated to the fight against addiction. Such advertising cannot be offered on websites that appear to be mainly targeting minors. In addition, any advertising for online gambling websites by way of radio or television is forbidden 30 minutes before and after the broadcasting of programmes specifically targeting minors.

7.　SOCIAL GAMING
7.1　We believe this to be a growing area. Please decide under what criteria social gaming is permitted in your jurisdiction. If games are free to play, or if there is no prize are they legal, without a licence? Please address circumstances where virtual currency is used and can be won: ie currency which is of no monetary or other value, save for as credits to take part in games.
Currently, there are no special provisions relating to social gaming under French law and no licence is required to provide social games to French residents. As a consequence, general provisions shall apply to social games, which shall in particular be analysed with respect to the general ban on commercial lotteries (please refer to section 2.3 above).

Nevertheless, there have been many discussions regarding the opportunities to create a social games regulation. We consider a better solution would be to not regulate social game, but to have self-regulation. In this way, it will be sufficient to adapt the legal framework to the nature of the game (paid, promotional campaign, etc).

Germany

Melchers Law Dr Joerg Hofmann, Matthias Spitz,
Danny Engelhardt & Martin Jarrett

1. OBJECTIVES AND STRUCTURE OF LEGISLATION

The German constitution (*Grundgesetz*) has a significant impact on the
structure of German gaming law. 'Classical' gaming law is considered to
be a matter of the 16 federal states of Germany (the *Länder*), in accordance
with their legislative powers for the law of public order. In 1970, the Federal
Constitutional Court (*Bundesverfassungsgericht*) held that the casino law
does not fall within the scope of the competing legislative powers of the
government for the law of economy pursuant to Article 74 (1) no. 11 of the
German constitution, but belongs to the law of public order (decision of 18
March 1970 – file no. 2 BvO 1/65). Based on these legislative powers, each
federal state (Land) has regulated gambling in state-licensed casinos in its
own Casino Act (*Spielbankgesetz*). Accordingly, the regulation of casinos in
Germany is controlled at state level.

In further exercising their legislative powers for the law of
public order, the Länder enacted an Interstate Treaty on Gambling
(*Glücksspielsstaatsvertrag*) with effect from 1 January 2008 (the Interstate
Treaty 2008). In September 2010, however, the Court of Justice of the
European Union (ECJ) ruled that the Interstate Treaty 2008 was non-
compliant with European Union law. This was a pivotal moment in the
development of the regulatory regime: while 15 Länder persevered with
restrictive gaming regulation, one, Schleswig-Holstein, chartered its own
course for a regulated market opening.

Another Interstate Treaty on Gambling (the Interstate Treaty) was
formulated after the striking down of the Interstate Treaty 2008. As
indicated above, 15 Länder signed up to this project. It took effect on 1 July
2012, after various amendments had been forced upon its drafters from
the European Union. Its objectives reflect the focus of 'classical' German
gaming law on public order. In particular, the Interstate Treaty aims at
preventing gambling addiction, channelling the population's 'natural desire
for gambling' to state-controlled gaming operations, ensuring youth and
player protection as well as preventing fraud. These objectives serve as a
justification for a monopoly of the Länder in lotteries, a limited number of
operators in sports betting and a prohibition on online casino gaming. A so-
called 'experimental clause' provides for 20 online sports betting licences. At
the time of writing, none of these licences had been granted; it is anticipated
that they will be granted in the second half of 2014 at the earliest.

Schleswig-Holstein was the only Land to pursue its own gambling
regulation and had passed a Gaming Act (*Glückspielgesetz*) in September

2011, which was derived from the Danish model. Though prescribing a state monopoly in lotteries similar to the Interstate Treaty, this legislation introduced a regulatory framework for the licensing of private operators of sports betting and online casino games for the first time ever in Germany. The first licences for sports betting were issued in early 2012. However, in May 2012, the government in Schleswig-Holstein, which had legislated for liberalised gaming regulation, was voted out. One of the first acts of the new government was to repeal this legislation and accede to the Interstate Treaty. The granting of licences continued until early 2013, when the repealment took legal effect. For a full list of gaming operators licensed under the Schleswig-Holstein regime, see section 2.4.

Amusement machines with prizes (AWPs) in arcade halls, bars and restaurants are regulated under the federal Trade Regulation Act (*Gewerbeordnung*), which again is based on legislative powers of the federal government for the law of economy. Private persons are allowed to operate AWPs due to this federal regulation, and the number of concessions is not limited yet, although the Länder intend to contain the proliferation of AWPs with restrictive rules under the Interstate Treaty.

A practical consequence of the fragmentation of German gaming regulation is that online gambling is largely prohibited in most of the Länder, whereas gambling with AWPs is possible at every corner in German cities, considering that a total number of 265,000 AWPs had been installed in arcade halls, bars and restaurants by December 2012 (see the ifo study, 'Economic Development of the German Coin-Operated Gaming and Amusement Machine Industry 2012 and Outlook for 2013', Munich, March 2013).

Another federal law on gaming and betting is the Race Betting and Lottery Act (*Rennwett- und Lotteriegesetz*), comprising provisions on the organisation of bets on events, where performance tests for horses are held, as well as taxation rules for lotteries and sports betting in general. On 1 July 2012, an amendment to the Race Betting and Lottery Act entered into force, prescribing a 5 per cent tax on stakes on all sports betting, including online sports betting, offered in Germany (see section 5 below).

Finally, the German Criminal Code (*Strafgesetzbuch*) comprises stipulations with respect to the organisation and advertising of games of chance within Germany. Pursuant to § 284 of the Criminal Code, the organisation or advertising of games of chance without an official permit may attract criminal liability, but the Code does not define which kind of permit is required, nor have the courts had the opportunity to decide on this conclusively. In practice, criminal enforcement in gambling-related matters against operators rarely occurs.

2. FRAMEWORK OF LEGISLATION

2.1 What is the legal definition of gambling and what falls within this definition?

Under German gaming law, the term 'gambling' refers to games of chance, whereas games of skill are not subject to gaming law, but may be subject to other stipulations of the federal Trade Regulation Act. A legal definition of 'games of chance' is given in § 3 (1) of the Interstate Treaty, which is widely accepted. As distinct from a game of skill, a game is considered to be a 'game of chance' if, in the context of a game, a consideration is paid for acquiring a chance to win, and the determination of winnings is entirely or predominantly a matter of chance. The predominant element of chance is assessed on the basis of the abilities of an average player. Games of chance also include betting in terms of wagers against payment on the occurrence or outcome of a future event.

2.2 What is the legal definition of online gambling and what falls within this definition?

Although prescribing restrictions on online gambling, a legal definition of online gambling is not given in the Interstate Treaty. Provisions of the Interstate Treaty relevant to online gambling simply make reference to 'gambling on the internet'.

The definition of online gambling in the Gaming Act of Schleswig-Holstein is linked to the distribution (equal to sales) of games of chance, and covered by the term 'distance sales', which again refers to sales solely made by using means of distance communication in terms of § 312b (2) of the German Civil Code (*Bürgerliches Gesetzbuch*). Generally, means of distance communication are means of communication which can be used to initiate or to enter into a contract between a consumer and an entrepreneur without the simultaneous physical presence of the parties, including, for example, telephone calls, emails and, obviously, the internet.

2.3 Please set out the different gambling products identified by legislation.

The following gambling products are, under at least one body of law regulating gaming in Germany, permitted gambling products:

- slot and other machine gaming (AWPs);
- horse betting;
- sports betting;
- casino games and poker;
- bingo; and
- lottery, including tote.

It should be noted that so-called fantasy betting (a betting type which contains real and fictional elements) as a special sub-type of sports betting is also permissible. Accordingly, most popular gambling products are permitted in one way or another in Germany. There are, however, certain gambling products which are not permitted in Germany. These include betting on other than sport, such as financial betting and social betting.

2.4 Please list the different requirements for each gambling product, including legal classifications for each; for example, is poker a game of skill or game of chance?

AWPs in arcade halls, bars and restaurants, also referred to as 'commercial automated games', are subject to federal legislation, specifically the Trade

Regulation Act and the Gaming Ordinance (*Spielverordnung*), issued on the basis of this Act. Pursuant to § 33c of the Trade Regulation Act, installing commercial automated games in arcade halls, bars and restaurants requires official permission. Such permission can usually be obtained from the municipal office for public order. The Gaming Ordinance prescribes that a maximum of three slot machines may be installed in bars and restaurants, and a maximum of 12 is prescribed for an arcade hall concession. In the past legislative period, the Federal Ministry of Economy, however, has suggested an amendment which involves, amongst others, the limitation of slots in bars or restaurants to only two. It remains to be seen whether the Ministry will resume this project in the legislative period from 2013 to 2017. A concept involving premises with multiple arcade hall concessions, multiplying the number of permissible slot machines, has been pervasive for more than a decade and was generally tolerated by local authorities. With the enactment of the Interstate Treaty, the Länder banned this practice; pursuant to §§ 25(1) and 29(4) of the Treaty multiple concessions are prohibited, with transitional periods between one and five years for existing arcade halls. As a consequence, an arcade hall with, for example, a quadruple licence would have to cease operation except for 12 AWPs under the single licence. The Interstate Treaty also contains a provision allowing the Länder to prescribe certain minimum distances between arcade halls, as well as between youth facilities and arcades. The Land Baden-Württemberg, for example, requires a 500 m beeline at the minimum. These restrictions, however, are subject to constitutional controversy (see also section 4.3).

Another gambling product identified by federal legislation is 'betting on performance tests for horses', as paraphrased by the Race-Betting and Lotteries Act, covering horse race betting and trotting as a subset. Under this Act, operating a totaliser on the race track is reserved for the horse race associations, but private persons may apply for a bookmaker licence for the distribution of bets on horse racing in Germany. Contrary to the prevailing opinion among bookmakers and regulators, the Federal Administrative Court (*Bundesverwaltungsgericht*) held in a judgment of 1 June 2011 that a bookmaker licence does not give the right to distribute bets on horse racing over the internet (file no. 8 C 5/10). The Interstate Treaty provides for licensing of bookmakers for horse-race betting on the internet under § 27 (2).

Sports betting is identified by both the Interstate Treaty and the former Gaming Act of Schleswig-Holstein, albeit the definition given by the Gaming Act – as well as regulation of betting in general – is more sophisticated. Sports betting is considered a game of chance. By the time of its accession to the Interstate Treaty in February 2013, Schleswig-Holstein had issued 25 online sports betting licences, eight of which allow holders to operate land-based betting in betting shops. The restrictions of the Gaming Act remain applicable for the licensees and their operational businesses. The licensees have been made public by the grantor, the Ministry of the Interior of Schleswig-Holstein. These are:

Sports Betting	Online Casino Gaming
NordwestLotto Schleswig-Holstein GmbH & Co. KG (brand 'Oddset')	888 Germany Ltd. (brand '888 Poker')
Polco Ltd. (brand 'Betfair')	bet-at-home.com Internet Ltd.
Personal Exchange International Ltd. (mybet Holding SE)	Hillside (Gibraltar) Ltd. (brand 'bet365')
Hillside New Media Ltd. (brand 'bet365')	Polco Ltd. (brand 'betfair')
bet-at-home.com Internet Ltd.	Electraworks (Kiel) Ltd. (brand 'Bwin')
Electraworks (Kiel) Ltd. (brand 'bwin')	Cashpoint Malta Ltd.
Tipico Company Ltd. (including land-based betting)	Ladbrokes International PLC
888 Germany Ltd.	Personal Exchange International Ltd. (brand 'mybet')
Cashpoint Malta Ltd. (including land-based betting)	OnlineCasino Deutschland GmbH
Ladbrokes International PLC	REEL Germany Ltd. (brand 'pokerstars')
Admiral Sportwetten GmbH (including land-based betting)	Tipico Company Ltd.
Admiral Sportwetten GmbH (Austria) (including land-based betting)	Skill on Net Ltd.
Victor Chandler (International) Ltd.	Betway Ltd.
bet90 Ltd. (including land-based betting)	OnGoingMedia GmbH
Interwetten Gaming Ltd.	Interwetten Gaming Ltd.
Spread Your Wings Germany Ltd.	World of Sportsbetting Ltd.
Primebet International Ltd.	Megapixel Entertainment Ltd.
OnGoingMedia GmbH	Victor Chandler (International) Ltd.
Nordbet GmbH (including land-based betting)	Greentube Malta Ltd.
World of Sportsbetting Ltd.	PlayCherry Ltd.
RULEO Alpenland GmbH	Trading Technologies Ltd. (merkur-win)
IBA Entertainment Ltd. (including land-based betting)	Unibet (Germany) Ltd.
Wettenleip GmbH (only land-based betting)	Löwen Play GmbH
Trading Technologies Ltd. (merkur-win)	
Cash-Line Sportwetten GmbH (only land-based betting)	

Betting within the scope of the Gaming Act means combination or single bets on the result or course of events, where 'event' expressly refers to the result of a sports competition, or a current or future occurrence during a sports competition. Consequently, in-play betting is permitted in Schleswig-Holstein. Betting other than sports betting, in particular social betting (eg bets on election results or on the outcome of a casting show) and financial betting, is not permissible under German gaming law. The Interstate Treaty generally prohibits live betting. An exception to this is live betting on the result of a sports event (final score, half-time score), excluding, however, bets on the result of a certain 'event' within a sport competition (eg corner balls, yellow cards, fouls). Although betting shops are a permissible channel for distribution, their number is subject to decentralised regulation and varies greatly between the Länder.

Even though horse races could also be considered sports competitions in the above sense, betting on these events is subject to § 27 of the Interstate Treaty, §§ 1–7 of the Race Betting and Lottery Act and the corresponding Implementation Ordinance. In § 27(2) the Interstate Treaty provides the legal basis for online operation and brokering of horse race betting. This, however, is 'subject to a uniform procedure for all Federal States' and under conditions which encompass, amongst others, restrictions with regard to the exclusion of minors and barred players, and a monthly stake limitation of EUR 1,000.

Casino games are generally subject to the laws of the Länder. The Casino Acts of each of the 16 Länder commonly distinguish between table games, such as roulette, bacarrat, poker and blackjack, and gaming machines. Operating casino games live is reserved for state-licensed casinos. In exception to this, Schleswig-Holstein has granted 23 licences allowing their holders to operate online casino games, including poker but excluding other bank-holder games (roulette, bacarrat and blackjack). All casino games are regarded as games of chance. As the abilities of the average player are the basis for determining the predominant element of a game (skill or chance), poker, too, is regarded as a game of chance throughout the German judicature.

The organisation of lotteries is reserved to the state-controlled lottery companies under both the former Gaming Act of Schleswig-Holstein and the Interstate Treaty. A lottery company for each Land exists, and all German lottery companies are joined together in the State Lottery and Tote Association (*Deutscher Lotto- und Totoblock*). Online distribution of lottery tickets of the state-organised lottery is permissible for lottery agents under the Interstate Treaty. Bingo and keno are specific lottery products and so are reserved to state lottery operators. Pari-mutuel (or tote) betting is considered a sub-type of lottery due to the totaliser principle. This principle involves the collection of player stakes in a pool from which lottery or tote prizes are paid. It is thereby subject to the monopoly of the State Lottery and Tote Association.

2.5 Explain the system of regulation of gambling; which regulatory or governmental body is responsible for the supervision of gambling? Which body issues licences? Which body examines enforcement powers? Is there any limit on the number or duration of available licences?

Generally, each of the Länder is responsible for supervising gambling in their respective territory, resulting in more than 16 competences for the supervision of gambling. Pursuant to the Interstate Treaty, the Länder have assigned certain competences to a specific regulator, resulting in a decentralised supervision structure. For example, the responsible authority for issuing sports betting licences is the Hessian Ministry of the Interior and Sports, whereas the authorities of Lower Saxony are responsible for payment blocking against illegal gambling on the internet. North Rhine-Westphalia is responsible for permitting TV and online advertising means with respect to lotteries and sports betting.

The individual issuing bodies of licences depend on the type of licence. As indicated above, permissions to operate AWPs in arcade halls, for example, must be obtained from the particular municipal office, whereas the licences for state-owned casinos are granted by the individual ministries of the interior. Online casino gaming and sports betting licences pursuant to the Gaming Act have been issued by the Schleswig-Holstein Ministry of the Interior.

A general restriction to a maximum of 20 licences is provided for in § 10a of the Interstate Treaty. Similarly, the number of potential betting shops is determined by the individual legislation of the Länder. Baden-Württemberg, for example, allows for a maximum of 600 betting shops spread equally between the sports betting licensees. Finally, the number of operational licences of state-owned casinos varies and is subject to the particular casino acts of the Länder. Schleswig-Holstein, before its accession to the Interstate Treaty, did not apply a limitation to the number of licences.

Limitations to the term of state-owned casino licences are usually provided in the Länder's casino acts. Schleswig-Holstein's Casino Act, for example, provides for a licence term of 15 years. Online licences for sports betting are valid for a period of seven years under the Interstate Treaty ('experimental clause', see section 1 above). This term begins with the entry into force of the Treaty on 1 July 2012. This time period has already been significantly reduced as a result of the ongoing licensing procedure. Operational licences are valid for six years from the time of their issuance under the Gaming Act of Schleswig-Holstein.

3. ONLINE GAMBLING

3.1 To what extent can online gambling be offered in your jurisdiction? Are licences available and, if so, for which gambling products? Please describe briefly the licensing process, who may apply, whether licences are limited in number and, if no licences are available, whether it is legal for online gambling to be offered. In the case of EU jurisdictions, please state whether there are any issues as

to the legality of the local law at EU level. Please refer to any relevant cases at ECJ level and explain any measures taken or pending by the European Commission.

Offering online gambling in Germany requires a licence, both under the Gaming Act of Schleswig-Holstein and the Interstate Treaty. Licences issued pursuant to the (revoked) Gaming Act allow their holders to operate online casino games and sports betting, respectively. The licensees are listed under section 2.4. Offering games of chance under a Schleswig-Holstein licence outside the territory of this Land is neither expressly legitimated nor expressly prohibited by the Gaming Act. Licensed operators of online casino gaming in Schleswig-Holstein have thus reason to argue that this is the only option to operate on a licensed basis in Germany, considering the ban on online casino under the Interstate Treaty. It could eventually turn out to be non-compliant with EU law. In a message of 20 March 2012 related to the notification of the Interstate Treaty to the European Commission, the Commission has already expressed its doubts with regard to a 'consistent and systemic' regulatory framework and emphasised its right to initiate infringement proceedings.

As mentioned above, only 20 licences for sports betting operations may be issued pursuant to the Interstate Treaty. Under § 4a(2) of the Interstate Treaty, the Länder claim that 'a legal entitlement to a licence does not exist'. Considering the judgments of the ECJ in *Engelmann* and *Costa and Cifone*, the generality of this statement is certainly incorrect (judgment of 9 September 2010 in Case C-64/08, Engelmann, and judgment of 16 February 2012 in Joined Cases C-72/10 and C-77/10, *Costa and Cifone*). In the latter judgment, the ECJ recalled that the obligation of transparency requires the licensing authority to ensure, for the benefit of any potential tenderer, a degree of publicity sufficient to enable the licence to be opened up to competition and the impartiality of the award procedures to be reviewed. As a consequence of these decisions, the ongoing licensing procedure has already been challenged by applicants for its lack of transparency before court. Further litigation, including competition claims, is expected once the licensees will be nominated.

The licensing procedures under both frameworks were split into tiers, with general requirements to licence applicants under tier one and enhanced requirements, particularly in the form of concept submissions, in tier 2. Although broadly identical, the Gaming Act provided more detail than the Interstate Treaty.

Within its two tiers, the Interstate Treaty requires the licence applicants to provide evidence for 'extended reliability', performance capacity, transparency and security of games of chance. Proving the 'extended reliability' requires disclosure of corporate structure and shareholders of the applying entity, as well as evidence for the individual reliability of statutory representatives, ie of the directors of the applying entity (such as CVs and criminal records). With regard to performance capacity, applicants have to prove sufficient funds and economic viability of the gaming operation. Transparency and safety inter alia means that the supervision of gaming operations may not be obstructed by third parties involved in the operation; furthermore, the applicants are eventually obliged to provide an interface which enables supervision of gaming transactions in real time. Finally, the Interstate Treaty requires the applicants to submit, amongst others, a security concept, a social concept and an economic viability concept.

Similar requirements for the Schleswig-Holstein licensees had been set out in the Gaming Act and the Licensing Ordinance. With regard to the performance capacity, applicants had to initially provide a security in the form of a bank guarantee, covering the amount of EUR 1 million for online operations. A SAFE-Server or digital vault, required for supervision purposes with regard to transparency and safety of games of chance, must be able to store payment and gaming transactions in near-real time (which means five minutes later at a maximum). In August 2013, detailed specifications to the SAFE-Server have been published by the regulator of Schleswig-Holstein in the Technical Guidelines (*Technische Richtlinie*). Similar to the Interstate Treaty, the second tier required of the applicant the submission of several concepts, including security, payment processing, AML, fraud prevention, social and economic viability concepts. The minimum requirement for going live is the installation of said SAFE-Server. Within 6 months of going live, licensees have to submit a testing laboratory certification and relevant certificates to the Ministry of the Interior, as detailed in the Technical Guidelines. Under both frameworks, a match with the player-barring database is mandatory.

The licence fees stipulated in the Interstate Treaty depend on the applicant's anticipated turnover for the first year; these are subject to a gradual increase. Licensing fees in Schleswig-Holstein range between EUR 2,500 and 15,000 for sports betting and between EUR 2,000 and 12,000 for online casino games.

3.2 Is there a distinction between the law applicable to B2B operations and that applicable to B2C operations?

Neither the Interstate Treaty nor the Gaming Act of Schleswig-Holstein draws a distinction between B2B and B2C operations, though this is common in other countries or in the gambling business in general. Under the Gaming Act, a distinction instead was made between the organisation of games of chance, ie the operator establishing the game on its own account, and the distribution (or sales) of games of chance, meaning anyone who is responsible for offering or facilitating the conclusion of gambling contracts. The licensing procedure prescribed in the Gaming Act accordingly distinguished between an organisation licence and a distribution licence for sports betting or online casino games. Pursuant to § 4 (1) of the Gaming Act, an organisation licence is only required if games of chance are organised within the (territorial) scope of the Gaming Act. As an example, an online operator resident outside of Germany, but within the EU and with a game server outside of Germany would require a distribution licence: the games of chance that are organised in another country and are to be offered under the Schleswig-Holstein licence would have to be evaluated during the licensing process for compliance with legal requirements of Schleswig-Holstein.

3.3 What are the consequences for B2C or B2B operators who are active in your jurisdiction without having obtained or applied for the required permits, licences and approvals? What penalties and enforcement powers are available in respect of the illegal operators? Please outline any significant domestic decisions or enforcement actions that have been taken by the relevant authorities in recent years.

In principle, operating games of chance without an official permit may be considered a criminal offence under § 284 of the German Criminal Code, although criminal prosecutors have been reluctant to initiate proceedings. This may be due to the legal uncertainty as to whether the Interstate Treaty complies with EU law or not, as well as the vagueness of this provision concerning the kind of required permit. In practice, regulatory measures based on § 9 of the Interstate Treaty are of relevance, such as interdiction orders of the responsible authorities of the Land concerned. Interdiction orders often are on pain of penalty payments between EUR 10,000 and EUR 50,000 per case or contravention. From an economic perspective, measures of competitors (ie potential licensed operators) may have more severe consequences. In a judgment of 29 November 2011, the Federal Court of Justice (*Bundesgerichtshof*) confirmed claims for damages of state-licensed lottery companies against operators of online sports betting, based on the prohibition of online gambling pursuant to § 4(4) of the Interstate Treaty 2008 and unfair competition law (file no. I ZR 92/09). The success of measures under unfair competition law, however, is dependent on the legal assessment and lawfulness of restrictions prescribed in the Interstate Treaty, which also serve as the legal basis for civil action.

3.4 What technical measures are in place (if any) to protect consumers from unlicensed operators, such as ISP blocking and payment blocking?

Following the criticism of the Interstate Treaty 2008, the current Interstate Treaty does not contain a legal basis for domain blocking. However, measures of payment blocking remain possible pursuant to § 9(1) of the Interstate Treaty. In particular, gambling regulators are authorised to prohibit banks and financial services providers from participating in payment transactions and pay-outs linked to unlawful gambling.

3.5 Has the legal status of online gambling changed significantly in recent years and, if so, how?

The protectionist model of the Interstate Treaty 2008 had already failed from an economic perspective, cutting the state operators off the internet and resulting in continuous losses. In 2009, one year after entry into force of the Interstate Treaty 2008, the market share of the state operator ODDSET was estimated to have diminished to 3 per cent, as compared to 94 per cent of the unregulated market (Goldmedia, Key Facts to the study *'Glücksspielmarkt 2015'*, Berlin, April 2010). It is estimated that, in 2017, the 20 companies regulated under the Interstate Treaty will accrue a mere EUR 400 million in stakes in online sports betting, as compared to stakes of EUR 4.529 billion in the unregulated market (Goldmedia, Key Facts to the study *'Glücksspielmarkt Deutschland 2017'*, Berlin, June 2013).

In recent years, new impetus to revise German gaming law was given by European institutions. The ECJ decisions of 8 September 2010 have been characterised as a major breakthrough from the perspective of the European gaming and betting industry. In *Carmen Media* (Case C-46/08), the ECJ concluded that the state monopoly on the organisation of sports betting and lotteries under the Interstate Treaty 2008 does not pursue the objective of combating the dangers of gambling in a consistent and systematic manner. Judgments in *Stoss and Others* (Joined Cases C-316/07, C-358/07 to C-360/07, C-409/07 and C-410/07) and *Winner Wetten* (Case C-409/06) concerned a transitional period before entry into force of this Interstate Treaty, but led to the same conclusion. In these judgments, the ECJ further indicated that, in terms of 'cross-sector consistency', restrictions to games of chance (eg sports betting) cannot be justified if other games of chance which pose a higher risk of addiction (such as AWPs or casino games) are regulated less strictly.

By way of background, restrictions to the freedom to provide services under Article 56 of the Treaty on the Functioning of the EU (TFEU), which is relevant to online gambling operations, may be justified by reasons of overriding general interest. As such, the objectives of consumer protection and the prevention of both fraud and incitement to squander on gaming, as well as the general need to preserve public order, have been recognised by the ECJ in constant jurisprudence (reference is made to the judgments of 24 March 1994 in Case C-275/92, *Schindler*, of 21 October 1999 in Case C-67/98, *Zenatti*, and of 6 November 2003 in Case C-243/01, *Gambelli and Others*). In a number of judgments, the ECJ emphasised that national legislation is appropriate for ensuring attainment of the objective pursued only if it genuinely reflects a concern to attain it in a consistent and systematic manner (eg judgment of 8 September 2009 in Case C-42/07, *Liga Portuguesa de Futebol Profissional*).

As a consequence of the decisions of 8 September 2010, restrictions sustaining the monopoly in sports betting have been considered inapplicable by a number of German administrative courts, and ultimately by the Federal Administrative Court. In a precedent decided on 24 November 2010, the Court concluded that restrictions on land-based sports betting were inconsistent and contravene EU law (file no. 8 C 15.09). This development urged the Länder to revise the Interstate Treaty, including regulation of online gaming and betting. Whether or not the internet ban under the Interstate Treaty sustains the monopoly and contravenes EU law has been discussed in depth since these verdicts of the ECJ and the Federal Administrative Court. This issue is also relevant to the regulation of online gaming under the Interstate Treaty of 2012, because it continues to ban online casino games. In a judgment of 1 June 2012, the Federal

Administrative Court held that the prohibition of online gambling under the former Interstate Treaty complies with EU law, since the corresponding provisions were separate from the monopoly on land-based betting and cover all sectors of gambling. However, it appears questionable whether this judgment is correct, in light of the later judgment in *Zeturf*. In *Zeturf*, the ECJ found that a betting market should in principle be considered in its entirety, independently of the question whether the bets concerned are offered by traditional channels, at physical locations, or by the internet; a restriction on the activity of collecting bets should be examined independently of the medium through which they are made (Case C-212/08).

As a result of the debate among the Länder on the future of gambling regulation, 15 Länder agreed on the Interstate Treaty concept, whereas Schleswig-Holstein made its own way by enacting the Gaming Act with effect from 1 January 2012. After a change of government, Schleswig-Holstein revoked the Gaming Act and acceded to the Interstate Treaty in February 2013. However, the Gaming Act continues to apply to the existing licences (see the table in section 2.4). Accordingly, these licences remain valid for the full licence term of 6 years and arguably may be extended for another licence term of 4 years pursuant to § 4(3) of the Gaming Act. Since the Gaming Act of Schleswig-Holstein entered into force, two regulatory regimes are applicable to online gambling in Germany. Whereas the gaming law of Schleswig-Holstein follows the concept of regulating the markets for both online sports betting and online casino games, the Interstate Treaty follows a rather prohibitive concept. These concepts are clearly divergent and, consequently, German gambling legislation in its entirety may be considered as inconsistent from an EU perspective.

In a message of the European Commission dated 20 March 2012 (see above), the Commission had acknowledged the commitment of the Länder to evaluate and demonstrate the suitability and proportionality of the Interstate Treaty concept for achieving policy objectives. The Länder were given 2 years from the entry into force of the Interstate Treaty (1 July 2012) for this evaluation, and a follow-up of the European Commission is expected in the second half of 2014.

3.6 Whilst acknowledging the inherent difficulty in predicting developments in gambling law, what are the likely developments in online gambling in your jurisdiction, both short term and long term? Are any specific amendments under consideration? Have there been any recent political developments, or do you envisage any in the near future? Are any specific amendments under consideration? Are they likely to be adopted and, if so, what is the time scale?

In the medium term, the principal development may be the grant of the sports betting licences under the Interstate Treaty. However, this is expected to occur in the second half of 2014 at the earliest. Aside from which gaming operators are granted licences, the industry will be closely watching the terms upon which such licences are granted. The regulatory authorities initially indicated that in-play betting would be prohibited, and monthly stakes limits on players of EUR 1,000 would be imposed. It remains to be seen whether regulators will be receptive to arguments against such terms. Accordingly, the final decision will be closely followed.

The other major development in the pipeline is the decision in the case of *Westlotto v Digibet*. This case, which is before the ECJ on referral from the Federal Court of Justice of 24 January 2013 (file no. I ZR 171/10), considers whether the current German regulatory regime for gaming is EU law compliant. A decision is expected to be handed down during 2014, and a finding that the German regulatory regime is non-compliant would have seismic consequences for the industry. The entire German regulatory regime would have to be reconstituted as a consequence, and this reconstitution could provide for general legalisation of online gaming.

3.7 Is the law the same in relation to mobile gambling and interactive gambling on television? If not, are there any headline differences?
Despite the remarkable impact mobile gaming has on the market, it has not been addressed as a major channel of distribution for gaming and betting by the German legislators yet. However, there exists an obvious trend in the gaming and betting industry. Where a draft version of the Interstate Treaty included a prohibition on gambling via text messages, this wording has been removed from the current version. Also, the Gaming Act of Schleswig-Holstein does not include specific provisions on mobile gaming. As a consequence, regulations on online gambling must apply to mobile gambling.

4. LAND-BASED GAMING
4.1 Please describe the licensing regime (if any) for land-based gaming, and what products are included. Please set out what licences are available, and the licensing regime for them.
A broad understanding of land-based gaming suggests that there are two main kinds in Germany: games offered in state-licensed casinos (bank holder games and gaming machines) and gaming machines in arcade halls, restaurants and bars (AWPs, see above).

Operating land-based casinos without a concession granted by the responsible authority – commonly the Ministry of the Interior – is not permitted. In some of the Länder, eg Berlin, privately owned legal entities are entitled to operate a casino. Permission to run branches or satellites can be included as part of the licence. In other Länder, licences may only be issued to companies if shares in the company are 100 per cent state-owned.

In a decision of 19 July 2000, the Federal Constitutional Court held that private companies should have the right to apply for a licence and may not be excluded from the market in favour of state-owned companies as long as they fulfil the requirements of the casino business (see BVerfG 102, 197). Following this decision, a public tender is usually conducted for the issuing of new or the extension of existing concessions.

Setting up gaming machines in arcade halls (AWPs) requires the operator to be reliable and to obtain a set of permissions. They include a general licence pursuant to § 24 of the Interstate Treaty, a certificate of technical approval issued by the German Physical-Technical Federal Institute (*Physikalisch-Technische Bundesanstalt*), clearance certificates from the fiscal authorities and a certificate declaring the particular location as suitable and compliant with the provisions of the Gaming Ordinance. The provisions of the Ordinance do not only restrict the number of gaming machines that may be set up; they also comprise limitations with regard to wagers, winnings and losses per time unit. Unlike gaming machines in arcade halls, machines installed in the state-owned casinos, although identically constructed, are not subject to any restrictions deriving from the Gaming Ordinance.

4.2 Please set out any particular limitations or requirements for (eg. casino) operators, such as a ban on local residents gambling.

Over decades, live gaming and slot machines have been strictly divided into separate areas. Entrance controls for players were only required for traditional live game customers. In late 2007 and finally at the beginning of 2008, when the former Interstate Treaty entered into force, full entrance controls became mandatory for slot machine areas in casinos. At the same time a statutory smoking ban was imposed on casino operations. These restrictions on casino operations, together with an advertising ban established under the Interstate Treaty (2008), have caused a significant decrease in gross gaming revenue. Compared to 2007, the gross gaming revenues (GGR) of all land-based casinos in Germany dropped from approximately EUR 920 million to approximately EUR 554 million in total.

Casino operators have to exclude addictive players and minors from all games of chance. Players are entitled to demand self-exclusion. by submitting a corresponding request to the operator. Mandatory reasons for banning players are the risk of gambling addiction and insufficient financial resources. In § 8(2), the Interstate Treaty also provides for barring initiated through reports by third parties (eg relatives).

As prescribed under §§ 8 and 23 of the Interstate Treaty, a centralised public database for player barring has been installed by the land-based casinos, which is frequently updated and synchronised with the casinos and the state-owned lottery companies. The Interstate Treaty originally intended to unite all forms of gambling operation, including AWPs, in a single barring database called 'OASIS'. However, on account of legal obstacles related to data-protection laws which result from individual Gaming Acts (eg the Hessian Gaming Act), arcade halls located in some Länder are obliged to synchronise with a different database which only encompasses the Land concerned.

4.3 Please address the questions in 3.5 above, but in relation to land-based gaming.

With respect to machine gaming in arcade halls, land-based gaming has experienced two significant changes since the entry into force of the Interstate Treaty.

First, certain stipulations of the Interstate Treaty enabled the Länder to enact minimum distances between arcade halls, as well as between youth facilities and such halls. The Länder have determined, for example, a 500 m beeline between arcade halls. Additionally, the Interstate Treaty contains a restriction for multiple licences, ie licences that are located in the same building or building complex. All permissions granted after 28 October 2011 are affected. Licensees, however, criticise the lack of an adequate transitional period allowing proper amortisation of their investments. Therefore, a number of constitutional claims have been brought before the constitutional courts of the Länder. Some claims have already been dismissed but others are still ongoing; decisions are expected by mid-2014.

Secondly, the above-mentioned Gaming Ordinance could be amended in the legislative period from 2013 to 2017. A revision of said Ordinance is likely to put further limitations on the operation of gaming machines outside state-owned casinos, as already proposed by the Federal Ministry of Economy during the previous legislative period. These proposals included a decreased number of permissible machines in bars or restaurants, the introduction of a non-personal player card and – in terms of requirements for the games themselves – a forced break in gaming after 3 hours.

5. TAX
5.1 Please summarise briefly the tax regime applicable to both land-based and online gaming.

Gaming products are taxed very differently in Germany. Land-based casinos are subject to a casino levy which is based on GGR. Progressive tax rates may apply depending on the economic capability of the casino operator. There used to be very high tax rates in the past amounting up to 91 per cent of annual GGR. As a consequence of continuous losses in annual GGR (see above), statutory tax rates were lowered in some of the Länder down to 25 per cent. A few Länder started to incorporate a system of combined gross gaming revenue and profit taxation, since the first casinos were not able to pay the stipulated tax rates or even went bankrupt, such as the casinos of Saxony-Anhalt in mid-2011. Casinos are exempt from corporate taxation under the Casino Acts of the Länder.

AWP operators are subject to an amusement tax of up to 20 per cent of the gross income generated from AWPs, in addition to regular corporate taxes. Amusement tax rates may be determined individually by each municipality through Local Billing Codes.

Companies with a licence to operate online casino gaming pursuant to the Schleswig-Holstein Gaming Act are obliged to pay 20 per cent (§ 36) of GGR. It should be noted that this levy accrues regardless of the legality of the offered products. Accordingly, operators who have not obtained a licence are still subject to this tax obligation. Generally, failure to comply with tax obligations may be a reason for the withdrawal of the licence and may induce prosecution for tax fraud.

Provisions for the taxation of sports betting have been incorporated in the Race Betting and Lottery Act. As set out in § 17(2) of the Race Betting and

Lottery Act, operators must pay 5 per cent tax on turnover from sports bets offered within Germany. This tax applies both to licensed and non-licensed operators. Since the sports betting tax is federal law, it supersedes the gaming levy of Schleswig-Holstein. The tax authorities of Frankfurt (Hesse) are responsible for collecting the sports betting tax.

Because of the tough competition and price elasticity of customers in online sports betting, the concept of 5 per cent taxation has been criticised as economically unviable by both operators and legal experts (see *Additional Opinion to the Legal Opinion on the constitutionality of the introduction of a concession system for organising sports betting* by Professor Hans-Jürgen Papier, Munich, December 2011).

It should be noted that the 5 per cent turnover tax does not have any effect on the operation of online casinos. Before going live, online casino operators have to register with the responsible fiscal authority, ie the fiscal authority Kiel-North.

6. ADVERTISING

6.1 To what extent is the advertising of gambling permitted in your jurisdiction? Again, this should cover both land-based and online gaming. To the extent that advertising is permitted, how is it regulated?

In principle, advertising of gambling may only be undertaken by licensed operators.

The principal body of law is the Advertising Guidelines (*Werberichtlinie*). The Advertising Guidelines apply to all gaming advertising published in Germany, except for such that is published in Schleswig-Holstein. Advertising for products offered under a Schleswig-Holstein licence is subject to the Code of Practice of the German Advertising Council (Verhaltensregeln des Deutschen Werberats). The Advertising Guidelines prohibit all gaming advertising unless it is published by a licensed operator. They contain detailed provisions on the permitted content of gaming advertising; for example, gaming advertising which makes gambling appear as a product of everyday life is prohibited. The media through which gaming advertising is published is regulated. Television and internet advertising is subject to prior permission. A permit may be either a general permit or an individual permit, both of which are granted by the authorities of North Rhine-Westphalia. Where an individual permit grants the right to launch single spots or advertising measures, a general permit authorises gambling operators to conduct whole advertising campaigns. In applying for a general permit, the advertising concept is the most critical feature. This document must include a description of the advertised gambling products, the target audience, and the frequency and duration of advertising broadcasts.

The advertising of gaming products which are offered under a Schleswig-Holstein licence is subject to the Code of Practice. Generally, the Code of Practice is a more liberal regime than that imposed by the Advertising Guidelines; most importantly, it does not require prior approval of advertising. In summary, it is a statement of 15 principles on what is prohibited content in gaming advertising, such as targeting minors or encouraging excessive gambling.

The third source of law for gambling advertising in Germany is the Unfair Competition Act (*Gesetz gegen den unlauteren Wettbewerb*). The Unfair Competition Act stipulates that 'unfair commercial practices' are not permitted if they cause tangible damage to competitors. Under section 4, examples are given of 'unfair commercial practices', with one example being infringement of statutory provisions intended to regulate market behaviour in the interest of market participants. Court decisions on this example have ruled that 'infringement of statutory provisions' also includes infringements of legal instruments such as the advertising restrictions under the Interstate Treaty. Accordingly, an infringement of the advertising restrictions of the Interstate Treaty as specified in the Advertising Guidelines is potentially actionable under the Unfair Competition Act. Further, courts have confirmed that 'market participants', such as gaming operators, have standing to sue. The principal remedy under the Unfair Competition Act for breaches of the Advertising Guidelines is 'cease-and-desist' orders. If a cease-and-desist order is not respected, the gaming operator exposes itself to penalties of EUR 250,000 per contravention or, if this amount cannot be paid, imprisonment for the directors of the relevant gaming operator.

7.   SOCIAL GAMING

7.1   We believe this to be a growing area. Please decide under what criteria social gaming is permitted in your jurisdiction. If games are free to play or if there is no prize, are they legal without a licence? Please address circumstances where virtual currency is used and can be won: ie currency which is of no monetary or other value, save for as credits to take part in games. The answer should address the question whether game credits or virtual money can be exchanged for other prizes. Is any change to regulation in the area proposed or envisaged?

Although social gaming is considered to be a growth sector in the industry, German gaming law does not comprise specific regulations for social gaming, and so general provisions apply. If games are free to play, or there is no prize with a monetary value involved (eg upgrades to a virtual farm that cannot be sold), a social game will not be considered to be gambling in terms of German gaming law. Similarly, a virtual currency does not alter a social game to a gambling game, if this virtual currency is of no monetary value. Where prizes have a monetary value, such as game points which can be exchanged for cash or goods, a social game may be considered to be gambling by regulators or competitors.

Gibraltar

Hassans Peter Montegriffo & Nyreen Llamas

1. OBJECTIVES AND STRUCTURE OF LEGISLATION

Gibraltar's first gambling statute was enacted in the 1950s and covered the provision of land-based gambling services. The legislation did not envisage the provision of gambling services through remote means.

However, in the 1990s, Gibraltar saw the first remote providers of gambling in the jurisdiction, most notably Victor Chandler and Ladbrokes, which commenced their telephone betting operations from here. The jurisdiction's reputation as a centre for remote operator business was consolidated in the early 2000s when the first internet gambling service providers established in Gibraltar. These initial licence arrangements were extended under the terms of the old legislation which did not provide for gambling through remote means. Therefore specific and bespoke arrangements were granted pursuant to individual licence agreements on terms contractually agreed between the operators and the Gibraltar Government as the Licensing Authority.

The increasing numbers of internet gambling providers relocating and establishing their business in Gibraltar, and the commercial pressures of some of the larger businesses who wished to list their shares on the stock exchange, gave rise to the enactment of the current Gibraltar Gambling Act 2005. This legislation is significantly modelled on the UK Gambling Act 2005. The statute not only makes provision for the licensing and regulation of land-based gambling but also gambling services through remote means (such as the telephone and internet).

2. FRAMEWORK OF LEGISLATION
2.1 What is the legal definition of gambling and what falls within this definition?

'Gambling' is defined in section 2(1) of the Gambling Act as including:
* betting (including pool betting) and bookmaking;
* gaming; and
* promoting or entering a lottery.

Furthermore, 'betting' is defined as follows:

'making or accepting a bet on –
* *the outcome of a race, competition or other event of any description;*
* *the likelihood of anything occurring or not occurring; or*
* *whether anything is or is not true – but does not include any bet made or stake hazarded in the course of, or incidental to, any gaming and the expressions bet, betting and bookmaking shall be construed accordingly'.*

'Gaming' is defined as: 'the playing of a game of chance for a prize' and a 'game of chance' includes:

'(a) a game that involves an element of chance and an element of skill;
(b) a game that involves an element of chance that can be eliminated by superlative skill;
(c) a game that is presented as involving an element of chance;
(d) a game where a computer generates images or data taken to represent the actions of another participant or participants in the game'.

Finally, a 'lottery' is defined as: *'any scheme for the distribution of prizes by chance or lot in which the participants or a substantial number of them make a contribution for the purposes of participation in the chances of the lottery and includes tombola, but does not include any gaming'.*

2.2 What is the legal definition of online gambling and what falls within this definition?

Under the Gibraltar Gambling Act, online gambling would fall within the definition of 'remote gambling'. This is described as:

'gambling in which persons participate by means of remote communication, that is to say, communication using –
(a) the internet;
(b) telephone;
(c) television;
(d) radio; or
(e) any other electronic or other technology for facilitating communication'.

2.3 Please set out the different gambling products identified by legislation.

As previously indicated, the legislation provides for the different categories of gambling which includes betting (including pool betting) and bookmaking, gaming and lottery. The 'gaming' element includes all types of casino games, poker, slots, machine gaming, bingo and all other number games without limitation.

2.4 Please list the different requirements for each gambling product, including legal classifications for each; for example, is poker a game of skill or game of chance?

See section 2.1 above. All types of gambling products can be offered in Gibraltar, with the exception of lotteries. In relation to the latter, the only lottery permitted under the Gambling Act is the Gibraltar Government Lottery and small bazaar, fete and fairground style lotteries (of the types identified in Schedule 2 of the Gambling Act).

With regard to non-remote betting and betting offices and gaming and gaming establishments, the licensee must conduct its business from approved premises and must maintain its licence in accordance with the conditions upon which it is issued. In the case of remote gambling, the licensee must ensure it complies with the provisions of the Act, its licence terms and the Codes of Conduct issued by the Licensing Authority, in particular the Remote Technical and Operating Standards for the Gibraltar Gaming Industry.

Quite apart from the specific obligations and conditions which a licence holder needs to comply with depending on whether it is offering remote or non-remote gambling services, all licence holders are obliged to:

- publicise its rules so that persons entering premises or accessing websites, as the case may be, can readily see these;
- establish and at all times maintain in operation an effective system of internal controls and procedures to monitor the activities authorised under its licence and for it to comply with its obligations under the Criminal Justice Act in respect of any transactions which may give rise to any suspicions of money laundering on the part of the participants;
- take all reasonable steps to prevent an underage person from participating in the gambling activities offered;
- nominate a place for the safekeeping of transaction records and keep true and fair annual financial records which have to be audited (these to be kept for at least five years and which are to be provided annually to the Gambling Commissioner);
- maintain approved banking and payment processing arrangements;
- promptly inquire into complaints; and
- pay all such charges, fees and gaming taxes as are prescribed by the Licensing Authority.

2.5 Explain the system of regulation of gambling; which regulatory or governmental body is responsible for the supervision of gambling? Which body issues licences? Which body examines enforcement powers? Is there any limit on the number or duration of available licences?

All licensing matters, including, most importantly, the substantive decision on licensing new applicants are determined by the Licensing Authority. The Licensing Authority pursuant to the Gambling Act is the minister with responsibility for gambling. All regulatory aspects (post licensing) are within the remit of responsibility of the Gambling Commissioner and his regulatory team. Although the roles are distinct and separate, the personnel and infrastructure organisations of both departments are merged into one. This ensures a more streamlined approach whereby the licensing and regulatory teams work closely to complement each other. This has brought synergies in the exercise of their duties which has benefited all operators.

Part VIII of the Gambling Act contains all the enforcement provisions in relation to the compliance by licence holders to the terms of their licences. Section 42 of the Gambling Act provides grants extensive powers of investigation, reporting and powers of entry where a licence holder is suspected of carrying on its activities contrary to the provisions of his licence, the Act or in a manner which is otherwise prejudicial to the public interest, the interest of any customer or potential customer or to the reputation of Gibraltar. This part of the Gambling Act also sets out the powers of the Licensing Authority to suspend or revoke a licence and enables a justice of the peace, if satisfied with the information laid before him, to grant the Gambling Commissioner and/or the police with a warrant to search premises.

Licences are issued for a period of 5 years, but must be renewed annually upon payment of a nominal licence fee. Upon expiry of the principal 5 year term, the licence can be renewed.

It should be noted that there are no limits on the number of licences granted in Gibraltar. However, the Gibraltar authorities apply a selective policy on licensing only operators which have a proven track record in the sector and who establish a real presence accountable to the regulator.

3. ONLINE GAMBLING
3.1 To what extent can online gambling be offered in your jurisdiction? Are licences available and, if so, for which gambling products? Please describe briefly the licensing process, who may apply, whether licences are limited in number and, if no licences are available, whether it is legal for online gambling to be offered. In the case of EU jurisdictions, please state whether there are any issues as to the legality of the local law at EU level. Please refer to any relevant cases at ECJ level and explain any measures taken or pending by the European Commission.

The Gibraltar Gambling Act 2005 establishes a licensing and regulatory framework for the provision of gambling services through remote means.

The first 'remote gambling' licences issued in Gibraltar however, pre-date the enactment of the 2005 legislation. There are currently only 28 licensed remote gambling operators in the jurisdiction and the Gibraltar Government has applied a very restrictive and selective policy towards the licensing of operators in the jurisdiction by requiring a substantive presence resulting in real accountability to the regulator, constant monitoring of operations and ensuring that gambling services are provided responsibly with appropriate measures to protect the young and problem gamblers.

Although there is no limit to the number of licences which may be issued in Gibraltar, given the current licensing policy which requires a bricks and mortar operation with key equipment in the jurisdiction, the numbers of licensees are selectively kept low and it is not anticipated that there will be a sharp increase in licences. There should nonetheless be a steady rise of licensees in Gibraltar as opportunities develop for medium-sized businesses with niche markets and products which have not partnered with other complementary operations or otherwise merged.

Whilst the legislation envisages that anyone can apply, there are various criteria applied by the authorities in determining whether to licence an operator. The principal one is that described above – real presence with senior individuals managing the business and with key technical equipment in the jurisdiction.

3.2 Is there a distinction between the law applicable to B2B operations and that applicable to B2C operations?

The legislation only envisages one type of remote gambling licence – the operator licence. There are however, sub-categories of this licence depending on the nature of the services provided, which are 'casino' (which includes poker, bingo, slots), 'betting' and 'lottery'.

Notwithstanding the single type of licence, the Licensing Authority recognises the B2B model and will extend a licence for such operations pursuant to the current Gambling Act and contractual arrangements agreed between the parties. At present, there are six licensed B2B operators in the jurisdiction which provide hardware and operational support to gambling operators. This number is likely to increase over the next year as B2B providers recognise opportunities for their business in the local market and as a hub for provision to operators in other regulated jurisdictions.

It should also be noted that most of the larger B2C operators also provide, as a significant element of their business, B2B services. The majority of these are white label services pursuant to which the operator provides the core gambling services, as well as customer services, registration and account handling, to a third party which owns a brand and websites. All white labels entered into by Gibraltar operators require prior Licensing Authority approval, which in most cases is a relatively straightforward procedure involving the submission of due diligence documentation on the white label partner.

3.3 What are the consequences for B2C or B2B operators who are active in your jurisdiction without having obtained or applied for the required permits, licences and approvals? What penalties and enforcement powers are available in respect of the illegal operators? Please outline any significant domestic decisions or enforcement actions that have been taken by the relevant authorities in recent years.

The Gambling Act imposes significant penalties on those persons providing remote gambling services without having previously sought and obtained the relevant approvals and licences (these penalties apply equally to B2B and B2C operators). On summary conviction, the penalty will include: (i) a fine of up to £5,000; and/or (ii) a maximum of three months in prison. On conviction on indictment, to a fine or to imprisonment for a term not exceeding one year or to both a fine and imprisonment.

3.4 What technical measures are in place (if any) to protect consumers from unlicensed operators, such as ISP blocking and payment blocking?

N/A.

3.5 Has the legal status of online gambling changed significantly in recent years and, if so, how?

Other than the introduction of the Gambling Act in 2005, there has been no other significant change to the online gambling legislative and regulatory framework in Gibraltar.

3.6 Whilst acknowledging the inherent difficulty in predicting developments in gambling law, what are the likely developments in online gambling in your jurisdiction, both short term and long term? Are any specific amendments under consideration? Have there been any recent political developments, or do you envisage any in the near future? Are any specific amendments under consideration? Are they likely to be adopted and, if so, what is the time scale?

The online gambling sector has seen exponential growth over the last decade and we anticipate that the next 10 years will see many further developments. The uncertain landscape in the EU will drive operators to streamline their businesses and at a commercial level, it is likely that more shall partner with each other to develop their operations further. Gibraltar is well positioned to handle these challenges given it is within the EU and has adopted a very conservative policy in the licensing of operations and has a well regulated industry in the jurisdiction. We consider that until harmonisation of rules on a pan-European basis, the most significant development will be regulatory cooperation.

In Gibraltar, we anticipate that in the short- to medium-term, there will be some legislative changes to accommodate the appropriate licensing of the different types of businesses in this sector, such as the B2B operator (hardware/software providers) and white label partners.

The Gibraltar government is determined to lobby against the proposed UK 'point of consumption' tax for the provision of gambling services. The Gibraltar Betting & Gaming Association has been actively lobbying against this and is reviewing the position with a view to potentially challenging in the English courts the introduction of the UK measures. The recent experiences in France, Spain and, over a longer period, Italy demonstrate that multiple and fragmented domestic licensing and regulation with uncompetitive taxation regimes can give rise to the proliferation of unlicensed and questionable operators providing services to consumers on a more profitable basis. Mainstream licensed and regulated businesses in Gibraltar and across the EU will only stand to lose with such arrangements and it would be ironic that operators outside the EU should become the unintended beneficiaries.

3.7 Is the law the same in relation to mobile gambling and interactive gambling on television? If not, are there any headline differences?

Both mobile gambling and interactive gambling on television fall within the remit of the Gambling Act. The legislation specifically catalogues these activities as forms of remote gambling.

Remote gambling is defined in section 2(1) of the Gambling Act as follows:

'gambling in which persons participate by means of remote communications, that is to say, communication using:

(a) the internet;

(b) telephone;

(c) television;

(d) radio; or

(e) any other kind of electronic or other technology for facilitating communication.'

It should be noted that this broad definition and in particular subsection (e) has been carefully drafted to catch any form of gambling service provided remotely.

4. LAND-BASED GAMING

4.1 Please describe the licensing regime (if any) for land-based gaming, and what products are included. Please set out what licences are available, and the licensing regime for them.

As indicated in question 1, the Gambling Act carefully prescribes the licensing regime applicable to land-based operators. Essentially, five different licence categories are available to those persons seeking to provide land-based services within Gibraltar. The following is a brief overview of the form of activity which an operator may seek to provide under each licence:

- Bookmakers licence – allows the holder to undertake, either on his own account or as agent, the business of receiving or negotiating bets. Furthermore, it should be noted that it shall be an offence for any person to keep or use any premises, or cause, or knowingly permit any premises to be used as a place where persons resorting thereto may effect any betting transactions without having previously obtained a bookmakers licence.

- Pool promoter's licence – allows the holder to run pool betting operations. Strict restrictions are imposed on the use of premises for the provision of pool betting services where the owner of such premises does not hold a pool promoters licence.

- Gaming operator's licence – allows the holder to conduct and/or provide gaming facilities (this includes the provision of games of chance for a prize, such as casino games). Restrictions are also imposed on the use of premises to conduct gaming operations.

- Lottery promoter's licence – allows the holder to promote and/or operate lotteries.

- Gaming machine licence – allows the holder to keep on his premises gaming machines for the purpose of land-based gaming services.

4.2 Please set out any particular limitations or requirements for (eg casino) operators, such as a ban on local residents gambling.

At present, no notable restrictions are imposed on land-based operators. Local residents are able to gamble.

4.3 Please address the questions in 3.5 above, but in relation to land-based gaming.
N/A.

5. TAX
5.1 Please summarise briefly the tax regime applicable to both land-based and online gaming.
The taxation of companies and individuals in Gibraltar is governed by one piece of primary legislation, the Income Tax Act. This is supported by subsidiary legislation enabled by the provisions of the Income Tax Act.

Previous legislation allowing for tax exempt companies (providing a 0 per cent rate) has been phased out with all exempt companies having expired on December 2010. The new corporate tax system was introduced on 1 January 2011 to provide a seamless transition for these companies into the new 10 per cent headline rate, though it may be possible to mitigate this significantly in appropriate circumstances.

In this regard, Gibraltar also transposed the EU Parent Subsidiary Directive under the Parent Subsidiary Company Rules 1991. Under these provisions a parent company is not liable in certain circumstances to tax in respect of dividend income paid by a subsidiary to its parent. Likewise a Gibraltar company making a dividend payment out would not have to withhold tax.

Furthermore, interest or royalty payments arising in Gibraltar are exempt in certain circumstances from any taxes imposed on those payments, provided the beneficial owner of the interest or royalties is either: (i) a company of a member state; or (ii) a permanent establishment situated in a EU member state of a company of a member state.

Quite separately, gambling operators in Gibraltar are also subject to gaming duty. This is levied at a rate of 1 per cent of turnover in respect of betting services and 1 per cent of gaming yield in relation to gaming services (casino and poker) but is subject to a minimum of £85,000 a year and a maximum of £425,000 a year.

6. ADVERTISING
6.1 To what extent is the advertising of gambling permitted in your jurisdiction? Again, this should cover both land-based and online gaming. To the extent that advertising is permitted, how is it regulated?
The Gambling Act empowers the minister responsible for gambling to prescribe rules governing the advertising of gambling activities authorised under a remote gambling licence after due consultation with the Gambling Commissioner, the Licensing Authority and individual remote gambling licence holders. Although to date no such rules have been published, these may prohibit under penalty advertisements that are:
- indecent, pornographic or offensive;
- false, deceptive or misleading;
- intended to appeal specifically to persons under the minimum permitted age, currently 18 years of age; or

- in breach of copyright laws.

However, it should be noted that copyright and intellectual property rights are specifically safeguarded by other legislative instruments.

7. SOCIAL GAMING

7.1 We believe this to be a growing area. Please decide under what criteria social gaming is permitted in your jurisdiction. If games are free to play or if there is no prize, are they legal without a licence? Please address circumstances where virtual currency is used and can be won: ie currency which is of no monetary or other value, save for as credits to take part in games. The answer should address the question whether game credits or virtual money can be exchanged for other prizes. Is any change to regulation in the area proposed or envisaged?

There is currently no legal definition of social gaming in Gibraltar. Social gaming can arguably be defined as a game featuring some degree of interaction with other human players over the internet. Most commonly, this would take place using a social media platform and would typically not involve a monetary or a cash-equivalent prize. A game may offer rewards and incentives for achievements, but these will not be of any ascertainable value outside the strict confines of the game and its platform.

In Gibraltar, there is no legislation which specifically or implicitly addresses the concept of social gaming within the parameters of the above definition. The Gambling Act is clear and unambiguous in that, to fall within the definition of 'gaming' (and thus fall within the gambling legislative and regulatory framework), the activity in question must involve a prize. As such, we take the view that if a game does not involve a prize element, it falls outside the regulatory regime and can generally operate from Gibraltar without obtaining a licence. The activity will not be treated as 'gambling' or 'gaming' and thus any operator or provider of such games would not require any specific licence in Gibraltar.

Some contemporary internet-based social games incorporate the use of a virtual currency unique to the particular game. In our view, a distinction must be drawn between those games where virtual currency can be exchanged for a prize with an ascertainable monetary value and those where the virtual currency remains within the confines of the game and is only a measure of a player's performance or exchangeable for in-game items. In the latter arrangement, we believe the better view is that no licensing requirements would be imposed on the operator who may therefore provide its services from Gibraltar without the need to obtain a remote gambling licence.

Greece

Constantinos N. Couccoullis and Associates
Constantinos N. Couccoullis & Alexia C. Couccoullis

1. OBJECTIVES AND STRUCTURE OF LEGISLATION

Gambling in Greece has a history dating back to antiquity where it had the support of an Olympian God, namely Mercury (Hermes). Contemporary Greece has an infrastructure for gambling-based tourism and casinos, and it is viewed by many as the best spot for casinos in Europe. Gambling is an important sector in the economy, and online gambling has grown rapidly in Greece over the past few years.

The Greek state supported land casinos with Law 2206/1994 but not gambling outside of casinos, a practice rendered illegal back in 2002 by Law 3037/2002 declared on July 30th 2002. The Greek state can take no less than 20-30 per cent of casino profits pursuant to Law no 2206/1994 Article 2(8) but no profit from any other sources. Under Law 3037/2002, all electrical games, electromechanical games and electronic games played in public places such as hotels, cafeterias or private places, were banned. Back then there was arguably a social backlash against teenagers spending all their money on slot machines, families losing their savings, and quasi-casinos could be found almost everywhere. It should be noted that the 3037/2002 law came as a reaction to a member of the ruling political party being videotaped in an illegal gambling establishment. The law instantly eradicated the arcade videogame market at that time. Internet cafes were allowed to operate, on the condition that no gaming took place in their establishments. There were several reactions against this law, given that it prohibited even the playing of chess in internet cafés. On 14 January 2004, the police raided several internet cafes in Larissa. The European Commission argued that the law was in conflict with EU legislation and that the European Court of Justice (ECJ) could take action against Greece. On 10 February 2005 the European Commission referred Greece to the ECJ. This law was enacted to fight illegal gambling, and was extended to all gaming because the government could not differentiate between 'regular' games and gambling machines. However, the result was quite the opposite, given that illegal gambling thrived in Greece back then.

In 2008, the EU Commission gave Greece a final warning before court action over restrictions on its gambling market. The European Gaming and Betting Association (EGBA) concluded that the national gambling legislation of that time was not serving *'any genuine consumer protection or public order interest has no future'*. The EU Commission ruled that Greece's 3037/2002 law contradicted the EU law on free trade and a fine of EUR 31,500 per day was imposed. Greece has been experiencing an economic crisis since 2010 and this motivated the government to lift the ban on internet casino gambling, ie in order to profit from a situation causing monetary losses since 2002. In 2010 things began to change.

The online gambling market in Greece was then estimated at EUR 2 billion per year, an amount that the Greek government could not afford to lose. This amount should undoubtedly have been collected to some extent via taxation and licensing fees. George Christodoulakis, the Ministry of Finance senior official said: *'The propensity for gaming in Greece is among the highest in Europe and the world…This has to do with our temperament and culture… The only thing one can do is set rules'*. Following the recession, the Finance Minister said: *'Our country today finds itself in the extremely unpleasant condition of paying around a million euros a month as a fine'*, and went on *to say 'we want a regulatory framework that is modern, compatible with European regulation, and that fortifies against illegal activity'*. It seemed only natural to announce the imminent release of a draft law on electronic gaming and internet betting. Betfair sent company representatives in Greece to discuss the proposed incoming legislation on online gambling in Greece with government officials. In 2010 the approach of the Greek government changed and finally Law 4002/2011, which was applicable to technical leisure games and to games of chance, was approved in August 2011. With legalisation realised in Law 4002/2011, the Greek state expected to gain EUR 700 million annually from taxing and licensing online casinos, ie by legalising online gambling and by introducing mini casinos, or gambling venues with gaming machines.

Lottery and sports betting are controlled by an organisation known as Organisation of Football Prognostics (OPAP), which has exclusive rights to all sports betting and lotteries in Greece until 2020. OPAP was founded in 1958, and has been publicly traded since 2001. OPAP's monopoly was challenged as being anti-competitive under EU regulations. OPAP is one of the major betting companies in Europe and under Law 4002/2011 it is expected to create 819 gaming venues within the next few years. Given that Greece is a member of the EU, it is subject to the requirements of the EU's free passage for trade and services from other EU states policy. However, gambling outside casinos remains OPAP's monopoly. OPAP had threatened in the past to prosecute Greek citizens who attempted to avoid its services and bet directly with foreign gaming companies online, though without offering more tempting odds.

Currently Law 4002/2011 follows the principles of responsible gaming and introduces the Individual Player Card, which assists in ascertaining the players' age and tax registration number, cash flows and maximum participation time, and in guaranteeing that any additional restrictions imposed by the players themselves are observed. The Individual Player Card may be issued by licence holders pursuant to the procedure and terms and conditions laid down in a decision of the Hellenic Gaming Commission (HGC) published in the Government Gazette. Gaming without an Individual Player Card is strictly prohibited. With this step it is evident that Greece is a pioneer when it comes to players' protection at European level, given that the Greek Government ensures that it will be able to receive money when appropriate, and protect players if necessary.

Law 4002/2011 allows land-based (wide area) games of chance via video lottery terminals (VLTs) and games of chance via the internet without excluding any type of games. The minimum amount payable for participating in games of chance played using gaming machines is EUR 0.10 and the maximum amount is EUR 2. Those amounts may be adjusted by decision of the HGC.

2. FRAMEWORK OF LEGISLATION
2.1 What is the legal definition of gambling and what falls within this definition?
Though there is no definition of gambling in Law 2206/1994, in Article 4(1)(a) it is forbidden for anyone to operate, keep or provide any means or material to conduct games promising monetary profit. Under this prohibition it would seem that gambling is understood as a game that promises monetary profit to the winners.

2.2 What is the legal definition of online gambling and what falls within this definition?
Under Article 25(b), games of chance are defined as games where the result is dependent on luck and where there are monetary profits for the winners. The Law also defines as games of chance, games where betting can be conducted. It would follow that online gambling includes games of chance where betting can be conducted online.

2.3 Please set out the different gambling products identified by legislation.
Pursuant the provisions of Law 2206/1994, there are no casino game limits when it comes to money that can be bet. There is however, a list of games allowed in land-based casinos under Article 3(7), ie blackjack, French and American roulette, baccarat, punto banco, craps, VLTs, chemin de fer and other games that exist in the US or in the EU following a decision by the Ministry of Development. For online casinos, the law provides no limits whatsoever.

2.4 Please list the different requirements for each gambling product, including legal classifications for each; for example, is poker a game of skill or game of chance?
Poker is not mentioned either in Law 2206/1994 or in Law 4002/2011. It is provided by online casinos and is considered *de facto* a game of chance, although there is no case law confirming that. Under Law 2206/1994 Article 3(7), other games existing in the US and in the EU can be played in land casinos. This is why poker can be played in Greece in land and online casinos. Law 4002/2011 is silent regarding mini casinos, and it can safely be concluded that there will be no poker played in mini casino establishments when they are created. No poker rules have been set in Greece so far.

Article 41 of Law 4002/2011 provides no rules for slot machines. It only provides that the specifications for game machines can be defined and modified by a decision of the HGC, ensuring their secure, lawful operation and their monitoring. The only categorisation of slot machines is mentioned in Article 39 of the Law 4002/2011 where it is provided that 35,000 licences will be issued for gaming machines; 16,500 of which will be given to OPAP with the other 18,500 to be sub-licensed to other enterprises following international tender. Under Law 4002/2011 Article 32(2) the minimum cost of participating in games of chance through game machines is10 cents and the maximum is EUR 2, and mini casinos may include only VLTs. The HGC may issue slot machine rules when it issues its Code on Gaming.

Law 4002/2011 provides no particular betting regulations; nonetheless online betting is allowed pursuant to the provisions of the Law.

There are no regulations on remote lottery offers like bingo.

There are also no provisions specifically on sports betting in law 4002/2011.

2.5 Explain the system of regulation of gambling; which regulatory or governmental body is responsible for the supervision of gambling? Which body issues licences? Which body examines enforcement powers? Is there any limit on the number or duration of available licences?

Article 3(1) of Law 2206/1994 provides for HGC to supervise the operation of land casinos. As it concerns mini casinos and online casinos, pursuant to Article 28 of Law 4002/2011, it is expected that the HGC will issue the rules on conducting and gaming control and a code on gaming. Under Article 31(5) the HGC determines the amounts that the licensees should have in a credit or payment institution which is located and legally operating in Greece. The licensee and the HGC are obliged to maintain the information received from the gaming machines or the online games for at least 10 years in a safe medium.

3. ONLINE GAMBLING

3.1 To what extent can online gambling be offered in your jurisdiction? Are licences available and, if so, for which gambling products? Please describe briefly the licensing process, who may apply, whether licences are limited in number and, if no licences are available, whether it is legal for online gambling to be offered. In the case of EU jurisdictions, please state whether there are any issues as to the legality of the local law at EU level. Please refer to any relevant cases at ECJ level and explain any measures taken or pending by the European Commission.

Online gambling can be offered by legal entities which have a licence. So far, however, there has been no competitive tender and companies that are registered in Greece and have paid taxes on their profits from 2010-2011 can legally operate for the time being. Operating games of chance over the internet shall only be permitted in Greece where a special licence has been obtained. The operating conditions and the technical characteristics of servers and software for such licensed games of chance are set by the

HGC. Members of the HGC were appointed by Ministerial Decision no. 55906/1673/20-12-2011 signed by the Minister of Finance.

For the issuance and renewal of a licence for gaming with game machines or via the internet, and for the operation of games machines, a fee for participation in the public licensing process should be paid pursuant to Articles 39 and 46 of the Law 4002/2011 along with the price for the licence, as set during the procurement process. For the certification of gaming services, game machines and shops in which technical entertainment gaming or gaming through game machines is conducted, a fee upon request should be paid along with a one-off fee for the certification of the game, game machine or shop.

As for the online betting licensing procedure, the Minister of Finance shall publish a decision announcing a contest for an unspecified number of licences. The licences shall be granted following an international highest bidder tender procedure. If all available licences are not awarded, the licences not awarded shall be put out to tender again by a decision of the Minister of Finance after at least one year. The licence for running online games shall be valid for five years from the date of award and shall include terms and conditions under which the activities for which it is issued may be carried on. At least one year before the end of each valid licence, the licence-holder may submit an application to the HGC requesting an extension of the licence for a period of time equal to or shorter than its term, under the same conditions but at a different price. In order to renew the licence it shall be essential that the terms of the licence were properly implemented, and that a reasonable price is proposed. The procedure for setting the new price shall be laid down by decision of the Minister of Finance.

No contractor may hold more than one licence. Licences are personal and non-transferable. The leasing or joint exploitation of a licence with third parties is prohibited. Participation in the tender procedure is open to capital companies with a paid-up share capital of at least EUR 200,000. In order to participate in the international tender procedure for a licence, it shall be necessary to submit a guarantee letter (participation bond) for EUR 100,000 from a bank established and operating lawfully in Greece.

Licence-holders shall be legal entities whose registered offices or permanent place of establishment is in Greece and shall be taxed in accordance with the general provisions of the Act.

The following amounts shall be paid in order for the licence to be issued: (i) the price of the licence; and (ii) an advance in lieu of the state's participation, in accordance with Article 32(6) of the Act.

Websites used to host online games are obliged to have a domain name ending in .gr.

As already mentioned, the licence holder shall be obliged to save data in real time on hardware located in Greece, such as data relating to the running of online games and data exchanged between the player, licence holder, internet service provider, and financial institutions relating to online gaming. Data shall be held on a secure medium, which permits the data saved to be accurately reproduced by the HGC; the retention period being at least 10 years. The Gaming Operations and Control Rulebook may specify a longer time period.

The person operating games of chance websites shall necessarily run those websites as well.

Ministerial Decision no. 1248/13-01-2011, which had been issued enforcing Article 50 of Law 4002/2011, provided clearly and explicitly for the companies providing online gaming services that are legally established in member states of the EU or within the European Economic Area (not in Greece) and simultaneously granted a legal licence for these purposes (ie from the state of their legal seat) that they would be able to continue to offer such services in Greece in the same way they did pending the international tender declaration and the granting of the licence by payment.

So far there are no available licences and a new ministerial decision is expected to that end. Companies not legalising their activities in Greece for years 2010 and 2011 would be put on an HGC 'black list', but if they do legalise them, they must 'keep the door open' by applying for a licence when the ministerial decision is issued, otherwise they will have severe difficulties getting a licence in the future.

All the requirements and the cost for a licence to operate over the internet will be specified by a new ministerial decision in the future. The said licences will be granted upon an international tender. The tender notice shall include the following information as a minimum:

- the number of licences to be issued;
- the deadline within which interested parties may request the relevant documents from the body responsible for the tender procedure;
- the body responsible for opening tenders, the date on which/place at which they will be opened, and the persons entitled to be present;
- the type, quantity, currency, and time at which participation bonds, and any other collateral which may be requested, are to be submitted;
- the information and supporting documents showing that the minimum financial and technical conditions laid down in the tender notice have been complied with;
- the deadline within which tenders may be submitted and the address to which they must be submitted;
- the period for which tenders remain valid;
- the inviolable terms which will result in a tender being rejected if that term is not complied with;
- the selection criteria relating to the personal status of candidates which will lead to their disqualification and the information required to demonstrate that candidates do not fall within the scope of those grounds for disqualification;
- the minimum start price for the highest bidder tender procedure;
- a draft version of the licence to be issued; and
- any other modalities relating to the holding of the tender procedure.

The Greek law 4002/2011 received several objections because it guarantees an unfair advantage to the state-owned online gambling monopoly of OPAP.

More specifically, the proposed law spoke of 25,000 game machines conducting games of chance, whereas Article 39(2) of the Act specifies 35,000 game machines. However, while OPAP was not mentioned in the proposed law, in Article 39 of the Act, OPAP's role is vital given that OPAP has been granted a licence for 35,000 game machines of which 16,500 are controlled by OPAP and the rest are given to tenderers by OPAP.

Moreover, the Act requires that operators are obliged to cease all forms of activity in Greece for six months before they can apply for a licence, a requirement presenting a huge unfair advantage to OPAP, ie an organisation which constitutes a state-owned online gambling monopoly.

The European Commission objected that the Act is contrary to EU practices, given that it limits the presence of foreign companies in the country, because it requires each company wishing to operate in Greece to use Greek financial institutions for all their translations.

The first company to react against the Act was the British gambling company Betfair, which filed a complaint to the European Commission indicating that the Act is extremely protectionist and infringes EC legislation. The Remote Gambling Association (RGA) has also questioned the legality of new gambling legislation in Greece. Clive Hawkswood, Chief Executive of the RGA, said: *'We are fully aware of the fiscal pressures on the Greek authorities at present, but they do not justify the imposition of anti-competitive tax provisions which benefit the existing monopoly gambling provider over private online operators soon to be licensed in Greece'*.

3.2   Is there a distinction between the law applicable to B2B operations and that applicable to B2C operations?

There is no distinction whatsoever between B2B and B2C operations.

3.3   What are the consequences for B2C or B2B operators who are active in your jurisdiction without having obtained or applied for the required permits, licences and approvals? What penalties and enforcement powers are available in respect of the illegal operators? Please outline any significant domestic decisions or enforcement actions that have been taken by the relevant authorities in recent years.

The Law provides severe criminal and administrative penalties for companies and individuals that gamble illegally.

Non licence-holders are prohibited from developing and running websites. The running of betting exchanges is also prohibited. The running of games of chance in Greece via other audiovisual or electromagnetic media shall only be permitted where a special licence is first obtained.

Pursuant to Article 51(3), operators conducting games of chance without using Individual Player Cards are punished with a fine of between EUR 5,000 to 7,000 per violation.

Under Article 51(5), ISPs legally seated in Greece are obliged to block access to illegal gambling sites. Under Article 51(6) licensees not establishing a connection with the 'Informational System of Supervision and Control via the Central Information System' are punished with a fine of between

EUR 100,000 to 500,000 and their licence may be recalled temporarily or permanently.

Under Article 52(2) criminal penalties are also provided for advertisers or advertisees of games of chance carried out without a licence, with imprisonment of two years minimum and a penalty of EUR 100,000 to 200,000. There are also criminal penalties for players participating in unlicensed games of chance pursuant to Article 52(3) who are punished with up to three months' imprisonment and a penalty from EUR 5,000 to 20,000.

There are administrative penalties pursuant to Article 51 of the Law for violation of its provisions or of its regulatory decisions issued under the motion or conditions of licences. The HGC can impose a fine of between EUR 1,000 to 2,000,000 or a percentage of gross receipts, per violation or per game machine, depending on the severity and frequency of the offence; or the licence can be recalled temporarily for up to three months, or permanently.

Moreover, illegal operators of games of chance face criminal penalties provided under Article 52, which states that anyone conducting gaming activities without having the necessary licence to do so will be punished with imprisonment of not less than three years and with a penalty of between EUR 100,000 to 200,000 per game machine or, in the case of gaming carried out through the internet with a penalty of between EUR 200,000 to 500,000. In the case of games of chance, the offence is punished with imprisonment of not more than 10 years.

3.4 What technical measures are in place (if any) to protect consumers from unlicensed operators, such as ISP blocking and payment blocking?

No one can provide online games in Greece without a .gr website. Any websites without a .gr domain name ending are blocked when found and put on a blacklist. This is the main technical measure ensuring consumers' protection from unlicensed operators, given that a website using a .gr domain name ending can be controlled at any time and may be blocked if deemed necessary. MasterCard, Visa and PayPal may be informed and block transactions between consumers and unlicensed operators; however, the government has not yet used such a measure.

3.5 Has the legal status of online gambling changed significantly in recent years and, if so, how?

No legal framework for online gambling existed before Law 4002/2011.

3.6 Whilst acknowledging the inherent difficulty in predicting developments in gambling law, what are the likely developments in online gambling in your jurisdiction, both short term and long term? Are any specific amendments under consideration? Have there been any recent political developments, or do you envisage any in the near future? Are any specific amendments under consideration? Are they likely to be adopted and, if so, what is the time scale?

The Law 4002/2011 constitutes new legislation and there are no amendments under consideration so far. There are no political developments yet as far as gambling law is concerned and no changes are envisaged in the future. It is thus rather unlikely that any amendments will be adopted any time soon.

3.7 Is the law the same in relation to mobile gambling and interactive gambling on television? If not, are there any headline differences?

The Law makes no distinctions, given that it is applicable to both mobile gambling and interactive gambling on television.

4. LAND-BASED GAMING

4.1 Please describe the licensing regime (if any) for land-based gaming, and what products are included. Please set out what licences are available, and the licensing regime for them.

Casinos have existed since 1994. These are also gambling venues that will open shortly providing gaming machines. There are two Laws that relate to casino gaming in Greece, namely Law 2206/1994 and Law 4002/2011. Casinos have legally operated in Greece since 1994 and online casinos began operating in 2010; however, a legal framework to cover the void concerning online casino operation, which simultaneously introduced provisions for the introduction of mini casinos, was only provided in 2011.

So far there are three types of casinos in Greece: land-based casinos; casino shops or mini casinos; and online casinos. Other than land casinos which include under Law 2206/1994 Article 3(7) blackjack, French and American Roulette, baccarat, punto banco, craps, VLTs, chemin de fer and other games that exist in the US or in the EU following a decision by the Ministry of Development, casino shops exist currently on paper and when created they will be shops containing VLTs (video lotto game machines). OPAP is expected to create casino shops to be known as 'GOLD'. So far no mini casinos exist yet. Other companies are expected to follow in 2013 to purchase VLT licences from OPAP and create their own casino shops. Online casinos have existed since 2010 though there was no legal framework supporting or prohibiting their operation. Certain of them (16 in total) have paid tax to the Greek Government for retrospective earnings in 2010 and 2011 and are allowed to operate legally in Greece until a tender procedure follows to issue online gambling licences. So far there has been no ministerial decision on any tender procedure.

Article 39(2) of Law 4002/2011 provides for 35,000 game machines (VLTs), 16,500 of which are controlled by OPAP, with the remaining machines subject to international tender. Pursuant to Article 42(2a) OPAP's shops are considered to be exclusive shops if they follow the terms and conditions set by the Code for Conducting and Monitoring of Games.

Pursuant to Article 39(4) the licence lasts for 10 years following its award. Licences are personal and non-transferable and they are issued on certain conditions; for example, under Article 31(5) of the Law the HGC determines by decision the amounts the licensees should have in a credit or payment institution located and legally operating in Greece. Article 38(3) determines that non-profit legal entities are not allowed to be issued a licence for technical entertainment games with game machines. As it concerns online betting the licence holder shall be obliged to comply with the player accounts terms and conditions as laid down in the Gaming Operations and Control Rulebook. Moreover, pursuant to Article 30(5) and (6), the licensee is obliged to maintain the information he receives from the game machines or the online game for at least 10 years in a safe medium allowing the accurate reproduction of the stored data by the HGC.

In any case, licence holders shall be legal entities whose registered offices or permanent place of establishment is Greece and they shall be taxed in accordance with the general provisions of Law 2238/1994 as in force at any given time. They also shall be prohibited from being affiliated companies. The Law provides that any *intra vivos* transfer of shares in a company holding a licence for games of chance played on gaming devices equal to or greater than 2 per cent of its share capital shall be notified to the HGC within a deadline of 15 days from such transfer. If a transfer could lead to a direct or indirect change in control of the company, the prior approval of the HGC shall be required, and where no such approval is provided the transfer shall not be deemed lawful and shall not generate legal consequences. The same obligation to notify the HGC applies when shares in the company are transferred on the basis of hereditary succession.

Payments of the amounts bet and the payouts resulting from participation in games of chance are conducted via financial institutions with head offices in Greece. The account number of every licence holder shall be assigned a special code which shall be notified to the HGC. Every banking transaction concerning online games of chance shall be independently recorded by the related financial institutions. The amount deposited in the players' account must, at least, be equal to the total amount which is credited to the online player accounts. If the amount deposited in the players' accounts is below the total amount credited to the online player accounts held by the licence holder, the licence holder will supplement that shortfall within three days. The amount bet to enable a player to participate in an online game of chance shall be paid to the authorised licence holder in a way safeguarding the identity of the player, in the manner specifically laid down in the Gaming Operations and Control Rulebook. Financial institutions whose registered head office is in Greece in accordance with the general provisions of Law 2238/1994, as in force at any given time, are prohibited from making payments of bets and winnings from participation in games of chance to accounts held at those institutions by illegal online gaming providers named in the relevant blacklist kept by the HGC.

4.2 Please set out any particular limitations or requirements for (eg casino) operators, such as a ban on local residents gambling.
There are no particular limitations or requirements for operators.

4.3 Please address the questions in 3.5 above, but in relation to land-based gaming.
There have been no significant changes to land-based gaming since the enforcement of Law 2206/1994.

5. TAX
5.1 Please summarise briefly the tax regime applicable both to land-based and online gaming.
Pursuant to Law 4002/2011 Article 50(5) the participation of the Greek Government, which is calculated on the turnover of the licence holder or the operator of the licence, upon the ongoing technical entertainment gaming and games of chance with game machines or via the internet is calculated at 30 per cent. Pursuant to Article 50(9) players are taxed at 10 per cent.

There was heavy criticism of the 30 per cent tax rate on gross profits amid fears that it would make the market unprofitable.

According to the provisions of the Law 4002/2011, the Minister of Finance has the power to legalise the previous activities of companies which offered internet gambling in Greece and which have their seat in the EU or within the EEA.

Indeed, the Minister of Finance issued Ministerial Decision no. 1248/13-12-2011, under which companies can retrospectively legalise their activities for 2010 and 2011 by voluntarily submitting to the Greek tax system.

These companies have been issued a Greek VAT number. They are obliged to submit annual tax returns and they must submit all the necessary documents proving their activities and their profits in Greece for 2010 and 2011.

The companies will pay to the Greek state 30 per cent of their gross gaming revenue gained in Greece and they will be free to act in Greece legally, until the final implementation of Law 4002/2011. There is also an obligation for the submission of annual tax returns and the specification of profits.

Players' winnings from games of chance played in Greece via the internet shall be subject to tax, computed at a rate of 10 per cent. This tax shall be withheld and paid over by companies to the competent tax authority the month after the date of payment of the profit to the players.

Although this decision came rather late many companies tried to comply with it in order to ensure that in the future they will be granted a gambling licence; nonetheless a ministerial decision to that end does not yet exist.

6. ADVERTISING
6.1 To what extent is the advertising of gambling permitted in your jurisdiction? Again, this should cover both land-based and online gaming. To the extent that advertising is permitted, how is it regulated?
The Law 4002/2011 regulates the conditions under which relevant gambling advertising and betting activities is tolerated, with a very strict level of

consumer protection. Article 35 entitled 'Commercial communication' provides limitations on advertisements for gambling games. Nonetheless there is no limitation for leisure games.

Pursuant to Article 29(4), advertising should provide a strict level of consumer protection, and should not be aimed at encouraging active participation based on ambiguous big expected profits. Advertising should provide a very strict level of consumer protection, and should not be aimed at strengthening the natural inclination of consumers to the games by encouraging active participation in them by making the games commonplace or projecting a positive image in relation to the fact that the proceeds are earned for general interest, or increasing the power of attraction of gaming through advertising which relies on expecting misleading significant profits.

Pursuant to Article 52(2), criminal penalties are also provided for advertisers or advertisees of games of chance carried out without a licence, with imprisonment for at least two years and a penalty of EUR 100,000 to 200,000. There are also criminal penalties for players participating in unlicensed games of chance under Article 52(3) who are punished with up to three months imprisonment and a penalty from EUR 5,000 to 20,000.

7. SOCIAL GAMING

7.1 We believe this to be a growing area. Please decide under what criteria social gaming is permitted in your jurisdiction. If games are free to play or if there is no prize, are they legal without a licence? Please address circumstances where virtual currency is used and can be won: ie currency which is of no monetary or other value, save for as credits to take part in games. The answer should address the question whether game credits or virtual money can be exchanged for other prizes. Is any change to regulation in the area proposed or envisaged?

No games are legal to play without a licence, and even technical entertainment games require one. Pursuant to Article 25 of Law 4002/2011 there are two kinds of games: technical entertainment games; and gambling games. All other games played outside casinos, even between families or at social occasions, are considered illegal if they involve money. However, these kinds of game are usually played on New Year's Eve and on that day they are considered a tradition. It is hardly likely that people will be prosecuted if they are found following this tradition. In other circumstances however, things may be different.

Although there should be provisions on social gaming differentiating these types of game, Law 4002/2011 barely scratches the surface. Virtual currency of no monetary value seems to be unregulated; however, as said before, even technical entertainment games require a licence, though not in social gaming.

Ireland

Arthur Cox Rob Corbet & Chris Bollard

1. OBJECTIVES AND STRUCTURE OF LEGISLATION

Gambling in various forms has been regulated in Ireland for centuries.
Ireland has always had a significant horseracing industry and there is a rich
cultural history of associated on-course and off-course betting. Bookmakers,
bookmakers' premises and wagering have been regulated since the 18th century
and beyond by various statutes and at common law (where, as with the United
Kingdom prior to 2007, the courts determined, as a matter of public policy,
that wagering contracts should be unenforceable). Ireland has not traditionally
had a casino industry although this has changed to a certain degree since the
early 2000s, with the emergence of 'private members' clubs' offering limited
gaming facilities. Ireland has had sweepstakes since the early part of the 20th
century (notably the Irish Hospitals Sweepstake). There is also a state regulated
prize bonds system and a state regulated national lottery which was launched in
1987, with a new 20 year national lottery licence being awarded in 2014.

From a legislative point of view, gambling in Ireland has primarily fallen
into one of two categories (i) betting or (ii) gaming and lotteries. The legislation
for both codes is under review as the current legislation is out of date and
significant legislative reform is expected in 2014/2015 (see section 3.6).

Betting
Betting is governed primarily by the Betting Act 1931, as amended (the 1931
Act). The 1931 Act was introduced to regulate the bookmaking industry
and it repealed the Betting Act 1926. It also relaxed certain prohibitions
on betting that were contained in the Betting Act 1853. The purpose of
the 1931 Act generally was to allow for and regulate the profession of
'bookmaking'.

Tote (pari-mutuel) betting is governed primarily by the Totalisator Act
1929 and the Irish Tote has been operated as a state monopoly since then.

Modern betting inventions such as betting exchanges have not
traditionally been specifically regulated although this is due to change (see
section 3.6).

Gaming and lotteries
Gaming and lotteries (aside from the National Lottery) are governed
primarily by the Gaming and Lotteries Acts 1956 to 2014, as amended (the
1956 Act). Under the 1956 Act, gaming in general is prohibited unless it falls
under one of two types of exemptions. The first type of exemption relates
to gaming which takes place in the context of circuses, travelling shows or

carnivals. The second type of exemption is more general and relates to the way in which the game is operated.

The 1956 Act was introduced to repeal and replace a series of individual 19th century gaming and lotteries acts. The 1956 Act was innovative in so far as it regulated both areas in a short single piece of legislation. Although generally viewed today as a rather archaic and unhelpful statute in its own right, it repealed much earlier legislation including an Act for Suppressing of Lotteries (1698) (10. Will. III, c. 23).

The 1956 Act is technically (and in some respects practically) applicable to online gaming, but it was obviously not drafted with online gaming in mind. Legislative changes are expected to fully regulate and tax online gambling in all forms (see section 3.6 for further details).

Lotteries, aside from the National Lottery, are permitted, though only to the narrow extent allowed for under the 1956 Act.

The largest and most lucrative lottery is the Irish National Lottery which has been historically operated by a subsidiary of the Irish Post Office (An Post). In 2013, the Irish government held a competitive tender process to award a new 20 year licence to operate the National Lottery. The winner of this process was a consortium involving An Post and led by the UK national lottery operator, Camelot. The licence was agreed and signed in February 2014, and very shortly thereafter the government commenced the National Lottery Act 2013 (the 2013 Act). The 2013 Act repealed and replaced the terms of the National Lottery Act 1986. The most notable feature of the 2013 Act is the establishment of a new office – the Regulator of the National Lottery. The primary functions of the Regulator of the National Lottery are to ensure that the National Lottery is run with all due propriety, to ensure that participants interests are protected and to ensure that the long-term sustainability of the National Lottery is safeguarded.

2. FRAMEWORK OF LEGISLATION
2.1 What is the legal definition of gambling and what falls within this definition?
As mentioned above, Irish law distinguishes between betting, gaming and lotteries.

'Betting' has not been tightly defined by statute. Section 1 of the 1931 Act simply provides that *'the word 'bet' includes wager, and cognate words shall be construed accordingly'*. The scope of this definition has fallen to be determined at common law by the courts although case law is relatively rare.

'Gaming' is defined in section 2 of the 1956 Act as meaning '... *playing a game (whether of skill or chance or partly of skill and partly of chance) for stakes hazarded by the players'*.

In turn, a 'stake' is defined in section 2 as including '... *any payment for the right to take part in a game and any other form of payment required to be made as a condition of taking part in the game but does not include a payment made solely for facilities provided for the playing of the game'*.

The 1956 Act defines 'lottery' as including *'all competitions for money or money's worth involving guesses or estimates of future events or of past events the results of which are not yet ascertained or not yet generally known'*.

A more detailed statutory definition of a lottery does not exist, but it has been accepted by the Irish Supreme Court (*Flynn v Denieffe* [1993] 2 IR) that *'a lottery consists of an arrangement for the distribution of prizes by chance where there is no element of skill on the part of the person participating and where there is some payment or consideration by or on behalf of the participant'*.

2.2 What is the legal definition of online gambling and what falls within this definition?

Irish gambling law does not at the present time address online gambling directly (see section 3.6 for details of significant future reform in this area).

2.3 Please set out the different gambling products identified by legislation.

Poker

Poker is not governed by any specific piece of law, but rather falls under the remit of the 1956 Act as a game (partly of skill and partly of chance) which is played for stakes hazarded by players.

Unlike in other common law jurisdictions, where there has been some debate as to whether poker was a game of skill or chance and consequently whether it could fall outside of legislation regulating games of chance, the law in Ireland is clear in that it makes no distinction between games of skill and chance or a combination of both. As such, it is not treated any differently from other types of gaming for the purposes of Irish law. It is nonetheless possible to operate poker games as 'lawful gaming' under the 1956 Act in certain circumstances.

Betting (other than sports betting)

The terms of the 1931 Act are drafted to cover betting which takes place in relation to any event of uncertain outcome. The 1931 Act does not define the act of 'betting' except to say that it includes activities such as wagering.

'Bookmaker' or the 'business of bookmaking' are not currently defined by statute (though see section 3.6 for the details of a proposed new definition of 'bookmaker' to be inserted as an amendment to the 1931 Act). The terms have been interpreted by the courts as requiring a person to enter into wagers as a matter of business and attempting to 'make a book' on a series of events. Another fundamental ingredient of bookmaking would seem to involve the assumption of some level of risk by the bookmaker in relation to the outcome of an event (notwithstanding that the bookmaker may manage this exposure to risk through laying some or all of the stakes received). In the High Court case of *Mulvaney & Ors v The Sporting Exchange Ltd trading as Betfair* [2009] IEHC 133 (18 March 2009), Clarke J observed as follows:

'While bookmaking is not defined in that legislation it seems to me that the term bookmaker derives from a person or body 'making a book' on an event. In other words, the person or body concerned offers odds on all or a significant

number of eventualities arising in respect of the same event (for example, offers odds on each horse winning or offers odds on either team winning a football game, or, indeed that game resulting in a draw). Thus, a person carrying on the business of bookmaking is someone who habitually offers to cover a range of possible eventualities on future uncertain events. Two private individuals entering into a wager on the same future uncertain event could not remotely be said to be engaged in the business of bookmaking.'

It is for this reason that a fixed odds bookmaker in Ireland who offers odds on a particular sports event is required to be licensed as a bookmaker (and to pay betting duty) whereas betting exchanges which simply offer facilities to allow punters to bet with each other have not to date been considered 'bookmakers' under Irish law. The bookmaker takes a position on an event and accepts wagers which he can then choose to lay or hedge if he so wishes. An exchange on the other hand assumes no risk in relation to the event and will simply take its commission regardless of the outcome of the matched bet.

The concept of a 'remote betting intermediary' was introduced by section 49 of the Finance Act 2011 to capture betting exchanges for tax purposes for the first time. The draft legislation which is required to licence and regulate remote betting service providers and betting intermediaries had not been enacted at the time of writing, but is expected to be passed shortly (see section 3.6 for further details).

Sports betting
Sports betting is treated in the same way as non-sports betting.

Casino games
Casino style games (such as blackjack or roulette) would fall under the broad definition of 'gaming' under the 1956 Act. They are not directly addressed by legislation however.

Anti-money laundering procedures in Ireland are governed by the terms of the Criminal Justice (Money Laundering and Terrorist Financing) Act 2010 (as amended) (the Criminal Justice Act). Section 25(1) of the Criminal Justice Act classifies, amongst others, the following categories of persons acting in the state as 'designated persons':
(a) casinos; and
(b) a person who effectively directs a private members' club at which gambling activities are carried on, but only in respect of those gambling activities.

This reflects the somewhat unusual position in Irish law whereby casinos (which are not technically permitted by the terms of the 1956 Act) are nevertheless regulated for anti-money laundering purposes.

Slot and other machine gaming
The prohibition on slot machines originally contained in the 1956 Act (section 10) was repealed in 1970. Section 43 of the Finance Act 1975 (as

amended) provides that a person who makes a gaming machine available for play must have a gaming machine licence for each gaming machine.

Bingo
Bingo is generally considered to be a lottery under Irish law.

Lottery
Lotteries (aside from the National Lottery) are addressed directly by the 1956 Act. The National Lottery is governed by the terms of the National Lottery Act 2013.

Tote betting
Pari-mutuel betting is governed by the Totalisator Act 1929 (as amended).

Prize bonds
The government backed 'Prize Bond' scheme was established by the Finance (Miscellaneous Provisions) Act 1956 and operates outside the scope of the 1956 Act.

Spread betting
Spread betting on financial instruments is governed by the Markets in Financial Instruments Directive (2004/39/EC) and regulated by the Irish Central Bank. The regulatory and tax treatment of spread betting on sports or other events is less clear pending the reform of the gambling laws.

2.4 Please list the different requirements for each gambling product, including legal classifications for each; for example, is poker a game of skill or game of chance?
Poker
As we have noted above, poker is regarded as a game partly of skill and partly of chance and therefore classified as a type of gaming. As a common law jurisdiction, Irish courts tend to be persuaded by case law in other common law jurisdictions. In this regard, cases such as the New Zealand case of *Aristocrat Gambling Technology Limited v Police* [1988] 1 NZLR 276 would support the contention that poker is a game of skill as well as chance. If the issue were ever to come before an Irish court (and it has not so far), this and similar cases would have persuasive value.

Betting (other than sports betting)
See section 2.3.

Sports betting
See section 2.3.

Casino games
See section 2.3.

Slot and other machine gaming

The Finance Act 1975 (as amended) defines a gaming machine as a machine:

(a) constructed or adapted for gaming;
(b) the player pays to play the machine whether by the insertion of a coin or token or in some other way; and
(c) the outcome of the game is determined by the action of the machine, whether or not provision is made for manipulation of the machine by the player.

The legislation excludes video game machines (which merely provide the player with the opportunity to play again if they win) and machines that offer non-monetary prizes or prizes of a low monetary value.

Bingo

Bingo is considered a lottery as it fulfils the definition of 'lottery' under the 1956 Act. Namely, it is a *'competition for money or money's worth involving guesses or estimates of future events or of past events the results of which are not yet ascertained or not yet generally known'.*

Lottery

See above.

Tote betting

Under the Totalisator Act 1929 'Totalisator' means *'an apparatus or organisation by means of which an unlimited number of persons can each stake money in respect of a future event on the terms that the amount to be won by the successful stakers is dependent on or to be calculated with reference to the total amount staked by means of the apparatus or organisation in relation to that event but not necessarily on the same contingency, and the said word includes all offices, tickets, recorders, and other things ancillary or incidental to the working of the apparatus or organisation.'*

The Totalisator Act provides for the establishment and regulation of the Totalisator by the Revenue Commissioners. Section 34 of the Irish Horse Racing Industry Act 1994 provided that the Irish Horse Racing Authority could apply for and hold a totalisator licence. This was later transferred to Horse Racing Ireland by the Horse and Greyhound Racing Act 2001. The licence is currently held by a subsidiary of Horse Racing Ireland called Tote Ireland. Tote Ireland's current licence is due to run until 2021.

Prize bonds

Government Prize Bonds are regulated separately from other forms of gaming and lotteries (see above at 2.3). They are described by the Finance (Miscellaneous Provisions) Act 1956 as non-interest-bearing securities which are *'subject to such conditions as to repayment, redemption or otherwise as [the Minister] thinks fit and in relation to which chance may be used to select particular securities for prizes.'*

Spread betting

As set out above, spread betting on financial services is governed by the Markets in Financial Instruments Directive (2004/39/EC) and regulated by the Irish Central Bank.

2.5 Explain the system of regulation of gambling; which regulatory or governmental body is responsible for the supervision of gambling? Which body issues licences? Which body examines enforcement powers? Is there any limit on the number or duration of available licences?

The primary enforcers of gambling law in Ireland are the Minister for Justice, An Garda Síochána (the Irish police force) and the Revenue Commissioners (the primary tax authority in Ireland). The National Lottery Act 2013 also established the office of the Regulator of the National Lottery, which has enforcement powers in respect of the National Lottery only.

Bookmakers' licences are issued by the Revenue Commissioners in accordance with the provisions of the 1931 Act.

Horse Racing Ireland is charged under statute with the overall administration of Irish horseracing, (apart from services operated by the Racing Regulatory Body – otherwise known as the Turf Club). Horse Racing Ireland also awards licences to 'on-course' bookmakers. These operate under a separate licensing regime from that which applies to bookmakers operating from licensed bookmakers' premises. On-course bookmakers are subject to the Racecourse Executives' Seniority and Pitch Rules.

It is not possible to obtain a gaming licence to cover casino activity in Ireland, though this position is expected to change in the medium term. The General Scheme of a new Gambling Control Bill proposes to introduce a limited number of land-based casino licences (see sections 3.6 and 4.3 for more detail).

Certain types of lotteries can be operated under a licence issued by a District Court, for which a maximum prize EUR 30,000 per week applies.

Certain other types of lotteries can be operated under a permit issued by a Garda Superintendent, for which a maximum prize EUR 5,000 applies (limited to one lottery per six month period). The prize limits in each case were slightly increased by section 51 of the 2013 Act.

3. ONLINE GAMBLING

3.1 To what extent can online gambling be offered in your jurisdiction? Are licences available and, if so, for which gambling products? Please describe briefly the licensing process, who may apply, whether licences are limited in number and, if no licences are available, whether it is legal for online gambling to be offered. In the case of EU jurisdictions, please state whether there are any issues as to the legality of the local law at EU level. Please refer to any relevant cases at ECJ level and explain any measures taken or pending by the European Commission.

Insofar as a form of gambling is legal under the 1956 Act or the 1931 Act, there is no prohibition per se to it being offered online. While these Acts do not expressly apply to online gaming, it is clear that the Irish authorities consider them to extend to online gaming.

There is at present no tax or regulatory framework which would apply specifically to gambling online. This position is due to change however, and a discussion of future reforms in this area is contained below in section 3.6.

Currently, it is very common for operators which are licensed overseas (for example, in the Isle of Man , Alderney, Malta or Gibraltar) to provide gambling services to Irish consumers. The purpose of locating offshore tends to be a dual one; to avoid the application of Irish betting duty and to ensure that the service is operated in a jurisdiction where it is licensed under a modern regulatory framework. Politically the Irish government has indicated that it is keen to establish a modern licensing regime to encourage reputable online operators to establish or to relocate in Ireland. Such companies could then avail of Ireland's attractive tax rates and various other benefits that arise in an English speaking EU member state located in the eurozone. While some online gambling operators have done so, the absence of a modern legislative regime has hindered development.

3.2 Is there a distinction between the law applicable to B2B operations and that applicable to B2C operations?

Irish law does not recognise a distinction between the law applicable to B2B versus B2C operators. In practical terms, white-labelling and other devices are used to ensure that online gambling activities are located and structured in a manner that does not offend Irish law. Obviously specialist local legal and tax advice is required.

The current text of the General Scheme of the Gambling Control Bill 2013 proposes that entities supplying certain equipment or services to the providers of licensed gambling services in Ireland would in future have to register with the Office for Gambling Control, Ireland (this assumes that the legislation is passed in its current form – see section 3.6 for further details).

3.3 What are the consequences for B2C or B2B operators who are active in your jurisdiction without having obtained or applied for the required permits, licences and approvals? What penalties and enforcement powers are available in respect of the illegal operators? Please outline any significant domestic decisions or enforcement actions that have been taken by the relevant authorities in recent years.

Offences under the 1956 Act are generally punishable by a small fine of EUR 127 and/or three months' imprisonment. We are not aware of any prison sentences in recent years for breach of the 1956 Act.

Section 45 of the 1956 Act provides that where an offence is committed by a body corporate or by a person purporting to act on behalf of a body corporate or an unincorporated body of persons and is proved to have been so committed with the consent or approval of, or to have been facilitated by any default on the part of, any person being, in the case of a body corporate, a director thereof, or, in the case of an unincorporated body, a member of the committee of management or other controlling authority thereof, that person will also be guilty of the offence.

Section 2 of the 1931 Act provides that any person who carries on business or acts as a bookmaker in contravention of the section and every person who holds himself out or represents himself to be a bookmaker or a licensed bookmaker in contravention of the section will be guilty of an offence and will be liable on summary conviction to an excise penalty of EUR 1,900. No term of imprisonment is provided for in the 1931 Act for an offence under section 2. Proposed reforms to the 1931 Act will increase these penalties (for further details, see section 3.6).

The most significant case in recent years which deals with regulation of lotteries is *Omega Leisure Ltd v Barry & ors* [2012] IEHC 23. Omega Leisure had entered agency agreements with various charities (who held charitable lottery licences) for the provision of lottery services. An Garda Síochána challenged the provision of lottery services in this manner by a large bingo-hall operator such as Omega Leisure. The case turned on whether an operator could provide lottery services for and on behalf of charities who held lottery licences. The High Court found that this did not offend the terms of the 1956 Act provided that the relevant prize limits and other conditions in the 1956 Act were adhered to.

The force of Irish laws and regulations generally do not apply to operators who are fully licensed overseas but whose services are available remotely in Ireland. This is dependent on a number of factors, including the requirement that the contract between the promoter and the player not be entered into in Ireland. This position as it relates to betting is subject to proposed reform however (see section 3.6 for further details).

The National Lottery Act 2013 considerably increased penalties for breaches of the national lottery legislation. For example, section 46 of the 2013 Act creates an offence for any person other than the National Lottery licensee using the term 'national lottery' and a breach is subject, in the case of conviction on indictment, to a fine of up to EUR 50,000, while section 35 enables the National Lottery Regulator to apply to the High Court to impose financial sanctions on the operator of the National Lottery.

3.4 What technical measures are in place (if any) to protect consumers from unlicensed operators, such as ISP blocking and payment blocking?

Currently, there are no technical measures in place to protect consumers from unlicensed operators. However, the package of reforms discussed below in section 3.6 includes a number of such technical measures. For example, under section 23 of the Betting (Amendment) Bill 2013 (as currently drafted), court orders may be obtained against unlicensed bookmakers, remote bookmakers or remote betting intermediaries which would prohibit credit institutions from transacting with them. Orders may also be obtained against ISPs and telecommunications service providers which would compel them to block access to unlicensed betting websites.

Financial transaction and ISP blocking are also provided for in the General Scheme of the Gambling Control Bill (discussed below); however, the scope and precise detail of the measures are yet to be finalised.

3.5 Has the legal status of online gambling changed significantly in recent years and, if so, how?

Currently online gambling does not receive any special treatment under Irish law, nor is it specifically taxed. This is due to change in the short term and draft legislation in relation to betting has been presented to government with a view to enactment in 2014/2015 (see below at section 3.6).

3.6 Whilst acknowledging the inherent difficulty in predicting developments in gambling law, what are the likely developments in online gambling in your jurisdiction, both short term and long term? Are any specific amendments under consideration? Have there been any recent political developments, or do you envisage any in the near future? Are any specific amendments under consideration? Are they likely to be adopted and, if so, what is the time scale?

The regulation of gambling in Ireland is currently in a state of flux and wholesale changes are expected in the short to medium term.

The Betting (Amendment) Bill 2013

In July 2012 the Government published the text of the Betting (Amendment) Bill 2013 (the Betting Amendment Bill). At the time of writing, the Betting Amendment Bill is entering Committee Stage in the Irish parliament. We would expect it to be passed by the Parliament's summer recess of 2014. The main purpose of the Betting Amendment Bill is to bring betting intermediaries (ie betting exchanges) and remote bookmakers (ie internet and mobile betting providers) within the scope of the existing licensing regime. The Betting Amendment Bill also proposes to tax them for the first time. It has been widely speculated that the bill is a temporary measure designed to tax operators in advance of the more sweeping changes which will be implemented by the Gambling Control Bill (discussed below).

Introducing the Betting Amendment Bill to the Houses of the Oireachtas (the Irish parliament), the Minister for Finance, Michael Noonan noted that; '[T]*he fact that off-shore bookmakers were not subject to the betting levy represented a competitive disadvantage to on-shore firms and also narrowed the state's yield from the levy'*.

The bill proposes to extend the existing 1 per cent turnover tax on bookmaker's activities to online and mobile bookmakers. It also proposes to introduce a 15 per cent commission tax on betting exchanges.

The Betting Amendment Bill's most notable features are as follows:
- The current licensing regime for bookmakers will be extended to now include 'remote bookmakers'. In the context of the Betting Amendment Bill, 'remote' includes betting conducted over the internet, the telephone and using telegraphy generally (including

wireless telegraphy). The initial fee for a remote betting licence will be EUR 5,000.

- A licensing regime will be introduced for remote betting intermediaries. They are proposed to be defined as '*a person who, in the course of business, provides facilities that enable persons to make bets with other persons (other than the first mentioned person) by remote means*'.
- The bill proposes to make it illegal to offer betting services (including intermediary betting services) over the internet to customers in Ireland without a remote bookmaker or remote betting intermediary licence.
- Breaches of the above provisions will be punishable by a EUR 5,000 fine on summary conviction. A conviction on indictment will carry a penalty of a EUR 150,000 fine or imprisonment for a term not exceeding five years or both. Interestingly, the bill also provides for prosecutions *in absentia*, in order to cater for prosecutions against overseas bookmakers who fail to present themselves before an Irish court.
- Where a licensing requirement is being breached by a bookmaker, remote bookmaker or remote betting intermediary, it is proposed that the Minister for Justice may seek the following orders in the District Court:
  - an order that credit institutions cease conducting business with the bookmaker, remote bookmaker or remote betting intermediary;
  - an order that advertising in the State on behalf of the bookmaker, remote bookmaker or remote betting intermediary be prohibited;
  - an order that any sponsorship of a sporting event by the bookmaker, remote bookmaker or remote betting intermediary be prohibited; and
  - an order that telecoms providers and internet service providers prohibit access to the websites of the offending remote bookmaker or remote betting intermediary.
- Traditional land-based bookmaking licences will now also allow limited remote betting. The value of remote betting on a standard bookmakers licence may not exceed the lower of EUR 200,000 or 10 per cent of that bookmaker's yearly turnover.
- The term 'bookmaker' is finally proposed to be defined under law as '*a person, who in the course of business, takes bets, sets odds and undertakes to pay out on winning bets*'.
- The Revenue Commissioners will establish and maintain Registers of Licenced Bookmakers and Remote Bookmaking Operations, both of which will be publicly accessible.
- Registered premises (licensed bookmaker's shops) will be permitted to open on any day except on Christmas Day or Good Friday. This will permit licensed betting to take place on Easter Sunday which has been sought by the industry for some time. Registered premises will be forbidden from operating outside the hours of 7.00am to 10.00pm, although this constitutes an extension to existing opening hours.
- The Betting Amendment Bill would also make it an offence for a person below the age of 18 to represent that they are over that age in order to enter into a bet with a bookmaker (including remote bookmakers).

The Gambling Control Bill

In September 2011, the Minister for Justice announced plans for a new gambling bill. In presenting his plans, the Minister noted that *'the present laws are not adequate to deal even with aspects of gambling which they were intended to cover'*. The overall purpose of the gambling bill therefore will be to generally modernise Irish law in this area.

On 15 July 2013, the government finally published the General Scheme for a Gambling Control Bill (the Heads). The Heads are the first step towards a bill which, if enacted, would modernise Ireland's legislative framework for all types of online and land-based gambling. The Heads are extensive, running to 90 pages, and will undoubtedly evolve over time (and this should be borne in mind – it is very unlikely that the Heads will be enacted into law until 2015 at the earliest).

The Heads are intended to bring almost all forms of betting, gaming and lotteries legislation under one new legislative roof and to create a granular licensing regime to cover all main forms of gambling. The Heads will also create a new gambling regulator, the Office of Gambling Control, Ireland (the OGCI), to be funded from licensing fees (the level of which will be determined by OGCI), and will introduce, for the first time, extensive player protection measures.

For the first time in Ireland, the Heads will make it possible to obtain a licence to operate a casino (including remote or online casinos), a new licensing regime will apply to all online betting and gaming operators who do business with Irish customers, and an updated regime will be introduced to govern charitable lotteries, bingo, prize competitions and gaming in retail and amusement locations.

The OGCI will be the licensing body for the 43 new categories of gambling licences and two categories of 'registrations' which are set out in the Heads. Gambling operators who offer any form of gambling by any means to persons in Ireland will require a licence from the OGCI. Those who locate equipment in Ireland may also be covered by a registration system even if they exclude Irish players from their services.

Bookmakers will be permitted to have gaming in their shops, although the provisions that will govern this are not clear at this point. Credit facilities for players are prohibited and the concept of 'player cards' (both physical and virtual) is included in the Heads, but the practicalities of how they will work is unclear.

The government has retained its stance against fixed-odds betting terminals, which would remain prohibited under the new regime. The Minister for Justice and Equality has the power to exclude other classes of games or machines on public policy grounds. Some as yet unspecified gaming machines will be permitted at such retail outlets as catering outlets, bars, shopping centres and airports.

While the Heads state that they are not intended to affect the National Lottery Act 2013, they do propose to introduce several new categories of lottery licences for lotteries that apply at least 25 per cent of the proceeds of sales in aid of a charitable or philanthropic cause. Certain smaller lotteries will be exempt. However, at the higher end, annual licences could be obtained for lotteries having a prize fund in excess of EUR 50,000 per week or EUR 250,000 per month (with a maximum prize fund limit of EUR 400,000 per month). Scratch cards would be subject to a separate annual licence requirement and a maximum prize limit of EUR 1,750. The Heads allow the Minister for Justice and Equality to alter the maximum amounts every 3–4 years.

In contrast with some EU member states, there is no appetite in Ireland to restrict reputable online operators from being licensed in Ireland. Accordingly, there will be no limit on the number of online casinos, bookmakers, betting exchanges, etc that can be licensed. The Heads also anticipate potential mutual recognition of licences held in other countries. However, assessments of applications will include criteria based on views submitted by An Garda Síochána, planning authorities and third parties who respond to the advertisement of a licence and competition law.

The OGCI will have the power to direct the taking of ISP blocking measures to prevent, disrupt or obstruct access to unlicensed remote services. A District Court procedure will be available to enforce internet blocking, and court orders may also include restrictions on advertising, payments services and the freezing of bank accounts.

The Heads allow the OGCI to introduce various player protection measures relating to combating problem gambling (including a self-exclusion register), underage gambling, match fixing, cheating, customer complaints processes and compensation procedures. The OGCI will be assisted by an advisory committee on responsible gaming.

3.7 Is the law the same in relation to mobile gambling and interactive gambling on television? If not, are there any headline differences?
Mobile gambling is treated in the same way as online gambling under Irish law. See section 3 generally.

4. LAND-BASED GAMING
4.1 Please describe the licensing regime (if any) for land-based gaming, and what products are included. Please set out what licences are available, and the licensing regime for them.
Bookmakers
Persons wishing to operate a bookmaking business must obtain a licence to do so in accordance with the conditions set down in the 1931 Act. Bookmakers' licences under the 1931 Act are personal in nature and cannot currently be granted to a company. In practice, employees of the large betting chains obtain them personally as agents for the company. It is proposed in the Betting (Amendment) Bill 2013 that companies be allowed to apply for betting licences.

There are two aspects to obtaining a licence. First, the applicant must obtain a Certificate of Personal Fitness from a member of An Garda Síochána not below the rank of Superintendent. Secondly, a Certificate of Suitability of Premises must be obtained in relation to the building from which the bookmaker will trade. This requirement does not apply to those obtaining 'on-course' only licences.

Under the 1931 Act, a bookmaker's licence can be revoked where a bookmaker is convicted of a crime which would render him or her 'unfit to continue to hold a bookmaker's licence'. The 1931 Act also allows the Minister for Justice to revoke any bookmaker's licence 'at his absolute discretion'. The conditions attaching to licence applications (and revocations) are subject to proposed amendment by the Betting (Amendment) Bill 2013 (see section 3.6 for more details).

Casinos

Ireland currently has no law specifically governing casinos. Mainstream commercial casino games generally constitute unlawful gaming and are generally prohibited under the 1956 Act unless certain narrow exemptions apply.

Though it is not possible to obtain a gaming licence to cover casino activity in Ireland, casinos do operate in Ireland under the auspices of 'private members' clubs'. However, the legal status of those operations is not clear as the private members' clubs exemption only applies to private lotteries, and there is no such 'private gaming exemption' provided for under the 1956 Act. Casinos are illegal if they promote or provide facilities for any kind of gaming that is deemed 'unlawful gaming' for the purposes of the 1956 Act. Section 4(1) of the 1956 Act provides that 'unlawful gaming' includes gaming in which by reason of the nature of the game, the chances of all the players, including the banker, are not equal, or gaming in which any portion of the stakes is retained by the promoter or is retained by the banker otherwise than as winnings on the result of the play.

As mentioned in section 2.3 above, the Criminal Justice (Money Laundering and Terrorist Financing) Act 2010 (as amended) classifies casinos and private members clubs as 'designated persons' for anti-money laundering purposes.

4.2 Please set out any particular limitations or requirements for (eg casino) operators, such as a ban on local residents gambling.

As per our answers above, the area is not currently regulated. Provision has been made in the General Scheme for the Gambling Control Bill for a limited number of small/medium sized casinos.

The Horse and Greyhound Racing Act 2001 repealed the provisions of the 1931 Act which prohibited Irish persons from entering into bets or wagers with persons outside of Ireland.

4.3 Please address the questions in 3.5 above, but in relation to land-based gaming.

The legal status of land-based gaming has not changed in recent years, but it will do quite significantly in the short to medium term. For a general summary, please see section 3.6.

There appears to be no political will to introduce super-casinos in Ireland. The Heads (discussed in section 3.6) instead propose to licence up to 40 casinos, with modest table limits (15) and gaming machine limits (25) per location. Planning permission will also be required for each premises and the location of casinos is subject to public policy restrictions (eg not near hospitals, places of worship or schools). Normal liquor licensing requirements and bar hours will apply.

5. TAX

5.1 Please summarise briefly the tax regime applicable both to land-based and online gaming.

Betting is taxed by way of an excise duty. Bets entered into by a bookmaker are currently taxed at 1 per cent. On-Course/tote bets are not taxed. Bookmakers must also be registered for betting tax before they begin to offer services to the public.

Online betting is not currently taxed unless the operator is established in Ireland and locates its online infrastructure within Ireland. This position is highly likely to change in the short term (see section 3.6 for full details). The Finance Act 2011 contained measures to allow for the extension of the 1 per cent betting duty to remote bookmakers. These taxation provisions are subject to a Ministerial Commencement order which can only be commenced when the Betting (Amendment) Bill 2013 is enacted (expected later in 2014).

When announcing the provision in the Finance Act 2011, the then Irish Minister for Finance estimated that the full year yield from the taxation of remote betting would be around EUR 20 million.

The General Scheme of the Gaming Control Bill 2013 was silent as to taxation and it is expected that considerable further debate on this issue will occur before this bill is passed.

6. ADVERTISING

6.1 To what extent is the advertising of gambling permitted in your jurisdiction? Again, this should cover both land-based and online gaming. To the extent that advertising is permitted, how is it regulated?

Betting

The 1931 Act places several restrictions on a bookmaker's ability to market to the public, in particular in relation to on-premises advertising.

Section 32 of the 1931 Act provides that it shall not be lawful for any person to write, print, publish or knowingly circulate any advertisement, circular or coupon advocating or inviting or otherwise relating to betting on football games, other than in a licensed betting office.

Section 20(1) of the 1931 Act prohibits a bookmaker from setting up or maintaining in or outside his shop *'any attraction (other than the mere carrying on of his business of bookmaking) which causes or encourages or is likely to cause or encourage persons to congregate in or outside such premises'*.

Further, it is prohibited under subsection (3) for a bookmaker to *'proclaim or announce or permit any other person to proclaim or announce in such premises to the persons there present the terms or odds on or at which he is willing to take bets in relation to any particular race, match, or other contest, or in respect of any competitor in any such contest'.*

Subsection (4) also prohibits a bookmaker from exhibiting (or permitting to be exhibited) in or outside his shop (or which is visible from the street) *'any lists or statements of the terms or odds on or at which he is willing to take bets in relation to any particular race, match, or other contest, or in respect of any competitor in any such contest, or lists or statements of the competitors entered for or withdrawn from or taking or likely to take part in any such contest, or statements of facts, news, or forecasts in respect of any such contest, or any other incitement or inducement to bet.'*

The level of compliance with these provisions is relatively low.

The Broadcasting Authority of Ireland (BAI) (an independent statutory organisation responsible for a number of key areas of activity with regard to television and radio services in Ireland) makes special mention of betting in its General Commercial Communications Code (the Code). The Code came into effect on 2 September 2013. It addresses standards with regard to all forms of commercial communication; advertising, sponsorship and teleshopping. Section 8.8.1 of the Code provides that commercial communications that seek to promote services to those who want to bet are acceptable.

Section 8.8.2 provides that such communications may contain the address of the service provider and factual descriptions of the services available but may not contain anything which could be deemed to be an encouragement to bet. Information detailing special offers, discounts, inducements to visit any betting establishment (including online), references to betting odds available or any promotional offer intended to encourage the use of services of this nature are not permitted.

Lotteries
In the case of gaming, the 1956 Act prohibits the promotion of unlicensed lotteries.

Gaming
Advertising commercial gaming websites hosted within Ireland will generally be prohibited as such gaming is unlawful. This would also apply to advertisements placed in the Irish media. Advertisements placed in Ireland, however, in respect of offshore operations made available to Irish residents would be acceptable on the basis that Irish legal jurisdiction would not extend to the offshore operations. There is an argument therefore that advertisements placed in Ireland by offshore operators may be legal as the gaming is not *per se* illegal as it is not taking place in Ireland.

As an EU member state, Ireland is also subject to the evolving case law emanating from the Court of Justice of the European Union in respect of the free movement of services, freedom of establishment etc. While gambling services are generally excepted from normal free movement provisions in the EU Treaty, the case law in this area continues to evolve.

There is no distinction made between sponsorship and affiliate marketing for the purpose of advertising regulations in Ireland and the principles described above under advertising generally will also apply to sponsorship arrangements.

Future Reform
Under the regulatory regime envisaged by the Heads, only the licensed operators would be permitted to advertise gambling services available to Irish players, and various restrictions would apply to how advertising, promotion or sponsorship could take place (with further rules to be issued by the OGCI in the future).

The Betting Amendment Bill contains provisions which would permit a District Court to make an order prohibiting advertising in the state in respect of a bookmaker, remote bookmaker or remote betting intermediary where the provisions of that bill have been breached.

7. SOCIAL GAMING
7.1 We believe this to be a growing area. Please decide under what criteria social gaming is permitted in your jurisdiction. If games are free to play or if there is no prize, are they legal without a licence? Please address circumstances where virtual currency is used and can be won: ie currency which is of no monetary or other value, save for as credits to take part in games. The answer should address the question whether game credits or virtual money can be exchanged for other prizes. Is any change to regulation in the area proposed or envisaged?
Social gaming is not addressed directly in the current Irish legislative regime. Therefore an analysis of social gaming must be done through the lens of the 1956 Act which regulates gaming generally. As a general statement, if social games are free to enter, there is no prohibition on them under Irish law for the simple reason that they would fall outside the definition of gaming under the 1956 Act due to the absence of a 'stake' (being defined as *'any payment for the right to take part in a game ...[but not including] a payment made solely for facilities provided for the playing of the game.'*).

If a social gaming promoter were to offer a game that required an 'entry fee' rather than a stake, this would be permissible but only on the conditions that:
• only one such charge is made per day;
• the charge is of the same amount for all players; and
• the promoter derives no personal profit from the promotion of the game.

In summary, if a game is free to play (or there is a charge but the above conditions are complied with) there will be no breach of the 1956 Act. The provision of prizes has no bearing on a game's legality.

There is no restriction on the use of virtual currency per se but if a player has to use real currency to buy it, it will likely push the game into the realm of illegal gaming.

There are no plans to address social gaming specifically in either of the two pieces of reforming legislation set out in section 3.6 above. That said, the Heads have quite a way to go before they become law, and it is possible that amendments to regulate social gaming could be introduced.

Isle of Man

MannBenham Advocates Limited Miles Benham

1. OBJECTIVES AND STRUCTURE OF LEGISLATION

On the Isle of Man both land-based and online gambling are legal licensable activities regulated by the island's Gambling Supervision Commission (GSC). As a small self-governing island located in the Irish Sea between England and Ireland, to stay economically competitive the Isle of Man has had to adapt to the demands of an ever-changing market. While originally created to provide entertainment to the summer tourists from the United Kingdom and Ireland, the gambling legislation has now been updated and adapted to cater for the internet generation.

The legislation was originally based upon English legislation and principles but it has evolved over time, and in areas such as online gambling the legislation is unique to the island. The legislation is split between land-based activities, such as bookmaking, casino, lotteries and pool betting, and gambling that takes place 'online'.

The first form of 'online' gambling was telephone betting, and a number of international bookmakers had large call centres on the island taking bets from around the world. At the time (the 1990s), there was a restriction upon the number of bookmakers' licences that could be issued, and this stifled growth in the sector as operators who could not obtain licences sought out alternative jurisdictions to operate from, which then quickly became the island's competitors.

In 2001, following demands from leading operators, the island brought in the Online Gambling Regulation Act to enable licences to be issued for regulated online gambling. The legislation proved extremely popular, and it has since been updated to enable most forms of online gambling to be licensed and regulated by the GSC.

The regulatory objectives of the GSC are:

- to ensure that gambling is conducted in a fair and open way;
- to protect children and the vulnerable from being harmed or exploited from gambling; and
- to prevent gambling from being:
  - a source of crime or disorder;
  - associated with crime or disorder; or
  - used to support crime.

Strong anti-money laundering rules are in place to deter the use of online gambling for criminal purposes. Operators are subjected to regular visits from the GSC Inspectors and, as would be expected in a small jurisdiction, a friendly but professional working relationship is maintained between operator and regulator.

2. FRAMEWORK OF LEGISLATION

2.1 What is the legal definition of gambling and what falls within this definition?

The Gambling Supervision Act 2010 gives the following definition of gambling:

'a) *gaming (within the meaning of the Gaming, Betting and Lotteries Act 1988);*
(b) *making, negotiating and receiving bets and wagers;*
(c) *organising, managing, promoting or participating in a lottery;*
d) *supplying or operating controlled machines (within the meaning of the Gaming (Amendment) Act 1984);'*

Gaming is defined in the Gaming, Betting and Lotteries Act 1988 as *'the playing of a game of chance for winnings in money or money's worth, whether or not any person playing the game is at risk of losing any money or money's worth'.*

A 'game of chance' does not include any athletic game or sport, but includes games of chance and skill combined, and pretend games of chance or of chance and skill combined.

2.2 What is the legal definition of online gambling and what falls within this definition?

The Online Gambling Act 2001 (OGRA), section 1 defines online gambling as:

'(a) *any gaming, where any player enters or may enter the game, or takes or may take any step in the game, by means of a telecommunication,*
(b) *the negotiating or receiving of any bet by means of a telecommunication, or*
(c) *any lottery in which any participant acquires or may acquire a chance by means of a telecommunication.'*

A person 'conducts' online gambling where:

'(a) *in the case of gaming or a lottery, he takes part in its organisation, management or promotion;*
(b) *in the case of a bet, he carries on any business involving the negotiating or receiving of the bet; or*
(c) *he maintains, or permits to be maintained, in the island any computer or other device on or by means of which the game or lottery is operated, or the bet is received, as the case may be.'*

A 'telecommunication' is defined as a communication sent, transmitted or received by means of a telecommunication system.

According to section 2 of the Telecommunications Act 1984, a 'telecommunication system' is a system for the conveyance, through the agency of electric, magnetic, electro-magnetic, electro-chemical or electro-mechanical energy, of:

'(a) *speech, music and other sounds;*
(b) *visual images;*
(c) *signals serving for the impartation (whether as between persons and persons, things and things or persons and things) of any matter otherwise than in the form of sounds or visual images; or*
(d) *signals serving for the actuation or control of machinery or apparatus.'*

Telecommunications apparatus which is situated in the island and *'(a) is connected to but not comprised in a telecommunication system; or (b) is connected to and comprised in a telecommunication system which extends beyond the island'* shall be regarded as a telecommunication system and any person who controls the apparatus shall be regarded as running the system.

The definition of online gambling is sufficiently wide to cover most, if not all, forms of online gambling.

2.3 Please set out the different gambling products identified by legislation.

The Gaming Betting and Lotteries Act 1988 identifies the following forms of gambling:
- gaming;
- amusements with prizes;
- betting;
- pool betting;
- totalisator; and
- lottery.

The Casino Act 1986 (and also the Casino (Amendment) Act 1990) relates to casino games. The following games are prescribed and may be played in the gaming rooms of a casino:
- roulette;
- blackjack;
- pontoon;
- punto banco;
- bingo;
- gambling on horse races shown on film or video;
- casino brag;
- poker;
- games of dice;
- baccarat;
- chemin de fer;
- backgammon;
- keno;
- playing on automatic machines;
- wheel of fortune; and
- super pan 9.

The Pool Betting Acts (Pool Betting (Isle of Man) Act 1961, Pool Betting (Isle of Man) Act 1965, Pool Betting (Isle of Man) Act 1970) cover pool betting.

The National Lottery Act 1999 extends the UK National Lottery to the Isle of Man.

2.4   Please list the different requirements for each gambling product, including legal classifications for each; for example, is poker a game of skill or game of chance?

All of the casino games listed above, with the exception of betting on horses, are games of chance or games of chance and skill combined, and fall under the definition of gaming.

Betting, sports betting, tote and pool betting, if conducted online, require the operator to hold an online gambling licence. When conduced by a land-based operator, the operator requires a bookmaker's permit and a betting office licence for betting and sports betting, and for pool betting a pool betting permit is required.

2.5   Explain the system of regulation of gambling; which regulatory or governmental body is responsible for the supervision of gambling? Which body issues licences? Which body examines enforcement powers? Is there any limit on the number or duration of available licences?

The GSC is the regulator of land-based and online gambling. The GSC was established in 1962 and is a statutory board. The GSC comprises the Inspectorate and the Commission. The Inspectorate is a division of the Isle of Man Treasury and is managed by its chief executive. The Commission comprises five independent members of the public who sit once a month and consider licence applications that have been prepared by the Inspectorate and other regulatory matters.

Online gambling licences are granted by the GSC and are issued for a period of five years. There are currently no restrictions on the number of online gambling licences that can be issued.

3.   ONLINE GAMBLING

3.1   To what extent can online gambling be offered in your jurisdiction? Are licences available and, if so, for which gambling products? Please describe briefly the licensing process, who may apply, whether licences are limited in number and, if no licences are available, whether it is legal for online gambling to be offered. In the case of EU jurisdictions, please state whether there are any issues as to the legality of the local law at EU level. Please refer to any relevant cases at ECJ level and explain any measures taken or pending by the European Commission.

Online gambling is legal licensable activity in the Isle of Man. With the exception of spread betting, all forms of online gambling are potentially licensable.

The following forms of gaming when conducted online require an OGRA licence:

- sports books;
- betting exchanges;
- online casino games (roulette, blackjack, slots, etc);
- live dealing;

- peer-to-peer games (poker, bingo, backgammon, mah-jong, etc);
- mobile phone betting;
- fantasy football (or similar);
- financial trading (but not spread betting);
- pari-mutuel and pool betting;
- network gaming;
- lotteries;
- certain spot-the-ball style games; and
- network services.

An application for an online gambling licence needs to be made by an Isle of Man company. The application process is well documented and supported by comprehensive guidance notes. Once completed, the application forms and the required supporting documentation are submitted to the GSC, together with the application fee. After the completion of a vetting process, the applicant is invited to a licensing hearing before the Commission, where the applicant will be advised if a licence will be granted. The successful applicant will need to pay the licence fee before going live.

3.2 Is there a distinction between the law applicable to B2B operations and that applicable to B2C operations?
There is no distinction in law between B2B and B2C operations, where the B2B is a white label with the players contracting with the licensed operator.

The situation as regards B2B providers of gambling services is different as, while potentially licensable, the Online Gambling (Exclusions) Regulations 2010 excludes a wide variety of gambling services from the requirement to hold an online gambling licence.

3.3 What are the consequences for B2C or B2B operators who are active in your jurisdiction without having obtained or applied for the required permits, licences and approvals? What penalties and enforcement powers are available in respect of the illegal operators? Please outline any significant domestic decisions or enforcement actions that have been taken by the relevant authorities in recent years.
If the B2C or B2B operators are actually conducting unlicensed online gambling (as defined in OGRA), then they will be guilty of an offence. Where the office has been committed with the connivance or neglect of any director, manager or secretary of the company, then that individual can be proceeded against and the punishment can be a term of imprisonment.

3.4 What technical measures are in place (if any) to protect consumers from unlicensed operators, such as ISP blocking and payment blocking?
None known.

3.5 Has the legal status of online gambling changed significantly in recent years and, if so, how?
No significant changes.

3.6 Whilst acknowledging the inherent difficulty in predicting developments in gambling law, what are the likely developments in online gambling in your jurisdiction, both short term and long term? Are any specific amendments under consideration? Have there been any recent political developments, or do you envisage any in the near future? Are any specific amendments under consideration? Are they likely to be adopted and, if so, what is the time scale?
None known.

3.7 Is the law the same in relation to mobile gambling and interactive gambling on television? If not, are there any headline differences?
The Isle of Man legislation makes no specific reference to the form of medium upon which the online gambling takes place. Legislative differences between the two mediums are likely to occur in the country where the consumer is based.

4. LAND-BASED GAMING
4.1 Please describe the licensing regime (if any) for land-based gaming, and what products are included. Please set out what licences are available, and the licensing regime for them.
With the exception of lottery and prize machines, land-based gaming is confined to casinos.

A maximum of two casino licences can currently be issued by the island's Council of Ministers. While the licence prescribes the types of games that can be played at the casino (the games are listed above), the island's regulators have adopted a fairly flexible approach, and new varieties of the traditional casino games have been trialled in the island's current sole casino.

Prize machines are subject to a separate licensing regime and low value jackpot slot machines are licensed in public houses.

The National Lottery is available on the island and, apart from small society lotteries, is the only legal lottery operating on the island.

4.2 Please set out any particular limitations or requirements for (eg casino) operators, such as a ban on local residents gambling.
Apart from the standard age restriction of 18, there are no significant limitations or requirements imposed upon operators.

4.3 Please address the questions in 3.5 above, but in relation to land-based gaming.
No significant changes.

5. TAX
5.1 Please summarise briefly the tax regime applicable to both land-based and online gaming.
The current corporate tax rate for Isle of Man gambling companies is 0 per cent.

The Gambling Duty Act 2012 came into force on 1 January 2014 and replaces the former general betting duty, pool betting duty and online gambling duty with a single duty of excise called 'gambling duty'.

Gambling duty is:
* for gross gaming yield not exceeding £20 million per annum = 1.5 per cent;
* for gross gaming yield more than £20 million, but not exceeding £40 million per annum = 0.5 per cent;
* for gross gaming yield exceeding £40 million per annum = 0.1 per cent; and
* for gross gaming yield from pool betting = 15 per cent.

Gross gaming yield is the total amount of all bets or stakes made and the price of all chances sold, less the value of all winnings and prizes due.

6. ADVERTISING
6.1 To what extent is the advertising of gambling permitted in your jurisdiction? Again, this should cover both land-based and online gaming. To the extent that advertising is permitted, how is it regulated?
The Gaming Betting and Lotteries Act 1988, section 7 provides that it is an office for a person to issue or cause to be issued any advertisement:
* that informs the public that gaming takes place on the premises;
* that invites the public to participate in any gaming that is to take place in premises on the island;
* that invites the public to subscribe money or money's worth to be used in gaming on the island or elsewhere; or
* that invites the public to apply for information about facilities for subscribing any money or monies worth.

This wide prohibition on the advertising of gaming is subject to an equally wide set of exemptions, the key ones of which are as follows.
* **Casinos** – a land-based casino may advertise itself and its games. The advertising is controlled and subject to specific casino advertising regulations.
* **Prize machines** – controlled machines, more commonly known as slot machines, may be advertised.
* **Online gambling** – the advertising of online gambling is subject to the provisions of the Online Gambling (Advertising) Regulations 2007.

The advertising of land-based bookmaking is also restricted and the advertising must be in a material form agreeable to the GSC.

Operators of online gambling sites must comply with the Online Gambling (Advertising) Regulations 2007. The regulations list the requirements that an advert must comply with, which includes the following:
* it must not be indecent or offensive;
* it must be based on fact;
* it must not be false, deceptive or misleading;

- it must not be directed at jurisdictions where online gambling is illegal; and
- it must not be directed at persons under 18.

The GSC has the power to direct an operator to stop an advertisement from being published or shown, or to change the advert to comply with the regulations. The penalty for non-compliance with the advertising regulations is a fine of up to £5,000.

7.   SOCIAL GAMING
7.1   We believe this to be a growing area. Please decide under what criteria social gaming is permitted in your jurisdiction. If games are free to play or if there is no prize, are they legal without a licence? Please address circumstances where virtual currency is used and can be won: ie currency which is of no monetary or other value, save for as credits to take part in games. The answer should address the question whether game credits or virtual money can be exchanged for other prizes. Is any change to regulation in the area proposed or envisaged?

While social gaming can be conducted both on- and offline, the real growth in social gaming is online through apps and websites. The definition of online gambling in the Online Gambling Regulation Act 2001 (see above) is, on the face of it, sufficiently wide to include some forms of social gaming.

The definition of bet is:

'"Bet" does not include any bet made or stake hazarded in the course of, or incidentally to, a game of chance'.

This definition implies that a bet does not need to involve the hazarding of a stake, ie risking the loss of money. If this interpretation is correct, then a bet could involve no stake of money or money's worth and the mere act of betting with another would fall within the definition of a bet. This would then catch social gaming that involves the player betting even if that bet uses virtual currency with no monetary value. However, this is just one interpretation; this is a grey area, and the opposite argument could be made to say that where no money is staked and no monetary prizes can be won the act carried out is not in the nature of a bet for the purpose of online gambling. In practice, a lot would turn upon the game itself, how it operates and the nature of the bets. It would be necessary to consider the full functionality of the game in order to determine if it was licensable.

If the game was free to play but included a game of chance as per the definition of gaming (see above), then it would be licensable if the player was able to exchange game credits or virtual money for other prizes as the game would then fall under the definition of gaming.

If the game were a game of chance that did not provide the player with any winnings in money or money's worth, then it would arguably fall outside the definition of gaming. Further, if the game also did not involve the negotiating or receiving of a bet and it was not in the nature of a lottery, then it would fall outside the definition of online gambling and would not be licensable.

Israel

Herzog Fox & Neeman Law Office
Yehoshua Shohat Gurtler, Itzhak Shragay & Ariel Yosefi

1. OBJECTIVES AND STRUCTURE OF LEGISLATION

The Israeli Penal Law 5737-1977 (the Law) prohibits the organising of lotteries, betting and games of chance, as well as operating venues where such activities take place.

Two exceptions to the general ban on gambling contained in Israeli criminal law were introduced over time:

*   in 1951 the Law was amended to allow for the implementation and operation of a national lottery (Mifal Hapayis) which offers scratch cards, a weekly subscription lottery, and various lotteries and raffles. The operations of Mifal Hapayis are supervised and regulated by the Ministry of Finance; and
*   in 1967 the Israel Sports Betting Board (ISBB) was awarded the exclusive right to organise and regulate sports betting for soccer and basketball games only. In recent years, the ISBB's right to conduct betting activities has been expanded to cover additional sporting activities (both local and foreign), as well as wagering on foreign (UK and Irish) horseracing events.

Any profits derived by Mifal Hapayis and the ISBB must be used for specific purposes set out by the law – profits made by Mifal Hapayis are used to fund hospitals, community centres, and educational institutions; the ISBB must allocate its profits to the advancement of amateur sport, the construction of infrastructure, and Olympic sports. Both Mifal Hapayis and the ISBB also offer their services online.

Despite several attempts by political parties and government committees to change the law to allow for the establishment of at least one casino in the country, there are currently no casinos or other terrestrial gambling venues legally operating in Israel. Draft bills introduced in this regard over the years were all eventually rejected by Israel's legislature.

2. FRAMEWORK OF LEGISLATION

2.1 What is the legal definition of gambling and what falls within this definition?

Chapter 12 of the Law, entitled 'Prohibited Games, Lotteries and Betting', contains several provisions related to gambling. The Law contains two main prohibitions relating to gambling, ie a prohibition on organising lotteries, betting and prohibited games (section 225) and a prohibition on participating in prohibited games (section 226). Section 225 provides that a person organising or conducting a prohibited game, lottery or betting is liable to a penalty of up to three years' imprisonment or a fine of up to

NIS 452,200. Section 226 provides that a person playing a prohibited game is liable to a penalty of up to one year's imprisonment or a fine of up to NIS 29,200. It should be noted that section 226 does not refer to betting or lotteries, ie the sanctions on participation are triggered only by playing a 'prohibited game'.

The Law provides the sole statutory definition of the different types of gambling, as follows:

'prohibited game' – a game at which a person may win money, valuable consideration or a benefit according to the result of a game, those results depending more on chance than on understanding or ability;

'place of prohibited games' – premises in which prohibited games are habitually conducted, whether open to the public or only to certain persons; it is immaterial whether those premises are also used for some other purpose;

'lottery' – any arrangement under which it is possible – by drawing lots or in another manner – to win money, valuable consideration or a benefit, more by chance than by understanding or ability;

'betting' – any arrangement under which it is possible to win money, valuable consideration or benefit, by guessing something, including lotteries based on the results of sports matches and contests.

(Translation from 'Penal Law 5737-1977' Aryeh Greenefield, 1996. As there is no official translation of the Israeli Penal Law, translations presented herein do not represent official translations. Adaptations to the translation by Aryeh Greenefield have been made to reflect recent amendments of the law.)

The Law defines three categories of gambling which include 'prohibited games', 'lotteries' and 'betting'. These terms have been given broad definitions which, cumulatively, cover practically all forms of gambling. It is worth noting that the definitions of these categories overlap and consequently certain gambling games may fit more than one category. Conceptually, the primary difference between 'lotteries'/'betting' and 'prohibited games' is that participation in the former is based on a specific arrangement or contract between the offeror and offeree whereas participation in the latter reflects the predetermined rules of a particular game. As such, for 'prohibited games', the chances of winning are determined by the game's rules and the nature of the players' participation in the game. In contrast, 'lotteries' and 'betting' are based upon agreements delineated between two or more parties in connection with an external occurrence or outcome. (Ya'akov Kedmi, *On Criminal Law*, 1995, pp. 1387–1392 (Hebrew).)

Although certain exceptions exist, as will be outlined herein, the Law deems all types of gambling to be illegal.

Israeli courts have recognised as gambling games, under Chapter 12 of the Law, *inter alia*, roulette, other casino games, bingo, slot machines, betting, lotteries, and sports betting.

As regards 'prohibited games', Israeli courts have established that to determine whether a game is 'based on chance more than understanding or ability' the predominance test will be used (ie whether the predominant element determining the outcome of the game is chance or skill).

In a March 2011 ruling related to 'betting', the Israeli District Court of Tel Aviv determined that in situations where a particular betting game consists of both skill and chance, the '*social interest and utility*' of the game in question should also be taken into account before considering its legality. (See, Class Action (Tel Aviv) 30284-01-10 *Simon Davush v Connective Group Ltd.* (Hebrew).)

2.2 What is the legal definition of online gambling and what falls within this definition?

No statutory provisions exist relating specifically to online gambling in Israel. Nevertheless, recent court decisions and official opinions of various government agencies, including the Ministry of Justice, the Israel Police, the State Comptroller and others, have clarified that the definitions and prohibitions found in the Law regarding traditional terrestrial gambling apply, *mutatis mutandis*, to online gambling. (See, for example, Special Requests, (Tel Aviv) 908617/07 *Carlton v The National Unit for the Investigation of Fraud* (Hebrew); Special Requests (Jerusalem) 1153/02 *The State of Israel v Aberg'il* (Hebrew); Annual Report 61B for the Year 2010 and the Accounting Year 2009, Jerusalem May 2011, Chapter 3 at p. 357. Published by the State Comptroller and Ombudsman of Israel.) For example, courts have applied the Law's prohibitions against gambling to an offshore operator offering its online gambling services to persons located in Israel while taking into account that this operator explicitly targeted the Israeli market. (Regarding the classification of foreign entities offering services in Israel (B2C Operators) see, Class Action (Tel Aviv) 30284-01-10 *Simon Davush v Connective Group Ltd.* (Hebrew), Special Requests, (Tel Aviv) 908617/07 *Carlton v The National Unit for the Investigation of Fraud* (Hebrew).)

2.3 Please set out the different gambling products identified by legislation.

- Poker – poker is not defined by any Israeli legislation. Nevertheless, in several decisions (few of them rendered many years ago) Israeli courts opined that certain forms of poker constitute 'prohibited games' as defined in section 224 of the Law.
- Betting (other than sports betting) – betting, as defined in section 224 of the Law, is generally illegal in Israel. However, in 1951 Mifal Hapayis was founded in Israel through a decision of the government. Section 231(a)(2) of the Law allows Mifal Hapayis to offer betting services upon permission by the Minister of Finance provided that the betting offered is not related to the outcome of sports events (see below regarding sports betting).
- Sports betting – sports betting is included in the general prohibition against the offering of betting in Israel (section 227 of the Law). As an exception to this prohibition, the Law for the Regulation of Sports Betting 5727-1967 established the Israel Sports Betting Board (ISBB or the Toto Winner). This statutory body is a state owned entity which has a monopoly on sports betting services. No other body may offer such services in Israel. Under the 1967 law the ISBB has enacted various secondary regulations. Specifically, in 1978 the ISBB passed regulations regarding a soccer betting programme and in 1996 similar regulations were passed regarding basketball. In

2011, the ISBB's right to conduct betting activities was expanded to cover additional sporting activities (both local and foreign), and in 2013 wagering on foreign (UK and Irish) horseracing events was introduced as well.

- Casino games – as with poker, there is no legislation which refers specifically to casino games. Nevertheless, various casino games (including, for example, blackjack and roulette) have been recognised by case law as 'prohibited games' under section 224 of the Law. (See, Class Action (Tel Aviv) 30284-01-10 *Simon Davush v Connective Group Ltd.* (Hebrew).)
- Slot and other machine gaming – slots are not specifically mentioned in Israeli legislation. As forms of lotteries, courts have considered these activities illegal in Israel. The Supreme Court of Israel ruled that slot machines constitute 'prohibited games' in Civil Appeal 813/88 *Astablismant Nahal Ltd. v Saul Barzri.*
- Bingo – bingo is not mentioned in Israeli legislation but Israeli courts have considered bingo to be an illegal form of gambling.
- Lottery – lotteries are given a broad definition in the Law (section 224). Together with betting services, lotteries may not be offered unless they meet the requirements stipulated in section 231 which include, *inter alia*, permission from the Minister of Finance. Under such permission Mifal Hapayis is entitled to offer lotteries, scratch cards, keno and similar fixed odds games. The permissible activities are clearly defined in the permit granted by the Minister of Finance.

2.4 Please list the different requirements for each gambling product, including legal classifications for each; for example, is poker a game of skill or game of chance?

There are two exceptions to the general prohibition on gambling in Israel. The first, as mentioned, covers activities offered by either Mifal Hapayis or the ISBB. The other exception is if the 'prohibited game, lottery or betting' meets three cumulative conditions as set forth in section 230 of the Law:

'230. The provisions of sections 225 to 228 shall not apply to any game, lottery or betting which fulfils the following three requirements:
(1) its conduct is intended for a particular circle of persons;
(2) it does not exceed the scope of amusements or entertainment;
(3) it is not held at a place of prohibited games or a place for the conduct of lotteries or betting.'

Poker – 'prohibited games' are defined as games in which one can win anything of value through a result determined more by chance than by skill. Israeli courts have established that to determine whether a game constitutes a 'prohibited game', the predominance test must be applied (ie is the predominant element determining the outcome of the game chance or skill). Such a determination is a question of fact. In determining whether a certain form of poker is categorised as a 'prohibited game' the court will consider the rules of play for that particular game. Using this approach, in several decisions (few of them rendered many years ago) Israeli courts opined that certain forms of poker constitute 'prohibited games'.

Casino games – like poker, each game must be considered in light of the predominance test used to define 'prohibited games'. There are only few binding court decisions in which the matter has been addressed, so a general categorisation is difficult to ascertain. Certain games (for example, blackjack, slots and roulette) have been definitively deemed – at various judicial levels – 'prohibited games'.

Other - all other forms of lotteries and betting (other than sports betting) may be offered exclusively by Mifal Hapayis and must conform to the permit granted by the Minister of Finance. Sports betting and horserace wagering may be offered exclusively by the ISBB according to conditions set forth in the applicable laws and regulations.

2.5 Explain the system of regulation of gambling; which regulatory or governmental body is responsible for the supervision of gambling? Which body issues licences? Which body examines enforcement powers? Is there any limit on the number or duration of available licences?

The Law grants the Minister of Finance the sole authority to issue permits for betting (other than sports betting) and lottery games in Israel. Pursuant to such a permit, Mifal Hapayis has been granted exclusive rights to offer non-sports based gambling games . The permit to conduct lotteries which was issued to Mifal Hapayis details the types of lottery schemes and scratch card schemes that Mifal Hapayis is authorized to organise and, in addition, Mifal Hapayis is obligated to prepare a detailed plan for each such lottery scheme, which is subject to the approval of the Ministry of Finance.

The Law for the Regularisation of Sports Betting 5727 – 1967 established the Israel Sports Betting Board (ISBB) which has the exclusive right to offer betting affiliated with sports events.

3. ONLINE GAMBLING

3.1 To what extent can online gambling be offered in your jurisdiction? Are licences available and, if so, for which gambling products? Please describe briefly the licensing process, who may apply, whether licences are limited in number and, if no licences are available, whether it is legal for online gambling to be offered. In the case of EU jurisdictions, please state whether there are any issues as to the legality of the local law at EU level. Please refer to any relevant cases at ECJ level and explain any measures taken or pending by the European Commission

The provisions of the Law explicitly refer to terrestrial gambling, ie the Law does not explicitly refer to online gambling. Nonetheless, online gambling is considered illegal to the same extent as terrestrial gambling. Recent court decisions and formal opinions of various government agencies, including the Ministry of Justice, the Israel Police, the State Comptroller, and others, have clarified that the prohibitions found in the Law regarding traditional terrestrial gambling apply, *mutatis mutandis*, to online gambling. Similar to the legal implications applicable to terrestrial gambling, the online gaming market is only open to the two state-owned monopolies exempted from the general ban on gambling – Mifal Hapayis and the ISBB. In practice, the only exception to the ban relates to the ISBB, which is allowed to operate an online betting platform. The Ministry of Finance has not given the approval required for Mifal Hapayis to sell its products online.

3.2   Is there a distinction between the law applicable to B2B operations and that applicable to B2C operations?
Not applicable.

3.3   What are the consequences for B2C or B2B operators who are active in your jurisdiction without having obtained or applied for the required permits, licences and approvals? What penalties and enforcement powers are available in respect of the illegal operators? Please outline any significant domestic decisions or enforcement actions that have been taken by the relevant authorities in recent years
B2C and B2B operators who are active in Israel may be exposed to criminal indictments by the local authorities (depending on the products they are offering and other considerations).

Section 225 of the Law provides for imprisonment of up to three years or a fine of up to NIS 452,000 for those organising or conducting a prohibited game, a lottery or betting. In recent years, Israeli law enforcement authorities have conducted a number of efforts aimed at cracking down on online gambling available in Israel. These included a number of high-profile arrests and subsequent legal proceedings.

3.4   What technical measures are in place (if any) to protect consumers from unlicensed operators, such as ISP blocking and payment blocking?
An attempt by the Israel Police to order Israeli ISPs to block access to online gambling sites was struck down by an Israeli Supreme Court for lack of explicit legal authority. However, a bill presently before the Israeli legislature would empower the Israel Police to issue orders aimed at preventing access from Israel to websites offering online gambling services.

In addition, payment processors have been targeted for processing funds deriving from Israeli residents for the purpose of conducting online gambling. The Israeli Central Bank issued a guidance note placing substantial burdens on financial transactions involving foreign online gambling. After being approached by the Israeli National Police, the Bank of Israel announced in January 2012 that Israeli financial institutions will be subject to stringent reporting requirements and are authorised (and in some cases may be required) to refuse transactions from online gambling sites.

3.5   Has the legal status of online gambling changed significantly in recent years and, if so, how?
While the formal legal status of online gambling has not changed in recent years, it should be noted that the practical application of the Law – as

applied by Israeli courts and authorities – has undergone some relevant changes.

First, as outlined above, Israeli courts have clarified in several decisions that the Law also applies to online gaming and not only to terrestrial gaming.

Secondly, in recent years, Israeli authorities have increased their enforcement activities against online gaming operators and third parties assisting operators in their provision of online gaming services, as detailed above.

While recognising the above changes in the Israeli online gaming landscape, it should be noted that enforcement actions have thus far only targeted online gaming websites that explicitly target the Israeli market as well as online gaming companies that were headed by local criminal organisations. Israeli authorities have never taken enforcement action against foreign operators with no presence in Israel which did not specifically target the Israeli market.

3.6 Whilst acknowledging the inherent difficulty in predicting developments in gambling law, what are the likely developments in online gambling in your jurisdiction, both short term and long term? Are any specific amendments under consideration? Have there been any recent political developments, or do you envisage any in the near future? Are any specific amendments under consideration? Are they likely to be adopted and, if so, what is the time scale?

Given the current social and political landscape in Israel, it is highly unlikely that the legislature will take active steps towards liberalisation and regulation of online gambling. In fact, we consider it likely that Israeli police and government agencies will take an even stricter approach to enforcing measures against illegal online gambling sites. As noted, Israel's legislature is presently considering a government-sponsored bill that would empower the Israel Police to issue orders aimed at preventing access from Israel to websites offering online gambling services.

3.7 Is the law the same in relation to mobile gambling and interactive gambling on television? If not, are there any headline differences?

The law does not distinguish online gaming from mobile or interactive gambling; therefore, the applicable legal framework is identical.

4. LAND-BASED GAMING

4.1 Please describe the licensing regime (if any) for land-based gaming, and what products are included. Please set out what licences are available, and the licensing regime for them.

Since terrestrial gambling activities may only be offered by the two state owned monopolies, Mifal Hapayis and the ISBB (for lottery games and sports betting, respectively), no licensing regime is currently in place.

4.2 Please set out any particular limitations or requirements for (eg casino) operators, such as a ban on local residents gambling.
Not applicable.

4.3 Please address the questions in 3.5 above, but in relation to land-based gaming.
Not applicable.

5. TAX
5.1 Please summarise briefly the tax regime applicable to both land-based and online gaming.
Under Israeli law the winners of prizes (including those who win prizes through the lotteries and betting organised by the state licensed monopolies) may be subject to taxation.

In the event that the value of any prize is more than approximately NIS 50,000 then the winner of such prize is subject to taxes in Israel and the organiser of the betting activity is required to withhold tax at source. The rate of tax varies for prizes between NIS 50,000 and NIS 100,000, and is set at 30 per cent for prizes above NIS 100,000. Furthermore, in the event that the prize is not a monetary prize, it is quite customary for the prize to be transferred to the winner only after the winner has provided the organiser with the required amount of tax.

6. ADVERTISING
6.1 To what extent is the advertising of gambling permitted in your jurisdiction? Again, this should cover both land-based and online gaming. To the extent that advertising is permitted, how is it regulated?
It is against the law to advertise gambling in Israel, other than the services offered by Mifal Hapayis and the ISBB. This is stated in section 227 of the Law, which reads: *'If a person offers, sells or distributes tickets or anything else that attests to a right to participate in any lottery or betting, or if he prints or publishes an announcement of a lottery or betting, he is liable to one year imprisonment or a fine of NIS 150,600.'*

7. SOCIAL GAMING
7.1 We believe this to be a growing area. Please decide under what criteria social gaming is permitted in your jurisdiction. If games are free to play or if there is no prize, are they legal without a licence? Please address circumstances where virtual currency is used and can be won: ie currency which is of no monetary or other value, save for as credits to take part in games. The answer should address the question whether game credits or virtual money can be exchanged for other prizes. Is any change to regulation in the area proposed or envisaged?
Contrary to many other jurisdictions, Israeli law does not only prohibit games of chance in which the player must pay consideration in order to participate in

the game, but – according to the definition of 'prohibited game' (see 2.1. above) – all games in which a person may win money, something of value, or a benefit according to the outcome of a game, if such outcome depends on chance more than on understanding or ability. Accordingly, the payment of consideration by the player is not a prerequisite in order for the game to be considered illegal. Therefore, a social game – even a game that is free to play – may be considered a 'prohibited game' under Israeli law, if the player is awarded something of value in accordance with the outcome of the game. Given that the prohibition encompasses any game of chance from which a player may glean a benefit, the legal conclusion is the same in cases where the player is able to win virtual currency which is of no monetary value, but may be used as credit to take part in other games. A different legal assessment may only be applicable if a social game does not involve any prizes of real world value, ie those games in which the player stands to gain no tangible benefit as a result of the outcome of the game.

The only exception to the aforementioned is provided for in section 230 of the Law, which states that the Law does not apply '*to a game, lottery or betting that meets the following three conditions:*
(1) its conduct is intended for a certain circle of persons;
(2) it does not exceed the scope of amusement or entertainment;
(3) it is not held in a place of prohibited games or a place for the conduct of lotteries or betting.'

Israeli courts have stated that the exception provided for in section 230 must be narrowly construed. In connection with online gaming special emphasis must be placed on the first requirement under section 230, limiting the game's targeted audience to a certain circle of persons. Online gaming by its nature may forfeit its 'social' aspect since it is typically characterised by the participation of a wide audience of potential players. Hence it is difficult to imagine a situation in which this exception would apply to online gaming.

Italy

SCM Lawyers Quirino Mancini

1. OBJECTIVES AND STRUCTURE OF LEGISLATION

The current status of gambling in Italy is quite peculiar as land-based gambling and 'remote' gambling (this wider notion including internet, mobile and interactive television gambling) are regulated in two substantially different ways. Indeed, land-based gambling was historically confined to only four brick-and-mortar casinos (Venice, Campione d'Italia, Saint Vincent and San Remo) that under the scope of an ad hoc regulatory regime dating back to the 1930s, were granted by the Mussolini-led government a unique and special status of fully-licensed gambling houses wherein a wide and unrestricted range of real money gambling products including poker, chemin de fer, baccarat, roulette and Vegas-style slot machines could be offered. Notably, all attempts made over the subsequent decades by various MPs to introduce fresh legislation aimed at expanding the scope of land-based gambling thus allowing the launch of more terrestrial casinos in Italy, have failed due to lack of strong parliamentary support, as a result of which the original casino-quadropoly is still in place today.

Apart from the full-purpose gambling offer available in the four terrestrial casinos; the historic yet declining presence of bingo halls and horse race betting outlets; and the sports betting outlets that mushroomed in Italy since their first licensing round in 2005, another form of very popular land-based gambling is that of street-side gaming machines. These were regulated only in 2004 when the Parliament decided to define what constituted a gaming machine and in the process introduced different classifications (collectively defined AWPs ie, 'amusement with prize') depending on the goal of the players; whether the game is for entertainment; or a combination of entertainment, skill or monetary reward. AWPs were allowed to be installed in public places such as bars, cafes and tobacco shops and devised a type of soft slot machine substantially different from the Vegas-style slot machines available within the four licensed casinos in terms of maximum coin-in and maximum pay-out requirements.

In 2009, in the wake of the earthquake that rocked large parts of a Central Italy region called Abruzzo, the government legalised and regulated videolotteries (VLTs) with the aim of using the related revenue to fund an ambitious reconstruction plan. VLTs are server-based terminals that can be installed in dedicated and highly regulated premises within betting shops, bingo halls and gaming houses. Due to a combination of factors including hefty licensing fees, high software development and setup costs, the VLTs market got into full gear only very recently yet it has quickly become an important revenue source for the Italian government.

Unlike land-based gambling, which was slowly and quite inconsistently regulated over several decades still featuring today a patchy and fragmented regulatory framework, remote gambling was legalised in a far more consistent, progressive and organic way. This process began in July 2006 when the then Prodi led cabinet, in an effort to heal the huge Treasury budget deficit and thus quickly raise new taxable revenues, decided to legalise and regulate a wide range of remote gambling services including sports and horse race betting, pool betting, skill gaming (including poker tournaments) and instant lotteries. To this end, a licence tender was called for the award of the first licences entirely and solely designed for the offer of 'remote' gaming services that were issued early in 2007. A second licence tender was then called in 2011 almost simultaneously with the legalisation and regulation of real money fixed odds games of chance (poker, casino, roulette and other table games).

With the regulation of online slots, online bingo, live betting, betting on virtual events and betting exchange that notably all occurred over the past three years, the remote gambling offer currently available in Italy is arguably the widest and most comprehensive across all regulated markets, in Europe and elsewhere in the world.

2. FRAMEWORK OF LEGISLATION

2.1 What is the legal definition of gambling and what falls within this definition?

Section 721 of the criminal code reads: '*Gambling is any for-profit game where a win or a loss is entirely or almost entirely determined by chance*'. It ought to be noted though that this definition, like all other gambling-related provisions set out in sections 718 to 723 of the criminal code, only applies to offline gambling as at the time the criminal code provisions were conceived and enacted back in the 1930s – online gambling obviously did not exist, nor have such provisions been updated since.

2.2 What is the legal definition of online gambling and what falls within this definition?

Gambling in Italy is regulated by the Agenzia dei Monopoli e delle Dogane (ADM, formerly known as Amministrazione Autonoma dei Monopoli di Stato or AAMS). Section 1.3(p) of the ADM Decree dated 10 January 2011 carries the following definition of real money fixed odds (online gambling): '*Any solitaire game played remotely where the possible outcomes which are the scope of the wager have a pre-determined and invariable chance to occur and the ratio between the possible win and the participation fee is known by the player at the time he places his bet*'.

2.3 Please set out the different gambling products identified by legislation.

- Poker. Live poker regulations are yet to be issued by ADM. Online poker is legal and regulated.
- Pool betting is legal and regulated (both offline and online).
- Sports/horserace betting is legal and regulated (both offline and online).

- Casino games. Unrestricted offline casino games are allowed only in the four terrestrial casinos. Online casino games are legal and regulated.
- Slots and other machine gaming. Offline slot games and AWP machines are legal and regulated by the ADM. Online slots are legal and regulated.
- Videolotteries are legal and regulated.
- Bingo is legal and regulated (both offline and online).
- Lotteries are legal and regulated (both offline and online).
- Skill games are legal and regulated (both offline and online).

2.4 Please list the different requirements for each gambling product, including legal classifications for each; for example, is poker a game of skill or game of chance?

Games regulated by ADM fall under two general categories: skill-based games and fixed odds games of chance.

The skill-based classification applies to all those games (whether card-based or not) where the ability of the player is the decisive and prevailing, yet not necessarily the sole factor, for purposes of determining the outcome of the game. Examples of skill-based games include: chess, burraco, gin rummy, and online poker tournaments.

The fixed odds games of chance include: poker and such other card games as baccarat; casino, slots and such other table games as roulette; lotteries, betting and bingo.

2.5 Explain the system of regulation of gambling; which regulatory or governmental body is responsible for the supervision of gambling? Which body issues licences? Which body examines enforcement powers? Is there any limit on the number or duration of available licences?

The ADM (see above section 2.2) is in charge of regulating games and enforcing the relevant provisions, issuing licences, monitoring the offer of gaming services, and collecting gaming taxes.

3. ONLINE GAMBLING

3.1 To what extent can online gambling be offered in your jurisdiction? Are licences available and if so, for which gambling products. Please describe briefly the licensing process, who may apply, whether licences are limited in number, and, if no licences are available, whether it is legal for online gambling to be offered. In the case of EU jurisdictions, please state whether there are any issues as to the legality of the local law at EU level. Please refer to any relevant cases at ECJ level and explain any measures taken by the European Commission.

When it comes to 'remote' gambling (including internet, mobile and interactive television), Italy is at present the most and probably also the best regulated gaming jurisdiction in Europe. So much so that the basic principles of the Italian regulatory model, which combines the possibility to offer a wide range of remote gaming services but only and strictly under the scope of an ADM-granted licence, have been largely imitated across the Alps by other jurisdictions (notably France, Spain and Denmark) that in recent years decided to open up their respective markets. The main characteristics of the Italian regulatory model can be summarised as follows:

- A licence granted by the ADM is strictly required in order to provide remote gambling services to Italian residents. Hence all offshore-based and other licensed EU operators who do not hold an Italian licence are not permitted to carry out cross-border services in Italy using their home licence.
- Since the opening of the Italian market, there have been two licensing rounds. The first took place over during 2006–08 when some 60 licences were issued, and the second in 2011 when 200 fresh licences were put up for award. The licensing window closed on 30 December 2011. Accordingly, any operators who wish to enter the Italian market now should not apply for a fresh licence but rather find an already trading one and then take it over (subject to ADM approval).
- A full purpose ADM remote gambling licence covers fixed odds/pool sports and horserace betting; skill gaming (including online poker and any other card tournaments which are all eligible for skill gaming classification); instant lotteries (subject to a sub-distribution agreement with the current exclusive licence holder); online bingo; online casinos; online poker and other cash games; online slots; and bets on virtual events and betting exchanges.
- The one-off cost of a full purpose ADM remote gaming licence is EUR 350,000 and it has a fixed validity period of nine years.
- The ADM licence is open to any applicant based in a European Economic Area jurisdiction. It can be granted directly to a foreign applicant provided he holds an EEA passport.
- The ADM licence may be issued even to a non-operator (such as a startup or a company coming from a totally different business) subject to: (i) release in favour of ADM of a EUR 1.5 million bank guarantee; and (ii) certification by an independent auditing firm that the applicant holds the required technological infrastructure and management resources to run a gambling licence.
- Remote gambling services may only be offered to Italian residents through a dedicated, ring-fenced platform to be certified by an ADM-approved testing laboratory that must be linked up the central control system ran by ADM so that each bet/wager placed by an Italian customer may be recorded, monitored, tracked, validated and taxed in real time.
- Provision of remote gaming services from a foreign-based '.com' platform to Italian residents is strictly forbidden and subject to the blacklist restrictions currently enforced by the ADM.
- Foreign-based ADM licensees are allowed to keep their servers abroad provided they are located in the EEA and a full, real time connection with the ADM central control system is in place.
- The gaming software of the poker and casino games available on the Italian platform must be certified by an ADM-approved testing laboratory.

Over the past eight years the Italian gambling regime, notably centred on the requirement to hold an ADM licence in order to legally and legitimately operate on the domestic market, has been repeatedly challenged before and tested by the European Court of Justice and has been ultimately found to be compatible with European law.

3.2 Is there a distinction between the law applicable to B2B operations and that applicable to B2C operations?

Unlike B2C operators, under ADM rules B2B service providers do not require a licence to do business in Italy.

3.3 What are the consequences for B2C or B2B operators who are active in your jurisdiction without having obtained or applied for the required permits, licences and approvals? What penalties and enforcement powers are available in respect of the illegal operators? Please outline any significant domestic decisions or enforcement actions that have been taken by the relevant authorities in recent years.

A B2C operator offering gambling services from a foreign-based platform and without holding an ADM licence faces imprisonment from six months up to three years. By the same token, whoever remotely organises, offers or takes bets from Italy on any games regulated by the ADM but in a way and through a channel other than those prescribed by the ADM rules, is subject to imprisonment from three months up to one year and to a fine ranging from EUR 500 to 5,000 even if the violator does hold an ADM licence. Moreover, the '.com' gambling site will be blacklisted by the ADM so that any customers trying to log on from an Italian IP address will be automatically re-directed to an ADM splash page with a notice that the gambling site in question is illegal.

As for B2B service providers, they do not require a licence, permit or authorisation from the ADM however they are restricted from having any direct dealings and relationship with Italian players.

The Italian law enforcement authorities recently stepped up their efforts to more effectively and consistently tackle the illegal gambling phenomenon, which resulted in some 5,000 'dot.com' gambling sites that were unlicensed in Italy being blacklisted by the ADM. As part of the clampdown, the Ministry of Finance began approaching individually each offshore-based operator and service provider offering illegal gambling services to Italian residents to demand that they immediately cease this activity, threatening that otherwise formal steps and legal initiatives would be taken directly with the authorities of the place where the offenders are based and locally regulated.

3.4 What technical measures are in place (if any) to protect consumers from unlicensed operators, such as ISP blocking and payment blocking?

As mentioned in the previous section, the ADM is proactively engaged in an ongoing fight against illegal (ie unlicensed in Italy) gaming operators. In addition to the sanctions discussed in section 3.3, the ADM regularly refreshes the '.com' blacklist and then distributes it to all local internet service providers (ISPs), who will be held directly liable for aiding and abetting should they fail to promptly and fully restrict access to all blacklisted sites from an Italian IP address. At this time, however, such restrictions do not apply to the means of payment associated with illegal gaming transactions.

3.5 Has the legal status of online gambling changed significantly in recent years and, if so, how?

Since the opening in 2006 of the Italian gaming market and with the ensuing introduction of ADM-granted licences as a strict legal condition to operating locally, online gambling has been officially legal and fully regulated.

3.6 Whilst acknowledging the inherent difficulty in predicting developments in gambling law, what are the likely developments in online gambling in your jurisdiction, both short term and long term? Are any specific amendments under consideration? Have there been any recent political developments, or do you envisage any in the near future? Are any specific amendments under consideration? Are they likely to be adopted and, if so, what is the time scale?

Following the regulation of slots, bingo, live betting, betting on virtual events and betting exchange, the ADM portfolio of games is almost fully complete. Specific measures are as follows:

(i) **Betting Exchanges.** On 11 December 2013, the ADM issued the operational guidelines relating to the launch of peer-to-peer interactive betting that is regulated by Ministerial Decree no. 47 of 18 March 2013. The first Italian betting exchange platform went live in early April 2014.

(ii) **Virtual Betting.** On 12 February 2013, the ADM published the technical rules concerning betting on virtual events. This service is already available on various Italian platforms.

(iii) **Online Bingo.** New game versions and rules for online bingo were introduced by the ADM Decree of 24 May 2011. However, the related ministerial decree required to implement them has not yet been enacted so they are not live as yet.

By Law no. 23 of 11 March 2014 (*Legge Delega*), the Parliament delegated the government, within one year from the date such law entered into force (that is, 27 March 2014), to review and amend the Italian tax legislation so as to make it more fair, transparent and growth-oriented. Section 14 thereof deals specifically with public games (both online and land-based), setting out the general policy guidelines aimed at harmonising the tax regime applicable to the various types of games, rationalising the gaming outlets network throughout the national territory, introducing more stringent anti-money laundering measures, preventing and tackling gambling addiction, restricting or banning altogether gambling advertising on radio, television and media in general, protecting minors and implementing more consumer-friendly operational codes.

3.7 Is the law the same in relation to mobile gambling and interactive gambling on television? If not, are there any headline differences?
The notion of 'remote gambling' includes internet, mobile and interactive television and is the subject of a single licence and set of regulations applying to each and all channels.

4. LAND-BASED GAMING
4.1 Please describe the licensing regime (if any) for land-based gaming, and what products are included. Please set out what licences are available, and the licensing regime for them.
The only venues where the offer of land-based gambling products is fully permitted in Italy are the four municipality-owned casinos of Venice, Campione d'Italia, Saint Vincent and San Remo, which have been operating off-licence under a special ministerial regime dating back to the 1930s.

As for the street-side slot machines available in bars, tobacco shops and gaming parlours, in 2004 the ADM introduced fresh regulations for the coin-operated machines with cash prizes establishing that all such machines had to be connected to the central control system in real time. This measure removed a significant number of illegal machines from the market and allowed the Italian government to control this highly profitable market. At present three types of gaming machines are available on the market:

- 'Comma 6' machines (AWPs also known as 'NewSlots'), which offer cash prizes and can be installed in licensed commercial premises and retail outlets (bars, coffee houses, gaming arcades) as well as in gaming houses, betting shops and bingo halls, which are linked to one another through remote networks and then all connected to a centralised system controlled by the ADM. Manufacturers, importers and distributors of NewSlots must be authorised or licensed (as the case may be) by the ADM in line with technical requirements and along with requirements established by the Department of Security/Public Safety in the Italian Ministry of Internal Affairs. NewSlots can distribute coin winnings up to EUR 100, the minimum payout is 75 per cent of the total coin-ins, and the machines cannot offer poker or games which are played in the same way as poker. The game must include elements of skill or entertainment in addition to the random element.
- 'Comma 7c' (skills without pay machines), available in commercial premises and subject to no particular restrictions. Examples of this type of machines include pool, juke boxes, table football, pinball and other gaming devices designed to test players' physical, mental or strategic skill. Prizes consist of small objects/gadgets, with a value of no more than 20 times the cost of playing (with a maximum of EUR 20). Prizes

cannot be exchanged for cash. Free games are not permitted and no games of chance are allowed to be provided.

- 'Comma 7a' (video lottery machines or VLTs) which were regulated by the ADM in 2009 with the aim of creating a nationwide terrestrial network of VLTs running alongside the very popular NewSlots, yet with much stricter logistical and operational requirements. Indeed, in view of the fact that VLTs are a type of sophisticated AWP machine which is much more rewarding and entertaining from a player experience viewpoint than a traditional NewSlot machine, can pay cash prizes of up to EUR 5,000 and can also award network jackpots of up to EUR 100,000, they can be installed only in appropriately designated and specially-equipped facilities within betting shops, bingo halls and gaming houses with a pre-set ratio of machines per square metre. Each VLT machine is connected in real time to the ADM central control system.

In 2010 the ADM called an uncapped NewSlot and VLT licence tender which resulted in 13 operators being provisionally awarded licences. However, early in 2012 the licensing process was challenged and the relevant proceedings are still pending. Based on their outcome, it is possible that ADM may have to call a fresh licence tender.

Licence tender for the award of 2000 licences to open new betting outlets (Legislative Decree 16/2012)
The scope of this licence tender is to redesign and rationalise the nationwide network of land-based betting and gaming outlets. The Council of State (ie the Italian supreme administrative court) applied to the European Court of Justice to seek an opinion as to whether the fact that the licences to be tendered will have a validity period shorter than that of the licences previously granted and still in full operation would pose any issues under European law. The ECJ ruling is pending.

Videolotteries and slot machines
On 1 January 2011, a register was introduced under the scope of section 1, paragraph 533 of Law 266/2005 as amended by section 1, paragraph 82, of Law no. 220 of 13 December 2010. This entails an official and mandatory name list kept by ADM for all companies engaged in the slot machines and video lottery business whether as manufacturers, importers, distributors or operators. Such list must be updated on an annual basis.

New licences
On 20 March 2013, ADM issued new licences to 12 operators running a nationwide network of AWP and VLT machines (also known as 'Comma 6' and 'Comma 6a', respectively) all remotely connected with the central control system monitored by ADM.

New technical standards
On 19 June 2013, ADM published on its website the new technical specifications and standards concerning slot machines. The new generation

of slots will have to run a mechanism to verify and double-check player's age, each component of the slot's hardware and software will have to be certified, and stricter rules will apply to the slot's maintenance. ADM is expected to publish any time soon an implementing decree setting out the timescale for the progressive withdrawal from the market of the old equipment and the simultaneous introduction of the new generation machines.

4.2 Please set out any particular limitations or requirements for (eg casino) operators, such as a ban on local residents gambling.

Under Italian law any form of gambling is prohibited to people under the age of 18. Moreover, residents of the municipalities where four Italian land-based casinos are respectively located are not allowed to access the premises.

The municipalities are entitled to establish a minimum 300 metres 'off-limit' restriction applying to VLT outlets located within sensitive venues like schools and churches.

Gambling operators are notably also subject to AML requirements under the scope of section 14, letters d), e) and e-bis) of Legislative Decree no. 231/2007. In this regard, by note dated 11 April 2013, ADM sent all licensees detailed instructions concerning all player transactions to be notified to the Bank of Italy for AML monitoring purposes. In particular, with respect to poker, cash and casino games, licensees are required to report players who open/close their game accounts with unusual frequency, any anomalous money transfers carried out by way of pre-paid card top-ups and any other money transactions that may look suspicious, bearing in mind the player's profile and his/her typical gaming pattern. Also, in case a player should wager more than EUR 1,000 in a single game session, the operator will be required to promptly monitor the situation in order to verify whether, over a one week period, the player ended up gambling an aggregate amount in excess of EUR 15,000. The same rule applies also to VLT and bingo operators, who will have to report any initial wagers exceeding EUR 1,000.

4.3 Please address the questions in 3.5 above, but in relation to land-based gaming.

Other than for the AWP and VLT regulations discussed above, the legal status of offline gambling has not substantially changed in Italy due to the status quo concerning the possibility of establishing new terrestrial casinos, which is not expected to see any breakthroughs in the foreseeable future, especially in the light of the very disfavourable political and social climate surrounding gambling.

5. TAX

5.1 Please summarise briefly the tax regime applicable both to land-based and online gaming.

With regard to land-based gambling such as sports betting, bingo and slot machines, the tax regime is turnover-based, ie it is levied on the total bets/ wagers collected by the operator. The applicable tax rate varies from one type of gaming product to another ranging from 3 per cent for VLTs, nearly 3.5 per cent (for sports betting), to 13.4 per cent for NewSlots.

As for online gambling, the tax regime devises a hybrid turnover-/profit-based model depending on the particular gaming product. For instance, an average 3.5 per cent turnover-based tax applies to sports betting; a 3 per cent turnover-based tax is levied on skill games (including poker tournaments); and a turnover-based tax rate of nearly 11 per cent is levied on bingo. By contrast, a flat 20 per cent profit-based rate is charged on gross gaming revenues associated with cash poker, casino and other table games as well as on betting exchanges.

6.   ADVERTISING
6.1   To what extent is the advertising of gambling permitted in your jurisdiction? Again, this should cover both land-based and online gaming. To the extent that advertising is permitted, how is it regulated?
Law Decree no 158 of 13 September 2012 (*Decreto Balduzzi*) – ADM Note dated 20 December 2012

Advertising restrictions were introduced applying to all TV and radio shows, as well as theatrical, editorial and internet publications aimed at minors. Moreover, gambling advertising via whatever transmission device is banned if: (i) the advertising claim lures or otherwise entices consumers into gambling practices; (ii) minors are featured in the advertising; (iii) no explicit warning is made to the risk of falling prey to gambling addiction problems; or (iv) players are not explicitly invited to check the win statistics and probabilities published on the ADM website. Operators are also required to warn in any piece and form of advertising that gambling is restricted to people under 18.

Pursuant to the requirements set out in the *Legge Delega* (refer to section 3.6 above), more stringent rules on gambling advertising on radio, television and the media in general are expected to be enacted, including a total ban on radio and television programmes, in the interest of minors, for real money games that may induce compulsive gambling problems. Online gaming advertising in particular will be closely monitored and substantially affected by such new and stricter rules.

7.   SOCIAL GAMING
7.1   We believe this to be a growing area. Please decide under what criteria social gaming is permitted in your jurisdiction. If games are free to play or if there is no prize, are they legal without a licence? Please address circumstances where virtual currency is used and can be won: ie currency which is of no monetary or other value, save for as credits to take part in games. The answer should address the question whether game credits or virtual money can be exchanged for other prizes. Is any change to regulation in the area proposed or envisaged?

Social games are currently not regulated in Italy. Accordingly, free-to-play games do not require a gaming licence provided no real money or non-token prizes are at stake. If the prize had a monetary value the related offer would not fall under the scope of the ADM regulations but, rather, under that of the ministerial rules concerning competitions with a prize. Therefore, as long as game credits or virtual money are used solely as play-on tools and cannot be converted into either real money (which would otherwise trigger the application of the ADM rules on real money gaming) or a valuable prize, such a journey, a smartphone or a shopping bonus (in which case the rules covering competition with prizes would apply), they are permitted.

Japan

Anderson Mori & Tomotsune Ko Hanamizu

1. OBJECTIVES AND STRUCTURE OF LEGISLATION

Gambling is generally prohibited in Japan unless special dispensation has been granted under law.

Article 185 of the Criminal Code of Japan (Act No. 45 of 1907, the Criminal Code) provides for the crime of 'simple gambling', and states that a person who gambles shall be charged with a fine of no more than 500,000 yen; however, this shall not apply when the bet is made only for momentary entertainment. In addition, item 2 of Article 186 of the Criminal Code provides that a person who opens a gambling house or assembles gamblers for gain shall be punished by a prison term of between 3 months and 5 years. Further, item 1 of Article 187 of the Criminal Code provides that a person who sells lottery tickets shall be punished by a prison term of no more than 2 years or a fine of no more than 1,500,000 yen.

In addition, a resident of Japan who bets habitually may be held liable for 'habitual gambling' pursuant to Article 186 of the Criminal Code, which provides that a person who indulges in gambling as a habitual practice shall be punishable with a prison term of up to 3 years.

Although gambling is generally prohibited under the Criminal Code, there are certain exceptions. These generally fall into two categories, as follows.

The first category of exceptions is pachinko and pachi-slot. Pachinko is a Japanese version of pinball and pachi-slot is a slot machine. Usually, both pachinko machines and pachi-slot machines are found in pachinko parlours, which are found throughout Japan. If you win balls or tokens in pachinko or pachi-slot, you can exchange them for goods that are available in the parlour's gift shop. Certain goods obtained from the parlour's gift shop can then be sold for cash at an exchange shop located near the pachinko parlour at a specified exchange rate. Although pachinko and pachi-slot are generally perceived as gambling by the general public, when operated in a specific manner, they are not legally prohibited under the Criminal Code since the betting in pachinko and pachi-slot is made 'only for momentary entertainment', as stated in Article 185 of the Code. Pachinko and pachi-slot are also regulated by the Act on Control and Improvement of Amusement Business, etc (Act No. 122 of 1948, the Amusement Business Act), the details of which regulation are explained below.

The second category of exceptions is gambling run by public bodies. Whilst pachinko and pachi-slot are gambling businesses operated by private companies, there are certain gambling activities run by public institutions under the supervision of certain governmental organisations. This category of gambling includes lottery (*takara kuji*), toto (football lottery), horse racing, boat racing, bicycle racing, local horse racing and motorcycle racing. There is special legislation for each of these gambling businesses, and a special corporation established under this legislation or supervised by a governmental organisation runs such gambling businesses.

Whilst casinos are legal in most countries, operating or playing in a casino is illegal under Japanese law. However, a bill entitled 'Act for Promotion of Development of Integrated Resort' is currently pending at the Diet for discussion. Once this bill has been passed by the Diet, it is expected that the prohibition on casinos will be lifted and one can operate a casino in an integrated resort by obtaining the necessary licence from the relevant authority. Since the bill only stipulates the basic framework of integrated resorts, another act which sets forth details of the operation of integrated resorts will also need to be enacted by the Diet. In the bill, this enforcement act is scheduled to be enacted within one year from when the act comes into force. To date, no draft of such an enforcement act has been disclosed to the public, and the details of integrated resorts and casinos are subject to future discussions. In the bill, 'integrated resort' is defined as *'complex facilities created and operated by a private operator in which casino and conference facility, recreation facility, exhibition facility, accommodation facility and other facility which would contribute to promotion of tourism are jointly operated'*. Therefore, even if the bill is passed by the Diet in the future, it is expected that a casino will be allowed to operate only in the form of an integrated resort in a special area designated by the government. The bill contemplates the establishment of a new governmental body, the Casino Control Committee, as a regulator to supervise the operation of casino businesses.

2. FRAMEWORK OF LEGISLATION

2.1 What is the legal definition of gambling and what falls within this definition?

Although the Criminal Code does not provide for a statutory definition of the term 'gambling', 'gambling' is generally interpreted as meaning the placing of things of value (including money, its equivalent, real and personal property, receivables, a 'stake') against the outcome of events, where the outcome is uncertain because it is subject to the element of chance. A game of skill, such as mah-jong, poker and blackjack, can be a means of gambling as wins or losses thereunder are ultimately decided by chance.

Under Japanese law, the act of gambling is carried out by the mere promise to place a stake; it is not necessary for the stake to have been actually offered, nor is it necessary for the outcome of the event to have been determined or the winnings to have been paid (Judgment of the Court of Great Judicature of 19 April 1925).

The act of betting an item 'only for momentary entertainment' (such as a pack of cigarettes, a bottle of beer or other relatively inexpensive items of immediate consumption or use) will not constitute criminally punishable gambling under Article 185 of the Criminal Code.

2.2 What is the legal definition of online gambling and what falls within this definition?

There is no legal definition of 'online gambling' under Japanese law. In addition, there is no statute which specifically regulates online gambling. In principle, the same regime will apply regardless of whether the gambling is online or land based.

2.3 Please set out the different gambling products identified by legislation.

N/A.

2.4 Please list the different requirements for each gambling product, including legal classifications for each; for example, is poker a game of skill or game of chance?

Pachinko and pachi-slot

As indicated above, the business of pachinko and pachi-slot parlours (collectively pachinko parlours) is not considered to be gambling or the offering of gambling places, since the pattern of such business can be described as follows:

(a) players rent pachinko balls from the pachinko parlours, paying cash at a rate which does not exceed the statutory rate (the Rate);

(b) the winning balls of players can be exchanged for premium goods (not cash) at the same rate as the Rate or so-called special premium goods at exchange rates which are often lower than the Rate, with the implicit understanding (which is never openly admitted by the pachinko parlours) that there are ways to exchange such special premium goods for cash at certain facilities described in (c) below;

(c) what makes the exchange of winnings at pachinko parlours possible is a system of exchange set up outside the pachinko parlours. The players take the special premium goods to an 'exchange' (an entity which, in order to run its business, obtained permits as second-hand dealers from the local public safety commissions), in most cases located near the pachinko parlour, where the players can exchange these special premium goods for cash. The exchange then sells the special premium goods purchased to a wholesaler, who in turn sells the special premium goods it purchased back to the pachinko parlour;

(d) currently, such recycling arrangements involving these three entities (ie the pachinko parlour, the exchange and the wholesaler) generally avoid the suspicion of law enforcement authorities and are not perceived to constitute gambling or the offering of gambling places where cash is used to settle wins and losses, because each of them are ostensibly independent operations and know nothing of what the others are doing; and

(e) essentially the same type of arrangements are used for the conversion of pachi-slot winnings to cash, even though tokens are used instead of pachinko balls.

It must be noted in this regard that it is only with pachinko parlour-related business that such avoidance of the suspicion of de facto gambling practices has been observed. Consequently, an attempt to set up similar arrangements for other casino games (roulette, baccarat, blackjack, slots other than pachi-slot, etc) or casual games (pinball, solitaire, etc) would promptly be subject to police raids and arrests for gambling or offering of gambling places, taking into consideration the fact that the Japanese National Police Agency has not made any positive reference to such similar arrangements.

As of 2012, there are 12,323 pachinko parlours in Japan, although this number is gradually decreasing. New entry into the pachinko and pachi-slot market is extremely difficult, since the market is heavily controlled by the authority.

Lottery

The Lottery Ticket Act (Act No. 144 of 1948) regulates the issuance of lottery in Japan. The lottery is called 'Takara Kuji' (literally 'treasure lottery' in Japanese). Only 47 prefectures and major cities are allowed to sell lottery tickets, subject to approval from the Ministry of Internal Affairs and Communications. Although selling lottery tickets is in general prohibited under item 1 of Article 187 of the Commercial Code, lottery tickets sold under the Lottery Ticket Act are exempt from the general prohibition of sales of lottery tickets. Since the Lottery Ticket Act is applicable only to lottery tickets issued in Japan in accordance with the Act, lottery tickets issued outside of Japan are not allowed to be marketed in Japan.

Toto – Japanese league soccer

Toto is a football lottery in which participants basically predict and bet on results of Japanese league soccer matches. The Act on Carrying Out, etc Sports Promotion Vote (Act No. 63 of 1998) regulates toto, and toto is occasionally sold in Japan by the Japan Sports Council.

Horse racing

Under the Horse Racing Act (Act No. 158 of 1948), only the Japan Racing Association (JRA) and 47 prefectures are allowed to hold horse racing. There are 10 national horse race tracks and 15 local horse race tracks in Japan. There are off-track ticket offices all over Japan at which betting slips for horse races can be purchased.

Boat racing

Under the Motorboat Racing Act (Act No. 242 of 1951), municipalities designated by Ministry of Internal Affairs and Communications are allowed to hold motor boat racing. There are 24 motor boat race tracks across Japan.

Bicycle racing
Under the Bicycle Racing Act (Act No. 209 of 1948), municipalities designated by Ministry of Internal Affairs and Communications are allowed to hold motor boat racing. There are 43 bicycle race tracks all over Japan.

Motorcycle racing
Under the Auto Racing Act (Act No. 208 of 1950), only 47 prefectures and major cities are allowed to hold motorcycle racing. There are six auto motorcycle race tracks in Japan.

2.5 Explain the system of regulation of gambling; which regulatory or governmental body is responsible for the supervision of gambling? Which body issues licences? Which body examines enforcement powers? Is there any limit on the number or duration of available licences?

Pachinko and pachi-slot
As explained above, the offering of pachinko or pachi-slot can be categorised as carrying on an entertainment and amusement business, which requires a permit or other authorisation issued by the local public safety commissions under the Amusement Business Act. Consequently, only those who have obtained such a permit or other authorisation from the local public safety commissions may offer pachinko or pachi-slot.

There is no fixed duration for licences under the Amusement Business Act and no renewal is required once a licence has been obtained.

The offering of pachinko or pachi-slot on the internet is subject to prohibitions against gambling and providing gambling places under the Criminal Code, but such offering is not governed by the Amusement Business Act or other laws.

Lottery
The Lottery Ticket Act regulates the issuance of lottery in Japan. Under the Act, only 47 prefectures and major cities are allowed to sell lottery tickets subject to approval from Ministry of Internal Affairs and Communications.

Toto – Japanese league soccer
Japan Sports Council is the operator of toto and the Council is under the supervision of the Ministry of Education, Culture, Sports, Science and Technology.

Horse racing
National horse racing is operated by JRA, whilst local horse racing is operated by each local municipality. The Ministry of Agriculture, Forestry and Fisheries supervises both national and local horse racing.

Boat racing

The Foundation of Japan Motor Boat Racing Association is the operator of motor boat racing in Japan. The Ministry of Land, Infrastructure, Transport and Tourism supervises the operation by the Foundation.

Bicycle racing

The JKA Foundation operates all bicycle racing, and this operation is under the supervision of the Ministry of Economy, Trade and Industry.

Motorcycle racing

The JKA Foundation is also the operator of motorcycle racing, and this operation is also under the supervision of the Ministry of Economy, Trade and Industry.

3. ONLINE GAMBLING

3.1 To what extent can online gambling be offered in your jurisdiction? Are licences available and, if so, for which gambling products? Please describe briefly the licensing process, who may apply, whether licences are limited in number and, if no licences are available, whether it is legal for online gambling to be offered. In the case of EU jurisdictions, please state whether there are any issues as to the legality of the local law at EU level. Please refer to any relevant cases at ECJ level and explain any measures taken or pending by the European Commission.

There is no statute which specifically regulates online gambling and there is no licensing regime for online gambling in Japan.

Although there is some discussion about whether or not online gambling is prohibited under the Commercial Code (especially in cases where an offshore operator is allowed to operate online gambling in accordance with the applicable laws and regulations of the country where the operator resides), it is most likely that Japanese residents who subscribe to online betting will be engaging in conduct that falls within the meaning of 'gambling' and therefore will be in breach of Article 185 of the Criminal Code. The crime will be committed in Japan as the bet is considered to be made in Japan by residents of Japan placing a bet online.

Article 185 of the Criminal Code provides for the crime of 'simple gambling' and states that a person who gambles shall be charged with a fine of no more than 500,000 yen; however, this shall not apply when the bet is made only for momentary amusement.

3.2 Is there a distinction between the law applicable to B2B operations and that applicable to B2C operations?

No.

3.3 What are the consequences for B2C or B2B operators who are active in your jurisdiction without having obtained or applied for the required permits, licences and approvals? What penalties and enforcement powers are available in respect of the illegal operators? Please outline any significant domestic decisions or enforcement actions that have been taken by the relevant authorities in recent years.

Although providing online gambling services towards Japanese residents is most likely to fall within an act of gambling prohibited under the Commercial Code, there are only a few instances where operators or service providers of online gambling have been arrested and charged in Japan. This is especially the case with offshore operators who provide online gambling services from outside of Japan. In fact, there are a number of online gambling websites which are written in Japanese and target Japanese residents as players. A number of cases where the Japanese police have taken action against online gambling operators or related business operators are presented below.

In September 2005, the Osaka District Court sentenced the Japanese operators of a website offering gambling on baseball game results to suspended jail terms of between 1 year and 2 months and 1 year and 8 months.

In February 2006, two Japanese internet café operators that were offering access to gambling through foreign gambling operators of Philippines-based websites were arrested and charged under item 1 of Article 186 of the Criminal Code. Two of their customers were also arrested and charged under Article 185 of the Criminal Code. The cafés had joined the online gaming websites and were in control of their customers' gaming accounts. The customers purchased points to be played online at a rate of 100 yen per point and were able to redeem said points against cash from the internet café operators; profits from customer losses were split between the operators and the online gaming websites. In January 2007, the Kyoto District Court sentenced the two operators to suspended jail terms of 2 years and ordered forfeit of over 100 million yen as a deemed profit from the illegal gambling.

We are also aware of the following two cases that are directly relevant to the issue of foreign company liability under the Criminal Code.

Manning, a UK bookmaker, appointed a booking agent in Japan whose role was to act as a liaison, accepting and relaying bets to Manning in the UK or elsewhere outside Japan. The National Police Agency gave an oral warning to the betting agent to the effect that, even if the bookmaking took place outside Japan, customers in Japan would be prosecuted for the crime of simple gambling and the booking agent for the crime of habitual gambling. The National Police Agency further warned that if the betting agent accepted any funds in Japan from customers it would commence criminal investigation.

The other case relates to another UK booking agent, SSP. According to a press report, SSP operated a website directed at Japanese residents whereby they could place bets via the internet, with all funds transferred through bank accounts situated in England. The National Police Agency stated that, even if the solicitation was made over the internet, the offer to accept bets made by the bookmaker via the internet to residents of Japan would be deemed to constitute an offer made in Japan. In this case, SSP had no presence in Japan, and to the best of our knowledge no action was taken against customers who placed bets with SSP.

3.4 What technical measures are in place (if any) to protect consumers from unlicensed operators, such as ISP blocking and payment blocking?
Some internet service providers block offshore online gambling websites. Also, some credit card companies use payment blocking in relation to some offshore online gambling websites.

3.5 Has the legal status of online gambling changed significantly in recent years and, if so, how?
Whilst a number of internet café operators which provided online casino services have been arrested and charged since 2006, there has been no significant change in relation to legal status of online gambling in Japan.

3.6 Whilst acknowledging the inherent difficulty in predicting developments in gambling law, what are the likely developments in online gambling in your jurisdiction, both short term and long term? Are any specific amendments under consideration? Have there been any recent political developments, or do you envisage any in the near future? Are any specific amendments under consideration? Are they likely to be adopted and, if so, what is the time scale?
As far as we know, there is no specific legislation currently under consideration in relation to online gambling. Although a bill for lifting the prohibition on land-based casino is pending at the Diet, the bill does not cover online casinos.

3.7 Is the law the same in relation to mobile gambling and interactive gambling on television? If not, are there any headline differences?
The law that is applicable to mobile gambling is also applicable to interactive gambling on television. Such online gambling is in principle prohibited under the Criminal Code.

4. LAND-BASED GAMING
4.1 Please describe the licensing regime (if any) for land-based gaming, and what products are included. Please set out what licences are available, and the licensing regime for them.
Since pachinko and pachi-slot are the only forms of gambling that private entities are allowed to operate by obtaining a licence in Japan, how the licensing regime for pachinko and pachi-slot is structured in Japan is discussed below.

The offering of pachinko or pachi-slot is categorised as carrying on an entertainment and amusement business under the Amusement Business Act, which requires a licence to be obtained from the local public safety commissions in accordance with the Amusement Business Act. Although in reality it is very difficult to newly obtain such a licence and penetrate the market, an outline of the statutory requirements under the Amusement Business Act is as follows.

First of all, the possible locations for a pachinko parlour are limited. In principle, opening a pachinko parlour in a residential area is prohibited. In addition, a pachinko parlour cannot be located within a certain distance from schools, universities, hospitals, public libraries, kindergartens, etc.

Secondly, there are certain disqualifying preconditions. If an applicant, its director or manager falls within such a precondition, the applicant will not be able to obtain the licence. The disqualifying preconditions include certain criminal records, addiction to drugs and having a relationship with *boryokudan* (Japanese mafia).

Thirdly, the building of a pachinko parlour must satisfy certain requirements in relation to floor space, noise and vibration in the building and visibility within the building, etc.

Fourthly, the pachinko or pachi-slot machines in the pachinko parlour must be inspected by police prior or to its operation. This inspection of machines is required whenever the parlour changes to new machines even after the commencement of its operation.

4.2 Please set out any particular limitations or requirements for (eg casino) operators, such as a ban on local residents gambling.

Other than purchasing lottery tickets, there is a specific age limit for each form of gambling in Japan (for instance, under-18s are prohibited from playing pachinko). There is no ban on local residents gambling, although such a ban may be introduced in relation to casinos once they have been legalised in Japan.

4.3 Please address the questions in 3.5 above, but in relation to land-based gaming.

For years there have been various discussions over lifting the prohibition on casinos in Japan. As mentioned in section 1 above, a bill for an 'Act for Promotion of Development of Integrated Resort' is currently pending at the Diet. Once the bill has been passed, it is expected that casinos will be allowed to operate in integrated resorts, which will need to obtain the necessary licence from the relevant authority.

5. TAX

5.1 Please summarise briefly the tax regime applicable to both land-based and online gaming.

To the extent that the entity is engaged in such activities through establishments located in Japan (or otherwise deemed to maintain a permanent establishment in Japan for tax purposes), all income attributed to those establishments will be taxed at normal rates, regardless of whether the activities are deemed illegal or otherwise prohibited.

There are no taxation statutes specifically directed to income gained through gambling activities.

Although, in most cases, income from gambling will be subject to taxation under the Income Tax Act (Act No. 33 of 1965), prize money won from the lottery is exceptionally exempt from such taxation under the Lottery Ticket Act.

6. ADVERTISING

6.1 To what extent is the advertising of gambling permitted in your jurisdiction? Again, this should cover both land-based and online gaming. To the extent that advertising is permitted, how is it regulated?

It is currently possible to find, in newspapers and magazines, advertising from overseas gambling entities (eg UK gambling, overseas lotteries), lawfully licensed under the laws of their country, that is directed at consumers residing in Japan. The Japanese police and consumer affairs bureaus caution against overseas lotteries and warn that participating in such overseas gambling may breach the Criminal Code. More importantly, because aiding in and soliciting gambling constitute crimes under Articles 61 and 62 of the Criminal Code, Japanese credit card companies do not allow their customers to use their credit cards for overseas lotteries.

There are no specific regulations under Japanese law as regards the advertising of online gaming services. There are, however, certain soft laws, such as the 2004 Guidelines on Advertising on the Internet issued by the Japan Internet Advertising Association. According to the Guidelines, as a problem unique to advertising on the internet, members should refrain from agreeing to advertise online gambling services offered by offshore online gaming operators to consumers residing in Japan even though the gaming operator may be lawfully licensed under the laws of its own country because Japanese residents who subscribe to online betting may be in breach of Article 185 or 186 of the Criminal Code.

For pachinko and pachi-slot, there are detailed regulations on advertising established by the Japanese National Police Agency. Such regulations basically prohibit advertisements which could arouse a passion for gambling.

7. SOCIAL GAMING

7.1 We believe this to be a growing area. Please decide under what criteria social gaming is permitted in your jurisdiction. If games are free to play or if there is no prize, are they legal without a licence? Please address circumstances where virtual currency is used and can be won: ie currency which is of no monetary or other value, save for as credits to take part in games. The answer should address the question whether game credits or virtual money can be exchanged for other prizes. Is any change to regulation in the area proposed or envisaged?

Social gaming is a huge industry in Japan. However, there is no statute which specifically regulates it. Therefore, social gaming is regulated by the same regime as applicable to gaming and gambling generally.

In general, if social games are free to play or if there is no prize, such games are legal and the operator of such social gaming does not require a licence.

If players in a social game win virtual currency which can be used as credits to take part in games, the issue becomes complicated. If the credits cannot be exchanged for cash and cannot be exchanged with other players, it is likely that such credits are not 'things of value' under the meaning of the Criminal Code, since it is practically impossible for a player to obtain a profit through dealing in such credits. If the credits are not 'things of value', such social games will not fall within the definition of 'gambling' under the Criminal Code. However, if the credits can be purchased for real money, there is an increased risk that they will be deemed as 'things of value', because this could create the appearance that the credits have the financial value of the purchased price.

However, even if there is a risk that the credits could be seen as 'things of value', such social gaming can still be justifiable via a different route. Under Article 185 of the Criminal Code, 'betting a thing which is provided for momentary entertainment' is excluded from the definition of 'gambling'. A typical example of 'betting a thing which is provided for momentary entertainment' is to bet a cigarette or lunch. Although obiter dictum, the Supreme Court of Japan held that a business that was licensed under the Amusement Business Act may fall within 'betting a thing which is provided for momentary entertainment' and therefore would not constitute 'gambling' (decision of Supreme Court dated 10 November 1953). As discussed above, pachinko and pachi-slot machines in pachinko parlours can be legally operated under the Amusement Business Act if such pachinko parlours satisfy certain conditions, including the condition that balls or tokens purchased for playing the machines cannot be directly exchanged for money. Taking into account that the Amusement Business Act allows pachinko and pachi-slot machines which are played with balls or tokens purchased with real money under certain conditions, it can be seen that playing social games with the credits that may be purchased with real money are unlikely to fall within the definition of 'gambling' on the condition that the credits cannot be exchanged for cash and cannot be exchanged with other players. In light of the obiter dictum in the 1953 Supreme Court decision, it can be argued that such games would fall within 'betting a thing which is provided for momentary entertainment'.

When the credits can be purchased for real money in relation to social games, the regulations under the Act on Financial Settlements (Act No. 59 of 2009) will also apply.

Under the Act, in principle, the operator of the game issuing the credits, who must hold over 10,000,000 yen (or equivalent amount in other currency) on each reference date (the last day of March and the last day of September), must:

(i)   notify its business and other statutory matters to the relevant Japanese authority within 2 months from the reference date;
(ii) deposit half of the total amount of the credits in a manner specified in the Act;
(iii) submit business reports on a semi-annual basis; and
(iv) disclose certain information about the operator and the credits to the holders of the credits through the internet or other means specified by the Act.

These regulations will not apply in a case where the effective period of the credits is limited to 6 months or less.

Luxembourg

Bonn Steichen & Partners Michaël Kitai

1. OBJECTIVES AND STRUCTURE OF LEGISLATION
Despite the conclusions reached by a European Parliament study issued in November 2008 according to which Luxembourg is the holder of the third highest gross gaming revenue per capital in the EU (UK ranked fourth), the country mainly has only two historical providers of gambling: (i) the 'Loterie Nationale' (the Loterie) organised by the *Oeuvre Nationale de Secours Grande-duchesse Charlotte* (the Oeuvre), a non-profit public institution under the supervision of the Prime Minister and State Minister; and (ii) one casino (the Casino '2000' Montdorf).

The Loterie Nationale
The Oeuvre, created by a Grand Ducal decree dated 25 December 1944 and the Loterie Nationale created by a Grand Ducal decree dated 13 July 1945, have played a leading role in organising solidarity in the Grand Duchy of Luxembourg. The initial objective of the Oeuvre was to help victims of the Second World War so that the net proceeds resulting from the organisation of lotteries, scratch tickets and other activities performed by the Loterie Nationale was shared between the Oeuvre on the one hand and other welfare offices on the other hand.

Considering that the initial purpose became a marginal activity over the passage of time and allied to the emergence of worthy new charitable needs in the country, the scope of the beneficiaries has been extended (lately by the Grand Duchy regulation dated 26 August 2005) so that the net proceeds resulting from the activities of the Loterie Nationale are currently distributed as follows:

- 30/72 – to the Oeuvre (redistributed to charitable institutions);
- 15/72 – to the *Oeuvres Sociales des Communes*;
- 12/72 – to the *Fonds National de Solidarité*;
- 5/72 – to the Luxembourg Red Cross;
- 5/72 – to the *Ligue Luxembourgeoise de Prévention et d'Action Médico-Sociales*;
- 5/72 – to the *Fondation Caritas*.

From an exclusive and enlarged competence (acting at the same time as organiser and regulator) at its creation, the Oeuvre has gradually seen its control diminished in relation to lotteries services:

- until 2005, any other private lotteries provider (exceeding EUR 15,000) had to, prior to the Ministry of Justice's authorisation, be granted a binding consent from the Oeuvre acting as a lottery regulator (in addition to its ordinary role of national lottery public provider);
- from 2005 to 2009, any private lotteries provider (exceeding EUR 15,000) had to, prior to the Ministry of Justice's authorisation, be granted

a simple consulting advice from the Oeuvre acting as a lottery regulator (in addition to its ordinary role of national lottery public provider);
* from 2009, private lotteries providers (exceeding EUR 15,000) need only ask for authorisation from the Ministry of Justice; the Oeuvre only has exclusivity in respect of the organisation of the national lottery, ie the Loterie Nationale.

Today, the exclusive right of the Loterie Nationale to operate its commercial channel of distribution of any forms of lotteries and sports betting products, including online, is regulated by the Law dated 22 May 2009 related to the Oeuvre and the Loterie Nationale (the 2009 Law).

The Casino '2000' Montdorf

Luxembourg has an old gambling history which began in the early 1880s when the Casino Bourgeois was built in the centre of the capital Luxembourg City.

Today, Casino '2000' Montdorf is the sole holder of authorisation, granted on 19 December 1980, and extended for a period of 20 years by decision of the Ministry of Finance taken on 8 June 1999. Such authorisation was given by virtue of Article 5 of the Law dated 20 April 1977 on the operation of a business of 'games of chance' (the 1977 Law) which states that '*notwithstanding legal prohibitions, it may be granted to casinos and similar establishments, installed in the interests of tourism, authorisation, to open to the public, special, separate and distinct premises, where some gambling will be practiced*'. The conditions related to this authorisation as well as the nature and listing of authorised games are defined in a Grand-Ducal regulation dated 12 February 1979, as modified from time to time.

In the parliamentary works of the 1977 Law, the legislature opined that '*by the installation of a casino in Luxembourg, there will be no more gamblers. Official casinos will prevent illegal and uncontrollable gambling joints*'. The legislature has therefore decided to implement one single casino in Mondorf-les-Bains for mainly two reasons: (i) this will augment local government financing and allow other town landmarks such as the spa to attract those tourists who have come primarily for the Casino '2000' Montdorf; and (ii) the size of the country does not justify more than one casino. Other casinos are today negotiating their access to Luxembourg market.

Current legal status

Article 1 of the 1977 Law perfectly describes the current legal status of gambling: '*the operation of a business of 'games of chance' is prohibited*'. Such principle of prohibition is based on the fact that the desire to gamble is understood in Luxembourg as creating a danger of irrational and destructive behaviour (Trib. Arr. Lux., 26 July 2000, Nationale Postcode Loterij, n°10605). Therefore, the exceptions to such prohibition (ie the granting of authorisation to suppliers who fulfil the conditions set forth by the laws) are limited in order to channel such desire to gamble.

The co-existence of the two historical providers and the restricted opportunities for other private gambling providers are the only exceptions to the principle of prohibition.

Luxembourg still needs a consistent legal system in relation to land-based and online gambling which should take into account the greater mobility of local residents and neighbouring populations, the increased market and demand due to new games and the cross-border nature of virtual games available.

2. FRAMEWORK OF LEGISLATION

2.1 What is the legal definition of gambling and what falls within this definition?

Neither the 1977 Law, nor any other laws or regulations, provides a legal definition of gambling.

However, 'gambling' or 'game of chance' is defined by a Luxembourg ruling as *'the game which, either by itself or by the conditions according to which it is performed, is characterised by a chance prevailing the physical or intellectual skills of the players …'* (Lux.13 November 1958, P. 17, 390). The aforementioned conditions are fulfilled 'when the gain is the result of chance and chance is the main factor of the game'.

Such definition of 'gambling' or 'game of chance' in Luxembourg as 'chance component prevailing skills' should be analysed at the level of the generality of the players. As a result, a game does not lose its character of 'game of chance' if skills can ensure gains to persons specially trained. Indeed, the special skills or ability acquired by a few should not be taken into account.

Lottery, sports betting, casino games, slot machines and poker (under some conditions) fall within this definition under some conditions as set forth by Luxembourg laws, especially the 1977 Law.

Mere competition games, free lotteries and raffles exclusively organised for marketing purpose are not considered to be 'gambling' and do not require any prior authorisation to be offered to Luxembourg residents.

2.2 What is the legal definition of online gambling and what falls within this definition?

'Online gambling' is indirectly defined in the 2009 Law as *'any form of lotteries and sports betting organised by the information society services/tools'*.

This 2009 Law only applies to online gambling organised by the Loterie Nationale.

However, the concept of 'information society tools/services' should apply mutatis mutandis to all online games which might be offered by any other authorised operators.

As a result, online gambling covers:
- any game which may be authorised according to the 1977 Law (subject to some restrictions in respect to sports betting);
- provided by the Loterie Nationale or Casino '2000' Montdorf or any authorised operator;
- for remuneration;
- at a distance (ie without the parties being simultaneously present);
- by electronic means (ie initially sent and received at its destination by means of electronic equipment for the processing (including digital compression) and storage of data, and entirely transmitted, conveyed and received by wire, by radio, by optical means or by other electromagnetic means);
- at the individual request of the gambler.

2.3 Please set out the different gambling products identified by legislation.

Poker

Luxembourg authorises two ways to organise poker games: (i) small stakes poker; and (ii) stud poker in casinos.

Since poker might result in addiction and in money laundering, the Luxembourg public prosecutor's department announced in 2007 a 'gentleman's agreement' agreed with the Ministry of Justice and poker organisers (in particular bars) enabling organisation of poker 'events' (any forms) if stakes paid in by players are low and under some conditions (approximately EUR 20 to 50 per player according to organisation's expenses).

Betting (other than sports betting)

Pure betting (other than sports betting and other than that organised as part of lotteries) is prohibited.

Sports betting

Article 4 of the 1977 Law empowers the Ministry of Justice to legally authorise sports betting. The conditions of the authorisation, the terms and conditions of the betting and applicable taxes are set forth by the Grand-Ducal regulation of 7 September 1987 on sports betting.

Neither the 1977 Law nor the Grand-Ducal regulation of 7 September 1987 take into consideration the differences between fixed-odds betting and pool betting; there are no restrictions as to the forms and types of sports betting : 'live betting', betting on the results or the winner etc.

Casino games

The only existing holder of a licence – Casino '2000' Montdorf – may offer the following casino games – as listed pursuant to the Grand-Ducal regulation dated 12 February 1979 (modified by the Grand-Ducal regulation dated 8 March 2002) by execution of Article 6 of the 1977 Law: roulette; 'American' roulette; 'English' roulette; trente-et-quarante; blackjack; craps; punto banco, and stud poker and pure table games, ie baccara chemins de fer, baccara à deux tableaux à banque limitée et l'écarté, baccara à deux tableaux à banque ouverte.

Authorisation for further casinos should only be granted by a decision taken by the Government Council after investigation and in accordance with specifications put in place by the Ministry of Finance and after the advice of the Council of State. The authorisation order fixes the duration of the licence and determines the nature of authorised games, the operation, monitoring and control measures of agents, conditions related to access into the gambling area, the opening and closing hours as well as the tax levy.

Slot and other machine gaming

Article 3 of the 1977 Law prohibits the organisation of slot and other machine gaming on the public highway and in public places and in particular in bars (outside casinos).

Authorised machines provided by the Casino '2000' Montdorf are defined in Articles 16 to 20 of the Grand-Ducal regulation dated 12 February 1979 (as modified by the Grand-Ducal regulation dated 8 March 2002) by execution of Article 6 of the 1977 Law.

The only agreed machine gaming are 'machines à rouleaux' and 'video games' and these devices should be previously agreed by the Ministry of Finance. A system of electronic gaming cards for slot machines was recently allowed by the Grand-Ducal regulation dated 22 January 2014.

Bingo
The legal regime of lottery applies to bingo. Otherwise, there is no specific regime for this game.

Lottery
Lotteries are defined in Article 301 of the Luxembourg criminal code as '*all operations offered to the public and intended to provide a gain by way of fate*'.

Lotteries are provided either by the Loterie Nationale by virtue of the 2009 Law (which has repealed the Grand-Ducal decree dated 13 July 1945), or by other providers by virtue of new Article 2 of the 1977 Law as amended by 2009 Law (which has repealed the Law dated 15 February 1882 on lotteries).

The organisation of lotteries is subject to authorisation from the Minister of Justice when the value of the tickets to be issued exceeds the amount of EUR 12,500. When the value of the tickets to be issued is equal to or less than this amount, the authorisation should be granted by the Board of Mayor and Aldermen (*Collège des Bourgmestre et Echevins*) of the municipality's principal place of ticketing.

Authorisation is granted to such lotteries only for – full or partial – purposes of general interest or public utility related to philanthropic, religious, scientific, artistic, educational, social, sport or tourism.

However, mere competition games, free lotteries and raffles exclusively organised for marketing purposes are deemed lawful and, as such, do not require authorisation from the Minister of Justice.

2.4 Please list the different requirements for each gambling product, including legal classifications for each; for example, is poker a game of skill or game of chance?
See section 2.3.

2.5 Explain the system of regulation of gambling; which regulatory or governmental body is responsible for the supervision of gambling? Which body issues licences? Which body examines enforcement powers? Is there any limit on the number or duration of available licences?
The 1977 Law (Articles 4 to 8) empowers the Ministry of Justice to authorise sports betting, casinos and lotteries. It is the sole authority in charge of delivering the required authorisation to private operators willing to offer gambling.

Terms and conditions of offered games – either by private operators or by the Loterie Nationale – should be previously agreed and controlled by several public bodies (Ministry of Justice, Ministry of Finance, the Police and Tax Administration) whose representatives may demand to be provided with all documents related to gambling and shall have access to all commercial premises.

Furthermore, by virtue of title IV of the Grand-Ducal regulation dated 12 February 1979 in execution of Articles 6 and 12 of the 1977 Law, the casinos are subject to a monitoring and a permanent control executed by officials of a special service from the *Gendarmerie* as well as by officials and agents of the tax administration designated by the Director of the Administration or any other officer appointed by a special decision taken by the Minister of Justice and the Minister of Finance.

Licences to private operators have a limited duration.

3. ONLINE GAMBLING

3.1 To what extent can online gambling be offered in your jurisdiction? Are licences available and, if so, for which gambling products? Please describe briefly the licensing process, who may apply, whether licences are limited in number and, if no licences are available, whether it is legal for online gambling to be offered. In the case of EU jurisdictions, please state whether there are any issues as to the legality of the local law at EU level. Please refer to any relevant cases at ECJ level and explain any measures taken or pending by the European Commission.

Currently, Luxembourg laws and regulations are not clear as to the regime applicable to online gambling.

Theoretical statements

It is worth noting that, unless otherwise foreseen in upcoming draft laws in respect of online gambling status, current Luxembourg laws do not distinguish between games offered 'online' or 'offline'. Consequently *'given the lack of precision in the 1977 Law, the Ministry of Justice could authorise online gambling activities … provided that some qualitative conditions are met by the gambling operator … within the limits of what is set by the current laws including the 1977 Law'* (taken from a Ministry of Justice joint statement with the author Michaël Kitai).

As a result, the application should theoretically include the criteria as specified under section 4.1 in line with the Ministry's practice with respect to land-based gambling. The Ministry should then check whether the introduction of the new game will not jeopardise the balance supplies/demands currently existing in the market.

Effective situations

Despite the above theoretical statement, the effective situation of online gambling shows that there are no online gambling companies which are operating in Luxembourg with the aforementioned authorisation, except the Loterie Nationale which is the sole organisation directly regulated by virtue of Article 9(1)2 of the 2009 Law. The Loterie Nationale is also entitled to operate its commercial channel of distribution of any forms of lotteries and sports betting products, including online.

Questions raised from our analysis
This raised a number of questions: has no operator been interested in offering online gambling in Luxembourg? Can no operator fulfil the aforementioned qualitative conditions to be authorised by the Ministry of Justice? Does that mean that Luxembourg implicitly establishes a monopoly in favour of the Loterie Nationale? Should this be taken to mean that the Ministry of Justice considers that its main objective *vis-à-vis* gambling law consists of maintaining moral controls over Luxembourg residents? If this is the case, is such a moral imperative incompatible with any supply of online gambling other than the one offered by the Loterie Nationale?

Compliance of Luxembourg law with EU gambling legislation
As to the legality of the current legal framework at EU level, there are three potential issues:
- Firstly, it is worth noting that Luxembourg is the only EU member state not to have notified any draft law or regulation relating to gambling to the European Commission by virtue of Directive 1998/34/EC, as amended by Directive 98/48/EC. Even if the 1977 Law does not expressly mention any rule applicable to online gambling services, it is clear that the 2009 Law contains one explicit provision related to online gambling services. Indeed, although Article 9(1)2 of the 2009 Law states that the Loterie Nationale is entitled to 'operate a commercial network of distribution of any form of lotteries and sports betting products, including through the information society services/tools', the legislature did not raise such draft provision to the European Commission.
  To our knowledge, the parliamentary works of the law (draft law n°5955) do not even mention any urgent reason or any serious and unforeseeable circumstances justifying the obligation for the country to enact and introduce such law without any consultation/notification being possible.
  Yet, it seems that such provision meets the requirements to be qualified as information society services by virtue of Directive 1998/34/EC, as amended by Directive 98/48/EC since it refers to a service normally provided by the Loterie Nationale for remuneration, at a distance, by electronic means and at the individual request of a recipient of services, ie the gambler.
  The European Commission has not received any complaints about the Luxembourg gambling law and has thus never investigated any potential doubt concerning the compliance of the national rules with EU law.
- Secondly, the European Commission condemned the former version of Article 2§5 of the law dated 14 August 2000 relating to electronic commerce (the 2000 Law). Indeed, such version stated that '*whenever the location of the providers of online services may be, Luxembourg law is applicable for gambling*

activities involving money (...)'. The European Commission considered
that an automatic and systematic application of Luxembourg law may
lead to an unjustified restriction on the principle of freedom of provision
of services, putting it at odds with Article 49 of the EC Treaty. Such
wording was replaced by the Law dated 5 July 2004 which now excludes
gambling activities from the scope of the Luxembourg law relating to
electronic commerce. Consequently, it is now difficult to assess whether
Luxembourg courts will apply its own laws including the well-known
prohibition on cross-border gambling activities deployed in Luxembourg.
Luxembourg administrations consider that, being a criminal law, the
1977 Law should apply to gambling activities offered by a Luxembourg
operator and should also apply when these activities are performed from
abroad but targeting Luxembourg residents. However, the country's
adopted policy of fair tolerance results in a lack of prosecutions.

• Thirdly, while assessing the legality of the monopolistic position of the
Loterie Nationale over non-casino gambling, one should be careful because
– apart from: (i) the Ministry of Justice current practice; and (ii) terms of
Article 9.2 of the 2009 Law – there is no law which precisely allows/forbids
private operators from offering online gambling to Luxembourg residents.
The Court of Justice (located in Luxembourg) recently recalled that, although
a monopoly over games of chance constitutes a restriction on the freedom
to provide services, such a restriction can, however, be justified by overriding
reasons in the public interest such as the objective of ensuring a particularly
high level of consumer protection, this being a question for the national
court.

In accordance with judgement dated 15 September 2011, Case C-347/09
Dickinger and Ömer, to be consistent with the objective of fighting crime
and reducing opportunities for gambling, national legislation establishing a
monopoly over games of chance should:

• be based on a finding that the crime and fraud linked to gambling and
addiction to gambling are a problem in the member state concerned
which could be remedied by expanding authorised regulated activities.
In specie, it is necessary to assess whether unlawful gambling activities
may constitute a problem in Luxembourg and whether the expansion
of authorised (eg casino games solely in favour of casinos) and regulated
(lotteries and sports betting solely in favour of the Loterie Nationale)
activities would be likely to solve such a problem:
(a) in order to limit the problem of unlawful activities, potential
fraud and addictions, the Ministry of Justice currently restricts the
suppliers to the existing need. However, several non-regulated games
(such as poker) correspond to an existing need and may not be offered
by any authorised provider so far (except (i) small stakes poker and (ii)
stud poker by casinos);
(b) the authorised and regulated gambling operators on Luxembourg
gambling market have voluntarily adopted and implemented
appropriate measures for the prevention of gambling addiction
so that public authorities have considered that no further action

is justified. Furthermore, Article 9(2) of the 2009 Law states that, alongside the development of commercial methods to promote lotteries and sports betting, the Loterie Nationale shall: (i) clearly inform the public of the real winning odds for each type of product; (ii) organise information campaigns on the economic, social and psychological risks in relation to gambling; and (iii) cooperate with the competent authorities and various associations specialised in the sector to an active and coordinated policy of prevention and assistance related to gambling addiction;

- allow only moderate advertising limited strictly to what is necessary for channelling consumers towards monitored gambling networks. In order for that objective of channelling into controlled circuits to be achieved, the Loterie Nationale aims to provide an alternative to non-authorised gambling providers, notably through the use of new distribution techniques according to Article 9(1)2 of the 2009 Law. Furthermore, although not foreseen in any laws, the Loterie Nationale states that the advertising of its products remains strictly limited to what is necessary and does not aim to encourage consumers' natural propensity to gamble which is understood in Luxembourg to create a danger of irrational and destructive behaviour. In addition, unlike in the cases C-72/10 Marcello Costa and C-77/10 Ugo Cifone, Luxembourg argues that its gambling and sports betting sectors have not been marked by a policy of expanding activity with the aim of increasing tax revenue. Indeed, since its statement issued on 20 October 1997, the Oeuvre emphasises that its main objective is to channel the desire to gamble and not to maximise profits for charity institutions. The monopolistic authority also asserted that it will refuse to exceed a turnover of EUR 100,000,000 unless additional forms of lotteries or gambling products are introduced.

As a result of the above, Luxembourg adopts a policy of fair tolerance towards EU operators performing cross-border gambling services since the country does not have the same technical means for controlling online gambling, nor the desire to implement a regulatory body in charge of monitoring such activities (for more information, see section 3.4). As things stand at the present, Luxembourg may not legitimately wish to monitor such economic online gambling activity which is carried on in its territory since the regulatory systems used in most of the other EU member states are determined by a level of protection with more sophisticated technical means.

3.2 Is there a distinction between the law applicable to B2B operations and that applicable to B2C operations?

Although the legal status and responsibility of online operators are generally different depending on whether they are performing B2C operations or B2B operations, the main laws excludes gambling activities from the scope of their application:

- The Consumer Code as introduced by a Law dated 8 April 2011 strictly regulates the agreements entered into between a professional and a consumer. However, chapter 2 related to distance agreements (i) excludes at Article 222.2 (e) from its scope the agreements concluded in relation to online betting services and (ii) prevents – at article 222-5 (f) – the consumer from exercising his right of withdrawal of seven working days concerning the service agreements related to betting and lotteries (unless otherwise agreed).

- The 2000 Law in relation to e-commerce, as modified by the Law dated 5 July 2004 excludes from its scope, the gambling activities which involve wagering with monetary value including lotteries and transactions on betting.

Luxembourg laws, however, impose some conditions on B2C operators, including: (i) the prohibition to assert that a product increases the chances of winning in games of chance (Article 122-4 of the Consumer Code) which is deemed to be an unfair deceptive marketing practice in all circumstances; and (ii) the obligations of the advertiser prior to the broadcast of the advertisement of lotteries, mere competitions games and free advertising raffles exclusively organised for marketing purpose (Article 21 of the law of 30 July 2002 regulating certain trade practices and penalising unfair competition).

The question related to the responsibility of gambling providers with respect to the processing and use of personal data is regulated by the data protection law dated 2 August 2002 as amended by the Laws of 31 July 2006, 22 December 2006, and 27 July 2007.

A B2C operator involved in gambling is likely acting as data controller whereas a B2B operator involved in gambling is deemed either as a data controller or as a data processor as appropriate under the data protection law. Indeed, in cases where a B2B operator has outsourced a particular function to a service operator (such as white labels), such B2B operator is likely to qualify as: (i) a data processor if the white label provider processes personal data on behalf of the B2B operator; or as (ii) data controller if the white label determines itself the purposes and methods of processing personal data.

Although the 2000 Law is not applicable to gambling services, one should advise B2C operators who provide (i) online services (ii) host the information (iii) to the consumer-gambler, to promptly remove illegal information or to disable the access to such illegal service. However, in any case, such operators are not obliged to monitor the information they host or transmit, nor seek facts or circumstances indicating illegal activity.

Furthermore, Luxembourg offers excellent incentives from a VAT perspective for non-EU internet service providers to establish B2C e-business companies within the European Union. Indeed, such non-EU internet service providers offering services to EU individuals must register and account for European VAT. VAT will be charged to their customers at the rate of their country of residence ranging from 15 to 25 per cent. Therefore, setting up a B2C sales company in Luxembourg can make non-EU providers benefit from the advantage of charging VAT to their EU customers at 15 per cent, the lowest VAT rate in the EU. As a result, to benefit from the competitive edge provided from a lower VAT rate, major US and other international entities such as Amazon, AOL, Microsoft, Apple I-tunes, eBay, PayPal, Vodafone, RealNetworks, Rakuten, Skype, have decided to establish their EU B2C e-business platform in Luxembourg. To be considered as established in Luxembourg a company needs to ensure that the effective place of management is located in Luxembourg and needs to have a minimum substance in terms of human and technical resources. One should further note that, from 1 January 2015, the so-called VAT place-of-supply rules will change for B2C telecommunications, broadcasting and e-services, including online gambling. Consequently, the place of supply for VAT purposes will be where the online player resides instead of the place of establishment of the Luxembourg gaming provider.

3.3 What are the consequences for B2C or B2B operators who are active in your jurisdiction without having obtained or applied for the required permits, licences and approvals? What penalties and enforcement powers are available in respect of the illegal operators? Please outline any significant domestic decisions or enforcement actions that have been taken by the relevant authorities in recent years.

According to Article 14 of the 1977 Law and Article 305 of the Luxembourg Criminal Code, the operators who illegally operate a business of 'games of chance' with a profit objective (the legislature aimed to punish the beneficiary of gambling's passion and not the player himself) are punished as follows: *'Persons who operate (either directly or by intermediary), in whatever place and whatever form, a business of 'games of chance' without legal authorisation either while taking part in it by themselves or through their employees, or by receiving people entitled to take part in a pecuniary payment or by operating a taking away on the stakes, or by getting directly or indirectly some other profit by means of these games, will be punished by imprisonment from eight days to six months and by a fine from EUR 251 to 25,000'.*

3.4 What technical measures are in place (if any) to protect consumers from unlicensed operators, such as ISP blocking and payment blocking?

Luxembourg applies:

* a no control policy on websites or blocking systems requiring internet service providers (ISPs) to block access to non-authorised gambling websites because, at the moment, the country does not intend to impede the activities of a service provider established in another member state where it is authorised to provide such service; and
* no blocking system of financial transactions related to betting or gambling.

3.5 Has the legal status of online gambling changed significantly in recent years, and if so how?

Luxembourg still needs to adopt a law on online gambling. Some informal discussions have taken place, but no formal draft law has been circulated mainly due to the policy of fair tolerance towards foreign operators, the small sizeof the country and lack of reaction of the European authorities.

3.6 Whilst acknowledging the inherent difficulty in predicting developments in gambling law, what are the likely developments in online gambling in your jurisdiction, both short term and long term? Are any specific amendments under consideration? Have there been any recent political developments, or do you envisage any in the near future? Are any specific amendments under consideration? Are they likely to be adopted and, if so, what is the time scale?

From the beginning of 2012 until the end of 2013, the Government Council held meetings, notably with the Ministry of Justice and under the chairmanship of former Prime Minister Jean-Claude Juncker, in order to adopt a consistent and systematic position in relation to online gambling.

Since the recent election (at the end of 2013), the newly appointed Minister of Justice (from the Green party) seems to consider the development of online gambling regulation as a non-priority matter.

3.7 Is the law the same in relation to mobile gambling and interactive gambling on television? If not, are there any headline differences?

There is no specific law regulating gambling on mobiles or interactive gambling on television.

The 1977 Law applies regardless of the medium used, be it television, mobile communications or otherwise. Being a criminal law, Luxembourg administrations consider that it should apply to media gambling services that are (i) operated by a mobile or TV provider situated in Luxembourg, as well as for such services when (ii) targeting Luxembourg residents wherever the TV or mobile provider is operating from.

Such interpretation of the scope of the 1977 Law with respect to mobile and TV gambling services results from the scope of the new version of the 2000 Law, as well as the scope of the law dated 27 July 1991 on electronic media as modified (the Media Law), which has implemented the 'Television without Frontiers Directive' as well as the 'Audiovisual Media Services Directive'. Indeed, such law and corresponding directives exclude gambling services from their scope so that the principle contained therein of freedom to provide media services from one authorised member state should not apply to such gambling services when targeting Luxembourg residents.

4. LAND-BASED GAMING

4.1 Please describe the licensing regime (if any) for land-based gaming, and what products are included. Please set out what licences are available, and the licensing regime for them.

Land-based gambling activities are prohibited except by authorisation pursuant to Articles 4 to 8 of the 1977 Law.

The 1977 Law does not provide a full list of necessary conditions to be met by the operator in order to be able to operate a land-based gambling business. Practically, it results from the Ministry's practice that the submitted application should inter alia include: (i) the nature and description of intended gambling activities to be exercised in Luxembourg; (ii) the integrity of the gambling operator; (iii) shareholder information of the operating company; (iv) description of the allocated parts of hazard/skill in the game; and (v) explanation of the utility of the proposed gambling supply (which may not jeopardise the balance supplies/demands currently existing in the Luxembourg gambling industry). The authorised suppliers are then limited in order to channel the desire to gamble. Furthermore, the Ministry of Justice restricts the suppliers to the existing need, which rejects the pure lure of money as the sole basis for application.

The Ministry underlines that: (i) it applies a policy of no discrimination based on nationality of applicants; and (ii) it takes into account the licences which have already been issued by other member state bodies in compliance with the principle of conditional mutual recognition.

In practice, regardless of the competence of the Loterie Nationale on lottery, scratch games and sports betting:

- according to the 2009 Law, an exclusive right is granted to the Loterie Nationale to operate its commercial channel of distribution of any forms of lotteries and sports betting products. In that respect, the Loterie Nationale recently entered into a commercial agreement with the French *Pari Mutuel Urbain* (PMU) in order to offer land-based betting on horse racing. According to this legal regime, the gambling product related to horse race betting remains in the ownership of the Loterie Nationale and the net proceeds generated by these products are solely (after repayment of PMU fees resulting from the agreement's terms and conditions) allocated to charity organisations; and
- according to the 1977 Law, two sorts of authorisations have been delivered so far: (i) a specific authorisation to Casino '2000' Montdorf (see above); and (ii) authorisations given by the Ministry of Justice since the early 1980s to German gambling companies providing German lotteries and sports betting in Luxembourg. Except where related to the Loterie Nationale, the 'German' authorisations expired in 2013–2014 and authorisation shall not be extended beyond their current term of validity (the appointment of a general agent domiciled in Luxembourg jointly liable for paying taxes and levies is still required for any authorised operator).

4.2 Please set out any particular limitations or requirements for (eg casino) operators, such as a ban on local residents gambling.

There are no particular limitations or requirements obliging the gambling providers to place a ban on local residents gambling. The only restrictions are those provided by laws and regulations, including the limitation and prohibition on employees of casinos to have: (i) part or interest in gambling products; (ii) for any reason whatsoever to have any discount on the gambling proceeds; and (iii) to participate in the game, either directly or through an intermediary. Minimum age for entrance is 18. Gambling providers and their employees shall not be entitled to grant credit or lend money for gambling or to pay gambling debts.

It is also required for casinos to reserve a special room, separate and distinct, for the installation of slot machines.

4.3 Please address the questions in 3.5 above, but in relation to land-based gaming.

A legal framework in relation to land-based gaming should be facilitated in the coming years. It is still uncertain whether this should be performed as part of the online introduction or independently.

5. TAX

5.1 Please summarise briefly the tax regime applicable both to land-based and online gaming.

The tax regime applicable to gambling is the same whether operated online or land-based.

The tax base applies to gambling proceeds as detailed in each following games:

Casino games

Gaming proceeds comprises:

- as to 'banking games' (which are defined as 'games where one player, the banker, competes against each of the other players individually' and listed as follows: roulette, trente et quarante, etc): the difference between the initial stake (together with any complementary stakes from time to time) put by the casino and the proceeds realised at the end of the game, such difference being diminished by the following deductions (25 per cent for the expenses and 10 per cent for the loss in relation to the artistic events organised by the casino);
- as to 'commerce games' (ie bridge, etc) and 'circle games' (ie baccarat, écarté, etc): the aggregate amount of charges or rakes withheld by the casino during the games.

'Sports betting' games and lotto

The tax base is the gross amount committed in the betting.

As to the tax rate, Luxembourg laws also distinguish according to the category of games:

Casino games

Withholding tax on the gross amount is 10 per cent up to EUR 45,000; 20 per cent from EUR 45,000.01 to 90,000; 30 per cent from EUR 90,000.01 to 270,000; 40 per cent from EUR 270,000.01 to 540,000; 45 per cent from 540,000.01 to 1,080,000; 50 per cent from 1,080,000.01 to 2,700,000; 55 per cent from 2,700,000.01 to 4,500,000; 65 per cent from EUR 4,500,000.01 to 6,300,000; 75 per cent from EUR 6,300,000.01 to 8,100,000; 80 per cent above EUR 8,100,000.

Sports betting and lotto

Tax rate: 15 per cent.

Tax exemptions

- Gambling proceeds are exempted from income tax, wealth tax and VAT.
- Special status of gambling products offered by the Loterie Nationale: since 100 per cent of the gains realised by the Loterie Nationale shall be

redistributed to charitable organisations, there is no tax on lotteries and no tax on sports betting products offered by the Loterie Nationale either.

6. ADVERTISING
6.1 To what extent is the advertising of gambling permitted in your jurisdiction? Again, this should cover both land-based and online gaming. To the extent that advertising is permitted, how is it regulated?

Advertising of gambling is generally allowed with one specific restriction set forth by law which concerns minors who shall not be targeted by advertisement. Other than that, advertisement of land-based and online gaming is not specifically restricted or regulated in Luxembourg. However, the general regulations regarding faithful, trustworthy and honest commercial advertisements are applicable to gambling.

Furthermore, the law of 30 July 2002 regulating certain trade practices and penalising unfair competition provides a list of conditions to be met by the advertiser-organiser of online and land-based lotteries, mere competition games and free advertising raffles exclusively organised for marketing purposes:

- prior to any broadcast of the advertisement, such advertiser-organiser should draw up a regulation stating the conditions and operation of the business transaction. This regulation and a copy of documents to be addressed to the consumers should be submitted to a ministerial officer who is in charge of ensuring their regularity. The full text of the regulation should also be sent, free of charge, by the advertiser to anyone who requests it;
- the advertising documents shall not cause confusion of any kind in the mind of their recipients or be misleading as to the number and value of prizes as well as on the conditions of their allocation;
- the entry form shall be separate from the order form of the product or the provision of the service;
- participation in the draw, whatever the conditions are, shall not be subject to any compensation of any kind or any necessary purchase;
- the advertiser-organiser who has created, through the design or layout of the communication, the impression that the consumer has won a prize, must provide this prize to the consumer.

7. SOCIAL GAMING
7.1 We believe this to be a growing area. Please decide under what criteria social gaming is permitted in your jurisdiction. If games are free to play or if there is no prize, are they legal without a licence? Please address circumstances where virtual currency is used and can be won: ie currency which is of no monetary or other value, save for as credits to take part in games. The answer should address the question whether game credits or virtual money can be exchanged for other prizes. Is any change to regulation in the area proposed or envisaged?

Located in the heart of Europe, Luxembourg is hosting some of the biggest ITC companies (Amazon, iTunes, eBay, PayPal, Vodafone, RealNetworks, Rakuten,

Skype, etc) and leading fast growing online cloud and social gaming companies (Innova, OnLive Inc, Zynga, Big Fish Games, Kabam, Nexon, Bigpoint and Mgame) that have elected the country as their European distribution platform.

These companies have chosen Luxembourg to install the technology centre of their European operations (eg OnLive Inc., Innova, Zynga or Mgame) and/or manage their operational activities for development, marketing and public relations for the European market (eg Nexon) and/or organise through Luxembourg their language customer support, marketing and business development (eg Kabam) and/or organise their accounting and marketing activities (eg Bigpoint).

Such financial, management and accounting activities, even if related to gambling, are not considered by the Ministry of Justice to be operating a gambling activity so that no prior authorisation is needed pursuant to the 1977 Law.

However, the operational or commercial activities performed in relation to social gaming are subject to receiving a right of establishment before setting up a business. The requested authorisation for establishing a business is issued by a decision of the Minister of the Middle Classes after an administrative investigation and after a reasoned opinion of a commission (Article 2 of the Law on business establishment of 1988). The right of establishment is granted to any individual who fulfils the double condition of honour and professional qualification.

As part of social gaming:

- if concerned games are free to play or if there is no prize, such games do not require prior authorisation or licence in order to be properly offered to residents of Luxembourg other than the aforementioned authorisation for business establishment if the case may be. Applying the same reasoning than the one with respect to slot machines by virtue of Article 3 al.2 of the 1977 Law, such social games shall not be prohibited if no 'chance of enrichment' or material advantage – other than the right to take part in further games – is given to the player;

- if virtual money involved in social games – where the concept of 'hazard' is present – can be exchanged for other prizes, one should analyse whether the gaming operator is operating and taking advantage of the player's passion or is simply offering an 'entertainment' game such as snooker or electronic flipper, in which case, no prior authorisation or licence from the Ministry of Justice is required. Such social games are deemed to be gambling activities requiring the prior authorisation from the said Ministry only if: (i) the game, either by itself or because of the conditions under which it is performed, is such that 'hazard' prevails over the intellectual or physical address of the players; (ii) the game requires real money from the players (considerable 'buy-in' exceeding the gaming operator's management and acquisition costs/expenses plus normal profits); and (iii) the game creates a risk of losing the buy-in and the hope of winning a prize or any direct/indirect financial consideration for the player or other material advantage (other than the right to play again).

Particular attention should be drawn to the organisation of social games in the form of lotteries, mere competition games and free advertising raffles organised exclusively for marketing purposes which should meet the conditions set forth by Article 21 of the law of 30 July 2002 regulating certain trade practices and penalizing unfair competition (see section 6 above).

The attractiveness of Luxembourg

The attractiveness of Luxembourg for ICT and 'social gaming' companies as an ideal distribution platform to access worldwide markets is a combination of its:

- ideal location in Europe;
- first class data centre infrastructure (Tier IV certification);
- pan-European connectivity and ultrahigh bandwith;
- installed client base;
- cutting-edge pro-technology financial and IP structures;
- very business friendly tax environment, notably: (i) the lowest VAT rates in the EU – 15 per cent (see above section 3.2); and (ii) exemption for IP rights introduced by the Law dated 21 December 2007 which provides for an 80 per cent tax exemption on income derived from IP as well as on capital gains realised on the disposal of such IP (attractive for brands having integrated social games into their marketing strategies);
- public incentives and financial assistance, notably through the law of 5 June 2009 relating to the promotion of research, development and innovation;
- tailor-made network provided by the Luxembourg administration agency supporting the various 'social games' actors in the field of information and communication technology and fostering business opportunities; and
- attractive corporate structures: (i) regulated investment vehicles (eg Undertakings for Collective Investment, SICAV, SICAF, FCP); (ii) semi-regulated investment vehicles (eg SICAR, SIF); and (iii) unregulated Luxembourg holding company (SOPARFI) which may benefit, under certain conditions, from full tax exemptions of dividends received, and of capital gains, realised on shareholdings held by the SOPARFI.

Macau

MdME Lawyers Luis Mesquita de Melo

1.   OBJECTIVES AND STRUCTURE OF LEGISLATION

We can trace gaming in Macau back as far as the XVI century, when
Portuguese navigators first set foot in the Pearl River Delta tiny territory. In
fact, gaming has been part of the social and cultural heritage of Macau from
when it was a small fishing village to now, when it is an important trading
city and a cultural melting pot well positioned between the East and West,
serving as a bridge between China and Europe. From the very early stages,
the local authorities have always been quite permissive and relaxed towards
gambling.

As many authors have put it, regulating the gaming industry in Macau
was always seen as something that was necessary (namely, to guarantee the
associated tax revenue), though not exactly a good thing. Thus, from as
early as 1850, the gaming regulations in Macau have been quite relaxed and
minimal, aimed solely at preserving public order and revenue, while laying
on the operators the responsibility, or freedom there of, to self-regulate
most of the day-to-day gaming issues that would arise from their business
activities.

From the Hao Xing Company to the Sociedade de Turismo e Diversões
de Macau (STDM), the gaming industry in Macau was, until very recently,
a monopolistic business operated substantially without a structured legal
framework or any type of regulatory supervision.

Only with the transfer of sovereignty from Portugal back to China in
1999, and with the STDM gaming concession due to expire in 2001, did the
government of the Macau Special Administrative Region of People's Republic
of China (MSAR) decided to end the previous monopoly system and to
liberalise the gaming market.

Launching an international open public tender for the award of
three gaming concessions carried this historical decision forward. This
undoubtedly marked the beginning of the modern times of gaming in
Macau under a new and more sophisticated legal regime.

The legal backbone of the liberalisation of the gaming market in Macau
consists of Law No. 16/2001, also known as the Macau Gaming Law, and
Administrative Regulation No. 26/2001, which contains the rules for
the international public tender for awarding the original three gaming
concessions.

Other relevant gaming rules are contained in:
* Administrative Regulation No. 6/2002 (containing the licensing regime
  applicable to the gaming promoters, also known as junkets);
* Law No. 5/2004 (Gaming Credit Law);

- Administrative Regulation No. 26/2012 (containing the electronic gaming machines manufacturers approval process); and
- executive orders and instructions issued by the Gaming Inspection and Coordination Bureau (DICJ).

We can summarise the most relevant highlights of the Macau gaming legal regime as follows:

- the operation of games of fortune, as well as electric and mechanic machines games, by an entity other than the MSAR is always subject to a prior concession (through a gaming concession agreement) granted by the MSAR government;
- the maximum number of concessions for the operation of games of chance in casinos is three;
- the granting of concessions for the operation of games of chance in casinos is preceded by a public tender;
- sports betting cannot be operated in casinos. The operation of sports betting also requires a concession from MSAR government;
- gaming concessionaires cannot operate interactive gaming (online or internet gaming), which is also subject to a specific concession mechanism; and
- there are no laws or regulations addressing interactive gaming.

I will now analyse the current basic structure of Macau gaming law, as it results from the applicable laws and administrative regulations, in more detail.

Law No. 16/2001, published in Macau Official Gazette No. 39-I of 24 September 2001 (Macau Gaming Law)

Law No. 16/2001 establishes the juridical system for the operation of casino games of fortune and further sets out the main legal framework concerning casinos in Macau.

The operation of casino games of fortune and other games of chance in Macau is reserved to the MSAR. (This means that the right to operate gaming in Macau belongs to the Special Administrative Region in a way similar to certain activities that can only be explored by the state. The MSAR can then grant concessions to private entities. This happens, for example, with electricity and telecommunications.) It is restricted to the locations and premises authorised by the MSAR government.

The operation of games of fortune, as well as electric and mechanic machine games (slot machines), by an entity other than the MSAR is always subject to a prior concession awarded by the MSAR government (Article 3 of Law No. 16/2001). Accordingly, the gaming regime restricts the operation of any such casino games of fortune to private companies incorporated in Macau that obtain concessions granted by the MSAR pursuant to the concession contracts and applicable gaming laws and regulations.

Pursuant to Law No. 16/2001 and Administrative Regulation No. 26/2001, the MSAR has granted gaming concessions to Galaxy Casino S.A. (Galaxy), Sociedade de Jogos de Macau S.A. (SJM) and Wynn Resorts Macau S.A.

(Wynn) under an international public tender. These are the three current gaming concessionaires.

The Macau government has also authorised three sub-concessions contracts, deriving from the above referred concessions: one granted by Galaxy to Venetian Macau S.A., one granted by SJM to MGM Grand Paradise S.A. (MGM) and one granted by Wynn to Melco Crown Jogos (Macau) S.A. (Melco). These are the current gaming sub-concessionaires.

The Macau Gaming Law, which became effective on 25 September 2001, established the legal framework and the principal rules for the operation of casino games of fortune or games of other forms in the MSAR. It sets forth the objectives of the legal system governing the operation of casino games of fortune and defines the permitted types of casino games, areas for the operation of games of fortune and periods of operation by considering MSAR as an area of continuous gaming, with casinos being opened for business every day of the year.

Law No. 16/2001 further sets forth principal rules for the gaming concession regime and obligations of the gaming concessionaires and sub-concessionaires, including, but not limited to, submitting their accounts and records to the Macau government and paying a special gaming tax to the MSAR. It also contains rules on the suitability of gaming operators, gaming promoters and obligations to provide information.

Law No. 8/96/M, published in Macau Official Gazette No. 30-I of 22 July 1996 (Law on Illicit Gaming)

The Law on Illicit Gaming, which came into effect on 28 July 1996, prohibits all forms of operation, promotion or assistance to gaming outside the areas that have been approved as casino or gaming areas by the MSAR government, as well as any fraudulent gaming in authorised areas, or any unlicensed granting of loans or gaming credits to players.

This law establishes the penalties for the illicit gaming offences.

Administrative Regulation No. 26/2001, published in Macau Official Gazette No. 44-I of 29 October 2001 (Gaming Tender Regulation)

The Gaming Tender Regulation, which became effective on 30 October 2001, mainly sets forth the terms of the public tender procedures for the granting of concessions for the operation of casino games of fortune and games of other forms, and rules for determining the suitability and financial capacity requirements of bidders (also applicable to the gaming sub-concessionaires). The Gaming Tender Regulation also contains relevant provisions applicable to the existing concessions and sub-concessions which impose information obligations on the gaming concessionaires and gaming sub-concessionaires, and grants the MSAR government approval rights in relation to the gaming concessionaires or sub-concessionaires obtaining loans or credit in an amount over MOP5.0 million.

Administrative Regulation No. 6/2002, published in Macau Official Gazette No. 13-I of 1 April 2002 (Gaming Promoters Regulation)

The Gaming Promoters Regulation, which became effective on 1 April 2002, sets forth the requirements and procedures to engage and operate casino gaming promotion activities which consists mainly in recruiting high-net-worth individuals (so-called high-rollers) and introducing them to the casinos in Macau, where they play in VIP rooms managed by these gaming promoters (junkets).

The gaming promotion business is nuclear to the gaming industry in Macau as it channels to the casinos in Macau well over 60 per cent (it used to be close to 75 per cent, a couple of years ago) of the total Macau gross gaming revenue (GGR).

All gaming promoters must be licensed by the DICJ, and can only provide gaming promotion services upon issuance of a gaming promotion licence by the DICJ. In order to obtain a licence, gaming promoters must be doing business with a gaming concessionaire or a gaming sub-concessionaire. The gaming promoters must also execute a junket representative agreement with one or more gaming concessionaires or sub-concessionaires after obtaining a gaming promoter licence.

The Gaming Promoters Regulation restricts the provision of gaming promotion services to licensed corporate entities, commercial partnerships or individuals that are registered as a single person enterprise with the MSAR Commercial and Moveable Assets Registry and the Finance Bureau and meet all the legal requirements. In order to obtain a licence to provide gaming promotion services, the applicant must submit an application for a suitability assessment by the DICJ, which also includes the assessment of the suitability of the gaming promoters' key employees.

When the gaming promoter is a commercial partnership or a company, the suitability of the gaming promoter's directors and shareholders holding 5.0 per cent or more of the share capital is also assessed.

A gaming promoter licence is valid until the end of the year in which it is granted and can be renewed on a yearly basis upon request to the DICJ. The renewal application must include a signed declaration by the legal representative of the relevant gaming concessionaire or sub-concessionaire with which such gaming promoter is doing business that the gaming concessionaire or sub-concessionaire intends to operate with such gaming promoter in the following year.

Gaming promoters that are a single-person enterprise are subject to compulsory assessment of their suitability every three years, whereas those that are commercial partnerships or companies are subject to compulsory assessment every six years. An extraordinary suitability assessment may also be conducted, at any time, by the DICJ.

The gaming concessionaires and sub-concessionaires are jointly liable to the Macau government for the activities conducted by their gaming promoters, and the gaming promoters' employees and collaborators, within their respective casinos. Gaming promoters are jointly liable for the activities of their employees and collaborators within the casinos of gaming concessionaires and sub-concessionaires, and for their compliance with applicable laws and regulations.

Breach by the gaming promoters or the gaming concessionaires or sub-concessionaires of their obligations under the Gaming Promoters Regulation may result in:

- the issuance by the DICJ of a non-suitability report;
- the refusal by the DICJ to grant a new gaming promotion licence or to renew an existing licence;
- suspension by the DICJ of the gaming promotion activities of gaming promoters upon notice by the gaming concessionaire or sub-concessionaire; or
- administrative liability arising out of violation of the Gaming Promoters Regulation without prejudice of contractual liability of the gaming promoter towards the gaming concessionaire or sub-concessionaire.

Gaming promoters are required to comply with the following obligations:

- to register with gaming concessionaires or sub-concessionaires and to operate under the terms agreed in a written contract submitted to the DICJ, including, in particular, the amount and payment method of commissions or other agreed remunerations, the nature of their activities in the casinos, including the designation of any VIP rooms or other premises within the casinos, the amounts and forms of required securities and guarantees, and the waiver indicating that gaming concessionaires or sub-concessionaires and gaming promoters agree to submit to the exclusive jurisdiction of the MSAR courts and defer to Macau laws;
- to execute written contracts with their collaborators and submit copies of such contracts to the DICJ;
- to submit annually, through the gaming concessionaires or sub-concessionaires, a list containing the identification of their chosen collaborators for the following year, and copies of their identification documents and certificates of no criminal record or equivalent documents to the DICJ for approval;
- to comply with laws and regulations relating to gaming promoters and the instructions issued by the DICJ;
- to accept auditing carried out by the DICJ and the MSAR Finance Department;
- to make all books and records available for inspection and review by the DICJ and the MSAR Finance Department, and provide any additional information and materials to them upon request;
- to perform all contractual obligations, especially obligations to players;
- to comply with the reasonable instructions issued by the gaming concessionaires or sub-concessionaires to the extent that such instructions do not interfere with the gaming promoters' autonomy; and
- to perform all contractual obligations stipulated in the written contracts with gaming concessionaires or sub-concessionaires.

Gaming concessionaires and sub-concessionaires are also required to comply with the following obligations with respect to the gaming promoters they engage in gaming promotion:

- to submit to the DICJ annually a list of gaming promoters with whom they intend to do business in the following year;
- to submit to the DICJ, prior to the 10th of each month, a detailed list of the amounts of commissions or other remunerations paid to each gaming promoter in the previous month, as well as the amounts of taxes withheld;
- to prepare and maintain an updated list of the names of registered gaming promoters, their directors, key employees and collaborators for submission to the DICJ quarterly;
- to inform the DICJ or proper authorities of any fact that may affect the solvency of the gaming promoters;
- to maintain and update the book records with the gaming promoters;
- to supervise the activities of the gaming promoters, in particular the gaming promoters' compliance with legal and contractual obligations;
- to inform the authorities of any potential criminal activity by their gaming promoters, in particular potential money laundering activities;
- to settle commissions or other remunerations agreed upon with their gaming promoters in a timely manner; and
- to pay withholding taxes for their gaming promoters in a timely manner.

Administrative Regulation No. 27/2009, published in Macau Official Gazette No. 32-I of 10 August 2009.

Administrative Regulation No. 6/2002 was amended by Administrative Regulation No. 27/2009, which came into effect on 9 September 2009, in order to foresee the introduction of a limitation to the amount of commissions payable to gaming promoters.

As a result of this change, the Secretary for Economy and Finance of the Macau government was granted the authority to issue a dispatch implementing the 1.25 per cent gaming promoter commission cap.

The amendment sets forth standards for what constitutes a commission to gaming promoters, including all types of payments, whether monetary or in specie, that are made to gaming promoters, such as food and beverage, hotel and other services, and allowances. The amendment also imposes obligations on gaming promoters, gaming concessionaires and sub-concessionaires to report regularly to the DICJ, and imposes fines or other sanctions for non-compliance with the commission cap or the monthly obligations to report and detail the amount of commissions paid to gaming promoters.

Through Secretary for Economy and Finance Dispatch No. 83/2009, published in Macau Official Gazette No. 38-I of 21 September 2009, the MSAR government has determined that the gaming commissions, or any other forms of remuneration for gaming promotion services provided by gaming promoters, cannot be higher than 1.25 per cent of the net rolling, notwithstanding the form of calculation used.

Law No. 5/2004, published in Macau Official Gazette No. 24-I of 14 June 2004 (Gaming Credit Law)

The Gaming Credit Law, which became effective on 1 July 2004, governs the granting of gaming credit in the MSAR and authorises the gaming operators, including the gaming concessionaires and sub-concessionaires and the gaming promoters who enter into a contract with gaming concessionaires and sub-concessionaires, to provide credit for gaming in casinos in Macau.

Pursuant to the Gaming Credit Law, the granting of gaming credit is limited to the following situations:

- a gaming concessionaire and sub-concessionaire may grant gaming credit to a gaming patron;
- a gaming promoter may grant gaming credit to a gaming patron; or
- a gaming concessionaire and sub-concessionaire may grant gaming credit to a gaming promoter.

The gaming promoters may only grant credit based on an approval to extend credit obtained from a gaming concessionaire and sub-concessionaire.

The Macau Civil Code determines in its Article 1171(1) that '*Gaming and betting are sources of civil obligations whenever special laws so provide, as well as in sports competitions in relation to the persons taking part on them; otherwise, if lawful, gaming and betting are a mere source of natural obligations*'.

The possibility of enforcing gaming debts constitutes an exception to the normal regime under civil law systems, which qualify gaming debts as 'natural obligations', as opposed to 'civil obligations'.

A natural obligation may be defined as an obligation that does not give rise to an action to enforce it but still has some cognisable legal effects. In fact, if the debtor pays the debt, such payment is recognised as extinguishing the obligation even though the creditor was not entitled to obtain fulfilment of such obligation by the debtor. Civil obligations, on the other hand, can be defined as those obligations which bind in law and which may be enforced in a court of justice.

Macau being a gaming jurisdiction, and considering that Macau's economy depends on the large scale of its gaming industry, the fulfilment of gaming debts could not be left to a 'moral or social duty', as it could undermine the basis of the gaming industry's business rationale and 'harmonious' development and sustainability.

Therefore, Law No. 5/2004 – the legal regime for the concession of credit for gambling in casinos – was enacted to address the specific issues raised by gaming debts, especially their enforceability.

The most common form of undertaking gaming debts arises out of the concession of credit for gaming purposes: in fact, it is quite normal across the gaming industry for gaming operators to grant credit to their players in the form of making available gaming chips without receiving their face value in money, as happens with an ordinary purchase of chips.

The most important features of the Gaming Credit Law are:

- recognising that the concession of credit for gaming purposes gives rise to civil obligations;
- the determination that the only form of gaming credit allowed is through the provision of gaming chips without a payment of the respective face value; and
- the restriction of the power to grant gaming credit to the gaming concessionaires, the gaming sub-concessionaries and the gaming promoters (junkets).

Any other deals or transactions with the scope of providing credit for gaming purposes that are made in violation of these rules are considered null in the eyes of Law No. 5/2004 and will not be recognised as creating civil obligations. They would therefore fall under the natural obligations regime as explained above, if not under other applicable legal provisions that incriminate a number of actions with respect to providing credit for gaming purposes (e.g. usury for gaming) as foreseen in Article 13 of Law 8/96/M, 22 July 2004, which regulates illicit gambling.

It is therefore quite easy and straightforward to obtain in Macau, under the regime instituted by Law No. 5/2004, a judicial decision enforcing payment of a gaming debt that has arisen out of unpaid credit for gaming purposes granted by a gaming operator or a junket.

Since the gaming credit is enforceable as a civil obligation, the granting of gaming credit is also subject to the restrictions established in the Macau Civil Code, namely the limits established in Article 1073 (Usury): these limits are triple the legal interest rate for remuneration of the loan, whereas for compensation the limit is five times the legal interest rate – currently 9.75 per cent, in accordance with Executive Order No. 29/2006, applicable ex vi Article 552 of the Macau Civil Code.

Credit agreements stipulating higher interests may be annulled as a result of usury or, alternatively, the interests charged may be mandatorily reduced to their legal limit (Article 1073, Nos. 3 and 4, Macau Civil Code).

Administrative Regulation No. 26/2012, published in Macau Official Gazette No. 48-I of 26 November 2012

This recent Administrative Regulation establishes a new set of rules concerning the approval of gaming manufacturers, and the approval of electronic gaming machines and related equipment and gaming systems supplied to the MSAR market.

The legal definition of gaming equipment under the scope of Administrative Regulation No. 26/2012 includes all devices, programmes or software that operate totally or partially by electronic and/or mechanical means and are conceived, adapted or programmed to run or store games of chance in which the player may receive a payment in cash or in equivalent tokens or values as the result of a bet placed.

The supply of slot machines and related equipment to the gaming concessionaries and sub-concessionaries, as well as slot machines distributors, is from now on reserved to approved (licensed) manufacturers.

The responsibilities of approving the gaming manufacturers, conducting suitability checks and approving the electronic gaming machines and related systems and equipment being supplied in Macau lies with DICJ.

There are four main principles that shape the legal framework of the new slot machines' regulations:

- the institution of an approval/licensing procedure for all gaming manufacturers doing business in Macau;
- a gaming manufacturers' corporate suitability check;
- an approval process for all the slot machines and related equipment being supplied in Macau; and
- a set of ongoing regulatory compliance obligations imposed on the gaming manufacturers.

In order to be approved/licensed as a gaming manufacturer by the DICJ, an initial request must be submitted together with required detailed information that includes, but is not limited to:

- the list of jurisdictions where the gaming manufacturer is authorised to do business;
- the certification by the jurisdiction elected as the main jurisdiction that the licence is valid in that jurisdiction and that there are no pending administrative procedures against the gaming manufacturer for violations in the previous 12 months;
- a description, by jurisdiction, of all the models of slot machines that the gaming manufacturer is authorised to supply, install, programme and maintain;
- the organisational chart of the gaming manufacturer and of all its shareholders, with 5 per cent or more of the share capital, up to the ultimate shareholder; and
- the composition of the gaming manufacturer corporate bodies.

The gaming manufacturers operating in Macau that are not branches of overseas companies shall be required to operate under the form of a joint stock company with nominative shares.

The licensing procedure of gaming manufacturers involves a suitability check on the applicant, its shareholders and directors. The suitability check may, however, be waived, following a request to that effect, if the gaming manufacturer is already licensed in one of the following jurisdictions: the US, Nevada, New Jersey & Mississippi, Australasia, New Zealand, Great Britain and Singapore.

All the slot machines being supplied in Macau must be approved by the DICJ. The electronic gaming machines must comply with the minimum standards set forth in Administrative Regulation No. 26/2012, and also with the Mandatory Gaming Machine Standard, approved by the DICJ's Instruction 1/2012, and the Electronic Gaming Machines Technical Standards, Version 1.0, with effect from 10 February 2012.

Administrative Regulation No. 26/2012 also imposes a number of periodical and occasional disclosure obligations concerning material information in relation to the gaming manufacturer's business activity.

The gaming manufacturers are now required to submit an annual corporate and business update including, but not limited to:
- a list of all the jurisdictions in which the gaming manufacturer is authorised to conduct gaming activities;
- a document issued by the regulator in the jurisdiction chosen as the primary certification validating the authorisation granted in such jurisdiction, the conditions to which it is subject, if applicable, and any procedures for administrative offence(s) of a similar nature, started within the previous 12 months;
- information, by jurisdiction, on the models of gaming devices which are authorised to manufacture, supply, assemble, install, programme, repair, adapt, modify, perform or provide technical maintenance; and
- a list of legal proceedings instituted against the gaming manufacturer with detailed information about the decision likely to materially impact its business.

Each gaming manufacturer is also required to provide to the DICJ each January detailed information of its activities in Macau during the previous calendar year, including the number of models and gaming devices supplied to each gaming operator, the site of installation and the identification of the gaming devices supplied to a distributor.

Administrative Regulation No. 26/2012 now makes it absolutely clear that gaming revenue sharing arrangements between a gaming concessionaire/ sub-concessionaire and a gaming manufacturer are not allowed and may result in the revocation of the gaming manufacturer's approval granted by the DICJ.

Casino games of fortune operational rules
Each of the casino games of fortune or games of other forms is subject to a specific set of operational rules. The operating rules for the casino games of fortune are approved through a Dispatch issued by the Secretary for Economy and Finance of the MSAR, upon proposal by the DICJ. Among others, the Dispatches of the Secretary for Economy and Finance Nos. 41/2003, 42/2003, 69/2003, 55/2004, 56/2004, 57/2004, 58/2004, 59/2004, 60/2004, 61/2004, 65/2004, 89/2004, 73/2005, 74/2005, 69/2006, 30/2007, 42/2007, 63/2007, 64/2007, 67/2007, 11/2008, 78/2008 and 71/2009 set out or renew the procedures and operating rules of certain casino games of fortune, including, but not limited to, football poker, wheel of fortune, baccarat, soccer poker, blackjack, craps, roulette, Q poker, fan-tan and stud poker.

Anti-money laundering regulations
Growing in importance worldwide as well as within the gaming industry, especially with the introduction of American gaming operators to Macau, are the anti-money laundering provisions and internal controls requirements imposed on the day-to-day gaming operations.

The new anti-money laundering law – Law No. 2/2006, published in Macau Official Gazette No. 14 -I of 3 April 2006 – came into effect on 12 November 2006.

The new anti-money laundering law requires gaming concessionaires and sub-concessionaires, gaming promoters and other entities, such as financial institutions, insurance companies, exchange houses, money-remittance companies and professionals, to assist the Macau government in its efforts to combat money laundering activities.

The entities mentioned must comply with the following duties as set out in section 7 of the new anti-money laundering law:
(i)   identify contracting parties, clients or users whenever any transactions with such parties may indicate money laundering practices or involve high transaction amounts;
(ii) identify the transactions and/or operations referred to in the preceding item;
(iii) refuse to carry on the transactions or operations whenever the relevant information necessary to fulfil the duties set forth in items (i) and (ii) is not provided;
(iv) maintain, for a reasonable period of time, documents and records relating to the duties set forth in items (i) and (ii);
(v) report transactions and/or operations when they indicate money laundering practices or transactions; and
(vi) collaborate with all authorities in charge of anti-money laundering measures.

The centralisation, analysis and general monitoring of compliance with these duties are entrusted to the Financial Intelligence Office of the MSAR government.

Under the new anti-money laundering law, corporate entities and associations are responsible and liable for money laundering when the crime is committed in their name and corporate interest by (i) their corporate body or representative or (ii) a person under their authority, when the crime became possible by virtue of an unlawful breach of the vigilance or control duties pending on such entity.

Administrative Regulation No. 7/2006, published in Macau Official Gazette No. 20 of 15 May 2006
Administrative Regulation No. 7/2006 sets out in detail the duties of relevant entities set forth in the new anti-money laundering law, establishing the supervision and monitoring mechanism and determining the penalties for non-compliance. The administrative regulation has been in force since 12 November 2006.

Instruction No. 2/2006, issued by the DICJ on 13 November 2006
The instruction was issued in relation to compliance with the provisions of section 2, No. 2 of Administrative Regulation No. 7/2006, to define the minimal compulsory duties, rules and procedures for gaming concessionaires and sub-concessionaires, including corporate entities entrusted by their

management, lottery or sports betting concessionaires, and gaming promoters, under the new anti- money laundering laws. Any breach of these duties can result in fines or administrative action from the DICJ, leading to heavy fines under the terms of Administrative Regulation No. 7/2006.

2. FRAMEWORK OF LEGISLATION

2.1 What is the legal definition of gambling and what falls within this definition?

There is no general legal definition of gambling/gaming in Macau, but the Macau Gaming Law, having set out its scope as the establishment of the juridical system for the operation of games of fortune in casinos in the MSAR, defines 'games of fortune' as those in which the outcome is contingent as it depends exclusively on the chance of the player – Article 2, paragraph 1(3).

Furthermore, the Macau Gaming Law lists, in its Article 3, paragraph 3, the following games of fortune authorised in the MSAR casinos: (1) baccarat; (2) baccarat 'chemin de fer'; (3) 'black jack' or 'twenty-one'; (4) 'boule'; (5) 'craps'; (6) 'cussec'; (7) 'twelve numbers'; (8) 'fantan'; (9) chinese dice game; (10) fish-prawn-crab dice game; (11) 13 card game; (12) 'mahjong'; (13) 'mahjong-bacará'; (14) 'mahjong-pai kao'; (15) 'pachinko'; (16) 'p'ai kao'; (17) 'two stone p'ai kao'; (18) 'three card poker'; (19) 'five card poker'; (20) roulette; (21) 'sap-i-chi' or 12 card games; (22) 'super pan 9'; (23) 'taiwan-p'ai kao'; and (24) '3-card baccarat game'.

Any other type of game of fortune must be approved by a dispatch issued by the MSAR Secretary for Economy and Finance at the request of one or more gaming concessionaires or sub-concessionaires based on an opinion issued by the DICJ.

Electric gaming machines (EGMs), including slot machines, may also be operated in MSAR casinos.

In order to better understand the definition of gambling and its legal and contractual framework in Macau, we must look at the scope of the gaming concessions and sub-concessions, since they really define the object of gaming operations in Macau as it currently stands.

The three gaming concessions contracts (SJM, Wynn and Galaxy), as well as the sub-concession contracts (Venetian, Melco and MGM), contain a contractual provision that states, in very similar terms:

'Article 1 – Object

1. The object under this License Contract is the operation of Games of Fortune or Chance or Other Casino Games in the Macao Special Administrative Region of the People's Republic of China (hereinafter referred to as 'Macao Special Administrative Region' or 'Grantor').

2. The license herein excludes the following gaming activities:

(1) Mutual gaming;

(2) Gaming activities provided to the general public, less those that interfere with the application of provisions in the seventh paragraph of Article 7 of Law No. 16/2001;

(3) Interactive gaming;

(4) Games of Fortune or Chance in Casino or other type of game, lottery or gaming services carried out on a ship or an aircraft, but all such shall not affect the application of provisions in Item (1) of the third and fifth paragraphs of Article 5 of Law No. 16/2001'.

2.2 What is the legal definition of online gambling and what falls within this definition?

Although there are no specific laws or rules and regulations addressing online gaming in MSAR, the Macau Gaming Law contains a definition of interactive gaming.

Under Law No. 16/2001, interactive gaming is defined as a game of fortune in which:

- a prize in money or kind is offered or can be won in accordance with the terms of the respective rules;
- the player enters or participates in a game by telecommunications, namely telephone, fax, internet access, data networks and transmission of video signals or digital data;
- the player makes or agrees to make payment in money or in kind; and
- the game is equally offered or approved as a game of fortune or as an electric or mechanic machine game in Macau casinos.

In summary, the qualification of interactive gaming (which includes internet gaming or online gaming) depends on the verification of the following cumulative requirements:

- the game made available is a game of chance;
- it is available (or approved) as a game of chance or an electronic game in Macau casinos;
- a prize (in cash or otherwise) is offered and can be won according to the applicable rules;
- the player accesses the game and plays through a telecom medium (phone, fax, internet, etc); and
- it performs or agrees to perform a payment in cash or otherwise.

Article 4 of the Macau Gaming Law states that the concessionaires operating gaming of fortune in casinos are not authorised to operate any interactive game (which also applies to the sub-concessionaires). This provision also states that the concessions for the operation of interactive games of fortune are autonomous from the concessions for operating games of fortune in casinos. Although there are no legal rules defining the type of connection that would render a certain online gaming operation subject to Macau's jurisdiction and therefore requiring a concession, we are of the opinion that the following indicators, not excluding others, should be considered:

- the management, administration or control of wagers that are initiated, received or made on an interactive gaming system takes place in Macau;
- the management, administration or control of the interactive games takes place in Macau;
- the operation of the software or hardware of the interactive gaming system takes place in Macau;

- the provider of the trade marks, trade names or other similar IP rights of the interactive gaming system is based in Macau; and
- the provider of services, products information or assets to an interactive gaming operator and receives a percentage of gaming revenue is based in Macau.

2.3 Please set out the different gambling products identified by legislation.

The main gambling products in MSAR are the land-based casino games of fortune and EGMs. Within the casino games of fortune, baccarat is the more popular table game and constitutes the source of all VIP gaming revenue and accounts for 90 per cent of the total GGR in MSAR.

The gambling products offered in MSAR also include greyhound racing, horse racing, Chinese lottery, instant lottery and sports betting (football and basketball).

2.4 Please list the different requirements for each gambling product, including legal classifications for each; for example, is poker a game of skill or game of chance??

Casino games of fortune

The Macau Gaming Law defines casino games of fortune as those in which the outcome is contingent as it depends exclusively on the chance of the player. All the table games listed in Article 3 of the Macau Gaming Law, which are approved to be operated at MSAR casinos, are considered games of fortune.

Greyhound racing, horse racing and the Chinese lottery are operated under exclusive concession agreements entered into between the MSAR government and the respective operators.

Sports betting

In 1989 a concession agreement was signed between MSAR (then the Territory of Macau) and a company called Sociedade de Lotarias e Apostas Mutuas de Macau, Limitada (SLOT) for the operation of instant lotteries. This concession agreement granted SLOT an exclusive right to operate instant lotteries.

In June 1998, SLOT requested permission to operate sports betting – football, which was granted, and in 2000 SLOT was approved to operate sports betting – basketball. SLOT was subsequently authorised to operate, on a trial period basis, sports betting – football and basketball, via internet betting.

On 27 May 2004, the concession agreement with SLOT was amended and renewed for another period of five years until 5 June 2009 and the scope of the concession became partially exclusive.

In fact, SLOT was granted the partially exclusive right to operate instant lotteries and sports betting – football and basketball in MSAR, excluding the areas used by the concessionaires and sub-concessionaires of casino games of chance or games of other forms for operating mutual betting and operations offered to the public (lotteries, raffles and tombola) within their developments and resorts approved by the government, in the form of cash betting.

The SLOT concession agreement was amended again in June 2009, but this time in order to reinstate the SLOT exclusive concession in relation to instant lottery and sports betting – football and basketball, eliminating the 'integrated resorts' exception.

The SLOT concession was then renewed under the same terms and conditions for a one-year term until 5 June 2010, and thereafter was renewed on a yearly basis. In July 2012, the SLOT concession was renewed for another term of three years, expiring on 5 June 2015.

In Macau, SLOT has therefore monopolised internet, telephone and over-the-counter betting on both soccer and basketball for over a decade. There is a clear expectation that the government will, sooner or later, open the sports betting market to other players, thereby ending SLOT's exclusive concession. According to an interview given to Macau Business in 2011, DICJ, through its deputy director, outlined that: *'maybe in the future sport could be liberalised, maybe have one more operator'*. In addition, the DICJ has made public that the government was *'still in the process of studying the feasibility of enhancing the current operational module of sports lottery in Macau'*.

On the other hand, Economy and Finance Secretary Francis Tam told Macau's Legislative Assembly during the last government policy address that the government intends to *'continue to strengthen administrative work in relation to the sports lottery ... [and] accelerate research into opening up the sports gaming monopoly, and, in 2012, establish a working group that will formulate an associated program'*.

The opportunity to increase public revenue and to implement the diversification of the economy and the gaming/entertainment offer, especially within the integrated resorts, should motivate the government to address, in the near future, the new challenges posed by the sports betting industry within a global transformation of the online gaming market.

2.5 Explain the system of regulation of gambling; which regulatory or governmental body is responsible for the supervision of gambling? Which body issues licences? Which body examines enforcement powers? Is there any limit on the number or duration of available licences?

In building the Macau gaming industry framework that resulted from the market liberalisation in 2001, and clearly aimed at providing the structure for the subsequent developments of the gaming legal regime, in 2003 the government of MSAR created the Gaming Inspection and Coordination Bureau (DICJ) (Administrative Regulation No. 34/2003).

The DICJ *'provides guidance and assistance to the Chief Executive of Macao SAR on the definition and execution of the economic policies for the operations of the casino games of fortune or other ways of gaming, Pari-Mutuels and gaming activities offered to the public'*.

The DICJ is the primary regulator and supervisory institution of the MSAR in respect of the gaming industry.

The duties and competences of DICJ include:

- to collaborate in the definition, co-ordination and execution of the economic policies for the operations of the casino games of fortune or other ways of gaming, pari-mutuels and gaming activities offered to the public;
- to examine, supervise and monitor the activities of the concessionaires, especially on their compliance with the legal, statutory and contractual obligations;
- to examine, supervise and monitor the eligibility and financial capability of the concessionaires or other parties stipulated by the law;
- to collaborate with the government in the process of locations and places authorisation and classification for the operations of casino games of fortune or other ways of gaming;
- to authorise and certify all the equipment and utensils used by the operations of the concessionaires approved in the respective concession;
- to issue licences for the junket promoters of casino games of fortune or other gaming activities;
- to examine, supervise and monitor the activities and promotions of the junket promoters, especially their compliance with the legal, statutory and contractual obligations, and other responsibilities stipulated in the applicable legislations;
- to examine, supervise and monitor the eligibility of the single or collective junket promoter(s), their partners and principal employees;
- to investigate and penalise any administrative infractions practised according to the appropriate substantial and procedural legislations;
- to ensure that the relationship of the concessionaires with the government and the public is compliant with the regulations and provides the highest interest to the MSAR; and
- to execute the competence which are not listed above but with similar nature according to the Chief Executive's order or the legal provisions.

Gaming concessionaires and sub-concessionaires are required to submit to the DICJ for record or inspection all significant documentation and periodic reports regarding their business and operation, as well as all matters requiring the MSAR government's approval or authorisation as required by laws, such as changes in shareholding structure, changes in control, directorship and key employees, gaming equipment, the concession or sub-concession contracts, as applicable, and other matters related to the operation of casino games.

Pursuant to Administrative Regulation No. 34/2003, which became effective on 4 November 2003, the DICJ is also entrusted with the responsibility to assist and support the Chief Executive of the MSAR in the definition and execution of economic policies for operation of casino games of fortune in the MSAR. The DICJ also collects and provides key information concerning the gaming industry in Macau, including gaming statistics, quarterly data of different gaming activities, and annual reports of gaming concessionaires and sub-concessionaires.

The DICJ is also responsible for assessing the gross daily income of the gaming concessionaires and sub-concessionaires. The DICJ continuously monitors the gaming concessionaires and sub-concessionaires' daily operations and tabulation of net-win generated from casino games, including casino table games and slot machines, through various control procedures conducted in the casinos.

The gaming concession agreements are entered into by and between MSAR, represented by the government, and the gaming concessionaires and gaming sub-concessions, and approved by the MSAR government.

As mentioned above, the Macau Gaming Law limits the number of concession to three. The three gaming concessions and the three gaming sub-concessions subsequently approved by the MSAR government have fixed terms, which, in the cases of the SJM concession and MGM sub-concession will expire on 31 March 2020, and, in the cases of the Wynn concession, Melco sub-concession, Galaxy concession and Venetian sub-concession, on 26 June 2022.

3. ONLINE GAMBLING

3.1 To what extent can online gambling be offered in your jurisdiction? Are licences available and, if so, for which gambling products? Please describe briefly the licensing process, who may apply, whether licences are limited in number and, if no licences are available, whether it is legal for online gambling to be offered. In the case of EU jurisdictions, please state whether there are any issues as to the legality of the local law at EU level. Please refer to any relevant cases at ECJ level and explain any measures taken or pending by the European Commission.

As mentioned above, although online gaming is foreseen as a gambling product in MSAR under the definition of interactive gaming, no operating rules have been enacted and no concessions have been awarded for this purpose by the MSAR government. Therefore, online gaming remains a mere concept within the Macau Gaming Law, which the MSAR government has shown very little interest in implementing and developing, considering the huge success of its land-based gaming industry.

3.2 Is there a distinction between the law applicable to B2B operations and that applicable to B2C operations?

Please refer to responses to questions 2.2 and 3.1 above.

3.3 What are the consequences for B2C or B2B operators who are active in your jurisdiction without having obtained or applied for the required permits, licences and approvals? What penalties and enforcement powers are available in respect of the illegal operators? Please outline any significant domestic decisions or enforcement

actions that have been taken by the relevant authorities in recent years.

Operating online gaming in MSAR without a concession granted by the MSAR government constitutes a breach of the Macau Gaming Law.

It is not clear if unauthorised online gaming would fall within the concept of illegal gambling and the sanctioning regime of the Illicit Gaming Law, as this law does not refer specifically to online gaming.

In any case, any online gaming operations that show a relevant connection with the MSAR jurisdiction, as outlined above, would be in contravention of the Macau Gaming Law and would face being shut down. We are not aware of any online gaming operations that have been developed based in the MSAR or with such a relevant connection, or any major enforcement actions that have taken place recently.

With respect to sports betting, any non-authorised operations that would also reveal a relevant connection with Macau jurisdiction, under the same parameters that we have established for online gaming, fall within the express provisions of the Illicit Gaming Law and constitute a criminal offence. They would therefore be subject to prosecution under Macau criminal laws.

From time to time, especially before a major international or world sports competition, it is quite common for the police, in an articulated effort between the Hong Kong, Macau and PRC Guangdong province authorities, to crack down on illicit sports betting syndicates.

3.4 What technical measures are in place (if any) to protect consumers from unlicensed operators, such as ISP blocking and payment blocking?

MSAR is a quite open and unregulated economy, and there is little or no control over payment platforms and internet access.

There are no obligations of geo-blocking imposed by Macau laws on its residents or on foreign countries in this regard. Each country will have its own rules in this respect.

The Macau residents/consumers can freely access any website and use the internet (including Facebook, other social media sites and even online gaming websites), without any type of restrictions or control.

3.5 Has the legal status of online gambling changed significantly in recent years and, if so, how?

Please refer to responses to questions 2.2 and 3.1 above.

3.6 Whilst acknowledging the inherent difficulty in predicting developments in gambling law, what are the likely developments in online gambling in your jurisdiction, both short term and long term? Are any specific amendments under consideration? Have there been any recent political developments, or do you envisage any in the near

future? Are any specific amendments under consideration? Are they likely to be adopted and, if so, what is the time scale?

The MSAR government has shown no interest in developing the online gaming business in MSAR. On the contrary, the DICJ has acknowledged, on a number of occasions, that they see online gaming as a segment of the gaming industry that would not add any value to the current gaming market in MSAR, which, for its scale, GGR results and complexity, keeps the government happy and the gaming regulator's hands full.

The development of online business in MSAR would require qualified resources, industrial know-how and technical sophistication that is clearly lacking in the current gaming regulatory structure. Land-based casinos are clearly the core business of MSAR's gaming industry, and will remain so for a long period of time. We do not anticipate any changes to the existing status quo of online gaming in MSAR.

We are not aware of any legislative initiatives aimed at regulating online gaming operations in MSAR, nor are we aware of any requests for online gaming concessions submitted by online gaming operators to the MSAR government.

3.7 Is the law the same in relation to mobile gambling and interactive gambling on television? If not, are there any headline differences?

There are no specific laws or rules and regulations in MSAR that are applicable to mobile gaming and interactive gaming at this stage.

4. LAND-BASED GAMING

4.1 Please describe the licensing regime (if any) for land-based gaming, and what products are included. Please set out what licences are available, and the licensing regime for them.

Gaming concessions are awarded by the MSAR government and materialised in a gaming concession agreement. The scope of the gaming concession agreements is the operation of casino games of chance or games of other forms, including electronic gaming machines, in casinos in the MSAR. The gaming concessions do not include mutual bets, gaming activities provided to the public, interactive gaming, or games of chance or any other gaming, betting or gambling activities on ships or airplanes.

The Macau Gaming Law only foresees the existence of three gaming concessions. However, in order to accommodate three more gaming operators, the MSAR government came up with the concept of gaming sub-concessions. Each gaming concessionaire was authorised by the MSAR government to enter into a sub-concession contract with a sub-concessionaire.

Although there are no legal rules regulating the gaming sub-concessions, it is nowadays generally accepted (and the government has recognised and acknowledged this in numerous correspondences exchanged with the gaming concessionaires and gaming sub-concessionaires) that the gaming sub-concessions are independent from the gaming concessions (in the sense that termination of one gaming concession will not affect the validity and existence of the associated sub-concession) and are subject to the same legal and regulatory regime.

The MSAR government has stated publicly that it has no intention in the near future – including the timeline of 2020/2022, when the existing gaming concessions and sub-concessions expire – to change the current number of gaming operators by awarding new concessions. Thus, we may consider the existing MSAR gaming market as a closed market with regard to new players, and it is expected to remain like this for the foreseeable future.

4.2 Please set out any particular limitations or requirements for (eg casino) operators, such as a ban on local residents gambling.

Macau residents can gamble in the local casinos and slot parlours without any restriction.

Article 24 of Macau Gaming Law determines the access restrictions to casinos and gaming areas. It should be noted that the restriction includes access to the casino or gaming area, as well as prohibiting gambling.

The most significant restrictions apply to MSAR civil servants and the employees of gaming concessionaires and sub-concessionaires in relation to the respective casinos and gaming areas.

Law 10/2012, published in the Official Gazette No. 35-I of 27 August 2012, increased the entry age to casino and gaming areas to 21.

In 2009, The MSAR stipulated commissions payable to junkets be set at a maximum of 1.25 per cent of rolling chip turnover. However, this cap or limitation only applies to the turnover-based commissions (rolling), not to revenue sharing arrangements.

The MSAR government has also capped the growth of annual table games at 3 per cent until 2022. This industry growth control measure was simply announced through a political statement issued by the Secretary for Economy and Finance of the MSAR government.

4.3 Please address the questions in 3.5 above, but in relation to land-based gaming.

The gaming legal system developed in MSAR in the light of the liberalisation of the gaming industry in 2001/2002 has remained basically unchanged for the last 12 or so years. The very few legislative initiatives that were taken during this period were motivated by political reasons rather than the desire to further complete and develop the MSAR gaming legal system and increase its juridical and regulatory sophistication. Quite important areas of the gaming industry remain to be regulated, and some of the existing rules and regulations require urgent updates to address the operational and regulatory issues that surfaced during the first 10 years of a new gaming system.

More relevant, perhaps, to the MSAR gaming industry are the decisions and procedures that, in the near future, will address the renewal of the current gaming concessions and sub-concessions.

One key question that has been recently raised on a number of occasions by the community of investors and gaming operators and analysts is what will happen when the Macau gaming concessions and the associated gaming sub-concessions expire in 2020 and 2022?

What we know at this stage:

- the term of gaming concessions/sub-concessions is an issue for the development of the Macau gaming industry and, in general, for the investment community;
- even if the current Chief Executive serves two terms, he will not be in office in 2020;
- it is a Macau official policy (reiterated by the current Chief Executive on various occasions) that Macau should seek to diversify its economy into non-gaming industries, such as conventions & exhibitions, leisure & entertainment and creative industries;
- Beijing exercises significant influence over Macau's gaming policy, and the central government has clearly indicated that Macau must control its casino growth; and
- if we consider the new projects planned for the Cotai Strip (Macau Studio City, Galaxy Phase 2, Louis XIII, Venetian Parcel 3, MGM, Wynn and SJM), which should come online from around 2015/2016, the normal payback period for financings of this type of development of 8/9 years will go beyond the 2020/2022 concessions/sub-concessions expiry dates.

It is true that the Macau Chief Executive has the prerogative to extend the concessions/sub-concessions' term for a maximum of five years, but this possibility can only be exercised once the 18 or 20 years' concession/sub-concession term has been fulfilled. It therefore does not help us to ascertain now what will happen then.

What we do not know:

- what the PRC's central government approach to gaming policies, travelling visa requirements, currency and capital flows will be, bearing in mind that each of these factors may, by itself, have a huge impact on the gaming sector in Macau, affecting the market circumstances under which the concessions and sub-concessions will be renegotiated;
- what will be the next MSAR Chief Executive's position in relation to the gaming industry and how the institutional relationship between Macau and China's central government will influence the policy-making process in Macau, considering the ongoing debate around the reform of the political system;
- how the Macau market will be affected by the new gaming developments around Asia including Singapore, Vietnam, Philippines, Cambodia, Korea, probably Taiwan and eventually Japan;
- where the Chinese economy will be in 2020 – specifically, that of the Guangdong province, economic performance of which has been proved to have a direct correlation with the gaming numbers in Macau as its most direct and immediate source of play; or
- what will be the outcome of some regulatory challenges (ongoing investigations in relation to FCPA, gaming licensing and listing rules

compliance) affecting some of the gaming operators in a very regulated industry.

Although we do not believe that, based on what we know today, any of the current gaming concessions and/or sub-concessions will be at risk of non-renewal, the renegotiation process will eventually open a window of opportunity for the MSAR government to:

- impose additional investment obligations to the gaming operators on non-gaming sectors of the economy and/or shorten the term of the gaming concessions/sub-concessions;
- increase the Special Gaming Tax (SGT) in order to retain more gaming revenue and to prevent the transfer of gaming profits to other jurisdictions;
- decrease the Special Gaming Tax in order to render the Macau gaming market more competitive in relation to other gaming jurisdictions around Asia;
- open the Macau gaming market to other key industry players who have showed a long-standing interest in investing in Macau;
- further control the gaming industry's growth by imposing contractual restrictions on the gaming operators (number of tables and slots); or
- enact legislation reviewing different aspects of the Macau gaming regime that have proved to have weak teeth and many loopholes.

We sincerely hope that the government and the regulator do not remain tight-lipped on these issues, and that well before 2020 we can see the legal path for business continuity being implemented with transparency and clear rules.

5. TAX

5.1 Please summarise briefly the tax regime applicable both to land-based and online gaming.

The bulk of casino taxation in Macau is centred on the SGT, which is calculated based on 35 per cent of the GGR.

In addition, the gaming operators (concessionaires and sub-concessionaires) are also subject to other two special levies:

- a contribution to a public foundation in Macau for the promotion, development and study of culture, society, economy, education, science and charity events: 1.6 per cent of GGR; and
- a contribution to the Macau government for urban development, tourism promotion and social security: 2.4 per cent of GGR (with the exception of the gaming concessionaire SJM, which is subject to only 1.4 per cent of GGR).

Common to all gaming operators is an annual fixed gaming premium in the amount of $3.8 million.

The gaming operators are also subject to a variable annual premium calculated as follows:

- $37,500 per VIP gaming table;
- $18,750 per mass market gaming table; and

- $125 per electric or mechanical gaming machine, including slot machines

All gaming operators are exempted from payment of Complementary Tax, which acts as a corporate tax or tax on profit in relation to gaming revenues. Such tax holiday has been granted pursuant to a Dispatch of the Chief Executive of Macau, which has so far been renewed for every five years in relation to each gaming operator.

As part of the gaming concessions/sub-concessions awarding process, the gaming operators were also subject to specific investment obligations in their integrated resorts/hotel/casinos, varying from $0.5 billion to $ 1.1 billion.

6. ADVERTISING

6.1 To what extent is the advertising of gambling permitted in your jurisdiction? Again, this should cover both land-based and online gaming. To the extent that advertising is permitted, how is it regulated?

The Macau Advertising Law (Law 7/89/M, Article 8, No. 1b) prohibits all advertising that contains as the main message any form of games of chance.

Considering that the Macau Advertising Law prohibits advertising gaming only as the main purpose of the message, a case-by-case analysis is required in order to assess if gambling is presented as the main purpose or direct call of the actual advertising message.

The fact that the advertisement message is not generated in Macau is irrelevant. As long as the gaming advertising message is displayed specifically in Macau in any format or support, it will be considered a violation of the Macau Advertising Law.

Advertisement online, displayed by websites accessible from Macau and available to Macau residents but not having a relevant connection with Macau (as defined above), would not qualify as an advertising message displayed in Macau for the purposes of the prohibition contained in Article 8, No. 1b of the Macau Advertising Law.

The relevant principle is that the gambling advertisement is displayed in Macau, not where it originates from. If the advertising message is displayed in Macau or is displayed online but there is a relevant connection between the online platform and Macau (as defined above), and gambling would constitute the main purpose of the advertising message, it is our opinion that such message would breach the Macau Advertising Law.

Sports betting advertising would not fall under the prohibition of Article 8, No. 1b of Law 7/89/M, since sports betting does not constitute a game of chance.

7. SOCIAL GAMING

7.1 We believe this to be a growing area. Please decide under what criteria social gaming is permitted in your jurisdiction. If games are free to play or if there is no prize, are they legal without a licence? Please address circumstances where virtual currency is used and

can be won: ie currency which is of no monetary or other value, save for as credits to take part in games. The answer should address the question whether game credits or virtual money can be exchanged for other prizes. Is any change to regulation in the area proposed or envisaged?

Once again, in MSAR there are no specific rules that address and regulate the new realities of social gaming.

Considering that there are similarities between social gaming and interactive gaming, namely on what concerns the internet platform supporting the gambling activity, one needs to consider the legality of social gaming by applying the criteria that the Macau Gaming Law established in relation to online gaming. If a specific social gaming product fulfils all the requisites contained in the definition of interactive gaming (please refer to question 2.2 above) and there is a relevant connection with MSAR jurisdiction, then a concession granted by MSAR government would be required and any operations carried out in the absence of such concession would breach the Macau Gaming Law.

On the other hand, if one of the elements of the definition of interactive gaming is missing, eg the game made available is not a game of chance or an electronic game offered in MSAR casinos, or there is no monetary element to the game either because there is no payment made by the player (bet or wager) or a prize (in cash or otherwise) is not offered, then this specific social gaming product would not fall under the definition of interactive gaming and, therefore, could be legally operated in MSAR. In other words, if the social game consists of a Macau casino game of chance or a slot machine, the player purchases credits that are redeemed for chips and plays with such chips, is able to win a prize in cash or otherwise, through a telecom medium (phone, tablet, internet, etc), this would constitute a situation qualified as interactive gaming under the Macau Gaming Law.

We do not expect any changes in the existing rules with respect to online gaming or the adoption of new rules with respect to social gaming in the near future.

Malta

CSB Advocates Dr Andrew Zammit, Dr Lynne Satariano & Mr Josef Cardona

1. OBJECTIVES AND STRUCTURE OF LEGISLATION

Lotto games are likely to have been operated in Malta since the end of the 17th and 18th century. However, it was only in 1922 that the Public Lotto Ordinance was enacted to establish the government monopoly for the organisation of lotto activities. The Racecourse Betting Ordinance was subsequently enacted in 1934 to regulate horse and dog racing licences.

The next milestone in the development of Maltese gambling history was in 1958 with the promulgation of the Kursaal Ordinance, which regulated casino activity. This statutory instrument was subsequently superseded by the Gaming Act 1998 which provided further controls and reinforcement of the regulatory framework for casinos.

In 2001 the Lotteries and Other Games Act (the Act) was enacted by the Maltese legislator. This Act established the Lotteries and Gaming Authority which was to replace the Director of Public Lotto and incorporated all gaming legislation into a single legislative instrument, with the exception of casinos which continue to be regulated by the Gaming Act.

The regulation of online gaming in Malta came into force in 2000 through amendments to the Public Lotto Ordinance. These regulations remained effective until 2004, when the Remote Gaming Regulations (the Regulations) came into force. The Regulations shifted regulatory focus from the 'games' to the 'means' by which the gaming was offered. The new Maltese regulatory regime became both game neutral (applicable to practically all types of games) and technology neutral (applicable to practically all types of technologies, namely internet, mobile, telephone and other types of remote gaming).

Today, Malta has established itself as a regulatory hub for online gaming. According to the Remote Gaming Update, to date over 430 licences have been issued to 280 remote gaming companies, making Malta one of the leading European jurisdictions within the sector. A number of interactive TV and mobile gaming operators are also based and licensed in Malta.

In terms of the information available on the Lotteries and Gaming Authority's website *www.lga.org.mt* relating to land-based gaming, Malta has one licensee with respect to the National Lottery, four licensed casinos, twenty-seven licensed gaming parlours and five licensed tombola (bingo) halls.

2. FRAMEWORK OF LEGISLATION

2.1 What is the legal definition of gambling and what falls within this definition?

There is no actual definition of 'gambling' *per se* under Maltese law, although the word 'gambling' is used in some parts of the various laws which regulate gaming in Malta. The law, however, does contain definitions for 'games' and 'gaming'.

For the purposes of the Lotteries and Other Games Act a 'game' means and includes a game of chance and a game of chance and skill, but does not include (i) a sport event (although it does include a sports bet and any other game of chance and/or game of chance and skill the operation or playing of which depends on a sport event or a set of sport events or the result or outcome thereof) and (ii) an amusement game.

A 'game of chance' means *'a game for money and/or prizes with a monetary value, the results of which are totally accidental'* and a 'game of chance and skill' means *'a game for money and, or prizes with a monetary value, the results of which are not totally accidental but depend, to a certain extent, on the skill of the participant'*.

A pure 'skill game', which is defined in the Lotteries and Other Games Act, as *'a game for money or money's worth the results of which depend, mainly, on the skill of the participant, other than a sport event'*, does not fall within the definition of 'game' as described above.

A 'bet' means *'a game in which the player is required to forecast any result or outcome in respect of one event or a set of events'*; and 'betting' means *'the playing of a bet'*.

It would also be pertinent to note that an 'amusement game' means *'a game played by means of an amusement machine'*, and an 'amusement machine' is *'a machine which is used for the purpose of playing games exclusively for amusement purposes and not for gambling purposes, where in the operation thereof, a successful player neither receives nor is offered any benefit other than the opportunity, if any, afforded by the automatic action of the machine, to play the game again without the insertion of other money or tokens'*.

The Remote Gaming Regulations furthermore define 'gaming' as *'an agreement, scheme, or arrangement between two or more parties to play together at a game of chance in which a prize or reward consisting of money or some other item of value, worth, advantage, or opportunity is offered or can be won and become the property of the winner under defined conditions established for the purpose of the game'*.

From the above definitions, therefore, it is clear that at the time of writing, any game (except a pure skill game) offering a monetary prize would fall within the definition of 'game' and 'gaming' under Maltese law.

2.2 What is the legal definition of online gambling and what falls within this definition?

The Remote Gaming Regulations define 'remote gaming' as *'any form of gaming by means of distance communications'*.

The same regulations specify that 'means of distance communication' includes *'any means which may be used for the communication, transmission, conveyance and receipt of information (including information in the form of data, text, images, sound or speech) or for the conclusion of a contract between two or more persons without the simultaneous physical presence of those persons'*.

The definition continues to state that such means may be *'unaddressed or addressed printed matter, a standard letter, telephone with or without human intervention (such as automatic calling machine, audiotext), radio, videophone (telephone with screen), videotext (microcomputer and television screen) with keyboard or touch screen, electronic mail, facsimile machine (fax), and television (teleshopping), and any other means of communication, transmission, conveyance and receipt of information by wire, radio, optical means, electromagnetic means or by any electronic means'*.

The Maltese definitions taken together therefore are very wide and cover all types of gaming (as defined in section 2.1 above) occurring through any means of distance communication, not merely those conducted through distance communication using electronic means.

2.3 Please set out the different gambling products identified by legislation.

Maltese Law regulates the following land-based gambling products:
- casinos and related games;
- gaming devices – defined in the Lotteries and Other Games Act as *'any electrical, electronic or mechanical device, ticket or any other thing which is used or intended for use in connection with the operation, promotion or sale of a game and, or in gaming'*. Slot machines are not specifically regulated under Maltese law; however, a slot machine would fall within the definition of a 'gaming device';
- racecourse betting, including betting on horse and greyhound racing;
- sports betting;
- the National Lottery, which includes the following games: Super 5, Lotto, Scratchers Instant Tickets, U*Bet, Quick Keno and Bingo 75;
- Advertising Lotteries and Not for Profit Lotteries; and
- bingo/tombola.

Maltese law regulates the following online gambling products:
- casino-type games;
- poker networks; and
- remote betting.

2.4 Please list the different requirements for each gambling product, including legal classifications for each; for example, is poker a game of skill or game of chance?

Land-based
- Land-based casinos and related games are primarily regulated under the Gaming Act. In order to operate a casino, a concession must be obtained from the Minister of Finance, together with a licence issued by the Maltese Lotteries and Gaming Authority. It should be noted that land-

based poker games are not regulated *per se* but would be considered as a type of casino game. Poker would generally be deemed to be a 'game of chance and skill' (as defined in section 2.1 above). The Gaming Act regulates the setting up of rooms dedicated to card games, which must be approved specifically within the casino licence or at a later stage by the Gaming Board.

- Gaming devices are primarily regulated under the Gaming Devices Regulations. In this respect, one should note the distinction between a 'gaming device' (which offers the possibility of winning a prize) and an 'amusement machine' (which, as mentioned in section 2.1 above, is for entertainment purposes only, without offering the possibility of winning a prize). The latter is therefore not considered to be a gambling product (and hence is excluded from the present analysis); however, it may be noted that 'amusement machines' are also regulated and licensed separately under the Amusement Machine Regulations. In relation to 'gaming devices', the relevant licence is also required in order to manufacture, assemble, service, supply, use, hosting or operation of such device. Four different categories of licence exist for gaming devices.

- Racecourse betting, including betting on horse and greyhound racing, is primarily regulated under the Lotteries and Other Games Act and the Racecourse Betting Ordinance. The requisite licence is required for on-course racecourse betting and is regulated by the Malta Lotteries and Gaming Authority. On-track bookmakers are licensed by the Malta Racing Club.

- Sports betting is primarily regulated under the Lotteries and Other Games Act and the Betting on Result of Football Matches Order. The latter provides a list of sports grounds, within the Maltese Islands, where betting on football matches is prohibited.

- The National Lottery, which is the main lottery in Malta, is primarily regulated under the Lotteries and Other Games Act. This Act provides that the National Lottery may be conducted under Ministerial authority or by any other person in whose favour a concession is granted for this purpose. Only one person in possession of a valid licence may operate the National Lottery at any given time.

- Advertising Lotteries and Not for Profit Lotteries require a specific permit and the request for such permit is made by means of a form (one for Advertising Lotteries and one for Not for Profit Lotteries organised by Non-Profit Organisations). The forms can be found on Lotteries and Gaming Authority website *www.lga.org.mt* and must be accompanied by specified information such as the nature and value of the prize that can be won or who would be eligible to participate in the game. The forms also set various conditions by which the applicant must abide.

- Bingo/tombola games are primarily regulated under the Lotteries and Other Games Act and the Commercial Tombola (Bingo) Regulations). The relative licence is required for a person to operate commercial tombola games in a tombola hall. There are two licences in this respect and the differences relate to the size of the tombola hall and the duration of the licence.

Online

- Casino-type games are primarily regulated under the Remote Gaming Regulations. A remote gaming casino would generally require a 'Class 1' remote gaming licence. The Remote Gaming Regulations Guidelines, issued by the Lotteries and Gaming Authority describe the Class 1 licence as a licence *'for operators managing their own risk on repetitive games. This covers casino-type games'*.
- Poker networks are primarily regulated under the Remote Gaming Regulations. In the case of P2P Remote Poker Networks, where players on the network play against each other, and the operator takes a percentage of the rake for organising and promoting the game, the operator would require a Class 3 remote gaming licence which is defined in Schedule 1 of the Remote Gaming Regulations as *'a licence to promote and, or abet remote gaming from Malta'*.
- Remote betting is primarily regulated under the Remote Gaming Regulations and would require a 'Class 2' remote gaming licence, which is defined as *'a remote betting office licence'*. The Remote Gaming Regulations Guidelines, issued by the Lotteries and Gaming Authority describe the Class 2 licence as a licence *'for operators managing their own risk on events based on a matchbook. Under this class operators can offer fixed odds betting.'*

2.5 Explain the system of regulation of gambling; which regulatory or governmental body is responsible for the supervision of gambling? Which body issues licences? Which body examines enforcement powers? Is there any limit on the number or duration of available licences?

The Lotteries and Gaming Authority is the primary regulatory body responsible for the governance of all gaming activities in Malta. Most gaming-related licences are issued by the Lotteries and Gaming Authority, although, as specified in section 2.4 above, a Ministerial concession is required for the operation of the National Lottery and of a casino. Moreover, the Department of Public Lotto is currently responsible for the licensing of commercial communications games, that is, games which are organised with the purpose of promoting or encouraging the sale of goods or services. These games do not in themselves constitute an economic activity, and any payments required to be made by the participant serve only to acquire promoted goods or services.

The Lotteries and Gaming Authority generally avoids taking a bureaucratic approach to the licensing of gaming operators, by adopting an industry-focused, practical attitude to the particular circumstances of each applicant or licensee, and by implementing measures to address issues which licensees may bring to their attention.

The license for the operation of all National Lottery games in Malta is exclusive, and was awarded to Maltco Lotteries Limited in 2012 for a 10 year period. Casinos licences in Malta are also granted for a period of 10 years. Remote gaming licences, on the other hand, are granted for a five year period, and may be renewed for further periods of five years. There is no limit imposed on the number of remote gaming licences that may be granted.

3. ONLINE GAMBLING

3.1 To what extent can online gambling be offered in your jurisdiction? Are licences available and, if so, for which gambling products? Please describe briefly the licensing process, who may apply, whether licences are limited in number and, if no licences are available, whether it is legal for online gambling to be offered. In the case of EU jurisdictions, please state whether there are any issues as to the legality of the local law at EU level. Please refer to any relevant cases at ECJ level and explain any measures taken or pending by the European Commission.

In accordance with Article 5 of the Lotteries and Other Games Act, a game of chance or a game of chance and skill, cannot be operated, promoted or sold by any person in Malta unless it authorised to be operated under any law in Malta.

An exception to this rule is made if the game is authorised to be operated under any law enacted by a member state of the European Union (EU), by a member state of the European Economic Area (EEA), or by any jurisdiction or territory approved by the Lotteries and Gaming Authority.

The amendments to the Remote Gaming Regulations, which came into force on the 1st March 2011, reiterate the same principle in Regulation 3 by stating that *'no person shall operate or promote or sell or abet remote gaming in or from Malta unless such person is in possession of a valid licence issued by the Authority or is in possession of an equivalent authorisation by the government or competent authority of an EEA member state, or any other jurisdiction approved by the Authority'.*

Malta has not had any issues as to the legality of the local law at EU level, primarily due to the fact that, as can be evidenced from the abovementioned section of the law, it employs a 'recognition' regime in terms of which a gaming licence issued by another EEA member state is permitted to offer its games in Malta, and also to enter into Business to Business (B2B) agreements with Malta-based licensees. This approach is based on the principle of the freedom to provide services within the EU, as established under Article 56 (ex Article 49) of Treaty on the Functioning of the European Union.

Malta also recognises a licence issued in respect of a remote gaming operator by a jurisdiction which falls outside of the EEA zone, but which is approved by the Lotteries and Gaming Authority. To date, the Authority has entered into bilateral Memoranda of Understanding with the Isle of Man, Jersey and Denmark.

In terms of the products which can be licensed and the licences available, these have been detailed in section 2.4 above, and due to the fact that the Remote Gaming Regulations are game neutral, the same regulations apply with respect to the various products.

There is no limitation imposed on the number of remote gaming licences which can be obtained in Malta; however, an applicant for a licence granted by the Lotteries and Gaming Authority must be a body corporate established in Malta in terms of the Companies Act. Furthermore, the individuals involved in the operation must be 'fit and proper persons' to carry out the licensed activities.

As a general rule under Maltese Law, an applicant for a licence must submit what is referred to as 'Know Your Customer' (KYC) information as part of the application process, in order to enable the Lotteries and Gaming Authority to carry out the relevant due diligence checks. With regard to individuals involved with the applicant entity, particularly shareholders (usually those with five per cent or more ownership of, or controlling interest in the applicant company), directors, and key employees, information requested would generally take the form of personal background and financial information; criminal record information; information relating to pecuniary, equity and other interests in the applicant entity and interests in any other commercial activity. This information is generally substantiated by the submission of birth certificates, passport copies, passport photos, police conduct certificates and bank and professional references. Forms which must be completed by individuals in this respect can be found on the Lotteries and Gaming Authority website *www.lga.org.mt*. Where a body corporate is a shareholder of the applicant, the Authority generally also requires the certificate, memorandum and articles of incorporation, a certificate of good standing, and bank and professional references in relation thereto. The Authority conducts probity investigations with other national and international regulatory bodies and law enforcement agencies.

An applicant for a licence granted must also submit evidence of possessing financial means and expertise available to carry out the operations in respect of which his application was submitted and to fulfil all its obligations under the law. As a matter of the Authority's policy, a business plan is generally provided by the applicant as part of an application process, which would normally include a marketing and sales plan, forecast balance sheets and a financing plan showing sources of finance, thereby distinguishing between shareholder funds and other funds (such as venture capital and bank guarantees). The various laws also provide that the licensee may be obliged to obtain (and maintain) a bank guarantee, which would generally be required to secure players' funds and winnings, payment of fees, taxes and any administrative penalties or other sums which may be due and payable by the licensee.

Depending upon the type of licence required, other information will be requested by the Authority such as specific details in relation to the gaming systems and control systems of the applicant. Examples of such information would include details relating to the games, the manufacturer of such games, certification by third parties, rules of the game, terms, conditions and procedures which players must abide by and the system architecture.

The Authority will evaluate an application for a gaming licence by considering, amongst other things, the financial position, financial background and business reputation of the applicant's promoters, shareholders and directors, whether the applicant has followed policies and will take affirmative steps to prevent money laundering and other suspicious transactions, and whether the applicant has the capacity and the internal control structures to enable it to comply with the policies and directives which the Authority deems appropriate.

If the audit is successful, the Authority will issue a licence with a validity period of five years, which is renewable after the licensee is submitted to further audits. In granting a licence the Authority always retains the discretion to impose such conditions as it may deem appropriate, and may from time to time after the granting of the licence, vary or revoke any condition so imposed, or impose new conditions.

3.2 Is there a distinction between the law applicable to B2B operations and that applicable to B2C operations?

Maltese law does create a distinction between B2B operations and B2C operations. The licences described in section 2.4 above in fact apply in the case of B2C operations. Vendors of remote gaming software who also intend to provide management and hosting facilities on their gaming platform to such B2C other operators, require a Class 4 remote gaming licence. The Class 4 remote gaming licence is described in Schedule 1 of the Remote Gaming Regulations as *'a licence to host and manage remote gaming operators, excluding the licensee himself'*.

The licensing or sale in Malta of remote gaming software, by itself, does not create the requirement for a Maltese licence unless the vendor is managing the software for the gaming operator.

In accordance with the policy laid down by the Lotteries and Gaming Authority, 'intermediaries' (also generally known in the industry as 'skins', 'affiliates' or 'white labels'), who partner up with a licensee for marketing purposes (generally referring traffic to the licensee's website through a link on its own website), are not required to possess a licence. However, notification to the Authority, prior to commencement of the intermediary's operations, is necessary. Such intermediaries would be considered by the Authority to be outside the scope of licensing if they merely act as referrers of player traffic to the licensee, without having a direct relationship with the player. Thus a licence is not required insofar as the intermediary does not register players, manage players' funds or undertake any gaming risk.

3.3 What are the consequences for B2C or B2B operators who are active in your jurisdiction without having obtained or applied for the required permits, licences and approvals? What penalties and enforcement powers are available in respect of the illegal operators? Please outline any significant domestic decisions or enforcement actions that have been taken by the relevant authorities in recent years.

As a general rule, it is an offence to engage in any form of gaming that is not duly licensed under the relevant laws. Any person so guilty of an offence will, on conviction, be liable to a fine of not less than EUR 6,988.12 and not more than EUR 232,937.34, or to imprisonment for a term of not more than two years, or to both such fine and imprisonment. Where the person convicted of such an offence is a recidivist, he will be liable to a fine of not less than EUR 11,646.87 and not more than EUR 349,406.01, or to imprisonment for a term of not less than six months and of not more than three years, or to both such fine and imprisonment. Where the person found guilty is the director, manager, secretary or other similar officer of a company or other undertaking, the said person will be deemed to be vested with the legal representation of the same company or other undertaking, and the said company or undertaking will be held jointly liable for the payment of the said fine.

The Zeturf case (*GIE Pari Mutuel Urbain (PMU) v Zeturf Limited*, 9 January 2007, Civil Appeal Number 92/2006/1) concerned the issue of whether a judgment given by the Paris Court of Appeal ordering Zeturf (the holder of a Maltese remote gaming licence) to cease taking online bets on horse races organised in France was enforceable in Malta in terms of Regulation 44/2001. The case originated from an action brought by GIE Pari Mutuel Urbain (PMU), a French company which had the primary object of safeguarding French public policy in respect of betting on horse races. Zeturf argued that the decision of the French court did not contain an order enforceable in Malta in terms of Regulation 44/2001, since it related to an administrative subject-matter. The Maltese Court of Appeal ultimately agreed with this reasoning and held that, although PMU was a private company, the laws under which it was incorporated and the scope for which it was incorporated went beyond those applicable between private persons insofar as the rights and obligations conferred on such company are concerned. The court held that, consequently, PMU had acted not within the ambit of the private law that regulates civil or commercial dealings between private persons, but within the ambit of the public law intended to safeguard French public policy. It went on to conclude on the basis of these considerations that the decision of the French court which PMU was seeking to enforce in Malta was one which (although formally or apparently of a civil or commercial nature) fell within the ambit of public law, and was consequently excluded from the remit of Regulation 44/2001. To date, Zeturf continues to retain its licence in terms of the Remote Gaming Regulations.

3.4   What technical measures are in place (if any) to protect consumers from unlicensed operators, such as ISP blocking and payment blocking?

There are no such technical measures in place at the time of writing.

3.5   Has the legal status of online gambling changed significantly in recent years and, if so, how?

The Lotteries and Other Games Act Remote Gaming (Amendment) Regulations, 2011, which were brought into force on the 1st March 2011, amended the Remote Gaming Regulations and gave effect to the recognition of a licence issued by the government or competent authority of an EEA member state, or any other jurisdiction approved by the Authority, as detailed in section 3.1 above. Although this concept was already established through the Lotteries and Other Games Act, these amendments clarified what could previously have been interpreted as a contradictory provision where both laws were compared, due to the fact that the Regulations, unlike the Parent Act, did not specifically recognise a licence that was not issued under Maltese law. A number of changes to the gaming taxes and licence fees were also effected through these amendments.

3.6   Whilst acknowledging the inherent difficulty in predicting developments in gambling law, what are the likely developments in online gambling in your jurisdiction, both short term and long term? Are any specific amendments under consideration? Have there been any recent political developments, or do you envisage any in the near future? Are any specific amendments under consideration? Are they likely to be adopted and, if so, what is the time scale?

As explained above, Malta's legislation is technology and game neutral, and compliant with the provisions on the freedom to provide services established by the Treaty on the Functioning of the European Union. No further significant changes to the remote gaming legislation in Malta are expected in the short term; however, we understand that the Lotteries and Gaming Authority continues to discuss and negotiate bilateral agreements with other gaming regulators both within and outside of the EU. The intended purpose behind such bilateral agreements would be the mutual recognition of a licence issued in either of the jurisdictions involved, as well as a common position on matters such as gaming tax, cross-border disputes, enforcement and sharing of information.

3.7   Is the law the same in relation to mobile gambling and interactive gambling on television? If not, are there any headline differences?

As mentioned above, the Maltese remote gaming legislation is technology neutral and therefore applicable to almost all types of technologies. The Remote Gaming Regulations, however, specifically exclude from the definition of 'remote gaming' games carried out by means of phone-ins during radio and television programmes.

A number of interactive TV and mobile gaming operators (not based on the phone-in model) are also based and licensed in Malta and have been licensed in accordance with the same processes outlined above.

The Authority may, moreover, impose additional conditions to ensure compliance with the Regulations in cases where the proposed business model is not commonplace; for example, the Authority may request an applicant to impose specific security measures to ensure that a minor would not be able to place bets through his parents' mobile phones.

4. LAND-BASED GAMING

4.1 Please describe the licensing regime (if any) for land based gaming, and what products are included. Please set out what licences are available, and the licensing regime for them.

The various land-based gaming products and the licensing regimes applicable thereto have been amplified in section 2.4 above. As a general rule, there is no limitation with regard to the number of licences which can be issued in relation to a particular product; however, the National Lottery, as mentioned above, can only be operated by one person at any given time, and is granted though a competitive process.

The licensing procedure is (with the exception of the National Lottery), in principle similar to that described in section 3.1 above in relation to online gaming, and requires the submission of KYC documentation, financing and information regarding the control system and gaming system of the activities being licensed.

Where the licensing process entails the licensing of a premises, information such as a description of the nature, location and dimension of the premises, architectural plans, relevant diagrams (for example, indicating where gaming devices are to be located) and development permits issued by the Malta Environment and Planning Authority in respect of the premises to be licensed, may be required.

In relation to the duration of licences granted, licences under the Gaming Devices Regulations are granted for one year; a casino licence remains in force for up to 10 years; the National Lottery licence is issued for such term as the Authority, after consultation with the Minister of Finance, may specify in the licence. Licences for tombola halls can be issued for six months or one year, depending on the type of licence required.

Licences may, in most circumstances, be renewed. On the other hand, the licence to operate the National Lottery is only renewable for a limited period and given the subsistence of specific circumstances.

4.2 Please set out any particular limitations or requirements for (eg casino) operators, such as a ban on local residents gambling.

As a general rule, players under 18 years of age cannot take part in any games offered by a licensee. With respect to casinos, however, Maltese citizens under the age of 25 years may not enter a casino. A game forming part of the National Lottery cannot be sold to a person under the age of 16.

A person may not be allowed to enter a casino if the person has asked for a ban or restriction on his own admission. A ban on, or restriction of, admission has effect during the period requested by the person concerned, which must not be less than six months and not more than one year. Any such ban or restriction cannot be cancelled before its expiry. Furthermore, a licensee must ensure that persons who may have a problem with pathological gambling are not given access to the gaming area.

4.3 Please address the questions in 3.5 above, but in relation to land-based gaming.

The legal status of land-based gambling has not undergone any significant changes in recent years.

5. TAX
5.1 Please summarise briefly the tax regime applicable both to land based and online gaming.

Land-based

With regard to the operation of casinos, taxes are paid to the Lotteries and Gaming Authority on a monthly basis and are calculated by the Authority based on the gross earnings of the casino. These can be set off against gross losses over two-month periods. In all cases, the tax must be paid within seven days from the end of the previous month. Furthermore, there is a tax payable on the income derived from the entrance fees of the casino.

The taxes related to gaming parlours are set out in the table below:

Description of licence or authorisation	Placement tax
Class 1 Licence	Nil
Class 2 Licence	Nil
Class 3 Licence	–€200 per relevant gaming device per month where the gross gaming revenue of each relevant gaming device does not exceed €1,000 for that relevant month; or –20% of the monthly gross gaming revenue generated by every relevant gaming device where the gross gaming revenue of each relevant gaming device exceeds €1000 for that relevant month
Class 4 Licence	Nil
Approval of relevant gaming devices	Nil
Approval of games	Nil
Approval of premises	N/A
Approval of employees	N/A

With respect to tombola halls, the Commercial Tombola Regulations provide that a licensee shall pay the Lotteries and Gaming Authority 10 per cent of the value of every scoresheet and/or 30 per cent of the total revenue on entrance fees. Where bingo is being offered by a non-profit organisation, a licensee must tender a duty of EUR 34.94 in respect of each session.

The licensee for a non-profit Lottery must pay the Ministry of Finance through the Lotteries and Gaming Authority, 25 per cent on the aggregate retail value of all prizes which can be won in such game.

Remote gaming

The taxes related to remote gaming are outlined in the following table:

Tax	EUR/per cent	
Class 1 Licence	4,660	For the first six months
	7,000	Per month for the entire duration of the licence
Class 1 Licence opening on a hosting platform in possession of a class 4 Remote Gaming Licence (class 1 on 4)	1,200	Per month for the entire duration of the licence
Class 2 Licence	0.5 per cent	Of the gross amount of bets accepted in remote betting operations
Class 2 Licence operation on a hosting platform in possession of a Class 4 Remote Gaming Licence (Class 2 on 4)	0.5 per cent	Of the gross amount of bets accepted in remote betting operations
Class 3 Licence	5 per cent	Of real income
Class 3 Licence operation on a hosting platform in possession of a Class 4 Remote Gaming Licence (Class 3 on 4)	5 per cent	Of real income
Class 4 Licence hosting and managing other remote gaming operators	Nil	For the first six months
	2,330	Per month for the subsequent six months
	4,660	Per month thereafter for the duration of the licence
Class 4 Licence hosting and managing an operator which is not in possession of the relevant Class 1, 2 or 3 Licence in terms of the regulations, though hosting as an EEA licensed Business to Consumer operator	1,165	Per month per operator, paid by the Class 4 Licensee
Remote Gaming Tax Capping per licensee per remote gaming licence	466,000	Per annum

6. ADVERTISING

6.1 To what extent is the advertising of gambling permitted in your jurisdiction? Again, this should cover both land based and online gaming. To the extent that advertising is permitted, how is it regulated?

As mentioned in section 3.1 above, a game of chance or a game of chance and skill cannot be promoted by any person in Malta unless such person is in possession of a valid licence issued by the Authority or is in possession of an equivalent authorisation by the government or competent authority of an EEA member state, or any other jurisdiction approved by the Authority.

It should be noted that the Code of Conduct on Advertising, Promotions and Inducements, which applies to all types of gaming, lays out the restrictions imposed on a licensee. The Code states generally that a licensee must not engage in advertising that:

- encourages anyone to contravene a gaming law;
- shows people under 18 years gambling;
- encourages or targets people under 18 years old to gamble;
- is false or untruthful, particularly about the chances of winning or the expected return to a gambler;
- suggests that gambling is a form of financial investment;
- suggests that skill can influence games that are purely games of chance;
- promotes smoking and, or the abuse of consumption of alcohol while gambling;
- implies that gambling promotes or is required for social acceptance, personal or financial success or the resolution of any economic, social or personal problems;
- contains endorsements by well-known personalities or celebrities that suggest gambling contributes to their success;
- exceeds the limits of decency;or
- tarnishes the goodwill and privilege that is associated or related in any manner whatsoever with being a licensee, or tarnishes the image or reputation of another licensee.

Furthermore, promotions (except junket gaming and tournaments) must not commit people to gamble for a minimum period of time or to gamble a minimum amount in order to qualify for player rewards. When a licensee publishes any advertising or conducts a promotion that encourages people to engage in any activity other than gambling, he must not refer, whether directly or indirectly, to the licensee's gambling facilities.

In relation to casinos, the Gaming Act sets out four forms of advertising that are prohibited, as follows:

- informing the public that any premises in Malta are being used as a casino;
- inviting the public to take part as players in any gaming which takes place in a casino, or to apply for information about facilities for taking part as players in a casino;

- inviting the public to subscribe any money or money's worth to be used in gaming in a casino or to apply for information about facilities for subscribing any money or money's worth to be so used; and
- inviting the public to take part as players in any gaming which takes place, or is to take place, in any casino outside Malta or to apply for information about facilities for taking part as players in any gaming which takes place, or is to take place, outside Malta.

With respect to the National Lottery, the Lotteries and Other Games Act states that it shall not be lawful for a person advertising, selling, offering for sale or offering the opportunity to participate in a game which does not form part of the National Lottery to give a false indication that it is a game which does in fact form part of the National Lottery.

The Remote Gaming Regulations place some restrictions on the manner in which a remote gaming company advertises its services. The law prohibits a licensee from engaging in advertising that:

- implies that remote gaming promotes or is required for social acceptance, personal or financial success or the resolution of any economic, social or personal problems;
- contains endorsements by well-known personalities that suggest remote gaming contributed to their success;
- is specifically directed at encouraging individuals under 18 years of age to engage in remote gaming; or
- exceeds the limits of decency.

Additionally, a licensee must not engage in any activity that involves sending of unsolicited electronic mail, whether it is through its own operation or by the intervention of third parties.

The Lotteries and Gaming Authority is responsible for the regulation of advertising of gaming in Malta.

7. SOCIAL GAMING

7.1 We believe this to be a growing area. Please decide under what criteria social gaming is permitted in your jurisdiction. If games are free to play or if there is no prize, are they legal without a licence? Please address circumstances where virtual currency is used and can be won: ie currency which is of no monetary or other value, save for as credits to take part in games. The answer should address the question whether game credits or virtual money can be exchanged for other prizes. Is any change to regulation in the area proposed or envisaged?

As mentioned previously, the gaming legislation in Malta is both technology and game neutral; therefore the same criteria mentioned above would be applicable to social gaming in the same manner as they would be applied with respect to any other game which is operated, sold or promoted, in any manner, in Malta, as long as it falls within the definition of 'game' or 'bet' as described in section 2.1 above.

The main issue as to whether a social game would require a licence relates to whether the prize which can be won through the playing of the game has a monetary value or otherwise. As concluded in section 2.1 above, it is clear that the definitions of 'game' and 'gaming' under Maltese law require that a monetary prize and/or a prize with a monetary value can be won through the playing of the game. Given a situation where the only prizes on offer through the playing of a game would be further credits to take part in the games, and where the prizes cannot be exchanged for cash, and credits cannot be exchanged with other players, then there is no monetary value to the prize being offered. The principle here is that an online game in which a successful player does not receive any benefit other than the opportunity to play the game again, should not be regulated in the same manner as game which could result in the winning of a prize with monetary value.

Finally, it should be noted that pure 'skill games' (as opposed to games of chance or 'hybrid' games which contain both an element of chance and an element of skill), are currently not regulated in Malta; however, the Lotteries and Gaming Authority plans to introduce the Digital Games Regulations to regulate skill games wherein there is a monetary benefit for the winner. The introduction of these Regulations is intended to complement the implementation of the Government of Malta's Digital Strategy.

Mexico

Bufete Carrillo Gamboa, S.C. César Morales Galán

1. OBJECTIVES AND STRUCTURE OF LEGISLATION

Gambling is currently a permitted activity in México, subject to the issuance of governmental authorisation to conduct gaming activities from the competent authority. It is also worth noting that gambling is an activity subject to regulation issued by the federal government and legislature and not to that enacted at the state or local level; with the exception of tax issues, which will be addressed later in this chapter.

The United Mexican States first adopted a federal system in the *Acta Constitutiva* of 1824; however, as a result of political instability in those times, Mexico changed from a centralist to a federalist system between 1824 and 1857. It was in the 1857 Constitution that Mexico adopted a federal system which was retained in the Political Constitution of the United Mexican States (the Constitution) now in effect and which dates back to 1917 and has not experienced any major amendment regarding the existence of México's federal government system. Pursuant to Article 124 of the Mexican Constitution, the authorities and competences not expressly assigned by the Mexican Constitution to the officials of the federal government shall be deemed reserved to the states.

The ability to legislate on gaming was not originally conferred on the federal legislature pursuant to Article 73 of the Mexican Constitution, which Article lists those activities or areas that fall within the scope of competence of the federal legislature for its regulation. Therefore, it could reasonably be argued that originally and even when the 1917 Constitution was adopted; it was for the state legislatures to regulate gaming. In fact, there are some precedents that go back to the commencement of the 20th century and some are subsequent to the 1917 Constitution, when various types of games, wagers and betting activities were regulated by the local legislatures, particularly those related to horse races and wager activities on those events.

As noted, the 1917 Constitution did not originally include the authority to regulate gambling by the federal legislature. Section X of Article 73 of the Constitution enacted as the 18th amendment to Article 73 of the Constitution, which was also the eighth amendment to section X of the Article in question, when through a Decree published on 29 December 1947, specifically granted authority to the federal legislature in Section X to legislate on games where bets are crossed (wagers) and games played involving draws of numbers or symbols.

Based on the amendment to section X of Article 73 of the Constitution, the federal legislature enacted the Federal Games and Draws Law (the Gaming Law), which was published in the Official Gazette of the

Federation (DOF) on 31 December 1947 and has been in effect since
5 January 1948, as per the First Transitory Article of the Gaming Law.
The Gaming Law continues to be the statute that currently governs and
regulates gaming activities in México. Originally, the problem with the
Gaming Law was that it was a very general statute that required either
legislative or regulatory supplementation to provide the detailed content
necessary for its adequate application and operability. However, it was
not until the Regulations of the Federal Games and Draws Law (Gaming
Regulations), which were published in the DOF on 17 September 2004
and came into effect 20 business days thereafter – almost 57 years after the
Gaming Law was enacted – that the Mexican federal government acted to
supplement the Gaming Law with a more detailed and thorough regulation
of gambling activity.

The Gaming Regulations have subsequently been amended (first on 19
October 2012, then on 23 October 2013). Although they attempted to clarify
the technical elements of slot machine gaming activities, specifically related
to skilful electronic games, the first amendments were so ambiguous that
many of them were again revised and clarified with the decree published
on 23 October 2013. For example, pursuant to the 2012 amendments, slot
machines (*máquinas tragamonedas*) were permitted so long as the conduction
of gaming activities via slot machines was authorised through an express
permit or authorisation issued by the Ministry of the Interior (SEGOB),
whereas now the conduction of such gaming activities is prohibited;
However, the same devices that under the 2012 amendments qualified
as slot machines and were permitted are now permitted and qualify as
electronic gaming devices for the conduction of number or symbol draws
through the definition of draw of numbers or symbols through devices.

Also, it was an important concern of the Regulator and the gaming
industry in general that many permit holders operated through third
parties that were not recognised by the Regulator nor had any reporting or
compliance obligations with the Regulator; therefore, the 2013 amendments
to the Gaming Regulations attempt to create rules and obligations for permit
holders for the purpose of preventing the operation of gaming facilities
by individuals or entities that are not supervised by the Regulator. This is
still a very common practice in Mexico and is known as 'permit-renting',
commonly under a fixed consideration or a revenue share scheme to be paid
by the unauthorised operator to the permit holder.

Nevertheless, since the *Partido Revolucionario Institucional* returned to
power in December 2012, and specifically as of February 2014, the House
of Representatives (*Cámara de Diputados*) and SEGOB have made multiple
commitments and communications stating that they will collaborate and
work closely together to draft a new legal framework that meets the needs
of a globalised gaming industry and addresses all regulatory needs based on
the technological developments now available, as well as to offer certainty
and clarity to permit holders, gaming operators and their customers,
incentivise growth and investment in the gaming industry, and facilitate

the application of such legal framework to SEGOB and any other competent authorities.

To summarise the current legal status of gaming activity in Mexico we should note that: (i) gambling regulation falls within the scope of authority of the federal government and the federal legislature; (ii) that gaming activity is currently regulated by the Gaming Law, which dates back to 1947, and by the Gaming Regulations, which were published in 2004 and amended in 2012 and 2013; (iii) that the current statute regulating gaming is outdated and as a result gives the Mexican regulator very broad discretion to issue gaming permits, allow gaming activities and expand or reduce the specific activities which could be considered as lawful gaming or gambling activities in Mexico, based on changes of criteria or interpretation; and (iv) that the Gaming Regulations of 2004 were an effort to comprehensively regulate gambling but themselves have many inconsistencies and are also outdated as they do not thoroughly or adequately address many recent business and technical developments in the gambling industry (eg online gambling).

2. FRAMEWORK OF LEGISLATION
2.1 What is the legal definition of gambling and what falls within this definition?

The Gaming Law does not include a legal definition of gambling or wagers.

Article 1 of the Gaming Law contains a general prohibition which states that within the national territory of Mexico, games of chance and games where bets are crossed are prohibited. Further, Article 2 of the Gaming Law gives some examples of what are considered to be games and expressly provides that '*the following games may be permitted: chess, dominoes and others of similar nature, dice, bowling, billiards, ball games in all their forms and denominations, races, horse races and car races, and in general all kinds of sports, and draws*' and that '*any other games not indicated shall be considered as prohibited for purposes of this law.*'

Notwithstanding the foregoing, the Gaming Law provides that the conduct of games where bets are crossed and draws of numbers or symbols occur, require a permit from SEGOB, Article 4 of the Gaming Law. In addition, Article 3 of the Gaming Law provides that '*the Federal Executive Power, through SEGOB, will regulate, authorise, control and supervise any kind of games where bets are crossed and draws (occur)...*'

In 2004, Article 3 of the Gaming Regulations included some legal definitions including the following:
- 'Wager or bet': means an amount which may be valued in Mexican currency and that is risked in a game contemplated by the Gaming Law and regulated by the Gaming Regulations with the possibility to obtain and win a prize, which amount, added to the risked amount shall be higher than such risked amount.
- 'Chance': means the uncertainty on which the result of a game is dependent and which is completely independent from the will of the player.

- 'Game where a bet is crossed': any kind of game where a bet is crossed, among those provided by the Gaming Law and the Gaming Regulations and authorised by SEGOB.
- 'Prize': payment in cash or in kind that is obtained by the winner of a game where a bet is crossed or a draw made.
- 'Draw': activity whereby the holder of a ticket through the prior selection of a number, combination of numbers or any other symbol, obtains the right to participate, whether gratuitously or through a payment, in a previously established procedure which has to be approved by SEGOB, pursuant to which a number, combination thereof, symbol or symbols is determined and the outcome of which results in the selection of one or more winners of a prize.
- 'Draw of numbers or symbols through devices': the activity in which the participant, through an apparatus or device of whatever nature, subject to chance, makes a bet, through the insertion of a note, coin or chip, or through an electronic payment device or similar object, for the purpose of obtaining a prize.

Based on the above definitions contained in the Gaming Regulations and considering there is no definition of 'gambling' in the Gaming Law, further definitions have generally fallen to the permit process, through which authorisation to conduct gaming activities is issued by SEGOB. SEGOB sets the parameters for what can be done and where and how such gaming activity shall occur pursuant to administrative gaming permits issued to each individual gaming permit holder. The end result set out in this paragraph is consistent with that set forth in Articles 3 and 4 of the Gaming Law, as the games where bets are crossed and draws are conducted are dependent upon the administrative permit issued by SEGOB.

2.2 What is the legal definition of online gambling and what falls within this definition?
There is no specific legal definition of online gambling in Mexican law.

2.3 Please set out the different gambling products identified by legislation.
As previously stated, Gaming Law does not specifically identify gambling products but lists what may be considered as games, and if bets are crossed in any of those games or for any draws, a permit from SEGOB is required. However, demonstrating the inconsistency of guidance, in some instances the Gaming Regulations do specify some gambling products, including but not limited to:

- horse races in formal horse race tracks;
- dog races in formal dog race tracks;
- *frontón* (racket games played in formal sport venues);
- horse races in provisional race tracks;
- cock fights in regional fairs;
- remote betting facilities or foreign books (locations for the taking and crossing of bets and wagers in sporting events and games permitted by

the Gaming Law, broadcasted in real time and simultaneously in video and audio, as well as for the conduct of number draws, which include bingo, lottery and electronic machine gaming);

- draws, which can be conducted in the following formats:
    (i)   draws with the sale of tickets;
    (ii) draws without the sale of tickets;
    (iii) instant draws;
    (iv) commercialisation system draws;
    (v)   draws of symbols or numbers; and
    (vi) draws broadcasted on mass communications media; and
- draws of numbers or symbols through devices (which is the same as slot machine gaming in other jurisdictions and was slot machine gaming pursuant to the amendment to the Regulations published in October 2012 and reverted in October 2013).

The amendment to the Regulations of 23 October 2013 authorised machine gaming; however, such activities are defined as draws of numbers or symbols through devices and, contrary to the 19 October 2012 amendments to the Regulations, 'slot' gaming is specifically prohibited by the amendment to Article 12 of the Gaming Regulations. Nevertheless, the element that differentiates the prohibited activities (ie slot machines) is the skill element, as slot machines are now defined as devices through which a user, subject to skill, makes a bet to obtain a specific or undetermined prize.

These recent changes were made to try to eliminate previous inconsistencies and clarify that machine gaming is permitted if the chance element and not the skill element is involved; however, there is still a great deal of confusion on the part of permit holders as to just what is and what is not allowed.

2.4   Please list the different requirements for each gambling product, including legal classifications for each; for example, is poker a game of skill or game of chance?

The Gaming Law and Gaming Regulations do not make a distinction between games of skill or games of chance. In any event, the element that would determine if any form of activity should be considered to be a gambling product, and thus be subject to authorisation from SEGOB, is if there is a wager, even if there are elements to classify any such game as a game of skill, or if there is chance in the determination of the winner of a prize.

The general requirements for obtaining a gaming permit are set out in Article 20 of the Gaming Regulations and are the following:
a)   permits for the taking of wagers in horse race tracks, dog race tracks, *fronton* venues, as well as for the installation of remote betting facilities and rooms for the conduct of number or symbol draws will only be granted to Mexican commercial companies;
b)   permits for the taking of wagers in regional fairs will only be granted to Mexican entities;

c)   permits for the taking of wagers in horse races in provisional or temporary race tracks and cock fights will only be granted to Mexican commercial companies and individuals;

d)   permits to conduct draws will only be granted to Mexican individuals or entities.

Article 21 of the Gaming Regulations contains the general rules applicable to any entity or individual requesting a permit for the offering of any of the gambling products previously described. However, those are only the general requirements, and other provisions of the Gaming Regulations set out additional specific requirements and documentation that will be necessary to request the relevant permit and will vary depending on the type of gambling product for which the permit is sought, in addition to those set out in Article 21 of the Gaming Regulations (eg: (i) Article 22 of the Gaming Regulations contains the specific requirements for the permits set out in letter (a) above; (ii) Article 24 of the Gaming Regulations contains specific requirements for the permits set out in letter (b) above; (iii) Article 25 of the Gaming Regulations contains specific requirements for the permits set out in letter (c) above; and (iv) Article 26 of the Gaming Regulations contains specific requirements for the permits set out in letter (d) above.

2.5   Explain the system of regulation of gambling; which regulatory or governmental body is responsible for the supervision of gambling? Which body issues licences? Which body examines enforcement powers? Is there any limit on the number or duration of available licences?

As previously stated, the Gaming Law provides that: (i) no games where bets are crossed, nor draws, of any kind, may be conducted without the authorisation of SEGOB (ie the issued permit), who will provide the requirements and conditions that the permit holder shall comply with; and (ii) the Executive Branch, exercised through SEGOB, has the authority to regulate, authorise, control and supervise the games where bets are crossed, as well as any form of draws and such authority is exercised through the Gaming Bureau, which is the competent authority to authorise, control, supervise and enforce all activities related to bets and draws and also to issue the relevant gaming licences. Further, it is useful to note that the authority/competence granted to SEGOB continues to be discretionary to a significant degree, as the scope of the Gaming Law and the Gaming Regulations, even after the 2012 and 2013 amendments, are still very broad and in many instances gaming activities are neither thoroughly nor consistently regulated resulting in a great deal of room for interpretation. Not surprisingly the latitude inherent in the ambiguous regulations has led to a series of allegations of unequal regulatory administration, favouritism and corruption on the part of SEGOB.

For the purposes set forth in this section, SEGOB acts through the competent bureaus or officials, as provided for in the Gaming Law, its Regulations or SEGOB Internal Regulations.

The Gaming Regulations also provide that SEGOB is the entity in charge of interpreting and applying the provisions of the Gaming Law and the Gaming Regulations for administrative purposes. Furthermore, the third paragraph of Article 2 of the Gaming Regulations provides that the General Gaming and Draws Bureau (the Gaming Bureau) is in charge of any hearings, regulatory proceedings and resolution of matters related to the supervision and surveillance of compliance with the Gaming Law and Gaming Regulations, the issuance of permits and other gaming related acts or activities. The Gaming Bureau, which is an administrative unit of SEBOG, is assisted by the Government Unit of SEGOB. The Consultation Council assists the Bureau in complying with public policies on transparency and accountability.

In addition, the Gaming Regulations (Article 3) provide that a permit is an administrative authorisation issued by SEGOB, which allows an individual or entity to conduct and operate games where bets are crossed and/or draws occur. Those administrative permits are issued for a set period of time, and their scope is restricted by the terms and conditions specifically determined in the permit itself, as determined and drafted by SEGOB or as a practical matter drafted by the permit applicant and approved by SEGOB.

The foregoing is consistent with section XII of Article 12 of the SEGOB Internal Regulations, which provides that it is within the powers of the Government Unit of SEGOB, to supervise, process and authorise the acts set forth in the Gaming Law and other applicable statutes and provisions, and that for such purpose the Government Unit may be assisted by the Director General of the Gaming Bureau.

Neither the Gaming Law nor the Gaming Regulations limit the number of available gaming licences, and in any case any such limitation to the issuance of new licences is more a *de facto* decision or government policy than a limitation set by the Gaming Law or the Gaming Regulations. In addition, the term or duration of the licences is determined by the Gaming Bureau.

3. ONLINE GAMBLING

3.1 To what extent can online gambling be offered in your jurisdiction? Are licences available and, if so, for which gambling products? Please describe briefly the licensing process, who may apply, whether licences are limited in number and, if no licences are available, whether it is legal for online gambling to be offered. In the case of EU jurisdictions, please state whether there are any issues as to the legality of the local law at EU level. Please refer to any relevant cases at ECJ level and explain any measures taken or pending by the European Commission.

Online gambling is not specifically regulated in México. References to online activity appear in a few articles of the Gaming Regulations indirectly addressing issues related to online gambling, and such references to online gambling cannot be considered as a thorough or precise regulation of online gambling activities.

Nevertheless and as previously noted, even though the Gaming Law and the Gaming Regulations exist, SEGOB's authority/competence to regulate, authorise, control and supervise gaming activities is discretionary, as the scope of the Gaming Law and the Gaming Regulations are still very broad and can be made more specific or even broadened by language included in a permit issued by SEGOB. This broad discretion has already appeared in some but not all issued permits granting specific authorisation for the conduct of internet gaming or online gambling as determined by SEGOB to be pursuant to the Gaming Law and Gaming Regulations.

In connection with online gambling pursuant to the Gaming Law, the statute is silent, which should not be considered as a prohibition on conducting or operating authorised gambling activities using a specific means of communication such as the internet, because: (i) the Gaming Law was published in the DOF on 31 December 1947 and the internet as a form of communication was non-existent; and (ii) if a gaming activity was authorised, as a result of the generality of the Gaming Law, SEGOB has as a matter of practice to set forth with reasonable specificity the terms and conditions of such authorisation in the corresponding gaming permits. Under these circumstances, conduct via the internet or similar technologies is not the authorisation of a form of gaming which is new, but rather just a different means by which a gambling activity is conducted which reflects the evolution of transmission technology.

In connection with online gaming pursuant to the Gaming Regulations, Article 85 provides that the remote betting gaming facilities may take bets over the internet, the phone or electronically, for which purpose they shall establish an internal control system for the transactions performed using those means of communication, describing in writing the proceedings and rules that give assurance that the integrity of the games is protected and to prevent the manipulation of the betting system. Such system shall record, at a minimum: (i) the account number and identity of the individual placing the bet; and (ii) the date, time, number of transactions, wagered amounts and a record of requested picks or selections. The Article also provides that the corresponding method (the method used to solicit bets using those means of communication) shall be previously approved by SEGOB.

Further, Article 86 of the Gaming Regulations provides that wagers/bets will only be taken or crossed in cash, except for those conducted/placed through the internet, via telephone or electronically, in which case it is considered that they were placed when payment confirmation is received from the corresponding banking institution, regardless of whether the confirmation is made to the player or the permit holder.

The Gaming Regulations further provide that certain permit holders (ie those that have a permit to operate a remote betting facility) shall comply with the requirements for the issuance of receipts and, specifically regarding internet, telephone or electronic wagers/bets, they provide that no ticket will be issued, but that the information will be recorded in the central betting system immediately after payment, and that the players shall have access to consult or print a certification of their folio number and be informed of their rights arising from the gambling transaction. With specific regard to telephone wagers there is a provision that they shall be recorded in an audio file.

In connection with the foregoing, the language used by the Gaming Regulations is ambiguous, thus subject to interpretation, as it only uses the word '*apuestas*' (bets/wagers generally on sporting events) while allowing the Remote Betting Facilities to use means such as the internet, telephone or any other electronic means to conduct the gaming activities they are authorised to conduct. The strict interpretation of this '*apuestas*' reference may lead one to consider that only bets on sporting events may be crossed using online means of communication. However, taking into account that pursuant to Article 104 of the Gaming Regulations, draws may be conducted via the internet or the telephone network it can reasonably be interpreted that any form of bet, which includes any form of authorised draw, may be conducted through those means of communication (ie internet, telephone or any other electronic means). The apparent contradiction in the Gaming Regulations has, as previously mentioned, been resolved in favour of broader internet wager on gaming through issuance by SEGOB of permits that are more inclusive of online games.

In addition, the Gaming Regulations provide that bets/wagers arising from remote betting facilities bets may be collected/crossed and prizes paid pursuant to that set forth in the permit holder's internal gaming regulations and the limitations to them allowed by SEGOB to each specific permit holder. Therefore, each permit holder's gaming regulations approved by SEGOB may limit or broaden the extent of the gambling activities or gambling offering that may be conducted via the internet or through other telecommunication means.

Furthermore, pursuant to the last paragraph of Article 85 of the Gaming Regulations, SEGOB has to approve the method used by the remote betting facility permit holder to solicit and conduct bets using any designated means of communication (eg the internet). As a result, the specific type of gambling products and the extent to which they may be conducted or offered via the internet will depend on the scope of each permit holder's permit, the permit holders internal gaming regulations approved by SEGOB, as well as the methodology to conduct gaming activities via the internet or using other means of communication approved by SEGOB.

Moreover, pursuant to the Gaming Regulations, any form of drawing may also be conducted through the internet. This situation arises pursuant to Article 104 of the Gaming Regulations, which is contained in Chapter I (*De las Modalidades de los Sorteos*; Types of Draws) of Book Four (*De los Sorteos*; Draws) of the Gaming Regulations. It provides that where draws are conducted in the Mexican territory in which participants are obtained through the internet or via telephone, a folio number must be given to the participant, and in each case the player or participant shall have access, via the internet to consult or print a certification of their folio number and the rights to which they are entitled as participants of the draw.

The Gaming Regulations further provide that the winner of the draw may be determined by the use of computer systems which, applied adequately, randomly determine the winning numbers. However, this system may only be used when the characteristics/computer system through which the winning numbers will be randomly determined are disclosed by the permit holder to SEGOB and SEGOB may conduct inspections to verify the correct functionality of such systems.

Based on what has been previously stated and discussed in this section 3.1, it can be stated that online gambling may be offered in México if the corresponding administrative authorisation (ie permit) allows for such online gambling activity to be conducted and the extent and scope of what such online gambling activities may entail will be limited directly by the permit and the game mechanics and regulations submitted to SEGOB by the corresponding permit holder.

3.2 Is there a distinction between the law applicable to B2B operations and that applicable to B2C operations?

No. Mexican Gaming Law and Gaming Regulations do not make a distinction between the law applicable to B2B operations and B2C operations.

In any event, the one that would be allowed to offer online gambling products to players in México shall only be an entity which is a duly authorised permit holder, that has obtained the corresponding permit from SEGOB, which should expressly allow the offering of any such online gambling products, and also such ability will be determined based on the permit holders' internal gaming regulations approved by SEGOB, as well as the methodology to conduct gaming activities via the internet or using other means of communication approved by SEGOB.

There is no restriction governing or regulating the offering of B2B services to a Mexican permit holder that has been authorised to offer online gambling products, so long as the ones contracting with the player are the directly authorised permit holders, even when such online gambling products are offered through a white label site run by a third party supplier. As the offering is in conjunction with the permit holders' authorisations, the activities of the B2B provider will be bound by the permit's requirements and approved methodologies for online play. As a result SEGOB may dictate server location and any and all technical aspects of the B2B providers' operations as they are derived from the permit holders' authorisation.

3.3 What are the consequences for B2C or B2B operators who are active in your jurisdiction without having obtained or applied for the required permits, licences and approvals? What penalties and enforcement powers are available in respect of the illegal operators? Please outline any significant domestic decisions or enforcement actions that have been taken by the relevant authorities in recent years.

As mentioned at the outset of this chapter no gambling activity in Mexico is lawful unless conducted pursuant to the Gaming Law or Gaming

Regulations and subsequent to the issuance of a permit. With that said, any unauthorised online activity is by its nature a violation of Mexican law.

Despite such prohibition the Mexican regulator and the country's prosecutors have been slow and permissive with unauthorised operators (eg individuals or entities not holding a valid permit to conduct and offer online gambling activities in México) offering B2C gambling products in México. Notwithstanding the foregoing, the Mexican regulator has informally expressed its intent to significantly reduce any informal or unauthorised offering of online gambling products in México. If the Government decides to move criminally against unlawful operators it can act to commence prosecutions under Mexico's criminal statutes or under the Gaming Law.

While the B2B offering of online gambling products in México does not require a permit, licence or approval, it does provide that any such offering of online gambling products or services to players, via the internet, is only to occur pursuant to the corresponding gaming permit. In addition, the reference to those services or online gambling products offered by the supplier to the permit holder should be disclosed in the corresponding permit holder's internal gaming regulations approved by SEGOB, as well as the methodology to conduct gaming activities via the internet or using other means of communication submitted for SEGOB's approval. Therefore the offering of online gambling in Mexico from anywhere in the world without a valid Mexican permit is a violation of law whether the party facilitating the activity acts in a B2B or B2C role.

The illegal gaming operations are sanctioned by the Gaming Law and can be separated into two groups of sanctions: (i) penalties or sanctions to the individuals (shareholders, managers, directors, etc) of illegal gaming operators, where such actions are considered as a crime and are sanctioned with imprisonment and fines; and (ii) sanctions imposed on the illegal gaming enterprise itself, which implies the seizure of all gaming devices, assets and cash of such gaming operations and the liquidation of the entity under which name the illegal gaming activity crime was committed.

The enforcement actions that have been adopted against legal gaming operations in recent years are most of the time related to the closure of the gaming venues or the seizure of gaming devices, the import documentation of which is not located within the gaming venue; nevertheless, given the discretionary authorities of the Regulator, as previously addressed, such closures are sometimes based on decisions of the municipal government or the state government and not the Gaming Bureau of SEGOB. Such closures are based on the lack of municipal permits (eg land use authorisation) and not on the lack of a gaming permit. In addition, on April 2014, the government revoked the gaming licence of a gaming permit holder and also declared a related licence obtained based on multiple judicial proceedings by a former operator of such permit holder as no longer valid. The grounds for these government actions are still uncertain due to their recency.

3.4 What technical measures are in place (if any) to protect consumers from unlicensed operators, such as ISP blocking and payment blocking?

There are no technical measures in the Gaming Law or Gaming Regulations in place to protect consumers from unlicensed operators.

3.5 Has the legal status of online gambling changed significantly in recent years and, if so, how?

No. It changed pursuant to the Gaming Regulations. But other than such statute, neither the regulator nor the legislature has changed the legal framework applicable to the offering of online gambling products. Furthermore, online gaming was not addressed through the decrees amending the Gaming Regulations published on 19 October 2012 and 23 October 2013.

3.6 Whilst acknowledging the inherent difficulty in predicting developments in gambling law, what are the likely developments in online gambling in your jurisdiction, both short term and long term? Are any specific amendments under consideration? Have there been any recent political developments, or do you envisage any in the near future? Are any specific amendments under consideration? Are they likely to be adopted and, if so, what is the time scale?

It is important to note that many draft bills submitted since the adoption of the 2004 Gaming Regulations for a new gaming law or new gaming regulations or that propose amendments to the existing Gaming Law and Gaming Regulations include, to some degree, references to the offering of online gambling products.

In recent months, there have been a number of official statements made by members of the House of Representatives and SEGOB about the political will and consensus regarding the need for a new legal framework that will totally reshape the legislation applicable to gaming activities, and the intention is for online gaming to be specifically addressed by such new legislation; therefore, even though it is difficult to predict, we foresee a significant change in the legal framework applicable to online gambling and to all gaming activities in general.

As in the past, common elements appear in the draft amendments, proposed new gaming law bills or new gaming law regulations that we have had access to, and also in the statements made by politicians in the press solely in connection with online gambling activities and products. These can be summarised generally as follows:

The concept of 'remote game through telecommunications' is included in some of the draft statutes or amendments to the existing statutes. Such concept is a possibility that gaming be conducted through the internet or any other telecommunications system.

There are suggested requirements for the control of games where bets are crossed or draws where monies are wagered over the internet, such as:

- Permit holders of gaming facilities may offer the authorised games by means of telecommunications, including the internet, and for such purpose a central system or management platform of games and draws and control, certified by the Gaming Bureau, will be necessary.
- The control, monitoring and auditing system for the operation of these games shall have at least the following information: (i) accounts system and accounts control processes; (ii) management systems and processes to be used; (iii) software to be used in the computer system, operation and telecommunications software; and (iv) mechanics that will be used in the operation of the game.
- The betting central and control system over the internet (eg the server) shall be physically located and operated within Mexico.
- The balance of a player account shall be reimbursed to the player whenever the players so requests it, but not later than the immediate calendar day following any such request.
- The permit holder shall maintain one or more accounts in financial institutions approved by the Bureau for their use in all banking and related transactions related to this type of gaming. These accounts shall be designated solely for these types of transactions and may not be used for any other purposes. The online gambling transactions would be subject to special scrutiny pursuant to the applicable money laundering provisions.
- The award of any prize shall be credited by the permit holder to the player account at the time of the win.

3.7 Is the law the same in relation to mobile gambling and interactive gambling on television? If not, are there any headline differences?
No. Further, please note that, as previously stated, the Gaming Regulations refer to the taking of bets/wagers for games and draws over the internet, telephone and other means of communication; however, it is dependent upon the scope of each permit holder's authorised activities; the permit holder's internal gaming regulations approved by SEGOB; as well as the methodology to conduct gaming activities via the internet or using other means of communication approved by SEGOB, that mobile and interactive gambling on television may be offered.

4. LAND-BASED GAMING
4.1 Please describe the licensing regime (if any) for land-based gaming, and what products are included. Please set out what licences are available, and the licensing regime for them.
Please refer to sections 2.3 or 2.4 above.

4.2 Please set out any particular limitations or requirements for (eg casino) operators, such as a ban on local residents gambling.
There is no specific particular limitation or requirement for permit holders, such as a ban on local residents gambling. The restrictions existent pursuant

to Gaming Law and Gaming Regulations are very general and can be summarised as follows:

- Pursuant to the Article 9 of the Gaming Law, a place where games and bets are crossed or draws are wagered may not be established close to schools or offices. Please note that this restriction is not in practice enforced by the Gaming Bureau nor SEGOB and is considered outdated but it is still in the Regulations.
- Article 5 of the Gaming Regulations lists general access restrictions on gaming facilities to individuals that: (i) are minors (under 18); (ii) are under the influence of alcohol; (iii) carry weapons of any kind; (iv) are police or military officials on duty; (v) alter the order and peace of the facility with their behaviour; (vi) are or have been caught cheating in a game; and (vii) do not comply with the permit holder's internal regulations previously approved by SEGOB.

4.3 Please address the questions in 3.5 above, but in relation to land-based gaming.

The legal status of land-based gaming, as previously discussed, has not changed significantly in recent years; however, we can see that there is the political will and a suitable environment to adopt a new gaming legal framework in the near future, which would impact not only online gaming, but also land-based gaming.

5. TAX

5.1 Please summarise briefly the tax regime applicable to both land-based and online gaming.

Gambling permit holders, whether in a land-based facility or online, are subject to a 30 per cent tax rate that results from the special tax on production and services (*Impuesto Especial Sobre Producción y Servicios* or IEPS). Under Article 2, Section II, item B), the tax applies to: games where bets are crossed and draws are made which require a permit pursuant to the Gaming Law and the Gaming Regulations; games of skill which employ the use of equipment and the development of those games using visual electronic displays (such as numbers, symbols, figures or other displays of a similar nature conducted in the Mexican territory); and games of chance.

The Mexican Supreme Court in *Amparo en revisión* 471/2001; *Distribuidora Liverpool, S.A.* de C.V. *9 de septiembre de 2003* decided that both the individual state and the federal government both have authority to impose taxes on games where bets are crossed and draws are made.

Even prior to the case referenced above, local governments imposed taxes on gambling permit holders. In general terms, the way these taxes or contributions are imposed is through local tax codes, fiscal statutes or municipal income and budget resolutions, which provide that gambling activities should be subject to a certain contribution, which is determined as a percentage of the amounts wagered, less the prizes paid (eg on the net win of the gambling permit holder), and even special taxes on the players that obtain prizes when participating in gambling activities.

For example, the 2014 Tax Code for the Federal District (Mexico City, D.F.), Articles 147 to 155, provides for a 12 per cent contribution to be applied on the net win of gambling permit holders and a 6 per cent contribution on the winnings or prize to be paid by the winner of a prize in a gambling activity.

In connection with gambling in electronic terminals, some states or municipalities charge a specific monthly contribution per each electronic gaming device in operation at the corresponding gaming facility, such as the municipalities of Rosarito, Ensenada and Mexicali, in the State of Baja California.

Recently the State of Yucatán passed an amendment to the local tax laws, creating a 10 per cent tax to customers of gaming venues on all transactions taking place at a gaming facility. The gaming terminals suppliers or providers are also jointly liable for the payment of such taxes, in addition to a monthly contribution for each gaming device at each venue. The consequence of such new taxes is that gaming operators are likely to close their venues in the State of Yucatán.

All local taxes need to be determined on a case by case basis, depending on the location where the gambling product is offered and the income generated. Finally, some gambling permit holders are currently pursuing legal actions to fight the imposition of certain local taxes as they may be inconsistent with the taxation principles of equity and proportionality.

Finally, gambling permit holders are subject to all the taxes required from any other Mexican corporation (ie income tax on the income arising from their gambling activities; flat rate corporate tax which is credited against the income tax paid; and value added tax (VAT) to be paid on services and products procured by the gambling permit holder and is also credited against the VAT collected by such gambling permit holder. However, in connection with the VAT, please note that the amounts wagered by players are not subject to VAT, thus the VAT collected by gambling permit holders is very limited, which could represent a problem to gambling permit holders as they have very small amounts of collected VAT to be credited against the VAT they should pay to procure products and services.

6. ADVERTISING
6.1 To what extent is the advertising of gambling permitted in your jurisdiction? Again, this should cover both land-based and online gaming. To the extent that advertising is permitted, how is it regulated

Advertising duly authorised gambling activities is permitted in México. The Gaming Regulations (Article 9 after the 2013 amendment to the Regulations) provide that the advertising and marketing of games where bets are crossed and draws are authorised under the Gaming Law and Gaming Regulations, as well as of the gambling facilities where those gambling activities are conducted, is permitted pursuant to the applicable provisions.

In any event, advertising and marketing of gambling activities may only be conducted when the corresponding gambling permit has been obtained and such advertising is subject to the following restrictions: (i) the authorised gambling activities may not be explicitly advertised; (ii) the advertising shall be clear and precise to prevent inducing by error, deceit or confusion the services offered; (iii) any advertising shall indicate the permit number authorising the conduct of such gambling activities; (iv) any such advertising shall indicate that minors may not participate in those activities; and (v) advertising shall include messages that invite players to play responsibly (responsible gaming) and for the primary purpose of entertainment.

7. SOCIAL GAMING

7.1 We believe this to be a growing area. Please decide under what criteria social gaming is permitted in your jurisdiction. If games are free to play or if there is no prize, are they legal without a licence? Please address circumstances where virtual currency is used and can be won: ie currency which is of no monetary or other value, save for as credits to take part in games. The answer should address the question whether game credits or virtual money can be exchanged for other prizes. Is any change to regulation in the area proposed or envisaged?

In the context of social gaming, or gaming content offered in social networks, if games are free to play, such gaming activity would not be subject to the Gaming Law or the Gaming Regulations, nor specifically regulated by any other statute in México.

Notwithstanding the foregoing, given the nature of Mexican gaming statutes (outdated, ambiguous and that give the regulator a great deal of discretion), some entities undertaking social gaming activities have approached the Gaming Bureau to obtain a ruling or written confirmation of criteria, but the Gaming Bureau has thus far taken the position that the corresponding activities fall outside the scope of its competence and therefore are not subject to Mexican gaming regulation.

Further, if those social gaming activities do not involve a wager which may result in the payment of a prize to the participant, as defined by the Gaming Regulations, such gaming activities would not be regulated as a gambling activity in Mexico.

In addition, in the event that players using social gaming products are allowed to purchase extra credits for real money, but there is no actual prize to be paid (ie if the player wins only the benefit of receiving additional credits which allow the player to continue playing), such 'prize/benefit' does not qualify as a prize under the Gaming Regulations and the Gaming Law, and thus it is still not regulated as a gambling activity in Mexico.

In the event that a new gaming legal framework is discussed, we envisage that social gaming will be addressed as part of the provisions of Online Gaming.

Monaco

Pinsent Masons LLP
Diane Mullenex & Annabelle Richard

1. OBJECTIVES AND STRUCTURE OF LEGISLATION

In the 1860s, gambling activities were prohibited in France, but the Principality of Monaco decided to authorise the opening of a casino. In 1848, the Prince of Monaco, Florestan I, was obliged to abandon his reign over the territories of Menton and Roquebrune, cities which accounted for 95% of the principality's territory. Being deprived of great sources of income, the principality was therefore confronted with a financial crisis.

In order to overcome this crisis, Prince Charles III, the successor of Florestan I, decided to turn to tourism. On 26 April 1856, Charles III granted an exclusive privilege of 35 years for the creation of a tourism facility housing a casino, which, unfortunately, was less successful than expected. In 1863, François Blanc, a major entrepreneur in the field of gambling, was granted a 50-year concession and founded the company Bains des Mers, which became the Monte-Carlo SBM Group (SBM). This group enjoyed a comfortable monopoly in Europe until 1907, the year in which the French law on casinos was adopted.

In 1966, the state of Monaco became the main shareholder of the SBM. On 12 June 1987, the Monegasque government adopted Law n° 1.103 on games of chance, the main purpose of which was to regulate land-based gambling, including new games and slot machines. Law n° 1.103 is a seminal text in the field of gambling regulation in Monaco.

Law n° 1.103 establishes the legal framework applicable to the activities of gambling houses, including the conditions under which authorisations and licences are granted, the terms of access and the operation of such gambling houses, and the supervision of land-based gambling. The scope of Law n° 1.103 is limited to land-based gambling and does not extend to lottery, betting or online gambling offers.

Lottery

On 6 June 1867, the General Police Law was passed. This prohibited lotteries, with the exception of lotteries offering movable items for the exclusive purpose of charity or art sponsoring, which were duly authorised by the governor general. However, according to governmental agreements entered into between France and Monaco, Monegasque citizens are allowed to participate in French lotteries offered by *La française des jeux*.

Betting
Monegasque law prohibits betting. However, an agreement between France and Monaco has authorised Monegasque citizens to participate in games offered by the French company PMU (a special legal entity created jointly by all French horse racing companies to manage their horse betting activities).

Online gambling
To date, there are no provisions applicable to online gambling in Monaco. A draft bill tabled in the National Council of Monaco on 24 September 2001 sought to regulate online gambling. The purpose of this draft law was to extend the regulations applicable to land-based gambling to online gambling. However, the draft bill was never adopted and there is no evidence to indicate that online gambling will be regulated in the near future in Monaco.

2. FRAMEWORK OF LEGISLATION
2.1 What is the legal definition of gambling and what falls within this definition?
Monegasque law prohibits the establishment of gambling houses and the organisation of lotteries or sales based on chance without legal authorisation. Pursuant to Article 350 of the Monegasque Criminal Code, gambling means *'games of chance, lotteries or sales based on chance and, in general, any operation offered to the public, regardless of its designation, in order to trigger the hope of a gain which would be acquired through chance'*.

However, in accordance with Article 351 of the Monegasque Criminal Code, *'games the result of which depends essentially on skills, strength or intellectual combinations are not considered games of chance'*.

2.2 What is the legal definition of online gambling and what falls within this definition?
Online gambling is prohibited in Monaco and there is no definition of online gambling under Monegasque law. However, the draft bill of 24 September 2001 provided a definition of online gambling: *'any game of chance located, hosted and executed in the Principality of Monaco by a licensed gambling house and providing, in accordance with the conditions specified by law, online gambling, the technical process of online betting and online earnings to internet users'*.

2.3 Please set out the different gambling products identified by legislation.
All gambling houses, including casinos, are entitled to offer the following products as land-based games:
- counterparty games: boule, roulette, 30 et 40, blackjack, craps, grande roue;
- baccarat games: chemin de fer, banque, punto banco;
- manual, mechanical or electronic games; and

- other games: pai gow poker, Carribean gold poker, casino stud poker, progressive stud poker, Texas hold'em ultimate, Texas hold'em no limit and three card poker.

2.4 Please list the different requirements for each gambling product, including legal classifications for each; for example, is poker a game of skill or game of chance?

Article 351 of the Monegasque Criminal Code distinguishes between games of skill and games of chance. However, Monegasque law does not provide such a qualification for each individual game.

Poker

According to Article 1 of Order n° 8.929 of 15 July 1987, gambling houses may offer seven different types of poker games: pai gow poker, Carribean gold poker, casino stud poker, progressive stud poker, Texas Hold'em Ultimate, Texas Hold'em No Limit and three card poker.

The conditions under which each of these poker games may be offered are provided in ministerial orders specifically adopted for each of these games and in the Ministerial Order n° 88.384 of 26 July 1988, which sets out the rules under which the games must be operated.

Betting

Monegasque law prohibits betting, but, according to governmental agreements entered into between France and Monaco, Monegasque citizens are authorised to participate in French betting offered by the company PMU on horse races.

Casino games

Casino games, together with gambling house games, are regulated by Law n° 1.103 and Order n° 8.929 of 15 July 1987, which sets out the rules of implementation for Law n° 1.103.

Law n° 1.103 defines the conditions for the authorisation, access, operation and control of gambling houses. Order n° 8.929 notably provides a list of authorised games as follows:

- counterparty games: boule, roulette, 30 et 40, blackjack, craps, grande roue;
- baccarat games: chemin de fer, banque, punto banco;
- manual, mechanical or electronic games; and
- other games: pai gow poker, Carribean gold poker, casino stud poker, progressive stud poker, Texas hold'em ultimate, Texas hold'em no limit and three card poker.

Games of chance, with the exception of poker games, are governed by Ministerial Order n° 88.348 of 26 July 1988, which sets out the rules for each game.

Regarding casinos' organisation, both Law n° 1.103 and Order n° 8.929 set out the rules for authorisations, casino staff and accounting rules.

Slot and other machine gaming

Casinos are authorised to use slot machines and other gaming devices. However, in accordance with Article 12 of Law n° 1.103, each machine requires an official authorisation. Slot machines and other gaming machines are regulated by Ministerial Order n° 88.348, which sets out the conditions for their operation.

Among the various requirements applicable to gambling machines, a written explanation is required for any technical intervention performed on gaming machines. Pursuant to Article 20 of the Ministerial Order n° 88.384, the intervention sheet must detail the stop time of the machine, the purpose of the intervention, the machine number and the engineer's signature.

Lottery

Pursuant to Articles 26 and 27 of the General Police Order of 6 June 1867, Monegasque law prohibits lotteries. However, according to governmental agreements entered into between France and Monaco, Monegasque citizens are allowed to participate in French lotteries offered by *La française des jeux* (in France, operation of the national lottery is granted to La Française des Jeux, which is structured as a public limited liability company).

2.5 Explain the system of regulation of gambling; which regulatory or governmental body is responsible for the supervision of gambling? Which body issues licences? Which body examines enforcement powers? Is there any limit on the number or duration of available licences?

Gambling in Monaco is regulated by the Ministry of Finance and the Economy through the Gambling Commission (*Commission des jeux*) and the Department of Gambling Control (*Service de contrôle des jeux*).

The Gambling Commission has overall responsibility for the supervision of gambling houses. The Commission issues advices on all matters relating to the functioning of gambling houses, gaming operations and the implementation of game regulations.

The Department of Gambling Control is responsible for ensuring compliance with the provisions of Law n° 1.103 and its implementing measures. Its agents are responsible for:

- supervising the operation of gambling houses by performing all investigations in this regard;
- controlling the operation of games and making all checks related thereto;
- supervising the control of access to gambling houses and that of their opening and closing hours; and
- ensuring the proper operation of the gaming and the correct employee behaviour.

The Ministry of Finance and the Economy is in charge of granting official authorisations which are required, in particular, in relation to

- working conditions;
- hiring of employees;

- gambling devices; and
- accounting rules.

These authorisations are issued by the Minister of State.

Pursuant to Article 2 of Law n° 1.103, all gambling licences are issued by Sovereign Order (*Ordonnance souveraine*), which specifies the name and qualifications of the licensee, the location of the licensed games, the number of gaming tables and the automatic equipment allowed. This licence is accompanied by specifications and does not apply to holders of a monopoly granted by sovereign order for the operation of games of chance (essentially the SBM).

In addition, pursuant to Article 1 of Law n° 1.103, these licences may only be granted under the conditions prescribed by the law and games must be executed in accordance with the provisions of Ministerial Decree n° 88-384 of 26 July 1988, which sets forth the mode of regulation governing the operation of each game. However, Law n° 1.103 does not apply to lotteries, mutual betting or prognosis competitions.

In fact, although the Monegasque legislation created a licensing system, the SBM is the sole gambling operator in Monaco. The only casinos sharing the gambling market in Monaco are SBM casinos and no other gambling house operates in such jurisdiction.

3. ONLINE GAMBLING

3.1 To what extent can online gambling be offered in your jurisdiction? Are licences available and, if so, for which gambling products? Please describe briefly the licensing process, who may apply, whether licences are limited in number and, if no licences are available, whether it is legal for online gambling to be offered. In the case of EU jurisdictions, please state whether there are any issues as to the legality of the local law at EU level. Please refer to any relevant cases at ECJ level and explain any measures taken or pending by the European Commission.

There are no provisions applicable to online gambling in Monaco. As a result, it is prohibited for online gambling operators to establish themselves in Monaco in order to provide online gambling offers in the jurisdiction. However, no specific provision prevents Monegasque users from playing on online gambling websites. In addition, gambling products are excluded from the scope of Law n° 1.383 of 2 August 2011 on the digital economy, which sets out the rules applicable to e-commerce and consumer protection.

The Monegasque legislators attempted to regulate online gambling offers in 2001 through a bill filed in the National Council of Monaco dated 24 September 2001. The purpose of the draft bill was to extend the regulations applicable to land-based gambling to online gambling. This project remained at the draft stage and there is currently no project to open the Monegasque market to online gambling in future.

3.2 Is there a distinction between the law applicable to B2B operations and that applicable to B2C operations?
N/A.

3.3 What are the consequences for B2C or B2B operators who are active in your jurisdiction without having obtained or applied for the required permits, licences and approvals? What penalties and enforcement powers are available in respect of the illegal operators? Please outline any significant domestic decisions or enforcement actions that have been taken by the relevant authorities in recent years.
N/A.

3.4 What technical measures are in place (if any) to protect consumers from unlicensed operators, such as ISP blocking and payment blocking?
N/A.

3.5 Has the legal status of online gambling changed significantly in recent years and, if so, how?
N/A.

3.6 Whilst acknowledging the inherent difficulty in predicting developments in gambling law, what are the likely developments in online gambling in your jurisdiction, both short term and long term? Are any specific amendments under consideration? Have there been any recent political developments, or do you envisage any in the near future? Are any specific amendments under consideration? Are they likely to be adopted and, if so, what is the time scale?
N/A.

4. LAND-BASED GAMING
4.1 Please describe the licensing regime (if any) for land-based gaming, and what products are included. Please set out what licences are available, and the licensing regime for them.
Gambling operator licence
Gambling operators must be authorised by the public authorities before starting operating. Pursuant to Article 350 of the Monegasque Criminal Code, any person who offers gambling without holding a licence shall be punished by imprisonment for one to six months and a fine of EUR 2,250–9,000. In addition, offenders may be deprived of their civil and family rights for a period of five to six years.

Under Article 2 of Law n° 1.103, all gambling licences are issued by Sovereign Order, which specifies:
• the name and qualifications of the licensee;
• the location of the licensed games; and
• the number of gaming tables and automatic equipment allowed.

This licence is accompanied by a requirements specification and does not apply to holders of a monopoly granted by sovereign order for the operation of games of chance (eg the SBM).

In addition, pursuant to Article 1 of Law n° 1.103, this licence may be granted only under the conditions prescribed by the law and only for games mentioned on the Sovereign Order list which sets out the mode of regulation governing the operation of each game. As such, the licence that is granted is necessarily subject to permanent supervision by the administration.

Meanwhile, Article 11 of Order n° 8.929 requires gambling operators to keep a special register detailing the dates and procedures of all interventions by the administrative authorities, ie the Gambling Commission and Gambling Control Department. Mainly, the administrative authorities may enter comments or instructions on this register which must be complied with within eight days by the employee responsible for the gambling premises.

Licence for employees

The rules regarding employment in gambling houses are set forth in Articles 6–8 of Law n° 1.103. Gambling operators may employ only individuals approved by official authorisation issued by the Minister of State. Moreover, the internal rules applicable to employees are also subject to this official authorisation.

Overall, employees of gaming houses must comply with various obligations, including the prohibition from frequenting other gambling houses or participating in gambling, even outside of the Principality of Monaco.

Gambling equipment licence

In accordance with Law n° 1.103, gambling operators are prohibited from using equipment which has not received an official authorisation issued by the Minister of State.

Ministerial Decree n° 88-384 of 26 July 1988 on gambling regulation contains provisions relating to: (i) specific material, such as playing cards and their equipment, dice or roulette equipment, and gambling machines (including slot machines); and (ii) the rules of each authorised game.

4.2 Please set out any particular limitations or requirements for (eg casino) operators, such as a ban on local residents gambling.

Under Articles 9–11 of Law n° 1.103, access to gambling houses is prohibited to minors (under age 18), excluded individuals, individuals under the influence of alcohol and/or drugs, members of the military, religious ministers, civil servants and other state employees.

Monegasque citizens are prohibited from gambling within the Principality of Monaco together with gambling house employees, for whom the prohibition goes even further, as the latter are also prohibited from gambling outside the jurisdiction of Monaco.

Pursuant to Article 10 of the law, excluded individuals are those who made a corresponding written request and those who are deemed undesirable. Any exclusion measure of more than one year requires official authorisation.

4.3 Please address the questions in 3.5 above, but in relation to land-based gaming.

There has been no major change in the status of land-based gaming in recent years.

5. TAX
5.1 Please summarise briefly the tax regime applicable to both land-based and online gaming.

According to Article 27 of the Monegasque Tax Code, the operating revenue from betting and gambling activities, including lottery and horse betting, are exempted from VAT.

This VAT exemption does not apply to the winnings perceived by operators and intermediaries taking part in the organisation of lotteries and horse betting.

Furthermore, lottery and/or betting tickets offered by French companies in the Principality of Monaco are subject to stamp duty.

6. ADVERTISING
6.1 To what extent is the advertising of gambling permitted in your jurisdiction? Again, this should cover both land-based and online gaming. To the extent that advertising is permitted, how is it regulated?

There are no specific provisions in this regard. However, advertising is permitted for operators offering services in Monaco legally.

7. SOCIAL GAMING
7.1 We believe this to be a growing area. Please decide under what criteria social gaming is permitted in your jurisdiction. If games are free to play or if there is no prize, are they legal without a licence? Please address circumstances where virtual currency is used and can be won: ie currency which is of no monetary or other value, save for as credits to take part in games. The answer should address the question whether game credits or virtual money can be exchanged for other prizes. Is any change to regulation in the area proposed or envisaged?

The Principality of Monaco has not adopted any law specifically on social gaming and does not plan to do so in the near future. However, other provisions may apply to social gaming, such as consumer protection regulation, and advertising and marketing law.

The Netherlands

Kalff Katz & Franssen Attorneys at Law
Dr Alan Littler & Justin Franssen

1. OBJECTIVES AND STRUCTURE OF LEGISLATION
Gambling in the Netherlands is regulated pursuant to the Betting and
Gaming Act 1964 (*Wet op de kansspelen* (BGA)), which embodies a
'prohibited unless licensed' approach. Licences are available on either a
permanent or semi-permanent basis and apart from the slot machine sector
all licences are exclusive. Each licence specifies the nature of the gambling
offer and to date no licence permits the holder thereof to offer online
gambling. Currently, the BGA provides no legal basis for the award of a
licence for online gambling and therefore the provision of such services
is prohibited in the Netherlands. However, this is due to change with
regulatory reform underway to introduce a local licensing regime for online
gambling, which officially should be operational in 2015. Details on the
regulatory reform, including the process to date, are found in section 3.6.

In terms of regulatory objectives, the present format of the BGA does not
refer to a core set. Objectives are provided for in the remote gaming bill as
notified to the European Commission on 5 March 2014 (remote gaming
bill), noting that the objectives include preventing gambling addiction,
consumer protection and combating fraud and criminality. As such, these
objectives reflect the position of the Ministry of Security and Justice (the
Ministry) on how it views the objectives of the existing legislation. In
2005 the Minister of Justice reported that the principal objectives of the
regulation and control of gambling were combating gambling addiction,
protecting consumers and combating illegality and criminality (Derde
voortgangsrapportage kansspelbeleid, *Kamerstukken II*, 2004–05, nr.47).

2. FRAMEWORK OF LEGISLATION
2.1 What is the legal definition of gambling and what falls within this definition?
Pursuant to Article 1(a) BGA it is prohibited to '*provide an opportunity to
compete for prizes or premiums if the winners are designated by means of any
calculation of probability over which the participants are generally unable to
exercise a dominant influence, unless a licence has been granted therefore,
pursuant to this law*'. Quite possibly in contrast to other jurisdictions, the
definition is not conditioned by the need for a player to have placed a stake;
consideration is not required. The opportunity to compete for prizes or
premiums encompasses those with an economic value and is not necessarily
restricted to prizes or premiums outside virtual gaming environments.
Section 7 details how these requirements can be of importance for social

and free play games. Thirdly, the outcome of the game must be determined by chance and over which participants are in general unable to exercise a dominant influence. Should such influence be exercisable, then the game will be one of skill and fall outside the scope of the regulatory regime.

2.2 What is the legal definition of online gambling and what falls within this definition?

No reference is made within the existing version of the BGA to online gambling. Pending legislative amendments to the primary legislation, no licences can be awarded for the provision of online gambling. Inherent in this situation is the lack of a definition of online gambling.

A definition of online gambling is proposed in the remote gaming bill, which refers to a gambling offer for the purposes of Article 1(a) BGA when provided at distance via means of electronic communication without physical contact between the provider and the customer (Article 31(1)). According to the draft explanatory memorandum, secondary regulation will determine which forms of electronic communications licensees will be able to use.

2.3 Please set out the different gambling products identified by legislation.

Poker

For the purposes of the BGA, poker is a game of chance and therefore the commercial offering of poker is restricted to Holland Casino, the public monopolist for the provision of casino gaming services in the Netherlands. The existing text of the BGA does not refer to poker and thus it remains undefined. Whilst the Supreme Court found poker to constitute a game of chance in 1998, some later rulings of lower courts have considered it to be a game of skill; to counter this, the remote gaming bill explicitly treats poker as if it is a game of chance and thus ensures it falls within the scope of Article 1(a) BGA. See section 2.4, 'Poker'.

Betting (other than sports betting)

The only form of betting other than sports betting is that on horseraces, including trot racing, with the provision of such totalisator betting being subject to a monopoly on the basis of a semi-permanent licence. Articles 23–27 BGA cover the provision of horserace betting with further conditions enumerated in the decision of the Gaming Authority of 30 September 2013 (*Vergunning Totalisator 2013/2014*), which is held by Sportech Racing b.v., operating under the name 'Runnerz'. This semi-permanent licence runs from 1 October 2013 until 31 December 2014 and defines what the licensee can offer. See section 2.4 for details.

Sports betting

Sports betting in the Netherlands is subject to monopoly-based supply pursuant to a semi-permanent licence. Under the BGA, generated revenues are destined for sports, culture, social well-being and public health.

Articles 15–22 BGA regulate the provision of sports betting, along with further conditions enumerated in the licence awarded by the Ministry on 14 January 2010 (*Beschikking Sporttotalisator*) as amended in December 2010 and July 2013. The Stichting de Nationale Sporttotalisator, which trades under the name De Lotto, has been the sole land-based provider of sports betting in the Netherlands since 1969.

Article 15(2) BGA defines sports betting as providing the opportunity for participants to guess or predict the results of sporting competitions other than those subject to the horse-race betting licence. The *Beschikking Sportotalisator* contains conditions which define the nature of the offer which De Lotto can supply. The current semi-permanent licence was originally set to expire in January 2012, but several amendments were made in December 2010, including an extension to its life expectancy to January 2015. This licence also permits the holder to offer lotto games and a numbers game (dealt with under respective sub-headings below).

Casino games
Article 27g BGA provides the legal basis for the offering of casino gaming in the Netherlands, with Article 27h(1) BGA establishing the basis for a single licence for the provision of such gaming to be awarded from which all revenues generated are for the benefit of the state (Article 27h(2) BGA).

Under the terms of the *Beschikking Casinospelen 1996*, the Nationale Stichting tot Exploitatie van Casinospelen in Nederland, operating under the name 'Holland Casino', has been awarded this single licence. In fact it has been the sole casino operator in the Netherlands since the first casino opened its doors in 1974 in Zandvoort. Over time casinos spread away from purely (domestic) tourist destinations and are now found in Amsterdam, Breda, Eindhoven, Enschede, Groningen, Leeuwarden, Nijmegen, Rotterdam, Scheveningen, Schiphol (Amsterdam) Airport, Utrecht, Valkenburg and Venlo. As noted in section 3.6, it is expected that Holland Casino will be privatised. However, at the time of writing, it is unclear how the future land-based casino market will be structured.

Slot and other machine gaming
The BGA has established a three-pronged system for the regulation of the slot machine sector, which is the only one in the Netherlands in which no cap is placed on the number of private operators permitted.

Pursuant to Article 30 BGA a licence is required to operate one or more slot machines in a given premise which is granted by the mayor of the relevant local authority. Such licences can only be awarded in relation to cafés and restaurants where no further activities are found and which are by and large directed towards those over 18 years of age. Alternatively they can be located within premises which are established primarily for the purpose of offering games via slot machines. Licences for premises can be granted for a limited or unlimited period of time.

A second licence is required for the exploitation of slot machines, which is granted to natural persons for a limited or unlimited period of time.

However an application will be denied to those who in the previous three years have breached conditions pertaining to slot machines or when there are concerns that the granting of such a licence will represent a danger for public order, safety and morality.

Finally, there is a type approval system in operation to determine which slot machines are permitted to enter the Dutch market. If lacking such approval, the presence of a slot machine type on the market will be deemed illegal. Slot machine types are approved according to rules pertaining to player protection and the exclusion of minors, game play and game duration, game process and the average amount which can be won and lost over a given period of time.

Small-scale gambling

Subject to certain conditions being satisfied, 'small-scale gambling' provides an exemption to the 'prohibited unless licenced' approach. Under this exception, bingo can be offered, for example. Article 7c BGA establishes this exception and the necessary conditions:

- only Dutch associations established for at least three years can organise such gambling;
- the association must have a clear objective (which cannot be the organisation of gambling and which is not contrary to the public interest);
- prizes and premiums can be up to EUR 400 per series and up to EUR 1,500 per gathering; and
- the offering of such gambling must be notified to the mayor at least 14 days in advance, including the location and time of the event.

State Lottery

Pursuant to Articles 9 and 10 BGA the provision of a national lottery is subject to the monopoly held by the Stichting Exploitatie Nederlandse Staatsloterij (Staatsloterij) under a licence awarded for an unlimited period of time. Sixty per cent of stakes must be returned to players as prizes or premiums and all profits arising from the State Lottery are destined to go to the state finances. Detailed provisions pertaining to the State Lottery are found in the *Beschikking Staatsloterij 1992*.

As discussed in section 3.6, the current government plans to privatise the Staatsloterij, following which indications have surfaced of a potential merger with De Lotto, which currently provides sports betting, lotto and an instant lottery (scratch cards).

Lotto

The provision of lotto is subject to a monopoly, with the exclusive licence being awarded to the same entity as that which provides sports betting. Therefore De Lotto provides lotto pursuant to the *Beschikking Sportotalisator*. Article 27a(2) BGA defines lotto as the opportunity for participants to predict a given quantity of symbols from a predefined range of symbols from which a draw is then made.

Instant lottery

Article 14b(1) BGA establishes the basis for an instant lottery and for which the current semi-permanent exclusive licence runs from 1 October 2011 until 31 December 2014 (*Beschikking instantloterij*). An instant lottery is defined in Article 14a(2) BGA as one whereby prizes are distributed prior to the sale of the tickets.

Charitable lotteries

There are currently three good causes lotteries in operation, pursuant to three separate semi-permanent licences, all of which are held by the Holding Nationale Goede Doelen Loterijen N.V. These lotteries and semi-permanent licences are:

- Nationale Postcode Loterij; currently licensed for the period 1 January 2013 until 31 December 2014 pursuant to the *Vergunning Nationale Postcode Loterij 2013/2014*.
- BankGiro Loterij; currently licensed for the period 1 May 2013 until 31 December 2014 pursuant to the *Beschikking BankGiro Loterij 2013/2014*, as amended in June 2013.
- VriendenLoterij; currently licensed for the period 1 January 2011 until 31 December 2014 pursuant to the *Beschikking Vriendenloterij 2011*, as amended in May 2013.

In contrast to other forms of gambling regulated pursuant to the BGA no provision defines these lottery forms but the competence to award licences for such lotteries is found in Article 3 BGA. Each licence defines the nature of the respective lottery draws:

- National Postcode Loterij – a combination of a Dutch postcode and a number between 001 and 499;
- BankGiro Loterij – a number lottery (previously the participant's bank account number was entered into the draw); and
- VriendenLoterij – participant's mobile phone number plus two letters.

Other gambling products

Although not identified by legislation, a Code of Conduct for Promotional Games of Chance 2014 (*Gedragscode Promotionele Kansspelen*) establishes rules for promotional games of chance. No licences are available for such games and, unless the Code is complied with, such offers are illegal. The central definition of a game of chance in Article 1(a) BGA defines the nature of such games. However, to benefit from the exemption to the licensing requirement, promotional games of chance must promote a product, service or organisation, and thus cannot form a stand-alone service.

Promotional games can only be temporary in nature with up to twenty draws being permitted annually per good, service or organisation. Participation must be free (except for communication costs, which are limited to EUR 0.45 per entry), minors must get permission from a parent or legal guardian, and the total value of the prizes or premiums must not be greater than EUR 100,000 per promotional game per year. Promotional games of chance, for which the associated prizes or premiums do not have a value greater than EUR 4,500, referred to as 'small promotional games of chance', do not have to adhere to the maximum of 20 draws, the cap on the value of the prizes or the general rules applicable to other promotional games of chance.

2.4 Please list the different requirements for each gambling product, including legal classifications for each; for example, is poker a game of skill or game of chance?
Poker
In 2010 the District Court of The Hague (*Rechtbank 's-Gravenhage*, BN0013, 2 July 2010) held in criminal proceedings that poker is a game of skill in contrast to an earlier Supreme Court (*Hoge Raad*) decision of 1998 (ZD0952, 3 March 1998). In short, the District Court was unconvinced by evidence provided by expert witnesses that the open standard of Article 1(a) BGA could be satisfied by poker and consequently the District Court found that 'there can be no conclusion other than that poker cannot be deemed a game of chance to the extent envisaged by the legislator'. This does not mean to say chance has no role in determining the outcome of poker games but rather that it cannot be shown 'in general' that chance plays the role which the 'prohibited unless licensed' approach requires. The decision is subject to appeal. Subsequent rulings from other district courts dealing with the taxation of winnings from remote poker have found poker to constitute a game of chance.

Horserace betting requirements
Bets can be taken on the following types of event in accordance with the *Vergunning Totalisator 2013/2014*:
- horseraces and trotting races organised under the auspices of the *Nederlands Draf- en Rensport*; and
- horseraces and trotting races organised under the auspices of the competent body in the relevant jurisdiction.

The monopolist can take bets in a variety of locations under the *Vergunning Totalisator 2013/2014*, notably:
- racetracks;
- betting offices – although food can be served, alcohol is prohibited;
- betting cafés;
- sales points;
- casinos – those operated by the monopolist Holland Casino;
- amusement arcades – conditional upon the approval of the appropriate local authority;
- e-commerce (replicating the offline offer).

There can be up 100 offices, cafés, casinos and arcades. All consumers must have reached the age of majority (18) according to the *Vergunning Totalisator 2013/2014*. There are two categories of betting product which can be offered, those with a maximum stake per game of EUR 250 and those with a maximum of EUR 1,000.

Betting requirements

Sports betting services can be offered via De Lotto's network of sales points which will also offer the other forms of gambling which De Lotto provides plus the 'e-commerce' route following the *Beschikking Sporttotalisator*. In contrast to the conditions attached to the horserace betting licence, a ceiling has been placed upon the number of sporting competitions and tournaments on which De Lotto can accept bets; 150 per week/7,800 per annum. Again, all participants must be 18 years or older.

Limits are set restricting how much participants can play, in terms of maximum stakes and weekly deposit limits. No single stake can be greater than EUR 22.69, according to the *Beschikking Sporttotalisator*, whether played offline or via the e-commerce route. However participation via the e-commerce route is subject to the following deposit limits:
- up to EUR 1,000 per week for participants over the age of 24 years; and
- up to EUR 100 per week for participants aged between 18 and 24 years.

Casino game requirements

Holland Casino is not free to offer any form of casino game but only those which are specified in the *Beschikking Casinospelen* namely French roulette, American roulette, blackjack, baccarat/chemin de fer, punto banco, sic bo, money wheel, red dog, keno and poker.

Holland Casino must ensure that the games offered satisfy the general requirement that no stake can be lower than EUR 5 or greater than EUR 10,000. However, there must be one game where the minimum stake is no higher than EUR 5 and at least one other game where the stake does not exceed EUR 2. In terms of slot machines located within Holland Casino venues, the highest possible stake permitted is EUR 50 and up to EUR 150 can be played in a single game. Prizes must be at least 80 per cent of the value of the stakes. However, where a chip card is used, a welcome gift of EUR 5 may be included and whilst anonymous cards may carry up to EUR 500, those held in a player's name have a limit of EUR 2,500. Should a player request otherwise this can be increased up to EUR 10,000.

Under the terms of the *Beschikking Casinospelen* Holland Casino is obliged to have a balanced policy in place for the prevention of gambling addiction, which in part, would appear to be reflected in the house rules which must be brought to the attention of all visitors. Such house rules must include information for consumers on the imposition of visit restrictions and entry bans.

State Lottery requirements

According to the *Beschikking Staatsloterij* there must be at least 10 draws per year spread evenly through a calendar year and the price for a whole lot is subject to a maximum amount of EUR 30. Should lots be sold in smaller divisions then the cost of each ticket should be reduced proportionately. The operator is required to ensure that there is good regional spread of sales points throughout the Netherlands which are accessible for all levels of society whilst advertising should be executed in a careful and balanced manner.

Lotto requirements
De Lotto is permitted to offer 422 lotto games on an annual basis, participation in which can also occur via the internet under the aforementioned guise of 'e-commerce' under the *Beschikking Sporttotalisator*. As with sports betting, the maximum single stake which De Lotto is permitted to offer is EUR 22.69 and for players who participate via the internet no more than EUR 100 can be staked per day, in contrast to the weekly limits applicable to sports betting.

Instant lottery requirements
De Lotto is permitted to offer up to 120 million scratch cards on an annual basis under the *Beschikking Instantloterij*. These are to be sold through up to 7,000 sales points, which cannot be in premises which are primarily focused on those below the age of 18 years. Whilst free scratch cards are permitted, no card can cost more than EUR 30. Over the course of a calendar year the amount returned to players as prizes must be between 47.5 per cent and 65 per cent of the stakes.

Charitable lottery requirements
Central to each of the lotteries' operations are the draws based upon the method previously indicated. The offerings of each of the lotteries are as follows:

- Nationale Postcode Loterij and the BankGiro Loterij can each offer:
  - 12 monthly lottery draws per annum consisting of one main draw and four or five weekly draws;
  - four extra draws per annum (one draw each);
  - a maximum of eight million tickets can be sold per lottery; and
  - the maximum nominal value of a ticket is EUR 22.69.
- Vrienden Loterij:
  - 52 weekly number lottery draws;
  - an additional game every month, which is a monthly (bingo) draw;
  - four extra number lottery draws per annum; and
  - the maximum nominal value of a ticket of EUR 22.69.

Each of these lotteries is required to direct at least 50 per cent of their revenues to good causes and each lottery is associated with funding different types of good causes. Whilst the operator of the lotteries enjoys discretion to determine which organisations receive funding, either on a structural or a one-off basis, the licence for each lottery specifies fields in which such organisations must belong. Respective fields per lottery are:

- Nationale Postcode Loterij – development cooperation and human rights; nature and environment; humanitarian assistance; civil, social and cultural work; and public health.
- BankGiro Loterij – culture; conservation; and social welfare.

- Vrienden Loterij – culture; social welfare; public health; sport and physical education; humanitarian assistance; and conservation.

2.5 Explain the system of regulation of gambling; which regulatory or governmental body is responsible for the supervision of gambling? Which body issues licences? Which body examines enforcement powers? Is there any limit on the number or duration of available licences?

On 1 April 2012 the Gaming Authority (*Kansspelautoriteit*), an independent regulatory authority, became operational. It is responsible for the issuing of licences, supervision and enforcement, and will issue online gambling licences once the necessary legislative amendments have been implemented. Policy formulation is the competence of the Ministry.

Licence award

Existing licences held by the current incumbent operators (licences are largely exclusive and are permanent or semi-permanent; see section 2.3 for details) have been awarded and renewed by the Ministry for awards and renewals made prior to the operationalisation of the Gaming Authority, and by the Authority from 1 April 2012 onwards. A key decision was rendered by the Council of State in March 2011 following a preliminary reference to the Court of Justice of the European Union (CJEU) with regard to the lack of transparency in the process for the award of the exclusive licences for sports betting and horserace betting. The CJEU clearly established that the obligation of transparency applied to the award of exclusive gambling licences, unless the operator in question is a *'public operator whose management is subject to direct State supervision or a private operator whose activities are subject to strict control by the public authorities'* (Case C-203/08, *Sporting Exchange*, paragraph 59).

The Council of State determined that De Lotto was not subject to sufficiently strict control to justify the lack of a transparent allocation process. This has been one of the key drivers behind the forthcoming introduction of a transparent licence allocation procedure for (offline) lottery licences, a system which should be in place as of 1 January 2015.

At the time of writing, the licence award process and conditions for online gambling licences are unknown. These will be determined in secondary legislation accompanying the remote gaming bill. The time line for this process is considered in section 3.6. Until such amendments enter into force, the Gaming Authority lacks the competence to award online gambling licences.

Supervision and enforcement

The Gaming Authority is responsible for the supervision and enforcement of the regulatory regime *vis-à-vis* licensed operators and also parties unlawfully offering gambling services in the Netherlands. For an overview of potential criminal and administrative sanctions see section 3.3.

In the transitional period pending the introduction of a regulatory and licensing regime for online gambling offerings available in the Netherlands remain in breach of the prohibited unless licensed approach. The prohibited unless licensed approach will prevail following regulatory reform. Enforcing the prohibition on promoting unlicensed gambling also falls within the Gaming Authority's remit; whilst it is understood that this prohibition encompasses the advertising of unlicensed gambling, differences of opinion prevail as to whether it reaches providers of other B2B services, such as payment processing. Clarification will follow from the remote gaming bill, which will probably establish that providers of payment services and internet service providers will fall within this prohibition. The Gaming Authority will acquire the competence to demand that such services are terminated on a case-by-case basis.

Until licensing for online gambling commences, the Gaming Authority is enforcing the prohibition on unlicensed online gambling on the basis of its so-called 'prioritisation criteria'. On this basis, the Gaming Authority will give priority to serving enforcement measures against those operators breaching at least one of the following three conditions:

- offering games of chance via a website available in the Dutch language;
- offering games of chance via a website with a .nl URL extension; and
- advertising via radio, television or print-based media directed towards the Netherlands.

According to the Gaming Authority's most recent press release on the matter, those operators who comply are not necessarily safe in terms of potential enforcement measures being sought against them (see *Handhaving online kansspelen, hoe doet de Kansspelautoriteit dat?* 14 February 2014). Adherence to the list of what not to do considerably reduces the risk of such measures, notwithstanding the fact that the underlying offer breaches the prohibition on unlicensed gambling.

3. ONLINE GAMBLING

3.1 To what extent can online gambling be offered in your jurisdiction? Are licences available and, if so, for which gambling products? Please describe briefly the licensing process, who may apply, whether licences are limited in number and, if no licences are available, whether it is legal for online gambling to be offered. In the case of EU jurisdictions, please state whether there are any issues as to the legality of the local law at EU level. Please refer to any relevant cases at ECJ level and explain any measures taken or pending by the European Commission.

Prior to the regulatory reforms coming into force, the Gaming Authority lacks the competence to award licences for online gambling. Given the absence of any such licences, all online gambling in the Netherlands is prohibited. Notwithstanding the lack of such a legal basis, several of the incumbent operators have been authorised to offer their services via the internet. Their online offer must reflect the services offered in the land-based sphere; for example, De Lotto cannot offer sports betting via its website on competitions which are not covered by its high-street offer. Such offerings have been deemed as merely constituting another 'distribution channel', and are considered as amounting to 'e-commerce' and thus not online gambling.

From the version of the remote gaming bill notified to the European Commission on 5 March 2014, it is expected that there will be no cap on the number of licences available. Whilst secondary legislation will provide precise details as to the forms of gambling permitted, it has already been indicated that online lotteries (including bingo) and spread betting will be excluded. Restrictions on live betting will follow in secondary legislation. International liquidity is foreseen for poker and exchange betting. Although the regime will regulate gambling provided via the internet, it is not to be expected that licences will enable the provision of gambling services via all forms of remote communication (television, smartphones). Secondary legislation will render clarification.

At the time of writing, the licensing process is unknown; again, this will be dealt with in secondary legislation. However, it appears that licence applicants must be established within the EU/EEA or another approved jurisdiction. Successful applicants will not be required to have their gambling servers located in the Netherlands if the servers are located in another EU/EEA member state or in an approved jurisdiction which regulates the activity in question (the bill refers to Alderney and the Isle of Man as examples). However, a control data bank will have to be located in the Netherlands. Licences are foreseen as being valid for a period of five years.

For provision of online gambling prior to the introduction of the forthcoming licensing regime see Supervision and enforcement in section 2.5.

3.2 Is there a distinction between the law applicable to B2B operations and that applicable to B2C operations?
In its present form, primary legislation does not recognise online gambling and therefore no distinction between B2B and B2C operations is made. Following the impending reform, it is anticipated that the regulation of online gambling will focus upon B2C operations, with only B2C entities being licensed whilst being responsible for ensuring compliance with local regulations by any B2B suppliers used.

3.3 What are the consequences for B2C or B2B operators who are active in your jurisdiction without having obtained or applied for the required permits, licences and approvals? What penalties and enforcement powers are available in respect of the illegal operators? Please outline any significant domestic decisions or enforcement actions that have been taken by the relevant authorities in recent years.
Following the decision of the Supreme Court in *De Lotto v Ladbrokes* (AR4841, 18 February 2005), a very low threshold has been set for determining whether gambling offered by an operator in another jurisdiction is offered in the Netherlands in breach of Article 1(a) BGA. It is irrelevant whether or not the operator is licensed in another jurisdiction. An

opportunity to participate in games of chance is considered as being offered in the Netherlands when access to such games is provided via a website which is also aimed towards the Netherlands and if Dutch residents are able to participate directly in games of chance through their computer and for such participation no further actions have to be performed other than those which can be performed on their computer (reference was made to a variety of actions, including, for example, the participant being able to receive the participation form on their computer and return the completed form from their computer to the operator's servers).

Furthermore, the BGA also prohibits the promotion of unlicensed gambling in Article 1(b). A narrow interpretation of 'promotion' is most probably restricted to covering advertising of prohibited gambling services to the exclusion of any other type of service which a B2B operator may provide and which facilitates the provision of unlicensed online gambling services in the Netherlands. Whilst opinion on the scope of Article 1(b) is somewhat divided, no grounds prevail in legislative history or case law to provide a foundation for a broader interpretation. Moreover, the remote gaming bill seeks to expand the scope of Article 1(b) so as to encompass intermediaries such as ISP and PSP providers, whilst providing the Gaming Authority with the competence to deliver binding instructions requiring that the provision of services to locally unlicensed online gambling operators ceases. See section 3.4 for further details.

An alternative, and currently wholly untested possibility, is that B2B operators are perceived as aiding and abetting the provision of unlicensed gambling services under Article 1(a) BGA. In this instance Article 1(a) would be read in conjunction with Article 48 of the Dutch Criminal Code which establishes the concept of complicity; it would have to be proven that a B2B operator intentionally aided and abetted the provision of unlicensed gambling or intentionally offered the opportunity, means and information to commit an offence, ie the unlicensed provision of gambling services.

In terms of criminal enforcement, breaching the prohibition contained in Article 1(a) could be met with the following sanctions:
- maximum imprisonment of two years and/or a fine of EUR 20,250;
- if the proceeds of the crime, or the worth of goods which were used to commit the crime, exceed one-fourth of EUR 20,250, a maximum fine per incident may be imposed of EUR 81,000;
- if the above fine is not a suitable punishment as far as it concerns legal persons, a fine of EUR 810,000 may be imposed; and
- for the offence of being an accessory (eg a B2B operator), the maximum penalty for the offence is reduced by one third.

Criminal penalties for breaching the prohibition on the promotion of unlicensed gambling are:
- maximum imprisonment of six months and/or a fine of EUR 20,250;
- EUR 81,000 if the proceeds of the crime, or the worth of goods which were used to commit the crime, exceed one quarter of EUR 20,250; or
- EUR 810,000 if the previous fine is not a suitable punishment, as far as it concerns legal persons.

It is generally understood that the authorities will prefer enforce the BGA by means of administrative sanctions, and pursuant to Articles 35 (a) and (b) the Gaming Authority has the competence to impose the following measures on all parties acting in breach of the BGA:

- fines: up to a maximum of EUR 810,000 or, if the annual turnover exceeds an amount of EUR 810,000, up to a maximum of 10 per cent of the turnover in the previous year;
- administrative orders; and
- incremental penalty payments.

As noted above, the Gaming Authority is managing enforcement of the prohibition on locally unlicensed online gambling on the basis of the prioritisation criteria. Nevertheless, a number of operators which failed to heed warnings from the Gaming Authority and adjust their offering accordingly have been served with fines on the basis of administrative proceedings. To date, fines in the range of EUR 100,000–200,000 have been awarded, with further fines in the pipeline. Once the licensing regime becomes operational, the prioritisation criteria will become obsolete.

3.4 What technical measures are in place (if any) to protect consumers from unlicensed operators, such as ISP blocking and payment blocking?

Under the current version of the BGA there are no such technical measures in place. However, the remote gaming bill (Article 34n) envisages that the Gaming Authority will be granted the competence to issue 'binding instructions' to those who promote participation in gaming which is offered in contravention of the prohibition on unlicensed gaming. Such a binding instruction may *'include a requirement for the provider of a payment service to take all reasonable steps to block payments used for organising gambling'* offered without a licence. Similarly, a binding instruction may also require *'the provider of a public electronic communications service to take all reasonable steps to render inaccessible certain information stored or transmitted'* for the purpose of organising, participating in or advertising unlicensed gaming.

3.5 Has the legal status of online gambling changed significantly in recent years and, if so, how?

Currently online gambling in the Netherlands is entirely unlawful, given the lack of a legal basis for licences to be awarded. The Gaming Authority is managing the enforcement of the prohibition on unlicensed gambling *vis-à-vis* online gambling operators in accordance with the prioritisation criteria until a regulatory and licensing regime is introduced in 2015. See Supervision and enforcement under section 2.5.

3.6 Whilst acknowledging the inherent difficulty in predicting developments in gambling law, what are the likely developments in online gambling in your jurisdiction, both short term and long term? Are any specific amendments under consideration? Have there been any recent political developments, or do you envisage any in the near future? Are any specific amendments under consideration? Are they likely to be adopted and, if so, what is the time scale?

Whilst the decision of the Council of State (*Raad van State*) in *Betfair* (BP8768, 23 March 2011) has been one driver of policy change towards the regulation of gambling, a change in government has also been highly influential. In March 2011, State Secretary for Security and Justice Fred Teeven sent a letter to Parliament in which he outlined plans for reforming the gambling market and establishing a regulated remote sector. State Secretary Teeven retained this position following general elections in September 2012, with the October 2012 coalition agreement of the PvdA (Labour Party) and VVD (Conservative Party) setting forth the cabinet's three-point plan to modernise the national gambling landscape. These three points are:

1.   introduction of a regulatory regime for online gambling;
2.   a transparent licence allocation procedure for semi-permanent lottery licences; and
3.   the privatisation of Holland Casino.

Officially, the necessary legislative amendments should be in place so as to enable the licensing of online gambling to commence in January 2015, although the final quarter of that year, or even the first quarter of 2016, would appear more realistic in terms of entities being able to submit online gambling licence applications. In terms of the transparent licence allocation procedure, it is likewise timetabled to become operational in 2015, and existing semi-permanent licences will expire on 31 December 2014. The time-frame for the privatisation of Holland Casino is less clear.

In relation to the introduction of a regulatory regime for online gambling, a draft bill was published for consultation purposes by the Ministry and the Ministry of Finance on 23 May 2013. A public consultation period ensued, with approximately 90 submissions being made by a variety of stakeholders, national and international alike. The Ministry revised the remote gaming bill during autumn 2013 with the amended version receiving the approval of the Council of Ministers (*Ministerraad*), resulting in the bill going the Council of State (*Raad van State*), which will deliver advice on the text. Its review of the bill is essentially technical in nature and, once the green light has been given, the bill will go to the House of Representatives, the lower chamber in Parliament. On 5 March 2014 the bill was notified to the European Commission, with the standstill period due to expire on 6 June 2014 in the absence of any detailed opinions being submitted. Debate on the floor of the House of Representatives, where the government has a narrow majority, will likely take place following summer 2014 and, once approved, it will be sent to the upper house, the Senate, where the government lacks a majority. However, the Senate can only accept or reject a bill. All things being equal, the bill will pass through the legislative process and reach the statute books in 2015. Once this stage has been reached, the Gaming Authority will subsequently be able to commence the licensing process in 2015/2016, as indicated above.

3.7 Is the law the same in relation to mobile gambling and interactive gambling on television? If not, are there any headline differences?

Given the current state of primary legislation, prior to the aforementioned regulatory reform to introduce a regulatory regime for online gambling, there is an absence of provisions regulating the provision of mobile gambling or interactive gambling on television. Within the forthcoming regulatory regime for online gambling, secondary legislation, which should be published before summer 2014, will set out how the law will apply to such forms of delivery. Indeed, the explanatory memorandum to the remote gaming bill indicates that not all forms of remote communication will be permitted.

4. LAND-BASED GAMING

4.1 Please describe the licensing regime (if any) for land-based gaming, and what products are included. Please set out what licences are available, and the licensing regime for them.

Please refer to conditions relating to casino and slot machine gambling as set out in sections 2.3 and 2.4.

4.2 Please set out any particular limitations or requirements for (eg casino) operators, such as a ban on local residents gambling.

Please refer to conditions relating to casino and slot machine gambling as set out in sections 2.3 and 2.4.

5. TAX

5.1 Please summarise briefly the tax regime applicable both to land-based and online gaming.

Taxation of gambling under Dutch law occurs pursuant to the aforementioned Law on Gambling Taxation (*Wet op de kansspelbelasting*).

Gambling tax at a rate of 29 per cent based on gross gaming revenue is applicable to both slots, offline casino games, and online games when provided by a party established in the Netherlands. This latter category is not restricted to casino-type games and could be somewhat theoretical in nature, as no entity established in the Netherlands can lawfully offer online gambling without being subject to the risk of enforcement measures. For all other offline games of chance, the participant is liable for tax at a rate of 29 per cent on prizes over EUR 454 without any deductions being permitted for stakes placed. Although the participant is liable, providers are required to withhold the amount due when paying out prizes.

When an online gambling operator is located outside the Netherlands and a Dutch resident participates in its offering, then the resident is liable for gambling tax, again at a rate of 29 per cent, based on gross earnings per month, and tax is due monthly.

Under existing proposals, online gambling licensees will be taxed at a rate of 20 per cent GGR; thus, the Netherlands will apply a differential tax rate when compared with the land-based sector, for which 29 per cent GGR will remain. In light of Denmark's experience, the Netherlands does not foresee any difficulties in having this measure approved under EU state aid rules. A variety of additional levies and fees are predicted to have the potential to push up the effective tax burden to around 25–27 per cent, whilst bonuses will not be deductible. Following licensing, residents playing on locally unlicensed sites will remain liable for tax at 29 per cent of gross earnings per month, as a means to dissuade patronage of such offerings.

6. ADVERTISING
6.1 To what extent is the advertising of gambling permitted in your jurisdiction? Again, this should cover both land-based and online gaming. To the extent that advertising is permitted, how is it regulated?

Rules governing the advertising of gambling are found in the Dutch Advertising Code (*De Nederlandse Reclame Code*, the Code) and secondary legislation, notably the decree regarding recruitment, advertising and addiction (*Besluit werving, reclame en verslavingspreventie kansspelen*), which entered into force on 1 July 2013 and the accompanying regulation of the same title (*Regeling werving, reclame en verslavingspreventie kansspelen*). The decree and regulation, based on Article 4a BGA, only apply to current licensees and their land-based offer. Examples of applicable provisions include: (i) a prohibition on 'tie-in' advertising, where services of the licensee are promoted in conjunction with goods or services of a third party if and when such goods or services are targeted at socially vulnerable people; and (ii) a prohibition on gambling related television advertising between 06:00 and 19:00, apart from neutral messages concerning the sponsorship of a television programme. Further, incumbents: (iii) have to report information to the Gaming Authority such as advertising methods used and the number of complaints received regarding advertising activities; and (iv) provide information to consumers such as the characteristics of the gaming offered and the cost of participation.

Broadly framed provisions found with the Code deal with three principal areas:
- advertising content;
- vulnerable groups; and
- sponsorship.

The Code is due to be revised in anticipation of the forthcoming licensing of online gambling. Indeed, on the basis of Article 4a BGA, specific conditions pertaining to the advertising of online gambling will become known following the publication of secondary legislation. However, the current explanatory memorandum indicates that B2C licensees will be responsible for ensuring that affiliates comply with local Dutch provisions in this regard.

7. SOCIAL GAMING

7.1 We believe this to be a growing area. Please decide under what criteria social gaming is permitted in your jurisdiction. If games are free to play or if there is no prize, are they legal without a licence? Please address circumstances where virtual currency is used and can be won: ie currency which is of no monetary or other value, save for as credits to take part in games. The answer should address the question whether game credits or virtual money can be exchanged for other prizes. Is any change to regulation in the area proposed or envisaged?

The question of social gaming in the Netherlands is one which, given the current legislative framework, is not explicitly addressed by Dutch law. In light of the definition of gambling as provided for in the BGA the conclusion should not be drawn that the scope of the existing law is not without relevance for social gaming.

First and foremost, central to any discussion as to the legality of unlicensed social or free play games in the Netherlands, is the definition of gambling as provided for in Article 1(a) BGA where two key elements are: (i) that the outcome is determined by chance; and (ii) a prize or premium is awarded.

In contrast to many other jurisdictions, particularly in the United States (for example in the gambling legislation of New Jersey, Nevada, Utah and Washington), consideration does not form part of the definition of gambling. Social games and free play games do not have to pass this particular hurdle to be considered as falling within the definition of a game of chance. Assuming that the outcome of a social game or free play game is determined by chance then the key element to consider is whether the prize awarded in a social or free play game constitutes a prize or premium for the purposes of the BGA.

No reference is made in legislative history to, nor has case law considered what 'prize or premium' entails. However, a clue to a possible interpretation of this provision is found within the Gambling Taxation Act (*Wet op de kansspelbelasting*) which defines prizes as all goods which are assigned a value in the course of trade (Article 3(2)). The seemingly wide reach of this definition finds some support in the legislation which the Gambling Taxation Act replaced, as the previous legislation read 'the definition of the term 'prizes' is very broad so that everything that participants win because of their participation in a lottery and such can be considered as a prize...'. (Explanatory Memorandum, Act of 14 September 1961, Stb. 1961, 313 (Lottery Tax Act', Parliamentary Papers II 1959/60, 5787, nr. 3, p.6). Support for relying upon the approach taken by the Gambling Taxation Act to fully understand the provisions of the BGA can be found in a 2011 decision of the Trade and Industry Appeals Tribunal which relied upon the tax legislation to define 'prize' as referred to in the BGA (Trade and Industry Appeals Tribunal, 7 April 2011, LJN BQ1786, paragraph 2.4).

Therefore, should a social or free play game result in no prize whatsoever then this condition will clearly not be satisfied. Virtual currencies and points are commonplace within social games and it cannot be conclusively concluded that such currencies or points do not amount to prizes or premiums.

Firstly, awarding successful players points which enable further play could be deemed to bring such points within the scope of the BGA. Although participation may be free at the point of entry some social games allow participants to purchase points, either on a one-time or subscription basis, which enable continued play once free play points have been utilised. A consumer who has been unsuccessful and spent all their allocated free points but wishes to continue playing may be provided the opportunity to continue playing upon purchasing further points, or drawing upon points secured on a subscription basis. What is of considerable significance is that the ability of consumers to purchase points to enable the continuation of play suggests that points won possess an economic value as these points enable play without the need for the consumer to part with money.

Should such points won form part of a virtual currency which can be used in a virtual environment to engage in (economic) exchanges then such points are more likely to constitute either a prize or premium. The fact that the exchange occurs wholly and only within a virtual environment with no opportunity for a player to 'cash out' (into the offline sphere) is unlikely to remove a game from the scope of the BGA should it otherwise fall within it.

Dutch criminal law also offers support for the positions taken above, more precisely a case regarding the theft of a virtual mask and amulet in the massively multiplayer online role-playing game (MMORPG) *Runescape*. In November 2009 the Leeuwarden District Court of Appeal found that these two items amounted to goods for the purposes of criminal law.

The goods acquired value from the effort and time invested in acquiring them. This position was confirmed by the Supreme Court which held in its decision in early 2012 that these items have an economic value (31 January 2012, LJN:BQ9251).

Therefore there is a chance that points or currencies earned in free play and social games will be considered as having an economic value and therefore will constitute a prize or premium for the purposes of Article 1(a) BGA.

Nevada (USA)

Lionel Sawyer & Collins
Dan R. Reaser, Mark A. Clayton & Robert D. Faiss

1. OBJECTIVES AND STRUCTURE OF LEGISLATION

Nevada has continuously licensed and regulated gambling as a commercial activity for more than 80 years. In 1931, commercial gaming was adopted by the Nevada Legislature as part of economic development measures during the Great Depression.

The state's comprehensive Gaming Control Act (the Act), was enacted in 1959 and substantially amended in 1967 and 1973 to add Nevada's corporate gaming statutes. Nev. Rev. Stat. §§ 463.010–790. The Act and five ancillary chapters of the Nevada Revised Statutes (the NRS) comprise the modern comprehensive legal scheme for the gaming industry established by the Nevada Legislature. See Nev. Rev. Stat. §§ 463A.010–260 (Gaming Employees' Labor Organizations); Nev. Rev. Stat. §§ 463B.010–280 (Supervision of Certain Gaming Establishments); Nev. Rev. Stat. §§ 464.005–100 (Pari-Mutuel Wagering); Nev. Rev. Stat. §§ 465.015–110 (Crimes and Liabilities Concerning Gaming); Nev. Rev. Stat. §§ 466.010–220 (Horse Racing). We provide more detailed discussions of the principal elements of the Nevada regulatory system in sections 2.5 and 4.1.

The Nevada Legislature has declared that the state's public policy objectives relative to commercial gambling are concerned with, among other things:

- the prevention of unsavoury or unsuitable persons from having a direct or indirect involvement with gaming at any time or in any capacity;
- the establishment and maintenance of effective controls over the accounting and financial practices of licensees, including the establishment of minimum procedures for internal fiscal affairs and the safeguarding of assets and revenues, providing reliable record keeping and requiring the filing of periodic reports with the gaming regulatory authorities;
- the prevention of cheating and fraudulent practices; and
- providing a source of state and local revenues through taxation and fees.

Nev. Rev. Stat. § 463.0129

Since 2001, the Nevada Legislature has authorised 'interactive gaming', which is the statutory term for online gaming. Nevada licenses and regulates interactive (or internet) gaming, which allows for gambling games to be played using communications technology so that a person can transmit information that aids in placement of wagers and receive information on game play and outcome. Nev. Rev. Stat. § 463.016425.

Different types of licences are required, depending on the aspect of interactive gaming business involved. Individuals and entities must apply for and obtain a nonrestricted licence to operate an internet game, manufacture equipment used for such games or act as a service provider for interactive gaming operations. Importantly, an operator's licence may only be held by a person directly or through an affiliate who also operates a gaming establishment that satisfies the resort hotel requirements of Nevada state law applicable in its geographical location, which establishment has been licensed for at least five years. Nev. Rev. Stat. §§ 463.745–785.

2. FRAMEWORK OF LEGISLATION
2.1 What is the legal definition of gambling and what falls within this definition?
'Gaming' or 'gambling' means to deal, operate, carry on, conduct, maintain or expose for play any 'gambling game' or to operate an 'inter-casino linked system'. Nev. Rev. Stat. § 463.0153. A 'gambling game' is expansively defined as:

'[A]ny game played with cards, dice, equipment or any mechanical, electromechanical or electronic device or machine for money, property, checks, credit or any representative of value, including, without limiting the generality of the foregoing, faro, monte, roulette, keno, bingo, fan-tan, twenty-one, blackjack, seven-and-a-half, big injun, klondike, craps, poker, chuck-a-luck, Chinese chuck-a-luck (dai shu), wheel of fortune, chemin de fer, baccarat, pai gow, beat the banker, panguingui, slot machine, any banking or percentage game or any other game or device approved by the Commission, but does not include games played with cards in private homes or residences in which no person makes money for operating the game, except as a player, or games operated by charitable or educational organizations which are approved by the Board...'

Nev. Rev. Stat. § 463.0152.

An inter-casino linked system is a *'network of electronically interfaced similar games which are located at two or more licensed gaming establishments that are linked to conduct gaming activities, contests or tournaments'*. Nev. Rev. Stat. § 463.01643. These systems are commonly known as wide area progressive games, such as the popular IGT Wheel of Fortune slot machine that is linked among participating casinos where players compete for common jackpots the value of which increments based on volume of play.

2.2 What is the legal definition of online gambling and what falls within this definition?
Interactive gaming is conducting gambling games, using communications technology that allows a person to transmit information aiding wager placement and receive information on the game play and outcome, through the medium of a computer. Nev. Rev. Stat. §§ 463.016425. In this context:

A 'gambling game' is any form of game allowed by state law to a casino licensee and specifically includes internet poker and explicitly excludes sports pools and race books. See Nev. Rev. Stat. §§ 463.0152 & .016425(1).

While the statute imposes no limitation on the form of gambling games that can be offered online, the Commission has limited interactive gaming to poker by regulation. Nev. Gaming Comm'n Reg. 5A.140.

'Communications technology' specifically includes the internet, but is broadly defined to capture any technology that facilitates information transmission. Excluded from this definition is the information and technology systems used to support sports pools and race books. Nev. Rev. Stat. § 463.016425(1).

A 'wager' is money or a 'representative of value' – like a casino chip – that a person risks on the outcome of an uncertain event. See, eg, *State v GNLV Corp.*, 108 Nev. 456, 834 P.2d 411 (1992).

2.3 Please set out the different gambling products identified by legislation.

The Act expansively defines gambling all of which is subject to the regulatory system prescribed by statute. Under state law, poker, specifically listed casino games, bingo, sports and race wagering, and slot machines are explicitly identified as permitted forms of commercial gaming subject to game approval and licensed operation. Section 463.0152 of the Act also empowers the state regulatory agencies to approve for licensing any other banking or percentage game, thereby encompassing virtually all forms of betting except a lottery.

Commercial lotteries are prohibited, whether conducted by the government or private entities. Nev. Rev. Stat. §§ 462.015–125 & .250–330. Nevada permits, subject to regulation, limited forms of charitable lotteries. Nev. Rev. Stat. §§ 462.015–125 & .130–200.

2.4 Please list the different requirements for each gambling product, including legal classifications for each; for example, is poker a game of skill or game of chance?

Nevada's expansive statutory definition of 'gambling' essentially allows licensees to expose for play any game that has been approved by the Nevada Gaming Commission (the Commission). See Nev. Rev. Stat. § 463.0152. Thus, for the purposes of Nevada's gaming regulatory system, with the exception of a lottery, a licensee may accept wagers on any game that has been approved by the Commission under the applicable game review process. The skill versus chance distinction recognised in some other jurisdictions, therefore, is not relevant except in the context of determining whether a person is engaged in an unlawful lottery. In that context, Nevada is a 'dominant factor' jurisdiction, meaning that skill must be predominant in a game to be so classified. See, eg, *Las Vegas Hacienda, Inc. v. Gibson*, 77 Nev. 25, 359 P.2d 85 (1961). See section 2.1.

2.5 Explain the system of regulation of gambling; which regulatory or governmental body is responsible for the supervision of gambling? Which body issues licences? Which body examines enforcement powers? Is there any limit on the number or duration of available licences?

The statutory plan in the Act is administered by the Commission and the State Gaming Control Board (the Board, and collectively with the Commission, the Nevada Gaming Authorities), which license and regulate the ownership and operation of gaming establishments located in the State of Nevada. The Board is the investigative and law enforcement agency within this two-tier regulatory structure. The Board is composed of three members appointed to four-year terms by the Governor, one of whom is designated to serve as Chairman. See Nev. Rev. Stat. §§ 463.030 & .1405. The Board members are full-time public officials and supervise approximately 400 agents and employees. The Board is organised into six divisions, namely Administration, Audit, Enforcement, Investigations, Tax & License and Technology.

The Commission is a five-member lay body appointed by the Governor to four-year terms. The Governor selects one of the Commissioners to serve as Chairman. The Commissioners serve in a part-time capacity and have other professions or occupations. A primary responsibility of the Commission is to act on the recommendations of the Board in licensing matters. The Commission is the final authority on licensing matters, holding the power to approve, restrict, limit, condition, deny, revoke or suspend any gaming licence. See Nev. Rev. Stat. §§ 463.022 & .140–143.

The Commission is also charged with the responsibility of adopting, amending and repealing gaming regulations consistent with, and to implement, the state's policies and objectives. See Nev. Rev. Stat. §§ 463.145–15995. In contested administrative cases the Board acts in a prosecutorial capacity and the Commission acts in a quasi-judicial capacity. The Commission decides disciplinary matters when the Board complains that a violation of statute or rule has occurred, and whether and what sanction to impose against a licensee or other regulated person for any such violations. See Nev. Rev. Stat. §§ 463.310–318. The Commission also resolves tax disputes, employee work registration cases and most other contested matters, but not disputes between patrons and licensed gaming establishment operators, which are determined by the Board. A person aggrieved by a final decision and order in a contested case is entitled to judicial review based on the factual record established before the regulators. See, eg, Nev. Rev. Stat. §§ 463.335–337, .366–3668 & .370–400.

The Commission may deny an application for licensing for any cause deemed reasonable. A finding of suitability is comparable to licensing, and is a determination of a person's suitability or qualification for particular affiliations with a licensed operation. Both require submission of detailed personal and financial information followed by a thorough investigation. Upon completion of the investigation, the Board will make a recommendation to the Commission. Nev. Rev. Stat.. § 463.1405. A decision of the Commission to deny an application for licensure, a finding of suitability or other approval generally is not subject to judicial review. Nev. Rev. Stat. §§ 463.1405, .170 & .318.

Nevada does not ration licences. Both state statute and local county or city ordinances, however, determine, through land use and zoning rules, the location and, in certain respects, the amenities for gaming establishments. See section § 4.2.

Although generally person and location specific, licences are perpetual unless expressly limited or conditioned by order of the Commission. See, eg, Op. Nev. Att'y Gen. No. 88-13 (Oct. 14, 1988). Limited licences are granted by the Commission when the Nevada Gaming Authorities determine that the applicant should only be allowed probationary entry into the privileged industry for a period of years during which the regulators can monitor conduct and operations under standards more stringent than provided by general standards and rules. At the conclusion of the limitation period, the licensed person must reapply *ab initio* for a new licence. See, eg, *Kraft v. Jacka*, 872 F.2d 862 (9th Cir. 1989). Typically, any licence granted must be activated or transactional approval given must be consummated within six months of receipt from the Commission. Nev. Gaming Comm'n Reg. 4.080.

3. ONLINE GAMBLING

3.1 To what extent can online gambling be offered in your jurisdiction? Are licences available and, if so, for which gambling products? Please describe briefly the licensing process, who may apply, whether licences are limited in number and, if no licences are available, whether it is legal for online gambling to be offered. In the case of EU jurisdictions, please state whether there are any issues as to the legality of the local law at EU level. Please refer to any relevant cases at ECJ level and explain any measures taken or pending by the European Commission.

Nevada strictly regulates and controls 'interactive gaming'. See sections 1 and 2.2. There are three types of licences, depending on the aspect of the interactive gaming business involved. Persons – this means either an individual or an entity – must apply for and obtain a nonrestricted licence to operate interactive games, manufacture equipment used in interactive gaming or act as a service provider for interactive gaming operations.

An interactive gaming operator's license is akin to licences held by a casino that owns and operates gambling games offered to the public. To be eligible for an interactive gaming operator's licence, the person applying must (i) satisfy resort casino requirements of Nevada state law applicable to its geographical location; or (ii) be an affiliate of such an establishment that has had a nonrestricted licensee for at least five years. Nev. Rev. Stat. § 463.750.

Licences are required of persons manufacturing interactive gaming systems for use in Nevada operations. A systems manufacturer licence is similar to that held by companies that design and produce slot machines for Nevada use or play. A related licence category exists for manufacturers of associated equipment used in interactive gaming. This is a licence to provide ancillary equipment or systems, such as an accounting records management software program, used to support a interactive gaming system. These licences are similar to Nevada's system for associated equipment findings of suitability or licences used today for those firms providing components and software supporting slot machines. Nev. Rev. Stat. § 463.750.

An interactive gaming service provider's licence is required of any business supporting a licensed interactive gaming operator by:

- managing wagers and games;
- providing intellectual property, customer information, assets or other products and services to the establishment operator for a percentage fee or otherwise; or
- maintaining interactive gaming computer system hardware or software. Nev. Rev. Stat. §§ 463.677(5) & .750.

Nevada does not ration the number of interactive gaming licences. Nev. Rev. Stat. § 463.750. The Nevada Legislature has specifically provided that patron debts incurred in connection with interactive gaming are enforceable. Nev. Rev. Stat. § 463.780.

3.2 Is there a distinction between the law applicable to B2B operations and that applicable to B2C operations?

Nevada's interactive gaming licensing system does distinguish between business-to-business operations and business-to-customer operations. Interactive gaming operators licences are required for those persons directly interfacing with patrons. Licensed interactive gaming manufacturers and service providers are those involved in providing goods and services to the licensed operators. See section 3.1.

3.3 What are the consequences for B2C or B2B operators who are active in your jurisdiction without having obtained or applied for the required permits, licences and approvals? What penalties and enforcement powers are available in respect of the illegal operators? Please outline any significant domestic decisions or enforcement actions that have been taken by the relevant authorities in recent years.

Persons engaged in unlicensed interactive gaming operations are guilty of a *'category B felony and shall be punished by imprisonment in the state prison for a minimum term of not less than 1 year and a maximum term of not more than 10 years or by a fine of not more than $50,000, or both'*. See Nev. Rev. Stat. § 463.750. Persons who transmit or receive Internet wagers into or from the state through unlicensed persons and where not lawful by interstate compact are guilty of a gross misdemeanour, punishable by up to one year in jail or a $2,000 fine, or both. Nev. Rev. Stat. §§ 193.140 & 465.091–094.

The Nevada Legislature has also enacted significant limitations on the eligibility for interactive gaming licences or findings of suitability for persons who owned or operated, after 31 December 2006, an internet gaming operation that involved patrons in the United States and was not licensed in compliance with domestic local, state and federal law, or used an asset that was employed in such operations. These limitations include an exclusion for five years after 21 February 2013, and a mandate that the person make themselves subject to criminal jurisdiction of state and federal courts, and waive certain defenses to prosecution. See Nev. Rev. Stat. § 463.750.

3.4 What technical measures are in place (if any) to protect consumers from unlicensed operators, such as ISP blocking and payment blocking?

The Commission has adopted a number of administrative rules to protect players and to protect the integrity of interactive games. Notably, these rules include a robust set of redundant requirements for registration of authorised players and the creation and oversight of wagering accounts. Nev. Gaming Comm'n Reg. 5A.110 & .120. The Commission's regulations mandate internal control procedures and technological systems that protect player information, ensure only natural persons who are not self- or governmentally excluded are allowed as players, and verify the age, identity and location of the player. Nev. Gaming Comm'n Reg. 5A.070, .110 & .140. Regulations also govern procedures for detection and prevention of criminal activities and a system of mandatory suspicious activity reporting. Nev. Gaming Comm'n Reg. 5A.080 & .160.

3.5 Has the legal status of online gambling changed significantly in recent years and, if so, how?

The 2001 statutes were significantly amended in 2011 and 2013. Statutory changes in 2011 included elimination of the predicate of action by the United States Government before interactive gaming could be operated, clarification of the requisites for service provider licences and changes to the fee requirements. See 2011 Nev. Stats. 213, 1283 & 1668–1669. In 2013, the Nevada Legislature passed provisions enabling the Governor, through a Commission-created process, to enter on behalf of Nevada interstate compacts for interactive gaming operations. The statutes were also amended to impose significant limitations on the eligibility for interactive gaming licences or findings of suitability based on the applicants involvement with internet gaming that violated federal and state law (see section 3.3), and allow for promotional activities supporting internet gaming operations. 2013 Nev. Stats. 3–4, 38, 3316 & 3307.

In December 2011, Nevada's regulatory authorities adopted implementing regulations, technical standards and internal control systems governing interactive gaming. See section 3.4. Nevada's first intrastate interactive gaming operation commenced on 25 April 2013. In the interactive gaming business, there are currently three firms licensed as operators, eight companies licensed as manufacturers and 16 entities licensed in various service provider capacities involved with interactive gaming.

3.6 Whilst acknowledging the inherent difficulty in predicting developments in gambling law, what are the likely developments in online gambling in your jurisdiction, both short term and long term? Are any specific amendments under consideration? Have there been any recent political developments, or do you envisage any in the near future? Are any specific amendments under consideration? Are they likely to be adopted and, if so, what is the time scale?

On 25 February 2014, Nevada and Delaware entered the first interstate agreement that allows interactive gaming to extend beyond the state's borders. New Jersey has also legalised internet gaming, and is likely to pursue similar agreements with Nevada and Delaware.

On 27 March 2014, the 'Restoration of America's Wire Act' bill was introduced in both the Senate and the House of Representatives of the United States Congress. If enacted, the purpose of the proposed federal legislation is to amend the Federal Wire Act (see 18 U.S.C. § 1084) to prohibit all internet gambling in the United States.

3.7 Is the law the same in relation to mobile gambling and interactive gambling on television? If not, are there any headline differences?

As governed by the Act, 'mobile gaming' is a form of gaming operation restricted to the 'premises' of eligible licensed gaming establishments. Nev. Rev. Stat. §§ 463.730–780. Mobile gaming operations may employ a wireless network, wireless fidelity, wire, cable, radio, microwave, light, optics or computer data networks, but cannot be conducted using the internet. Instead, this form of technology is restricted to:

'[T]he conduct of gambling games through communications devices operated solely in an establishment which holds a nonrestricted gaming license and which operates at least 100 slot machines and at least one other game by ... communications technology that allows a person to transmit information to a computer to assist in the placing of a bet or wager and corresponding information related to the display of the game, game outcomes or other similar information.'

Nev. Rev. Stat. § 463.0176.

Mobile gaming may be operated within any approved premises of a licensed establishment. Players must first open an account with the casino in person, and that process and the technology associated with the games must provide secure access restricted to the approved premises that includes measures to prevent minors from gambling. Nev. Gaming Comm'n Reg. 5.220.

Interactive gaming operations can be accessed through mobile devices, such as smart phones, tablets and laptop computers. To the extent that it is configured to access the internet, a television can also be utilised by players to participate in licensed interactive games. Nevada law broadly defines the systems that can be used for interactive gaming to include any *'collective hardware, software, communications technology, and proprietary hardware and software specifically designed or modified for, and intended for use in, the conduct of interactive gaming'*. Nev. Gaming Comm'n Reg. 14.010(16). The Commission generally requires that the servers and databases running the games and storing game and account informationt be located in the State of Nevada.

4. LAND-BASED GAMING

4.1 Please describe the licensing regime (if any) for land-based gaming, and what products are included. Please set out what licences are available, and the licensing regime for them.

The Nevada Gaming Authorities have extensive discretion to require persons involved with gaming to apply for and obtain a licence or finding of suitability. This discretionary authority augments the mandatory licensing requirements imposed by the Act for persons engaged in the operation of a gaming establishment or who receive revenues from gaming, and may be exercised when necessary to accomplish the public policy of the State of Nevada to strictly regulate and control the licensed gaming industry. See, eg, Nev. Rev. Stat. §§ 463.0129, .162, .165, .1665, .167–169, .530, .569, .5735 & .637.

Nevada law extends mandatory licensing to certain officers, directors, employees and beneficial owners of business entities seeking licensing or that are licensed for gaming, as well as discretionary licensing or suitability determination for lenders, underwriters, key executives, agents, consultants, business associates (eg vendors and contractors) and other individuals or entities that influence the management and control of a gaming establishment or gaming operation. See id.; see also, eg, Nev. Rev. Stat. §§ 463.160, .161, .520, .568, .5734 & .635. Mandatory licensing requirements also are imposed by the Act on manufacturers and distributors of gaming devices or cashless wagering, mobile gaming or interactive gaming systems; interactive or mobile gaming operators; slot route and inter-casino linked system operators; cash access and wagering instrument providers; interactive gaming service providers and certain other service providers; licensees operating international gaming salons or as information service providers; and disseminators of racing information and operators of off-track pari-mutuel wagering systems. Nev. Rev. Stat. §§ 463.160, .430, .650, .730, .750 & 464.010(2); Nev. Gaming Comm'n Reg. 5A.220 & 5.240. Licences are generally classified as restricted (operation of 15 or fewer slot machines at a location where gaming is incidental to the primary business) and nonrestricted (operation of 16 or more slot machines or any number of gaming devices with any other game; manufacturers or distributors; and slot route, mobile gaming, interactive gaming or inter-casino linked system operators, or interactive gaming and other service providers). Nev. Rev. Stat. §§ 463.0177, .0189, .160 & .161; Nev. Gaming Comm'n. Reg. 4.030 & 5A.030.

Licensing of landlords

Nevada law requires licensure of any person who furnishes services or property, real or personal, on the basis of a contract, lease or licence, pursuant to which that person receives payments based on earnings or profits from any gambling game. Nev. Rev. Stat. § 463.162(1)(c); see also

Nev. Rev. Stat. § 463.167(1). This requirement does not apply to persons receiving payments that are a fixed sum determined in advance on a bona fide basis for the furnishing of services or property other than a slot machine. Nev. Rev. Stat. § 463.162(2)(a). The Act states, however, that the Nevada Gaming Authorities may require a finding of suitability or the licensing of any person who owns any interest in the premises of or real property used by a licensed establishment, whether the property is leased directly to the licensee or through an intermediary. Nev. Rev. Stat. § 463.162(5)(a).

Licensing of owners and operators
In general, businesses or persons that commercially operate any gambling game, gaming device, slot machine, race book or sports pool, or that receive any revenues from such gaming operations in the State of Nevada, must receive and maintain state and local gaming licences prior to commencing operations or receiving revenues. See, eg, Nev. Rev. Stat. §§ 463.160, .161 & .162. For this reason, a person or business entity must be prepared to apply for and obtain a gaming licence, finding of suitability, registration or other approval, as appropriate, if they intend to operate gaming or obtain a legal interest in the revenues from gaming, even if only as a landlord or lender.

Licensing and regulation of business entities
As it relates to business entities, the Act envisions that gaming licenses usually will be held by private corporations, publicly traded corporations, limited partnerships or limited liability companies. See, eg, Nev. Rev. Stat. §§ 463.490, .564, .5731 & .635.

Private corporations
A private corporation that owns or operates a Nevada gaming establishment must be licensed by the Commission. Nev. Rev. Stat. §§ 463.489–560; Nev. Gaming Comm'n. Reg. 15. Likewise, every director and officer of a corporate licensee must be individually licensed or found suitable. Nev. Rev. Stat. § 463.530. However, only shareholders owning more than five per cent interest in the corporation must be licensed or found suitable, while shareholders with five per cent or less ownership need only go through a less stringent registration process, even though they remain subject to the discretionary licensing authority of the Commission. Nev. Gaming Comm'n Reg. 15.530–1.

Public corporations
Publicly traded corporations are also eligible to hold a gaming licence or own an entity that is a gaming licensee. The Commission may investigate and require a finding of suitability of any holder of any class of a public company's voting securities or debt securities at any time. Nevada law requires any person who acquires more than five per cent of any class of a public company's voting securities to report the acquisitions and

such person may be required to be investigated and found suitable at the discretion of the Commission. Any person who becomes a beneficial owner of more than 10 per cent of any class of the voting securities of a public company must apply for a finding of suitability by the Commission within 30 days after the Board Chairman mails a written notice requiring such filing. Officers, directors and key employees of the public company who are actively and directly involved in the gaming activities may be required to be licensed or found suitable by the Nevada Gaming Authorities. Typically, with respect to public companies, the Nevada Gaming Authorities will require licensing of the chairman of the board of directors; chairman of the audit committee; directors owning more than five per cent of any class of the public company's voting securities; directors serving on a committee delegated authority by the board of directors to act on gaming matters; lead directors; directors who are also employees involved in gaming; the president; the principal executive or operating officer; the principal financial officer; and persons functioning as the chief technology or information officer. The Nevada Gaming Authorities nevertheless maintain the discretion to require any officer, director, or shareholder of a public company to be investigated and found suitable. See generally Nev. Rev. Stat. §§ 463.625–643; Nev. Gaming Comm'n. Reg. 16.

Regulations of the Commission provide that control of a registered publicly traded corporation cannot be changed, whether through merger, acquisition of assets, management or consulting agreements, consummation of tender offer or any other form of takeover, without the prior approval of the Commission. Persons seeking approval to control a registered publicly traded corporation must satisfy the Commission as to a variety of stringent standards prior to assuming control of such corporation. The failure of a person to obtain such approval prior to assuming control over the registered publicly traded corporation may constitute grounds for finding such person unsuitable. Commission rules also prohibit certain repurchases of securities without the prior approval of the Commission. The regulations of the Commission also require prior approval for a 'plan of recapitalisation'. Generally, a plan of recapitalisation is a plan proposed by the board of directors of a registered publicly traded corporation that contains recommended action in response to a proposed corporate acquisition that requires prior approval of the Commission and is opposed by management of the corporation.

Limited partnerships

The Commission is authorised to issue a gaming licence to a limited partnership. Every general partner and limited partners with more than five per cent ownership interest are subject to mandatory licensing. Limited partners who have five per cent or less ownership interest must still register in advance with the Board, but remain subject to being investigated and found suitable at the discretion of the Nevada Gaming Authorities. The Commission may waive licensure and grant applications for deferred or delayed licensing to limited partners who own no more than 10 per cent of the partnership. Delayed licensing decisions entail the applicant's filing of personal history and financial disclosure statements and thereafter an assessment by the Nevada Gaming Authorities of several criteria that relate to the nature and extent of the limited partners' involvement in the licensed gaming operation and the passivity of their investment. See generally Nev. Rev. Stat. §§ 463.563–572; Nev. Gaming Comm'n. Reg. 15A.

Limited liability companies

Similarly, the Commission is authorised to issue a gaming licence to a limited liability company. Every manager and members with more than five per cent membership interest in a limited liability company are subject to mandatory licensing. Members of a limited liability company that is an applicant for a gaming licence or a licensee who owns five per cent or less interest must register with the Board in advance of acquiring such interest, but are also subject to discretionary licensing by the Nevada Gaming Authorities. The Commission may waive licensure and grant applications for deferred licensing to members who own no more than 10 per cent of the limited liability company. The Nevada Gaming Authorities apply the same criteria in formulating deferred licensing decisions for members of a limited liability company that are applied to deferred licensing rulings for limited partners. See generally Nev. Rev. Stat. §§ 463.573–5737; Nev. Gaming Comm'n. Reg. 15B.

Institutional investors

Under certain circumstances, an 'institutional investor', as such term is defined in the regulations of the Commission, that acquires up to 15 per cent of the voting securities of a private corporation, limited partnership or limited liability company may apply to the Commission for a waiver of the required equity-holder finding of suitability requirements if such institutional investor holds the voting securities for investment purposes only. An institutional investor in a public company licensed by or registered with the Commission may own up to 25 per cent of voting securities with a waiver. Nev. Gaming Comm'n. Reg. 15.430, 15A.070, 15B.070, 16.430.

Holding company regulation

A holding company of a gaming licensee must qualify to conduct business in the State of Nevada and register with the Commission. Officers, directors, partners, principals, employees, members, managers, trustees, and direct or beneficial owners of the holding company who the Commission determines are engaged in the administration or supervision of, or have any other significant involvement with, the gaming activities of a licensee must also be found suitable. Owners of more than five per cent interest in a holding company must be found suitable, while those with five per cent or less ownership interest in a holding company must register with the Board but remain subject to being investigated and found suitable at the discretion of the Nevada Gaming Authorities. See, eg, Nev. Rev. Stat. §§ 463.575–615; Nev. Gaming Comm'n. Reg. 15, 15A, 15B & 16.

Transaction reporting

Licensees must report on a broad range of transactions, including, but not limited to, certain leases, instalment contracts, loans, lines of credit, credit extensions and guarantees, within 30 days following the end of the quarter when the transaction is consummated. The reportable loan transaction may be investigated in any manner the Board deems appropriate. If, after such investigation, the Commission finds that the transaction is against the public health, safety, morals, good order or general welfare of the people of the State of Nevada, or would reflect, or tend to reflect, discredit upon the State of Nevada or the gaming industry, the Commission may order the transaction rescinded on any terms and conditions the Commission deems appropriate. See generally Nev. Gaming Comm'n. Reg. 8.130.

Local government gaming regulation

In addition to regulation by state regulators, commercial gaming is licensed by local governments in Nevada. For instance, the Clark County Board of County Commissioners, sitting as the Liquor and Gaming Licensing Board, actively regulates the gaming industry on the Las Vegas Strip and other areas of unincorporated Clark County. The gaming ordinances of cities and counties in Nevada vary in complexity and approach. Some local jurisdictions will defer to the state's Gaming Board for a gaming license investigation.

4.2 Please set out any particular limitations or requirements for (eg casino) operators, such as a ban on local residents gambling.

The primary limitation of note upon the issuance of nonrestricted 'casino' licences relates to locational restrictions. Generally, these gaming establishments may not be near schools and churches, and in Nevada's urban areas the casinos may only be within certain zoning districts and must have amenities qualifying the facilities as resort hotels. For restricted licences, the licensed location must be dedicated to a non-gaming business, such as a tavern, restaurant or convenience store, and gaming must be incidental to that business. See, eg, Nev. Rev. Stat. §§ 463.1605, & .3072– 3094; Nev. Gaming Comm'n Reg. 3.010; Clark County Code 8.04.070. See also sections 1 and 4 above.

4.3 Please address the questions in 3.5 above, but in relation to land-based gaming.

On 21 November 2013, the Commission adopted immediately effective regulations that authorize the operation of multi-jurisdictional progressive prize systems. See Nev. Gaming Comm'n Reg. 14.010, .030 & .100. This type of system allows slot machines operated in Nevada to be linked through a wide area network, where lawful, together with slot machines operated in another state or tribal casino for the purpose of participating in a common progressive jackpot prize. The Board and Commission are processing applications that will allow in 2014 the first of these multi-jurisdictional prize systems to operate between Nevada and New Jersey.

5. TAX
5.1 Please summarise briefly the tax regime applicable both to land-based and online gaming.
As to land-based licensees, the Act imposes six primary types of gaming fees or taxes upon licensees. These fees and taxes include: (i) licence fees on monthly gross gaming revenues; (ii) quarterly flat fees on slot machines; (iii) an annual excise tax on slot machines; (iv) quarterly and annual fees on table games; (v) annual licence renewal fees; and (vi) a live entertainment tax (formerly the casino entertainment tax). The Act also imposes certain miscellaneous taxes including race wire fees, parimutuel fees, manufacturer and distributor licence fees and slot route operator licence fees. See generally Nev. Rev. Stat. §§ 463.370, .373, .380, .383 & .385.

Nevada imposes significant initial and renewal licence fees on licensed interactive gaming businesses. Nev. Rev. Stat. § 463.750. An initial licence fee of $500,000 is imposed on operators. The initial term of an operator's licence is two years, after which the licence must be renewed every year and a renewal fee of $250,000 is imposed. Manufacturers must pay an initial fee of $125,000. Manufacturer licences must be renewed annually and require a $25,000 annual fee. Interactive gaming associated equipment manufacturers must pay an initial fee of $50,000 and renew the licence annually, which also includes a $25,000 renewal fee. Unless duplicative of a federal tax on interactive gaming, Nevada imposes a monthly fee on total gross revenue earned from operating interactive gaming. Nev. Rev. Stat. § 463.770. The operating licensee is obligated to pay the fee subject to a reimbursement right of 6.75 per cent of amounts earned by any manufacturer pursuant to contract with the establishment.

6. ADVERTISING
6.1 To what extent is the advertising of gambling permitted in your jurisdiction? Again, this should cover both land-based and online gaming. To the extent that advertising is permitted, how is it regulated?
A Nevada licensee may be disciplined for failing *'to conduct advertising and public relations activities in accordance with decency, dignity, good taste, honesty and inoffensiveness, including, but not limited to, advertising that is false or materially misleading'*. Nev. Gaming Comm'n Reg. 5.011(4).

7.   SOCIAL GAMING
7.1   We believe this to be a growing area. Please decide under what criteria social gaming is permitted in your jurisdiction. If games are free to play or if there is no prize, are they legal without a licence? Please address circumstances where virtual currency is used and can be won: ie currency which is of no monetary or other value, save for as credits to take part in games. The answer should address the question whether game credits or virtual money can be exchanged for other prizes. Is any change to regulation in the area proposed or envisaged?

Generally, 'social gaming' is evaluated under Nevada's existing statutory schemes to determine whether it is: (i) an activity for which licensing is required under the Act or the Commission's regulations; (ii) a form of permitted promotion by a licensee subject to administrative regulatory approval; or (iii) structured in a manner that violates Nevada commercial lottery prohibition. The Nevada Attorney General has opined that *'in order to find gaming or gambling activity, a wager must be made'*. Op. Nev. Att'y Gen. 2000-38 (29 December 2000). A 'wager' is defined as *'a sum of money or representative of value that is risked on an occurrence for which the outcome is uncertain'*. Nev. Rev. Stat. § 463.01962. A wager requires at least two parties, who each have a risk of loss and a chance of gain. *State v. GNLV Corp.*, 108 Nev. 456, 834 P.2d 411 (1992). Nevada generally defines a 'prize' for the purpose of gambling as *'money, property, or anything of value'*. Nev. Rev. Stat. § 463.0152 & .0191.

Even if a party bets free credits (the equivalent of a no-purchase option) on a chance game with the possibility of winning a prize, a wager has occurred. Op. Nev. Att'y Gen. 2000-38 (29 December 2000). Based on the current status of Nevada law, therefore, a social gaming operation should not be viewed as gambling or a lottery where no consideration is risked by the player (ie a 'wager') and no 'prize' can be won from the game or activity.

New Jersey (USA)

Michael and Carroll Guy S. Michael

1. OBJECTIVES AND STRUCTURE OF LEGISLATION

Atlantic City, New Jersey has a long and colourful history. Beginning in the late 19th century, a congruence of factors made Atlantic City one of the most popular resorts in the country. There was the proximity of the City to major population centres such as New York, Philadelphia, Baltimore and Washington. There were the cooling summer sea breezes, and there was the convenient rail transportation that rendered the City accessible. And so Atlantic City became the place to be for some sixty years. It was called 'The Playground of the World' and the 'Queen of Resorts.' It was in Atlantic City where the Miss America Pageant was held for many years. It was in Atlantic City where Dean Martin met and began to perform with Jerry Lewis. Anyone who has seen the American television series, 'Boardwalk Empire' is aware of the heyday of the town – where people came to play, sometimes within the law and sometimes outside of it.

Then, when air travel made it easier to go to places like Florida or the Caribbean, the factors that had made Atlantic City prosper began to dissipate. The economy of the town had been built around tourism and the tourists were no longer coming. This author can speak to the decline of Atlantic City from personal experience. My first appearance in court, in December of 1974, happened to be in Atlantic City. I arrived the night before and stayed at what then was the Holiday Inn. I worried that I might not be able to get a room, but my worries were needless. I was one of only three rooms then being used. When I went to dinner at the hotel's top-floor restaurant I was basically alone. I recall only one other diner.

Groups in Atlantic City who wanted to restore their town latched onto an idea. What if casinos could be built there? Wouldn't that bring the people back? But, there was a problem, though. Casinos were illegal. They were prohibited in New Jersey by the State Constitution.

The first attempt was made to amend the Constitution to allow casinos in Atlantic City in 1970. A Bill to do so failed in the Legislature. Then, in 1973, another effort similarly failed. Later, in 1974, a Bill passed and this time was placed on the November 1974 ballot. This amendment would have allowed casinos throughout the state pending local approval. Voters rejected it. Still, even this third failure did not deter the Atlantic City leaders. A referendum was again placed on the 1976 ballot. This time, the proposal limited casinos to just Atlantic City and it further created a fund of casino tax revenue that would be dedicated to benefit the elderly and the handicapped throughout the state. That referendum passed. See N.J. Const., Article IV, section VII, paragraph 2(D). A subsequent amendment allowed simulcasting of horse races. Article IV, section VII, paragraph 2(E) and (F).

Now authorised by Constitution, the Legislature passed the Casino Control Act in 1977. The objectives of the law are spelled out in its initial section, N.J.S.A. 5:12-1. In summary, the purpose of the law is:

- the rehabilitation and redevelopment of existing tourist and convention facilities in Atlantic City and the fostering and encouraging of new construction there in order to expand and encourage New Jersey's hospitality industry;
- the use of casino gambling in order to accomplish this goal;
- the restriction of casino licences to major hotel facilities;
- ensuring public trust and confidence in casinos with strict regulation and control; and
- the exclusion from casinos of people who cannot establish their good character, honesty and integrity.

With these objectives in mind, the legislation was originally structured with two regulatory agencies – the Casino Control Commission and the Division of Gaming Enforcement. It was intended for the regulatory powers to be divided between the two agencies. The Commission would serve as the quasi-judicial agency and the arm of the system that would promulgate the controlling regulations. The Division would be the investigative agency that would conduct background and operational investigations and report the results to the Commission for necessary licensing and enforcement decisions. In theory, this created a clear separation of responsibility between the two agencies. In practice, it did not turn out that way.

Duplication of efforts between the two agencies became common. In the early 1980s, recognising this problem, the two agencies set up a 'Duplication Committee' to study how to avoid unnecessary overlap. Rather than solve the problem, The 'Duplication Committee' duplicated its reports – each agency issuing its own.

This bureaucratic problem continued until 2011 when the Act was amended to place the bulk of regulatory responsibility with the Division of Gaming Enforcement. The Casino Control Commission retains a critical role. Generally, it is the Commission that deals with all matters involved in the issuance of casino licences and it hears appeals from decisions made by the Division. All other licences are issued by the Division, and that agency promulgates and enforces all rules.

2. FRAMEWORK OF LEGISLATION
2.1 What is the legal definition of gambling and what falls within this definition?

New Jersey courts have adopted the generally recognised view of what constitutes 'gambling'. New Jersey courts agree with the traditional definition of gambling as an activity that must contain three component parts – consideration, chance, and prize. *See Boardwalk Regency Corporation v The Attorney General of the State of New Jersey*, 188 N.J. Super. 372 (L. Div. 1982) citing *Carll & Ramagosa, Inc. v Ash*, 23 N.J. 433 (1957).

More specifically, the New Jersey Legislature has defined 'gambling' in its criminal statutes as: '...*staking or risking something of value upon the outcome of a contest of chance or a future contingent event not under the actor's control or influence, upon an agreement or understanding that he will receive something of value in the event of a certain outcome'* (N.J.S.A. 2C:37-1(b)).

In addition, the law further defines the term, *'something of value' as: '…any money or property, any token, object or article exchangeable for money or property, or any form of credit or promise directly or indirectly contemplating transfer of money or property or of any interest therein, or involving extension of a service, entertainment or a privilege of playing at a game or scheme without charge. This definition, however, does not include any form of promise involving extension of a privilege of playing at a game without charge on a mechanical or electronic amusement device, other than a slot machine as an award for the attainment of a certain score on that device'* (N.J.S.A. 2C:37-1(d)).

The Casino Control Act contains its own more specific definitions of what constitutes gambling for its purposes. At N.J.S.A 5:12-22 it says that 'gaming' or 'gambling' is: *'The dealing, operating, carrying on, conducting, maintaining or exposing for pay of any game'*.

By itself, that doesn't help much. But the Act clarifies this standard with another – N.J.S.A. 5:12-21. It says that a 'game' or 'gambling game' is: *'Any banking or percentage game located within the casino or simulcasting facility played with cards, dice, tiles, dominoes, or any electronic, electrical, or mechanical device or machine for money, property, or any representative of value'*.

A more detailed discussion of what constitutes gambling for purposes of social gaming is discussed in section 7.

2.2 What is the legal definition of online gambling and what falls within this definition?

'Internet gaming' is defined as: *'the placing of wagers with a casino licensee at a casino loicated in Atlantic City using a computer network of both federal and non-federal interoperable packet switched data networks through which the casino licensee may offer authorized games to individuals who have established a wagering account with the casino licensee and who are phyusically present in this State, as authorized by rules established by the Ddivision'* (N.J.S.A 5:12-28.1).

2.3 Please set out the different gambling products identified by legislation.

The New Jersey Casino Control Act identifies the types of games allowed to be played in Atlantic City casinos at N.J.S.A. 5:12-5. It defines the term, 'authorised game.' That definition reads, in pertinent part: *'Roulette, baccarat, craps, big six wheel, slot machines, minibaccarat, red dog, pai gow and sic bo; any variations or composites of such games, provided that such variations or composites are found by the division suitable for use after an appropriate test or experimental period under such terms and conditions as the division may deem appropriate'*.

In addition, this section allows the Division to authorise *'any other game which is determined… to be compatible with the public interest'* after an appropriate test period.

Gaming tournaments involving any otherwise authorised game are also permitted.

While this chapter concentrates on casino gambling, other forms of gambling are also permitted in New Jersey. New Jersey allows horse racing, including harness racing; bingo; raffles; amusement games; and operates a state lottery.

The New Jersey Racing Commission regulates horse racing. The Commission is part of the State Attorney General's Office. The controlling statute is N.J.S.A 5:5-22 et seq. The governing regulations for horse racing are found at N.J.A.C. 13:70-1 to 32, and for harness racing at N.J.A.C. 13:71-1 to 30.

The Legalized Games of Chance Commission, also a part of the State Attorney General's Office, regulates bingo, raffles, and amusement games. This form of gambling is authorised in the State Constitution by Article IV, section VII, paragraph 2(A) and (B). The controlling statute is N.J.S.A. 5:8-1 et seq. The regulations are found at N.J.A.C. 13:3-1.1 et seq.

Finally, the state operates a lottery as authorised in the State Constitution at Article IV, section VII, paragraph 2(C). This activity is regulated by the Division of State Lottery as part of the Department of the Treasury. The governing statute is N.J.S.A. 5:9-1 et. seq. and the regulations are contained in N.J.A.C. 17:20-1.1 et. seq.

2.4 Please list the different requirements for each gambling product, including legal classifications for each; for example, is poker a game of skill or game of chance?

The regulations of the Division of Gaming Enforcement establish the rules for the proper method by which all table games are offered for play. As explained above in section 2.1, whenever any new game is offered, the rules must be submitted for approval by the regulators. Then, once approved they become regulations. These rules are found at N.J.A.C. 13:69F-1 to 37. They range from craps (N.J.A.C. 13:69F-1) to Mini-Tex 3 Card Hold 'Em (N.J.A.C. 13:69F-37) and everything in between. Poker is included and is considered a game of chance.

In addition, the operation of gaming equipment is regulated at N.J.A.C. 13:69E-1.1 et seq. The internal and accounting controls for the operation of the games are found at N.J.A.C. 13:69D-1.1 et seq.

The Division of Gaming Enforcement also operates its own laboratory in which it conducts all testing of gaming equipment, including slot machines that are proposed for use in the casinos. The lab ensures that all the equipment meets all required standards. In addition to the use of its own lab, the Division is authorised to utilise the services of an independent lab and then, in its discretion, utilise the data developed by the independent lab, including adopting its conclusions. See N.J.S.A. 5:12-100(h).

2.5 Explain the system of regulation of gambling; which regulatory or governmental body is responsible for the supervision of gambling? Which body issues licences? Which body examines enforcement powers? Is there any limit on the number or duration of available licences?

As described in section 1, there are two agencies in New Jersey that regulate casinos. They are the Casino Control Commission and the Division of Gaming Enforcement.

The Casino Control Commission is considered in but not of the Department of the Treasury. This means that because all agencies must be assigned to one State Department or another, the Commission is assigned to the Treasury Department, but it retains its independence from control by the Treasurer. The Commission consists of three members appointed by the Governor and confirmed by the State Senate for five-year terms. They serve on a full-time basis. One member is appointed as the Chair. The Commissioners, among themselves, select a Vice-Chair to serve a one-year term. No Commissioner can serve for more than two terms. The Commission has a staff of administrators and attorneys. Key staff includes a General Counsel and an Executive Secretary.

Commissioners are subject to background investigations prior to appointment. Commissioners automatically forfeit their office upon conviction for any crime. They may also be removed from office for misconduct, wilful neglect of duty or other conduct evidencing unfitness for office, or incompetence. Removal for these reasons must be done through a proceeding in court. Commissioners, as well as supervisory and policy-making staff, are prohibited from making political contributions.

The Commission must promulgate a code of ethics under which it must operate. No Commissioner may have any direct or indirect interest in or be employed by any applicant or any person licensed by or registered under the casino law (except for non-gaming service industries) for a period of four years after they leave office. No Commission member or person employed by the Commission may represent any party before the Commission for a period of two years after they leave office.

Commission's duties include the obligations to:
- hear and decide applications for casino licenses, including all subsidiary approvals necessary for a casino licence;
- review and decide appeals from decisions on enforcement actions and licence applications made by the Division;
- promulgate regulations necessary for the conduct of hearings;
- refer matters to the Division for investigation or investigative hearings, as necessary;
- review and rule on complaints filed by casino licensees against the Division regarding investigative procedures;
- take all necessary actions, along with the Division, for the implementation of internet wagering, when that form of gaming is permitted by state and federal law;
- along with the Division, remain up to date on the development of the casino industry and report to the Legislature on any defect in the New Jersey law and any suggestions for changes.

The Division is an agency within the State Attorney General's office. It is led by a Director who is appointed by the Governor with the advice and consent of the State Senate. The Director is under the supervision of the Attorney General. The Director serves under the term of office of the Governor. The Director hires staff, which typically includes a Deputy Director. The Division Director may not hold any direct or indirect interest in, or be employed by, any applicant or by any person licensed by or registered under the Act for a period of four years after he or she leaves office. For other policymaking employees, the restrictions run for two years and then, for another two years, those people must request permission to assume any such positions. All other Division employees, other than secretarial and clerical employees, have similar prohibitions, but for only two years. For a complete recitation of all conflict restrictions of both the Commission and Division, reference can be made to N.J.S.A. 5:12-60.

The functions delegated to the Division under the statute at N.J.S.A. 5:12-76 are:

- initiate and decide actions against licensees for violations of the act and regulations and impose penalties therefore;
- to enforce the provisions of the Act and the regulations;
- to investigate all applications;
- to report to the Commission regarding all applications involving casino licences;
- to review and approve all casino service industry enterprise licences;
- to accept and maintain registrations for casino employees and vendor registrants;
- to take action against all casino service industry enterprise licensees and registrants for violations of the Act and regulations and initiate or defend appeals therefrom;
- to promulgate necessary regulations in order to administer its responsibilities;
- to review casino operations and observe such operations on-site;
- to receive referrals from the Commission and take appropriate action;
- to conduct audits of casino operations;
- to receive complaints from the public;
- to certify casino revenue;
- to create and maintain a list of persons excluded from the casino;
- to administer involuntary exclusions;
- to issue operation certificates to casino licensees;
- to make recommendations to the Commission for the issuance or revocation of statements of compliance;
- to accept impact statements from casino licensees; and
- to utilise private contractors to conduct background investigations.

New Jersey licences casino owners and operators, casino key employees, and vendors providing gaming services and those that provide non-gaming services designated for licensing by the Division. All such licences last for a duration of five years and are then subject for renewal for additional five-year terms.

3. ONLINE GAMBLING

3.1 To what extent can online gambling be offered in your jurisdiction? Are licences available and, if so, for which gambling products? Please describe briefly the licensing process, who may apply, whether licences are limited in number and, if no licences are available, whether it is legal for online gambling to be offered. In the case of EU jurisdictions, please state whether there are any issues as to the legality of the local law at EU level. Please refer to any relevant cases at ECJ level and explain any measures taken or pending by the European Commission.

After years of various failed bills and other efforts, New Jersey authorised online gambling on 26 February 2013. In November 2013, online gambling went live in New Jersey for the first time. The essential statutory elements of online gambling in New Jersey as found at N.J.S.A. 5:12-95.17, et seq. are:

- all online gaming may only be conducted by a casino licensee;
- a casino licensee must obtain an Internet Gaming Permit in order to offer online gaming;
- online gambling is intra-state only. All wagers must be made within the territorial boundaries of New Jersey;
- all online gambling facilities and equipment must be located within a restricted area on the premises of the casino licensee in Atlantic City, New Jersey;
- all wagers must be placed directly with the casino licensee by the holder of a wagering account;
- the casino licensee must verify the identity of and the location of the person placing the wager; and
- online gambling is taxed at the rate of 15 per cent of gross revenues. There is also an additional 5 per cent investment alternative tax (see section 5.1 below).

The Division of Gaming Enforcement has also promulgated regulations further governing Online gambling. They can be found at N.J.A.C. 13:69O-1.1 et seq. The essential elements of these rules include:

- general standards of use;
- requirements for internal controls;
- location of equipment;
- requirements for establishing accounts;
- patron file contents, including encryption requirements;
- standards for the transfer of funds;
- operational controls;
- table game simulcasting; and
- communication standards.

The rules also address the licensing of 'internet gaming operators'. These are entities that operate the online system for the casino. Finally, the rules authorise New Jersey to enter into reciprocal agreements with other jurisdictions. These agreements would allow players and those in that other jurisdiction to play on the same systems. As of the time of writing, no such agreements have been entered into by New Jersey.

3.2   Is there a distinction between the law applicable to B2B operations and that applicable to B2C operations?
See above.

3.3   What are the consequences for B2C or B2B operators who are active in your jurisdiction without having obtained or applied for the required permits, licences and approvals? What penalties and enforcement powers are available in respect of the illegal operators? Please outline any significant domestic decisions or enforcement actions that have been taken by the relevant authorities in recent years.
See above.

3.4   What technical measures are in place (if any) to protect consumers from unlicensed operators, such as ISP blocking and payment blocking?
N/A.

3.5   Has the legal status of online gambling changed significantly in recent years, and, if so, how?
See above.

3.6   Whilst acknowledging the inherent difficulty in predicting developments in gambling law, what are the likely developments in online gambling in your jurisdiction, both short term and long term? Are any specific amendments under consideration? Have there been any recent political developments, or do you envisage any in the near future? Are any specific amendments under consideration? Are they likely to be adopted and, if so, what is the time scale?
The effort to revitalise New Jersey's gambling industry by introducing sports betting is continuing. At present, sports betting in New Jersey is barred by the federal Professional and Amateur Sports Protection Act (PASPA) passed by Congress in 1992. As part of an initiative led by State Sen. Raymond Lesniak, a lawsuit was filed alleging that PASPA is unconstitutional as applied to New Jersey. That complaint was dismissed as premature because New Jersey, at the time, had no sports betting law that it was being prevented from implementing.

Thereafter, in order to meet that jurisdictional obstacle, a referendum to amend the state Constitution to allow sports betting was placed on the ballot for the 2011 election. That referendum passed, and its provisions are now part of the Constitution. See Article IV, section VII, paragraph 2(D) and (F). Pursuant to that authority, the Casino Control Act has been amended to allow sports betting at both casinos and racetracks. N.J.S.A. 5:12A-2.

However, before any sports betting regime could be implemented, the law was challenged by certain professional sports leagues. In March 2013, the United States District Court for the District of New Jersey ruled in favor of the Leagues. The state appealed. In September 2013, the United States Court of Appeals for the Third Circuit upheld the District Court ruling and in the same month denied the state's request for a re-hearing. In February 2014, the state appealed to the United States Supreme Court. That appeal is pending.

There have also been recent discussions among lawmakers about authorising casino gambling in other parts of New Jersey. The main location discussed is the Meadowlands Sports Complex in the northern part of the state, where Met Life Stadium I is located. These talks are at a very preliminary stage.

3.7 Is the law the same in relation to mobile gambling and interactive gambling on television? If not, are there any headline differences?

Interactive gambling on television is not allowed in New Jersey, but a limited form of mobile gambling has recently been proposed for the State's casinos.

Mobile gaming is now allowed in New Jersey. It is defined as a *'server based gaming system at a casino located in Atlantic City using a computer network through which the casino licensee may offer authorized games to individuals who have established a wagering account with the casino licensee and who are physically present within the property boundaries of an approved hotel facility'.*

More specifically, mobile gaming can only occur within the property boundaries of an approved casino hotel facility. For purposes of this limitation, the approved casino hotel facility shall include any area located within the property boundaries of the casino hotel facility, including any recreation area or swimming pool, where mobile gaming devices may be used by patrons, but excluding parking garages or parking areas. A mobile gaming system must disable all gaming activity on a client terminal whenever it is removed from the property boundaries.

4. LAND-BASED GAMING

4.1 Please describe the licensing regime (if any) for land-based gaming, and what products are included. Please set out what licences are available, and the licensing regime for them.

Other than the recently enacted online gaming which may only be conducted by Atlantic City land-based casino operators, all gaming in New Jersey is land-based and so the descriptions otherwise contained in this chapter apply to this section.

4.2 Please set out any particular limitations or requirements for (eg casino) operators, such as a ban on local residents gambling.

'No applicant for or holder of a casino license, nor any holding , intermediary or subsidiary company thereof, nor any officer, director, casino key employee or principal employee of any of those companies, nor any person or agent on behalf of any of those persons or entities is allowed to contribute any money or thing of value to a candidate for nomination or election to a public office in New Jersey or any committee of a political party in New Jersey or any group organized in support of any such candidate.' This rule, however, does not prevent candidates for the governing body of Atlantic City from contributing to their own campaigns. N.J.S.A. 5:12-138.

4.3   Please address the questions in 3.5 above, but in relation to land-based gaming.

5.   TAX
5.1   Please summarise briefly the tax regime applicable to both land-based and online gaming.

There are a number of taxes and fees imposed by the Casino Control Act. They include:

Taxes
- An 8 per cent annual tax on gross revenues (Gross Revenue Tax) N.J.S.A. 5:12-144a;
- an additional 2.5 per cent tax on gross revenues (Investment Alternative Tax) N.J.S.A. 5:12-144.1. This tax can be reduced to 1.25 per cent depending on whether a casino makes certain qualified investments as calculated by a very complicated statutory formula administered by a separate agency, the Casino Reinvestment Development Authority. The tax on internet gaming is set at 15 per cent of gross revenues and 5 per cent for the Casino Reinvestment Tax.

Principal fees
- A casino licence application fee of not less than $200,000 to cover the cost of investigation. Upon application, a non-refundable deposit of $100,000 is required, (N.J.S.A. 5:12-139);
- an initial Internet Gaming Permit application fee of not less than $400,000 to cover the cost of investigation. Upon application, a non-refundable deposit of $100,000 is required. The Internet Gaming Permit is to be renewed on an annual basis. The renewal fee is not less than $250,000 to cover the cost of maintaining enforcement, control and regulation of internet gaming wagering. Permit holders must also pay an annual Responsible Internet Gaming Fee of $250,000 (N.J.S.A. 5:12-95.29);
- for testing gaming equipment based on hourly rates of the Division of Gaming Enforcement with an initial minimum charge of $500, (N.J.A.C. 13:69A-9.5);
- an annual slot machine fee of $500 per machine, (N.J.A.C. 13:69A-9.6);
- a Casino Hotel Alcoholic Beverage Licence Fee: (i) hourly and out-of-pocket expenses of the Division of Gaming Enforcement's activities; (ii) $1,000 for each location within the casino hotel if the licensee is not affiliated with the casino (N.J.A.C. 13:69A-9.7) and for Casino Hotel Alcoholic Beverage Casino Service Industry Enterprises a $3,500 fee (N.J.A.C. 13:69A-9.9);
- Casino Service Industry Enterprise Licence Fee of $5,000 at the outset and then: (i) an additional $5,000 when the total number of hours of Division professional staff time exceeds 333 hours; (ii) an additional $5,000 when that staff time exceeds 667 hours; and then (iii) additional hourly rates for time exceeding 1,000 hours, (N.J.A.C. 13:69A-9.8);

- a Labor Organization Registration Fee of $250 every two years, (N.J.A.C. 13:69A-9.10);
- a one-time casino employee registration fee of $95.00, (N.J.A.C. 13:69A-9.15);
- a fee for conversion of a licence to a registration of $95.00, (N.J.A.C. 13:69A-16); and
- a fee for non-credentialed employment of $95.00, (N.J.A.C. 13:69A-9.18).

6. ADVERTISING

6.1 To what extent is the advertising of gambling permitted in your jurisdiction?

Advertising by casino licensees is regulated. 'Advertising' is defined as *'any notice or communication by an applicant or licensee to the public of any information concerning the gaming-related business of an applicant or licensee through broadcasting, publication, or any other means of dissemination'.* Communications such as notices of rules of the games, gaming guides, information on gaming tables and slot machines, directional signs and news of general interest are not considered 'advertising'. N.J.A.C. 13:69C-14.1.

All on-site advertising must contain the phrase, 'Bet With Your Head, Not Over It.' All advertising that appears on billboards or in print must contain the words, 'If you or someone you know has a gambling problem and wants help, call 1-800-GAMBLER' or some comparable language approved by the Division. N.J.A.C. 13:69C-14.2(c). Advertising must be based on fact and cannot be false, misleading or obscene. N.J.A.C.13:69C-14.2(d). No advance approval of advertising by the regulators is required. N.J.A.C. 13:69C-14.3.

7. SOCIAL GAMING

7.1 We believe this to be a growing area. Please decide under what criteria social gaming is permitted in your jurisdiction. If games are free to play, or if there is no prize are they legal, without a licence? Please address circumstances where virtual currency is used and can be won: ie currency which is of no monetary or other value, save for as credits to take part in games.

As was touched upon in section 2.1, New Jersey adopts the traditional definition of what constitutes a gambling transaction. Such a transaction must include the combined elements of consideration, chance, and prize. In the area of social gaming, it is clear that all such activities involve chance and prize. The issue in New Jersey, as it would be in many other jurisdictions, is whether or not in a particular situation, the element of consideration is present. The answer to this question has evolved over the years.

This evolution is well described in a Formal Opinion of the Office of the Attorney General of New Jersey. In *Formal Opinion No. 9 – 1978* (1978 N.J. AG LEXIS 4), the Attorney General was asked whether a cable television company could transmit a game characterised as bingo. In concluding that it could, the Attorney General distinguished an earlier State Supreme Court decision entitled, *Lucky Calendar Co. v Cohen*, 19 N.J. 399 (1955). In that case, the Court interpreted a statute at that time that forbade lotteries as not requiring consideration of any kind in order for a game to be a lottery as that statute then defined it. Importantly, for the purposes of this analysis, the Court then went on to say that even if consideration were required, it would be satisfied by any consideration necessary to sustain a simple contract. That would include mere inconvenience. In *Formal Opinion No. 9*, the Attorney General refused to adopt the Lucky Calendar standard. It said that the Court there was only interpreting a particular statute, not the general Constitutional prohibition against gambling. The Opinion took the broader, more modern view of 'consideration' that mere inconvenience would not be enough. See 1978 N.J. AG LEXIS at 7–8.

This modern view was further refined in the *Formal Opinion of the Office of the Attorney General of New Jersey No. 6 – 1983* (1983 N.J. AG LEXIS 2). There, the Attorney General reviewed various forms of promotions being offered by casinos. It concluded that casino promotions should only be considered gambling if a participant 'risks something of value'. It then cited to the statutory definition of that term as the *'risking of money or property or tangibles as well as personal effort standing in their stead'*. Finally, the Opinion said that this definition does not include lesser acts of personal inconvenience. 1983 N.J. AG LEXIS at 13. The opinion then further notes that whether something of value is risked in any given situation can only be ascertained by *'considering all of the relevant circumstances'* (1983 N.J. AG LEXIS at 13).

Thus, whether a particular type of social gaming would be considered legal would depend on how that gaming is structured. The closer to the line the structure gets to requiring any form of cost to play, the more difficult it will be to sustain. This author is not aware of any prosecutions in New Jersey against any national social gaming websites at this time.

Ontario (Canada)

Dickinson Wright LLP Michael D. Lipton, Q.C.,
Kevin J. Weber & Jack I. Tadman

1. OBJECTIVES AND STRUCTURE OF LEGISLATION

Canada inherited the English law of the 19th century, which contained a near-total prohibition on gambling. In 1892, the Canadian Criminal Code (the Code) was enacted by the Parliament of Canada, and it remains the federal legislation governing gambling in Canada.

Since 1892, major amendments to the Code include:
*   the regulation of horse-racing (1910);
*   the Joint Committee Report examining the need for reform of lotteries (1956) and subsequent introduction of federal and provincial regulated lotteries (1969);
*   the transfer of power of lotteries from a shared provincial-federal power to an exclusively provincial power (1985); and
*   the removal of the prohibitions on dice games in the Code (1999).

At present, the Code generally prohibits commercial gaming and betting activity within Canada. There are a few exemptions to this prohibition, the most important of which is the exemption permitting provincial governments to conduct, manage and regulate gaming and betting, and to license and regulate gaming and betting conducted and managed by charitable and religious organisations.

Other exemptions to the general prohibition on commercial gaming and betting include those permitting:
*   the federal government to supervise pari-mutuel horse race betting;
*   gaming and betting on international cruise ships (provided their operators meet certain qualifications);
*   private bets between individuals not engaged in any way in the business of betting; and
*   persons or associations becoming the custodian or depository of any money, property or valuable thing staked, to be paid to:
    (i)   the winner of a lawful race, sport, game or exercise;
    (ii) the owner of a horse engaged in a lawful race; or
    (iii) the winner of any bets between not more than ten individuals.

Certain types of gaming and betting are prohibited in all circumstances, including offering:
*   three-card monte;
*   punch board;
*   coin table; and
*   bets on any race or fight, or on a single-sport event or athletic contest.

Certain types of gaming and betting are not prohibited by the Code, namely the playing of games of skill for stakes.

The gaming and betting provisions of the Code apply equally to land-based and online gambling.

From a public policy perspective, protection of the public interest is Parliament's foremost consideration with respect to gaming and betting. Historically, Parliament has seized upon public ownership, operation and regulation as the most effective method of protecting the public interest with respect to gaming and betting, while at the same time allowing government and private industry to best utilise gaming and betting revenues for the benefit of the public.

In Ontario, gambling is regulated by the Alcohol and Gaming Commission of Ontario (the AGCO). Commercial gambling is conducted and managed by the Ontario Lottery and Gaming Corporation (the OLG), whereas charitable gambling is conducted and managed by licensed charitable and religious organisations. Both the AGCO and OLG are provincial government organisations. The primary provincial legislation for regulating gambling in Ontario is the Ontario Gaming Control Act (the Act).

2. FRAMEWORK OF LEGISLATION
2.1 What is the legal definition of gambling and what falls within this definition?
Gaming
Part VII of the Code addresses disorderly houses, gaming, and betting. 'Gambling' is not defined in the Code; however, it is clear from many reported cases that the terms 'gambling' and 'gaming' are synonymous (*R. v Gardiner*, [1971] 2 W.W.R. 728, 2 C.C.C. (2d) 463, paragraph 9).

'Game' is defined in the Code as a *'game of chance or mixed chance and skill'*. The Supreme Court of Canada has read in additional elements of what is considered a 'game' for the purpose of the gaming and betting provisions of the Code.

With respect to whether a 'game' has taken place, according to the common law, *'it is not sufficient for the prosecution to prove only the elements required by the plain and literal meaning...[of 'game']...the prosecution must also prove that the participants in the game or operators of the game have a chance of both (i) winning and (ii) losing money or money's worth by (iii) participating in a game of chance or mixed chance and skill'* (*R. v Irwin*, (1982), 1 C.C.C. (3d) 212 (Ont. C.A.), p. 225, cited with approval in *Di Pietro et al. v The Queen*, [1986] 1 S.C.R. 250, paragraph 8).

In other words, for a game to be a 'game' for the purposes of the Code, it must contain the following three elements:
(i) winning money or money's worth – covers any game where there is a chance to win money or money's worth (the 'prize element');
(ii) losing money or money's worth – covers any game where there is a chance to lose money or money's worth (the 'consideration element'); and

(iii) participating in a game of chance or mixed chance and skill – covers any game where there is an element of chance, provided that chance does not refer to *'the unpredictables that may occasionally defeat skill'* (*R. v Ross*, (1968), 70 D.L.R. (2d) 606, [1968] S.C.R. 786, 1968 CarswellOnt 16 (S.C.C.)). 'Chance' as contemplated by the Code refers to the *'systematic resort to chance involved in many games such as the throw of dice, the deal of cards'* (ibid) (the 'chance element').

Only when all three of the above elements are present and satisfied will a game fall within the provisions of the Code and be classified as 'gaming'.

As noted in section 1, a 'game of skill' is not prohibited by the gaming and betting provisions of the Code. At the same time, one particular prohibition in the Code that was initially enacted to combat 'pyramid schemes' (subsection 206(1)(e)) has been interpreted by the Supreme Court of Canada to be applicable to any 'scheme, contrivance or operation,' even where winners are determined by the application of skill (*Roe v The King*, [1949] 2 D.L.R. 785 (S.C.C.) and *R. v Dream Home Contests (Edmonton) Ltd*, [1960] S.C.R. 414 (S.C.C.)). However, to interpret subsection 206(1)(e) of the Code so broadly as to cover games of 'skill alone' would introduce an internal inconsistency into Part VII of the Code as between the 'common gaming house' provisions of the Code and subsection 206(1)(e). The rules of statutory construction require that a line be drawn between the skill-based 'schemes, contrivances or operations' prohibited by subsection 206(1)(e) and the 'games of skill' explicitly permitted by other provisions of the Code.

Roe v The King and *R. v Dream Home Contests (Edmonton) Ltd* dealt with situations involving betting, not gaming (see definition of 'betting' from decision in *R. v Lebansky*, below). Participants in those schemes were not paying money *'for the right or privilege of participating in any event, in the hope of winning a prize'*. In both schemes, participants were paying money to back their forecasts of an event of a doubtful issue; in the first case, of the amount of time it would take a barrel to travel a distance down a river, in the second, of the value of a house and its contents. This is the usual form of betting: stakes put forward on the outcome of an event between non-participants in that event.

From this we conclude that subsection 206(1)(e) of the Code can apply to 'schemes, contrivances or operations' that are akin to betting. However, subsection 206(1)(e) cannot be interpreted so as to render unlawful activities that relate to the playing of 'games' of 'skill alone'.

Betting

'Betting' is not defined in the Code. However, 'bet' is defined in the Code as a *'bet that is placed on any contingency or event that is to take place in or out of Canada, and without restricting the generality of the foregoing, includes a bet that is placed on any contingency relating to a horse-race, fight, match or sporting event that is to take place in or out of Canada'*.

Due to the circuitous nature of the Code definition of 'bet' (ie a 'bet' is defined as a 'bet that is…'), Canadian courts have elaborated to state that 'betting' is *'the backing of a forecast by offering to forfeit, in the case of an adverse issue, a sum of money or article of value to one who maintains the opposite opinion and who backs his opinion by a corresponding stipulation; it is the staking of money or other value on the event of a doubtful issue...The payment of money for the right to participate in an event is not a 'bet,' even where the entry monies form a prize pool are to be paid out to winning players'* (R. v Lebansky, [1940] 3 W.W.R. 374; affirmed [1941] 2 D.L.R. 380 (Man. C.A.)).

2.2 What is the legal definition of online gambling and what falls within this definition?

Online gambling is described in 207(4)(c) of the Code as a *'game...that is operated on or through a computer, [or] video device'.*

Only provincial governments are authorised to provide this type of gambling.

2.3 Please set out the different gambling products identified by legislation.

The federal government is responsible for supervising the following products:
- pari-mutuel betting on horse racing.

Certain gambling products are entirely prohibited, and may not be provided by anyone. These are:
- bookmaking, pool selling or the making or recording of bets, including bets made through the agency of a pool or pari-mutuel system, on any race or fight, or on a single sport event or athletic contest;
- three-card monte;
- punch board; and
- coin table.

Other gambling products are restricted, in the sense that only a provincial government can provide them (ie the provincial government may not license a charity to provide these products). These gambling products are:
- bets or games operated on a computer, video device or slot machine (207(4)(c)); and
- dice games (207(4)(c)).

2.4 Please list the different requirements for each gambling product, including legal classifications for each; for example, is poker a game of skill or game of chance?

As noted in section 2.2, a game is classified as a game of skill, a game of chance, or a game of mixed chance and skill.

In order for a game to be a game of skill (and thus not prohibited by the gaming and betting provisions of the Code), there must be no systemic element of chance whatsoever involved in determining the outcome of the game. Any systemic element of chance, however small, is sufficient to make a game a game of mixed chance and skill. The element of chance does not refer to *'the unpredictables that may occasionally defeat skill'.*

Against this background, we note the following classifications in Canada of gambling products:

- poker – game of mixed chance and skill;
- betting – a bet; is also considered a game of mixed chance and skill for the purpose of a lottery scheme;
- sports betting – a bet; is also considered a game of mixed chance and skill for the purpose of a lottery scheme;
- casino games – generally considered games of mixed chance and skill;
- slot and other machine gaming – traditional slot machine gaming is a game of chance. If there are decisions exercisable by the player which have an impact on the success of the game, the machine gaming may be a game of mixed chance and skill;
- bingo – game of mixed chance and skill;
- lottery – game of chance; and
- pari-mutuel betting on horse racing – a bet.

2.5 Explain the system of regulation of gambling; which regulatory or governmental body is responsible for the supervision of gambling? Which body issues licences? Which body examines enforcement powers? Is there any limit on the number or duration of available licences?

Games of chance and games of mixed chance and skill are permitted under the provincial government's authority to conduct and manage 'lottery schemes'. The game of bingo is conducted and managed pursuant to licences issued to charitable and religious organisations.

Each province has a regulatory body in charge of the supervision of gambling. In Ontario, this provincial regulatory body is the AGCO. As part of the AGCO's responsibilities, it issues gambling-related licences and registrations. Licences are issued to charitable organisations to conduct and manage gaming. Registrations are issued to both gaming- and non-gaming-related suppliers. These suppliers may supply services to the OLG or to charitable and religious organisations.

In certain situations a municipality, under the supervision of the AGCO, may be delegated the authority to issue gaming licences to charitable and religious organisations.

The AGCO has certain enforcement powers in relation to its licensees and registrants. However, if a person or organisation is providing gaming or betting services without being licensed or registered by the AGCO, that person or organisation is acting unlawfully, and may be subject to investigation by the police and prosecution under either the Code or the Gaming Control Act, 1992.

Horse racing is regulated federally by the Canadian Pari-Mutuel Agency and provincially by the Ontario Racing Commission. The Ontario Racing Commission is responsible for issuing licences relating to horse racing in Ontario.

3.1 ONLINE GAMBLING

3.1 To what extent can online gambling be offered in your jurisdiction? Are licences available and, if so, for which gambling products? Please describe briefly the licensing process, who may apply, whether licences are limited in number and, if no licences are available, whether it is legal for online gambling to be offered. In the case of EU jurisdictions, please state whether there are any issues as to the legality of the local law at EU level. Please refer to any relevant cases at ECJ level and explain any measures taken or pending by the European Commission.

In Canada, online gambling refers to the conduct and management of lottery schemes by means of a computer or video device. This type of gaming may only be offered by the provincial government. Unlike other forms of gambling, the AGCO cannot issue a licence to a charitable organisation to conduct and manage lottery schemes by means of a computer or video device.

3.2 Is there a distinction between the law applicable to B2B operations and that applicable to B2C operations?

There is a distinction between the law applicable to B2B operations and that applicable to B2C operations with respect to gaming and betting operations authorised by the provincial government. Only provincial governments may provide B2C services, whereas licensed suppliers may provide B2B services to provincial governments that conduct and manage land-based and online gambling.

As noted, the provincial government must conduct and manage online gambling. In Ontario, this has been interpreted as the OLG being the 'guiding mind', requiring it to own the online gambling site and have control of certain aspects of the online gambling site, such as player funds, budgeting and forecasting, and all of the strategic decision-making that is involved in the conduct and management of the gambling business.

A B2B may not contract directly with players, as this would violate the OLG's conduct and management obligations. However, a B2B may licence its products to the OLG without directly contracting with customers, and may provide any online gambling services to the OLG, provided that such B2B is registered by the AGCO as a gaming-related supplier and none of the B2B's actions impinge on the OLG's obligation to conduct and manage its own gambling operations.

There is also a distinction between the law applicable to B2B operations and that applicable to B2C operations with respect to online gaming and betting operations not authorised by the provincial government. However, this distinction relates to *which* of the gaming and betting provisions of the Code are being violated by the B2B or B2C. From a practical perspective, it is illegal to provide online B2B and B2C services that are not authorised by the provincial government as long as a 'real and substantial connection' exists between Canada and the alleged violation of the gaming and betting provision(s) of the Code.

3.3 What are the consequences for B2C or B2B operators who are active in your jurisdiction without having obtained or applied for the required permits, licences and approvals? What penalties and enforcement powers are available in respect of the illegal operators? Please outline any significant domestic decisions or enforcement actions that have been taken by the relevant authorities in recent years.

B2C or B2B operators who are active in Ontario without having applied for or obtained the required permits, licences and approvals are in violation of the gaming and betting provisions of the Code, provided that a 'real and substantial connection' exists between Canada and the alleged violation of the gaming and betting provisions of the Code.

Offences under sections 201, 202 and/or 206 of the Code relating to gambling are punishable criminally as indictable offences, and upon conviction the penalty is a term of imprisonment not exceeding two years. A minimum sentence of 14 days applies under section 202 for a second offence under that section, and a minimum sentence of three months applies to all subsequent offences under that section.

As is the case with all offences under the Code, a criminal fine may be imposed in addition to and/or in lieu of the terms of imprisonment noted above. The only limitation on the amount of the fine is that the court must be satisfied that the offender is able to pay the fine. Further, the offender may be subject to a forfeiture order under the 'proceeds of crime' provisions of the Code.

These operators may also have difficulty obtaining registration with the AGCO and contracting with the OLG as their conduct in acting in violation of the Code may impugn their integrity.

Since August 2010, gambling offences under sections 202 and 206 of the Code have been among those classified as 'serious offences'. A conviction for a 'serious offence' can result in the offender being deemed to be part of what the Code calls a 'criminal organisation': a group composed of three or more persons in or outside Canada that has as its main purpose or activity the facilitation or commission of one or more 'serious offences' that, if committed, would likely result in the direct or indirect receipt of a material benefit by the group or any of the persons who constitute the group.

Among the consequences of being deemed to be a criminal organisation are the increased sentences available to a prosecutor. For example, a person may be imprisoned for up to five years for participating in or contributing to the activity of a criminal organisation for the purpose of enhancing its ability to formulate or commit a serious offence, imprisoned for up to 14 years for committing a serious offence for the benefit of, at the direction of or in association with a criminal organisation, or imprisoned for life if, as a part of a criminal organization, knowingly instructs directly or indirectly any person to commit a serious offence for the benefit of, at the direction of or in association with the criminal organisation. Another consequence is that law enforcement agencies are granted a greater ability to obtain judicial authority to tap telephones when investigating cases involving alleged criminal organisations.

The activities of companies associated with offshore online gambling may be sufficient to characterise such companies as being part of a criminal organisation. While the government has indicated its intention to use the powers granted by these regulations to prosecute unlawful gambling that is operated by 'organised crime', there is nothing preventing their use against offshore online gambling even where that online gambling is licensed by a foreign jurisdiction.

The only three known Code prosecutions of entities involved in online gambling have involved entities that carried out their activities while being physically located in Canada. The first case involved an online gambling website that was operated from servers located in Vancouver. The second involved a company which was located in Montreal and provided assistance to the operation of an online gambling website from servers located on the Territory of Kahnawà:ke Mohawks in Quebec, Canada. The third involved owners of an online gambling website located in Ontario with alleged ties to organised crime operating a credit betting website using Ontario-based agents from servers and a call centre located in Costa Rica.

Canadian law enforcement authorities have not initiated any prosecutions against 'truly' offshore online gambling operators, regardless of whether they have actively promoted themselves in Canada or whether they have merely passively made their services available to persons in Canada. Nor have any prosecutions been initiated against Canadian-based third parties who have actively assisted offshore online gambling operators in their operations, such as marketing affiliates who assisted in attracting Canadian-resident customers to gambling websites, payment service providers who allowed persons in Canada to conduct transactions related to online gambling or software suppliers who provided gambling software to offshore online gambling operators which was then used to offer online gambling services to persons in Canada.

Starnet Communications International Inc. (Starnet)

Starnet was the first online gambling company to be prosecuted in Canada. It was an online gambling operation that was physically based in Canada and was a publicly traded company, incorporated in the State of Delaware. Through a number of wholly owned subsidiary companies, Starnet conducted an online gambling operation from the premises of a Vancouver address.

On 17 August 2001, Starnet pleaded guilty to one count of keeping a device for gambling or betting contrary to subsection 202(1)(b) of the Code, was fined C\$100,000 and forfeited approximately US\$3,925,000 as proceeds of crime pursuant to subsection 462.37 of the Code.

Because the Starnet conviction was obtained by way of a guilty plea, there is little in the way of judicial reasoning to be gleaned from the case, but the facts are instructive. Police authorities in B.C. were suspicious that Starnet was accepting online bets from Canadians and as a result set up a police sting operation. As part of the sting, police gambled nearly US$3,000 on the company's site.

Starnet initially anticipated that all online gambling activities would be done in Antigua, where one of its wholly owned subsidiaries (World Gaming Services Inc.) was incorporated and licensed to provide online gambling services. A group of Caribbean companies were formed to facilitate the withdrawal and deposit of monies by customers, using credit cards. While Starnet kept many of its servers in Antigua, some were being operated from its Vancouver office. The Vancouver servers were the ones that customers would access in order to reach Starnet's web pages. The gambling websites were physically located in Vancouver. The customers accessed and downloaded the 'casino-side software' via these Vancouver websites. This casino-side software and the modifications to that software necessary to allow it to function on customers' computers were both located in Vancouver. The Crown prosecutors focused their attention on whether *'the components of the systems that enable persons to engage in gambling or betting… were…present in Vancouver'*.

It would be an error to characterise Starnet's operations in Canada during this period as B2B. While Starnet did license software to third-party online gambling operators, the charges against Starnet were based primarily on its B2C activities, specifically the fact that *'patrons accessing the betting and gaming products offered by the Starnet gaming system did so via servers in [its Vancouver] server room'*. Starnet was not prosecuted for the simple act of entering into a licensing agreement with third-party online gambling operators; it was prosecuted because of actions it took in support of its licensees' operations that went well beyond B2B activity, and involved Starnet's computers and personnel in Canada dealing directly with the customers of its licensees. Customers downloaded gambling software from Starnet's Vancouver servers, and cheques payable to customers were signed by Starnet personnel in Vancouver and mailed to customers from the Vancouver offices.

Cyber World Group
There were no further prosecutions under the Code involving online gambling until 25 January 2007, when 3370861 Canada Inc., also known as Cyber World Group, was charged with two counts under Part VII of the Code in connection with activities relating to the conduct of the business of an online gambling website, GoldenPalace.com, through a server located on the Mohawk Territory of Kahnawà:ke.

On 26 September 2007, Cyber World Group pleaded guilty to these charges and paid a fine of C$2,000,000. The prosecution did not become public knowledge until two months after the conviction, through a story broadcast by the Canadian Broadcasting Corporation on 29 November 2007. Neither the prosecution nor the conviction was publicised by the Quebec police, the Quebec government, the authorities of the Mohawk Territory of Kahnawà:ke, Cyber World Group or GoldenPalace.com.

The charges in the information sworn commencing the prosecution referred to 'virtual casinos and computers' kept and operated in Kahnawà:ke. However, the police did not collect the evidence to support those charges by conducting a raid on the Kahnawà:ke reserve; rather, the evidence in question was obtained from a raid at the offices of Cyber World Group, in the Ville St Laurent District of Montreal, nowhere in the vicinity of the Mohawk Territory of Kahnawà:ke. No charges were laid against any person or entity residing on the Kahnawà:ke reserve. Chuck Barnett, a member of the Board of Supervisors for MIT, states that no Mohawk person or entity *'was even remotely contacted'* in relation to the police action during the months following the raid in Ville St. Laurent, adding:

'As somebody who lives, breathes, eats and sleeps every day of my life in Kahnawà:ke Mohawk Territory, I can easily say there have been no policing actions from external police forces here relative to this or any other I-gaming related issue'.

Since 1996, the Mohawk Council of Kahnawà:ke (the Mohawk Council) has claimed the right to conduct, manage and regulate online gambling conducted within the Mohawk Territory of Kahnawà:ke. The Kahnawà:ke claim jurisdiction to issue gambling licences for lottery schemes, notwithstanding the offences found in Part VII of the Code, as an incident of their self-proclaimed status as a sovereign nation. In addition, the Mohawk Council alleges that the Kahnawà:ke have an inherent aboriginal right to conduct and regulate commercial gambling, protected by section 35 of the Constitution Act, 1982. They take the position that the plain wording of the Code, which states that only a provincial government can lawfully conduct and manage gambling that is *'operated on or through a computer or video device'*, is inapplicable to the Kahnawà:ke. The Quebec and federal governments and the provincial police have investigated the activities at Kahnawà:ke, and in 2001 the Quebec Minister of Public Security stated publicly that online gambling activity operating from Kahnawà:ke is unlawful. However, no police action has ever been taken, possibly due to residual tensions dating from the summer of 1990, when a police raid at Kahnawà:ke led to a stand-off with the Canadian military.

The prosecution and conviction of Cyber World Group was carefully framed in such a way as to refrain from openly challenging the constitutional position taken by the Mohawk Council. Cyber World Group operated from Canadian offices outside the Kahnawà:ke Mohawk reserve. Moreover, the Kahnawà:ke gambling regulatory authority had granted a permit to Golden Palace Ltd, not Cyber World Group, and accordingly the jurisdiction to grant that permit was never directly challenged. Had the authorities wished to challenge the jurisdiction of the Kahnawà:ke to regulate the activities of GoldenPalace.com, it would have been a simple matter to charge the Kahnawà:ke with aiding and abetting Cyber World Group (contrary to subsection 202(1)(j) of the Code), or with doing things not authorised by section 207 of the Code in the conduct, management or operation of a lottery scheme (contrary to subsection 207(3)(a)).

Project Amethyst & Platinum SB

On 9 November 2012, the Royal Canadian Mounted Police (RCMP) issued a press release stating that 21 people (primarily in the Ottawa area) had been charged with a variety of offences relating to unlawful gaming, bookmaking, extortion, the production of marijuana and offences related to organised crime. The RCMP indicated that the arrests were part of Project Amethyst, a partnership between three levels of Canadian law enforcement formed for the purpose of investigating the criminal activities of a particular organised crime group.

On 3 February 2013, police raided an invitation-only 2,300 person Super Bowl party north of Toronto, Ontario. Six men were charged with offences relating to their alleged roles in betting taking place at the party, and in connection with an alleged illegal online gambling operation in relation to the website PlatinumSB.com. The police indicated that these arrests were also part of Project Amethyst.

Based on the allegations available through media reports, PlatinumSB appears to be an online version of the conventional sports betting rings that have long been operated by organised crime. It does not resemble the typical online gambling operation, most of which are licensed and regulated by the gambling authorities of a recognised jurisdiction. PlatinumSB was not licensed or regulated in any jurisdiction.

While the alleged events leading to the PlatinumSB prosecutions have an online gambling dimension, it appears that PlatinumSB was not truly an 'offshore' online gambling operation from a Canadian perspective. Although the PlatinumSB website used a server located outside Canada, the prosecution appears to contend that it was operated by Canadians in Canada and that, through activities such as the invitation-only Super Bowl party that took place in Markham, Ontario, it exclusively targeted Canadians. Unlike typical offshore online gambling operations, which accept funds through electronic transfers of funds or through credit card payments, in the PlatinumSB operation it appears that bets were made on credit, and thereafter Canadian agents collected money locally from Canadian customers. As mentioned above, PlatinumSB was not licensed by any jurisdiction, and the individuals arrested are alleged to have ties to organised crime in Canada.

Therefore, the arrests of 9 November 2012 and 3 February 2013 relating to Project Amethyst and PlatinumSB do not in and of themselves signal a shift in the priorities of Canadian law enforcement towards expanding the scope of the prosecutions of offshore online gambling operators. On their face, these arrests appear to involve an online gambling operation that is alleged to have had considerable ties to Canada, including controlling mind and management located in Canada, and a great deal of activity 'on the ground' in Canada relating to the promotion of online gambling and the settlement of funds relating to online gambling. In other words, the matter as presented appears similar in some respects to the cases of Starnet and Cyber World Group, in that Canadian law enforcement has pursued an operation that is alleged to have a great many links to Canada, rather than a true offshore operation whose sole activity in Canada is to passively accept persons in Canada as customers.

3.4 What technical measures are in place (if any) to protect consumers from unlicensed operators, such as ISP blocking and payment blocking?

There are no ISP blocks in place that prevent Canadians from accessing the websites of foreign-based online gambling operators, either in law or in practice. There are no payment blocks in law. While it is unlawful in Canada for anyone to have under their control any money or other property relating to a transaction that is contrary to the gaming and betting provisions of the Code, there is no legislation in Canada explicitly prohibiting financial services providers from processing gaming and betting transactions, which are identified by a merchant category code of 7995. However, for various reasons, including the concern that the gambling activity may be illegal under the Code, certain banks in Canada refuse to process transactions coded 7995.

3.5 Has the legal status of online gambling changed significantly in recent years and, if so, how?

The legal status of online gambling has not changed significantly in recent years.

3.6 Whilst acknowledging the inherent difficulty in predicting developments in gambling law, what are the likely developments in online gambling in your jurisdiction, both short term and long term? Are any specific amendments under consideration? Have there been any recent political developments, or do you envisage any in the near future? Are any specific amendments under consideration? Are they likely to be adopted and, if so, what is the time scale?

There are two likely developments with respect to laws related to online gambling in Canada.

Charities conducting various aspects of lotteries through the use of a computer

In its 2014 Economic Action Plan (ie the federal budget), the Canadian government stated that '*in order to reduce administrative costs associated with charitable lotteries and allow charities to modernise their lottery systems, Economic Action Plan 2014 proposes to amend the Criminal Code to allow charities to conduct various aspects of lotteries through the use of a computer. The use of a computer will also allow charities to use modern e-commerce methods for the purchasing, processing and issuing of lottery tickets and issuing of receipts to donors*' (Economic Action Plan, p. 215). This budget measure will likely be passed in the near future.

Betting on single-sport events, fights and races
Under the Code as presently written, lawful sports betting conducted and managed by provincial governments is restricted in that they cannot offer betting on the results of single sporting events – all betting must be in parlay format – nor can provincial governments offer betting on fights and races.

A private member's bill (Bill C-290) to amend the Code to allow for authorised groups (ie provincial governments) to provide betting offers on single sporting events, fights and races was passed unanimously by the House of Commons in 2012. In order to become law, it will need to be passed by the Canadian Senate. The bill, however, has been before the Senate since 2012, and has not gone to a vote. Bill C-290 has been criticised by certain Senators as promoting gambling and match-fixing. Media outlets have recently reported that Bill C-290 is stalled in the Senate because it does not have enough support to survive a vote.

If the amendments enacted by Bill C-290 come into force, the various provincial lottery corporations are expected to expand their sports betting offerings, including online betting on sports. Ontario, which anticipates offering online gambling in 2014, could potentially launch full-scale online sportsbook operations in response (offering services solely to persons physically located in Ontario).

3.7 Is the law the same in relation to mobile gambling and interactive gambling on television? If not, are there any headline differences?
The law is the same with respect to mobile gambling and interactive gambling on television.

4. LAND-BASED GAMING
4.1 Please describe the licensing regime (if any) for land-based gaming, and what products are included. Please set out what licences are available, and the licensing regime for them.
The Ontario government (through the OLG) does not require a licence to conduct and manage a lottery scheme in Ontario.

The OLG conducts and manages all commercial casino gambling in Ontario.

A charitable or religious organisation may obtain a licence to conduct and manage a lottery scheme in Ontario, provided that the proceeds from the lottery scheme are used for a charitable or religious object or purpose. The recognised common law categories of 'charitable purpose' are
* relief of poverty;
* advancement of education;
* advancement of religion; and
* other purposes that are beneficial to the community.

Accordingly, there is a clear distinction between how provincial governments may use the proceeds of gambling and how a charitable organisation may use such proceeds. The provincial government may treat the proceeds of gambling as general government revenue that may be applied to whatever ends the government sees fit. Proceeds from licensed gambling must be used for a charitable or religious object or purpose.

Another major difference between gambling conducted and managed by the provincial government and gambling conducted and managed by charities is that under the Code only the provincial government may conduct and manage slot machine gambling. The Great Blue Heron Casino, located approximately 60 km east of Toronto, is a licensed charity casino at which the Mississaugas of Scugog First Nation conducts and manages table games, while the OLG conducts and manages the slot machines.

The AGCO licenses a number of activities, including the following:
- a charitable gaming event (an event at a bingo hall where proceeds are pooled, for which a licence is issued to conduct and manage one or more lotteries, including bingo and break open tickets);
- bingo;
- break open tickets;
- a raffle lottery;
- a Monte Carlo event; and
- a fair or exhibition gaming event.

4.2 Please set out any particular limitations or requirements for (eg casino) operators, such as a ban on local residents gambling.

In Ontario, players must be 19 or older to enter a casino, and 18 or older to enter a charitable gambling site.

Individuals who appear to be intoxicated are not permitted to access a casino.

4.3 Please address the questions in 3.5 above, but in relation to land-based gaming.

The last major amendment with respect to the legal status of land-based gaming occurred in 1999. It was to amend the Code so as to permit provincial governments to conduct and manage dice games.

5. TAX
5.1 Please summarise briefly the tax regime applicable to both land-based and online gaming.

There is no tax regime applicable to the proceeds of commercial gaming operations in Canada because those proceeds flow to either the provincial governments or charitable organisations. Revenue from government-operated commercial gaming operations is spent on government services. Revenue from charitable gaming operations is spent by the charity earning the revenue, and the revenues of a charitable organisation are not subject to income tax. The revenues of gaming and non-gaming suppliers registered by the AGCO are generally subject to federal and provincial income tax.

As a general rule, a player's gambling winnings is treated as a windfall under the Income Tax Act. In circumstances where a taxpayer is found to pursue gaming as a professional or business activity, the winnings from such gambling will be considered income from a business and will thus be taxable.

6.   ADVERTISING

6.1   To what extent is the advertising of gambling permitted in your jurisdiction? Again, this should cover both land-based and online gaming. To the extent that advertising is permitted, how is it regulated?

Gambling authorised by the provincial government

Provided that a gaming operation is authorised by a provincial government (ie conducted and managed by a provincial government or conducted and managed by a charity and licensed by a provincial government), there are no limitations in the Criminal Code with respect to advertising.

Advertising and marketing materials of authorised gambling providers in Ontario must comply with the AGCO's Registrar's Standards for Gaming.

Specifically, advertising and marketing materials and communications shall not target underage or self-excluded persons to participate in lottery schemes and shall not include underage individuals. At minimum, materials and communications shall not:

- be based on themes, or use language intended to appeal primarily to minors;
- appear on billboards or other outdoor displays that are directly adjacent to schools or other primarily youth-oriented locations;
- contain cartoon figures, symbols, role models and/or celebrity/ entertainer endorsers whose primary appeal is to minors;
- use individuals who are, or appear to be, minors to promote gambling; or
- appear in media and venues directed primarily to minors or where most of the audience is reasonably expected to be minors.

Further, according to the AGCO's Registrar's Standards for Gaming, advertising and marketing materials and communications shall not be misleading. At minimum, materials and communications shall not:

- imply that playing a lottery scheme is required for social acceptance, personal success, financial success or resolving economic, social or personal problems;
- contain endorsements by well-known personalities that suggest that playing lottery schemes has contributed to their success;
- encourage play as a means of recovering past gambling or other financial losses;
- present winning as the most probable outcome, or misrepresent a person's chances of winning a prize;
- imply that the chances of winning increase:
    (i)   the longer one plays; or
    (ii) the more one spends; or
    (iii) by suggesting that skill can influence the outcome (for games where skill is not a factor).

Gambling not authorised by the provincial government
Criminal Code
With respect to offshore online gaming operations, subsection 206(1)(a) of the Code, which applies to games of chance alone, applies to render it unlawful to advertise casino games that contain no element of skill, such as roulette or slots, in Canada. The advertisement of foreign lotteries is specifically prohibited by subsection 206(7) of the Code.

Some have argued that advertising for games of mixed chance and skill (ie poker and blackjack) may be prohibited by the Code, but this is subject to some controversy.

Subsection 202(1)(g) of the Code relates to information or writing that *'is likely to promote gambling'*; however, it is restricted to situations where information or writing that promotes or is of use in sports betting is imported or brought into Canada. The act of exporting that same material is not criminalised; also, advertising and marketing material that originates in Canada does not offend against this provision.

Subection 202(1)(i) of the Code makes it an offence to send, transmit, deliver or receive *'any message that conveys any information relating to book-making, pool-selling, betting or wagering, or that is intended to assist in book-making, pool-selling, betting or wagering'*.

These prohibitions would apply to all forms of marketing, whether on foreign websites, on foreign TV channels transmitted to Canada or via direct advertising to consumers.

Consumer Protection Act
The Province of Ontario has enacted a specific consumer protection law specifically directed at advertising for online gambling. Section 13.1 of the Consumer Protection Act, 2002 (Ontario) (the CPA) purports to ban the advertisement of 'internet gaming sites'. Section 13.1 of the CPA applies to advertisements that either originate in Ontario or are primarily targeted at residents of Ontario.

The offence created by section 13.1 of the CPA states that *'no person shall advertise an internet gaming site that is operated contrary'* to the Code. If the site is operating contrary to the Code, and any advertisements for the site offering the games either originate in Ontario or are primarily targeted at residents of Ontario, such activity will be subject to prosecution under section 13.1 of the CPA.

Summary
In summary, in relation to casino games of pure chance, it is illegal to send electronic marketing communications to existing or prospective customers in Canada, pursuant to subsection 206(1)(a) of the Code. In relation to games of chance and games of mixed chance and skill, it is illegal to import or bring into Canada information or writing that is likely to promote such gaming. Judicial opinion is unsettled as to whether it is illegal to send such marketing communications to persons in Canada, where those communications refer to games of mixed skill and chance, such as poker and

blackjack. In Ontario, advertisements of online gambling sites originating in Ontario or primarily targeting residents of Ontario are illegal, if such online gambling site is operating contrary to the Code

In practice, almost all radio and television broadcast advertising of online gaming in Canada, including for games of mixed skill and chance such as poker, is restricted to 'freeroll' websites. Such advertising is accepted as lawful by Telecaster Services of the Television Bureau of Canada (Telecaster), the body responsible for pre-approving the content of nearly all television advertisements in Canada. Telecaster does not allow advertisements for 'real money' games of chance or mixed chance and skill.

7. SOCIAL GAMING

7.1 We believe this to be a growing area. Please decide under what criteria social gaming is permitted in your jurisdiction. If games are free to play or if there is no prize, are they legal without a licence? Please address circumstances where virtual currency is used and can be won: ie currency which is of no monetary or other value, save for as credits to take part in games. The answer should address the question whether game credits or virtual money can be exchanged for other prizes. Is any change to regulation in the area proposed or envisaged?

Social gaming is not directly addressed in any Canadian legislation; however, it is lawful to offer social gaming throughout Canada as long as one or more of the elements of gambling in Canada (prize, consideration and chance), as described in section 2.1, are not satisfied.

If games are free to play, the consideration element is not satisfied and the game is lawful.

If games have no prize (other than a virtual prize which has no monetary value), the prize element is not satisfied and the game is lawful.

If games have virtual currency which players may win or lose, and the virtual currency has no real-world value (eg it cannot be sold and is not directly redeemable for prizes of money or money's worth), the consideration element is not satisfied and the game is lawful.

If games have virtual currency which players may win or lose and the virtual currency has a real-world value (eg it is redeemable for real prizes), the chance, consideration and prize elements are all satisfied and the game is unlawful (assuming the game is not a game of skill). However, case law has held that, where the only possible reward is the provision of free games (eg replays on a pinball machine), that is not a sufficient prize to render the activity unlawful gambling pursuant to the Code even if the consideration and chance elements are satisfied.

If games have virtual currency available for purchase, and such virtual currency may be won or lost, if such purchase is used for the purpose of the enhancement of gameplay which is otherwise free (eg advanced features, functionality or virtual goods provided by a game provider using a freemium business model), the consideration element is not satisfied and the game is lawful.

If a game is not prohibited by the Code, an entity or individual offering such game does not need to obtain a licence from a gaming regulatory authority.

There are no proposed or envisaged changes to regulation in this area.

Panama

Blandon & Young Attorneys
Herbert Young Rodriguez & Lizi Rose Archer

1. OBJECTIVES AND STRUCTURE OF LEGISLATION
History of gambling in Panama
The legality of gambling in Panama was addressed in 1904 at the constitutional level. Article 37 of the Constitution of Panama of 1904 prohibited gambling. Following this constitutional mandate, Law 25 of 1906 was passed to prohibit all forms of gambling. Thirty-seven years later, in the Constitution of 1941, Article 154 established that gambling could be exploited by the state or through concessions granted by the state to private enterprises. Gambling was exploited by private enterprises without the intervention of the government until 1946, when Article 238 was introduced into the Constitution of Panama to limit the exploitation of gambling to the state only and to its own benefit. Decree No. 822 was passed in the same year, creating a board that would issue gambling rules and regulations and also study and resolve all problems that could arise due to the exploitation of gambling by the state. Decree Law No. 19 was passed in 1947, and the board that was created under Decree No. 822 was named the Gaming Control Board. The Gaming Control Board then and now functions as a dependency of the Ministry of Economy and Finance. The Gaming Control Board is the entity that regulates the exploitation of gambling in Panama on behalf of the state.

For around 50 years from 1947, casinos and slot parlours in Panama were operated directly by the state through the Gaming Control Board. In 1996, the state decided to modernise this sector to foment and develop tourism, and it called for a public bid to transfer the operation of the existing casinos and slot parlours to private companies by granting them a contract of administration and operation under the supervision and control of the Gaming Control Board.

In 1997, new guidelines for the operation of casinos and slot parlours were enacted by means of Resolution No. 92 and the Gaming Control Board functions were also restructured by Decree Law No. 2 of 1998. Both of these regulations are still in effect and are the main rules applicable to the exploitation and regulation of gaming in the country.

Decree Law No. 2 of 1998 gives the Gaming Control Board the faculty to determine which activities fall within gaming (excluding lottery); to regulate and control the existing administrators/operators of gaming establishments; to collect gaming revenue; to evaluate and approve or deny new applicants for a contract with the state; to operate a gaming establishment; to issue gaming licences; and to modify and approve gaming regulations.

The Resolution No. 92 of 1997 is applicable to casinos and slot parlours only. Resolution No. 65 of 2002 is applicable to online gaming.

2. FRAMEWORK OF LEGISLATION

2.1 What is the legal definition of gambling and what falls within this definition?

Definition of games of chance, bet and wagering activities

Decree Law No. 2 of 1998 provides a definition of the following concepts:

- 'Wagering activities' are those in which ordinarily, the bets are the object, purpose or main base of the activity.
- 'Bet' is the obligation acquired by one or several people to commit a sum of money or anything else that will be lost in favour of another person or persons, if the uncertain outcome of an event or future event is favourable to them.
- 'Games of chance' are all those in which the adverse or favourable outcome of the game does not depend mainly on the talent or skill of the player, including any game with cards, dices or with any device, mechanical, electromechanical or electronic machine to win money or other item of value. Such games include, but are not limited to, type A slot machines and also roulette, keno, Yan-tan, twenty-one, blackjack, craps, check-a-luck (*dai-shu*), Wheel of fortune, chemin-de-fer, baccarat, Paigow and pangini poker. Also included are: clubs of goods, travel clubs, bingo halls, type C slot machines, raffles, horse racing, betting agencies and commercial promotions involving the performance of an activity that results in bets determined by the Gaming Control Board.

2.2 What is the legal definition of online gambling and what falls within this definition?

Definition of online gambling according to Resolution No. 65 of 2002

Resolution No. 65 of 2002 defines the following concept:

- Electronic wager: the wager performed in a game through a system of electronic communication authorised to operate in Panama.

Games of chance and wagering activities performed through systems of electronic communication operating in or from the Republic of Panama shall be subject to the provisions of this regulation. The activities understood to be performed pursuant to this regulation include casinos and wagering agencies of sports events that are via the internet or by international telephone calls.

2.3 Please set out the different gambling products identified by legislation.

Decree Law No. 2 of 1998 regulates the following gambling products:

- Table games (includes poker and type A slot machines): to be operated only within a casino. Table games must be submitted to the Gaming Control Board for prior approval.
- Slot parlours or type A slot machines: only slots are allowed. The parlour must be located in a touristic area classified by law as such and outside the designated area. The designated area is the area located within the following limits: to the north: the Colon District, Portobelo and Saint Isabel, Colon Province; to the south, the area bordering the

Bay of Panama; and to the west: the District of La Chorrera in Panama province. Territorial waters are not included in the areas described.

- Type C slot machines: the maximum bet allowed per play is $3.00 and the maximum payout cannot exceed $200.00. This kind of activity requires a liquor licence and is forbidden to children.
- Bingo halls are regulated by Resolution No. 25 of 2003.
- Online casinos are regulated by Resolution No. 65 of 2002.
- Online sportsbooks are regulated by Resolution No. 65 of 2002.
- Sports betting agencies are regulated by Resolution No. 77 of 1999.

2.4 Please list the different requirements for each gambling product, including legal classifications for each; for example, is poker a game of skill or game of chance?
Classification of gaming halls that can be operated in Panama
A) Full casino
Decree Law No. 2 of 1998 only allows the installation of table games in a casino. Decree Law No. 2 of 1998 refers to a casino as a 'full casino' and defines it as the game hall that offers a combination of table games and type A slot machines, together with any combination of other games or gaming devices. The Administrator-Operator shall provide services to complement entertainment and fun as it deems necessary for the better development of the game hall. Poker is considered a game of skill and the casino will only charge a commission as a charge to the player for the right to play. Poker can only be offered inside a full casino duly licensed to operate in Panama. It is required that the applicant applies for a contract with the state.

B) Type A slot parlour
Only slots are allowed. The parlour must be located in a touristic area classified by law as such and within the designated area. The designated area is the area located within the following limits: to the north: the Colon District, Portobelo and Saint Isabel, Colon Province; to the south, the area bordering the Bay of Panama; and to the west: the District of La Chorrera in Panama province. Territorial waters are not included in the areas described. It is required that the applicant applies for a contract with the state.

C) Bingo hall
Bingo is a game of chance consisting of a draw made on the basis of numbers that gives every player the chance to win in the various game modes according to the numbers printed on their card or cards. Bingo halls can be operated in any part of the country. There is no legal restriction in place as far as geographical area is concerned. The traditional Spanish Bingo as a public spectacle has been the way of operation. Notwithstanding the above, the Gaming Control Board recently issued a resolution allowing licensed bingo halls to request a special licence for bingo machines. Such bingo halls with machines can only operate in international airports.

Also, a televised bingo operation, which is very similar to the lottery game, was approved by the Gaming Control Board. Because this game is very similar to the lottery game, the National Lottery of Beneficence, which is a state institution, was supposed to have a monopoly on its operation; however, the concession of this game was acquired by a private company. This was possible because the National Lottery was not taken into account or consulted over the viability of the operation prior the granting of the authorisation.

D) Operation of type C slot machines
These can only be operated in bars. Only slots are allowed. The maximum bet allowed per play is $3.00 and the maximum payout cannot exceed $200.00. In the last five years, these kinds of machine have proliferated under the auspices of the Gaming Control Board. The authorisation of slot machines has been increased all over the Republic, without any scientific study of the detriments to the poorest in the population with regard to compulsive gambling.

E) Sports betting shop
Bets can be taken on any sporting event, greyhound races and any other races with the exception of horses. Only local bets can be accepted. It is prohibited to accept bets placed by international telephone calls or via the internet.

F) Internet gambling
For casino games and sports betting, lotteries or any other game.

2.5 Explain the system of regulation of gambling; which regulatory or governmental body is responsible for the supervision of gambling? Which body issues licences? Which body examines enforcement powers? Is there any limit on the number or duration of available licences?

The Gaming Control Board of Panama, which is a multidisciplinary government body comprising the Minister of Finance, a member of the Congress and the Controller of the Republic of Panama, took control of granting concessions to private enterprises, and regulating the gaming activity and all of the relations with the authorised operators. The Gaming Control Board of Panama regulates gaming activities that generate gambling and is the authorised entity which qualifies each game as a game of chance or if a specified game originates gambling.

In order to operate a gaming room or a casino, it is necessary to enter into an administration/operation contract with the Gaming Control Board and to obtain a gaming licence granted by the referred authority allowing the administrator/operator to manage a full casino. The process requires that each applicant obtains a resolution authorising the Minister of Economy to sign a contract with the operator, posting an insurance bond (the amount of the bond, depends on the gaming activity), and that each party sign the contract, which will come into effect with the final signing of the General Controller of the Republic.

3. ONLINE GAMBLING

3.1 To what extent can online gambling be offered in your jurisdiction? Are licences available and, if so, for which gambling products? Please describe briefly the licensing process, who may apply, whether licences are limited in number and, if no licences are available, whether it is legal for online gambling to be offered. In the case of EU jurisdictions, please state whether there are any issues as to the legality of the local law at EU level. Please refer to any relevant cases at ECJ level and explain any measures taken or pending by the European Commission.

By means of Resolution No. 65 of 25 October, the Gaming Control Board of Panama, which is in charge of the authorisation, regulation and supervision of wagering activities, approved the statute named 'For the operation of games of chance and wagering activities performed through electronic communications systems that allows online bets in Panama'.

The operation of companies aimed to capture all kinds of internet wagering, including casinos, sports books, poker rooms and electronic lotteries, and any other game. This regulation found its way out without generating the conflicts caused in other countries where the established casinos and sports books are against these activities, considering them to be unfair competition. Legally, the regulation is open, and there is no limit in terms of quantity of operators.

Documentation required by Resolution No. 65 to be filed with the application for obtaining the contract

- the name of the applicant;
- the name of the supplier of the software or hardware for the System for Electronic Communication Games;
- name of each person directly or indirectly involved in the proposed operation and his/her capacity;
- complete and detailed information on the personal data of the applicant and its trusted employees, including the criminal history, commercial activities, financial and commercial matters, within at least a 10 year period prior to the filing date of the referred to application;
- for corporations, the information required must be also submitted for all directors, officers, legal representatives and shareholders;
- business plan details, including projections for the next seven years;
- corporations must submit a certificate issued by the Public Registry Office evidencing its legal existence, legal representative, constitution date, directors and officers, and initial capital of the corporation;
- authenticated copies of documents evidencing the constitution of the corporation or authenticated copies of documents certifying the identity of the natural person, depending on each case;
- a description of the financial structure of the corporation, including a list of all the shares that were issued, all the outstanding shares, and a list of the related rights;

- certification issued by the corporate secretary indicating the names of every shareholder of the corporation;
- certification issued by the corporate secretary or the applicant, as is the case, indicating all outstanding loans, mortgages, trusts, encumbrances and obligations and any other liability incurred;
- certification issued by the corporate secretary or the applicant indicating the names of the persons employed whose benefits, wages or fees correspond to the 10 highest amounts on the payroll, whether or not reliable directors, officials, officers or employees;
- a description of the procedures used by the applicant to grant bonds and profit-sharing;
- a photocopy of the agreements or sub-agreements executed or to be executed in relation to the operation of the game or other activity that requires a licence;
- a general profit and loss statement certified by an authorised public accountant for at least three fiscal years prior to the date of the application. In the case of the applicant not having three years of operations, the statement must include the complete operation period;
- a copy of the income tax returns for the last three years. In the case of the applicant not having operated for a complete fiscal period, an estimated income tax return must be submitted;
- a manual of the internal control procedures to be used, prepared according to the minimum standards of internal control procedure adopted in the regulation;
- documentation evidencing the organisational experience and/or personnel experience in the development of the operation, including, without limitation, experience and knowledge in the administration of information systems; and
- any other information or documentation that the Director may consider necessary and convenient to guarantee the public health, security, morale, good reputation, public order and general interest of the residents of the Republic of Panama and of the gambling industry.

Once the contract has been approved, the applicant must post a bond to guarantee compliance with its obligations.

Additionally, the applicant must manage its operations in accordance with technical standards approved by the Gaming Control Board, this mainly involves identifying players, identifying the source of the funds received as gambling, establishing an escrow account with a local bank to guarantee the payment of the prizes and not capturing players located in jurisdictions where virtual or electronic gambling is prohibited.

Licences are available for all of the gambling products and all of the corporations to which the regulations apply. It is possible to include several products in the same licence. Some operators use their licence for just one game (eg, poker) but one licence allows the inclusion of several games.

What is needed is an immediate review of the policy with respect to the granting of licences. While there is no such thing as a master licence, the last two consecutive governments have maintained only one operator.

The authorised operator company is allowed to grant sub-licences with the authorisation of the Gaming Control Board. This process is very fast since the company could be initiating operations within 30 days, including the time taken by the Gaming Control Board to grant the approval.

It is our opinion that the prohibition of national gaming should be eliminated so that, as in other jurisdictions, internet gaming operators are allowed to associate with land-based casino operators to achieve the full development of this industry, which, as a consequence of wrong policies, has failed to capture the attention of respected international operators and has failed to achieve the sustained growth achieved by other countries that do have all the attractions that can be found in Panama.

3.2 Is there a distinction between the law applicable to B2B operations and that applicable to B2C operations?
N/A.

3.3 What are the consequences for B2C or B2B operators who are active in your jurisdiction without having obtained or applied for the required permits, licences and approvals? What penalties and enforcement powers are available in respect of the illegal operators? Please outline any significant domestic decisions or enforcement actions that have been taken by the relevant authorities in recent years.
N/A.

3.4 What technical measures are in place (if any) to protect consumers from unlicensed operators, such as ISP blocking and payment blocking?
The regime has been the same since 2002, and no changes are predicted at this time.

3.5 Has the legal status of online gambling changed significantly in recent years and, if so, how?
N/A.

3.6 Whilst acknowledging the inherent difficulty in predicting developments in gambling law, what are the likely developments in online gambling in your jurisdiction, both short term and long term? Are any specific amendments under consideration? Have there been any recent political developments, or do you envisage any in the near future? Are any specific amendments under consideration? Are they likely to be adopted and, if so, what is the time scale?
N/A.

3.7 Is the law the same in relation to mobile gambling and interactive gambling on television? If not, are there any headline differences?

Mobile gambling and interactive gambling on television are not regulated in Panama. It is necessary to issue new regulations to allow such games. In accord with the Decree Law, each game will require a specific regulation; in the meantime, these activities are not permitted.

4. LAND-BASED GAMING

4.1 Please describe the licensing regime (if any) for land-based gaming, and what products are included. Please set out what licences are available, and the licensing regime for them.

There are only two kinds of licence regime: complete casino and type A slot machine rooms. The next bid will be in 2017. The contract issued is for a period of 20 years.

Procedure to obtain a contract

In order to operate a Gaming Room or a Casino, it is necessary to enter into an Administration/Operation Contract with the Gaming Control Board and to obtain a Gaming License granted by the referred to authority allowing the Administrator/Operator to manage a Complete Casino

Documentation required for obtaining a contract

- name of the applicant;
- name of all persons directly or indirectly involved in the proposed operation and his/her capacity;
- complete and detailed information on the personal data of the applicant and its reliable employees, including the criminal history, commercial activities, financial and commercial matters, within an at least 10 year period prior to the filing date of the referred to application;
- for corporations, the information required must be also submitted for all directors, officers, legal representatives and shareholders;
- business plan details, including projections for the next 10 years;
- corporations must submit a certificate issued by the Public Registry Office evidencing its legal existence, legal representative, constitution date, directors and officers, and the initial capital of the corporation;
- authenticated copies of documents evidencing the constitution of the corporation or authenticated copies of documents certifying the identity of the natural person; depending on each case;
- a description of the financial structure of the corporation, including a list of all the shares that were issued, all the outstanding shares and the related rights;
- certification issued by the corporate secretary indicating the names of every shareholder of the corporation;
- certification issued by the corporate secretary or the applicant, as is the case, indicating all outstanding loans, mortgages, trusts, encumbrances and obligations, and any other liability incurred;
- certification issued by the corporate secretary or the applicant indicating the names of the persons employed whose benefits, wages or fees

correspond to the 10 highest amounts of the payroll, whether or not reliable directors, officials, officers or employees;

- a description of the procedures used by the applicant to grant bonds and profit-sharing;
- a photocopy of the agreements or sub-agreements executed or to be executed in relation to the operation of the game or other activity that requires a licence;
- a general profit and loss statement certified by an authorised public accountant for at least three fiscal years prior to the date of the application. In the case of the applicant not having three years of operations, the statement must include the complete operation period;
- a copy of the income tax returns for the last three years. In the case of an applicant not having operated for a complete fiscal period, an estimated income tax return must be submitted;
- a manual of the internal control procedures to be used, prepared according to the minimum standards of internal control procedure adopted in the regulation;
- documentation evidencing the organisation's experience and/or personnel's experience in the development of the operation, including, without limitation, experience and knowledge of five years in the gaming industry. This can be proved by filing a copy of a licence issued by the proper authorities in charge in the country in which a casino is operated by the applicant and a copy of the documents of incorporation of the corporation in the referred to country;
- solvency certification reflecting that the applicant counts with financial facilities for the project; and
- any other information or documentation that the Director may consider necessary and convenient to guarantee the public health, security, morale, good reputation, public order and general interest of the residents of the Republic of Panama and of the gambling industry.

It is possible for Panamanian Authorities to prepare the necessary documentation, but the applicant must provide them with the documents related to the experience of the corporation and any other documents requested.

Once the contract has been approved, the applicant must post a bond of $1 million in the city of Panama (the designated area) to guarantee compliance with its obligations.

Additionally, the applicant must manage its operations in accordance with technical standards approved by the Gaming Control Board.

Gaming rooms have to be located at a distance of more than 100 metres from educational institutions, churches, health centres and hospitals. Casinos cannot be located in national parks or natural monuments, or in other places officially declared as fauna reserves.

Geographical location

It is important to point out that our gaming rules have established as designated areas Panama City in general to the Chorrera border and the Colon border, not including territorial waters.

The casinos which are planned to operate 'within the designated area' have to be located in a new hotel having at least three hundred rooms, a swimming pool, 24/7 night entertainment, 24/7 restaurants and room service with international luxury standards classified with at least four stars.

Hotels located outside the designated areas will be evaluated by the Gaming Board, which can allow some adjustments when issuing the licence.

Contracts for type A slot machine rooms can be approved outside the designated area, in the interior of the Republic, eg in the Province of Chiriqui (David, Boquete, Cerro Punta), Bocas del Toro Province, Farallón and Coronado.

4.2 Please set out any particular limitations or requirements for (eg casino) operators, such as a ban on local residents gambling.

Once the operator obtains a contract, the land-based casino can take bets from citizens, residents and/or tourists without any restriction. The gamein Panama is forbidden to minors (players must be at least 18 years old) and those individuals on the Gaming Control Board-approved list of excluded people.

5. TAX

5.1 Please summarise briefly the tax regime applicable both to land-based and online gaming.

Although our law provides a formula for calculating the taxes that must be paid directly to the Gaming Control Board, the Congress approved the amendment of the Gaming Law with a flat fee of 18 per cent of the gross income per month since April 2012, per slot. This is the Gaming Tax for type A slot machines located in casinos or in slot parlours. The tables will pay 12.5 per cent of the gross income per month.

This tax has produced a distortion in the industry, to wit: a corporation that maintains the contractual monopoly of 26 rooms of type A slot machines, with approximately 7,250 installed machines and 1000 employees, pays the same tariff as 19 complete casinos with 5,375 installed machines and 4000 employees. Evidently, the operating expenses of the rooms with the type A machines cannot be compared with the those incurred by the complete casinos. Nevertheless, they are liable to the same tributary treatment.

Gross income in our industry shall be understood as the sum of the total amount in coins or tokens in the drop box of all the slots machines, plus the bills in the stacker of the referred to slots, minus the prizes paid to the players, minus the refills of coins, tokens and bills. Regarding the gross incomes of tables, the same principle is applied using the appropriate formulation for this kind of games.

Type C slot machines paid a flat tax of $125.00 per month, per machine.

Also, the new operator must pay to the government a sole tax (licence tax) established by the Gaming Control Board in the amount of $500,000 per type A slot machine room and $1,000,000 for casinos.

Taxes related to the profits of the operators of online gambling were excluded. The gaming taxes for internet operations are flat rates which amount to the sum of $20,000 per year for each operation licence and $10,000 for the concept of right key (paid once).

As stated above, under this regulation, it is prohibited to capture bets from Panama; hence the revenues generated by the System for Electronic Communication Games are considered to be foreign source income, therefore, these operations are not subject to income taxes and revenue sharing taxes.

The particularities of our country and the tax system created for the establishment of international companies was conceived with the purpose of increasing the enrolment of Panamanian labour in call centres; the leasing of commercial stores; and the establishment of corporations and organisations of high technology in places such as the City of Knowledge in Panama's Business, Scientific and Technological Park located in Howard , which in the past was a military base inside the Panama Canal Zone controlled by the United States government.

6. ADVERTISING

6.1 To what extent is the advertising of gambling permitted in your jurisdiction? Again, this should cover both land-based and online gaming. To the extent that advertising is permitted, how is it regulated?

Land-based operations have no restrictions on advertising in Panama. The Congress has approved rules restricting cigar advertising, but no regulation has been issued on gaming.

Regarding internet gaming, only the System for Electronic Communication Games duly authorised by the Gambling Control Boards shall be published; thus, it is our opinion that the publicisationof internet gaming sites located in other countries is forbidden.

If the Director considers that the advertising is inappropriate, he may order its discontinuance or amendment. The Director shall notify the administrator/operator in writing and the administrator/operator shall immediately comply with the order of the Director.

The failure to conduct advertising and public relations activities with decency, dignity, good taste and honesty, and without being offensive or against the good image, shall be considered an inappropriate operational method.

7.   SOCIAL GAMING

7.1   We believe this to be a growing area. Please decide under what criteria social gaming is permitted in your jurisdiction. If games are free to play or if there is no prize, are they legal without a licence? Please address circumstances where virtual currency is used and can be won: ie currency which is of no monetary or other value, save for as credits to take part in games. The answer should address the question whether game credits or virtual money can be exchanged for other prizes. Is any change to regulation in the area proposed or envisaged?

Social gaming is allowed as a private activity, without publicity, bets or prizes. The Gaming Control Board needs to draw up the rules for social gaming to bring this activity up to the level of other countries.

Romania

Nestor Nestor Diculescu Kingston Petersen
Ana-Maria Baciu, Oana Albu & Lucian Barbu

1. OBJECTIVES AND STRUCTURE OF LEGISLATION

With a real need to have the expanding gambling market regulated through
more elaborated legislation and with authorities beginning to see this
sector as an important source of revenue to the state budget, Romania,
having discussed the subject for many years, managed to replace its former
gambling legislation dating back to 1998 with the adoption in 2009, of
Government Emergency Ordinance No. 77 regarding the organisation and
exploitation of gambling activities (EGO 77/2009) and Government Decision
No. 870 for the approval of the methodological norms for the application of
EGO 77/2009 (GD 870/2009).

Upon its issuance, the new regulatory framework was declared to be
focused on protecting minors and preventing their access to gambling,
preventing fraud, money laundering and financing of terrorist actions, and
ensuring the integrity and transparency of gambling activities, as well as a
constantly supervised fair gaming system.

However, while the purpose of the new legislation was reflecting the
technological and conceptual developments in this sector and at the same
time significantly increase the fees for organising and exploiting gambling
activities in Romania, which had remained unchanged since 2000, the 2009
regulatory framework seemed to run counter to the consumers' demand
with respect to remote gambling, which was deemed illegal and qualified as
a criminal offence.

Nevertheless, since 2009, the gambling legal framework has suffered
several important amendments and, as of 24 December 2010, Romania has
opened its doors to online gambling operators, reflecting the market reality.
Unfortunately, until now, this has only remained valid as pure theory.

Thus, while currently the same legislation applies to both land-based and
online gambling, in the past, the online gambling market was practically
closed. First, the secondary regulations specific for the licensing operation
of online gambling in Romania entered into force at late August 2011, and,
secondly, until the issuance of Emergency Ordinance No. 20/2013, which
established the National Gambling Office, there was no authority to act
as a monitoring and reporting operator for online gaming, as required by
the 2011 legislation. As a direct consequence, lawfully conducted online
gambling is still practically non-existent in Romania, as no operator holds a
licence and authorisation for this activity.

2. FRAMEWORK OF LEGISLATION

2.1 What is the legal definition of gambling and what falls within this definition?

Under Romanian legislation, gambling is defined as the commercial activity that cumulatively fulfils the following conditions: (i) material winnings, usually in money, are granted as a result of the public offer of the organiser of a potential earning and of the acceptance of the offer by the participant, (ii) with the perception of a direct or dissimulated participation cost, (iii) the winnings being attributed through the random selection of the results of the events making the object of the game, irrespective of the way they happen.

2.2 What is the legal definition of online gambling and what falls within this definition?

Romania's legal framework defines online gambling as all gambling activities other than: (i) lotto games and bingo games taking place in game rooms or organised through television network systems and (ii) online betting representing fixed odds betting and bingo games, organised through communication systems such as the internet, or landline or mobile telephony systems, which are carried out by methods other than those which require the physical presence of the gamblers, which are organised and transmitted by communication systems, and for which an organiser of gambling activities has obtained authorisation and a licence.

2.3 Please set out the different gambling products identified by legislation.

The gambling products identified by the Romanian legislation in force are:
- lotto games;
- betting (including sports betting);
- gambling specific to casino activities;
- slot machines games;
- bingo games; and
- online gambling.

2.4 Please list the different requirements for each gambling product, including legal classifications for each; for example, is poker a game of skill or game of chance?

Each gambling product is subject to authorisation and licensing requirements. For details, refer to sections 3.1 and 4.1 below.

Lotto games

Lotto games are qualified as gambling products in the case of using the purely random results of certain events consisting in the draw of numbers, letters, tickets or symbols, irrespective of the procedures and characteristics of the means used for the draws (urns, wheels, cups and other similar means) that are conducted in or without the physical presence of the players. This category includes: lotteries, including instant lotteries, as well as any gambling games that are not carried out in the presence of the players and

consist of number, letter, symbol, form or ticket drawings, by means of
which various winnings can be obtained which are determined by events
that are not carried out in the physical presence of the players except for the
gambling games defined hereinafter.

It should be noted that, under Romania's legal framework currently in
force, lotto games (both offline and online) are under the legal monopoly
of the National Company Loteria Romana (Compania Naţională Loteria
Română, Loteria Romana), which is the sole entity entitled to organise and
exploit such gambling products.

According to the gambling legal framework, the lottery games category
includes, but is not limited to, the following types of games:

- **lottery games with completely random number draws**, including,
  but not limited to, 5/40, 6/49, 3/90, 5/55, 5/45 + 1/20 (JOKER), dream
  number, bingo lotto, keno;
- **lottery games with completely random pre-draws of numbers and/
  or symbols**, including, but not limited to, pull tabs, tear opens, sealed
  lottery tickets, wrapped lottery tickets, scratch cards;
- **lottery games – passive lotteries**, which are based on the completely
  random drawing of tickets, numbers and/or ticket identification data,
  including, but not limited to, Lottery Run; Lottery Present; Winter
  Holidays Lottery; Zodiac Lottery; and
- **video lottery** – a lotto-type game by which winnings are randomly
  obtained; the result of the game is revealed to the player via the video
  lottery terminal, and the dexterity or ability of the player does not have
  any influence/relevance in winning the prize.

Bets
Bets are qualified as gambling products in the case of using the results of
certain events that take place without the organisers being involved. Betting
is a gambling game in which the participant must indicate the results of
certain events that are going to take place or which are randomly generated
by an independent computer system. This category includes:

- **mutual bets**, in which the prize is distributed between the participants
  who are declared to be the winners proportionally to the number of
  winning combinations each of them holds, with the organiser only
  involved in the participation fee collection process and the distribution
  of the prize. Note: as in the case of lottery games, mutual bets (both
  offline and online) are under the legal monopoly of the Loteria Romana,
  which is the solely entity entitled to organise and exploit such gambling
  products; and
- **fixed-odds bets**, carried out in well-defined locations called betting
  agencies in which the organiser, based on its own criteria, establishes
  the stake multiplication quota should the combinations that are
  played be declared to be the winning ones, and communicates it to the
  participants in accordance with the provisions stipulated in the rules
  of the respective games. The amount of each prize is determined by the

rules (a fixed amount or a multiple of the stake), regardless of the total number of stakes.

In addition, **online bets** are defined as the fixed-odds betting activities organised via internet communication systems, as well as landline or mobile telephone systems.

Casino-type gambling games

Casino-type gambling games are qualified as gambling products if events take place using specific means of gambling in the physical presence of the participants, with or without their direct participation. The specific means of gambling used can be cards, dice, roulette balls, roulette and gambling tables, including their auxiliary systems, as well as other means of gambling.

Operators holding a licence and authorisation for casino gambling activities may organise poker tournaments under a regulation approved by the supervisory committee, an entity part of the National Gambling Office.

Note that, prior to the amendments to gambling legislation as of July 2013, poker games could only be played in casinos. Currently, gambling operators may organise and exploit poker games in poker clubs, consisting of establishments dedicated exclusively to the operation of cards games, with a minimum of 10 gambling tables in Bucharest and five gambling tables in locations outside of Bucharest. Moreover, such operators may organise poker tournaments outside the approved premises as long as they notify the gambling regulator, at least 30 days before, about the location where the tournament is to be conducted, the time schedule of the event, the participation cost and the timetable of the tournament.

Slot-machine games

Slot-machine games are qualified as gambling products if the events are organised in the physical presence of the participants via specific machines, equipment and installations, and the winnings depend on luck.

The means of gambling included in the slot-machine games category are specific machines, equipment and installations that, from a constructive point of view, are assembled within a unit by which random elements (based either exclusively on luck or on luck together with the dexterity or ability of the game participants) are generated on an independent basis, without the organiser, their personnel or other persons being involved in any way or by any means in the process of selecting or generating the luck and determining the results of the game.

Economic operators who hold a licence to organise gambling games and operate slot-machine games, on the basis of an authorisation to operate gambling games, can organise jackpot systems by interconnecting the slot-machine games within a location if using mystery gambling systems, or machines of the same type if using progressive gambling systems. However, only slot-machine games belonging to the same economic operator can be interconnected within the jackpot system, and only for the period for which there is a valid authorisation to operate gambling games for these machines. In order to organise a jackpot system, it is necessary to meet all of the following minimum requirements: the same online connecting system for the means of gambling with the same communication protocol, specialised software and a random algorithm for awarding the prize.

Bingo games
Bingo games are classified as follows:
* **bingo games carried out in game rooms**, with winnings generated by random elements, which are organised through the use of complex lottery-type drawing equipment and are characterised by successive drawings and awarding of prizes in the physical presence of the players;

    A bingo game carried out in a gaming room is understood to be a gambling game characterised by successive random number draws and prize awards, using complex lottery-type drawing equipment. The game participants are deemed to be the winners provided that they announce that the game card provided by the organiser in exchange for the participation fee bears the full combination of numbers from those drawn up until that moment, which corresponds to the following successive prizes: line, bingo, accumulated bingo, maximum ball and special prizes from the reserve funds.
* **bingo games organised via television network systems**, with winnings generated by random elements, which are organised through the use of complex lottery-type drawing equipment and are characterised by successive draws and awarding of prizes without the physical presence of the players;
* **bingo games organised via internet communication systems, as well as landline or mobile telephone systems**.

Online gambling
Online gambling is defined as all gambling activities other than: (i) lotto games and bingo games taking place in game rooms or organised through television network systems; and (ii) online betting representing fixed odds betting and bingo games, organised through communication systems such as the internet, or landline or mobile telephony systems, that are carried out by methods other than those which require the physical presence of the gamblers, organised and transmitted by communication systems, and for which an organiser of gambling activities has obtained authorisation and a licence.

2.5 Explain the system of regulation of gambling; which regulatory or governmental body is responsible for the supervision of gambling? Which body issues licences? Which body examines enforcement powers? Is there any limit on the number or duration of available licences?
According to the Romania's gambling legislation in force, the National Gambling Office (the Office), an entity subordinated to the Romanian government, is the regulatory authority for the gambling industry and acts as the licensing authority, as well as the monitoring and reporting operator (MRO), for online gambling industry.

The Office was established in April 2013 as an independent authority in the gambling sector, preserving the rights and duties of the former Gambling Commission within the Ministry of Finance. By creating the new authority, the Romanian government tried to cover the lack of supervision of online gambling, to find a better way to control the accuracy and legality of gambling transactions.

One of the key prerogatives entrusted to the Office by the current legislation in force is to request and receive information from other entities – payment institutions and internet services suppliers – having direct or indirect connections with the gambling industry.

In addition, a supervisory committee (the Committee) has been set up within the Office to grant to gambling operators the licences/authorisations required by law, to issue certificates to operators for the manufacture of various gambling machines (either for their own use or to place them on the market), and to enforce gaming regulations and internal rules applicable to such operators.

For each type of gambling activity that the applicant intends to operate as detailed in section 2.4 above, a licence must be obtained from the Office. The licence is valid for five years, and is subject to the payment of annual fees ranging between approx. EUR 5,500 and EUR 110,000. In addition, an authorisation must be obtain annually and implies payment of fees ranging between approx. EUR 1,800 and EUR 180,000, or, for certain activities, a fee expressed as a percentage of the amounts collected from the respective activity.

The organisers of gambling activities must also create a security fund for each electronic machine, casino gambling table or location, in order to cover risk of non-payment of their financial obligations to the Romanian state. In addition to all of the above, the organisers of a gambling activity must have a subscribed and paid-up share capital ranging between approx. EUR 6,700 and EUR 450,000, depending on the type of activity for which the licence is requested. Furthermore, the current gambling framework imposes a minimum number of game means, locations and technical equipments for which an authorisation may be requested.

3. ONLINE GAMBLING
3.1 To what extent can online gambling be offered in your jurisdiction? Are licences available and, if so, for which gambling products? Please describe briefly the licensing process, who may apply, whether licences are limited in number and, if no licences are available, whether it is legal for online gambling to be offered. In the case of EU jurisdictions, please state whether there are any issues as to the legality of the local law at EU level. Please refer to any relevant cases at ECJ level and explain any measures taken or pending by the European Commission.

Prior to 2009, online gambling could no be lawfully offered in our jurisdiction as there was no legislation covering such activities. Moreover, starting with 2009, the Romanian gambling legislation qualified as criminal offence organisation of online gambling. The first draft of 2009 gambling legislation was late notified to the European Commission which issued a detailed opinion against it but Romania ignored it and went on, as the respective legal deed was already in force. Further, the second proposed draft legislation allowing online gambling to take place in our country had been notified by Romania to the European Commission on July 2, 2010. While the standstill period was to expire on October 4, 2010, EC issued a detailed opinion against the second draft legislation, which extended the standstill period until November 4, 2010. Consequently, as of December 2010, online gambling was allowed to take place in the country, but only in theory.

From the very beginning, the legislation opening Romania's doors to online gambling operators encountered several issues as to the legality of the local law at EU level, but mostly because licences for gambling were (and still are) available only to operators established in Romania.

Furthermore, even if the EC's opinion was based on the fact that the Romanian online gambling draft of legislation was creating obstacles to the free movement of services and/or the freedom of establishment of service operators within the internal market, and despite the repeated signals received so far from the European Commission that the Europe does not agree to Member States imposing disproportionate restrictions on foreign operators, Romania went ahead and implemented the second draft gambling legislation anyway.

Currently, the following online activities are regulated in Romania:
- bingo games organised through communications systems such as internet, landline or mobile telephony systems;
- online betting representing the fixed odds betting activity, organised through communications system such as internet, landline or mobile telephony systems;
- online gambling representing all the gambling activities, other that lotto games and bingo games taking place in game rooms or organised through television network systems and the gambling activities mentioned under items (a) and (b) above, that are carried out by methods other than those which require the physical presence of the gamblers, organised and transmitted by communication systems and for which an organiser of gambling activities has obtained authorisation and a licence.

Note should be made that Poker game is not regulated as a separate gambling product in Romania.

Moreover, lotto games and mutual betting, both offline and online, are placed under the legal monopoly of Loteria Romana.

For the moment, betting exchange is kept outside the Romanian online gambling market.

The authorisation to operate online gambling games shall be valid for 1 year from its date of issue, for the entire activity involving their organisation, carrying out and operation, and for all technical equipment used for this purpose. The licence for organising online gambling shall be valid for 5 years, subject to payments of annual fees.

An economic operator applying for a licence and authorisation to organise online gambling games must meet the following general requirements:

- the economic operator must be set up as a Romanian legal entity in accordance with the law, with 'gambling and betting' activities as its main object of activity and the share capital subscribed and paid-in to the amount stipulated by the law (despite the EC's opinion that such creates obstacles to the free movement of services and/or the freedom of establishment of service operators within the internal market);
- an economic operator which, directly or through a shareholder/partner, holds a licence to organise and an authorisation to operate gambling games characteristic to casinos with at least 20 authorised game tables, slot-machine games for a minimum 500 game stations, fixed-odds betting games with a minimum 100 agencies or bingo games organised via television network systems, can apply to be licensed and authorised as an organiser of the gambling games (it seems that such requirement was introduced in our legislation in furtherance to the lobby of certain influential land-based operators, which were trying to close the market);
- to own the means of gambling and technical equipment that provide the support for organising, operating, and broadcasting gambling games;
- to have specialised personnel trained and experienced in the field of information technology;
- to register as a personal data operator at the National Supervisory Authority for Personal Data Processing;
- to conclude a monitoring contract with a monitoring and reporting operator (MRO) authorised in accordance with the law; (in practice, a MRO never existed, effectively meaning that online gambling has been impossible to carry out legally);
- all their technical equipment that provides the support for organising and broadcasting these types of gambling games must be located in Romania. However, economic operators who are authorised for this field in a Member State of the European Union and have the technical equipment needed for operation in a Member State of the EU are exempt from this provision.

The applicant shall have a subscribed and paid-up share capital of approx. EUR 110,000 for bingo games organised through internet communication systems fixed on mobile telephony systems and of approx. EUR 225,000 for online betting or for online gambling.

Further, the organisers of online gambling activities must pay the annual fees for licences due for the newly gambling activities as it follows: (i)for bingo games organised through internet communication systems or landline or mobile telephony systems or for on-line betting – approx. EUR 22,500; (ii) for online gambling – approx. EUR 90,000.

In addition, the annual fees related to the authorisation to exploit gambling activities must be paid as follows: (i)for bingo games organised through internet communication systems, landline or mobile telephony systems – 10 per cent of the amounts collected by the organiser, but no less than RON 400,000 (approx. EUR 90,000); (ii)for on-line betting — 5 per cent of the amounts collected by the organiser, but no less than RON 250,000 (approx. EUR 56,000); (iii)for online gambling – 1.5 per cent of the amounts collected by the organiser, but no less than RON 400,000 (approx. EUR 90,000).

On top of that, the organisers of online gambling activities must create a security fund (either in cash, or by providing a bank guarantee letter) until the date of submission of the documentation to cover the risk of non-observance of their payment obligations towards the state budget.

Note should be made that while the authorities decided – most probably following the intervention of the European Commission – to uniform the annual licence and authorisation fees to be paid for online gambling with the already existing ones for offline activities, as well as the minimum subscribed and paid-up share capital, not the same principle appears to apply to the security fund to be created in order to cover the risk of non-payment of the operator's financial obligations to the Romanian State.

Currently, the amount of the security fund that must be created by the organiser of the on-line gambling activities is of approx. EUR 225,000 for gambling activities such as online bets and online gambling activities organised by means of communication systems such as internet, landline or mobile telephony systems and of approx. EUR 135,000 for bingo games organised by means of communication systems such as internet, landline or mobile telephony systems.

3.2 Is there a distinction between the law applicable to B2B operations and that applicable to B2C operations?

The same legal provisions apply to B2B and B2C operations carried out in Romania.

3.3 What are the consequences for B2C or B2B operators who are active in your jurisdiction without having obtained or applied for the required permits, licences and approvals? What penalties and enforcement powers are available in respect of the illegal operators? Please outline any significant domestic decisions or enforcement actions that have been taken by the relevant authorities in recent years.

According to the Romanian gambling legislation in force, the deed committed by the administrator, director or any other legal representative of a legal entity (or even by a natural person) of carrying out any of the activities in the gambling sector without a licence or authorisation is considered a criminal offense and is punished with a one month to one year prison sentence or criminal fine. Moreover, the sanction applied to a legal entity for committing such criminal is a fine ranging between approx. EUR 2,250 to 22,500 and the additional sanction of dissolving the legal entity.

In addition, marketing, advertising, publicity or other promotional activities regarding online gambling or related activities, not authorised in Romania, are qualified as minor offence and sanctioned with an administrative fine ranging from approx. EUR 11,200 to EUR 22,500. Under the same sanction, gambling legislation expressly forbids the promotion, through permitted online gambling activities, of any services, means or activities that are forbidden, or are not regulated by the Romanian legislation. In the latter situation, the authority may also revoke the license granted for the organisation of the respective activity.

Also, gambling law in force expressly provides the prohibition of natural persons to participate from Romania to online gambling activities not authorised on the Romanian territory. Such act is qualified as criminal offence and sanctioned with imprisonment for a period of six months to two years or criminal fine.

To the best of our knowledge, no significant domestic decisions have been taken by the relevant authorities in recent years. However, note should be made that the first sanction for TV advertising was imposed in November 2013, with respect to two ads for online poker. Thus, the National Gambling Office has sent a report to the National Audiovisual Council together with a letter stating that it has not yet issued any licenses for online gambling, and therefore, online operators were promoting gambling activities which are not authorised in Romania. Following such, the Board members of the National Audiovisual Council found that the respective ads were broadcast in violation of the Romanian Code of Regulation for the Audiovisual Content in what concerns the provisions for protection of minors and as well of the legal provisions according to which *'gambling services may be broadcast in an audiovisual program or may be subject of an audiovisual commercial communication only if they have been authorised under the terms of the Law'* and thus, forbade them.

From our view, this is a first sign that the recently established gambling regulator intends to improve coordination, cooperation and information exchanging between institutions and ensure a better coordination and management of surveillance and control in the field of gambling.

3.4 What technical measures are in place (if any) to protect consumers from unlicensed operators, such as ISP blocking and payment blocking?

In order to protect consumers from unlicensed operators, the National Gambling Office in its capacity of monitoring and reporting operator for online sector has the responsibility and obligation to identify the websites that enable access to online gambling games which do not hold a licence to organise/an authorisation to operate gambling games in accordance with the Romanian legislation.

Moreover, the Office shall identify the websites used for carrying out marketing, advertising, and publicity activities or any other promotional activities relating to the online gambling games, or activities and services related to these, which are not authorised in accordance with the Romanian legislation.

In such cases, the Office shall immediately communicate all information regarding any unauthorised activities identified to the Internet providers, so that access to these websites can be blocked, and in addition shall also communicate the information about these unauthorised websites to payment institutions and services so that any payments to and from these unauthorised websites can be blocked.

In practice, the National Gambling Office has already begun sending letters to the Internet service providers, in order to help detect and further stop the infringements of the Romanian gambling legislation with respect to on-line gambling.

By such letters, the Internet Service Providers have been requested (i) to take all necessary measures in order to block the access to illegal online gambling websites available for players located in Romania and (ii) to provide information related to: total number of distinct IP addresses accessed from the Romanian territory, details regarding such IP holders, the registration date of the users, how many times they accessed the listed websites and other data of interest (IP domain name for gaming website, domain name holder, website owner, server location, country etc (to the best of our knowledge, such action was carried out for 22 considered websites). However, the ISPs informed the National Gambling Office that they are not able to provide such information, as they do not have access to this data.

3.5 Has the legal status of online gambling changed significantly in recent years, and if so how?

The legal status of online gambling has changed significantly in recent years given that, in 2009, the Romanian gambling legislation qualified as criminal offence organisation of gambling activities through the Internet or Intranet communication systems, as well as through other communication systems (landline or mobile telephony) or similar systems, transforming, thus, the already existing *de facto* passive prohibition of online gambling into a regulated active prohibition.

Further, such restriction was removed in theory in 2010 when the Romanian authorities have passed legislation allowing gambling operators to legally offer remote services to customers in Romania, though licences for online gambling were (and still are) available only to operators established in Romania.

Thus, since 2010, Romania has had legal framework regulating online gambling but the legislation did not contain, at that time, any specific conditions related to licensing and operation of online gambling in Romania, being expressly stated that such licensing conditions would be provided through secondary regulations. Such secondary legislation entered into force on 31 August, 2011. Even so, online gambling activity could not be legally conducted ever since as, in practice, there was no person authorised to monitor the activity, effectively meaning that remote gambling has been impossible to carry out legally. The monitoring was supposed to be performed either by an economic operator duly authorised by the then Gambling Commission within the Ministry of Finance to perform such activity or by a state authority to be further established. For a long time, no state authority was empowered to monitor online gambling and no economic operator applied for an authorisation to monitor online gambling.

In March 2013, the Government seemed to have decided that it is finally the time to unblock the online gambling market in Romania, and, as a first step, it issued the Government Emergency Ordinance No. 20/2013 (GEO 20/2013), intended for the creation of the National Gambling Office (the Office). The Office will not only monitor online operators but also issue authorisation for remote operators wishing to provide their services to Romania. Still, in practice, no improvement of the online gambling operator occurred.

The authority is not entitled to conduct the monitoring agreements that are required in order for a valid application for licence and authorisation to be filed. Thus, while in theory (again) things seem to look better having been in practice for three years after this activity turned legal, there is still no possibility for such to be lawfully conducted in Romania.

3.6 Whilst acknowledging the inherent difficulty in predicting developments in gambling law, what are the likely developments in online gambling in your jurisdiction, both short term and long term? Are any specific amendments under consideration? Have there been any recent political developments, or do you envisage any in the near future? Are any specific amendments under consideration? Are they likely to be adopted and, if so, what is the time scale?

According to some recent legislatives proposal now under debate, it seems that the authorities are currently discussing important changes of the legislation in force, so that the major online gambling organisers to be willing (and able) to enter a market that they (or at least some of them) constantly refused to unlawfully target.

In December 2013, after the circulation of several unofficial versions, a legislative proposal was published on the Ministry of Public Finance website. Subsequently, the legislative proposal on gambling was retracted, most likely because the notifying proceedings to EC were not meet.

What the new legislation announces to bring, is the removal of the land-based requirement (allowing the operators established in EU countries to carry out gambling activities in Romania, this time without being required to establish a legal entity headquartered in Romania), amendments to the tax models and level of taxes, and also the revision of the rules regarding tax on winnings, which under current legislation should be withheld by the organisers, on the basis of daily winnings.

Moreover, it is expected to regulate new activities or new products for Romanian gambling market such as (i) land-based and online betting exchange, (ii) online casino-type games (iii) poker games carried out in poker clubs and (iv)temporary gambling activities carried out in resorts.

In addition, it is expected for mutual betting activities, both online and land-based, to be exiting the monopoly of Loteria Romana in order to allow the economic operators to organise such activities.

Moreover, the operators carrying out unauthorised online gambling activities shall be literally blacklisted, along with their unlawfully websites.

With regards to taxation requirements, it appears that in the near future the gambling legislation will be amended and the authorisation fee will be established at 16-17 per cent of the organiser's gross gaming revenue.

In addition, a new vice tax will be introduced for specific types of gambling activities, such as 2 per cent of winnings in case of land-based betting. The vice tax will normally be borne by the players. Concurrently, it appears the income tax on players' gains in case of on-line gambling will be abolished, except for lottery and bingo winners which will continue to be taxed 25 per cent of any amount exceeding RON 600 (approx. EUR 135).

Unfortunately, in case the above mentioned legislative proposal will be adopted in its current form, the new legislation to come will not suffice to unblock online gambling in Romania. The reason is that the legislative proposals provides that the verification and reporting functions will still be outsourced to companies to be licensed by the National Gambling Office, thus ignoring previous attempt of the Romanian government to outsource monitoring of the gambling market under the existing gambling legislation which has contributed to the legislation not being successful.

Also, another legislative proposal for amending the gambling legislation is aimed at fighting against gambling addiction by forbidding the gambling operators to place their slot-machine games in cinemas, theatre halls, sports halls, art halls and the like (such placing is currently permitted). Moreover, the draft provides that it shall be expressly prohibited for the National Lottery to organise and operate slot-machines games at all. In our view, this last proposal has low chances of being passed through the legislative body in Romania.

3.7 Is the law the same in relation to mobile gambling and interactive gambling on television? If not, are there any headline differences?

The only gambling product in Romania that may currently be lawfully organised via television network systems is bingo. And while lotto games, mutual bets and bingo games organised via Internet communication systems, as well as landline or mobile telephone systems were forbidden until December 2010 but allowed ever since (at least, in theory), the history of TV bingo is more restless.

Thus, for the whole period between 1992 and 2002, TV bingo was a legal activity. In 2002, TV bingo was banned by government decision. This ban lasted until June 2009, when the EGO 77/2009 came into force. In 2012 the Romanian Government prohibited again bingo games organised through television network systems. All until now, when the Government used GEO No. 20/2013 as an instrument to amend the existing gambling legislation and make TV bingo legal once again.

Besides the technical aspects that differentiate mobile gambling from interactive gambling on television, another distinguishing side of mobile gambling and interactive gambling on television is a financial one, proving than Bingo TV is more expensive for organisers. For example, while an applicant for mobile bingo games shall have a subscribed and paid-up share capital of approx. EUR 112,000, an applicant for TV bingo games must double that. Moreover, the annual fees due for the newly gambling activities for TV bingo are three times higher than the annual fees for mobile bingo.

4. LAND-BASED GAMING
4.1 Please describe the licensing regime (if any) for land-based gaming, and what products are included. Please set out what licences are available, and the licensing regime for them.
According to the current legal framework, the licensing regime for land-based gaming covers the following products: lotto games, bets, casino-type gambling games, bingo games carried out in gaming halls, slot-machine games and poker games in poker clubs.

In order to apply for a gambling license, the economic operator must meet the legal and financial requirements related to: (i) licensing (ii) authorisation (iii) share capital and (iv) security fund.

Licensing
In order to obtain the licence to organise gambling games, the applicant economic operators are obliged to meet the specific requirements with respect to the minimum number of means of gambling (eg for slot-machine games, the minimum number of means of gambling that can be operated by the same economic operator is 50 machines, which can be used within the same location or in different locations), location (eg for the betting activity, the minimum number of locations in which the activity can be carried out by the same economic operator is 15) or technical equipment for which an authorisation can be requested.

In case an economic operator intends to organise two or more activities of those stipulated above (except for lotto games and mutual bets), such is obliged to apply for a licence to organise gambling games for each individual activity.

Note should be made that out of permitted gambling activities, lotto games and mutual betting (both land-based and online) are placed under the legal monopoly of Loteria Romana, which shall be issued a licence and an authorisation by the effect of the law, provided that it pays the fees for obtaining the licences to organise gambling games or authorisations to operate gambling games.

The licensing fee is a fixed fee payable annually for obtaining/maintaining the gambling license, and ranges between approx. EUR 5,600 for slot machine games and approx. EUR 112,000 for land-based lottery.

Authorisation

The organisers of land base gambling activities must pay the annual fees related to the authorisation to exploit gambling activities. The authorisation fee is payable annually for obtaining/maintaining the gambling authorisation, and is generally established as a fixed fee (eg: approx. EUR 180,000 for lotto games, approx. EUR 1,800 for each slot machine) or as a percentage of the amount cashed by gambling organisers from players (eg: 5 per cent of the amounts collected by the organiser, but no less than approx. EUR 56,000 for fixed-odds bets)

In what concerns the activities specific to poker clubs, the fee for authorisation to exploit such gambling activities shall be paid not annually but monthly, as it follows: approx. EUR 5,600 for each poker club in Bucharest and approx. EUR 1,800 for each poker clubs in locations other than Bucharest.

The Authorisation to operate gambling games shall be valid for 1 year from its date of issue, as follows:
- for lotto games: for the entire activity that involves drawing numbers, letters, tickets or symbols, regardless of the procedures or characteristics of the means used to carry out the drawings (urns, wheels, cups and other similar means) which are not carried out in the presence of the players;
- for bets (mutual bets or fixed-odds bets): for the basic means of gambling used to ensure the unified organisation and operation of each individual activity at the organiser level;
- for casino-type gambling games/activities specific to poker clubs: each organiser is granted a single authorisation to operate gambling games for the location where these activities are organised and carried out;
- for bingo games carried out in gaming halls: for each location where these activities are organised and carried out; and
- for slot-machine games: for each means of gambling.

Share capital

In what concerns share capital of the organisers of land-based gambling activity applying for a gambling license, such applicant shall have a subscribed and paid-up share capital of:
- approx. EUR 450,000 for lotto games;
- approx. EUR 225,000 for mutual bets, fixed-odds bets, casino-type gambling games;
- approx. EUR 22,500 for bingo games carried out in gaming halls;
- approx. EUR 6,700 for slot-machine games; and
- approx. EUR 11,000 for poker clubs.

Security fund

Furthermore, the organisers of land-based gambling activities must create a security fund (either in cash, or by providing a bank guarantee letter) until the date of submission of the documentation to cover the risk of non-observance of their payment obligations towards the state budget.

Currently, the amount of the security fund that must be created by the organiser of land-based gambling activities is:

- approx. EUR 62,5 for each electronic prize-winning machine or station, as applicable, that is owned by the organiser, or approx. EUR 125 for each electronic prize-winning machine or station, as applicable, held by the organiser in any other way, as applicable, but not more than approx. EUR 62,500 for a single organiser;
- approx. EUR 12,500 for each gambling table inside a casino, but not more than RON approx. EUR 18,750 for a single organiser;
- approx. EUR 5,000 for each hall where bingo games are organised, but not more than approx. EUR 6,250 for a single organiser;
- approx. EUR 6,250 for the activity carried out by an economic operator who organises fixed-odds bets and approx. EUR 125 for each work place (agency) where they are carrying out their activity, but not more than approx. EUR 125,000 for a single organiser; and
- approx. EUR 17,500 for each poker club in Bucharest and approx. EUR 8,750 for each poker club in locations outside of Bucharest, but no more than approx. EUR 26,250.

4.2 Please set out any particular limitations or requirements for (eg casino) operators, such as a ban on local residents gambling.
N/A.

4.3 Please address the questions in 3.5 above, but in relation to land-based gaming.
The 2009 gambling legislation, replacing former gambling legislation dating back to 1998, has brought a significant increase in the authorisation fees and introduced the licensing fees, together with making compulsory the owning of a higher share capital and of some money guarantees (security fund), and has led to more rigorous selection of organisers operating on the gambling market.

Further, the 2013 amendments to the existing gambling legal framework introduced poker clubs, consisting of establishments dedicated exclusively to the operation of cards games, subject to a specific legal regime. The same year, a specific type of gambling game, namely bingo games carried out via television networks, was reintroduced in the legislation. The legal regime of TV bingo has been repeatedly modified since their initial classification as lawful gambling games in 1992. The most recent prohibition of bingo games carried out via television networks had been introduced in August 2012.

5. TAX
5.1 Please summarise briefly the tax regime applicable both to land-based and online gaming.
Gambling activities are generally subject to the following taxes and fees:

Annual licensing fee
This is a fixed fee payable annually for obtaining/maintaining the gambling license, and ranges between RON 25,000 (approx. EUR 5,600) for slot machine games and RON 500,000 (approx. EUR 112,000) for land-based and on-line lottery.

Annual authorisation fee
This is a fee payable annually for obtaining/maintaining the gambling authorisation, and is generally established as a percentage of the amount cashed by gambling organisers from players. Depending on the type of gambling, the percentage ranges between 1.5 and 10 per cent. In some cases, the authorisation fee is established as a fixed fee (eg, in case of casinos or slot machines).

Both the annual licensing fee and the annual authorisation fee need to be paid for being able to operate gambling activities in Romania.

Corporate tax
The general corporate tax rate is 16 per cent, applied to the taxable profit (ie, accounting profit adjusted with non-taxable revenues and non-deductible expenses). Taxpayers carrying out activities in the nature of casinos or sports betting must pay as corporate income tax at least 5 per cent applied on the revenue derived from those activities.

Income tax on players' gains
Gambling revenues derived by players are subject to income tax at 25 per cent. The taxable income is the net revenue calculated as the difference between the gross revenue and the non-taxable amount of RON 600 (approx. EUR 135), obtained from the same gambling organiser in one day. The gambling organiser is liable to compute, withhold and pay the individual income tax to the state budget.

6.   ADVERTISING
6.1   To what extent is the advertising of gambling permitted in your jurisdiction? Again, this should cover both land-based and online gaming. To the extent that advertising is permitted, how is it regulated?
Advertising for all types of gambling is permitted to the extent that such games are legal in Romania. As a practical consequence of the fact that currently no licence and authorisation for online gambling have been issued yet, online gambling sector does not allow marketing, advertising, publicity or any other promotional activities, at least for now.

Special advertising rules are made with respect to organisers of fixed odds, slot machines and bingo games organised in games rooms.

7.   SOCIAL GAMING
7.1   We believe this to be a growing area. Please decide under what criteria social gaming is permitted in your jurisdiction. If games are

free to play or if there is no prize, are they legal without a licence? Please address circumstances where virtual currency is used and can be won: ie currency which is of no monetary or other value, save for as credits to take part in games. The answer should address the question whether game credits or virtual money can be exchanged for other prizes. Is any change to regulation in the area proposed or envisaged?

The Romanian legislation currently in force does not expressly regulate social gaming. However, given Romania's definition of gambling activities, we may say that any game (including social games) that lacks any of the elements falling within the legal definition of gambling, shall not be deemed as gambling and thus, shall be permitted in our jurisdiction without authorisation for such.

Therefore, any social game not involving (i) material winnings or (ii) participation cost or (iii) hazard making the object of the game shall not be regarded as gambling activity.

*Authors' disclaimer: this chapter was written based on the Romanian legislation in effect as of 15 April 2014.

Singapore

Quahe Woo & Palmer LLC
Lawrence Quahe & Yeo Khung Chye

1. OBJECTIVES AND STRUCTURE OF LEGISLATION
How gambling legislation came about
Gambling is a regulated activity in Singapore today. Since Singapore was founded in 1819, gambling has either been legalised or banned, depending on the authorities' prevailing school of thought. The practical versus moral considerations on gambling presented competing priorities – gambling, despite generating revenue for the government, created social problems. Today, the legislative position combines elements of both considerations. The rationale can be gleaned from former Minister for Finance Dr Goh Keng Swee's words at a 1960 Parliamentary debate on the Betting Bill:

'[We are] realists. We do not pretend that ... we shall be able to suppress completely gambling in all forms. The only alternative then is to see that such an activity carries on under controlled and well regulated conditions ... [otherwise] you will merely reduce the administration of the law to ridicule and contempt ...'

This statement should not, however, be construed as the Singapore authorities condoning illegal gambling. In *Poh Soon Kiat v Desert Palace Inc* [2009] SGCA 60, the Court of Appeal discussed Singapore's public policy position on gambling and concluded (at [98]) that:

'Controlled casino gambling may not be contrary to the legal policy of Singapore and also the public policy of this country (in so far as legal policy reflects public policy), but gambling in general, especially unregulated gambling at large and gambling on credit, is, in our view, contrary to Singapore's public policy. This is evident from the retention of s 5 of the CLA in the statute book.'

For a summary of Singapore's legislative development in relation to gambling, please see our response to question 4.3 below.

Basic structure of legislation
Section 5 of the Civil Law Act (Cap 43, 1999 Rev Ed) (CLA) sets out Singapore's general legal position on gambling, providing the general rule that all wagering or gaming contracts are null and void and gambling debts are irrecoverable. This provision does not apply to betting activities that are regulated and hence legal, as shall be discussed below.

In conjunction with the CLA, the Betting Act (Cap 21, 2011 Rev Ed) (BA) and the Common Gaming Houses Act (Cap 49, 1985 Rev Ed) (CGHA) operate to provide a general ban on gambling. The BA primarily deals with betting in relation to 'any horse race or other sporting event', which appears to address more specifically sports-type betting, while the CGHA focuses on betting of 'games of mixed chance and skill', which appears to be linked more to casino-type betting.

Under the BA and CGHA, the Singapore authorities have the power to exempt persons or organisations from the said statutes' prohibitions. Examples of such exempted organisations are the Singapore Totalisator Board (Tote Board), the Tote Board's agent and proprietary club, ie the Singapore Turf Club (Turf Club), and the Tote Board's agent and wholly owned subsidiary – the Singapore Pools (Private) Limited (Pools). The Singapore Totalisator Board Act (Cap 305A, 2012 Rev Ed) (STBA) governs the Tote Board and provides for the making of its bye-laws, which govern these agents in their conduct of betting activities, including games of chance, such as Toto, 4D, sports betting and horse racing.

Another example of an exemption from the BA and CGHA would be ad hoc gambling events that would otherwise be prohibited, such as the Betfair Asian Poker Tour that was held in Singapore in 2006.

Two other statutes are relevant. They are the:
* Private Lotteries Act (Cap 250, 2012 Rev Ed) (PLA);
* Casino Control Act (Cap 33A, 2007 Rev Ed) (CCA).

The PLA regulates lotteries that are conducted for members of a society that is established for purposes not connected with gaming, wagering or lotteries. This covers, for example, slot or jackpot machines in clubhouses, in which the proceeds go towards the club fund.

The CCA regulates the licensing, establishment, management and operation of casinos in Singapore.

Policy objectives

As discussed above, Singapore adopts a general prohibitory approach against gambling, but provides exemptions and licences for certain regulated gambling activities. Such an approach seeks to reconcile the Singapore government's concerns with the social costs of gambling while allowing the state to enjoy the economic benefits of gambling activities. On the former objective, Mr S. Iswaran, the Second Minister for Home Affairs, succinctly explained at the 3rd Singapore Symposium on Casino Regulation and Crime in November 2013 that Singapore imposes *'strict laws on gambling [so as] to maintain law and order and to minimize the potential harm, especially to the young and vulnerable'*, while the latter objective may be gleaned from Singapore's legislative developments in relation to gambling over the last 40 years.

Whether the same legislation applies to land-based and online gambling

The BA and CGHA were enacted in 1960 and 1961, respectively, before the advent of the internet, and do not directly address online gambling. However, these laws may apply to some extent in relation to certain aspects of online gambling.

For example, section 5(3)(a) BA provides that a person who acts as a bookmaker in any place shall be guilty of an offence. In *PP v Kathiresan s/o Thangavelu* [2012] SGDC 361, a man was charged under section 5(3)(a) BA read with section 109 of the Penal Code (Cap 224) for abetting a bookmaker by issuing a user ID and password to an online betting website to a user for betting. He was imprisoned for 5 months and fined $30,000. It would appear, however, that his situation would differ from one in which a user uses his own user ID and password to access the gambling website.

In *PP v Peh Chye Heng* [2009] SGDC 100, a man was convicted under section 4(1)(a) CGHA for operating a cybercafé that provided online casino gaming services to its customers. The court held that the cybercafé fell within the meaning of 'common gaming house' as any member of the public may access to engage in betting activities. This situation may, however, differ from one in which a person bets from the privacy of his own home, where the public would not have access.

In this regard, it is also to be noted the 2010 Report of the Law Reform Committee on Online Gaming and Singapore (the LRC) had observed in 2010 that *'the current legal framework in Singapore adopts a prohibitive stance towards online gambling ... and both [CGHA and BA] contain inadequacies in dealing with certain issues unique to the phenomenon of online gambling'.* Consequently, Mr Iswaran announced in November 2013 that new laws will be introduced to restrict online gambling. These new laws will also accord enforcement powers against providers or facilitators of online gambling services.

Until the new laws are passed, however, it is unclear whether the current legislation will be applied to online gambling.

2. FRAMEWORK OF LEGISLATION

2.1 What is the legal definition of gambling and what falls within this definition?

The Singapore legislation defines terms such as 'gaming', 'game', 'lottery' or 'common betting-house'.

'Gaming' is defined as:

'with its grammatical variations and cognate expressions, means the playing of any game of chance or of mixed chance and skill for money or money's worth' (section 2(1) CGHA); and

'the playing of any game of chance or mixed chance and skill for money or money's worth' (section 2 STBA).

'Game' is defined as:

'a game of chance or a game that is partly a game of chance and partly a game requiring skill' (section 2(1) CCA).

A 'lottery':

'means any game, method, scheme or device whereby money or money's worth is distributed or allotted in any manner depending upon or to be determined by chance or lot, whether the same is held, drawn, exercised or managed either in whole or in part within or outside Singapore' (section 2 PLA).

'includes any game, method, device, scheme or competition whereby money or money's worth is distributed or allotted in any manner depending upon or to be determined by chance or lot' (section 2 STBA).

A 'common betting-house':

'means any place kept or used for betting or wagering on any event or contingency of or relating to any horse-race or other sporting event to which the public or any class of the public has or may have access' (section 2(1) BA).'

2.2 What is the legal definition of online gambling and what falls within this definition?

In Singapore, there is presently no legal definition of online gambling.

2.3 Please set out the different gambling products identified by legislation.

The schedule of N2 (Games of Chance and Skill) of the CGHA sets out the games that shall be regarded as games of chance and skill for the purposes of the CGHA. The schedule lists the following products:

*   pai kowor pan toing;
*   tien kow;
*   tau ngau;
*   chap ji kee panjang;
*   fan tanor thuahn;
*   pohor poh kamor lien poh;
*   pek bin;
*   belankas;
*   mahjong;
*   'roulette';
*   rajah kena;
*   tikam tikam;
*   'three cards' or pa kauor sam cheong or daun tiga;
*   'pair';
*   'poker';
*   'Russian poker';
*   'twenty-one' or yee sap yator ji it tiamor dua pulah satu;
*   main terope;
*   minta daun;
*   'fishing'or ang tiam or tiew yue;
*   'five cards' or tan;
*   si-ki-phuay;
*   see goh lak;
*   ta kai;
*   chong yuen chow;
*   tai sai;
*   hoo, hey, how;
*   soo sikor see sek;
*   chi kee;
*   seong kumor pin kum;
*   luk foo;
*   sap ng hor;

- tung koon; and
- oh peh.

In addition, the Singapore Totalisator Board (Prescribed Lotteries, Betting and Gaming Activities) Regulations 2004 (STBR) sets out the gaming products that may be provided by the Tote Board and its agents. As provided in Regulation 2(a)–(c) these are:

- Singapore Big Sweep Draw;
- Toto Games Draw;
- 4-Digit Numbers Games Draw; and
- Scratchit.

In relation to sports betting, the STBR further identifies the following betting products, addressing betting in connection with:

- any S. League football match in Singapore;
- any other football match in Singapore that is organised, sanctioned in writing or hosted by the Football Association of Singapore; and
- any football match outside Singapore that is organised, sanctioned or hosted by FIFA or its successor.

The gambling products that are available in each of the two casinos in Singapore are approved in separate legislation meant for that specific casino. The Casino Control (Approved Games – Resorts World Sentosa) Order 2011 identifies the following approved products for the casino in Resorts World Sentosa:

- Blackjack (RWS);
- Caribbean Stud Poker (RWS);
- Casino War (RWS);
- Commission Baccarat (RWS) (Version 2);
- Commission Baccarat with Insurance (RWS) (Version 3);
- Commission Baccarat with Super Six (RWS) (Version 2);
- Mini Dice (RWS) (Version 2);
- Money Wheel (RWS);
- Non-Commission Baccarat (RWS) (Version 2);
- Non-Commission Baccarat with Insurance (RWS) (Version 3);
- Non-Commission Baccarat with Super Six (RWS) (Version 2);
- Non-Commission Three Pictures (RWS);
- Pai Gow (RWS);
- Poker (RWS);
- Pontoon (RWS);
- Progressive Texas Hold'em (RWS) (Version 2);
- Roulette (RWS);
- Tai Sai (RWS) (Version 2); and
- Three Card Poker (RWS);

The Casino Control (Approved Games – Marina Bay Sands) Order 2011 identifies the following approved products, some of which replicate the abovementioned products, for the casino in Marina Bay Sands:

- 7 Up Baccarat (MBS) (Version 2);
- Baccarat (MBS) (Version 2);
- Blackjack (MBS) (Version 2);

- Blackjack Lucky 8 (MBS);
- Double Zero Roulette (MBS);
- Let it Ride (MBS) (Version 2);
- Money Wheel (MBS);
- No Commission Baccarat (MBS);
- Pontoon (MBS) (Version 2);
- Pontoon Pandemonium (MBS);
- Power Baccarat 98 (MBS) (Version 2);
- Roulette (MBS);
- Roulette Complete Bet (MBS);
- Roulette with Racetrack (MBS);
- Sic Bo (MBS) (Version 2);
- Singapore Stud Poker (MBS) (Version 2);
- Texas Hold'em Bonus Progressive (MBS) (Version 3);
- Three Card Poker (MBS) (Version 2); and
- Three Pictures (MBS) (Version 2).

2.4 Please list the different requirements for each gambling product, including legal classifications for each; for example, is poker a game of skill or game of chance?

Please refer to our responses to questions 2.1 and 2.3. Under Singapore law, the above gambling products are considered games of chance or games of mixed skill and chance.

2.5 Explain the system of regulation of gambling; which regulatory or governmental body is responsible for the supervision of gambling? Which body issues licences? Which body examines enforcement powers? Is there any limit on the number or duration of available licences?

In general, gambling activities in Singapore are supervised by different regulatory bodies.

In relation to illegal gambling, the Singapore Police Force (SPF) is the main body responsible for its supervision. For example, section 8 CGHA provides powers for police officers to arrest any person found gaming in a public place without a proper warrant. Police officers are also empowered (as provided in sections 13–16 CGHA and sections 11–13 BA) to enter and search premises or persons and conduct arrests. The Ministry of Home Affairs is also involved as the body that has the authority, as provided in section 24(1) CGHA and section 22(1) BA, to exempt any person or organisation from the provisions of the BA and CGHA that prohibit gambling.

In relation to Pools and Turf Club, the Tote Board, which is a statutory board under the purview of the Ministry of Finance, is the main body responsible for their supervision. Section 4 STBA provides for the Minister of Finance to issue or approve rules in relation to the operation or conduct of any totalisator, lottery, betting or gaming activity that is established or conducted by the Tote Board.

For private lotteries, the relevant bodies, as prescribed in the PLA, are the Ministry for Home Affairs and the Ministry of Finance. The former is responsible, as provided for in section 4(1) PLA, for appointing the permit officer who decides whether a permit application for a private lottery may be granted. The latter is responsible, pursuant to section 5(1) PLA, for appointing a commissioner to oversee matters in relation to betting duties.

For casinos, the relevant bodies that supervise gambling are the Casino Regulatory Authority (CRA) and law enforcement agencies (as provided for in section 186(1) CCA) such as the SPF, the Central Narcotics Bureau and the Corrupt Practices Investigation Bureau. The CRA licenses and regulates the operation of casinos in Singapore. At present, it is statutorily provided that only a maximum of two licences (each licence to apply to one casino only) may be granted. Section 13(6) CCA provides the authority for the CRA to authorise any person to hold powers of enforcement pursuant to section 181 CCA. Section 186 CCA allows the CRA to direct the casino operator to provide it with any manner of information relating to the casino's operations, which can be made available to the law enforcement agencies. Notwithstanding this, the SPF may also prescribe an exclusion order to prohibit a person from entering or remaining on any casino premises.

3. ONLINE GAMBLING

3.1 To what extent can online gambling be offered in your jurisdiction? Are licences available and, if so, for which gambling products? Please describe briefly the licensing process, who may apply, whether licences are limited in number and, if no licences are available, whether it is legal for online gambling to be offered. In the case of EU jurisdictions, please state whether there are any issues as to the legality of the local law at EU level. Please refer to any relevant cases at ECJ level and explain any measures taken or pending by the European Commission.

Please refer to our response in section 1 in relation to online gambling. At present, online gambling cannot be legally offered in Singapore.

3.2 Is there a distinction between the law applicable to B2B operations and that applicable to B2C operations?

At present, whether or not the operations are carried out via B2B or B2C, the illegality of online gambling remains the same. Leaving that aside, however, there are differences in the way Singapore broadcasting laws apply to B2B and B2C operators.

In Singapore, the Media Development Authority (MDA) is a statutory board that promotes and regulates the media sector, primarily through the Broadcasting Act (BCA).

First, the BCA provides that no person may provide any licensable broadcasting service in or from Singapore without a broadcasting licence granted by the MDA. Additionally, the Broadcasting (Class License) Notification 2001 (BCLN) requires that computer online services that are provided by internet content providers (ICPs) or internet service providers

(ISPs) are subject to a class licence. ICPs and ISPs who provide licensable broadcasting services as specified in the BCLN are automatically licensed and subject to the terms of the licence as set out in the BCLN.

The BCA and BCLN cover both B2B and B2C operators, as the BCLN defines an ICP to mean:

'any corporation or groups of individuals (including any association, business, club, company, society, organisation or partnership, whether registrable or incorporated under the laws of Singapore or not) who provides any program on the World Wide Web through the Internet, and includes any web publisher and any web server administrator.'

Both B2B and B2C operators would therefore fall foul of the BCLN as its licensing terms require that licensees *'ensure that its service is not used for, or in furtherance of games and lotteries, the conduct of which is an offence under the CGHA'.*

It appears that differences in application would, however, arise in relation to the BCA's powers against foreign broadcasting services. As against B2C operators, these regulations would apply directly against them, as they would have a website presence in Singapore. However, as against B2B operators, the regulations would likely apply only to the third party (through which the gambling operator operates through), who would be the licensee.

3.3 What are the consequences for B2C or B2B operators who are active in your jurisdiction without having obtained or applied for the required permits, licences and approvals? What penalties and enforcement powers are available in respect of the illegal operators? Please outline any significant domestic decisions or enforcement actions that have been taken by the relevant authorities in recent years.

Please refer to our response in relation to online gambling in section 1.

B2B and B2C operators may face liability under the BCA and BCLN. The terms of the automatic licence require that the B2B and B2C operators ensure that its service is not used for, or in furtherance of, games and lotteries. While the BCLN does not appear to provide for any sanctions that may be applied to such a breach, the operators may, by virtue of section 12 BCA, have their broadcasting licence cancelled or suspended, or be fined.

In relation to solely B2C operators, section 29 BCA allows the MDA to proscribe a foreign broadcasting service if it considers that the content in the broadcasting service is prejudicial to public interest and order or offends against good taste and decency.

To date, we are not aware of any overseas ICPs, including offshore operators, offering online gambling products to Singapore-based players being prosecuted by the Singapore authorities for breaching the BCA or BCLN, though it was reported in 2013 that, since 1996, the MDA had issued two takedown notices for inappropriate gambling-related content which were fully complied with.

3.4 What technical measures are in place (if any) to protect consumers from unlicensed operators, such as ISP blocking and payment blocking?

Internet users are blocked from accessing certain online gambling websites, but these are not foolproof measures against gambling operators. According to a report in the newspaper *The Straits Times* in 2008, the MDA only requires the ISPs to block a specific number of websites. It is likely that the ostensible reason for such an approach is that it is practically impossible to control the internet sphere. In any event, as indicated above, the Second Minister for Home Affairs Mr S. Iswaran has publicly announced that Singapore intends to develop measures against online gambling, including measures such as banning advertisements promoting remote gaming as well as restricting access and payment to gambling websites.

3.5 Has the legal status of online gambling changed significantly in recent years and, if so, how?

Please refer to our response in relation to online gambling in section 1.

3.6 Whilst acknowledging the inherent difficulty in predicting developments in gambling law, what are the likely developments in online gambling in your jurisdiction, both short term and long term? Are any specific amendments under consideration? Have there been any recent political developments, or do you envisage any in the near future? Are any specific amendments under consideration? Are they likely to be adopted and, if so, what is the time scale?

As explained in section 1, the Singapore government has announced that it will introduce new legislation in relation to online gambling. The Singapore government has expressed concerns about the social risks associated with online gambling, but it is to be noted that the estimated online gambling market in Singapore is valued at US$300 million and is expected to grow at 6–7 per cent annually. In view of the trend in which land-based gambling laws have evolved in Singapore and the potentially substantial returns to the Singapore treasury, it appears that the new laws would similarly outlaw online gambling but provide specific exemptions with licensing requirements.

While it is unclear as to what specific amendments will take place, it was announced that the new legislation would generally involve a slew of measures to block advertising on and access to online gambling websites, and payment to online gaming operators. It is further to be noted that the LRC's 2010 report had proposed that any legislative reform:

'(a) *provide clarity on the types of online gambling and ancillary activities that should be addressed by legislation;*

(b) *consider whether to impose criminal sanctions on operators, Internet service providers (intermediaries), the individual gamblers, advertisers and/ or financial intermediaries who are either engaged in or who facilitate the [provision of illegal gambling activities]; and*

(c) *consider whether to extend the enforcement of criminal sanctions against persons that are not domiciled in Singapore and who are engaged in or who facilitate'* the provision of illegal gambling activities in Singapore.

Further, from the end of November 2013 to early January 2014, the Ministry of Home Affairs conducted a public consultation exercise on the proposed legal framework to restrict remote gambling, in which various stakeholders, including community and grassroots organisations, religious and social services groups, industry players and members of the public, provided feedback. The majority of respondents welcomed and supported the Singapore government's move to restrict remote gambling and for the Singapore government to take proactive measures to deal with remote gambling, including the implementation of measures to block access to remote gambling websites and payments to remote gambling operators.

There were, however, mixed views as to whether the Singapore government should allow a limited form of remote gambling through a strictly regulated authorised entity. Those who supported a limited form of remote gambling felt that there was a need for a tightly regulated entity that could divert demand away from illegal and unregulated gambling operators. They cited the Hong Kong model, where the operator was a locally based not-for-profit entity the surpluses of which were channelled to support social and community causes, as a possible model for Singapore to consider. Others called for a complete ban on remote gambling on the basis that existing terrestrial gambling options were sufficient and no new forms of gambling should be allowed in Singapore, given the social impact of gambling.

Until the new laws are enacted, however, it is not clear if any interim measures will be imposed. Mr Iswaran, in response to a parliamentary question on whether interim measures may be imposed till the new laws are enacted, responded to say that *'it is a question not just of the will but also the ability to follow through. But we are looking at it and we will take the necessary steps and if we can do it effectively, then we will also look at some interim measures'*.

3.7 Is the law the same in relation to mobile gambling and interactive gambling on television? If not, are there any headline differences?

At present, there is no specific legislation that addresses mobile gambling and interactive gambling. However, Mr Iswaran, in responding to questions on online gambling at a 2012 parliamentary sitting on the Casino Control (Amendment) Bill, commented that online gambling included *'gambling on social media platforms and mobile devices'*. Accordingly, the Singapore government is aware of this branch of gambling, and it is anticipated that this area may eventually be addressed together with the new law.

4. LAND-BASED GAMING
4.1 Please describe the licensing regime (if any) for land-based gaming, and what products are included. Please set out what licences are available, and the licensing regime for them.

The Singapore licensing regime for land-based gaming may be broadly categorised as follows:
- licensing for lotteries, sweepstakes, football betting, etc;
- licensing for private lotteries; and
- licensing for casino-based gaming.

These licences are granted in respect of the gambling products that were listed in section 1 above.

Licensing for lotteries, sweepstakes, football betting, etc

We have mentioned above that the BA and CGHA set out the general prohibitions against gambling in Singapore. Section 22(1) BA and section 24(1) CGHA allow for the provision of exemptions that allow certain persons or organisations to provide gambling services in Singapore. Pursuant to these provisions, the Minister for Home Affairs subsequently exempted the following from the said Acts' prohibitions:
- Turf Club in respect of betting in connection with horse races and public lotteries; and
- Tote Board and Pools in respect of betting in connection with public lotteries and footballs matches.

In addition to the Tote Board and its agencies, the Minister for Home Affairs can and has also conferred ad hoc exemptions for organised gambling events held in Singapore. For example, the Common Gaming Houses (Exemption) (No. 4) Notification 2006 exempted the organisers of the 2006 Betfair Asian Poker Tour (Singapore) from the CGHA's provisions.

Licensing for private lotteries

Section 7 PLA requires a permit to be granted by a permit officer (as appointed by the Minister for Home Affairs) before a person may promote or conduct a private lottery. *'Additionally, section 8 PLA requires that the application is to be submitted in a specific manner and form required and accompanied by the prescribed fee, as well as any information and documents that may be required.'* The application is to be submitted to the Commissioner of Estate Duties for processing.

For all permits granted, section 9(1) PLA imposes the following conditions:

'(a) no profit shall accrue to any individual person from the conduct of such lottery; and

(b) no commission either in money or money's-worth including by way of free tickets or chances shall be payable in respect of the sales of tickets or chances.'

Section 9(2) PLA provides the permit officer discretion to grant additional conditions that specify:

'(a) the amount and number of the prizes to be offered;

(b) the number of tickets or chances to be offered for sale in such lottery and the prices and denominations of those tickets or chances;

(c) the persons by whom, the manner in which and the places at which, those tickets or chances may be sold or distributed and the persons or classes of persons to whom the tickets or chances may be sold or distributed;

(d) the time, place and manner at or in which the winners of prizes therein will be determined;

(e) the opening and closing dates for the sale or distribution of tickets or chances in such lottery;

(f) the conditions subject to which any ticket or chances may be offered for sale;

(g) the costs, charges and expenses which may be deducted by the person promoting such lottery from the funds raised by the lottery;

(h) the percentage of the gross proceeds raised by the lottery that shall be applied to the object for which such lottery is promoted;

(i) the manner in which the names of the winners of prizes in such lottery shall be advertised; and

(j) requirements in respect of machines and equipment to be used, including fruit machines.'

While the permit officer retains the discretion whether or not to grant a permit, an aggrieved applicant may, pursuant to section 8(6) PLA, appeal within 14 days of being notified to the Minister for Home Affairs, whose decision shall be final. Section 9(4) PLA allows a permit holder to appeal against the above-mentioned additional conditions that may be imposed on him in the same manner.

Successful applicants who apply to operate fruit machines are required by the Private Lotteries (Fees) Regulations 2011 to pay $195 for the permit for the first year, and $33 for every yearly renewal thereafter.

Licensing for casino-based gaming

There are generally two types of licensing in respect of casino-based gambling. The first relates to the establishment of the casino, while the second and third relate to the day-to-day operation of the casino.

First, section 41 CCA restricts the number of casino licences in force to two at any particular time, limiting each casino licence to a single casino. The licence may, as provided by section 54 CCA, be cancelled or surrendered before the duration granted by the licence has run out. The applicant is required by section 44(1) to be the owner of the designated site on which the casino is intended to be located, or a person nominated by the owner.

The licensing regime sets out the factors to be considered in each application, which broadly relates to matters in relation to financial resources, business ability and good reputation. Section 45 CCA requires the applicant to be a 'suitable person' to manage and operate a casino, which considers whether:

'(a) each such person is of good repute, having regard to character, honesty and integrity;

(b) each such person is of sound and stable financial background;

(c) in the case of an applicant that is not a natural person, the applicant has, or has arranged, a satisfactory ownership, trust or corporate structure;

(d) the applicant has or is able to obtain financial resources that are adequate to ensure the financial viability of the proposed casino and the services of persons who have sufficient experience in the management and operation of a casino;

(e) the applicant has sufficient business ability to establish and maintain a successful casino;

(f) any of those persons has any business association with any person, body or association who or which, in the opinion of the Authority, is not of good repute having regard to character, honesty and integrity or has undesirable or unsatisfactory financial resources;

(g) each director, partner, trustee, executive officer and secretary and any other officer or person determined by the Authority to be associated or connected with the ownership, administration or management of the operations or business of the applicant is a suitable person to act in that capacity;

(h) any person proposed to be engaged or appointed to manage or operate the casino is a suitable person to act in that capacity;

(ha) the applicant is a suitable person to develop, maintain and promote the integrated resort (of which the casino is a part) as a compelling tourist destination which meets prevailing market demand and industry standards and contributes to the tourism industry in Singapore; and

(i) any other matter that may be prescribed.'

An evaluation panel will be formed under section 45A CCA, consisting of three or more persons, to assess whether the applicant may suitably ensure that the integrated resort will satisfactorily contribute to the tourism industry in Singapore. Any person who operates a casino without a casino licence is liable to a maximum fine of $200,000 and further fines of up to $20,000 for every day that the offence continues.

Secondly, ancillary licences form part of the licensing regime. Special employees and international market agents are to hold valid licences in order to exercise their functions.

A special employee is one who, pursuant to section 2 CCA:

'(a) is employed or working in a casino in a managerial capacity or who is authorised to make decisions, involving the exercise of his discretion, that regulate the operations of a casino; or

(b) is employed or working in a casino in any capacity relating to any of the following activities:

   (i) the conduct of gaming;
   (ii) the movement of money or chips about the casino premises;
   (iii) the exchange of money or chips to patrons of the casino;
   (iv) the counting of money or chips on the casino premises;
   (v) the security and surveillance of the casino;
   (vi) the operation, maintenance, construction or repair of gaming equipment;
   (vii) the supervision of any of the above activities;
   (viii) any other activity relating to the operations of the casino that is specified by the Authority for the purposes of this definition by notice in writing given to the casino operator.'

Special employees are required by virtue of section 80(1) CCA to hold a licence. Any person found in contravention of this requirement is liable, pursuant to section 80(4) CCA, to a maximum fine of $25,000 and a further fine of up to $2,500 per day that the contravention continues after conviction. Any casino operator who employs any person to function as a special employee without a licence shall be liable to disciplinary action as provided for in section 80(5) CCA.

Separately, an international market agent is required by virtue of section 110A CCA to hold a licence. The functions of an international market agent, as provided by section 110A(2) CCA, include generally the organising or conducting of a casino marketing arrangement, in which the agent extends credit to or organises, promotes or facilitates the playing of any casino game by a patron, in consideration of some form of reward.

Any person who contravenes this licence requirement is liable, pursuant to section 110A(5), to a fine from $30,000 to $300,000 and a maximum prison term of four years for the first offence. Subsequent offences are liable to a fine from $30,000 to $300,000 and a maximum prison term of up to seven years. If the casino operator is a party to this offence, it shall be liable to disciplinary action.

4.2 Please set out any particular limitations or requirements for (eg casino) operators, such as a ban on local residents gambling.

In addition to the licensing requirements discussed in section 4.1, there are additional requirements and/or limitations that are imposed on the Tote Board and its agents, private lotteries and casinos.

Section 15 STBA provides that agents and agencies of the Tote Board may provide their services only for persons of at least 18 years old. A quick survey of the bye-laws for clubs or associations suggests that the same age restriction also applies for private lotteries.

There are various restrictions that casinos operators must comply with, including the following:

First, section 116 CCA requires operators to levy a tax on citizens or permanent residents to enter the casino. An amount of $100 is to be charged for every consecutive period of 24 hours or, alternatively, an amount of $2,000 for an annual membership of the casino. The casino operator may not refund or reimburse this entry levy once paid.

Secondly, section 132 CCA provides that persons below 21 years old may not enter the casino premises.

Thirdly, section 108 CCA provides that credit on chips may not be provided to citizens or permanent residents of Singapore unless they are patrons who have a deposit account with the casino operator with a credit balance of at least $100,000 (ie a 'premium player').

Fourthly, section 109 CCA prohibits the casino operator from allowing any automatic teller machine from being provided within the boundaries of the casino premises.

Fifthly, casino operators are restricted in the form of exclusion orders that may be imposed by the following classes of person: the relevant authorities, the patrons and family members. In relation to the first, the following classes are excluded from entering the casino by law, by virtue of section 165A CCA: a person who is on a social assistance programme or subsidy scheme funded by the government, or an undischarged bankrupt. The relevant authorities may also exclude persons with poor credit records or persons who, because of gambling, are determined to be vulnerable to financial harm (section 165(1) CCA). Separately, the Commissioner of Police has the power the power to prescribe a written exclusion order by virtue of section 122(1) CCA. The casino operator must, pursuant to sections 126(1) and 127 CCA, prohibit excluded persons from entering or remaining on the casino premises.

Sixthly, casino operators are required by section 129(1) CCA to take all appropriate steps to ensure that acts such as soliciting for immoral purposes, eg prostitution, unlicensed moneylending, or illegal betting or gaming activities, are not committed within the casino premises.

Lastly, casino operators are required by section 170B CCA to establish and implement a responsible gambling programme that is approved by the relevant authorities. The Casino Control (Responsible Gambling) Regulations 2013 require that the programme covers, among others, the following:

- procedures and guidelines to identify patrons with suspected gambling-related problems;
- procedures and guidelines on availing information or intervention services to any patron on gambling-related problems;
- a system to enable patrons to set limits on gambling expenditure and on visits a patron may make per month;
- training curricula for casino employees in adopting responsible measures in the conduct of gambling; and
- the appointment of people to implement the responsible gambling programme.

As may be observed, the restrictions that apply to the different forms of betting differ in strictness and comprehensiveness. This may presumably be due to, among other reasons, to the notion that one is more susceptible to casino-based gambling than other forms of gambling. This may be set to change. In October 2013, it was announced by the Singapore authorities that the relevant Singapore ministries are reviewing the minimum age for gambling at private jackpot clubs and other gambling venues.

4.3 Please address the questions in 3.5 above, but in relation to land-based gaming.

The legal status of land-based gambling in Singapore is observed to have evolved over the years to permit an expanding range of gambling products. The development of the legal status of the Singapore land-based gambling landscape may be summarised as follows:

- The BA was enacted in 1960 to prevent illegal betting and bookmaking.
- The CGHA was enacted in 1961 to prevent illegal gaming houses and lotteries.

- In 1968, the first state operator, Pools, was established to counter illegal gambling and provided legalised gambling in the form of lottery, 4D and toto games.
- In 1988, the Tote Board was established as a statutory board under the Ministry of Finance, which took over the conduct of totalisators and 4-digit forecast draws from Turf Club. (As mentioned above, the Tote Board today oversees the operations of its agent and proprietary club, Turf Club, and the operations of its agent and wholly owned subsidiary, Pools.)
- In 1999, football betting on Singapore's domestic football league was introduced by Pools.
- In 2002, Pools extended its coverage to include external football games such as the World Cup, the English Premier League and other international matches.
- In 2005, the Singapore government lifted its ban on casinos in Singapore, which paved the way for the construction of two integrated resorts which had casinos.
- In 2006, the CCA was enacted to license and govern the two casinos in Singapore.
- In 2008, in conjunction with Singapore's first Formula One race, Pools further expanded its gambling services to offer betting on Formula One races.

5. TAX
5.1 Please summarise briefly the tax regime applicable to both land-based and online gaming.
We refer to our response to section 1. At present, online gaming is not permitted under Singapore law. As regards land-based gaming, the tax regime broadly addresses the following areas:
- gambling *vis-à-vis* an exempt organisation;
- private lotteries; and
- casino gambling.

Gambling *vis-à-vis* an exempt organisation
The Betting and Sweepstake Duties Act (BSDA) applies to an 'exempt organisation', which means, pursuant to section 2 BSDA:
  'any person or organisation that is exempt from all of the provisions of the Betting Act (Cap. 21) under a notification made under section 22(1) of that Act, or from all of the provisions of the Common Gaming Houses Act (Cap. 49) under a notification made under section 24(1) of that Act.'

As explained above in section 1, the Tote Board and its agents, Pools and Turf Club, are exempted organisations. The BSDA therefore applies to these organisations, as required by section 12(1)(a) STBA. Sections 3 and 4 BSDA are relevant, charging duties for:
- any betting on a totalisator;
- sweepstakes; and

- betting at fixed odds on any football game or sporting event where betting is promoted in Singapore.

The tax rates are set out in the Betting and Sweepstake Duties Act (Cap 22, Sections 3, 4 and 6) Betting and Sweepstake Duties Order (BSDO). They are set out as follows:

BSDO	Betting activity	Tax rate	Organisation liable
Order 2(1)	Betting on a totalisator, pari-mutuel or in any other system	25 per cent* of every bet	Tote Board; Singapore Pools
Order 2(2)	Betting on a totalisator in connection with any horse race	25 per cent of gross betting profit	Tote Board; Singapore Turf Club
Order 3(1)	Sweepstake	30 per cent of amount contributed to sweepstake	Tote Board
Order 4(1)	Betting at fixed odds on any football game or sporting event promoted in Singapore	25 per cent of gross betting profit	Tote Board; Singapore Pools

*The government has announced that the betting duty rates in relation to the totalisator, pari-mutuel and any other system will be increased from 25 to 30 per cent from 1 July 2014.

In addition to the above, the Entertainments Duty Act applies by virtue of section 14(1) STBA, which requires Turf Club to pay a duty when an admission fee is charged.

Private lotteries

The PLA sets out the tax obligations in relation to private lotteries, but, as provided for by section 3(1) PLA, to the exclusion of any bets that are already subject to the BSDA. This means that any bet made in relation to a lottery via the Tote Board or its agents is not subject to taxation under the PLA.

The promoter of the private lottery is liable to pay this tax, by virtue of section 16(1) PLA. The promoter, as defined in section 2 PLA:

'in the case of a lottery promoted by a society, means the individual who, the secretary (or similar official) of the society who, promotes the lottery, and in the case of a lottery promoted, held, drawn or managed outside Singapore, the principal official of the local or affiliated branch or section of the society.'

The taxes imposed are set out in section 15(1) PLA. There are two categories of taxes. The first relates to private lotteries not conducted using a fruit machine. The promoter will be charged a duty of 30 per cent on the total amount raised from any such private lottery. The second relates to private lotteries conducted using fruit machines. The promoter will be charged a duty of 9.5 per cent on the total amount wagered by players of each fruit machine, without deduction of any winnings that might have been paid out.

The penalty for late payment is provided for in section 15(7) PLA, in which the promoter is liable to pay a penalty of 5 per cent of the unpaid duty. In the event that this duty is not paid within the following seven days, a further penalty of 5 per cent of the unpaid duty shall be added.

Casino gambling
Part IX of the CCA governs the casino operator's tax obligations. Section 146 CCA provides that a casino operator is to pay a casino tax amounting to 5 per cent of the monthly gross gaming revenue from premium players and 15 per cent of the monthly gross gaming revenue from any other player. (See section 4.2 for the definition of a 'premium player'.)

The penalties applicable for late payment are provided for in section 147 CCA. A penalty of 5 per cent of the amount of casino tax payable shall be added. In the event that this duty is not paid in the next calendar month, an additional penalty of 5 per cent of the outstanding tax shall be payable for each completed month that the tax remains unpaid, subject to a total additional penalty cap of 50 per cent of the amount of casino tax outstanding.

6. ADVERTISING
6.1 To what extent is the advertising of gambling permitted in your jurisdiction? Again, this should cover both land-based and online gaming. To the extent that advertising is permitted, how is it regulated?
We refer to our response in relation to online gambling in section 1. As regards Singapore land-based gaming, the advertising regime may be categorised into two broad categories – unregulated gambling and regulated gambling activities. In relation to unregulated gambling activities, the BA and CGHA govern the prohibitions on their advertising. In relation to regulated gambling activities, they may be categorised as follows: gambling *vis-à-vis* Tote Board and/or its agents; private lotteries; and casino gambling.

Unregulated gambling activities
The BA and the CGHA prohibit the advertisement of unregulated gambling activities. The applicable provisions are set out as follows:

Section 3(1)(e) BA provides that any person who:

'announces, exhibits or publishes, or causes to be announced, exhibited or published, either orally or by means of any letter, circular, telegram, placard, handbill, card, print, writing, design, sign, advertisement or otherwise that a place is opened, kept or used as a common betting-house or betting information centre in Singapore or elsewhere, or in any other manner invites or solicits any person to commit a breach of any of the provisions of this Act, shall be guilty of an offence and shall be liable on conviction to a fine of not less than $20,000 and not more than $200,000 and shall also be punished with imprisonment for a term not exceeding 5 years.'

Section 4(1)(d) CGHA provides that any person who:

'announces or publishes or causes to be announced or published, either orally or by means of any print, writing, design, sign or otherwise, that any place is opened, kept or used as a common gaming house, or in any other manner invites or solicits any person to commit a breach of section 7, 8 or 9 [ie gaming in a common gaming house, gaming in public, or buying a ticket] ... shall be guilty of an offence and shall be liable on conviction to a fine of not less than $5,000 and not more than $50,000 and shall also be punished with imprisonment for a term not exceeding 3 years.'

Gambling *vis-à-vis* Tote Board and/or its agents

Section 21 STBA empowers the Singapore authorities to make regulations in relation to advertising of any betting activity by the Tote Board and its agents. These regulations are found in the Singapore Totalisator Board (Advertisements) Regulations 2010) (STBAR).

The STBAR addresses 'gaming advertisements', which are defined in Regulation 2 STBAR to mean:

'any advertisement which

a. *expressly or impliedly leads to, induces, urges, promotes or encourages participation in any totalisator, lottery, betting or gaming activity of an operator; or*

b. *being designed to publicise or to promote participation in any totalisator, lottery, betting or gaming activity of an operator, mentions, illustrates or depicts –*

    (i) *any brand name, trade mark or service mark relating to such totalisator, lottery, betting or gaming activity; or*

    (ii) *any pictorial device commonly associated with any such brand name, trade mark or service mark.'*

The following definitions as defined in Regulation 2 are of note, as they define the principal manners in which gaming advertisements are advertised:

'distribute':

'(a) in relation to a printed notice or publication, means deliver or send to any person, or leave on any premises or vehicle; and

(b) in relation to any electronic message, means transmit to any person using electronic mail, short message service (SMS) or any other form of electronic transmission'.

'publish', in relation to a gaming advertisement, means:

'(a) publish the advertisement in a newspaper, magazine, journal, periodical, directory or other printed publication or printed notice or on any object;

(b) disseminate the advertisement by radio, television or other mass medium;

(c) disseminate the advertisement by the public exhibition or broadcast of a photograph, slide, film, video recording, audio recording or other recording of images or sound;

(d) publish or disseminate the advertisement electronically, including (but not limited to) publishing the advertisement on the Internet or in any way that renders it accessible from the Internet;

(e) *publicly exhibit the advertisement in, on, over or under any building, place,*
     vehicle, vessel, train, aircraft or in the air; or
(f) *make known the advertisement to the public or a section thereof in any other*
     manner or by any other means,
but excludes the distribution of the advertisement'.

The STBAR regulates advertising for betting activities carried out by the
Tote Board and its agents in the following broad manners:
*   restriction on time, frequency and duration of gaming advertisements;
*   restriction on contents of gaming advertisements; and
*   restriction on manner of publication or distribution of gaming
    advertisements.

Restriction on time, frequency and duration of gaming advertisements
Regulation 3(1) STBAR restricts gaming advertisements of a new betting
activity from being published or distributed past an initial period
determined by the relevant minister.

In addition, Regulation 3(3)–(4) STBAR provides that all gaming
advertisements may not be published or distributed beyond 60 discrete days,
whether or not consecutive, in any one year.

The above rules do not, however, apply to a gaming advertisement
'published in a newspaper, magazine, journal, periodical directory, or other printed
publication or printed notice or on any object', pursuant to Regulation 3(6)
STBAR.

Restriction on contents of gaming advertisements
Regulation 4 STBAR provides that operators may neither publish, or cause
to be published, nor distribute, or cause to be distributed, restricted gaming
advertisements in Singapore. A 'restricted gaming advertisement' generally
contains content that target vulnerable persons or induce gaming by making
suggestions on the prospects of winning. It is defined in Regulation 4(2), as:
   'one which
(a) *depicts a vulnerable person or person who appears to be a vulnerable person*
     participating in a totalisator, lottery, betting or gaming activity;
(b) *includes any personality, character, animation, music or anything who or*
     which is likely to have a particular appeal to minors;
(c) *depicts a criminal act, violence or other anti-social behaviour;*
(d) *depicts or promotes excessive or reckless participation by any person in a*
     totalisator, lottery, betting or gaming activity;
(e) *suggests that winning a prize will be a definite or likely outcome of*
     participating in a totalisator, lottery, betting or gaming activity;
(f) *offers any form of gambling tip;*
(g) *suggests that a player's skill can influence the outcome of a totalisator, lottery,*
     betting or gaming activity;
(h) *suggests that participating in a totalisator, lottery, betting or gaming activity*
     will improve the financial prospect of a person;
(i) *offers free bets or their equivalent in cash which can be used for participation*
     in a totalisator, lottery, betting or gaming activity;

(j)   exploits the susceptibility of a vulnerable person;
(k)   is false, misleading or deceptive; or
(l)   does not contain, in a clear and conspicuous part of the advertisement, a responsible gambling message.'

Restriction on manner of publication or distribution of gaming advertisements

Regulation 5 STBAR governs the manner in which a gaming advertisement may be published in Singapore. It may be observed that the regulations restrict advertisements from reaching the masses via channels such as newspapers or locations readily viewable or accessible by the public, such as cinema screenings, buildings or transport. Specifically, Regulation 5(1) provides that:

'an operator shall not publish or cause to be published in Singapore a gaming advertisement:

(a)   in any free-to-air broadcasting service within the meaning of the Broadcasting Act (Cap. 28);

(b)   in any cable programme other than one included in a cable channel that is dedicated to participation in a totalisator, lottery, betting or gaming activity of an operator;

(c)   in any printed publication (other than a newspaper) the principal market of which is Singapore and which is principally directed at minors;

(d)   on the front and back pages of a printed newspaper the principal market of which is Singapore or any section of such printed newspaper;

(e)   in any electronic document (including but not limited to an Internet website or webpage) that is principally directed at minors, including making it or causing it to be made accessible in any way from that electronic document;

(f)   in, on, over or under any building, place, vehicle, vessel, train, aircraft or in the air where it is visible or audible to members of the public or any section thereof; or

(g)   in any film, video recording or other recording of images shown in a cinema or theatre in Singapore which the public or any section of the public has access.'

Lastly, Regulation 5(3) provides that a gaming advertisement may be distributed in the form of a printed notice or publication or as an electronic message only if the relevant minister approves it, and if the person who receives it gives prior written consent.

Any person who contravenes the above-mentioned restrictions will, pursuant to section 21(2)(c) STBA, be liable to a fine of up to $5,000 for a first conviction and up to $10,000 for a subsequent one.

Private lotteries

The PLA governs the advertising of private lotteries broadly in two ways. First, section 9(1)(a)–(b) mandates that there shall be no profit accrued to any person from the conduct of such lottery, nor commission made either in money or money's worth in respect of ticket sales. This provision presumably has the effect of constraining participation rates in private lotteries by not encouraging advertising effort that may be increased by incentive of monetary reward.

Secondly, section 9(2) provides for the imposition of discretionary conditions on the grant of the private lottery permit. These conditions generally relate to the manner in which persons may be reached. The relevant conditions are set out as follows:

'*the Permit Officer may, in granting any permit under this Act, impose conditions specifying –*

(a) *...;*

(b) *...;*

(c) *the persons by whom, the manner in which and the places at which, those tickets or chances may be sold or distributed and the persons or classes of persons to whom the tickets or chances may be sold or distributed;*

(d) *...;*

(e) *...;*

(f) *...;*

(g) *the costs, charges and expenses which may be deducted by the person promoting such lottery from the funds raised by the lottery;*

(h) *...;*

(i) *the manner in which the names of the winners of prizes in such lottery shall be advertised; and*

(j) *... .*'

The consequences on contravening any condition of the permit granted is provided by section 21(2)(b), which holds convicted persons liable to a maximum fine of $20,000 and/or a maximum imprisonment term of 12 months.

Casino gambling

Casino operators and licensed international market agents, among others, are subject to section 170A CCA and the Casino Control Act (Cap 33A) Casino Control (Advertising) Regulations 2010 (CCAR), which prohibit advertising or promotional activities relating to a casino. The definitions of 'casino advertisement' and 'casino promotion' are set out as follows:

'*"casino advertisement" means any writing, object, still or moving visual image or message or audible message, or any combination of them, which –*

(a) *contains any express or implied inducement, suggestion or request to visit any casino;*

(b) *expressly or impliedly leads to, induces, urges, promotes or encourages the playing of any game in any casino;*

(c) *being designed to publicise or to promote the casino or the playing of any game in the casino, mentions, illustrates or depicts –*

   (i) *any brand name, trade mark or service mark of a casino;*

   (ii) *any pictorial device commonly associated with any brand name, trade mark or service mark of a casino; or*

   (iii) *any pictorial representation, or any brand name, trade mark or service mark, of a game which may be played or gaming equipment which may be used in a casino; or*

(d) publicises a casino promotion.'
    '"casino promotion" means –
(a) any membership or loyalty programme by which –
    (i)   points, credits or rewards may be earned from the playing of any game in
          a casino; or
    (ii) points, credits or rewards may be redeemed within the casino premises
          (whether for the playing of any game or otherwise);
(b) any contest, lucky draw or tournament in which –
    (i)   a prize may be won directly or indirectly as a result of visiting any casino
          or playing any game in a casino; or
    (ii) a prize may be redeemed on or used for the playing of any game in a
          casino;
(c) the offering of any transportation or other amenity or service which gives
    publicity to, or otherwise promotes or is intended to promote –
    (i)   the visiting of any casino; or
    (ii) the playing of any game in any casino; or
(d) any other activity, programme, service or incentive (other than the winnings
    from a game), or any combination of them, which gives publicity to, or
    otherwise promotes or is intended to promote –
    (i)   the visiting of any casino; or
    (ii) the playing of any game in any casino.'

The advertising regime on casino gambling may be broadly categorised as
follows:
* restrictions on what content may be used for advertisement;
* restrictions on what persons may be subject to advertisement; and
* restrictions on the manner in which advertisements may take place.

Restrictions on what content may be used for advertisement

The CCAR makes a further distinction between 'casino advertisements' and
'limited advertisements'. Limited advertisements, as provided in Regulation
4(3) CCAR, have the characteristics of:
* containing factual information only that is capable of being
  substantiated;
* not containing information on the games available in the casino,
  winnings or testimonials of the winnings of the patrons; and
* not containing any express or implied inducement, suggestion or
  encouragement to play any game in a casino.

Stricter conditions in relation to content are imposed on limited
advertisements than on casino advertisements, but such content may be
placed in other locations. These specific locations are discussed below.

Restrictions on what persons may be subject to advertisement

In relation to casino advertisements and casino promotions, Regulation
4(1A) CCAR provides that publication or distribution may be approved if:
* the printed publication's principal market is not Singapore; and

- in relation to a casino advertisement, that it occurs within the casino premises but is not visible or perceptible to persons outside the casino premises; or
- in relation to a casino promotion, that it is directed primarily at tourists; or
- in relation to a casino promotion, that it occurs within the casino premises even if the points, credits or rewards may be redeemed outside the casino premises.

Limited advertisements may generally be approved, pursuant to Regulations 4(1A) and 4(2) CCAR, if:

- in relation to a casino advertisement, the publication (including where it is accessible from the casino operator's internet website) is not directed primarily at or has particular appeal to persons resident in Singapore; or
- its publication is in the form of a printed notice or printed publication that is directed primarily at or has particular appeal to tourists.

Restrictions on the manner in which advertisements may take place

While casino advertisements may generally be distributed only within the casino premises, limited advertisements may be publicised or distributed outside casino premises but only at locations where tourist traffic is predominant.

Regulation 4(2) CCAR provides that limited advertisements may be approved when they are exhibited on billboards or signboards placed within the premises of Changi Airport, Marina Bay Cruise Centre Singapore, International Passenger Terminal at HarbourFront Centre, or within the premises of a tourist information centre managed or approved by the Singapore Tourism Board. These premises also apply to the distribution of limited advertisements in the form of printed notices or publications, in addition to the premises of a designated tourist attraction or any designated site.

Regulation 4A CCAR separately prohibits the publishing or distributing outside the casino of any information in relation to any winning casino patron or his winnings.

Lastly, Regulation 5 CCAR restricts casino operators, licensed international market agents, etc, from giving interviews or media releases via any channel of print or broadcast media that contains or operates as a casino advertisement.

Contravention of the above regulations attracts a liability of a maximum fine of $10,000.

7. SOCIAL GAMING

7.1 We believe this to be a growing area. Please decide under what criteria social gaming is permitted in your jurisdiction. If games are free to play or if there is no prize, are they legal without a licence? Please address circumstances where virtual currency is used and can be won: ie currency which is of no monetary or other value, save for as credits to take part in games. The answer should address the question whether game credits or virtual money can be exchanged for other prizes. Is any change to regulation in the area proposed or envisaged?

Social gaming is, at present, not legally defined in Singapore. Informally, however, social gaming may be broadly categorised into non-virtual social gaming and virtual social gaming.

As regards the former, such gambling, usually in the form of mahjong or blackjack, is usually carried out in the context of a private social activity between family, friends and acquaintances. Taking into consideration the cultural heritage of Singapore, it is not uncommon for such gambling activities to take place, especially during the Lunar New Year festive period. As mahjong is a statutorily identified gambling product when it is played for 'money or money's worth', it should technically fall within the CGHA's meaning of 'gaming' as discussed in section 2.1. Notwithstanding this, in 2011, the SPF released a press statement in *The Straits Times* announcing that, *'playing mahjong among a small group of friends and relatives is generally allowed'*. However, the aforesaid announcement was qualified to also provide that *'it is an offence under the Common Gaming Houses Act for any person or establishment to operate gambling activities (including mahjong) for the purpose of making a profit, or for any person to gamble inside a common gaming house'*. Our view is that the Singapore authorities take a practical approach towards this form of social gambling in recognition of our cultural heritage, and would generally tolerate such activities so long as they are kept private and members of the public are not seen as having unrestricted access to them.

As regards virtual social gaming, such as 'free-to-play' websites, the position is unclear. At present, the existing legislation does not expressly address this form of gambling. It should also be noted that such social gaming comes in various forms, which may attract different legislative treatment; a 'free-to-play' website that does not permit any use of monies and points that are awarded cannot be exchanged for anything is likely to be viewed more positively than one where players are able to convert their points into cash. It also cannot be ruled out that the Singapore authorities may determine all forms of such social gaming to be illegal on the basis that they facilitate or encourage gambling. We are hopeful that the proposed new legislation dealing with online gambling will clarify the legal position on this issue.

South Africa

Whitesmans Attorneys Garron Whitesman

1. OBJECTIVES AND STRUCTURE OF LEGISLATION

Prior to 1996, all forms of gambling other than betting on horseracing were outlawed in South Africa. The philosophy behind this was that betting on horseracing involved the application of skill, rather than being dependent on luck or chance, which was viewed as a defining element of gambling.

During the period preceding the legalisation of gambling in the country, the apartheid regime had resulted in the creation of the so-called independent homelands, also referred to as the TBVC States (Transkei, Bophuthatswana, Venda and Ciskei), which were given nominal independence from South Africa. In these states, gambling was legalised, resulting in the operation of a number of casinos. Following upon the democratisation of the country in 1994, the TBVC States were reintegrated into South Africa, with the licences allocated to the various casinos remaining valid, despite the ongoing prohibition on gambling in the remainder of the country. This was regarded as an unwarranted anomaly, which needed to be addressed.

In addition, the ban on gambling in South Africa had resulted in the emergence of a plethora of illegal operations, which by their nature were unregulated and untaxed. It was recognised that the licensing and regulation of gambling in the country could generate significant economic benefit to the country, create meaningful employment opportunities, and contribute towards the advancement of persons previously disadvantaged by discrimination on the basis of race.

These considerations, together with others, ultimately resulted in the legalisation of other forms of gambling in South Africa, which was carried into effect by the enactment of the National Gambling Act, No. 33 of 1996. This Act set forth the broad policy parameters within which gambling was to be licensed and regulated. It established a National Gambling Board, which in essence, had no regulatory function, but was charged with ensuring the development and application of uniform norms and standards in relation to gambling throughout the country. This approach was informed by the fact that, under the new constitutional dispensation, casinos, racing, gambling and wagering would be areas in which the national and various provincial legislatures would enjoy concurrent legislative competence.

Accordingly, each of the nine provinces of South Africa has the power to enact legislation regarding the licensing and regulation of gambling within its geographical area. The various provincial legislatures have enacted such legislation, which has brought into being nine different provincial licensing authorities, each with its own licensing and regulatory dispensation.

The legislative model which has been adopted in South Africa is a sumptuary one, under which the licensing and regulation of gambling are intended to satisfy only the existing demand for gambling and to prevent the over-proliferation of opportunities to engage in gambling, by placing limits on the number of licences available and imposing certain restrictions in respect of the advertising of gambling. As such, the national framework provides for a maximum of 40 casino licences throughout South Africa, specifying the distribution of such licences per province, as well as placing limits on the number of limited payout machines available for play in the country (50,000), also on a per province basis.

The year 2004 saw an overhaul of the National Gambling Act, which was replaced in its entirety by a new National Gambling Act, No. 7 of 2004 (the 2004 Act). The primary objective behind the remodelling of the national legislation was twofold: on the one hand to define with greater precision and therefore to coordinate activities relating to the concurrent exercise of legislative competence, and to provide for the licensing and regulation of interactive gambling by the National Gambling Board.

Accordingly, while the National Gambling Board remains the entity charged with ensuring the necessary degree of uniformity between the legislative and regulatory dispensations of the various provinces, it has also been vested with a regulatory function which it did not previously enjoy. It is contemplated that, while the various provincial licensing authorities will continue to license and regulate all forms of gambling (other than interactive gambling), the National Gambling Board will license and regulate interactive gambling. The amended National Gambling Act provided for the bulk of the regulatory framework in respect of interactive gambling to be laid down in regulations to be made under the 2004 Act.

In 2009, a set of proposed regulations in relation to interactive gambling was published. These proposed the licensing of no more than 10 interactive providers in the country, as well as a range of significant harm minimisation requirements. When the proposed regulations were considered by the relevant Portfolio Committee of the National Parliament, legislators expressed grave reservations regarding the appropriateness of licensing and regulating interactive gambling, despite the provisions of the 2004 Act to this effect, and recommended a comprehensive review of the legislative and regulatory framework in force in the country in respect of gambling in general.

In accordance with these recommendations, the proposed interactive gambling regulations were put on ice, and a five-person Commission (the Gambling Review Commission) was established to conduct the relevant review. The review focused on both formal and informal (licensed and illegal) forms of gambling throughout the country, across all industry sectors, as well as the effectiveness of provincial licensing authorities and the National Gambling Board and the legislative scheme in place in relation to gambling.

The Gambling Review Commission produced its final report during the third quarter of 2011, which recommended, inter alia, the licensing and regulation of interactive gambling on a national level in South Africa. Having considered the report of the Commission, the relevant Portfolio Committee of the national Parliament has endorsed this recommendation in principle; however, a number of constitutionally mandated processes are yet required to be followed in relation to proposed amendments to the 2004 Act, so that finality regarding the matter is conservatively estimated to be forthcoming in 2013, at the earliest.

2. FRAMEWORK OF LEGISLATION

2.1 What is the legal definition of gambling and what falls within this definition?

The 2004 Act defines a 'gambling activity' as being an activity involving:
* placing or accepting a bet or wager under section 4(1);
* placing or accepting a totalisator bet, under section 4(2); or
* making available for play, or playing: (i) bingo or another gambling game under section 5; (ii) an amusement game, to the extent that applicable provincial laws require such games to be licensed, or (iii) an interactive game.

A bet or wager occurs when a player stakes money or any other thing of value on a bet with a bookmaker on any contingency, or when a bookmaker either accepts such a stake on a bet from a player or itself stakes money or anything of value on a bet with another bookmaker. A bet or wager is also taken when any person stakes money or a thing of value on any contingency with any other person, as well as when any person expressly or implicitly undertakes, promises or agrees to do anything described in the relevant definition.

A totalisator bet is taken when a player stakes money or anything of value on any event or combination of events by means of a system in which all the amounts bet or staked are pooled, with the holders of winning tickets sharing proportionately in the pool, after all deductions permitted by law have been made.

A 'gambling game' is defined as a game which is played upon the payment of any consideration, with the chance that the player may become entitled to, or may receive a pay-out, irrespective of whether the result of such game is dependent on skill, or chance, or any combination thereof, and includes any bet or wager which is placed in a casino and which conforms with the definition.

Bets and wagers, as well as totalisator bets and amusement games are defined as being gambling activities, but are not gambling games.

2.2 What is the legal definition of online gambling and what falls within this definition?

Online gambling is referred to the 2004 Act as 'interactive gaming'. Interactive gaming is essentially the engaging in or making available of an 'interactive game'. An *'interactive game'* is defined under the 2004 Act as *'a gambling game played or available to be played through the mechanism of an electronic agent accessed over the internet other than a game that can be accessed for play only in licensed premises, and only if the licensee of such premises is authorised to make such a game available for play'*.

A *'gambling game'* is as defined above. All games of chance or skill or mixed chance and skill which are played upon payment of any consideration and which may result in potential or actual pay-out (prize) are classed as gambling games. These include traditional casino games, poker, slot and other related machine gaming and bingo. Betting, sports betting, totalisator betting, betting exchanges and amusement games are dealt with separately and are not regarded as 'gambling games' for the purposes of 'interactive gaming'.

Indeed, online bookmaking or sports betting is licensed under provincial legislation and has been for over a decade. Betting exchanges are not licensed. Sports pools are regulated by the Lotteries Act, No. 57 of 1997 (the Lotteries Act).

2.3 Please set out the different gambling products identified by legislation.

South African legislation is not preoccupied with listing the individual properties of particular gambling products, but groups them in accordance with the defining characteristics of the transactions which they involve. The overarching approach accords relevance to the question of whether any particular product or equipment conforms to the definition of 'gambling device', which is defined as meaning any 'equipment, software or any other thing that is used, or at the time of its manufacture was designed to be used, in determining the result of a gambling activity'. All gambling devices are in turn required to be registered on a national database, and such registration updated on an ongoing basis, as and when ownership or possession of such device changes hands, providing a full audit trail, and a conclusive indication of the ownership, use and location of that gambling device at any given point in time.

In addition, there are national standards in place in respect of defined gambling devices, with which any such gambling device must comply before being exposed for play. Such devices are submitted to licensed testing agents, which must test them against the requirements of the applicable standards, whereafter a letter of certification must be issued, and furnished to the relevant provincial regulator.

In accordance with this approach, South African gambling legislation does not contain individual references to poker or other classes of games, such as blackjack or roulette, commonly found in the casino environment.

Similarly, there is no substantive distinction drawn between the defining characteristics of betting as a generic activity, on the one hand, and sports betting on the other, except inasmuch as the tax dispensation applicable to betting on sporting events differs from that which applies to betting on horseracing.

Slot machine gaming may be offered by licensed casinos and route operators. Whereas the slot machines found in casinos may be linked to local or wide area progressive jackpots and may contain additional gamble and/or double-up features, with no limits being placed on the jackpots which may be won, the slot machines offered for play outside of casinos by route operators are subject to fixed limits on the amounts which may be staked and won by players on a per-game basis. For this reason, the slot machines exposed for play by a route operator are called 'limited payout machines'. A player may stake no more than R5.00 on a single game on a limited payout machine, and may receive no more than R500 in winnings in respect of any such game. The Gambling Review Commission has recommended that these amounts be increased to R30 and R3,000 respectively.

The game of bingo, which is commonly offered under authority of a separate bingo licence, is defined in national legislation, with reference to the defining characteristics of the traditional game of bingo, although the legislation in force in certain provinces has made provision for electronic forms of this game. In the recent case of *Akani Egoli (Pty) Ltd and Others v Chairperson of the Gauteng Gambling Board and Others* [2008] ZAGPHC 262, the Gauteng Provincial Division of the High Court of South Africa found that electronic bingo terminals (EBTs) do not offer the game of bingo, as defined in the 2004 Act, but that these terminals are in effect slot machines, which may be exposed for play only in licensed casinos. The Gambling Review Commission has recommended that EBTs should not be permitted to be offered by the holders of bingo licences, and that any provincial legislation providing the contrary should be revised and aligned with the national legislation.

The National Lottery in South Africa is licensed and regulated by the National Lotteries Board under the provisions of the Lotteries Act. The licensed operator of the lottery enjoys a monopoly in the market, and is required to pay a defined percentage of the revenue generated from the conduct of the Lottery into the National Lottery Distribution Trust Fund, which is managed by the National Lotteries Board. A distribution agency appointed under the Act considers applications for the allocation of a portion of such funds to various causes, including charities, projects for the development of sport and recreation, the arts, culture and the like.

The National Lottery Licensee has the exclusive statutory right to conduct sports pools in South Africa. Notwithstanding the foregoing, the Gauteng Gambling Act, No. 4 of 1995 (the Gauteng Act) (the provincial gambling legislation for the Gauteng province) makes provision for the holder of a totalisator licence issued by it to conduct betting pools.

Wagering record-keeping systems used by the licensed betting industry to record and store wagering transactions, as well as electronic monitoring systems used in the casino and limited payout machine environments are regarded as gambling devices, and required to be tested against the requirements of the applicable national standards and certified as complying with such standards before they can be utilised in gambling operations.

2.4 Please list the different requirements for each gambling product, including legal classifications for each; for example, is poker a game of skill or game of chance?

The definition of a 'gambling game' under section 5 of the 2004 Act is wide and all-encompassing. As such, each gambling product that falls subject to definitional scrutiny as a 'gambling game' does not per se have different individual requirements. It can be accepted that for the purposes of the Act, virtually every type of game in which there is an element of skill or chance or a mixture of these elements and which falls within the scope of the relevant definition, will be subject to the Act and its regulation. Poker, therefore, is to be regarded as a 'gambling game'. In amplification thereof, under the Gauteng Act, for example, the definition of a 'casino game' specifically includes poker.

There are, however, nationally applicable and enforceable technical standards in place in respect of the following gaming and gaming-related equipment:

SANS NO	Year	Edition	Title
SANS 1718-1	2008	2.02	Part 1: Casino equipment
SANS 1718-2	2005	3.00	Part 2: Limited payout gaming equipment
SANS 1718-3	2003	2.00	Part 3: Monitoring and control systems for gaming equipment
SANS 1718-4	2008	2.00	Part 4: Wagering record-keeping systems
SANS 1718-5	2009	1.00	Part 5: Local area and wide area jackpot and progressive jackpot equipment
SANS 1718-7	2007	2.00	Part 7: Tokens
SANS 1718-8	2007	1.00	Part 8: Roulette wheels
SANS 1718-9	2005	2.00	Part 9: Central monitoring system for limited payout machines
SANS 1718-10	2009	1.00	Part 10: Server-based gaming systems

The above products must all be tested and certified as complying with the requirements of the relevant standards before they may be lawfully used in a licensed gambling environment.

2.5 Explain the system of regulation of gambling; which regulatory or governmental body is responsible for the supervision of gambling? Which body issues licences? Which body examines enforcement powers? Is there any limit on the number or duration of available licences?

The provincial licensing authorities issue licences in respect of casinos, route operators, bookmakers, the totalisator, bingo operators, the manufacturers of gaming devices and/or equipment (including the maintenance and repair thereof) and license or register employees engaged in work in the gambling industry on various levels.

In order to avoid duplication of cost and effort, national licences may be applied for in respect of the manufacturing sector, as well as in relation to employment licences. National licences are issued by provincial licensing authorities, but authorise the licensee to engage in the activities authorised by the licence throughout the country.

The National Lotteries Board licenses and regulates the operations of the National Lottery Operator.

It is contemplated that the National Gambling Board will license and regulate the interactive gambling sector.

3. ONLINE GAMBLING
3.1 To what extent can online gambling be offered in your jurisdiction? Are licences available and, if so, for which gambling products? Please describe briefly the licensing process, who may apply, whether licences are limited in number and, if no licences are available, whether it is legal for online gambling to be offered. In the case of EU jurisdictions, please state whether there are any issues as to the legality of the local law at EU level. Please refer to any relevant cases at ECJ level and explain any measures taken or pending by the European Commission.

Unlicensed online gambling is prohibited under section 11 of the Act. In addition thereto, sections 7 and 8 of the Act contain general prohibitions against gambling in relation to illegal activities and unlicensed activities respectively. The operation of an online bookmaker is permissible if licensed and falls to be dealt with under provincial legislation.

Section 11 of the Act provides as follows: *'A person must not engage in or make available an interactive game except as authorised in terms of this Act or any other national law'.*

It should be noted further that section 15 of the Act prohibits the advertising of unlawful gambling. In contracted form it reads as follows: *'A person must not advertise or promote any gambling activity...that is unlawful in terms of this Act or applicable provincial law...'.*

Finally, it should be noted that sections 82 and 83 of the 2004 Act make it a statutory offence to contravene sections 11 and 15 of the Act and that any person convicted of a breach thereof shall be liable to a fine not exceeding R10 million or to imprisonment for a period not exceeding 10 years or to both a fine and such imprisonment.

Provincial gaming legislation also contains certain prohibitions against unauthorised or unlicensed gaming and the advertisement or promotion thereof.

The application of the prohibitions (both national and provincial) to offshore-based online casinos and poker rooms has remained vexed for many years and was the subject of litigation that lasted approximately eight years between the national and provincial gambling authorities and Casino Enterprises Swaziland (Pty) Ltd (*Casino Enterprises v The Gauteng Gambling Board* (653/10) [2011] ZASCA 155 (28 September 2011)) (the Casino Enterprises case).

In casu Casino Enterprises offered online poker, casino games and slots from premises and servers situated in Swaziland (an independent neighbouring kingdom to South Africa) under a gambling licence issued by the Kingdom. Its gaming offering proved extremely popular with the South African public and it advertised prolifically in South Africa. During its lifetime a number of other casino operators started targeting the South African public and they too proved popular. In or around 2004, Casino Enterprises ran radio advertisements in the province of Gauteng, the economic hub of the country. The Gauteng Gambling Board (the relevant provincial authority) (the GGB) notified these radio stations that they were prohibited from running the advertisements on the basis that, in the GGB's view, they contravened certain provisions of its provincial legislation (sections 76 (unauthorised gambling illegal) and 71(1) (prohibition on advertising unauthorised gambling) of the Gauteng Act). Casino Enterprises disagreed with the GGB's stance and applied to the relevant provincial High Court for a declaratory order.

In issue, was whether: (i) when persons in Gauteng gamble using the internet casino, such gambling takes place and is made available to them on Casino Enterprises servers in Swaziland and not in Gauteng in any manner that contravenes the Act; and (ii) the advertising occurring in South Africa in respect of a Swaziland-based casino was unlawful and contravened section 15 of the NGA or 71(1) of the Gauteng Act.

After a number of hearings on technical legal issues, the matter was heard in the North Gauteng High Court (Pretoria) in August 2010. Tuchten, AJ found against Casino Enterprises (*Casino Enterprises (Pty) Ltd (Swaziland) v Gauteng Gambling Board and Others* 2010 (6) SA 38 (GNP)). After hearing expert evidence from both sides, the learned Judge found that: (i) the legislature did not purport to create extra-territorial prohibitions but rather to regulate the conduct of parties within South Africa; and (ii) 'section 11 does not merely prohibit engaging in or making available the game as a whole. It matters not...whether the critical elements are to be found or generated within the borders of South Africa or not. *Section 11 proscribes... both engaging in the game, which happens each time a gambler presses the spin button, and making available the game, which takes place at least when the plaintiff's servers in Swaziland make it possible for the gambler in Gauteng to connect interactively with them through the internet*' (para 66 of Tuchten, AJ's judgment).

Casino Enterprises appealed to the Supreme Court of Appeal (essentially the highest court in South Africa on non-constitutional issues) (the SCA). In September 2011 the SCA finally disposed of the matter when it confirmed the applicability of the prohibitions and the judgment of the court of first instance.

According to the South African gambling authorities and courts it is unlawful to offer interactive gaming in or to South Africa or for South Africans to engage or participate in the activity, unless such activities are offered pursuant to a licence granted under the 2004 Act. As at this juncture it is not yet possible to apply for a licence to offer interactive gaming, such activities are currently illegal.

The above prohibition does not apply to bookmakers who are licensed in South Africa and who trade online. There are a number of well-known international and local bookmaking operations with local websites. A bookmaker licence issued by a provincial licensing authority may permit the holder thereof to trade online across provincial boundaries and to accept bets from persons throughout South Africa. As noted above and below, however, there is disparity between the application of certain advertising rules and rates of tax, depending on the province in which the relevant licence was issued.

3.2 Is there a distinction between the law applicable to B2B operations and that applicable to B2C operations?

There is no formal legal distinction between B2B and B2C operations.

3.3 What are the consequences for B2C or B2B operators who are active in your jurisdiction without having obtained or applied for the required permits, licences and approvals? What penalties and enforcement powers are available in respect of the illegal operators? Please outline any significant domestic decisions or enforcement actions that have been taken by the relevant authorities in recent years.

The consequences are untested as a matter of law. Notwithstanding, it is speculated that the B2C operator would have a similar liability to the white label site but that it is unlikely (barring exceptional circumstances) that the B2B operator would have any liability. To the extent that there may be any allegation that any such activity contravenes any statutory prohibition, such allegation would have to pass the conventional common law tests for determining liability to be sustained. The position is however likely to become somewhat clearer once interactive gambling is licensed.

3.4 Has the legal status of online gambling changed significantly in recent years and, if so, how?

Not *per se*, in that the law has not changed, but yes, insofar as the uncertain position in law has now been settled by the SCA. See the above commentary in respect of the Casino Enterprises case.

3.5 Whilst acknowledging the inherent difficulty in predicting developments in gambling law, what are the likely developments in online gambling in your jurisdiction, both short term and long term? Are any specific amendments under consideration? Have there been any recent political developments, or do you envisage any in the near future? Are any specific amendments under consideration? Are they likely to be adopted and, if so, what is the time scale?

As mentioned above, it has long been contemplated that South Africa may license interactive gaming.

Accordingly, the 2004 Act contains transitional provisions including provisions relating to the *'[d]evelopment of interactive gambling policy and law'*, which are to be found in Item 5 of the Schedule to that Act and which direct the Minister of Trade and Industry within two years after the Committee furnished its report to *'introduce legislation in Parliament to regulate interactive gambling within the Republic'*. Pursuant to these provisions, a committee was established to *'consider and report on national policy to regulate interactive gambling within the Republic'*. The Committee rendered its report (recommending the legalisation of interactive gambling) in September 2005 and a draft bill to amend the NGA was published shortly thereafter. Draft regulations were thereafter produced and parliamentary and departmental hearings took place on the topic.

The full history of the process is beyond the scope of this Chapter and is largely irrelevant given the more recent history, which is canvassed below, but the following salient issues emerged from the process:

(a) the government is concerned about the over-proliferation of gambling and the stimulation of the latent demand and accordingly built into the draft regulations certain player reality checks and daily limits;

(b) the government was/is circumspect about person-to-person gambling and betting and seemed to be confused as to how to regulate such activities. On that basis, both poker and betting exchanges were omitted from regulation (and by inference subject to the omnibus prohibition);

(c) certain persons within the government appeared to be doing a policy about-turn on permissive, regulated gambling as a general proposition.

The process remained in regulatory and political limbo until December 2009 when the Minister of Trade and Industry appointed the Gambling Review Commission with a 'broad remit to *"consider if the currently legalised gambling activities can/should be expanded or curtailed considering the number of casinos, limited payout machines and bingo outlets already licensed"*, having regard for the *"socio-economic consequences attached to gambling, such as problem gambling, youth gambling and other social concerns"'*. In addition the *'Commission was further tasked with... considering licensed and unlicensed activities and technological developments and the viability of new gambling activities'. (Gambling Review Commission Report, 2011, p8).* After national Gambling Review Commission public hearings and numerous public and closed session Parliamentary and Portfolio Committee hearings, the Gambling Review Commission submitted its report (the GRC Report) to the Minister of Trade and Industry in the third quarter of 2011.

The GRC Report (pp. 23 through 25) recommended in relation to interactive gambling, *inter alia*, that the following activities be licensed and regulated:

- online poker, regulated through online gambling legislation, provided that the same rules should apply as are in place in relation to land-based forms of the game;
- betting exchanges;
- virtual racing;
- online casino-style games;
- all forms of remote gambling such as telephone or cellphone gambling.

Further, the Gambling Review Commission recommended (*GRC Report,* pp 24 and 25) that, *inter alia*:

- current licensed forms of remote betting (for example, online bookmaking and totalisators) be brought within the purview of a national interactive licence rather than provincial licence;
- a maximum number of licences be stipulated and a restriction on the number of operators and games should be considered. (It is interesting to note that prior to this, 10 licences had been contemplated or discussed and that the GRC has noted that *'(c)are should, however, be taken not to make the number of licences too few or restricted, as the intention of a licensing regime would be to attract operators, not to exclude them')*;
- the current requirement that the server should be hosted in South Africa should be reviewed; and

- a single regulator should regulate online gambling (including the national lottery and sports pools, which are currently regulated separately by the Lotteries Board under the National Lotteries Act).

On 6 March 2012 the Parliamentary Sub-Committee responsible for considering the Gambling Review Commission's recommendations presented its report to the Minister of Trade and Industry. In essence, it endorsed the recommendations of the Gambling Review Commission.

As at the time writing in the last edition of this publication, the Gambling Review Commission's recommendation were to be considered by the National Council of Provinces (a parliamentary chamber for the provinces) whose approval is a necessary part of the legislative process.

The debate lay in limbo once again until December 2013, when the official opposition's Shadow Minister for Trade and Industry introduced a private member's bill (PM Bill) seeking to repeal certain aspects of the NGA that regulated interactive gambling and replace the same with wide-ranging stand-alone legislation to regulate all forms of remote gambling in line with the GRC Report. The PM Bill not only proposes to change the forms of remote gambling that are desired to be regulated and licensed, but also seeks to create a new regime for the administrative regulation thereof at a centralised national level with certain functions being undertaking by the provincial gambling authorities. A private member's bill has the same legal status as any other form of bill introduced to Parliament for its consideration.

After an initial round of public comment, a further rendition of the PM Bill was published for public comment, which closed in late May 2014.

South Africa held national elections in May 2014 and it will likely take some weeks, if not months, before the PM Bill is considered at parliamentary level.

I am of the view that, whilst changes may be made over the coming months to the PM Bill, the same is likely to provide impetus to the creation of a licensing regime which will cover a wide range of remote gambling and betting activities. Notwithstanding this renewed impetus, I do not foresee the new regime being implemented in full before the second haf of 2015.

3.6 Is the law the same in relation to mobile gambling and interactive gambling on television? If not, are there any headline differences?

The law is the same.

4. LAND-BASED GAMING

4.1 Please describe the licensing regime (if any) for land-based gaming, and what products are included. Please set out what licences are available, and the licensing regime for them.

Each provincial licensing authority enjoys exclusive jurisdiction, within its province, to license and regulate the operations of all gambling industry sectors other than the interactive gambling sector.

While the legislation of certain provinces limits the period of duration of certain licence types, in most cases licences are issued on an indefinite basis, subject to ongoing compliance with the law, and are renewable at regular intervals.

Over and above the licences issued by provincial licensing authorities in respect of casinos, route operators, bookmakers, the totalisator, bingo operators, the manufacturers of gaming devices and/or equipment and employees engaged in work in the gambling industry on various levels, licences are also issued in respect of the various sites on which limited payout machines are exposed for play. In most cases, such site licences authorise the exposure for play of no more than five limited payout machines on a site, although in certain cases licences may be issued for the placement of more than five, but no more than 40 limited payout machines on a site. Applications of this nature must be approved by the National Gambling Board.

The legislation in force in certain provinces also requires other categories of premises on which gambling activities are conducted, such as bingo, bookmaking and totalisator operations, or the conduct of horseracing meetings, to be separately licensed.

4.2 Please set out any particular limitations or requirements for (eg casino) operators, such as a ban on local residents gambling.

As a result of the history of the country and the need to correct institutionally entrenched imbalances between persons of different races, national legislation earmarks black economic empowerment as a key objective to which the holders of gambling licences must conform. The 2004 Act requires any provincial licensing authority considering an application for a licence (other than an employment licence) or for the transfer of a licence, to consider the commitments, if any, made by the applicant or proposed transferee, in relation to the promotion of broad-based black economic empowerment.

The relevant provincial licensing authority may impose reasonable and justifiable conditions on the licence in this regard. In addition, the relevant commitments, as well as the achievements of the licensee regarding those commitments, must be reviewed on an annual basis and where necessary, the relevant authority may impose different or additional conditions on the licence in this context.

In respect of licensed route operations, the regulations made under the national legislation require a phased rollout process in relation to limited payout machines, with a view to preventing and containing possible negative social impact. In this regard, the rollout of the 50,000 limited payout machines authorised to be exposed for play in the country is required to be managed in three separate phases, namely:

- Phase 1, under which a provincial licensing authority may roll out no more than 50 per cent of the total number of limited payout machines allocated to the province;
- Phase 2, which must be preceded by the conduct of a socio-economic impact study, focusing on the actual and projected impact of the rollout of limited payout machines in the relevant province, and provided that based on the results of the study, the National Minister (of Trade and Industry) authorises the further rollout of limited payout machines in the relevant province, entailing the rollout no more than a further 35 per cent of the total number of limited payout machines allocated to the province; and

- Phase 3, which must follow the same processes as are contemplated in relation to Phase 2, involving the rollout of the balance of the total number of limited payout machines allocated to the province.

Of the 40 casino licences provided for by national legislation, 37 have been issued.

5. TAX

5.1 Please summarise briefly the tax regime applicable to both land-based and online gaming.

In the context of play on slot machines and banking games offered in the licensed casino environment, taxes are levied at a rate of a defined percentage of adjusted gaming revenue (essentially hold). The various tax rates differ from province to province and in some cases, are calculated using a sliding scale. In respect of non-banking casino games, taxes (at the applicable rates) are payable in respect of any rake or similar fee or commission charged by the casino operator.

The taxes payable by the holders of route operator and bingo licences are similarly based on adjusted gaming revenue, but different tax rates apply.

The holders of totalisator licences are required pay a defined percentage (which may differ from province to province) of the amounts deducted by them from the gross betting pool (prior to the payment of dividends) and applied towards the costs of administration of the horseracing industry (on average roughly 25 per cent of all amounts staked by patrons).

The holders of bookmaker licences are required to recover from winning patrons a withholding tax (generally 6 per cent) of the total amount of such winnings, in relation to betting on horseracing or any betting transaction of which a bet on horseracing is a component. These withholding taxes are generally split between the relevant provincial fiscus and the totalisator operator. The provision for the diversion of a portion of these taxes to the totalisator is intended to provide a mechanism for the subsidisation of the horseracing industry by the bookmaking sector.

In relation to sports betting, licensed bookmakers are generally required to pay taxes at an average rate of 6.5 per cent of the gross profit generated by betting transactions.

Many of the provinces are currently reviewing their gambling tax dispensations. In addition, the Gambling Review Commission has noted the lack of harmonisation of tax rates as between the various provinces. It is accordingly possible that an initiative may be taken to standardise tax rates in respect of various industry sectors, as a component of the impending legislative reform.

In addition to the above, the National Minister of Finance has recently announced the proposed introduction of an additional tax, payable by all licensed gambling operators, at the rate of 1 per cent of adjusted gross revenue, with effect from the 2013 fiscal year.

No finality has as yet been reached as to the rates of taxation which will be payable in the context of interactive gambling operations albeit that a bill placed before Parliament in June 2008 contemplated that the activity would be taxed at a rate of 6 per cent of gross gambling revenue (wagers less payouts). This money bill lies in legislative limbo until the main issue of regulating interactive gambling is resolved.

6. ADVERTISING

6.1 To what extent is the advertising of gambling permitted in your jurisdiction? Again, this should cover both land-based and online gaming. To the extent that advertising is permitted, how is it regulated?

In South Africa, the holders of gambling licences are permitted to advertise their gambling-related offerings, subject to the provisions of regulations made under the 2004 Act, which set certain broad requirements with which such advertising should comply. Briefly, these provisions require inter alia that advertising in relation to gambling should not be misleading, be directed at, placed in media aimed at, or designed to attract persons under the age of 18 years, or contain false or misleading information in relation to the probability of winning.

In addition, advertisements in respect of gambling are required to include cautionary statements regarding the phenomenon of problem gambling and to provide additional mandatory information, in the form of the name, toll free counselling line number and slogan of the National Responsible Gambling Programme, as well as a reference to the prevailing age threshold requirement of 18 years for participation in gambling.

The situation in relation to the advertisement of gambling products in South Africa is, however, complicated by reason of the fact that the provisions of provincial legislation dealing with the matter are not uniform, with certain provinces having imposed more onerous requirements (in law and/ or in practice), under which licence holders are required to submit any proposed advertisement in relation to gambling to the relevant provincial licensing authority for prior approval.

In addition, there is an inherent tension between the provisions of the National Lotteries Act, which allow the operator of the National Lottery to advertise extensively and without any restraint as to form and content, and other forms of gambling, which are subjected to significantly higher levels of scrutiny and regulation.

It is anticipated that the impending amendment of national legislation in relation to gambling will give further attention to standardising the approach towards the advertising of gambling products and services.

7. SOCIAL GAMING

7.1 We believe this to be a growing area. Please decide under what criteria social gaming is permitted in your jurisdiction. If games are free to play or if there is no prize, are they legal without a licence? Please address circumstances where virtual currency is used and can be won: ie currency which is of no monetary or other value, save for as credits to take part in games. The answer should address the question whether game credits or virtual money can be exchanged for other prizes. Is any change to regulation in the area proposed or envisaged?

The legislation in force in certain provinces deals with the concept of 'social gambling'. However, this is the exception rather than the rule. In the rare instances where social gambling is permitted, however, this concept excludes the playing of a slot machine or any other gambling game in respect of which a gambling device (other than playing cards or dice) is required to be utilised, as gambling devices cannot be lawfully possessed otherwise than under the authority of a licence. In addition, social gambling may not be conducted or operated for profit and no person may receive any form of compensation or remuneration whatsoever for making such an activity available.

Where permitted, social gambling may also take the form of the playing of bingo, provided that it is conducted for genuine fund-raising purposes by a church, a school, a sporting club or other entity duly registered for such purposes, and provided that the relevant provincial licensing authority has authorised the relevant activity.

Amusement games, which are played against payment of a consideration and may entitle the player to a prize, are permitted without being required to be licensed, provided that any such prize is limited to a non-cash item with a market value not exceeding R50.00.

More generally, there is currently no distinction in South African gambling law between games in respect of which the consideration is payable by way of cash, virtual currency, or any other thing of value, or the prize takes either of these forms. Provided that something of value is staked and something of value is available to be won in the course of playing a game, that game will be classified as a gambling game, unless it is an amusement game, as alluded to above. The sole exception to this is a situation where a player may, as a result of successfully playing a game, win an opportunity to play a further game, which is defined as an opportunity to continue playing the same type of game, without interruption, on the same machine on which the opportunity was won, which cannot be distributed or transferred to the winner thereof or to any other person, or converted into any other thing of value.

Accordingly, if game credits are capable of being converted to anything of value, including the opportunity to play the same type of game which is held over or postponed until a later occasion, the game in question will for all intents and purposes, qualify as a gambling game, and be unlawful unless conducted under the authority of the appropriate licence.

South Korea

Kim & Chang Jeffrey D. Jones, Hyun Ho Eun,
Jin Ho Song, Michael S. Lee, Mi-Ryoung An, John K. Kim
& Junhee Choi

1.   OBJECTIVES AND STRUCTURE OF LEGISLATION

The general prohibition against gambling was made part of the Criminal
Code with its enactment on 18 September 1953. The purpose of the
prohibition was to preserve good public morals and prevent the furtherance
of speculative spirits, which has been interpreted to include incitement
of excessive behaviour seeking profits based on games of chance to
the detriment of society, by legally controlling gambling with certain
permissible activities as exceptions. The law has evolved to include certain
exceptions for permissible activities, which are addressed in greater detail in
section 2.1 below. However, it is noted that the general prohibition against
gambling is still enforced in Korea, and the legal trend has been to subject
those who are in violation of the laws to strict sanctions, further addressed
below.

2.   FRAMEWORK OF LEGISLATION

2.1   What is the legal definition of gambling and what falls within this definition?

The Criminal Code, which generally prohibits gambling, also provides for
a limited number of exceptions pursuant to separate laws which regulate
specific types of permissible betting activities. Although gambling itself
is not specifically defined under the Criminal Code, gambling has been
interpreted by the Korean courts to mean any act of determining monetary
gain or loss by wagering property on chance or luck. This has been broadly
construed by the courts. According to Article 246 (Gambling, Habitual
Gambling) of the Criminal Code, a person (i) who gambles or wagers for
the purpose of gaining property is punishable by a fine of up to KRW 10
million and (ii) who does so habitually is punishable by imprisonment of up
to three years or a fine of up to KRW 20 million, except for gambling that
is merely 'for occasional amusement'. Some examples of illegal gambling
include betting or wagering on card games such as poker, mah-jong, go-
stop, billiards, slot machines and dice games, unless such opportunity to
participate in such activities are provided by a licensed and approved gaming
(casino) business operator.

However, certain betting activities are permissible to the extent that they
are specifically provided for and permitted by other laws. For example, a
gaming business is permissible under the Tourism Promotion Act and subject
to strict regulation requiring approval and licensing by the Ministry of

Culture, Sports and Tourism (the MCST). A gaming business is defined as the business of operating an exclusive business facility in which players make a profit while other players sustain a loss as a consequence of probabilities, playing with specific implements such as dice, cards and slot machines.

Further, the following activities are permissible as long as they are operated in accordance with their respective laws: lotteries (regulated by the Lottery Tickets and Lottery Fund Act) and other specified speculative activities, such as prize contests and sweepstakes (as regulated by the Act on Special Cases concerning Regulation of Speculative Acts); betting on horse racing (as regulated by the Korean Racing Association Act); cycling and motorboat racing (both as regulated by the Cycling and Motorboat Racing Act); traditional bullfighting (as regulated by the Traditional Bullfighting Act); and other specified sports betting operated by the Korea Sports Promotion Foundation and its trusted operators (as regulated by the National Sports Promotion Act). However, any betting activity which is outside the scope of these regulated and permitted activities is subject to the prohibition against gambling as set forth in the Criminal Code.

2.2 What is the legal definition of online gambling and what falls within this definition?

There is no distinction between online gambling and land-based gambling under the laws of Korea. As such, any activity which falls within the broad scope of gambling under the Korean courts' interpretation of the Criminal Code will likewise be prohibited if such activity occurs online. Therefore, any online activity which determines monetary gain or loss by wagering property on chance or luck is prohibited, including online card games, slot machines, dice games, etc. In addition, although land-based gaming businesses are permitted to a certain extent under the laws, there are no licensed online gaming businesses in Korea.

Furthermore, online games, including card games, slot machines and other games which incorporate betting elements, are subject to rating requirements. Pursuant to the Game Industry Promotion Act (the Game Act), all games, including online games, must be rated prior to release in Korea by the Games Ratings Board (GRB), with certain exceptions for games which are developed and distributed for non-commercial purposes (eg education, religious or public interest activities). The GRB's rating categories are as follows: (i) all ages; (ii) ages 12 and older; (iii) ages 15 and older; and (iv) not suitable for minors (ages 18 and older). Additionally, the GRB may issue a 'no-rating' designation when it deems that a game at issue violates Korean law, in which case the distribution of such game is prohibited in Korea. Games which are also deemed to be 'speculative games' are subject to a 'no-rating' designation in Korea and distribution of such speculative games is prohibited.

In this respect, speculative games include any game which may provide financial gain or may cause financial loss depending on the outcome and possesses any of the following characteristics: (i) a game that involves wagering or payouts; (ii) a game of which the outcome depends on a method of chance; (iii) a game which imitates land-based gaming business, horse-racing, cycling and/or motorboat racing as defined under the relevant laws; or (iv) all other games as determined by the Presidential Decree to the Game Act (as a subordinate regulation under a specific main body of law). The Presidential Decree to the Game Act has included games which imitate traditional Korean bullfighting, lotteries and other speculative activities defined under the relevant Korean laws.

Therefore, any game which contains betting for cash or financial gain or loss (ie 'cash betting') will likely be deemed to be a speculative game and will likely receive a 'no rating' designation, in which case the release in Korea will not be permitted. However, even if cash betting is not involved, such game may not be deemed to be a speculative game, and may rather receive an age-restrictive rating.

2.3 Please set out the different gambling products identified by legislation.

Gambling is primarily regulated and generally prohibited under the Criminal Code, unless specifically exempted and regulated under other specific laws. The Criminal Code further prohibits the operation of a gambling place other than as set forth in other laws, such as the Tourism Promotion Act, which regulates gaming business operators. As such, the categories mentioned above – that is, poker and betting (other than permitted sports betting), casino games, slot machines and other machine gaming – are prohibited by the Criminal Code as illegal gambling, unless operated by a licensed gaming business operator.

Sports betting is permitted subject to heavy regulation under the National Sports Promotion Act and exclusively operated by the Korea Sports Promotion Foundation and its entrusted operators. Bingo, sweepstakes and prize contests, etc, may fall under the scope of 'speculative activities' which are regulated by the Act on Special Cases concerning Regulation of Speculative Acts and permitted with the approval of the relevant local authorities. The national lottery is regulated by the Lottery Tickets and Lottery Fund Act, and lottery tickets may only be issued by the Korean Lottery Commission and other authorised governmental or quasi-governmental entities. In addition, betting on horse racing, cycling, motorboat racing and traditional bullfighting are permitted and regulated under their respective laws, as addressed in section 2.1 above.

2.4 Please list the different requirements for each gambling product, including legal classifications for each; for example, is poker a game of skill or game of chance?

The laws of Korea do not distinguish between so-called games of skill and games of chance. In other words, both games of skill and games of chance may be deemed to be illegal gambling. Therefore, regardless of whether a game contains skill elements, such game may still be deemed to be illegal gambling in accordance with the interpretation by a court of the Criminal Code.

For example, the Korean Supreme Court held that betting on golfing activities where golfers settled in cash depending on their scores was deemed to be within the scope of gambling (see Supreme Court Case No. 2006Do736 (23 October 2008)). The Supreme Court reasoned that, although a golfer's skill would affect his/her score, the element of chance or luck of gambling existed since the outcome of betting on golfers' scores could not be predicted by the betting individuals.

2.5 Explain the system of regulation of gambling; which regulatory or governmental body is responsible for the supervision of gambling? Which body issues licences? Which body examines enforcement powers? Is there any limit on the number or duration of available licences?

As noted above, permissible gambling and speculative activities are regulated pursuant to the specific laws mentioned in section 2.1.

With respect to gaming businesses, approval and licensing is required from the MCST pursuant to the Tourism Promotion Act. Meanwhile, the Jeju Special Self-Governing Province is separately regulated under the Special Act on the Establishment of Jeju Special Self-Governing Province and the Development of Free International City. Pursuant to this law, the Governor of the Jeju Special Self-Governing Province has independent authority to approve and license gaming businesses in the Jeju Special Self-Governing Province, separate from the MCST and Tourism Promotion Act.

With regard to the duration of the gaming business licence, the Tourism Promotion Act is silent on an expiry date to a licence and the licence also does not specifically define an expiry date. The licence, therefore, is currently without an expiry date. There may be amendments to the law in the future introducing an expiry and renewal protocol according to the recent (March 2014) announcement by the MCST, in which the MCST publicly announced that it is currently reviewing and considering the introduction of an expiry date and/or renewal protocol for gaming business licences as a method to strengthen regulation on casinos). As to the limit on the number of available gaming business licences, reference is made to the 600,000 Rule and the exceptions thereto in section 4.1 below.

Other permissible gambling activities and their respective regulatory schemes are described in section 4.1 below.

3. ONLINE GAMBLING

3.1 To what extent can online gambling be offered in your jurisdiction? Are licences available and, if so, for which gambling products? Please describe briefly the licensing process, who may apply, whether licences are limited in number and, if no licences are available, whether it is legal for online gambling to be offered. In the case of EU jurisdictions, please state whether there are any issues as to the legality of the local law at EU level. Please refer to any relevant cases at ECJ level and explain any measures taken or pending by the European Commission.

Online gambling activities which involve cash payouts are prohibited as Korean law does not distinguish between online gambling and land-based gambling. Further, online games which imitate or mimic gambling activities are subject to the ratings requirement by the GRB prior to its release in Korea. As discussed in section 2.2, online gambling which contains betting for financial gain or loss will be deemed to be a speculative game and subject to a 'no-rating' designation by the GRB, in which case distribution of such game in Korea is prohibited. If cash betting is not involved, then it is possible that the game may receive an age-restrictive rating. There is no separate licensing regime for online gambling.

3.2 Is there a distinction between the law applicable to B2B operations and that applicable to B2C operations?

There is no distinction between B2B and B2C operators, and all online gambling activities involving betting for financial gain or loss will be viewed as speculative games subject to the no-rating designation.

3.3 What are the consequences for B2C or B2B operators who are active in your jurisdiction without having obtained or applied for the required permits, licences and approvals? What penalties and enforcement powers are available in respect of the illegal operators? Please outline any significant domestic decisions or enforcement actions that have been taken by the relevant authorities in recent years.

While criminal penalties for violations under the Criminal Code depend on the type of gambling activity at issue, sanctions for establishing an unlicensed gambling place for the purpose of profit may generally include imprisonment of up to five years or a fine of up to KRW 30 million. In terms of the foregoing criminal penalties, the type of gambling place is irrelevant to the determination of criminal liability, and there is no requirement that the business place be found as permanent or even a physical location. With respect to operation of gambling services offered through the web or internet, there is precedent where the Supreme Court held that the operation of a website offering games to engage in gambling was found to be within the scope of 'establishing a gambling place' as set forth under Article 247 of the Criminal Code. Therefore, given the Supreme Court's decision, the operation of a website offering games to engage in gambling would fall within the scope of prohibited gambling activities under the Criminal Code.

3.4 What technical measures are in place (if any) to protect consumers from unlicensed operators, such as ISP blocking and payment blocking?

The MCST may order an ISP to refuse, suspend or restrict contacting a website which provides a speculative game product, such as online gambling services which have been denied a ratings classification. The Korea Communications Commission may likewise order an ISP to refuse, suspend or restrict contacting a website which provides online gambling services as information with content that falls within speculative activities prohibited by the laws of Korea and other subordinate regulations.

3.5 Has the legal status of online gambling changed significantly in recent years and, if so, how?

Online gambling has generally been prohibited in Korea since the inception of online gambling on the internet within the scope of prohibited gambling under the Criminal Code without any significant changes.

3.6 Whilst acknowledging the inherent difficulty in predicting developments in gambling law, what are the likely developments in online gambling in your jurisdiction, both short term and long term? Are any specific amendments under consideration? Have there been any recent political developments, or do you envisage any in the near future? Are any specific amendments under consideration? Are they likely to be adopted and, if so, what is the time scale?

It is difficult to forecast the potential or future development of the laws and regulations relating to gambling, online gaming and gaming businesses in Korea. Any such developments will generally reflect various considerations such as government policy, public perception, trends and demand in the tourism industry, political discussion, global and local economic circumstances and the necessity to promote foreign investment, among others. Although there has been discussion on whether to ease or maintain certain restrictions (or in some cases strengthen said restrictions) in the relevant laws and regulations which would result in minor amendments to the relevant laws as above, it is still difficult to predict any future developments to those laws and regulations at this time.

3.7 Is the law the same in relation to mobile gambling and interactive gambling on television? If not, are there any headline differences?

While interactive gambling on television does not have a significant presence in Korea as of February 2014, generally, online gambling, mobile gambling and interactive gambling are all subject to the same prohibitions as illegal gambling under the Criminal Code.

4. LAND-BASED GAMING

4.1 Please describe the licensing regime (if any) for land-based gaming, and what products are included. Please set out what licences are available, and the licensing regime for them.

Land-based gaming is regulated by the specific laws depending on the type of activity at issue.

For gaming businesses, the MCST has the authority to grant gaming (casino) business licences to gaming business operators pursuant to the Tourism Promotion Act. The licences are granted on a national level, although the licence is limited to the facilities which are registered under the licence itself. Any person who intends to operate a gaming business shall have certain facilities and machines, including an exclusive business facility, and submit a licence application to the MCST. The MCST may, upon receiving an application for a gaming business licence, grant it only when the applicant intends to operate a gaming business in the facilities of a hotel business operated in a Special Metropolitan City, a Metropolitan City, a Province or a Special Self-Governing Province having an international airport or an international passenger ship terminal or in a special designated zone, or in a subsidiary facility to the facility of international conference business. In addition, a gaming business must possess certain facilities and equipment in compliance with the rules of the MCST (eg machines that comply with the minimum payout ratio and retention of game records). Under the Tourism Promotion Act and its Presidential Decree, the MCST may grant a new licence when the total number of foreign tourists who have entered into a specific area of Korea has increased by 600,000 persons or more since the previous licence was granted, and such licence may be granted to the extent of no more than two licences per each increase of 600,000 foreign tourists. The MCST may also take into account: (i) the trend in the increasing number of foreign tourists; (ii) the increasing trend in the number of gaming business visitors; (iii) the total capacity of the existing gaming business operators; (iv) the total results of foreign exchange earnings by existing gaming business operators; and (v) any other matters necessary for the sound development of a gaming business. Even if the above requirements are met, the MCST may restrict permission as it deems necessary for the maintenance of public peace and order or for the sound development of the gaming industry.

A similar regulatory regime over gambling and speculative activities as regulated by the MCST under the Tourism Promotion Act exists in the Special Act on the Establishment of Jeju Island Special Self-Governing Province and the Development of Free International City, which specifically provides a rule similar to the '600,000 Rule' for the Jeju Special Self-Governing Province with different thresholds based on foreign tourists visiting Jeju Island. It should be noted, however, that the 600,000 Rule provides that a new casino business licence will be granted at the discretion of and through the initiative of the MCST. The MCST or the Governor of the Jeju Special Self-Governing Province has not issued any new casino business licences since 2005.

The Special Act on Designation and Management of Free Economic Zones (the Special Act on FEZ) as a separate regulatory regime imposes additional requirements to those set forth in the Tourism Promotion Act for investors, such as (i) a minimum investment or (ii) the application for and the securement of a licence for certain zones designated as Free Economic Zones. However, it is especially noted that the Special Act on FEZ waives the 600,000 Rule for investors/applicants. For example, if an investor/applicant who seeks a licence as a gaming business operator under the Special Act on FEZ can make a minimum investment of $500 million towards the tourism industry in a Free Economic Zone, then the MCST may issue and grant a gaming business licence without consideration of the 600,000 Rule. Recently (in March 2014), the MCST approved (not a gaming licence issuance itself but) a pre-certification application for a gaming business licence submitted by a foreign-invested joint venture by issuing a conditional 'suitability notification'.

For lotteries, the Commissioner of the Metropolitan Police Agency or the Chief of the National Police Agency may grant a licence, or the Lottery Commission may consign certain functions related to the lottery, including issuance of lottery tickets, to an organisation or a private individual, and a consignee may re-consign the lottery related functions to another organisation or private individual after the Lottery Commission has issued its approval pursuant to the Act on Special Cases concerning the Regulation of Speculative Acts.

With respect to other speculative businesses, such as sweepstakes and prize contests, the Commissioner of the Metropolitan Police Agency or the Chief of the National Police Agency has the authority to grant a licence for such activities pursuant to the Act on Special Cases concerning the Regulation of Speculative Acts.

Other speculative activities are permitted and regulated by the local authorities (eg the police) in the province or district in which such activities are to occur. The following businesses may be permitted upon obtaining permission: (i) lottery ticket issuance business in which money is collected from purchasers by issuing tickets, after winners are given financial gain while the other customers suffer losses; (ii) prize competition business where money is collected from customers who participate in suggesting or selecting an answer with regard to a particular question, after which all or some winners are given financial gain while the other customers suffer losses; (iii) other speculative businesses determined by Presidential Decree which utilise for-profit implementations or methods such as wheel-spinning, drawing lots, awarding prizes, etc, which may incite speculative spirits.

With respect to sports betting, the National Sports Promotion Act permits certain types of sports betting, although it does not specify the types of sports for which betting may be permissible. Rather, the business plan of the relevant operator must be submitted along with the licence application to the MCST and the types of sports subject to betting may be determined through the procedures of the MCST. Currently, betting on domestic and overseas football (soccer), basketball, baseball, volleyball, golf and Korean sumo wrestling are operated by the Korea Sports Foundation and its entrusted operator.

Traditional bullfighting is regulated by the Ministry of Agriculture, Food and Rural Affairs (the MAFRA), pursuant to the Traditional Bullfighting Act. Traditional bullfighting may be held by any local government that obtains a permit from the MAFRA. However, a local government may entrust part of its authority over business affairs related to traditional bullfighting, such as sales of betting slips, the operation and management of a bullfighting arena, and public relations activities, to an organisation or a private individual approved by the MAFRA.

Horse racing is operated exclusively by the Korean Racing Authority, a non-profit organisation established pursuant to the Korean Racing Association Act. It is the sole horse racing authority in Korea and operates under the MAFRA. Pursuant to the Korean Racing Association Act and its lower regulations, the MAFRA may grant a licence to the Korean Racing Association to install horse racing tracks only where there are appropriate facilities (circular or oblong horse racing track which is no more than 1,000 meters in length, more than 16 meters wide, with a referee spot, betting ticket agency, etc).

Cycling and motorboat racing are operated exclusively by the local government or the Korea Sports Promotion Foundation licensed by the MCST pursuant to the Cycling and Motorboat Racing Act. The MCST may grant a licence for a local government or Korea Sports Promotion Foundation to install cycling racetracks only where there are appropriate facilities (circular or oblong cycling race road which are more than 300 meters in length, more than seven meters wide, with a referee spot, betting ticket agency, etc) and motorboat facilities only where there are appropriate facilities (a water path which is more than 450 meters in length, more than 70 meters wide, with a referee spot, betting ticket agency, etc).

4.2 Please set out any particular limitations or requirements for (eg casino) operators, such as a ban on local residents gambling.

Currently, under the Tourism Promotion Act, gaming businesses (ie casino operators) licensed under the same act are not allowed to permit the entrance of local residents into the gaming facilities. Thus, for local residents, land-based gaming is limited to one licensed gaming business facility in Korea, ie Gangwonland, for which the requirement to restrict the entrance of local residents under the Tourism Promotion Act is relaxed pursuant to the Special Act on Support of Development of Abandoned Mine Area in order to support the development of a disused mine area.

Also, the minimum age for participation in legitimate, licensed betting activities is 19 years of age.

Otherwise, sports betting is permitted for certain sports. The National Sports Promotion Act does not specify the types of sports; however, betting on domestic and overseas football (soccer), basketball, baseball, volleyball, golf and Korean sumo wrestling is currently in operation. The betting activities must be conducted at certain facilities which are operated by the Korea Sports Foundation and/or its entrusted operator.

4.3 Please address the questions in 3.5 above, but in relation to land-based gaming.

In general, the recent changes to the regulatory regime with regard to land-based gaming is as explained above in section 4.1. Further, it is understood that the MCST is considering strengthening of the existing regulations on casinos (eg requirements for mergers/acquisitions, a licence renewal system).

5. TAX
5.1 Please summarise briefly the tax regime applicable both to land-based and online gaming.

The general corporate income tax regime applies to land-based and online gaming. The relevant corporate income tax rates are 10 per cent for those companies which earn up to KRW 200 million per annum, 20 per cent for those companies which earn over KRW 200 million and up to 20 billion per annum, and 22 per cent for those companies which earn over KRW 20 billion. Other than certain fund contribution requirements under the respective gaming related laws such as the Tourism Promotion Act (described below), there are no special regulations on taxes related to gambling. In addition, revenue from illegal gambling sources may be taxable as regular income as if the revenue were gained from legitimate sources.

With respect to individual income tax, any proceeds earned from gambling are subject to the individual's income tax rate.

As a separate matter, gaming businesses (ie casino operators) licensed under the Tourism Promotion Act are obligated to make certain payments to funds (eg tourism promotion funds) and pay individual consumption taxes for a certain portion of its revenue as prescribed under the relevant laws.

6. ADVERTISING
6.1 To what extent is the advertising of gambling permitted in your jurisdiction? Again, this should cover both land-based and online gaming. To the extent that advertising is permitted, how is it regulated?

Advertisement of gambling activities is permissible to the extent that the activity being advertised is a legal activity provided that the method and contents of the advertisement are in accordance with the relevant laws and regulations. On the other hand, if the gambling activities are prohibited by the laws of Korea, then any advertisement would be illegal. Therefore, the advertisement of licensed gaming businesses, lotteries, etc, is permitted under the laws of Korea to the extent that such advertisement is released in accordance with the relevant laws and regulations. In this regard, 'licensed' gaming businesses, lotteries, etc, mean only those businesses licensed under the laws of Korea. Therefore, advertising of gaming businesses, lotteries, etc in Korea by businesses licensed in other jurisdictions but not in Korea are not permitted and may be punishable as 'aiding and abetting' in illegal gambling.

Online advertisements are regulated by the Act on Promotion of Information and Communications Network Utilisation and Information Protection Act, etc, which similarly permits advertisement of gambling activities to the extent that the activity being advertised is a legal and permitted activity. Furthermore, the Juvenile Protection Act prohibits the placement of certain online advertisements which are deemed to be harmful to minors on websites which are not adequately equipped to restrict access by minors. It is likely that an advertisement for gambling activities would be deemed to be materially harmful to minors and therefore prohibited unless the website in which the advertisement were placed was adequately equipped to restrict access to minors.

However, it is noted that there are certain restrictions on the advertisements of permissible betting activities. Under the Tourism Promotion Act, the advertisement or public relations activity of a gaming business cannot excessively instigate speculative spirit or undermine good public morals. However, the restrictions against instigating speculative spirits or undermining good public morals are vague and there is no clear guidance or precedent to interpret such provisions.

For other 'speculative' activities (eg lotteries, contests and sweepstakes), the Act on Special Cases concerning Regulation of Speculative Acts similarly prohibits any advertisements or propaganda that may be detrimental to good morals by inciting excessive speculative spirit.

7. SOCIAL GAMING

7.1 We believe this to be a growing area. Please decide under what criteria social gaming is permitted in your jurisdiction. If games are free to play or if there is no prize, are they legal without a licence? Please address circumstances where virtual currency is used and can be won: ie currency which is of no monetary or other value, save for as credits to take part in games. The answer should address the question whether game credits or virtual money can be exchanged for other prizes. Is any change to regulation in the area proposed or envisaged?

All games, including social games, are subject to the ratings requirement pursuant to the Game Act administered by the GRB, subject to certain limited exceptions, such as games which are developed and distributed for non-commercial purposes (eg education, religious or public interest activities).

The GRB's rating categories are as follows: (i) all ages; (ii) ages 12 and older; (iii) ages 15 and older; and (iv) not suitable for minors (ages 18 and older). Additionally, the GRB may issue a 'no-rating' designation when it deems that the game at issue violates Korean law, in which case the distribution of such game will be prohibited in Korea.

As threshold matter, any game which contains the exchange of real money or game money which is obtained while playing a betting game is prohibited under Korean law as a speculative game. According to the Game Act, games (including social games) are deemed to be speculative games if a game provides financial gain or causes financial loss depending on the outcome, and is any one of the following: (i) a game that involves wagering or payouts; (ii) a game of which the outcome depends on a method of chance; (iii) cash or other materials which are to be provided or obtained as a result of play; (iv) game credits/points which can be redeemed for tangible or intangible compensation through direct or indirect trading; (v) other detailed restrictions in the case of physical gaming locations; or (vi) game credits/points which may be used for in-game betting and are transferable between players and purchased directly with cash. If none of the above criteria have been met, then it is possible that such games will not constitute speculative games (which receive a 'no rating' designation) when rated by the GRB. In such case, a game may be rated with an age restriction.

For gaming products, the GRB reviews gambling-like activities in accordance with the following guidelines and examples of speculative games: (i) non-standard service fees; (ii) game credits/points which can be redeemed for cash or other property; (iii) game credits/points which can be redeemed for tangible or intangible compensation through direct or indirect trading; (iv) game credits/points which may be used for in-game betting and are transferable between players and purchased directly with cash. If none of the above has been met, then it is possible that such games may not constitute speculative games (which receive a 'no rating' designation) when rated by the GRB. In such case, the games may be rated with an age restriction.

In the case of non-betting games, the exchange of game money is not expressly prohibited under Korean law. However, the existence of a cash trade system which permits the exchange of game money for real money may have an effect on the GRB's review of a game for the purpose of the age ratings.

Spain

Asensi Abogados SLP
Santiago Asensi & Alla Serebrianskaia

1. OBJECTIVES AND STRUCTURE OF LEGISLATION
Gambling in Spain is currently divided into games that are played at
federal level and games that are played only in one specific region. In
both cases, the operator is subject to obtaining a licence or authorisation
in order to legally operate in Spain. However, the legislation applicable to
both cases is different. The online gaming activities referred to in the first
case are regulated by a recent federal law and consequently are subject to
obtaining a federal licence, while the land-based games are regulated by
each autonomous region and are subject to the corresponding regional
authorisation.

However, in order to provide a better understanding of the situation,
it is crucial to have a clear overview about the history and background of
the gaming regulation in Spain, since the online games that are developed
in more than one autonomous region (commonly at federal level) were
a non-regulated matter, until the end of May 2011, when a new Spanish
Gambling Act (*Ley 13/2011, de 27 de mayo, de regulación del Juego*) was
finally published. On the other hand, the competences on land-based
gambling matters were transferred to the different autonomous regions
during the 1980s and 1990s.

However, the traditional concept of gaming has unquestionably changed
in recent years as well as the scope of its exploitation and marketing
activities.

The main reason for this fundamental change was the decriminalisation
of gaming that took place in 1977 and the inrush of new electronic
communication services such as the use of interactive gaming services
through the internet. In this regard, the quick development of technology
in the 21st century, has left behind the traditional regulatory instruments
in Spain, and the regulation was not adapted to deal with reality.
Consequently, the regulation became insufficient for operators and
participants as well as for the regulatory bodies.

The fact is that online gambling at federal level was not regulated and
cross-border gaming was not expressly forbidden by the law. In this regard,
the situation was quite controversial because the gaming regulations
prohibited unauthorised or unlicensed gaming businesses operating from
Spain, but they did not prohibit online businesses operating from abroad.

Things started to change in late 2007, when the Spanish Parliament
passed the Law on Measures in order to Develop the Information Society
(*Ley 56/2007, de 28 de diciembre, de Medidas de Impulso de la Sociedad de la*

Información). The 20th Additional Provision of which obliged the Spanish Government to regulate online betting and gambling in Spain, including a list of principles, which would govern the future – at that time – gambling act.

Although the abovementioned principles were expected to be developed in a law during 2008/2009, this regulatory process did not start until September 2010 once the state lotteries' monopoly entity, *Loterías y Apuestas del Estado* (LAE), started to lead the process.

After a total of six different versions of the draft Gaming Act, the last one became a Bill in February 2011, when the Spanish Congress published it in its gazette. The Bill was approved by the Congress on 12 April and was passed to the Senate, the Spanish Lower House, where some amendments were introduced on 5 May. These amendments were definitively approved by the Congress on 12 May.

The Gaming Act was finally published in the Spanish State Gazette (BOE – *Boletín Oficial del Estado*) on 28 May, and became enforceable the day after.

The main aim of the federal Gaming Act, as stated in its introductory preamble, is to harmonise the regulation of online gambling in Spain, an activity which clearly transcends beyond regional boundaries, while regional gambling continues to be regulated by each one of the autonomous regions.

2. FRAMEWORK OF LEGISLATION

2.1 What is the legal definition of gambling and what falls within this definition?

The Gaming Act defines the concept of 'gambling' as: *'Activity in which amounts of money or economically measurable objects in any way, are put in risk upon uncertain or future events, dependent to some extent on chance, regardless that it predominates in them the degree of skill of the players or are exclusively or primarily games of luck or gambling stakes. The awards may be in cash or kind depending on the type of game'.*

According to this, there are three essential facts that must concur within the game in order to fall within the definition, which are: (i) a component of chance; (ii) pay-to-play; and (iii) the existence of a prize.

If one of these factors is not involved within the game, it should be considered outside the definition of 'gambling' and consequently, the Gaming Act or any secondary gaming regulation will not be applicable.

2.2 What is the legal definition of online gambling and what falls within this definition?

The Gaming Act defines games performed through electronic channels, IT and interactive systems as follows: *'Games that take place when any device, equipment or system is employed to produce, store or transfer documents, data or information, including any open or restricted communication networks such as television, internet, land lines, mobile phones or any other interactive communication system, either in real time or recorded'.*

Therefore, and according to the legislation, online gambling is the activity of the games performed through electronic channels, IT and interactive systems where on-site means have a secondary roll.

2.3 Please set out the different gambling products identified by legislation.

Considering the division established between online gaming offered at federal level and land-based gaming, the offer of gambling products subject to licence depends on the regulation that is in place in each one of the regions or the ones available at federal level. Thus, each regional regulation contains its own Catalogue of Games where the gambling products are regulated and only those that are included in the catalogues are allowed to be offered by the operator. On the other hand, the Gaming Act does not establish a Catalogue of Games. Instead, each type of game subject to licence needs to have its own regulation and therefore, if a game is not regulated, it is forbidden.

In this regard, the gambling regulations at federal level have approved the following games providing specific regulation for each of them: pools on sports betting; fixed odds sport betting; pools on horse racing; fixed odds horse racing; other fixed odds betting; contests; poker; bingo; roulette; complementary games; blackjack; and baccarat.

With regard to lotteries offered at federal level, LAE maintains the monopoly on this game as well as ONCE (the National Organisation of Spanish Blind people). Exceptionally, only charity organisations may be allowed to organise lotteries.

Currently, online slots and any other game that is not expressly regulated by the federal legislation is not subject to licensing and is therefore banned. However, in the case of online slots and exchange betting, the draft regulation has already been drawn up by the DGOJ and, as will be explained in later sections of this questionnaire, the very early approval of these two products is expected.

At regional level, and taking as an example the Catalogue of Games offered by the Madrid Region, the following gaming products are authorised and can be offered by operators: roulette; blackjack; boule; thirty and forty; craps; baccarat; poker; slots and other machine gaming; bingo; raffles; tombola or charity raffle; betting; sports betting; and horse racing.

2.4 Please list the different requirements for each gambling product, including legal classifications for each; for example, is poker a game of skill or game of chance?

As stated before, all the operators that are interested in developing games that are approved, whether by the federal legislation or by any regional regulation, and that are exclusively or essentially games of chance or mixed with a player's skill, are subject to obtaining the corresponding licence or authorisation. Those games that are exclusively games of skill do not need a gaming licence in order to be offered.

2.5 Explain the system of regulation of gambling; which regulatory or governmental body is responsible for the supervision of gambling? Which body issues licences? Which body examines enforcement powers? Is there any limit on the number or duration of available licences?

Regarding the federal licences derived from the Gaming Act, the competent body for issuing the licences, supervising the games and examining enforcement powers is the General Directorate for Gambling Regulation (Dirección General de Ordenación del Juego).

With regard to the regional authorisations, the body in charge of issuing and supervising the licences and games as well as of examining enforcement powers is the corresponding regional competent body, which in most cases will be subject to the competences of the regional departments of finance or interior.

Neither the Gaming Act nor the regional regulations include a limit on the number of licences available. However, this is a condition that can be included on the basis of the tender, once a call for a public tender in order to apply for gaming licences has been launched by the corresponding gaming authority.

3. ONLINE GAMBLING

3.1 To what extent can online gambling be offered in your jurisdiction? Are licences available and, if so, for which gambling products? Please describe briefly the licensing process, who may apply, whether licences are limited in number and, if no licences are available, whether it is legal for online gambling to be offered. In the case of EU jurisdictions, please state whether there are any issues as to the legality of the local law at EU level. Please refer to any relevant cases at ECJ level and explain any measures taken or pending by the European Commission.

Online gambling in Spain can be offered in one specific autonomous region or in more than one or at federal level, the latter being the most common case for online gaming.

In this regard, the aim of the Gaming Act is to regulate all types of games that take place at federal level in order to protect public order; combat fraud; prevent addictive behaviours; protect minors; and safeguard players' rights, without affecting what is established in the regional statues.

According to the Gaming Act, entities which are interested in operating need to obtain a general licence per category of game. General licences per se are not valid to offer games. To do so, the operator will also need to obtain a single licence for each type of game within its category.

General licences are granted for the term of 10 years, extendable to 10 more years, while single licences will be granted for a minimum term of one year and a maximum of five (depending on each game), extendable for identical periods of time.

In this regard, the Royal Decree 1614/2011, of 14 November, developing the regulation of the Gaming Act 13/2011, on Licences, Authorisations and Gaming Registries, as well as the different ministerial orders approving the specific regulation of each kind of game, establish the following categories for the single licences in accordance with each type of general licence:

General licences	Single licences
Betting	Pools on sports betting
	Fixed odds sports betting
	Pools on horse racing
	Fixed odds horse racing
	Other fixed odds betting
Raffles	
Contests	Contests
Other games	Poker
	Roulette
	Blackjack
	Bingo
	Baccarat
	Complementary games

For instance, should an operator wish to commercialise fixed odds sports betting and poker games, it will need to be granted two general licences (betting and other games). Furthermore, the operator will also need to obtain a single licence for each game that it is going to commercialise. Following the example above, it will also need to obtain two single licences (fixed odds sports betting and poker).

The licences must be obtained through a public tender process. The first public tender was convoked by the General Directorate for Gambling Regulation on 18th November 2011 and the deadline to submit the applications was due on 14th December.

The tender did not limit the number of operators to be granted a licence. In other words, all those operators that met the requirements established within the tender had obtained a licence. However, all those that have not been granted the licence, are banned from operating in Spain, at least until the following public process is convoked.

The licensing process established a large list of requirements and documents that the applicants needed to file.

In this regard, the main requirements that the gaming operators should comply with are:
- the operator can only be a company based in Spain or anywhere else in the European Economic Area;
- should the operator not be based within the Spanish territory, it needs to have, at least, a permanent representative in Spain with capacity to receive notifications and e-notifications (physical address and e-mail account);
- the operators need to be under the formula of a *Sociedad Anónima*, or the analogous form of the EEA; and

- the corporate purpose of the company must be limited to the organisation, commercialisation and exploitation of gaming/betting activities.

The documents filed together with the applications were mainly distinguished in three different groups in order to prove the following aspects:

- legal solvency: within this group of documents the applicant should have to provide, among others, corporative documents and proof of being up-to-date with payments to the Spanish Tax Agency and Social Security and the corresponding administrative fees;
- economic solvency: among the documents required to prove financial solvency, the annual accounts of the last three years are required as well as a description and the origin of the own and external resources planned to be used for the development of the activity subject to the licence. Furthermore, the constitution of economic guarantees which amounts are significant (EUR 2 million for betting, EUR 2 million for other games and EUR 500,000 for contests). It is important to highlight that these are the amounts for guarantees that operators must deposit for the first year. However, for the second year and after, the total amount in guarantees is reduced since the amount that a gaming operator needs to fulfil all its general and single licences is provided by the sum of the percentage legally established on GGR (gross gaming revenue) of all the single licences that the operator has been granted. In any case, the regulation states that the minimum amount for all of the general and single licences shall not be less that EUR 1 million unless only the licences are only for contest games, in which case the amount shall not be less than EUR 250,000. According to that and in relation to 2014, all the guarantees linked to operators that obtained a gaming licence during the first licensing process have recently been amended and the excess amount has accordingly been returned to each operator; and
- technical solvency: the technical solvency should have been proved through a large list of documents and certifications, which independent labs were also involved in. The technical project related to the licence as well as the Internal Control System has to be certified and other documents in accordance with the basis of the tender need to be provided, as an anti-money laundering policy, an operating plan or the definitive agreements performed with third parties, for instance.

Fifty-nine companies applied for different licences during the first licensing process, with 93 general licences and 189 single licences being granted to 55 companies.

On 15 June 2012 the official list of licenced operators was published by the General Directorate for Gambling Regulation and the sanctioning regime consequently entered into force. All of those operators without a Spanish gaming licence had to stop operating in Spain.

3.2 Is there a distinction between the law applicable to B2B operations and that applicable to B2C operations?

One of the most controversial points during the drafting of the secondary regulation on Licences, Authorisations and Gaming Registries, was how the concept of 'gaming operator' should be defined.

The last definition that was approved by the Royal Decree 1614/2011, of 14 November, developing the regulation of the Gaming Act 13/2011, on Licences, Authorisations and Gaming Registries, and concluded that both the B2C and B2B operators are included in the concept of gaming operator. Therefore, there is no distinction between the law applicable to the operations of one operator or the other. In this regard, both operators are required to obtain a gaming licence in order to legally operate in Spain.

The definitive concept of 'gaming operator' is as follows:

Article 3.2. *'Operator shall mean, those individuals or legal persons that, wholly or partly, run a gaming activity as far as their incomes derived from such activity are linked to the gross or net revenue, commissions, as well as whatsoever any other amounts related to gaming services and, at the same time, they perform any commercializing gaming activity, as it may be, for instance and not limited to, determining the prizes or tournaments, managing player's rules, transactions and payment settlements, managing the gaming platform or the registration of users.'*

Article 3.3. *'hose meeting the requirements established in the previous paragraph, that also manage gaming platforms, in which they are members or which other gaming operators join and where they put in common stakes coming from their respective users, will be considered as operator and gaming co-organizers. Under the terms of the call of the public tender for the licences or through the specific regulation for this purpose, the General Direction on Gambling will be entitled to adapt or to establish exceptions to certain requirements demanded to gaming operators if, from a objective perspective, these rules are not justified according to the nature of the activity performed as gaming co-organizers as well as limit their liability regime.'*

Article 3.4 *'No licence is requested to those companies that exclusively perform an affiliation activity, consisting of a promotion activity or by obtaining new clients for the gaming operator, as far as they do not register clients or maintain an agreement or gaming account with them (the clients [the users]).'*

Therefore, the regulation includes software providers in the definition of gaming operators required to obtain a licence.

3.3 What are the consequences for B2C or B2B operators who are active in your jurisdiction without having obtained or applied for the required permits, licences and approvals? What penalties and enforcement powers are available in respect of the illegal operators? Please outline any significant domestic decisions or enforcement actions that have been taken by the relevant authorities in recent years.

Both B2C and B2B operators that are actively organising, commercialising and exploiting gaming activities without having obtained the corresponding licence are legally seen as committing a very serious infringement that carries a fine from EUR 1 to 50 million.

Apart from the applicable economic sanctions, it is possible to apply additional measures, such as the blocking of illegal activities, the interruption of financial transactions and the withdrawal of advertising campaigns.

The fight against illegal gambling has been one of the main objectives of the Spanish Administration since June 2012, when the opening of the legal market took place. In this regard, the first sanctioning proceeding against an illegal operator was initiated in October 2012. However, the General Directorate for Gambling Regulation continuously carries out inspections and currently there are around 250 websites that have been identified as operating illegally in Spain, with more than a dozen sanctioning proceedings opened against illegal portals.

From our point of view, the sanctioning regime establishes fines that are disproportionate to the seriousness of the punishable activity and the regime, in general terms, is also quite imprecise and vague at the time of defining each particular infringement.

3.4 What technical measures are in place (if any) to protect consumers from unlicensed operators, such as ISP blocking and payment blocking?

There are no technical measures, though there are enforcements which could lead to the blocking of IP addresses by Spanish ISPs.

3.5 Has the legal status of online gambling changed significantly in recent years and, if so, how?

Considering all the foregoing, the legal status of online gambling has clearly changed in recent years, since the sector was unregulated until May 2011. Until then, online gaming operators had almost no obligations, however currently, the companies that have not been granted the licence are prohibited from operating. Additionally, those that are legally operating will need to attend to all the duties and obligations derived from the gaming legislation.

3.6 Whilst acknowledging the inherent difficulty in predicting developments in gambling law, what are the likely developments in online gambling in your jurisdiction, both short term and long term? Are any specific amendments under consideration? Have there been any recent political developments, or do you envisage any in the near future? Are any specific amendments under consideration? Are they likely to be adopted and, if so, what is the time scale?

The main changes demanded by the operators are related to the approval of a wider offer of games, especially the regulation of online slots and exchange betting.

The General Directorate for Gambling Regulation had been evaluating the possibility of regulating these two new types of games for months until finally, at the end of April 2013, the regulator announced his decision in favour of authorising these two products. Consequently, the proper regulatory process has been initiated. In fact, on 13 February 2014 the confidential first draft regulation for online slots and exchange betting games, prepared solely by the General Directorate for Gambling Regulation, was leaked and published in several Spanish publications. Later, on 10 March 2014, the draft regulation for online slots and for exchange betting was officially published by the General Directorate for Gambling Regulation for public consultation for the term of 15 working days. Moreover, and in parallel, the draft Ministerial Orders were submitted on 18 March to the European Commission for its review and also for consultation at the European level. Interested parties may provide comments and arguments about this process by the deadline of 19 June 2014.

According to the drafts, one of the main provisions that we consider essential to highlight in both cases is the one related to the entry into force of the Ministerial Orders approving these two new games. Both drafts state that they will enter into force on the same day that a new call for a public tender to apply for general licences is published. Therefore, those operators that currently hold a general licence will be entitled to apply for the relating single licence while those operators without any kind of online licence in Spain will be allowed to apply for the corresponding general and single licences and enter into the Spanish market. The upcoming regulation for online slots and exchange betting games as well as the upcoming call for a new licensing process was officially confirmed by the Ministry of Finance in a press release published on 19 February 2014. Therefore, this is a development that will definitely take place in a short term.

Anther relevant matter that must be taken into consideration and amended is the federal gaming tax regime. The current tax rate applicable to online casino games and fixed odds betting games is of 25 per cent on GGR, in contrast to the 10 per cent applicable by the regional authorities on gaming at the regional level. The 25 per cent on GGR rate is considered by the industry to be excessive and as a consequence it generates a lack of competitiveness. This rate should be homogenised in line with the regional rates applicable to the online games or at least reduced to the much more economically viable rate of 15 per cent. However, even though the tax rate is being reviewed by the General Directorate for Gambling Regulation, it will need to be approved by a different authority body within the Ministry of Finance and it is likely to be adopted in the long term – or, rather, it will not happen in a short term, but it is already in progress.

3.7 Is the law the same in relation to mobile gambling and interactive gambling on television? If not, are there any headline differences?

The Gaming Act is also applicable to mobile gambling and interactive gambling on television.

4. LAND-BASED GAMING
4.1 Please describe the licensing regime (if any) for land-based gaming, and what products are included. Please set out what licences are available, and the licensing regime for them.

As it has been previously stated, the licensing regime for land-based games depends on each regional regulation. In this regard, each of the 17 autonomous regions in Spain have their own licensing regime based on allowing the companies to operate under authorisation. Also the regions have their own catalogue of games approving the offer of gaming products than can be developed by the operator.

In general terms, with some small differences between the regions, the gaming products that are included within the several regional catalogues of games are the following: French roulette; American roulette; blackjack; boule; trente et quarante; craps; baccarat; poker (different forms); slots and other machine gaming; bingo; raffles; tombola or charity raffles; betting; sports betting; horse racing and wheel of fortune.

The companies that are interested in organising and commercialising games in any of the regions must first apply for the corresponding administrative authorisation, which in most of the cases must be done through a call for a public tender process. One of the requirements that is commonplace to all the regional regulations is that the company should be registered in the General Registry of Gaming Companies belonging to the corresponding region.

Additionally, the companies that are interested in obtaining regional authorisation should submit to the regional competent authority a large list of documents which, as in the federal regulation, are required mainly in order to prove legal, economic and technical solvency.

Among the large list of documents the most significant are as follows:
*   the operator needs to deposit the corresponding economic guarantees. It is relevant to note that the economic guarantees that are requested in some regions are very high. (Eg: the authorisation for the organisation and commercialisation of betting games in the Madrid region requires the operator to submit an economic guarantee of EUR 12,000,000);
*   the operator needs to prove that it is up to date with Social Security payments and with the Tax Agency;
*   the operator needs to comply with all the technical requirements and needs to provide documents in order to prove technical solvency. Subsequently, the corresponding competent authority evaluates and homologates the system; and
*   documents in order to prove economic and legal solvency (eg annual accounts, bank certificates, articles of association, deeds of incorporation of the company, etc).

Simultaneously with the application for authorisation to commercialise and exploit games, the companies can also apply for authorisation related to the gaming establishments and businesses, where there are different and additional requirements that the operator should comply with. Some regions provide a more restrictive approach and a good number of requirements are established like the number of slots/betting terminals, the number of establishments or installations, minimum number of square meters in the gaming premises, etc.

4.2 Please set out any particular limitations or requirements for (eg casino) operators, such as a ban on local residents gambling.

In general terms, there are no particular limitations or requirements for land-based gaming operators other than the ban on gambling to minors under the legal age.

With regards to online gambling at regional level and continuing with the example of the Madrid region, there is a limitation that states that only individuals that are tax residents in the Madrid region are allowed to play. However, this is a controversial condition since, in practical terms, this means that an individual who is a Madrid tax resident player is entitled to play on the Madrid's operator website from any different location (different than Madrid), just because that individual is a Madrid tax resident. The point here is that the autonomous regions have territorial competences, not personal ones (ie autonomous regions are competent in their own territory and have no competences in others regions where the Madrid tax resident goes). Therefore, there is a clear conflict of regional competences against the State.

4.3 Please address the questions in 3.5 above, but in relation to land-based gaming.

In general terms, the legal status of land-based gaming has not undergone any significant changes in recent years. Despite this, the different regional regulations include a number of minor changes that make them less restrictive and more flexible to operators. It is thus likely that, in the medium term, there will be a convergence between the territorial regulations and the federal ones.

Probably the most significant regulatory changes that have been taking place within the land-based sector in recent years is the growth of the sports-betting regulations. Thus, eight different regions have developed regulations for this type of product (Aragon, Castilla la Mancha, Galicia, Madrid, Murcia, Navarra, Basque Country and Valencia), while five others have draft regulations (Baleares, Canary Islands, Castilla y Leon, Cataluña and Extremadura).

5. TAX

5.1 Please summarise briefly the tax regime applicable both to land-based and online gaming.

Pursuant to the division of the gaming regulation in Spain, the taxes are also different according to the applicable law. In this regard, the tax regime applicable to online games subject to the Gaming Act are established as indicated in the following table:

Game	Rate
Pool betting on sports	22 per cent on turnover
Fixed odds sport betting	25 per cent on gross gaming revenue (GGR)
Betting exchanges for sports	25 per cent on GGR
Pool betting horse betting	15 per cent on turnover
Fixed odds horse betting	25 per cent on GGR
Other forms of pool betting	15 per cent on turnover
Other forms of fixed odds betting	25 per cent on GGR
Other forms of exchange betting	25 per cent on GGR
Raffles	20 per cent on turnover 7 per cent on turnover (non-profit associations)
Contests	20 per cent on turnover
Other games (poker, casino, bingo, etc)	25 per cent on GGR
Random combination games	10 per cent of the prize's market value

Additionally, the Gaming Act establishes that the autonomous regions will be able to raise up to 20 per cent over the abovementioned rates in relation to the players that are tax resident within their boundaries and where the operator is also based in its region.

The tax on gaming activity has been approved by the Gaming Act. Since its approval, the active operators who are currently developing their activity in Spain, are paying quarterly taxes in order to be up to date with the Tax Agency.

On the other hand, the taxes applicable to land-based games are approved by each regional regulation. In the case of the Madrid region, the taxes are as follows:

Tax rates
- The general tax rate is 20 per cent on GGR.
- The tax rate applicable to bingo is 15 per cent on GGR and to electronic bingo is 30 per cent on GGR.
- The tax rate applicable to online games developed in the Madrid region is 10 per cent on GGR.
- The general tax rate for betting games is 13 per cent on GGR and on sports betting, horse racing and other betting games is 10 per cent on GGR.
- The tax rates applicable to casino games are as indicated in the following table, based in tranches:

Portion of the tax base (in euros)	Rate
Between 0 and 2,000,000	22 per cent
Between 2,000,000 and 3,000,000	30 per cent
Between 3,000,000 and 5,000,000	40 per cent
More than 5,000,000	45 per cent

Fixed rates
In the cases of operating betting terminals or automatic appliances suitable for the development of games, there are fixed rates that will be applied in accordance with the classification of the types of terminals or devices provided by each regulation.

6. ADVERTISING
6.1 To what extent is the advertising of gambling permitted in your jurisdiction? Again, this should cover both land-based and online gaming. To the extent that advertising is permitted, how is it regulated?

Since licences were granted on 1 June 2012, the general rules are as follows:

- advertising and sponsoring activities are only allowed for those operators that have been granted a Spanish licence and have been awarded authorisation to advertise;
- a self-regulatory code of conduct has been drafted by the General Directorate for Gambling Regulation and subscribed to by the majority of gambling operators, advertising agencies, media operators and communication services providers. This code of conduct and the general Spanish law regarding advertising and eCommerce are the applicable framework in this regard; and
- unauthorised gaming advertising has been explicitly banned. According to Article 40.d of the Act, unauthorised advertising activities, or those outside the limits established in the certificate, by whatsoever means, will be considered to be a serious infraction. Serious infractions could be sanctioned with fines from EUR 100,000 to EUR 1 million plus cancellation of the activity in Spain for six months.

With regard to land-based games, there are also advertising rules drafted by each autonomous region. In most regions, prior authorisation for advertising activities is required; however, other regions that seek to liberalise the sector and reduce the regulatory rigidity are removing this independent authorisation for advertising activities. Some of the most recent regional regulations are in Canary Islands and Valencia. This latter regulation has not been approved yet to date. However, it has already been passed to public consultation, and will be finally approved once this period has finished. Instead of the prior independent authorisation, these regulations establish general principles and prohibitions that ensure that the use of the advertising tool is held in all cases respecting the guarantees of citizens, in particular the protection of youth, childhood and the consumer's health. The draft regulation for Valencia, for instance, establishes general prohibitions on the advertising activities and special conditions applicable to advertising inside betting shops, advertising through radio or by audiovisual means (allowed from 11pm to 6am), advertising in magazines, press or brochures, and advertising on websites.

Unauthorised advertising activities or those outside the limits established in the certificate or regulation, by whatsoever means, will be considered to be a very serious infraction.

7. SOCIAL GAMING

7.1 We believe this to be a growing area. Please decide under what criteria social gaming is permitted in your jurisdiction. If games are free to play or if there is no prize, are they legal without a licence? Please address circumstances where virtual currency is used and can be won: ie currency which is of no monetary or other value, save for as credits to take part in games. The answer should address the question whether game credits or virtual money can be exchanged for other prizes. Is any change to regulation in the area proposed or envisaged?

The concept of gambling requires the existence of three essential components which are: (i) the chance; (ii) pay-to-play; and (iii) the existence of a prize.

If one of these factors is not in place, it would fall outside the definition of 'gambling'. Consequently, the Gaming Act would not be applicable and the game would not be subject to licensing. This means that if games are free to play or if there is no prize, it is compliant with the law to carry out this activity without obtaining a gaming licence. The same rule applies to games where virtual currency which is of no monetary value is used and can be won, or even if credits can be purchased for real money but the player cannot win anything of value other than additional game plays, chips, coins or other virtual items.

With regard to social games, the federal regulation has approved regulation for a type of game called 'complementary games' (being in the previous draft versions of the regulation wrongly named 'social games').

The complementary games, are defined as those types of game which include games with a different nature (combining chance with skill, culture and knowledge) having a common denominator – which is that the performance of these games is not solely based on obtaining an economic profit – but above all they should be played for fun.

The maximum amount that the player can risk on this kind of game (per hand) is EUR 1. The maximum prize that the player can win is 40 times the amount risked.

With regard to the offer of this gaming product, a general catalogue of the complementary games or a list of the games included within this category does not exist. Each operator should produce a catalogue including and proposing all the complementary games that it intends to commercialise within the platform. This catalogue, jointly with the particular rules of each of the proposed complementary games, should be notified to the General

Directorate for Gambling Regulation as a minimum within a period of 15 days prior to the start date of commercialising the games.

Once the General Directorate for Gambling Regulation analyses the catalogue, it shall be entitled reasonably to suspend it, or to demand that the operator introduce changes in order to guarantee the participant's protection.

The General Directorate for Gambling Regulation will focus on ensuring that there are no games within the catalogue which include games or bets not corresponding with the definition and/or which according to the name of the game, nature, rules or mechanisms, could correspond to any of the other games defined in another specific Gaming Regulation.

According to the definition provided for complementary games, those games determined as skill games where the design of the games dictate that the skill of the participants is not due to any fortuitous actions that determines the results (as games of chance, like different types of poker, bingo etc, where the results of the games have, at least, an element of chance) are excluded from the Gaming Act and therefore, are not subjected to licence.

Therefore, and as previously explained, pure skill games are excluded from the definition of 'gambling' since this requires that 'some degree of chance' takes place during the game. Therefore, skill games do not require a licence nor regional authorisation in order to be organised and commercialised.

Sweden

Hansen Advokatbyrå KB Dr Ola Wiklund

1. OBJECTIVES AND STRUCTURE OF LEGISLATION

At first sight, Swedish gambling legislation presents a monopolistic regime, closed to commercial providers. However, this is a false perception of the practical legal reality, in which the nationally permitted providers compete against remotely based – but often 'truly' Swedish – operators. Despite the formal impression of the gambling legislation, the situation may be summarised as follows. The legislature and jurisprudence respects the EU right to provide cross-border services – or at least, they lack the means to restrict a remotely-based operator. Consequently, gambling services may be offered from a distance to Swedish residents – ie online gambling. Meanwhile for land-based gambling the onerous national legislation still applies – reserving the market to state-owned/controlled companies and non-profit associations. Profit-making companies are not permitted, other than for small-scale restaurant casinos and the economically insignificant amusement games and goods gambling machines. An important feature, framing the legal status for gambling in Sweden, is the prohibition, in commercial operations or otherwise for the purpose of profit, to promote the participation in an unlawful domestic lottery or a foreign lottery.

From the 1970s and onwards, an already restrictive gambling regime became even more strict. Private profit-making providers were shut out from the market, which was reserved to state companies – Svenska Spel and ATG – or non-profit associations. This constitutes the historical and rhetorical background behind the main purpose underlying the Swedish gambling policy. This is to provide for a healthy and safe gambling market, in which social protection interests and the demand for gambling are provided for in controlled forms. Profits from gambling should be reserved for objectives which are in the public interest or socially beneficial, that is, the activities of non-profit associations, equestrian sports and the state. As has been the case hitherto, the focus should be on prioritising social protection considerations whilst offering a variety of gambling options and taking heed of the risk of fraud and unlawful gambling. Over the years the government has claimed that these objectives also require that the offering of internet gambling services should be entrusted to state controlled companies. But as described above, the emergence of online gambling has substantially changed Swedish gambling policy and withered down the monopoly in terms of internet gambling.

By now the Swedish government and jurisprudence acknowledge that it is not illegal for private operators established in another EU member state to offer gambling services to Swedish customers. And, consequently, it is permitted to engage in internet gambling for Swedish residents. Consumers are free to choose between a wide variety of brands and products. The private operators can even legally market their services in Sweden through television (though broadcasted from abroad) and internet. Through a coherent legal strategy, and by avoiding obvious violations, commercial online gambling operators may target the Swedish market, although a formalistic reading of the Swedish gambling legislation gives another impression.

2. FRAMEWORK OF LEGISLATION
2.1 What is the legal definition of gambling and what falls within this definition?

Gambling in Sweden is mainly governed by the Lotteries Act (Code of Statutes no 1994:1000). Consequently, most legal definitions are to be found within this act. The most important definition is that of 'lottery', for it establishes what is comprised by the act. A lottery is *'an activity where one or more participants may, with or without a stake, obtain prizes of a higher value than that which each and every one of the other participants may obtain'*. This definition explicitly includes drawing of tickets, guessing, betting and similar procedures, amusements at fairs and amusement parks, bingo games, gaming machines, roulette games, dice games, card games, chain letter or similar games.

The Lotteries Act separates skill games from lotteries. A gambling arrangement which is decided by an element of chance is to be considered a lottery, whilst a gambling arrangement which is decided by skill is considered to be a game/competition and hence falls outside of the scope of the Lotteries Act. As noted above, despite the elements of skill the Swedish legislator considers card games (such as poker) to be more of a lottery than a skill game. But the element of chance is not decisive alone for whether the arrangement is a lottery or not. Depending on the general character of the activity, it may be a lottery even if the winning opportunity to little or no part depends on chance. Furthermore, the Lotteries Act only applies to lotteries arranged for the public. This probably excludes small and closed gatherings were the participants have a mutual connection – other than the gambling.

The broad definition and scope of lotteries is complemented by a catch-all provision in section 9 of the Lotteries Act, stipulating that unless the act provides otherwise, lotteries shall only be arranged after a permit has been obtained. However, the situations where the act actually provides exceptions are not insignificant, and furthermore the scope and jurisdiction of the Lotteries Act also has practical limitations.

An important feature of the Lotteries Act is its refined definition of 'true lotteries'. 'True lotteries' are specified as drawing of tickets, guessing, betting and similar procedures and amusements at fairs and amusement parks. Horse racing and betting in connection with sports competitions undertaken in more than one municipality are not covered by 'true lotteries'.

2.2 What is the legal definition of online gambling and what falls within this definition?

There is no legal definition of online gambling. Such gambling is covered by the general definition and it is apparent from the actual permit to arrange a certain lottery whether it relates to an online offering. Certain differences may occur in the permit procedure depending on whether the gambling is arranged online or offline. Yet the Lotteries Act contains provisions relating to lotteries communicated by means of electronic waves – which comprise, eg radio, television, internet and mobile phones. According to this provision such lotteries shall be deemed 'true lotteries', but certain regulations may be issued, such as age limits.

2.3 Please set out the different gambling products identified by legislation.

The different gambling products identified by legislation are:

* lotteries;
* special lottery permits;
* poker;
* betting (other than sports betting);
* sports betting;
* casino games;
* slot and other machine gaming; and
* bingo.

2.4 Please list the different requirements for each gambling product, including legal classifications for each; for example, is poker a game of skill or game of chance?

Lottery

The Lotteries Act's definition of lotteries comprises a lot of different gambling products. These includes drawing of tickets, guessing, betting and similar procedures, amusements at fairs and amusement parks, bingo games, gaming machines, roulette games, dice games, card games, chain letter or similar games. Still, the broad definition of lotteries and its scope is fundamental to Swedish gambling legislation.

As mentioned above the definition of 'true lotteries' comprises a broad range of gambling services. There are four different categories of 'true lotteries': those that may be arranged by non-profit associations and require a permit (section 15, Lotteries Act); those that may be arranged by non-profit associations and do not require a permit but must be registered (section 17, Lotteries Act); those that may be arranged by non-profit associations and do not require a permit (section 19, Lotteries Act); and those that may be arranged by any entity under certain circumstances (section 20, Lotteries Act).

Permits to arrange a 'true lottery' must generally only be granted to non-profit associations which have as their principal purpose the promotion of objects of public benefit. The major players amongst these non-profit associations are A-lotterierna (owned by the Social Democratic Party and its youth league); IOGT-NTO (the Swedish temperance movement), several patient's rights organisations; and the Swedish Postcode Lottery (inspired by the Dutch concept). For such 'true lotteries' the value of the prizes must correspond to at least 35 per cent and not more than 50 per cent of the value of the stakes. While the former follows from the general provisions in section 15, the latter follows from the special provisions relating to such lotteries in section 16.

There are vast restrictions concerning 'true lotteries' in the Gaming Board's general recommendations, ie limiting the size of the highest prize to one Price Base Amount (ie the official economic amount set every year – during 2014 amounting to SEK 44,400 – by the Swedish Statistics Bureau for the purpose of indicating amounts in, eg legislation).

In 'true lotteries' not requiring permits, arranged by non-profit associations, the Lotteries Act limits the stakes to 1/6000 and the highest prize to 1/6 of the Price Base Amount. For 'true lotteries' that may be arranged by any entity, more onerous conditions apply. They may only be arranged in connection with a public amusement event or a public event in support of an object of public benefit (or a gathering for performance of an artistic work in support for such an object). The prizes may only consist of goods or services and the stakes are limited to 1/6000 and the top prize to 1/60 of the Price Base Amount.

Special lottery permits
According to section 45 of the Lotteries Act, the government may issue special lottery permits. The provision entitles the government to grant special lottery permits in other cases and according to other procedures than provided in the Lotteries Act. There are no statutory rules for special lottery permits. However, such limits and regulations are provided together with the decision to grant a permit.

Poker
Under the Lotteries Act, poker is considered a card game. Only Svenska Spel – and its casino-running subsidiary Casino Cosmopol – is granted a permit to arrange poker games. Internet poker is regulated by the Lotteries Act and Live poker is regulated by the Casino Act (Code of Statutes no 1999:355). It should be observed that the Swedish Supreme Court in 2011 (see NJA 2011 s. 45) ruled that a certain form of poker (Texas Hold'em), under certain conditions, when arranged in a large tournament is not a game of chance. Consequently, such arrangement does not fall within the scope of the Lotteries Act and the provisions in the Penal Code targeting illicit gambling. The Court particularly focused on the rounds played in such a tournament and the effect it has on the hazard.

In the permit to arrange internet poker granted to Svenska Spel, certain conditions are prescribed including: players must be above 18 years old; a limit on losses and time spent playing; the ability to see the time spent playing; and participation in an information programme. Furthermore the stakes are limited to two Price Base Amounts. Live poker is regulated by the Casino Act.

Betting (other than sports betting and horse racing)
Betting is generally considered a 'true lottery', under the definition provided by the Lotteries Act (see above).

Sports betting
Sports betting in connection with competitions undertaken in more than one municipality is separated from other sorts of betting by the definitions provided in the Lotteries Act. Consequently, there is no specific provision in the act governing sports betting and the licensing of such arrangements. Instead sports betting is permitted by the government under section 45 of the Lotteries Act. Currently, Svenska Spel has the sole right to arrange sports betting.

Horse racing
Along with sports betting, horse racing is specifically distinguished from other forms of betting in the Lotteries Act. As with sports betting, this means that the Lotteries Act contains no specific provision governing horse racing and the licensing of such arrangements. Horse racing is permitted by the government under section 45 of the Lotteries Act. ATG (the Swedish Horse Racing Totalisator Board) has the sole right to arrange horse race betting.

Casino games
There are two legal categories of casino operations, informally denominated 'international casinos' and 'restaurant casinos'.

International casinos are governed by the Casino Act, and they basically operate international casino rules with higher stakes and higher prizes. The Casino Act restricts the number of international casinos to six. They must be operated by companies wholly-owned by the state, and their permit is granted by the government. Currently there are four international casinos in Sweden, located in Stockholm, Gothenburg, Malmö and Sundsvall. All of them are operated by Casino Cosmopol AB, a subsidiary of Svenska Spel.

Restaurant casinos include games of card, dice and roulette arranged in relation to certain public amusements, eg hotels and restaurants (with table licences), amusement parks and ships in international traffic. Restaurant casinos are regulated in detail under sections 32 and 33 of the Lotteries Act, strictly limiting the stakes and prizes. A permit is mandatory, and it is permitted by the Swedish Gaming Board. According to the Gaming Board there are currently approximately 600 such restaurant casinos.

Slot and other machine gaming
In terms of slot machines, the Lotteries Act differentiates between goods gaming machines, cash machines and token machines. Furthermore the act on arrangements for certain gaming machines (Code of Statutes no 1982:636) regulates games in mechanical or electronic gaming machines that do not provide winnings or which only provide winnings in the form of free games on the machine – so-called 'amusement games'

For goods gaming machines the stakes are limited to 1/7000 and the prizes to 1/300 of the Price Base Amount. Such machines may be permitted in relation to public amusement events.

For cash and token machines stricter rules apply. They are only allowed to be placed in relation to hotels and restaurants that hold a table licence under the Alcohol Act, or in connection with bingo games. Only five machines may be placed in the same premises. According to the Lotteries Act such permits may only be granted to state-owned companies, eg Svenska Spel. For cash machines and token machines the stakes are limited to 1/7000 of the Price Base Amount and the prize to 100 times the stake.

Currently Svenska Spel has a permit for 7,000 machines in relation to hotels and restaurants and 500 in relation to bingo games. Essentially there are only token machines, since that is what Svenska Spel holds and have a permit for – the model used is called 'Vegas machines'. This permit and the Gaming Board's guidelines relating to the permit prescribe further detailed rules for such machines.

A judgment by the Supreme Court in December 2011 (case no. B 2350-10) concerned non-permitted gaming machines running on remotely-based servers. Without connection to this server the machines were useless for gaming purposes. The defendants in these cases have been the proprietors of the premises where the machines have been exhibited. The jurisprudence overlooked the importance of the internet connection for the purpose of establishing liability for the proprietor, *inter alia*, for the exhibition of the machines and involvement in any distribution of prizes.

Bingo games

There are certain provisions in the Lotteries Act applicable to bingo games. Basically these provisions correspond to the ones applicable to 'true lotteries', which require permits (section 15, Lotteries Act). However, the rules for bingo games take into account that bingo halls are one of two categories of venues where token machines may be placed – the other venue category being establishments with table licences.

2.5 Explain the system of regulation of gambling; which regulatory or governmental body is responsible for the supervision of gambling? Which body issues licences? Which body examines enforcement powers? Is there any limit on the number or duration of available licences?

The general principle behind the system is that the body responsible for the granting of licences is also in charge of supervision. In addition, however, there are a few special provisions.

As regard permits under the Lotteries Act, these are issued by four categories of bodies; municipalities, regional, the Gaming Board and the government. Municipality permits are granted by the appointed municipal committee and regional permits are granted by the county administrative board.

The municipality grants permits for municipality lotteries. The county administrative board grants permits for regional lotteries and bingo games conducted in one county.

The Gaming Board grants permits for national lotteries, bingo games conducted in more than one county (or if the top prize is set according to section 22), gaming on goods machines, gaming on cash machines and token machines on maritime vessels in international traffic and restaurant casinos. The Gaming Board also determines matters relating to the mandatory 'type approval' concerning lottery tickets, bingo cards and technical equipment used for stakes, drawing of prizes or monitoring of true lotteries and bingo games. The Gaming Board also grants permits to possess cash, token and goods gaming machines – without holding a permit to arrange gaming. Furthermore the Gaming Board grants permits for 'amusement games'.

The government grants permits for token machines and for international casinos. Most importantly the government also grants special lottery permits in other cases and according to other procedures than as provided for in the Lotteries Act.

The Gaming Board is charged with central monitoring of compliance of the Lotteries Act and regulations issued pursuant to it. It is also charged with more detailed supervision of lotteries – and international casinos – arranged under permit from the Gaming Board or the government. The municipal authority and the county administrative board are charged with more detailed supervision of lotteries that are arranged under the permit of, or registration with, that authority.

Attached to this supervisory role, the responsible supervisory authority is also charged with the ability to issue orders and prohibitions required for compliance with the Lotteries Act, and any directions and conditions issued pursuant to the act. Breaches of such order or prohibition may be subject to conditional fines.

There is no limit on the number of permits that can be granted, albeit that the number of international casinos is restricted to six. A permit under the Lotteries Act shall be granted for a specific time, usually six months. Special lottery permits from the government are also granted for a certain period.

3. ONLINE GAMBLING

3.1 To what extent can online gambling be offered in your jurisdiction? Are licences available and, if so, for which gambling products? Please describe briefly the licensing process, who may apply, whether licences are limited in number and, if no licences are available, whether it is legal for online gambling to be offered. In the case of EU jurisdictions, please state whether there are any issues as to the legality of the local law at EU level. Please refer to any relevant cases at ECJ level and explain any measures taken or pending by the European Commission.

The Lotteries Act includes certain provisions relating to lotteries communicated by means of electromagnetic waves. According to these provisions such lotteries – with the exception of horse racing and sports betting – are to be deemed 'true lotteries', and for the purpose of permits, treated accordingly. The application process is also, through a reference to section 15, the same as that of ordinary permits for 'true lotteries'. For such lotteries certain regulations may be issued concerning age limits and population registration for participation or other requirements or the arrangement or the equipment used by the arranger.

As described above, Swedish authorities acknowledge that Swedish residents are unimpeded when participating in foreign gambling and that online gambling operators duly licensed in another EU member state are allowed to offer such services. So far, no commercial provider has been granted a Swedish permit, despite their attempts. Irrespective of each other, Ladbrokes and Betsson a few years ago applied to the Swedish government to be permitted to provide online gambling. Both companies legally challenged the government's refusal by claiming incompatibility of the Swedish gambling legislation with EU law (see RÅ 2005 not 54 and RÅ 2007 not 72). The court concluded that there could, in some areas, be doubts as to the consistency between the outspoken objectives and actual business policy implementation of the permitted operators. This was, however, not serious enough to conclude that the Swedish system as a whole was in breach of the EU rules as applicable at the time of the decisions.

The cases with Betsson and Ladbrokes underline an important feature of gambling legislation. There are no formal restrictions for the government to issue special lottery permits to private, commercial providers. These special lottery permits are granted by discretion of the government and they may involve specific rules and/or conditions pertaining to the particular permit.

3.2 Is there a distinction between the law applicable to B2B operations and that applicable to B2C operations?

No legal framework separates B2B and B2C operations. They are both subject to the Lotteries Act – or any other relevant legislation for the purpose of a certain gambling service separately regulated (see above). However, B2B operations stretch the applicability of the Swedish legislation and jurisdiction. This is barely adapted to the technological shifts in gambling services and not at all adapted to online B2B services. As a consequence any B2B operation deserves to be assessed on a case-by-case basis.

Nonetheless it must be concluded that B2B operators can, to a vast extent, operate without impeding any restrictions provided by the gambling legislation, as the prohibited activities are arrangement of a lottery or promotion of an unlawful or foreign lottery.

Sweden-based B2B operators are market leading and provide some of the most successful software on the market. However, it is generally recommended to keep any servers on which participants from Sweden might participate out of Swedish territory.

3.3 What are the consequences for B2C or B2B operators who are active in your jurisdiction without having obtained or applied for the required permits, licences and approvals? What penalties and enforcement powers are available in respect of the illegal operators? Please outline any significant domestic decisions or enforcement actions that have been taken by the relevant authorities in recent years.

The Swedish Lotteries Act prohibits the arrangement of unlicensed lotteries (a wide ranging concept under the act) and the – in commercial operations or otherwise for the purpose of profit – promotion of participation in unlawful domestic lotteries or a foreign lotteries. Consequently, the legal question of relevance is whether any of the services performed in Sweden amount to either of these prohibited acts.

According to section 54 of the Lotteries Act a fine or a maximum of six months' imprisonment may be imposed on persons who intentionally or by gross negligence unlawfully arrange a lottery or possess a cash machine, token machine, goods gaming machine or skill machine. If the offence is serious, two years imprisonment may be imposed, while there shall be no convictions for trivial offences.

Furthermore, according to section 54 of the Lotteries Act a fine or a maximum of six months' imprisonment may also be imposed on persons who, in commercial operations or otherwise, for the purpose of profit intentionally unlawfully promote participation in gambling arranged outside the country, if the participation particularly relates to participation from Sweden. As outlined below, the Supreme Court has concluded that the promotion prohibition is in conflict with the prohibition of discriminatory measures under EU law, meaning that penal sanctions may not be applied in relation to unlawful promotion of participation in gambling arranged outside Sweden (Case no. B 3559-11). The Gaming Board may still, however, issue orders in conjunction with conditional fines for promotion.

As mentioned, the Gaming Board is charged with the ability to issue orders and prohibitions, subject to conditional fines, required for compliance with the Lotteries Act, and any directions and conditions issued pursuant to the act. Persons in breach of an order or prohibition subject to a fine under the Lotteries Act cannot be sentenced to punishment pursuant to the penal provision in the Lotteries Act for acts covered by the order or prohibition.

There is also a provision in section 14, Chapter 16 of the Penal Code regarding *illicit gambling*, which prescribes imprisonment for up to four years. If the Penal Code is applicable then sections 54 and 56 of the Lotteries Act are not.

Such illicit gambling is at hand if a person unlawfully organises for the public a game or other similar activity the outcome of which is entirely or essentially dependent on chance and, if in view of the nature of the activity, the financial value of the stakes and other circumstances it appears hazardous or of a nature to bring considerable financial gain to the organiser. The sentence is either a fine or imprisonment for at most two years. The same applies to a person who permits such activity in an apartment or other premises which he has opened to the public. For gross illicit gambling the sentence is imprisonment for at least six months and at most four years.

These Penal Code provisions strongly resemble the penal provisions in the Lotteries Act. The legislator's intention is that only more qualified cases are to be sentenced under the Penal Code, or cases falling outside the scope of the Lotteries Act.

Arrangement

The Lotteries Act does not contain any stipulations as to what constitutes an arrangement of a lottery within Sweden. However, the government bill *Lotteries over the Internet, etc.* elaborates on the concept (Prop. 2001/02:153, p. 15f.). In discussing which circumstances to consider when determining whether a lottery which is attainable on the internet, is 'arranged' in Sweden or not, it is noted that the arrangement of internet gambling often may be connected to several different countries. For instance, the arranger may have its company registered in one country, its principal office situated in a different country and the gambling server in a third country.

According to the bill, it does not seem appropriate to let the location of the technical equipment serve as the starting point in determining where a lottery is arranged – partly because it is difficult to determine the geographical location of the equipment and partly because it is simple and quick to relocate. Instead, it is argued that the arrangement of a lottery over the internet should be determined to take place in the country in which the main business is carried out. In answering the question of where the main business is carried out, significant importance should be accorded the location where the organisation and management of the business takes place. However, the bill concludes stating that it is for the courts to decide these issues when trying cases.

The concept of arrangement was further elaborated upon in the Swedish Government Official Report *Gaming in a changing world*, according to which a single measure alone – while being part of a gambling arrangement as such, within the broader sense of the word – might not necessarily constitute arrangement in the Swedish context. It was pointed out that the existence of a lottery is established through accomplishment of several measures, eg the selling of a ticket, receiving of bets, marketing of the lottery, etc. Meanwhile it was concluded that the possibility to participate in Sweden in a lottery arranged abroad, is not necessarily enough to also render the lottery as arranged in Sweden. Overall, it was concluded that arrangement within the meaning of the law comprises the situation where a lottery is organised within the country and made accessible to Swedish participants (Swedish Government Official Report 2006:11 *Gaming in a changing world* p. 206f.).

The issue whether a lottery is arranged in Sweden or abroad has not yet been authoritatively settled by Swedish courts. The level of restrictiveness of the concept of arrangement to be applied by Swedish authorities therefore remains uncertain.

Promotion

The Lotteries Act does not provide any guidance on what may constitute unlawful promotion of foreign lotteries. It is clear that the promotion ban leaves without notion whether the promoted lottery holds a licence in another country (Swedish Government Official Report 2006:11 *Gaming in a changing world* p. 270).

The government bill *New Lotteries Act* defines 'promotion' as the offering, selling or supply of lottery tickets or evidence of participation, the collecting or intermediary of stakes or intermediary of winnings. Furthermore it includes the distribution of invitations, plans or lottery-lists regarding the lottery (Prop. 1993/94:182, p. 78). This was elaborated in the government bill *Criminalisation of promotion of participation in lotteries arranged abroad*, which indicates that promoting a lottery is a far-reaching notion (Prop. 1998/99:29, p. 8 f.). The bill mentions, *inter alia*, the marketing or advertising of lotteries, selling of tickets, receipt of stakes and passing on of prizes. Furthermore, it is noted that in the event the arranger of a foreign lottery establishes a business in Sweden, that could in itself be seen as 'promoting'. Moreover, a case from the Svea Court of Appeal from 1997 (Case no. B 2482-97) is cited, in which a betting company established in Great Britain had a representative in Sweden, who collected bets and transferred them to the company in Great Britain. The court found that the activities carried out in Sweden were not sufficient to constitute the arrangement of a lottery in Sweden, however, it amounted to promoting a foreign lottery. To arrive at that conclusion, the Svea Court of Appeal took into account that the company was registered in Great Britain, carried out legal business there and that the central computer, through which communication with the computers located in Sweden was possible, was located in London. Furthermore the Swedish courts have regarded the supply and publication of links and banners as 'promotion' (Judgments of the Svea Court of Appeal case no. B 864/99 and the Supreme Administrative Court, see RÅ 2004 ref. 96).

In the Swedish Government Official Report *From tombola to internet*, it was concluded that purely passive supply of services necessary for participation in a foreign lottery (ie internet providers, postal and bank services) is not covered by the prohibition.

Jurisdiction

The Lotteries Act comprises every measure regarding gambling and lotteries within the Swedish territory, thus comprising both the situation where a lottery is arranged here and where a lottery arranged abroad is promoted – through marketing, selling or otherwise. According to the Swedish Government Official Report *Gaming in a changing world*, the Lotteries Act is applicable to lotteries in Sweden, but it is not decisive as to where the activity originally derives from. In order to be considered as taking place in Sweden it is necessary that the lottery is accessible in Sweden and – furthermore – that the activity is somehow targeting the Swedish market. The connecting link with the Swedish market must be clear. Such connecting links can include: presentation of the activity in Swedish; betting on Swedish events without international interest; marketing of the activity in Sweden; customer relations provided in Swedish; and the outspoken ambition to target Sweden. An overall assessment of such connecting links is needed. Yet the tendency within EU law is that the law of the sending state applies, and this is respected by Swedish authorities.

3.4 What technical measures are in place (if any) to protect consumers from unlicensed operators, such as ISP blocking and payment blocking?

There are no technical measures, such as ISP or payment blocking, in place to protect Swedish consumers from unlicensed operators.

3.5 Has the legal status of online gambling changed significantly in recent years and, if so, how?

Commercial game operators are provided with the opportunity to offer their services to Swedish customers through the fundamental EU right to provide services. This clash between the onerous national gambling legislation and the possibilities offered under EU law have, during the last decade, caused rather fierce activity in the Swedish courts, where the effects stemming out of this contradiction have been reviewed. To a large extent the courts have upheld EU law, however, without striking down the Swedish legislation as such. Generally Swedish authorities also respect the fundamental rights provided by the EU treaties and, hence, show a rather relaxed attitude to foreign entities targeting their gambling services at the Swedish market.

In 2004 the Supreme Administrative Court examined compliance with EU law of the Gaming Board's authority to issue orders in conjunction with conditional fines (Case RÅ 2004 ref 95). While confirming the compliance of this authority, the Court also confirmed that the state-sanctioned gambling companies, despite being in a monopoly situation, *de facto* operate in a competitive market, since Swedish residents are unimpeded in participating in foreign arranged lotteries.

Gambling companies licensed elsewhere within the EU can thus more or less freely pursue an internet-based gambling business on the Swedish market. The preconditions for this development, however, are lame legal sanctions and the open-ended obligations of EU law. Moreover, these endeavours have been launched against the emergence of a political movement advancing ideas of free access to information on the internet. At the end, this movement has been reinforced by powerful media owners who have found a way to effectively use old freedom of the press and free speech arguments to protect vast advertisement revenues. These media houses hold a substantial financial interest in the revenues stemming from gambling operators, and have actively been campaigning – both in the field of public opinion and in the courts – against provisions in the Swedish legislation restraining promotion of foreign lotteries. One such case of a decisive nature (Case no. B 3559-11) has been settled by the Swedish Supreme Court, following a preliminary ruling by the European Court of Justice.

Consequently two public opinions have been of big relevance in terms of limiting the practical scope of Swedish gambling legislation. First of all, there has been a strong notion in Sweden that the internet should be 'free', ie opposed to IP blocking and/or limits on electronic monetary transfers. Second of all, freedom of speech and freedom of opinion is traditionally deeply founded in Sweden and enjoys old constitutional protection, ie censorship and prohibition of (almost) any messages is highly controversial. Jointly, these views have played out together when it comes to understanding why Swedish legislators have not been able to shut out foreign online gambling operators from the Swedish market.

3.6 Whilst acknowledging the inherent difficulty in predicting developments in gambling law, what are the likely developments in online gambling in your jurisdiction, both short term and long term? Are any specific amendments under consideration? Have there been any recent political developments, or do you envisage any in the near future? Are any specific amendments under consideration? Are they likely to be adopted and, if so, what is the time scale?

In December 2008 the Swedish Government Official Report *A Proposed New Gaming Act* was handed over to the government, marking the third such official report on gambling legislation during the 2000s. However, the findings and conclusions of the report have yet not been implemented. Among the proposals was a cautious opening for new providers on the gambling market.

There is, however, a rather broad consensus among most political parties in Sweden that reform, involving licensing of commercial operators, is needed. Despite this, difficult issues remain to be solved, eg concerning the future role of the entities today permitted on the Swedish market and how to maintain attractiveness in Swedish licences, given the vast opportunity to offer cross-border gaming services within the EU. The Swedish government wants to study the effects of how Denmark and other neighbouring countries have handled their gaming markets, not least the issue whether monopolies should be replaced with the licensing of gaming companies. The Minister of Financial Markets, Peter Norman, had stated to the press that: *'The problem is that these gaming companies are often located in tax havens and send out the games by air to Sweden. We need to ask ourselves why these companies would ever leave a tax haven, come to Sweden where we pay real taxes, and pay for a license, when you might as well send it through the air. This we must be clear about so that a potential licensing system is not only an empty blow in the air.'* Reformed gambling legislation is unlikely to be introduced before the next general election in September 2014.

3.7 Is the law the same in relation to mobile gambling and interactive gambling on television? If not, are there any headline differences?

Such forms of gambling are covered by the provisions relating to lotteries communicated by means of electromagnetic waves (see above). However, such gambling may also be subject to a special lottery permit granted by the government. In both cases important restrictions and regulations may be delivered in connection with the actual permit.

4. LAND-BASED GAMING

4.1 Please describe the licensing regime (if any) for land-based gaming, and what products are included. Please set out what licences are available, and the licensing regime for them.

Land-based gambling is the very premise for the gaming legislation. The permits, and the system for granting permits, are set forth above.

4.2 Please set out any particular limitations or requirements for (eg casino) operators, such as a ban on local residents gambling.

No general criterion applies to a potential operator, outside of the rules that restrict the potential operator's legal identity (eg state-owned company or non-profit association) for each gambling category.

Lottery permits may only be granted if it can be assumed that the operations will be conducted in a manner appropriate from a general point of view and in accordance with directions, conditions and regulations issued. When applying for a permit such an assessment is made by the supervisory authority, eg the Gaming Board. For this purpose, rather extensive documentation must be provided in connection to the application, and these depend on the type of gambling operation applied for.

For several forms of gambling the permit may be linked to, or even conditional on, a table licence on the premises. In such cases gambling may not be operated outside of the hours prescribed by the table licence. Since the hours prescribed by the table licences are generally rather strict, this effectively restricts the operational hours for land-based gambling.

4.3 Please address the questions in 3.5 above, but in relation to land-based gaming.

The legal status of land-based gaming has remained materially unchanged in recent years.

5. TAX

5.1 Please summarise briefly the tax regime applicable both to land-based and online gaming.

The Lottery Tax Act (Code of Statutes no 1991:1482) prescribes a 35 per cent tax on the surplus from lotteries after disbursement of all prizes. There are important exemptions, ie such non-profit associations as specified in section 15 of the Lotteries Act.

Roulette games, card games and dice games are also exempted, but are instead subject to another applicable law namely the Tax on Games Act (Code of Statutes no 1972:829). Basically it is aimed at restaurant casinos and prescribes a tax on each gambling table. This tax increases up to a certain level depending on the number of such tables, ranging between SEK 2,000-5,000 per table/month.

6. ADVERTISING

6.1 To what extent is the advertising of gambling permitted in your jurisdiction? Again, this should cover both land-based and online gaming. To the extent that advertising is permitted, how is it regulated?

Under Swedish law, it is only legal to advertise permitted Swedish lotteries. There is currently no specific law applicable to marketing of betting, gambling and comparable activity in Sweden. However, the Marketing Act applies to marketing of permitted gambling services.

According to the Marketing Act's general clause (section 5, Marketing Act) marketing practices shall be consistent with generally accepted marketing practices. Generally accepted marketing practices is a broad concept consisting among other things of the International Chamber of Commerce's (ICC) Consolidated Code of Advertising and Market Communication Practice.

A few providers within the Swedish gambling market – ie Svenska Spel and ATG – have agreed on general guidelines for the marketing of gambling. These guidelines probably constitute such accepted marketing practices as stated in the general clause of the Marketing Act. To a large extent these rules coincide with ICC's Consolidated Code of Advertising and Market Communication Practice.

It is in relation to marketing and advertising that it becomes apparent that commercial providers are not permitted under Swedish legislation, since one of the prohibited acts under the Lotteries Act is the promotion of foreign lotteries. Effectively, the advertising possibilities for remotely-based online operators are limited. As mentioned, for the Lotteries Act to apply, the promotional activities must be considered to be situated in Sweden. Several of the most influential television channels broadcast from abroad (mainly the UK) – and on these channels the operators may market their services. Operators can also market on the internet. As set out below, it has recently been established that event marketing in Sweden has a wide area of activity from a legal perspective.

Most importantly, the Swedish media is reluctant to agree to the restrictions provided by the legislation. The media houses have actively challenged the prohibition on promotion in court. In the most important case two former editors-in-chief of the major evening papers *Expressen* and *Aftonbladet* were prosecuted for breaching the prohibition. In December 2012, the Supreme Court acquitted them (Case no. B 3559-11).

The editors were prosecuted for violating the promotion prohibition by publishing advertisements for unlicensed foreign lotteries. Meanwhile, the same promotion of unlicensed Swedish lotteries would not be a penal act or, as such, criminal, according to current legislation. The Court of Appeal asked the European Court of Justice for a preliminary ruling on the legality of such legislation. In its preliminary ruling, the European Court of Justice made it clear that Article 56 TFEU – the freedom to provide services – must be interpreted as precluding legislation of a member state which subjects gambling to a system of exclusive rights, according to which the promotion of gambling organised in another member state is subject to stricter penalties than the promotion of unlicensed gambling operated on national territory (Case C-448/08).

The Supreme Court aligned with the Court of Appeal and the European Court of Justice, concluding that the promotion prohibition is in conflict with the prohibition of discriminatory measures under EU law. The Supreme Court focused on the legal fact that, had the advertisements published in the evening papers been promoting an unlicensed Swedish lottery, no penal sanctions, but merely administrative sanctions, would have been available against the editors. Thus, the current Swedish legislation is discriminatory and rendered inapplicable by the supremacy of the EU. It should be noted, however, that the formal possibility for the Gaming Board to issue orders in conjunction with conditional fines for promotion still apply.

In another important judgment (Case no. HFD 7800-07) in June 2011 the Supreme Administrative Court stated that the prohibition in the Lotteries Act on promoting participation in lotteries does not include broadcasted sponsored messages. With regard to the comparison of odds, it held that such comparisons (in the circumstances of the present case) were not to be regarded as commercial messages and hence broadcasting of the odds was protected by the Fundamental Law on Freedom of Expression. This outcome aligns with the outcome in administrative proceedings brought to the Supreme Administrative Court by *Expressen* and *Aftonbladet* against conditional fines issued against them (Case no. RegR 3582-07). The Gaming Board claimed that the evening paper's publication of odds from foreign gambling companies constituted promotion and issued fines. The court found that the odds were editorial material since the intent behind the publication was to satisfy the readers' interest. It was not considered to be commercial advertising, which is not fully covered by the Freedom of the Press Act. That act is of a constitutional nature and, thus, the Gaming Board's order and conditional fine were deemed unlawful.

Furthermore, it has recently been established that event marketing in Sweden has a wide area of activity from a legal perspective. Although promotion of foreign lotteries cannot be prosecuted following the Supreme Court's judgment, as set forth above, the Gaming Board may still issue conditional fines prohibiting such promotion. The Gaming Board contemplated issuing such a conditional fine against the arranger of the Stockholm Open 2013 (the Swedish ATP tournament), prohibiting the arranger from displaying any trademarks, logos and domain names of Unibet. Prior to the opening of the Stockholm Open, however, the Gaming Board announced that it has closed the case against the arranger. The main reason given was that the tournament would be long over when the decision gained legal force. Thus it has been confirmed that a decision on conditional fines has significant restrictions, as outlined below.

A final decision by the Gaming Board has to be preceded by a period of consideration (usually three weeks), during which the addressee can submit its view. When the Board has taken its final decision, the addressee has three weeks to appeal the decision to an administrative court. The decision of the administrative court can then be appealed to an appeal court and finally to the Supreme Administrative Court. No private undertaking can be sentenced to pay a conditional fine until the decision has passed through the court system. Hence, the decision of the Board lacks the capacity of being directly enforceable. Moreover, the Board cannot render a decision before a violation of the prohibition has taken place.

The above-mentioned restrictions with regard to the sanction powers of the Gaming Board means that event marketing has a wide area of activity from a legal perspective.

7. SOCIAL GAMING
We believe this to be a growing area. Please decide under what criteria social gaming is permitted in your jurisdiction. If games are free to play or if there is no prize, are they legal without a licence? Please address circumstances where virtual currency is used and can be won: ie currency which is of no monetary or other value, save for as credits to take part in games. The answer should address the question whether game credits or virtual money can be exchanged for other prizes. Is any change to regulation in the area proposed or envisaged?

As specified above, a lottery is defined as an activity where one or more participants may, with or without a stake, obtain prizes of a higher value than that which each and every one of the other participants may obtain. Consequently, it does not matter whether the games are free to play or not, ie whether there is a stake or not. When assessing whether an activity constitutes a lottery, the general nature of the activity shall be taken into account and not just the greater or lesser degree of chance present in the individual case. A right to continue the game constitutes a prize (winning) under the Lotteries Act. But if the game has no prize at all, it cannot fall under the statutory definition of lottery. In this sense, the prize becomes the determining factor for whether the Lotteries Act is applicable or not.

Consequently, virtual currencies or credits to continue or participate in other games may very well be considered a prize under the Lotteries Act.

In this area, the Penal Code should be kept in mind because it may target cases falling outside the scope of the Lotteries Act. The provision in section 14, Chapter 16 contains several prerequisites but the key for the purpose of social gaming would probably be whether it is hazardous or not.

Finally, such modern forms of gambling, such as social gaming, involve the abovementioned issue of whether activities on the internet fall under Swedish jurisdiction. The current legislation has not been properly adapted to these gambling services. Consequently, the determining factor may be whether Swedish authorities can exercise any sanctions or not. For this reason, eg the location of servers is decisive. No change to the regulation of social gaming has been proposed.

Switzerland

MME Partners Luka Müller-Studer & Andreas Glarner

1. OBJECTIVES AND STRUCTURE OF LEGISLATION

It is essential to understand that Switzerland's political frame is based on a federal system. This means that law is always governed on a national level as well as on a member state level (cantons).

In 1874, the Swiss Federal Constitution for the first time set forth the legislative responsibilities for gambling in Switzerland. Ever since then, the Swiss gambling industry has been regulated by the Federal Justice and Police Department. Held to be dangerous to public morality, the Swiss Constitution banned games of luck for money for more than a century. It was only in 2000 that the prohibition was lifted and Switzerland's land-based casino industry started to flourish. Subsequently, the Swiss Constitution distinguishes between two kinds of gaming: (i) games offered in casinos; and (ii) bets and lotteries (Article 106 of the Swiss Federal Constitution). Therefore, there are currently two separate laws in force. Whereas gaming in casinos (terrestrial and online) is based on and regulated by the Federal Act on Games of Chance and Casinos of 18 December 1998 (SR 935.52; FGA), any other games – such as lotteries, bets and bingo – are governed by the Federal Act on Lotteries and Commercial Betting of 8 June 1923 (SR 935.51; LLB). Skill games and prize competitions (as far as they do not fall under the LLB – see below) do not fall under these federal laws but are regulated by cantonal law.

The key objectives of the Swiss gaming legislation are the following:

- ensuring transparent and safe gambling operations;
- tackling organised crime and money laundering in or through gambling operations; and
- preventing of the socially harmful impacts of gambling operations, by allowing gambling only inside of casinos.

There is not only a federal and cantonal legislation, but also a federal and cantonal supervisory body. The federal supervisory body is the Swiss Federal Gaming Board (SFGB). The situation is slightly different on the cantonal level. Since the Conference of Cantonal Lottery Directors approved the Intercantonal Agreement on Supervision and Licensing in 2005 (IKA), the lottery and betting market, as well as its supervision, is harmonised within Switzerland. Only since then has the Intercantonal Betting Board, Comlot, been responsible for the supervision of betting and lotteries within Switzerland. Before Comlot was established, the lottery and betting market was the responsibility of the cantons, and was monitored by each canton individually. As there was no national authority responsible, the sole competency lay with the various cantonal administrative departments.

The gaming market in the industrialised nations of the West has grown considerably in the last few decades. Not only has Switzerland's gaming market been transformed, but so has the Swiss gambling market as a whole. Specifically, the process of deregulation in Switzerland began in 1993, when Swiss voters decided by a 75 per cent majority to reintroduce casino gambling after the ban. Since 2000, the casino market has witnessed significant changes, going from small slot halls and illegal card rooms to a well-established industry, which by 2010 encompassed seven large A-type casinos and 12 small B-type casinos. Whereas the A-type casinos are located in urban areas, the small B-type casinos are in resort towns or smaller communities. Together, these 19 casinos generated gross revenues of nearly 900 million Swiss francs in 2010. The golden age of the early 2000s seemed to have vanished quickly, with the industry suffering a significant decline since 2007.

Nevertheless, the federal government decided to announce two new casino licences in June 2011: one A-type licence to Swiss Casinos, for a casino to open in Zurich in late 2012, and one B-type licence to FBAM Neuchatel SA, to open in Neuchatel. With the launching of these two new casinos, the market seems to be saturated. As stated by a media release by the Federal Casino Federation in May 2013, gross revenues further declined in 2012 to 757 million Swiss francs, an 8.2 per cent fall compared to the previous year. Currently, with 21 casinos in operation, Switzerland has one of the highest casino densities in the world.

The lottery market, however, was not affected much by the decline. According to the annual report of Swisslos from 2012, it generated gross revenues of 532 million Swiss francs, 16 million of which are allocated to bets. This result did not vary much compared to 2011 (534 million Swiss francs; 17 million generated by bets).

2. FRAMEWORK OF LEGISLATION

2.1 What is the legal definition of gambling and what falls within this definition?

There is no actual definition of gambling in Switzerland. Under the general heading of gambling, two segments can be summarised, each with its own legislation. The casino sector is based on and regulated by the FGA, whereas the lottery and betting sector is governed by the LLB.

The FGA defines games of chance as games that cannot be influenced by any skill factor (Article 3 FGA); for example, slot machines, roulette, blackjack, baccarat and poker are encompassed by the terminology of games of chance.

Games of skill are defined as games where the outcome depends to a certain extent on the player's skill, eg chess.

However, pure games of chance, as well as pure games of skills, are rare. Games depending on money or other financial benefits are usually a mixture of both luck and skill, and it is not always obvious which of the two factors is dominant. Regarding the regulatory consequences, however, it is crucial whether a game is defined as one of chance or one of skill. Since cash games of chance outside licensed casinos in Switzerland are illegal but games of skill are permitted, the question whether a cash game depends on skill rather than on luck is of utmost importance.

2.2 What is the legal definition of online gambling and what falls within this definition?

Organising online games of chance is illegal (Article 5 FGA). Moreover, each and every activity which supports funds or simply facilitates online gambling is illegal. Article 5 FGA assumes that the terms internet and telecommunication-based are known. Article 5 FGA is based on the traditional concept of understanding, whereupon the distribution channel to the customer is significant in determining whether a game is classified as remote gaming or as online gaming. A clear definition does not exist in the law.

The prohibition in Article 5 FGA typically includes online casinos, ie cash games of chance offered online. Depending on the specific circumstances of the individual case, the following activities have been prosecuted or are deemed illegal by the SFGB:

- operation of a gaming server;
- processing certain financial transactions in connection with online gambling;
- advertising or marketing for online games (also hypertext linking); and
- management and/or financing of online gambling.

This means that both operators as well as suppliers can be prosecuted.

The SFGB recently ruled, in an unpublished opinion letter, that it makes a difference whether the online gaming services target Swiss residents or not. The FGA intends to protect gamblers in Switzerland. If Swiss residents could be effectively blocked by technical measures from accessing the online gaming services, supporting activities for remote gambling would be allowed.

However, participating in online games of chance is generally not illegal. According to prevailing doctrine, the mere accessibility of a foreign online service in Switzerland does not qualify as an activity on Swiss territory and the Swiss gambling prohibition does not apply. Thus, the individual Swiss player accessing foreign online casinos does not need to fear sanctions. Furthermore, it is legal for an international online gaming operator to set up its corporate headquarters in Switzerland to consolidate its operation. It is also permitted for an internationally operating online gaming operator to organise all its group internal financial transactions to be undertaken by Swiss banks. In both cases the SFGB decided that these 'links' do not fall under the territorial ambit of the FGA if any online gaming attempts of Swiss residents can be blocked from accessing the gambling websites.

The same applies to online lotteries: while provision of internet-based lottery or betting services is principally illegal, the cantons may grant licences. However, as of today, only Swisslos and Loterie Romande have obtained the necessary permissions and allow players to take part in online games (a duopoly situation). As a result, both of them have made use of their permissions by developing a wide range of online lottery and sports betting services.

2.3 Please set out the different gambling products identified by legislation.

On the level of national legislation the FGA, LLB and the Executive Ordinances to the FGA (SR 935.521) and the LLB (SR 935.511) regulate the following gambling products:

- lotteries;
- betting;
- lottery-like games;
- casinos;
- poker;
- gaming machines; and
- online gambling.

Skill games and prize competitions such as tombolas are subject to cantonal law.

2.4 Please list different requirements for each gambling product, including legal classifications for each; for example, is poker a game of skill or game of chance?

Lotteries

Lotteries are defined as events where players have to pay money in advance to participate in a game and winners are chosen by the drawing of lots. Therefore lotteries can be qualified as a game of chance. The lottery market is regulated by the LLB. The implementation of the LLB is subject to cantonal law.

According to Article 1 LLB, lotteries of any kind, as well as lottery-like undertakings such as snowball, hydra, gella, multiplex, house draws, auctions as lottery-like events and internet-based lotteries, are generally prohibited. The law exempts lotteries serving not-for-profit or charitable purposes from the prohibition, provided they are permitted by cantonal law. Cantonal law may permit, limit or prohibit such kinds of non-profit-making activity. Permissions in the form of licences can only be issued to corporations and public-law institutions, as well as associations of individuals and foundations, under private law, and all must have their primary address in Switzerland. The licences are not transferable to any third party. However, in Switzerland there is a lottery duopoly: only Swisslos and Loterie Romande have been granted a licence to date (see sections 2.1 and 4.1).

Since 2005, the LLB has been complemented by the IKA. Previously, all cantons had their own licensing authorities, distribution offices (for the net profits) and representations within their lottery organisations. Now the IKA has harmonised this separation of powers by establishing the Swiss Lottery and Betting Board (Comlot) to supervise the Swiss lottery and betting market (see section 1.1).

Bets

Bets are defined in the Swiss Code of Obligation. The LLB itself does
not contain a definition of a bet. At the time the law was written, it was
obviously assumed that there was no need to define a bet. Betting is
governed by the LLB, according to which commercially offering, selling and
accepting bets on horse races, boat races, football matches and similar events
is prohibited in Switzerland. The prohibition also includes the marketing
and advertising of bets in oral or written form, ie by announcements,
billboards, newspaper articles, letters or any other means.

The LLB prohibits betting only if it is offered commercially. However, the
Swiss law does not make clear what exactly the term 'commercial' means.
Following the factual situation, betting will only be authorised if such
business activity is not aimed at profit making. Any offering, acting as an
agent for and entering into bets on sporting events without any commercial
aim is permitted provided the event is limited with regard to its duration
and the persons participating.

Lottery-like games

Lottery-like games are a new genre of gambling. Because of the variety
of terms for such games, an exact definition of the term is not possible.
According to Comlot and to the standards laid down in Article 43 LLB
lottery-like games include the so-called pyramid systems, gift circles, contests
or competitions that require payment of a fee or are subject to obligation
to purchase, and the purchase or extent of winnings of which depends
significantly on chance or on circumstances unknown to participants. With
entry into force of the new Article 3 section r of the Federal Act against
Unfair Competition (SR 241) in April 2012, all pyramid systems became
illegal. Hence, any pyramid systems are subject to the jurisdiction of the
State Secretariat for Economic Affairs.

Casino

While all other gambling operations are subject to cantonal law, all games
offered in a land-based casino, such as blackjack and roulette, fall under
the federal jurisdiction. The SFGB determines which games of chance may
be offered by the casinos, as well as the maximum stake that can be set.
Moreover, the licensed casinos are obligated to draft and implement a social
concept, including measures to avoid gambling addiction. The main legal
references in Switzerland are the FGA and its complementary executive
ordinance.

The FGA differentiates between two different types of casinos in terms of
the possible types of games of chance to be offered, the winnings and the
maximum number of slot machines (A-type and B-type). A-type casinos are
casinos with no limits in stake and may offer 14 different table games, with
unlimited stakes, jackpots and maximum winnings at all slot machines.
An A-type casino is only allowed in an area with a population of at least
one million people. B-type casinos are usually spa or resort casinos, with
a maximum of three kinds of table games and limited stakes, jackpots

and maximum winnings at all slot machines. The maximum number of gambling tables operated per casino is three, and for slot machines the maximum is 250. While for the A-type casinos there are no limitations, the limit per stake in B-type casinos is 25 Swiss francs and the maximum jackpot offered is 25,000 Swiss francs.

Poker cash games
As poker cash games are defined by the SFGB as games that are predominantly depending on luck, the FGA applies. Therefore, poker cash games can only be permitted and played in licensed casinos (Article 4 FGA). The organisation and commercial offering of poker cash games outside licensed casinos is illegal.

Tournaments were handled identically to cash games until late 2007. The SFGB had issued an important and widely discussed exception rule enabling legal poker tournaments with cash prizes to take place outside of casinos, provided cantonal law did not prohibit such tournaments. The argument of this ruling was that single poker cash games refer to luck in principal whereas the same does not apply to gambling in tournaments. However, on 20 May 2010, the Supreme Court of Switzerland classified Texas Hold'em poker as a game of chance and therefore Texas Hold'em poker tournaments could no longer be organised outside licensed casinos. According to media information published by the SFGB on 2 June 2010, the organisation of poker tournaments outside casinos has become illegal again.

Gaming machines
The cantons are responsible for the licensing of gaming machines involving an element of skill (Article 106, paragraph 4 SFC). If the element of chance is predominant, gambling machines are subject to Article 3, paragraph 4 FGA and are only allowed to be operated in licensed casinos. Accordingly, machines that offer games of skill may be operated outside of casinos if permitted by cantonal law. The cantonal permission may only be granted in case the SFGB has qualified the respective gaming machine as skill-based.

Gaming machines and slot machines
Basically, there are two main categories of slot machines: first, gaming machines, which have the sole purpose of entertainment and have no benefit in view, such as table football, pinball and any kind of sports simulators; and secondly, slot machines, which give the player an opportunity to win money or other prizes of monetary value (points, chips or goods). Equivalent to casino rules, the casino may adopt rules for its slot machines and submit them to the SFGB for approval. The rules need to be summarised in plain language and placed on the table game area or on each slot machine, and released on demand.

2.5 Explain the system of regulation of gambling; which regulatory or governmental body is responsible for the supervision of gambling? Which body issues licences? Which body examines enforcement powers? Is there any limit on the number or duration of available licences?

Organising games of chance, lotteries or bets in Switzerland is subject to a governmental permission (licence, concession), and all gambling operations are supervised and controlled by the competent authorities:

- The SFGB acts as an independent public authority board, which is administratively affiliated to the Federal Department of Justice and Police. The SFGB has regulatory oversight over casinos and a general mandate to enforce Switzerland's gaming laws. It is therefore responsible for supervising Swiss casinos and monitoring compliance with the country's gambling regulations. Since April 2000 the SFGB has acted as the authority for casinos, and supervises their compliance with the FGA and other applicable regulations. Furthermore, the SFGB is in charge of deciding whether a game should be qualified as a game of chance or as a game of skill and thus subject to the FGA. Casino licences are issued by the Federal Counsel, which also determines the number of licences that may be issued and their duration.

- The Swiss Lottery and Betting Board Comlot was established by the cantons in 2006 and is the global licensing and supervising body for lotteries and betting in Switzerland (see also section 2.4). Comlot evaluates the licence applications of lottery operators and supervises compliance with laws, regulations, licensing requirements and the like. The Appeals Commission is in charge of guaranteeing appropriate legal protection. Lottery operators can appeal decisions of Comlot at this Intercantonal judicial authority. Nevertheless, each canton retains the right to prohibit certain lottery products on its territory even if they have previously been acknowledged by Comlot. The enforcement of the LLB is subject to the cantons, particularly to Comlot.

- The cantonal governments and their appointed departments have the right to enforce the rule of law within their territories. Hence, despite the prohibition of betting according to the LLB, cantonal law may provide for exceptions for its own territory. Accordingly, any offering of commercial bets, such as commercial selling and accepting of totalisator bets on the sports categories defined above, is subject to a cantonal permission (Article 34 LLB). The competent authority to assign such permits is also Comlot.

3.   ONLINE GAMBLING

3.1   To what extent can online gambling be offered in your jurisdiction? Are licences available and, if so, for which gambling products? Please describe briefly the licensing process, who may apply, whether licences are limited in number and, if no licences are available, whether it is legal for online gambling to be offered. In the case of EU jurisdictions, please state whether there are any issues as to the legality of the local law at EU level. Please refer to any relevant cases at ECJ level and explain any measures taken or pending by the European Commission.

Since remote gambling and remote lotteries are illegal in Switzerland, there is no licensing framework (aside from cantonal law; see section 2.5).

Since Switzerland is not part of the EU, there are no direct regulatory issues regarding compatibility with EU law. However, particularly in the drafting process of the new law, legislators have to raise the issue as to what extent EU licensed operations might be accepted in Switzerland.

3.2   Is there a distinction between the law applicable to B2B operations and that applicable to B2C operations?

Since online gaming is illegal in Switzerland and no regulation regarding online gaming exists, there is no distinction between B2B operations and B2C operations regarding the applicable law. However, the SFGB has adopted a practice which allows certain B2B activities (see above), whereas all B2C activities are still strictly prohibited.

3.3   What are the consequences for B2C or B2B operators who are active in your jurisdiction without having obtained or applied for the required permits, licences and approvals? What penalties and enforcement powers are available in respect of the illegal operators? Please outline any significant domestic decisions or enforcement actions that have been taken by the relevant authorities in recent years.

Because online gaming is illegal in Switzerland, there are no licences, concessions or approvals for any online gambling operators available at this point in time. However, the FGA contains a set of enforcement actions against unlicensed operators:

Online cash games of luck

Articles 55 and 56 FGA provide the legal foundation for the punishment of online cash games of luck. Accordingly, infringements are sanctioned with penalties. Additionally, freezing of illegal asset allocation and seizure of any materials and documents involved may also be part of the means of police enforcement. No distinction is made between foreign players and Swiss nationals. The decisive criterion is where the crime was committed. Article 56 FGA provides for a fine of up to one million Swiss francs if the illegal act was performed intentionally. In serious cases, sanctions are imprisonment of up to five years and a fine of up to two million Swiss francs. In addition, the authorities may confiscate the facilities of any online gaming provider or supporter.

Very view enforcement decisions have been taken by the FGA. To the best of the authors' knowledge, the FGA has never initiated investigations against offshore/foreign companies providing online gaming to Swiss users from abroad. The same applies to their representatives or local partners. However, the FGB sanctioned the hyperlink setting to gambling providers with a fine of CHF 2,000 (Decision of FGB of 6 December 2007).

Illegal betting
Illegal betting activities may be punished with a monetary penalty (up to 90 daily rates) or a fine of up to 10,000 Swiss francs. All assets relating to the criminal activity could be confiscated. As Comlot is not authorised to prosecute, the prosecution and violation of the LLB is subject to the cantonal authorities. However, Comlot will report to the criminal prosecutor anyone who operates or advertises illegal lottery or betting activities in Switzerland. Legal advice from Comlot does not bind the cantonal authorities.

3.4   What technical measures are in place (if any) to protect consumers from unlicensed operators, such as ISP blocking and payment blocking?
There are currently no regulated technical measures (such as payment or ISP restrictions) in place to protect consumers from unlicensed gaming operators.

3.5   Has the legal status of online gambling changed significantly in recent years and, if so, how?
Even though concerns regarding online gaming operations – particularly those relating to the protection of gamblers (addiction, youth protection, etc) – data protection and money laundering are still present, the Swiss government realised in 2009 that banning online gambling is not the appropriate way to tackle them (press release of the Federal Department of Justice, 22 April 2009). Because consumers have always been free to visit gambling websites from non-Swiss operators, unlicensed, untaxed and uncontrolled foreign operators have established a strong presence in the Swiss market. This has made the Swiss online gambling ban untenable in the long run. Accordingly, the Swiss Federal Council announced in early 2013 that it would present a first draft of a new gaming law (see question 3.6 below).

3.6 Whilst acknowledging the inherent difficulty in predicting developments in gambling law, what are the likely developments in online gambling in your jurisdiction, both short term and long term? Are any specific amendments under consideration? Have there been any recent political developments, or do you envisage any in the near future? Are any specific amendments under consideration? Are they likely to be adopted and, if so, what is the time scale?

On 30 April 2014, the Swiss Federal Council released its draft of a revised gambling law for consultation. The revised act proposes to replace the current online gambling ban with a system that allows online gambling based on a concession. However, only a holder of a licence for a land-based casino (type A and B) qualifies to apply for an online licence and to thereby extend its services. Online gaming, however, shall only be offered to Swiss residents. Illegal (not licensed) offers shall be reduced more effectively through appropriate technical measures (and not financial blocking measures). In particular, the Federal Counceil intends to technically block the access to foreign online gaming providers if their services have not been licensed in Switzerland. Gaming as such on platforms of unlicensed gaming providers will still be legal.

Furthermore, the draft bill provides for a tax exemption for all money games and introduces new guidelines for the charitable use of the incomes from lotteries and sports betting services. The revised act also proposes to strengthen the player's protection and contains a number of provisions to guarantee secure and transparent gaming operations. Finally, the draft legislation foresees the creation of a coordinating body to support the cooperation between the authorities of the federal government and the cantons on an institutional level.

The revised legislation proposed by the Swiss Federal Council is now in consultation (until August 2014). The cantons, political parties and other interested groups are invited to offer their opinions on the draft. The purpose of the consultation is to check the acceptance of the planned revision and conduct amendments prior to releasing it to Parliament for deliberation. Accordingly, it is not clear yet which system Switzerland will finally adopt. It seems unlikely that a revised law will enter into force prior to 2018.

3.7 Is the law the same in relation to mobile gambling and interactive gambling on television? If not, are there any headline differences?

Switzerland does not have any special rules for mobile gambling and interactive gambling on television. To the extent that such offers qualify as remote access games within the meaning of the FGA or the LLB, the provision of such services is illegal.

4. LAND-BASED GAMBLING

4.1 Please describe the licensing regime (if any) for land-based gaming, and what products are included. Please set out what licences are available, and the licensing regime for them.

Licences are issued only to legal entities under public law and to joint stock companies organised in accordance with Swiss law whose share capital is split into registered shares, provided the members of these companies' administrative boards have their primary residence in Switzerland. Moreover, licences may also be issued to cooperatives organised in accordance with Swiss law if their members have their primary residence in Switzerland. Further, a licence may only be granted if the applicant and its most important business partners, as well as its beneficial owners and the shareholders, have sufficient capital, a good reputation and guarantee a proper business.

Applications for casino licences must be submitted to the federal government. Applicants must present a social concept, including strict security concepts and measures to prevent gambling measures. The SFGB reviews the applications and issues a recommendation to the federal government. The application will be released to the public, which will be invited to comment on the planned casino.

Licences for casino location

Licences for casino locations may be granted only if the appropriate canton and local community support the application. Therefore, the applicant in a report has to outline the economic benefit of the planned casino for the region.

There are two types of casino licences: A-type and B-type. The difference between the licences lies mainly in the games available. B-type casinos are subject to limitations of both stakes (CHF 25) and wins (CHF 25,000), may only have a limited number of slot machines and gambling tables, and are subject to a limited total jackpot for slot machines. A-type casinos are not subject to such limitations.

Operation licences

Operation licences may only be granted if the applicant guarantees the independence of the management and supervision of the gaming operation. Casinos can be operated only after the licence has been granted by the federal government and issued by the SFGB. The usual term of casino licence is 20 years, though, in certain cases, the federal government can set a shorter or longer term.

The lottery market

The lottery market is regulated by the LLB. The implementation of the LLB is subject to cantonal law. According to Article 1 LLB, lotteries of any kind, as well as lottery-like undertakings, auctions as lottery-like events and internet-based lotteries, are generally prohibited. The law exempts lotteries serving not-for-profit or charitable purposes from the prohibition provided they are permitted by cantonal law. Cantonal law may permit, limit or prohibit such kinds of non-profit-making activities. Permissions in the form of licences can only be issued to corporations and public-law institutions, as well as associations of individuals and foundations, under private law, and all must have their primary address in Switzerland. The licences are not transferable to any third party. However, in Switzerland there is a lottery duopoly: currently, only Swisslos and Loterie Romande have a licence (see section 2.4).

4.2 Please set out any particular limitations or requirements for (eg casino) operators, such as a ban on local residents gambling.

According to Article 21, paragraph 1 FGA, the following persons are subject to a general ban on casino gambling:

* persons under 18 years;
* persons who are suspended from casinos;
* board members or members of the SFGB;
* casino employees who are involved in the daily business;
* representatives of companies that manufacture or deal in gaming facilities; and
* representatives of casinos.

Casino employees who are not involved in the daily business, shareholders holding more than 5 per cent of the share capital of the casino and corporate members are also subject to exclusion. However, the casino can refuse access to persons without indicating any reason.

One of the main objections of deregulation of the casino market was the assumption that deregulation would result in an increase in gambling addiction. Therefore, applicants must present a social concept, including measures to prevent gambling addiction and strict security concepts.

Players that are insolvent or fail to meet their financial obligations must be blocked from casino gaming operations. The same holds true for players who risk wagers that are disproportionate compared to their income or their assets, as well as players who negatively affect the operation of a casino. A clear understanding of a player's income or assets is not necessary to block a player; an assumption is sufficient so long as it is based on the casino's own perception or on the basis of reports of third parties. However, the casino itself is not allowed to instigate investigations into a player's financial circumstances. Moreover, the player can also apply for a block. The casino must register the blocked players and notify all of the other casinos in Switzerland. However, the block must be cancelled as soon as the reason for the block has ceased.

The prevention of problem gambling was one of the main goals of the IKA when it came into force. In particular, the IKA includes regulations regarding the obligation to clarify the potential of problem gaming before granting a licence for lottery or betting operations.

4.3 Please address the questions in 3.5 above, but in relation to land-based gaming.

Since the FGA entered into force in 1998, there have not been any major regulatory developments related to land-based casino gaming that need to be pointed out.

5. TAX
5.1 Please summarise briefly the tax regime applicable to both land-based and online gaming.

As the gambling market is divided into the casino sector and the lottery and betting sector, the tax system for each sector has to be handled separately.

In accordance with the Swiss constitution, casino gross revenues are taxed. The collected tax funds flow into Switzerland's pension system. The tax rate can vary from 40 to 80 per cent of gross revenues, but casinos may request a reduction in the rate in the case of exceptional economic conditions.

Type-A casinos pay 40 per cent tax on gross revenues up to 10 million Swiss francs. If gross revenues exceed this sum, the tax rate rises by 0.5 per cent per million Swiss francs. Type-B casinos pay 40 per cent tax on gross revenues up to 10 million Swiss francs. If gross revenues exceed this sum, the tax rate rises by 1 per cent per million Swiss francs. The federal government is, however, free to change the actual level of taxation and set taxation rates of up to 80 per cent.

According to a press release of the SFGB, in 2008 around 517 million Swiss francs were collected as tax from gross revenues. This sum was distributed as follows: 85 per cent went into the Swiss pension system and 15 per cent was allocated to the cantons where the type-B casinos operate. The average tax rate for the two types of casino (type A and B) combined was above 52 per cent in 2008.

As lottery and betting winnings in most cantons are considered as income, such winnings are not tax free. Betting and lottery winnings of 50 Swiss francs or more are taxed at 35 per cent (the so-called withholding tax) in every canton of Switzerland. The tax amount is subtracted automatically when the betting or lottery winnings are claimed; the tax amount can then be reclaimed by the player on his or her tax return. In addition to the withholding tax due, betting winnings are taxed differently in each canton (eg subject to the income tax).

According to Article 18 IKA, the organisers of grand lotteries, ie Swisslos and Loterie Romande, are obligated to pay a tax of 0.5 per cent of their gross revenues to the cantons. The cantons, on the other hand, are obligatedto use this tax for the prevention of and fight against gambling addiction.

Casino winnings are tax free.

6. ADVERTISING

6.1 To what extent is the advertising of gambling permitted in your jurisdiction? Again, this should cover both land-based and online gaming. To the extent that advertising is permitted, how is it regulated?

According to Article 33 FGA, any advertisement for the commercial offering of games of chance with regard to licensed land-based casinos is prohibited if made in an obtrusive way. With regard to unlicensed casinos or foreign online operators, marketing measures are generally considered as illegal.

According to Article 33, paragraph 2 LLB, any promotion for bets within Switzerland's borders for betting/lottery services which are not licensed by the Swiss authorities is prohibited. If any person or company were to pursue such promotion activity in Switzerland, Comlot would, if notified, open an investigation against such person or company. Any illegal promotion, including the transport and distribution of the promotional material in Switzerland, can be sanctioned with up to a three-month prison sentence and a fine of up to 10,000 Swiss francs.

7. SOCIAL GAMING

7.1 We believe this to be a growing area. Please decide under what criteria social gaming is permitted in your jurisdiction. If games are free to play or if there is no prize, are they legal without a licence? Please address circumstances where virtual currency is used and can be won: ie currency which is of no monetary or other value, save for as credits to take part in games. The answer should address the question whether game credits or virtual money can be exchanged for other prizes. Is any change to regulation in the area proposed or envisaged?

Switzerland does not have a special regulatory regime for social gaming. Thus, it must be decided on a case-by-case basis whether a specific social game qualifies as a lottery, bet or casino game within the meaning of the FGA or the LLB.

As long as such games are free and/or there is no monetary advantage to be won, the provision of social gaming services is not subject to a licence requirement. The same applies if the participants may purchase gaming credits but may not gain any monetary advantage. However, if the participant purchases credits and has the possibility to gain a monetary profit (eg money, credits that may exchanged for cash, prizes or further gaming activities that are otherwise only accessible after payment), it is likely that such service qualifies as a lottery, bet or casino game, and is therefore considered as illegal.

United Kingdom

Harris Hagan Julian Harris & John Hagan

1. OBJECTIVES AND STRUCTURE OF LEGISLATION

From the 1960s until 2005, the principal forms of gambling were governed by different legislation. By the early 1990s however, the pace of change in a number of fundamental respects led to calls for new legislation.

Aside from these physical changes, there had also been a change in attitude since the legislation of the 1960s had been passed. It was felt that new legislation would be needed to reflect the metamorphosis of gambling from a vice that could not be prevented, but would be strictly regulated and controlled, into an acceptable form of adult entertainment. The government set up the Gambling Review Body (the GRB), under the Chairmanship of economist Professor Sir Alan Budd, which was asked to consider the state of the gambling industry and its social impact, how the industry might change and what new regulations would be appropriate.

The GRB Report was published in July 2001 with recommendations designed to simplify the regulation of gambling and to extend choice for adult gamblers on the one hand, whilst on the other, seeking to ensure gambling is crime free and honest, that players could know what to expect and should be free from exploitation, and that there should be protection for children and vulnerable persons. It stressed the need to ensure that any system of regulation should be flexible enough to incorporate technological developments and to enable adjustments to be made to regulations in the light of practical experience. Most significantly, it recommended that all gambling regulation should be incorporated into one act of Parliament, that all gambling activities should be regulated by a single regulator (the Gambling Commission), though the National Lottery should continue to be separately regulated.

In November 2003, the government published the first draft of the Gambling Bill incorporating many of the Budd Committee's recommendations. The Committee was reconvened to consider policy on regional casinos and Parliament made a number of significant changes to the Bill, in particular to the proposals relating to casinos.

The Gambling Bill had proposed four sizes of casino, namely 'regional' or 'resort' casinos, 'large casinos', 'small casinos' and 'below the minimum size for a licensed casino', the last category being to accommodate casinos existing at the date of the passing of the 2005 Act. The Bill introduced a clause enabling local authorities to resolve not to issue casino premises licences in their own areas. Subject to that, the government's view was that there should be no statutory limit on the number of casinos, which should be determined by market forces.

In the face of determined opposition, both from Parliament and in the press, the government announced that it proposed to limit the number of licences for small, large and regional casinos to eight each. However, due to time pressure, the government was forced to change the Bill in some significant respects in order to persuade opposition parties to allow the Bill to be enacted. In particular, the government agreed to reduce the number of regional casinos in the first instance from eight to one. The Bill then received Royal Assent on 7 April 2005.

Towards the end of 2006, the Casino Advisory Panel recommended to Government the locations for the 17 licensing authorities to be granted power to award premises licences for new casinos and a draft Order was laid before Parliament. They were chosen as the best areas in which to test the social impact of the new casinos. Following rigorous debate, this Order was defeated. Meanwhile, the new Prime Minister, Gordon Brown, added to the uncertainty when he announced in Parliament in July 2007 that he would look at alternative methods for regeneration to areas earmarked for regional casinos. The new Secretary of State laid a draft Order in Parliament in February 2008 seeking approval for the 16 local authorities selected by the Casino Advisory Panel. He further confirmed that there would be no regional casino.

In two key respects the scheme of the new framework for casino gaming in Great Britain recommended by the Budd Report and the Joint Committee had been derailed, at least for the foreseeable future. These were that there would be only a small number of new casinos, instead of a free market, and that there would be no resort-style casinos at all. The Order was approved by Parliament.

The 2005 Act sets out three objectives:
- preventing gambling from being a source of crime or disorder, being associated with crime or disorder or being used to support crime;
- ensuring that gambling is conducted in a fair and open way; and
- protecting children and other vulnerable persons from being harmed or exploited by gambling.

These are of fundamental importance to the regulation of licensed gambling, in that the Gambling Commission must aim to pursue and, if appropriate, have regard to the objectives when carrying out any functions under the 2005 Act. For their part, licensing authorities are required to permit the use of premises for gambling insofar as the authority thinks it reasonably consistent with the objectives.

The government announced in July 2011 that it was proposing to amend the provisions of the 2005 Act that allowed offshore remote gambling operators to enjoy an advantageous position over those based and licensed in the UK. The 2005 Act permits operators based in the EEA (of which Gibraltar is treated as a part) and selected 'white-listed' jurisdictions (Alderney, the Isle of Man, Antigua & Barbuda and Tasmania) to advertise their services in the UK without holding a UK operating licence or paying UK gaming duty. By 2011, the government had acknowledged that its position was at odds with the trend in much of Europe that required online gambling operators to obtain a local licence. Following a consultation period with the industry, the Gambling (Advertising and Licensing) Bill was issued on 3 December 2012.

The Bill proposed a fundamental change to the basis on which remote gambling is regulated from a point of supply basis to a point of consumption basis. After a slow start, the Bill was approved by the House of Commons on 26 November 2013 and then progressed quickly through the remaining stages. At the time of writing, the changes to the 2005 Act have not yet gone live, but this is expected to happen in or around July 2014. This will follow an application window, during which operators with an existing permission to advertise in the UK will be invited to make an application for an operating licence. Provided such operators make their application during this window, they will be given permission to continue targeting the UK pending a full determination of their application.

Once the changes go live, all operators advertising gambling services in the UK and/or transacting with customers physically located in Great Britain will be required to hold a licence from the Gambling Commission, and will therefore be subject to the provisions of the 2005 Act, its regulations and the Gambling Commission's social responsibility and technical standards requirements.

A further key change is that, from 1 December 2014, all operators (regardless of their location) will be required to pay UK remote gambling duty on all transactions with customers whose normal place of residence is in the UK.

2. FRAMEWORK OF LEGISLATION

The 2005 Act is divided into various 'Parts'. Part 1 interprets key concepts and contains definitions of important terms. Part 2 establishes the Gambling Commission and sets out its powers and duties, Part 3 deals with offences and Part 4 protection of children and young persons. Parts 5, 6, 7 and 8 deal with the various types of licences. There are then a number of Parts dealing with specific types of gaming and other matters, such as advertising.

2.1 What is the legal definition of gambling and what falls within this definition?

In contrast with previous legislation, the 2005 Act defines critical definitions, enabling a number of questions to be applied to the relevant facts:

1. Do the facts constitute gambling? If not, the regime of the 2005 Act will not apply.
2. If so, which type of gambling? Is it
   a. gaming? If so, is it:
      i. casino gaming; or
      ii. equal chance gaming (eg bingo);
   b. betting? Or
   c. a lottery?
3. In any event, does the activity involve remote gambling?
4. In all cases, is any person providing facilities for gambling?

With answers to the above questions, it is then possible to decide whether a licence is required, and if it is, the type of operating licence which is relevant.

'Gambling' is defined as

(a) gaming;
(b) betting; and
(c) participating in a lottery.

'Gaming' means playing a game of chance for a prize. It includes a game which involves both chance and skill, even where the chance element can be eliminated by superlative skill. 'Game of chance' includes games where the element of chance can be eliminated by superlative skill.

Chess is an example of a game of pure skill. Card games generally offer more scope for the role of chance, given the random deal of cards, as do games involving the roll of dice. Poker gives rise to different approaches in different jurisdictions, but in the UK the element of chance introduced by the deal of cards, notwithstanding the skill element, dictates that it will fall within the definition of gaming, thereby giving superior odds to some players.

The concept of playing includes a sole participant, even if a computer represents the actions of other players.

'Prize' is defined as including money or money's worth, and playing for a prize encompasses requiring a chance of winning, whether or not the player risks any loss. It follows that gaming, which involves playing a game for a prize does not, in contrast with a lottery, necessarily involve the player making a stake or bet on the game, and this is a common misconception. It becomes important in looking at social gaming, or 'free play', which can still constitute gaming which, if provided commercially, requires a licence. It will not do so if there is still no prize, and it is generally accepted, certainly in the UK, that the mere opportunity to play a game again does not constitute a prize, as it is not recognised as having any monetary value.

'Equal chance gaming' exists if the game does not involve playing or staking against a bank, and if chances are equally available to all participants.

A person is said to provide facilities for gambling if he:
(a) invites others to gamble in accordance with arrangements made by him;
(b) provides, operates or administers arrangements for gambling by others; or
(c) participates in the operation or administration of gambling by others.

In order to deal with activities which do not fall clearly into one of the above categories, the 2005 Act provides guidance, as follows:

- A transaction falling both within the definition of betting and that of gaming will be treated as betting, but only if it is also pool betting under section 12. All other cases which appear to be betting and gaming will be considered as gaming.

- There are complex provisions for arrangements satisfying both the definition of a game of chance and a lottery. If a person paying to join a group amongst whose members prizes are allocated is required to participate or be successful in more than three processes before acquiring that entitlement, the 2005 Act will treat the arrangement as a game of chance and not a lottery. If it satisfies the lottery definition, or is promoted in reliance on a lottery operating licence it will be treated as a lottery. Any other arrangement would be treated as a game of chance.

- Activities satisfying both the definition of a lottery and that of pool betting or betting where it falls within the definition of a prize competition: if a transaction falls within those parts of Schedule 11 (lotteries) identified in section 18(2) it will be treated as a lottery. Otherwise it will qualify as betting.

2.2 What is the legal definition of online gambling and what falls within this definition?

'Remote gambling', the term used throughout the 2005 Act to include online gambling, means gambling in which people participate by means of remote communication which is itself defined as communication using the internet, the telephone, television, radio or any other kind of electronic or other technology for facilitating communication. Importantly, the Secretary of State may by regulation provide that a specified system or method of communication is or is not to be treated as a form for remote communication under the 2005 Act.

A significant amendment to the 2005 Act has recently been passed by Parliament which alters the basis upon which a licence to operate remote gambling is required. In relation to remote gambling, the offence of providing facilities for gambling without a licence now applies to situations where:

(a) at least one piece of remote gambling equipment used in the provision of the facilities is situated in Great Britain; or

(b) no such equipment is situated in Great Britain but the facilities are used there.

Situation (b) was added by the recent amendment to the law and significantly extends the requirement for a UK licence to all operators who wish to transact with British customers. The offence occurs where the person providing the facilities knows or should know that the facilities are being used, or are likely to be used, in Great Britain. Facilities for gambling are deemed to be used in Great Britain where the customer is physically located in Great Britain at the time of using the facilities.

'Remote gambling equipment' means *'electronic or other equipment used to store information relating to a person's participation in gambling, presenting to those participating in a virtual game, virtual race or other virtual event by reference to which gambling is conducted, determining all or part of a result or storing information relating to the result'*. The definition is potentially wide enough to cover any electronic or other equipment, for example a computer system, which stores any information whatever relating to a customer's participation. On a literal interpretation, this may include a customer username, email address, account balance, hours played, sessions played and favourite games. It is not however the intention of the legislation to catch equipment which stores information for marketing and promotional purposes. Importantly, the Gambling Commission does not adopt such a strict and unduly literal interpretation. The Commission considers that a piece of equipment is remote gambling equipment only if it is *'used in the provision of facilities for gambling'* and the components deployed on it to perform the functions set out in section 34(a)–(d).

2.3 Please set out the different gambling products identified by legislation.

The 2005 Act regulates the following gambling products:

- arcades;
- betting;
- bingo;
- casinos;
- gambling software;
- gaming machines;
- lotteries (raffles); and
- remote (online gambling).

2.4 Please list the different requirements for each gambling product, including legal classifications for each; for example, is poker a game of skill or game of chance?

Arcades

There are three types of amusement arcade:

1. adult gaming centres;
2. licensed family entertainment centres; and
3. unlicensed family entertainment centres.

The three different types of amusement arcade can offer specific categories of gaming machine. No one under the age of 18 years is allowed to enter an adult gaming centre or the adult-only section of a licensed family entertainment centre.

Bingo

Bingo is equal chance gaming. There is no legal definition, nor is there a standard set of rules governing the game. However, bingo has developed to a point that the game is broadly similar throughout the UK.

Betting

'Betting' is defined as the making of or acceptance of bets on the outcome of an event, or on the likelihood of anything occurring or not, or whether anything is true or not. Pool betting is betting made on terms that all or part of the winnings will be determined by reference to the total stakes played by those betting, will be divided amongst the winners or may be something other than money.

Casinos

'Casino' is an arrangement whereby people are given an opportunity to participate in one or more casino games. Casino games are those which are not equal chance gaming.

The definition of a casino as *'an arrangement whereby people are given an opportunity to participate in one or more casino games'* applies equally to casinos located physically in buildings in which the games are played, and to online casinos offering casino games by some form of remote communication, though for obvious reasons only the former will require a premises licence.

Premises licences for casinos can be obtained for one of two types of casino: large and small, in the specified areas.

A casino is a small casino if the combined floor area of parts of the premises used for providing facilities for gambling exceeds 500 square metres, but is less than 1,500 square metres. Minimum table gaming area is 250 square metres.

A large casino is one where the floor area used for providing services for gambling exceeds 1,500 square metres, but is less than 3,500 square metres. Minimum table gaming area is 1,000 square metres. Non-gaming at least 500 square metres.

Casino premises licences also allow the licensee to make available any number of games of chance other than casino games, such as equal chance card room games. They also permit licensees to provide automated table games such as automated roulette, being a version of the game played with a wheel controlled electronically rather than with a croupier.

Schedule 9 of the 2005 Act sets out the process for applying for small, large and, possibly in the future, regional casino premises licences.

Gambling software

Section 41 states that a person commits an offence if in the course of a business he manufactures, supplies, installs or adapts gambling software unless he acts in accordance with an operating licence.

'Gambling software' means:

* computer software for use in connection with remote gambling; but
* does not include anything for use solely in connection with a gaming machine.

A person does not supply or install gambling software by reason only of the facts that he makes facilities for remote communication or non-remote communication available to another person, and the facilities are used by the other person to supply or install gambling software.

Gaming machines

The definition of gaming machine is deliberately broad, covering a wide range of gambling activities which can take place on a machine, including betting on virtual events. Section 235(1) defines a 'gaming machine' as: '*A machine which is designed or adapted for use by individuals to gamble (whether or not it can also be used for other purposes*'.

Part 10 of the 2005 Act contains the main gaming machine provisions. The manufacture, supply, maintenance, repair, installation and adaption of a machine, including its software are all regulated activities. Part 10 applies to gaming machines whether situated in Great Britain or if anything is done in Great Britain in relation to a machine, wherever it may be situated. A gaming machine manufactured in Great Britain for export overseas will be covered by the provisions or require a gaming machine technical operating licence. However, such machines need not comply with the categorisation regulations under section 236.

The categories of machines set out in the regulations are as follows:

	Maximum stake	**Maximum prize**
Category A	Unlimited	Unlimited
Category B1	£2	£4,000
Category B2	£100	£500
Category B3	£2	£500
Category B3A	£1	£500
Category B4	£1	£250
Category C	£1	£70
Category D These can be non-money prize only machines, money prize machines or both.	Non-money: 30p Money: 10p Hybrid: 10p	Non-money: £8 Money: £5 cash Hybrid: £8 (£5 maximum in cash)

Lottery

A 'lottery' is defined as a 'simple' lottery if:

(a)   payment is required to participate;

(b)   one or more prizes are allocated to one or more members of a class; and

(c)   the allocation of prizes relies wholly on chance.

A 'complex' lottery exists if in addition to (a) and (b) above, prizes are allocated by a series of processes, the first of which relies wholly on chance. The definition thus includes events which contain an element of skill after the initial process.

2.5   Explain the system of regulation of gambling; which regulatory or governmental body is responsible for the supervision of gambling? Which body issues licences? Which body examines enforcement powers? Is there any limit on the number or duration of available licences?

The 2005 Act establishes two gambling regulators: the Gambling Commission and 'Licensing Authorities'. In England and Wales these are local authorities, operating through Licensing Committees. The Gambling Commission replaced the Gaming Board for Great Britain, which was set up under the 1968 Act, but only to regulate casinos and bingo clubs, gaming machines and lotteries. In contrast with the Gaming Board, the Gambling Commission has a duty to regulate all gaming, betting and lotteries, except spread betting. Its primary functions are to:

- issue operating licences to authorise a licensee to provide facilities for gambling;
- issue personal licences to authorise the licensee to perform functions of a specified management role (personal management licences), or specified operational function (personal functional licences);
- specify general licence conditions for each type of licence, and any individual licence conditions which it considers appropriate;
- issue Codes of Practice concerning the way in which facilities for gambling are to be provided;
- regulate licence holders;
- investigate and prosecute illegal gambling and other offences under the 2005 Act;
- issue guidance to local authorities on their role; and
- advise the Secretary for State on the incidence of gambling, how it is carried out, its effects and its regulation.

The Gambling Commission is required to publish at least one code of practice, being the social responsibility code. The Gambling Commission has now issued codes on a number of matters, but most importantly its licence conditions and codes of practice, of which a revised version is due to be published shortly.

Gambling Commission codes may be revised or revoked, subject to consultation with trade associations and those likely to be affected by the code or revision. The Gambling Commission has wide powers to consult other bodies and members of the public. Failure to comply carries no automatic penalty, but the Gambling Commission has the power to insist on compliance with the terms of its codes, compliance with which is likely to be a condition of a licence.

In practice, the most important functions of the Gambling Commission are its consideration of applications of operating licences, the specification of conditions attached to such licences, the power to review, suspend and revoke licences, or to impose a financial penalty for their breach, and it has similar powers in respect of personal licences. In contrast with its predecessor, the Gaming Board for Great Britain, the Commission has the power to investigate and prosecute offences directly.

There is no limit on the number of operating licences available and they are of unlimited duration. There is also no limit on the number of premises licences, with the exception of casino licences. Only 16 premises licences for casinos were made available under the 2005 Act and each licence is subject to a public competition, with the Local Authority determining which bidder will be awarded the licence.

3. ONLINE GAMBLING

3.1 To what extent can online gambling be offered in your jurisdiction? Are licences available and, if so, for which gambling products? Please describe briefly the licensing process, who may apply, whether licences are limited in number and, if no licences are available, whether it is legal for online gambling to be offered. In the case of EU jurisdictions, please state whether there are any issues as to the legality of the local law at EU level. Please refer to any relevant cases at ECJ level and explain any measures taken or pending by the European Commission.

The licensing regime for gambling applies equally to remote and non-remote gambling, so that for every type of gambling listed below at 4.1 there are both remote and non-remote operating licences. Licences are available to operators located anywhere in the world; however, the Commission would need to be satisfied as to the suitability of the location of key gambling equipment.

Please see 4.1 for the licensing process.

3.2 Is there a distinction between the law applicable to B2B operations and that applicable to B2C operations?

The 2005 Act does not specifically distinguish between B2B and B2C businesses, with different requirements for each. Rather, it specifies different forms of licences for specific activities.

A B2B operator which provides a white label service or a gambling platform, would require the same operating licence as that required by a B2C operator as it is providing facilities for gambling. This would be the case even if the B2B operator and its equipment were located offshore, as an operating licence is required if the gambling facilities are used by customers located in Great Britain.

It is also an offence to manufacture, supply, install or adapt gambling software without an operating licence. The Gambling Commission considers any software, which is designed for use in connection with remote gambling that is intended to be used or is used by a gambling operator, to be gambling software. The Gambling Commission issued guidance in May 2011, detailing what activities are covered by the term 'manufacture, supply, install, or adapt' for gambling software. Towards the end of 2014 it is expected that a new condition will be applied to all operating licences to the effect that all gambling software must be provided by a supplier licensed by the Commission.

Where an individual or company is supplying or offering the same off-the-shelf gambling software to a number of different operators, or making amendments to their off-the-shelf product for a specific gambling operator the activities need a gambling software licence. In these circumstances it would be expected that the software developer retains intellectual property rights.

Where an individual is contracted by a gambling operator to contribute to software development and where the individual's work is only part of the development process, or a company is sub-contracted to contribute to software development, or to provide custom software, the activities are unlikely to need a gambling software licence. In these circumstances the gambling operator would be expected to hold intellectual property rights to the software.

3.3 What are the consequences for B2C or B2B operators who are active in your jurisdiction without having obtained or applied for the required permits, licences and approvals? What penalties and enforcement powers are available in respect of the illegal operators? Please outline any significant domestic decisions or enforcement actions that have been taken by the relevant authorities in recent years.

It is a criminal offence for a B2C or B2B operator to provide facilities for gambling if it does not hold the required operating licence. The offence applies to operators who have remote gambling equipment in Great Britain and/or transact with customers located in Great Britain. It is also a criminal offence to advertise facilities for gambling in Great Britain and Northern Ireland if the operator does hold the appropriate operating licence.

Until very recently, operators located in EEA states and whitelisted jurisdictions were permitted to advertise their services in the UK without holding an operating licence. Operators located anywhere in the world were permitted to transact with British residents without holding any kind of licence. Following the change in the law, it is not yet known to what extent the authorities will pursue operators who continue activities in the UK without holding the appropriate licence. We anticipate that, in the first instance, the Commission would contact operators in breach of the law and request that they cease their activities and/or immediately make an application for an operating licence. For those who persist in operating illegally, the Commission may use its powers to initiate prosecutions however this may be difficult where operators have no presence in the UK.

The offence of providing facilities for gambling carries a maximum penalty of imprisonment for up to 51 weeks and an unlimited fine. The maximum penalty for the offence of advertising unlawful gambling is the same.

3.4 What technical measures are in place (if any) to protect consumers from unlicensed operators, such as ISP blocking and payment blocking?

In debating the recent amendments to the 2005 Act, the government considered the introduction of measures such as ISP and payment blocking to enforce the new provisions but decided against it for the time being. There are currently no technical measures to protect consumers from unlicensed operators.

3.5 Has the legal status of online gambling changed significantly in recent years and, if so, how?

For obvious reasons, the legislation governing all forms of gambling prior to the 2005 Act did not deal with use of the internet for gambling. However, since the early 1960s, it had been legal to place bets by telephone, and, given that the internet was merely another form of remote telephonic communication, it was automatically legal to use it for the placing of bets.

Bookmakers holding a bookmaker's permit in the UK could therefore supply British customers with betting products.

In relation to gaming, the position was more complicated. It was not possible under the 1968 Act to obtain a licence for online gaming, given that only licences for specific premises were available, and there was a requirement for those participating in the gaming to be present on the premises where gaming is taking place. The Gaming Board took the view that gaming took place where the server was located and that it was not illegal for British residents to participate in gaming offshore, from the privacy of their own homes. Gaming could be offered to British residents, from overseas, though it could not be licensed in the UK. Ironically, the strict rules in the 1968 Act against advertising, did not apply to foreign gambling, so that foreign operators whether licensed in any jurisdiction or not, were free to advertise in Great Britain.

Prior to the passing of the 2005 Act, it was unlawful to offer remote gaming from within the UK. As a result, UK operators offered remote gaming through subsidiary or associated companies from outside the UK mostly from tax friendly offshore jurisdictions.

The most significant change to the legal status of online gambling since the 2005 Act came into force has been the recent amendment which means that all operators who wish to transact with customers located in Great Britain or advertise their services in the UK must hold an operating licence. Prior to this change in the law, operators located in EEA states and whitelisted jurisdictions were permitted to advertise in the UK and there were no restrictions on operators located anywhere in the world transacting with British residents.

3.6 Whilst acknowledging the inherent difficulty in predicting developments in gambling law, what are the likely developments in online gambling in your jurisdiction, both short term and long term? Are any specific amendments under consideration? Have there been any recent political developments, or do you envisage any in the near future? Are any specific amendments under consideration? Are they likely to be adopted and, if so, what is the time scale?

Following the recent amendments to the Gambling Act 2005, which require all operators to hold a UK licence if they provide gambling facilities to, or advertise in, the British market, even if they are based abroad, we do not anticipate any further significant developments in the near future. Any developments in the coming months will revolve around the implementation and enforcement of the new requirement. The Gambling Commission is expected to introduce a new licence condition in the coming months which will require all operators to ensure that all gambling software that they use has been supplied by the holder of a gambling software licence.

3.7 Is the law the same in relation to mobile gambling and interactive gambling on television? If not, are there any headline differences?

The 2005 Act is applicable to all types of technologies.

4.   LAND-BASED GAMING
4.1   Please describe the licensing regime (if any) for land-based gaming, and what products are included. Please set out what licences are available, and the licensing regime for them.

The 2005 Act creates categories for operating licences as follows:

*   Casino Operating Licence;
*   Bingo Operating Licence;
*   General Betting Operating Licence;
*   Pool Betting Operating Licence;
*   Betting Intermediary Operating Licence;
*   Gaming Machine General Operating Licence (for Adult Gaming Centres);
*   Gaming Machine General Operating Licence (for Family Entertainment Centres);
*   Gaming Machine Technical Operating Licence;
*   Gambling Software Operating Licence; and
*   Lottery Operating Licence.

In each case, there are two types of licence, one for remote and one for non-remote operating licences. In the case of operators applying for non-remote, or land-based, facilities, they will need a premises licence to authorise use of these specific premises. Operators wanting to offer both remote and non-remote will need two operating licences.

Applications for licences are made to the Gambling Commission who will determine the application, following extensive investigations, having regard to the licensing objectives, to determine whether the applicant is a suitable person to carry on the licensed activities.

The Gambling Commission publishes on its website its statement of principles for licensing and regulation, which it will apply to applications. These include:

*   assessing integrity by requiring relevant individuals to undergo criminal records checks; in some cases information will be sought from public agencies;
*   assessing the competence of applicants to operate a gambling business, particularly with reference to social responsibility issues;
*   enquiring about the financial position of applicants, including directors and business partners of applicants; and
*   investigating the source of funding for the proposed business.

The Gambling Commission has discretion to specify conditions to be attached either to all operating licences, or to those falling within a specified category, or to individual operating licences. These conditions will only be lawful if they are necessary to uphold the licensing objectives. The Commission has wide discretion as to how they will regulate operating licences through conditions. The licence conditions and codes of practice set out:

*   the general conditions to be attached to operating licences;
*   the general conditions to be attached to personal licences;
*   the principal codes of practice relating to social responsibility and other ordinary/general provisions; and
*   the code of practice attaching to casino premises licences concerning access to children and young persons.

The Gambling Commission will also enquire into the suitability of any gaming machine, equipment or software to be used in connection with the licensed activities. Following the grant of a licence, the Gambling Commission will require equipment to be tested by a recognised third party testing house. Following investigation, in some cases the applicant will be interviewed in private by a panel of Commissioners.

An annual fee is payable, but licences are granted in perpetuity, subject to lapse, revocation, surrender or suspension. Licensees can apply to vary the licence in order to:
- add, amend or remove a licensed activity;
- amend another detail of the licence; and
- add, amend or remove the condition attached to a licence.

The procedure is similar to that for a new licence.

The Gambling Commission has the important regulatory power to call in licences for review. The Gambling Commission will investigate in order to establish whether its conditions are being complied with, or where it fears that a licensee has been convicted of a relevant criminal offence, or where the Gambling Commission takes the view that the licensee may be unsuitable to continue to keep a licence, or simply where it considers that a review is appropriate.

The Gambling Commission has the power to suspend or revoke licences, or to impose financial penalties for various infractions, but one of the following conditions must apply:
- the licensed activity is being or has been undertaken in breach of the licensing objectives;
- a condition of the licence has been breached;
- the licensee has failed to cooperate with a review; or
- the licensee is unsuitable to carry on the licensed activities. This may involve circumstances where the integrity, confidence or financial standing of the licensee is questioned.

Personal licences

While the operating licence authorises an individual, company, or other form of association to operate a particular type of gambling, those responsible for the management of the business, for compliance and for the control of gambling, will need Commission approval in the form of a personal licence. For each operating licence there must be at least one personal licence holder.

The application for a personal licence must specify the specific functions for which the applicant is applying, be made in the form required by the Gambling Commission and be accompanied by the prescribed fee and any required supporting documentation. Functions include, for example regulatory compliance, head of gambling IT, and overall strategy. The Gambling Commission will enquire into suitability of the applicant, and in particular his integrity and competence. A licence may be refused where the applicant has a relevant criminal conviction (in Great Britain or abroad) but it is not automatic.

A personal licence is required by anyone exercising an operational function capable of influencing the outcome of gambling, receiving or paying money in connection with gambling, or manufacturing, supplying, installing, maintaining or preparing gambling equipment. There is a requirement for those exercising functions at every level of the company from relevant directors to croupiers in a casino to be licensed.

Personal licence holders are under a duty to report suspicion of offences, to report 'key events' and to provide certain regulatory information to the Gambling Commission pursuant to a request.

Individuals may only hold one licence, though that may authorise more than one function, and there is the ability to vary to incorporate additional functions.

Premises licence

This is granted by the relevant local authority for premises authorising their use for one or more specified forms of gambling. There are five types of licence to enable premises to be used for:
- casino gaming;
- bingo;
- as an adult gaming centre for making Category B gaming machines available for use;
- as a family entertainment centre, for Category C gaming machines; or
- as betting premises.

A premises licence is not required in order to provide facilities if they are to be used only by those who:
- are acting in the course of the business; or
- are not on the premises.

Only one premises licence can apply to a particular premises at a time, limiting the type of gambling permitted to the particular type authorised by the licence. The rule is subject to exceptions, most notably in relation to betting tracks, but no more than one premises licence can operate in relation to any area of the track.

Different gaming machine entitlements apply to different types of premises licences.

Application is made to the licensing authority in whose area the premises are located. The applicant must hold, or have applied for, an operating licence authorising the type of gambling for which the premises are sought. The applicant must have a right to occupy the premises to which the application relates. This may be a freehold, leasehold or tenancy.

4.2 Please set out any particular limitations or requirements for (eg casino) operators, such as a ban on local residents gambling.

There is no ban on local residents gambling in Great Britain. There are strict social responsibility requirements set out in codes of practice and licence conditions from the Gambling Commission in pursuance of the licensing objectives.

4.3 Please address the questions in 3.5 above, but in relation to land-based gaming.

The legal status of land-based gaming has not changed significantly since the introduction of the 2005 Act and no significant developments to the legal status of land-base gaming are expected in the near future.

The government is currently giving serious consideration to whether restrictions should be placed upon fixed odds betting terminals, due to concerns about problem gambling and criminality. A key development has been the issue of a new code of conduct by the Association of British Bookmakers, the Code for Responsible Gaming and Player Protection (the ABB Code). This was issued in September 2013 and fully came into effect from 1 March 2014. The ABB Code contains a number of obligations which are specifically aimed at operators of FOBTs, together with more general obligations that will also apply to any bookmaker (irrespective of whether they have FOBTs on their premises). These obligations include reminders when customers have played for a certain length of time or through a certain amount of money, the option for customers to set limits on their play by way of time or money spent and training for staff in recognising problem gambling.

5. TAX

5.1 Please summarise briefly the tax regime applicable both to land-based and online gaming.

Currently, HMRC operates different regimes for:

	Tax year 2012–2013
Bingo duty	
Percentage of bingo promotion profits	20 per cent
General betting duty	
Percentage of 'net stake receipts' for fixed odds bets and totalisator bets on horse or dog races	15 per cent
Percentage of 'net stake receipts' for financial spread bets	3 per cent
Percentage of 'net stake receipts' for all other spread bets	10 per cent
Lottery duty	
Percentage of the price paid or payable on taking a ticket or chance in a lottery	12 per cent
Remote gaming duty	
Operators based in the UK: Percentage of remote gaming profits	15 per cent
Operators based outside the UK	0 per cent
Machine games duty from 1 February 2013	
Percentage of net takings from dutiable machine games with a maximum cost to play not more than 10p and a maximum cash prize not more than £8	5 per cent
Percentage of net takings from all other dutiable machine games	20 per cent
Gambling at a casino in the UK ('gaming duty') on or after 1 April 2012	
Gross gaming yield – £2,175,000	15 per cent
Gross gaming yield – £1,499,500	20 per cent
Gross gaming yield – £2,626,000	30 per cent
Gross gaming yield – £5,542,500	40 per cent
Gross gaming yield – Remainder	50 per cent

The majority of gambling activities are exempt from VAT.

In Budget 2012, the government announced that it will move to taxing remote gambling on a point of consumption basis. The new provisions are currently scheduled to take effect from 1 December 2014 and at a rate of 15 per cent. Neither the rate nor the implementation date is set in stone, but we do not consider that they are likely to change.

6. ADVERTISING
6.1 To what extent is the advertising of gambling permitted in your jurisdiction? Again, this should cover both land-based and online gaming. To the extent that advertising is permitted, how is it regulated?
Meaning of advertising
Section 327 of the 2005 Act defines 'advertising' as:

(a) doing anything to encourage one or more persons to take advantage (whether directly or through an agent) of facilities for gambling,

(b) with a view to increasing the use of facilities for gambling, bringing them or information about them to the attention of one or more persons, or

(c) participating in or facilitating an activity knowing or believing that it is designed to:

    i. encourage one or more persons to take advantage (whether directly or through an agent) of facilities for gambling, or

    ii. increase the use of facilities for gambling by bringing them or information about them to the attention of one or more persons.

This definition is extremely wide and covers most forms of advertising and marketing, including potentially online advertising and emails to customer databases.

The 2005 Act reformed virtually all the previous restrictions on the advertising of gambling and provides the basis framework for regulation. It is a condition of both non-remote and remote gambling operating licences issued by the Commission that the licensee complies with the relevant codes of practice.

The Secretary of State has the power to pass regulations relating to gambling advertising by controlling the form, content, timing and location of advertisement for gambling, including requirements for specified words to be included in advertisement. At the time of writing, no Secretary of State has exercised this power since the 2005 Act came into force on 1 September 2007.

Relevant offences
It is an offence under section 46 for a person to invite a person under 18 to gamble, and section 330 of the 2005 Act makes it an offence to advertise 'unlawful gambling'. Gambling is 'unlawful' if, in order for it to take place as advertised without the commission of an offence under the 2005 Act, it would or might be necessary to rely on a licence or exception under the Act. This effectively means that, if the provision of facilities for gambling would be an offence as the appropriate licence is not held, the facilities may not be advertised in the UK.

The Gambling Commission may take enforcement action against those not permitted to advertise if illegal advertising occurs, and may seek to prosecute.

The Codes

The CAP and BCAP codes, which are administered by the Advertising Standards Authority (ASA), cover the content and placement of advertising to ensure that all gambling advertising is conducted in a socially responsible manner. Thus, the rules ensure that gambling advertising is conducted in pursuance of the licensing objectives by not being aimed at children or young people and by not leaving vulnerable people open to exploitation and harm. The Codes apply to marketing communications for 'play for money' gambling products and marketing communications for 'play for free' gambling products that offer the chance to win a prize or that explicitly or implicitly direct the consumer to a 'play for money' gambling product, whether onshore or offshore.

All gambling advertising must also follow the general rules for advertising set out in the entire CAP or BCAP Code. All advertisements must also be *'legal, decent, honest and truthful'* and *'prepared with a sense of responsibility to consumers and to society'.*

The marketing provisions of the LCCP provide, *inter alia*, that *'licensees should only offer incentive or reward schemes in which the "benefit" available is proportionate to the type and level of a customer's gambling.'* Also, when offering inducements and bonuses, such as free bets or points, the value of the inducement must increase at a rate no greater than the amount spent.

The ASA does not have criminal sanctions at its disposal to enforce the Codes. However, if an advertiser failed to comply with a direction to withdraw an advertisement which was in breach, this could be a reason for the Commission to review the operator's licence. Further, the ASA issues a list of non-compliant advertisers to media outlets, so failure to comply with a direction is likely to lead to the operator being unable to advertise in the UK in the future.

7. SOCIAL GAMING

7.1 We believe this to be a growing area. Please decide under what criteria social gaming is permitted in your jurisdiction. If games are free to play or if there is no prize, are they legal without a licence? Please address circumstances where virtual currency is used and can be won: ie currency which is of no monetary or other value, save for as credits to take part in games. The answer should address the question whether game credits or virtual money can be exchanged for other prizes. Is any change to regulation in the area proposed or envisaged?
Unsurprisingly, the Commission is taking a keen interest in social gaming because of the element of chance in these games, in particular those that mimic gambling games. An increasing number of games in the UK now incorporate virtual currency that can either be obtained by registering to play or purchasing virtual money using PayPal or a credit card.As set out above, the 2005 Act defines gaming as *'playing a game of chance for a prize'*. Social gaming sites can offer real money prizes, providing their games are purely skill-based. Social gaming sites offering poker and casino games avoid attracting regulation by not offering prizes which are reducible to monetary value.

Matters are complicated when social games of chance offer prizes in virtual money. In a nutshell, if no real money is paid out to players and winnings have no monetary value, social games will not attract regulation under the 2005 Act because the virtual money does not constitute money's worth within. This is on the basis that it is not exchangeable for any goods or services and cannot be traded for anything other than additional play. However, regulators are showing a keen interest in this area and it remains to be seen what further developments may result.

The Commission is carrying out a review to investigate potential risks of social gaming and issues such as whether winning virtual currency is equivalent to winning real prizes. In October 2013 the Commission published a preliminary report which explored the evidence for potential risk factors and called on the social gambling industry to build on this work using their existing player data to further explore the size and potential impact of these risks. The Commission has said that it would recommend regulation in this area if its review raised significant concerns in relation to such games misleading players or exploiting the young or vulnerable.

The Commission has also formed a group on social gaming, with the Office for Fair Trading (OFT), the Committee of Advertising Practice, Ofcom, PhonepayPlus and the Information Commissioner's Office, to share knowledge, learning and research.

In January 2014, the OFT came to the end of an investigation into social gaming and warned operators that they must give up-front information to players as to costs and in-game advertising. Reacting to concerns about in-game payments being racked up by children playing on their parents' devices, the OFT has said that such payments will only be permitted where the account holder has given informed consent.

Contact details

ALDERNEY
Julian Harris
Harris Hagan
6 Snow Hill
London EC1A 2AY
UK
T: +44 20 7002 7636
F: +44 20 7002 7788
E: harris@harrishagan.com
W: www.harrishagan.com

AUSTRALIA
Jamie Nettleton, Justine Munsie &
Jessica Azzi
Addisons
Level 12
60 Carrington Street
Sydney NSW
Australia
T: +61 2 8915 1000
F: +61 2 8916 2030
E: jamie.nettleton@addisonslawyers.
    com.au
E: justine.munsie@addisonslawyers.
    com.au
E: jessica.azzi@addisonslawyers.
    com.au
W: www.addisonslawyers.com.au

AUSTRIA
Walter Schwartz
Schwartz Huber-Medek und Partner
Rechtsanwälte OG
1010 Wien
Stubenring 2
Vienna
Austria
T: +43 1 513 5005-20
F: +43 1 513 5005-50
M: +43 699 100 600 92
E: w.schwartz@s-hm.at
W: www.s-hm.at

BELGIUM
Pieter Paepe
Astrea
Avenue Louise 235 Louizalaan
B-1050 Bruxelles-Brussel
Belgium
T: +32 2 215 97 58
F: +32 2 216 50 91
E: ppa@astrealaw.be
W: www.astrealaw.be

BRAZIL
Fabio Kujawski &
Juliana Gebara de Sene
Mattos Filho, Veiga Filho, Marrey Jr.
e Quiroga Advogados
Al. Joaquim Eugênio de Lima, 447
01403-001 São Paulo SP
Brazil
T: 55 11 3147 2795
E: kujawski@mattosfilho.com.br
W: www.mattosfilho.com.br

COLORADO (USA)
Roger M. Morris
Roger M. Morris, LLC
1775 Sherman St.
Suite 1445
Denver, CO 80203
USA
T: +303 329 0141
F: +303-321-8106
E: rmorris@rogermorris.com
W: www.rogermorris.com

Richard L. Nathan
Robinson Waters & O'Dorisio, P.C.
1099 18th Street, Suite 2600
Denver, CO 80202, USA
T: +303 297 2600
F: +303 297 2750
E: rnathan@rwolaw.com
W: www.rwolaw.com

CYPRUS

Alexia Couccoullis
Law Office 'G. & A. Ladas'
Athienitis Kennedy Park Building,
3rd Floor, Suite 301
67 Kennedy Avenue
Nicosia 1080
Cyprus
&
Law Offices 'Constantinos N.
Couccoullis & Associates'
58 Panepistimiou Av, 106 78
Athens
Greece
T: +30 210 3803323 [6 lines]
F: +30 210 3302058
M: +30 6974479301
E: couclaw@couclaw.com
W: www.couclaw.com

CZECH REPUBLIC

Jan Kozubek & Veronika Žánová
Becker & Poliakoff s.r.o.
U Prašné brány 1078/1, 110 00
Prague 1
Czech Republic
T: +420 224 900 000
F: +420 224 900 041
M: +420 731 609 502
E: kozubek@becker-poliakoff.cz
W: www.becker-poliakoff.cz

DENMARK

Nina Henningsen & Mikkel Taanum
Horten
Philip Heymans Allé 7
2900 Hellerup
Copenhagen
Denmark
T: +45 3334 4000
F: +45 3334 4001
E: nhe@horten.dk
E: mta@horten.dk
W: www.horten.dk

ESTONIA

Silja Elunurm

Law Firm Indela & Elunurm
Tartu mnt 84a-25
Tallinn 10112
Estonia
T: +372 5186578
E: silja@indela.ee
W: www.indela.ee

FRANCE

Diane Mullenex & Annabelle Richard
Pinsent Masons LLP
21-23, rue Balzac
75008 Paris
France
T: +33 1 53 53 02 80
F: +33 1 53 53 02 81
E: diane.mullenex@pinsentmasons.
com
E: annabelle.richard@
pinsentmasons.com
W: www.pinsentmasons.com

GERMANY

Dr Joerg Hofmann, Matthias Spitz,
Danny Engelhardt & LL.M. &
Martin Jarrett, B.A. LL.B. (1:1)
Melchers Rechtsanwaelte
Partnerschaftsgesellschaft mbB
Im Breitspiel 21
69126 Heidelberg
Germany
T: +49 6221-18 50 0
F: +49 6221-18 50 100
E: gaming@melchers-law.com
W: www.melchers-law.com

GIBRALTAR

Peter Montegriffo & Nyreen Llamas
Hassans
57/63 Line Wall Road
PO Box 199
Gibraltar
T: +350 200 79000
F: +350 200 71966
E: peter.montegriffo@hassans.gi
E: nyreen.llamas@hassans.gi
W: www.gibraltarlaw.com

GREECE

Constantinos Couccoullis & Alexia
Couccoullis
Constantinos N. Couccoullis and
Associates
58 Panepistimiou Av, 106 78
Athens
Greece
T: +30 210 3803323
F: +30 210 3302058
E: couclaw@couclaw.com
W: www.couclaw.com

IRELAND

Rob Corbet & Chris Bollard
Arthur Cox
Earlsfort Centre
Earlsfort Terrace
Dublin 2
Ireland
T: +353 1 618 0566 (Corbet)
T: +353 1 618 0649 (Bollard)
E: rob.corbet@arthurcox.com
E: chris.bollard@arthurcox.com
W: www.arthurcox.com

ISLE OF MAN

Miles Benham
Advocate
MannBenham Advocates Limited
49 Victoria Street
Douglas
Isle of Man
E: milesbenham@mannbenham.
   com
W: www.mannbenham.com

ISRAEL

Yehoshua Shohat Gurtler, Itzhak
Shragay & Ariel Yosefi
Herzog Fox & Neeman Law Office
Asia House, 4 Weizmann St
Tel Aviv 64239
Israel
T: +972 3 692 2020
F: +972 3 696 6464
E: gurtlery@hfn.co.il

E: shragayi@hfn.co.il
E: yosefia@hfn.co.il
W: www.hfn.co.il

ITALY

Quirino Mancini
SCM Lawyers
Via Pasquale Stanislao Mancini 2
00196 Rome
Italy
T: +39063221485
F: +39063613266
E: qmancini@scm-partners.it
W: www.scm-partners.it

JAPAN

Ko Hanamizu
Anderson Mori & Tomotsune
Akasaka K-Tower
2-7, Motoakasaka 1-chome
Minato-ku, Tokyo 107-0051
Japan
T: +81-3-6888-1127
F: +81-3-6888-3127
E: ko.hanamizu@amt-law.com
W: http://www.amt-law.com/en/

LUXEMBOURG

Michaël Kitai
Bonn Steichen & Partners
2, rue Peternelchen
Immeuble C2
L-2370 Howald
Luxembourg
T: +352 26025-256
F: +352 26025-999
E: mkitai@bsp.lu
W: www.bsp.lu

MACAU

Luis Mesquita de Melo
MdME Lawyers
Avenida da Praia Grande, 409
China Law Building, 21st Floor
Macau
T: +853 66485575/+853 28333332
F: +853 28333331

E: lmm@mdme.com.mo
W: www.mdme.com.mo

MALTA

Dr Andrew Zammit, Dr Jackie Scerri
& Dr Richard Bernard
CSB Advocates
The Penthouse
Tower Business Centre
Tower Street
Swatar, BKR 4013
Malta
T: +356 2557 2300
F: +356 2557 2310
E: ajz@csb-advocates.com
E: js@csb-advocates.com
E: rb@csb-advocates.com
W: www.csb-advocates.com

MEXICO

César Morales Galán
Bufete Carrillo Gamboa, S.C.
Parque Reforma
Campos Elíseos No. 400, Piso 16
Col. Polanco
11000 México, D.F.
T: +52 55 52 02 70 00
F: +52 55 52 02 00 05
E: cesarmorales@bcarrillog.com
W: www.bcarrillog.com

MONACO

Diane Mullenex & Annabelle Richard
Pinsent Masons LLP
21-23, rue Balzac
75008 Paris
France
T: +33 1 53 53 02 80
F: +33 1 53 53 02 81
E: diane.mullenex@pinsentmasons.
com
E: annabelle.richard@
pinsentmasons.com
W: www.pinsentmasons.com

THE NETHERLANDS

Dr Alan Littler & Justin Franssen

Kalff Katz & Franssen Attorneys at
Law
Concertgebouwplein 9
1071LL Amsterdam
The Netherlands
T: +31 20 676 07 80
E: littler@kalffkatzfranssen.nl
E: franssen@kalffkatzfranssen.nl
W: www.kalffkatzfranssen.nl

NEVADA (USA)

Dan R. Reaser, Mark A. Clayton &
Robert D. Faiss
Lionel Sawyer & Collins
300 S. 4th Street
Suite 1700
Las Vegas, NV 89101
USA
T: +702-383-8888
F: +702-383-8845
E: rfaiss@lionelsawyer.com
E: dreaser@lionelsawyer.com
E: mclayton@lionelsawyer.com
W: www.lionelsawyer.com

NEW JERSEY (USA)

Guy S. Michael
Michael & Carroll
1125 Atlantic Avenue, Suite 619
Atlantic City, New Jersey
USA
T: +609-441-9292
F: +609-441-9110
E: guysmichael@aol.com

ONTARIO (CANADA)

Michael D. Lipton, Kevin J. Weber &
Jack I. Tadman
Dickinson Wright LLP
199 Bay Street, Suite 2200
Commerce Court West
Toronto, ON M5L 1G4
Canada
T: +1 416 856 2929
M: +1 416 528 1285
E: MDLiptonQC@dickinson-wright.
com

E: KWeber@dickinson-wright.com
E: JTadman@dickinson-wright.com

PANAMA
Herbert Young Rodriguez
Blandon & Young Attorneys
Vía Argentina, Ph Cristal Park, No.
1, Corregimiento de Bella Vista
Cíty of Panama
Republic of Panama
T: +507 2698827
F: +507 2698675
E: hyoung@blandonyoung.com
W: www.blandonyoung.com

Lizi Rose
Veneto Hotel & Casino
El Cangrejo, Eusebio A. Morales Ave.
Republic of Panama
T: +507 340 8880 Ext.: 4273
F: +507 340 8882
E: lrose@vwgrand.com
W: www.vwgrand.com

ROMANIA
Ana-Maria Baciu, Oana Albu &
Lucian Barbu
Nestor Nestor Diculescu Kingston
Petersen
Bucharest Business Park
1A Bucuresti-Ploiesti National Road
Entrance A, 4th Floor, 1st District
Bucharest 013681
Romania
T: +40 21 201 1200
F: +40 21 201 1210
E: Ana-Maria.Baciu@nndkp.ro
W: www.nndkp.ro

SINGAPORE
Lawrence Quahe & Yeo Khung Chye
Quahe Woo & Palmer LLC
180 Clemenceau Avenue
#02-02 Haw Par Centre
Singapore 239922
T: +65 6622 0366
F: +65 6622 0377

E: lawrence@quahewoo.com
W: www.quahewoo.com

SOUTH AFRICA
Garron Whitesman
Whitesmans
1st Floor, Hill House,
43 Somerset Road
Green Point, Cape Town 8005
South Africa
PO Box 661, Green Point
T: +27 (0)21 425 3093
F: +27 (0)867 168071
E: garron@whitesmans.com
W: www.whitesmans.com

SOUTH KOREA
Jeffrey D. Jones, Hyun Ho Eun, Jin
Ho Song, Michael S. Lee, Mi-Ryoung
An, John K. Kim & Junhee Choi
Kim & Chang
39, Sajik-ro 8-gil
Jongno-gu
Seoul 110-720
Korea
T: +82-2-3703-1114
F: +82-2-737-9091~3
E: lawkim@kimchang.com
E: jdjones@kimchang.com
E: hheun@kimchang.com
E: jhsong@kimchang.com
E: michael.lee@kimchang.com
E: mran@kimchang.com
E: John.kim@kimchang.com
E: junhee.choi@kimchang.com
W: www.kimchang.com

SPAIN
Santiago Asensi & Alla
Serebrianskaia Asensi Abogados SLP
Gran Via Puig Del Castellet, 1
Bloque 2, 1ª
07180 Santa Ponsa
Islas Baleares
Mallorca
Spain
T: +34 971 909 219

E: santiago@asensi.es
W: www.asensi.es

SWEDEN
Dr Ola Wiklund
Hansen Advokatbyrå KB
Hovslagargatan 5B
SE-111 48 Stockholm, Sweden
Sweden
T: +46 76 888 18 09
E: ola@hansenlaw.se
W: www.hansenlaw.se

SWITZERLAND
Dr Andreas Glarner, LL.M. &
Dr. Luka Mueller-Studer, LL.M.
Partners/Attorneys at Law
MME|PARTNERS
Kreuzstrasse 42
CH-8008 Zurich
Switzerland
T: +41 44 254 99 66
F: +41 44 254 99 60
E: andreas.glarner@mmepartners.ch
E: luka.mueller@mmepartners.ch
W: www.mmepartners.ch

UNITED KINGDOM
Julian Harris
Harris Hagan
6 Snow Hill
London EC1A 2AY
UK
T: +44 20 7002 7636
F: +44 20 7002 7788
E: harris@harrishagan.com
W: www.harrishagan.com